Butterworths Guide to
US/UK Private Wealth Tax Planning

Butterworths Guide to US/UK Private Wealth Tax Planning

Robert L Williams

Richard P Layman

Dawn Nicholson

Tottel Publishing   Maxwelton House, 41–43 Boltro Road, Haywards Heath, West
                      Sussex, RH16 1BJ

© Robert L Williams, Richard P Layman and Dawn Nicholson 2004

All rights reserved. No part of this publication may be reproduced in any material form (including photocopying or storing it in any medium by electronic means and whether or not transiently or incidentally to some other use of this publication) without the written permission of the copyright owner except in accordance with the provisions of the Copyright, Designs and Patents Act 1988 or under the terms of a licence issued by the Copyright Licensing Agency Ltd, 90 Tottenham Court Road, London, England W1T 4LP. Applications for the copyright owner's written permission to reproduce any part of this publication should be addressed to the publisher.

Warning: The doing of an unauthorised act in relation to a copyright work may result in both a civil claim for damages and criminal prosecution.

Crown copyright material is reproduced with the permission of the Controller of HMSO and the Queen's Printer for Scotland. Parliamentary copyright material is reproduced with the permission of the Controller of Her Majesty's Stationery Office on behalf of Parliament. Any European material in this work which has been reproduced from EUR-lex, the official European Communities legislation website, is European Communities copyright.

A CIP Catalogue record for this book is available from the British Library.

ISBN 1-84592-027-9

Typeset by Letterpart Ltd, Reigate, Surrey

Printed and bound in England by Antony Rowe Ltd, Chippenham, Wilts

Preface

A long time ago, when the authors of this book first started working together in London on international private wealth planning, we discovered not only many similarities in the framework of US and UK tax and trust laws but also fundamental differences in tax methodology and terminology. In an age of increasingly international families, estates and lifestyles, we quickly learned the limitations of advising on one's own country's tax rules without knowing the different reach of another country's overlapping rules.

As there seemed to be a good many US taxpayers based in the UK who were blissfully unaware of either the application or the conflicts in the two systems, not to say the possibilities of integrated tax-effective planning, we set out to compare the two systems side by side in terms of income, capital gains, gift, estate, generation-skipping and inheritance tax rules. From that perspective, we identified and analyzed the most common integrated planning scenarios, including techniques to remove assets from US or UK transfer taxes, to plan for emigration to either country, to structure income tax effective non-resident trusts and distributions for US and UK beneficiaries and to plan for families of mixed nationality and/or domicile, including American spouses and children.

That effort led to several law review articles published by BNA Tax Management Inc in 1992 as a book called *US/UK Integrated Tax Planning: Estates, Gifts and Trusts*. As no one else had dared to write in this area, that book was found in a number of City firms and its cover, being almost a monotonous green, gained a certain reputation as the 'Green Book'.

Time passed and laws changed, substantially in both the UK and the US. Within the last two years, a number of users or colleagues asked us whether an update of the book would be done. We decided to do a complete rewrite, the result of which is the present, much larger book (incorporating the original green in a more interesting cover).

The level of complexity and sophistication of tax legislation in one country alone can today be daunting enough, but where tax exposures arise in more than one country, integration of any asset and income structuring, as well as avoiding the numerous pitfalls which exist, can be a minefield. The present book is intended as a guide through that minefield, not as a final resource or substitute for tax advice on specific client situations.

Because this book is pitched to a wider audience, including offshore trustees, financial advisers and other professionals who deal with clients with families, assets or residences in either or both countries, we have attempted to explain the logic and the reasoning behind the applicable rules and planning, illustrating both with a number of examples involving characters, some of whom you may think are recognizable but who are entirely fictitious.

Preface

We also caution you that we have deliberately avoided notions of politically correct terminology or prose. As to gender, our UK colleague seems to think that all clients are men, while on the US side we know that women own 70% of the wealth and you will see a lot references to female clients. On the differences in spelling and vernacular, please don't tell us we don't know how to spell or use grammar. At least one of us was educated in the Queen's English and the others recognize that Americans would never accept as credible an explanation of US tax laws which was not in the American vernacular. You will find both styles used in this book and readers on both sides of the Atlantic can read about their own tax systems in home prose, comfortable in the knowledge that we are truly two countries divided by a common language.

However, we do have compassion for those on each side of the Atlantic who have to confront the other's tax system for the first time. Therefore, the rest of this Preface is a summary (generally written by the other side) of the key concepts and terminology of the two systems, including some fundamental 'Look right, not left!' signpost concepts for the UK system of which American advisers should be aware before using this book. This is a useful section to bookmark, as you read and use this book, a kind of familiar explanation in one place of 'what's going on'.

Two caveats remain. First, while this book seeks to review the principal issues of which practitioners should be aware in US and UK private wealth planning, it is not intended to be an exhaustive exposition of the provisions in either jurisdiction (both of which are lengthy and highly complex). Rather, we seek through a side-by-side comparison of some of the more fundamental aspects of income, capital gains, trust and transfer taxes and tax planning, to highlight the potential areas of conflict and those areas where the laws in each country are complementary. In both countries, there are whole books written on subjects we cover in a few pages. Give us credit, however, for breadth of coverage.

Second, we cannot over emphasize that the laws in this field are highly complex and subject to frequent change. Therefore, any planning should be undertaken only with appropriate local advice on both the US and UK side and with a thorough understanding of the current legislative provisions of each country, as well as those of any other country whose laws may have an impact.

The comments in this book are based on the law as at September 2004.

A. The US system

1. Wealth transfer tax system

In the US, gratuitous wealth transfers are taxed under the gift tax, estate tax, and generation-skipping tax regimes. The *gift tax* is imposed on transfers during life. The *estate tax* is imposed on assets transferred at the decedent's death. The *generation-skipping tax* (or GST) is a tax – imposed in addition to any gift or estate tax – on transfers that skip generations (for example, gifts from grandparents to grandchildren). These regimes are briefly described in **Chapter 1**.

Preface

US citizens are subject to US transfer tax, regardless of where they live or the location of the transferred assets. The same rule applies to US domiciliaries. Non-domiciled aliens (referred to in this book as 'NDAs') are only taxed on US situated assets. The scope of the US transfer tax rules is addressed in **Chapter 2**.

The US transfer tax rules include relatively high (but finite) exemptions. The gift tax exemption (for cumulative lifetime gifts) is fixed at $1 million. The estate tax exemption is currently $1.5 million (less the amount of gift tax exemption used during life). The GST exemption is also currently $1.5 million. Both the estate tax and GST exemptions are scheduled to increase to as much as $3.5 million by 2009. Exemptions for NDAs, however, are severely limited, in the absence of treaty relief. These and other exemptions, deductions and credits are covered in **Chapter 3**.

Transfers to spouses are generally exempt from gift and estate tax because of the so-called *marital deduction*. Tax-free gifts and bequests to spouses who are not citizens of the US are, however, severely restricted. These topics are explored in **Chapter 4**.

The US gift and estate tax share the same rate schedule. The highest marginal gift and estate tax rate is currently 48%, but the top rate is scheduled to be reduced in coming years. The GST is imposed at the highest marginal gift and estate tax rate. The rate schedule, as well as nuances in computing these various taxes, are summarized in **Chapter 5**.

US transfer taxes are generally imposed only on the transferor – the donor (with respect to a lifetime gift) or the decedent's estate (with respect to transfers at death). In some instances, however, the tax can be charged against certain trusts. These topics are covered in **Chapter 6**.

Bilateral US estate and gift tax treaties can provide considerable relief from US transfer taxation of domiciliaries of the other country. These treaties are discussed in **chapter 7**, with particular emphasis on the US-UK and US-Canada treaties.

2. Capital gains and basis issues

Unlike the UK, the US generally does not impose a capital gains tax on gratuitous transfers. There are limited exceptions, perhaps the most important of which in the international setting is the imposition of a capital gains tax on the transfer of appreciated property by US taxpayers to certain foreign trusts. This topic is discussed in some detail in **Chapter 8**.

US residents are taxed on worldwide capital gains. The US residence rules are discussed in **Chapter 9** while deductions and exclusions from capital gain taxation are discussed in **Chapter 10**.

The donee of a lifetime gift will generally take the donor's tax basis, and the beneficiary of a decedent's estate generally receives his inheritance with a new basis equal to fair market value at the date of death. The basis rules are found in **Chapter 11**.

Preface

3. Taxation of trusts and beneficiaries

The US income tax system has a complex scheme for taxing trusts, estates, beneficiaries and, in the case of trusts, the *grantor* (the person who funded the trust). In some instances, the grantor is taxed on trust earnings. In other instances, the trust or estate will be taxed on its gains and income. In still others, the income and gains earned in a trust or estate will be taxed to the beneficiary (and not the trust or estate) by reason of certain distributions. These rules are sorted out in **Chapter 12**.

4. Trusts often used in US tax planning

In US tax and estate planning, a variety of trusts are used for a variety of purposes. These trusts are referred to throughout the book, so we thought it useful to briefly introduce the reader to some of these key types of trusts.

Marital trust: A trust designed to qualify a gift or bequest to a spouse for the US marital deduction.

QTIP trust: A qualified terminable interest property ('QTIP') trust is a form of marital trust for the surviving spouse's sole benefit during her life in which she is given a life interest but need not be given a power to specify the disposition of the remainder.

QDOT: Not a candy treat, but a qualified domestic trust ('QDOT') is the only form of trust that will qualify a bequest to a non-citizen spouse for the US marital deduction. These trusts must have at least one US trustee and could include other security arrangements to ensure that the deferred US estate tax is collected at the survivor's death.

Grantor trust: This is an income tax concept. A grantor trust is a form of trust in which the person who funded the trust (the 'grantor') is taxed as if he remained the owner of the underlying trust assets. A grantor trust is transparent for income tax purposes. There are various ways in which a trust might be considered a grantor trust – including where the grantor retains certain interests in or powers over the trust. In some instances, irrevocable trusts for others will include intended 'defects' so that they will be considered grantor trusts (causing the grantor to be taxed on income that actually flows to other beneficiaries). These trusts are sometimes referred to as 'defective grantor trusts' (DGTs) or 'intentionally defective grantor trusts' (IDGTs), but there is really nothing defective in their design or operation.

Non-grantor trust: Any trust that is not considered a grantor trust for income tax purposes. The income or gains of a non-grantor trust will be taxed either to the trust or to the trust's beneficiaries, depending on distributions.

Simple trust: A non-grantor trust that is obligated to distribute all of its income to beneficiaries (who, in turn, are taxed on that income). A trust that makes a principal distribution will not be a simple trust *in that year*.

Complex trust: A non-grantor trust that is not a simple trust.

Preface

Drop off trust: A trust (discussed in **Chapter 16**) which can be used by a NDA who is planning to immigrate to the US and wishes to set some portion of his estate aside in an irrevocable trust (often for the benefit of himself and his family) that will be exempt from US estate tax and also from the claims of creditors. The same type of irrevocable trust can also be used by a NDA to remove assets from US estate tax even if he doesn't intend to immigrate to the US, and this trust is also called a drop off trust (discussed in **Chapter 14**). The immigrant drop off trust will usually be a grantor trust during the settlor's period of US residence.

Crummey trust: This is a form of irrevocable trust used by US taxpayers for tax-free annual gifts. Under the gift tax annual exclusion, a donor can make gifts of up to $11,000 per year to an individual, but the gift must be of a 'present interest'. A Crummey trust (named after the court case) confers temporary withdrawal rights on the beneficiary in order to give the beneficiary a present interest in the trust.

2503(c) trust: A form of trust (named after the relevant tax code provision) used by donors to make gifts in trusts for minors that qualify for the gift tax annual exclusion. (Also see Crummey trust.)

GST exempt (or dynasty) trust: Taxpayers, using their GST exemptions, can set up trusts for intervening generations that will not be subject to gift tax, estate tax or the GST as the property passes from generation to generation. Funded with life insurance, dynasty trusts can produce substantial income tax free proceeds on death of an insured beneficiary. Many US states (and some foreign countries) have eliminated the rule against perpetuities, thus allowing trusts to potentially last for many generations without artificial rules that mandate the termination of the trust after a certain number of years.

Irrevocable life insurance trust (ILIT): The proceeds of life insurance owned by an insured at death will be taxed in his estate. Conversely, if the policy is owned by someone other than the insured at death, the proceeds will generally escape tax. ILITs are used to hold life insurance and keep the proceeds from being taxed in the insured's estate.

Revocable trust: Often a key tool in an individual's estate plan, allowing maximum flexibility and control during the settlor's life, but setting out the terms of the disposition of his estate at death. In some sense, a revocable trust will serve as a substitute for the individual's will. Revocable trusts are often used to hold an individual's assets during life in order to avoid probate at death. The settlor retains the power to revoke and modify the trust (and thus to modify or revoke his estate plan). For US income tax and transfer tax purposes, the trust is transparent: the settlor will be taxed on all trust income/gains and property held in the revocable trust at death will be included in the settlor's taxable estate.

5. Tax administration and enforcement

The body responsible for administering and enforcing the US federal tax rules is the Internal Revenue Service. In practice and in this book, they are commonly referred to as the *IRS* and the *Service*. (Taxpayers often have other words and adjectives for the IRS, but we've chosen here to be a bit more diplomatic.)

Preface

The US tax laws are consolidated in the Internal Revenue Code of 1986, as amended, which we refer to as the *Code*. (Perhaps Dan Brown – the author of the best selling book, *The DaVinci Code* – might devote his next effort to deciphering the hidden meaning in the US Tax Code. For example, if the Code section numbers were added together and then divided by the number of pages in the Gutenberg bible, does the result offer some clue about the next Super Lotto numbers?)

The Treasury Department (or *Treasury*) – of which the Service is a part – from time to time issues *regulations* that offer the Treasury's more detailed view of the meaning and operation of the specific provisions of the Code. The official citation we use for these regulations is 'Treas Reg' (which stands for Treasury Regulations). Practitioners often refer to the regulations as the 'regs', although we think we've steered clear of that usage.

In some instances, the Code invites the Treasury to promulgate regulations to flesh out rules and exceptions that Congress was not prepared to include in the Code. In most instances, however, the regulations simply expand upon the provisions in the Code. Regulations are issued in proposed form, with the Treasury inviting comment from others (practitioners, academics, taxpayers). Sometimes these proposed regulations sit for years before they are finalized. Regulations often become outdated after new legislation is enacted (and before the Treasury has an opportunity to amend the regulations). Courts will generally give deference to the regulations, but from time to time courts will overturn certain regulations, that is find that they do not properly interpret the Code and thus do not properly define the implications to the taxpayers.

The Service also communicates its opinion on specific tax issues by issuing *Revenue Rulings* (cited as 'Rev Rul'). Revenue Rulings are defined by the Service as 'an official interpretation by the Service of the internal revenue laws and related statutes, treaties, and regulations, that has been published in the Bulletin. Revenue rulings are issued only by the National Office and are published for the information and guidance of taxpayers, Service officials, and others concerned.' These rulings typically define a hypothetical fact pattern (or series of related fact patterns) and then address specific tax issues related to those facts. In reaching their conclusions, the rulings cite relevant provisions of the Code and regulations, and, where relevant, prior rulings and court cases. Like regulations, Revenue Rulings often become outdated with the enactment of new laws. From time to time the Service will purge obsolete rulings or update rulings to reflect changes in the law. Finally, although rulings are typically upheld by courts, on occasion courts will strike down Revenue Rulings that they find to be an improper interpretation of the law.

Revenue Procedures (or 'Rev Procs') are described by the Service as 'an official statement of a procedure published in the [Internal Revenue] Bulletin that either affects the rights or duties of taxpayers or other members of the public under the Internal Revenue Code and related statutes, treaties, and regulations or, although not necessarily affecting the rights and duties of the public, should be a matter of public knowledge.'

Taxpayers can also seek *private letter rulings* (or 'PLRs'), in which the Service is asked to address the specific tax implications of a completed or proposed transaction. There are areas upon which the IRS will not rule. Not all ruling requests

Preface

ultimately result in PLRs: a taxpayer is given the opportunity to withdraw his request before the IRS issues an unfavorable ruling. PLRs effectively bind the Service, but only with respect to that taxpayer. Redacted copies of PLRs are periodically published, giving the world an insight on the IRS's current thinking on particular issues. However, PLRs cannot be cited as precedent, but are cited by authors (including us) to reflect what appears to be the Service's currently ruling position. Taxpayers (other than those receiving the ruling) thus rely on PLRs at their own risk.

Finally, the court system. The courts are the final arbiters of the meaning and application of the tax laws. The US has a *Tax Court* that hears disputed tax assessment cases brought by the IRS. Alternatively, the taxpayer can pay the disputed tax and sue for a refund in federal district court or the Court of Claims. Both Tax Court and district court/Court of Claims refund cases can be appealed to the *federal circuit courts of appeal*. In rare cases, the *US Supreme Court* will hear appeals of tax cases.

Stop Press: As this book was going to press the US Congress enacted the American Jobs Creation Act of 2004, two sections of which impact a few sections of this book. These are identified in **Appendix IX**.

B. The UK system

UK inheritance tax is a very complex regime, replete with concepts unfamiliar to US tax practitioners. Like an American newly landed in Britain, you will discover the rules have changed as soon as you cross the road or get into a car. What is needed to understand the UK transfer tax system is a basic overview of its most fundamental 'Look right, not left!' signpost concepts. These are summarized in the following. Remember, this is an overview and we are oversimplifying – there are whole books written on these basic concepts.

1. Wealth transfer tax system

In the UK, gratuitous wealth transfers both in lifetime and on death are taxed under a single regime – inheritance tax. This is briefly described in **Chapter 1**.[1]

UK domiciliaries (see below) are subject to UK inheritance tax, regardless of where they live or the location of the transferred assets. Non-UK domiciliaries are only taxed on UK sited assets. The scope of the UK inheritance tax rules is addressed in **Chapter 2**.

Subject to a small 'nil rate' band (effectively an exemption, which for 2004/05 stands at £263,000), chargeable ('taxable') transfers which are deemed to be made by a deceased immediately before his death are taxed at 40%. Chargeable transfers made in one's lifetime are taxed at 20%, subject to an increase in the tax rate if death

---

[1] Section 100 of the Finance Act (hereinafter 'FA') 1986.

Preface

occurs within the following five years[2] (tapered to take account of the period between the gift and the date of death). However, transfers during lifetime escape tax if made as outright gifts, or to an 'interest in possession' trust or to an 'accumulation and maintenance' trust for beneficiaries under 25 – provided the donor/settlor survives the transfer by seven years and retains no reserved benefit over the transferred property.[3] Such lifetime transfers are called potentially exempt transfers. These concepts and other exemptions, deductions and reliefs are covered in **Chapters 1** and **3**.

Transfers to spouses are generally exempt from inheritance tax. Tax-free gifts and bequests by UK domiciliaries to spouses who are not domiciliaries of the UK are, however, severely restricted (unless, in the case of lifetime gifts, they qualify as potentially exempt transfers). These topics are explored in **Chapter 4**.

As noted above, the lifetime rate of tax on chargeable transfers is 20%, whereas the rate at death is 40%. Certain intermediate rates can apply for lifetime gifts made within seven years of death. These issues are summarized in **Chapter 5**.

UK transfer taxes are generally imposed on the transferor – the donor (with respect to a lifetime gift, unless the donee agrees to pay the tax) or the decedent's estate (with respect to transfers at death). In some instances, however, the tax can be charged to the trustees of trusts. These topics are covered in **Chapter 6**.

2. Capital gains and basis issues

Unlike the US, the UK generally imposes a capital gains tax on gratuitous transfers, which are treated as deemed disposals. There are some exceptions to this but the UK capital gains tax regime is highly complex, particularly as it applies to trusts. This topic is discussed in some detail in **Chapters 8–10** (**Chapter 13** as it relates to trusts).

The donee of a lifetime gift will generally take, as his cost base, the market value of the asset at the date of a lifetime gift (unless one of the above-mentioned exceptions applies), whilst the beneficiary of a decedent's estate generally receives his inheritance with a new cost basis equal to open market value at the date of death. The cost basis rules are found in **Chapter 11**.

3. Taxation of trusts and beneficiaries

As in the US, the UK income and gains tax regimes are complex as they apply to the taxation of trusts, estates and beneficiaries. Again, as in the US, complex rules in the case of trusts can also tax the settlor/grantor (the person who funded the trust) in certain circumstances. In some cases the settlor/grantor is taxed on trust income

---

[2] Strictly the period is seven years but the tapering mechanism creates no effective increase in the tax after a period of five years.
[3] Confusingly, the reservation of benefit rules do not apply to the donor's retention of a separate interest which has previously been 'carved out' of the asset (eg a life interest 'retained' is not a reserved benefit for this purpose), subject to exceptions created by certain avoidance legislation.

whilst in other instances, the trust or estate will be taxed on its gains and income. In still others, the income and gains of a trust will be taxed to the beneficiary (and not the trust) if he is entitled to receive such income or receives certain discretionary distributions. These rules are covered in **Chapter 13**.

4. **Trusts often used in UK tax planning**

   a. *An interest in possession trust*

An 'interest in possession' (IIP) is a fixed-income right of a beneficiary, to receive the income of the trust as it arises during his lifetime, net of trust expenses. The trustees must have no discretion to divert the income from the beneficiary once it has arisen. However, an IIP can exist currently, even if it may be taken away *prospectively* by the trustees, pursuant to their exercise of an overriding power to appoint trust income and capital to others at their discretion. In this sense, it is similar to a US revocable life interest, though in this case the trustees have the power over the assets, not the settlor.

Fundamental UK income tax and IHT consequences flow from an IIP:

- Not only is an IIP holder taxable on trust income, whether or not distributed (subject to remittance rules if he is non-UK domiciled), but he is deemed to own the entire underlying principal for IHT purposes (in contrast to the US tax system where estate tax inclusion would only apply to a *settlor* retained life interest).

- As a consequence, death of an IIP holder or termination of his interest in whole or in part by the trustee can be an IHT chargeable (taxable) event with generally the same consequences as though the IIP holder held the property outright.

- Finally, transfers to an IIP trust are potentially exempt from an IHT charge to the transferor, ie such transfers will be exempt if the transferor survives the transfer by seven years.

Example: Oliver settles a country property in the Cotswolds on trust with an interest in possession for his son, Charles. Oliver is excluded from benefiting and survives the settlement by seven years. On Charles' death the trust assets are deemed included in his taxable IHT estate (though the tax is payable by the trustees). No IHT is imposed on Oliver.

Example: Charles leads an increasingly profligate life. The trustees decide to revoke Charles' interest, appointing one half of the trust assets to Charles' son and granting an interest in possession in the other half to his UK domiciled wife. The creation of an interest in possession for Charles' wife is an exempt spousal transfer (deemed to be made by Charles). The appointment of trust assets to Charles' son is a 'potentially exempt transfer' (deemed to be made by Charles), exempt if Charles survives this appointment by seven years. There are no IHT consequences to Oliver from these transfers.

Preface

The bottom line: in US terms, an IIP trust is like a beneficiary grantor trust for transfer tax purposes. The reason transfers to IIP trusts are 'potentially' exempt IHT transfers is that in the UK system giving assets to an IIP trust is deemed to be the same as giving them to an individual (the IIP holder). As long as the donor survives the gift by seven years the gift is exempt from IHT with respect to the donor.

b. *'Discretionary' trusts – the decennial IHT tax regime*

In IHT terms, a 'discretionary' trust is any trust which is *not* an interest in possession trust. The term is confusing to American practitioners who would view most IIP trusts as 'discretionary' trusts with a revocable life interest. Not so to UK practitioners. The IIP holder is deemed to own all trust assets for IHT purposes and the 'discretion' of the trustees to make capital distributions to other beneficiaries, including termination of his IIP interest, is irrelevant in characterising the trust as an IIP or a discretionary trust. Only the nature of the beneficial entitlement over income is taken into account in determining whether the trust is discretionary.

Because, unlike the IIP trust, the assets of a discretionary trust are not deemed to be comprised in any person's estate, lifetime transfers to such a trust are not 'potentially exempt', but are instead chargeable and subject to IHT at half the normal rate, or 20%. In addition, if the transferor reserves a benefit over the transferred assets (see below) within seven years of his death, the trust assets may be included in his estate under the IHT 'gifts with reservation of benefit' rules. Double charges may be relieved in certain cases.

Since the assets of discretionary trusts are not attributed to individual donees, they are true 'generation-skipping' trusts since they avoid tax in the estates of intervening generations. To compensate for this, discretionary trusts are subject to a special IHT tax regime – the 'decennial IHT regime'. Under this regime, the assets of a discretionary trust are deemed subject to a separate IHT charge every ten years, or to an 'exit' charge on earlier transfers out of the trust, between ten-year anniversaries. This charge, at its highest, is 6% of the relevant trust asset value (computed by reference to a formula). The distribution of trust assets between decennial anniversaries is subject to an 'exit' charge which broadly amounts to a proportion of the ten-yearly charge depending on the period which has elapsed since the last charge.

c. *'Accumulation and maintenance' (A&M) trusts*

An 'accumulation and maintenance' trust is a special type of discretionary trust for children, grandchildren or other descendants of a common grandparent (such as nieces and nephews). Like the IIP trust, it also qualifies as a 'potentially exempt transfer'. It must start out as a discretionary trust for the benefit of the specified class, all of whom must either be distributed their putative share of trust assets on or before reaching age 25, or receive an interest in possession in such share by age 25 (or earlier if required under the UK trust rule allowing income to be accumulated for limited periods of time, usually 21 years). The applicable IHT rules are stringent

Preface

and great care needs to be taken in the drafting to avoid the trust being categorised as a discretionary trust, and hence creating a chargeable lifetime transfer. Provided the trust qualifies, special rules preclude IHT charges which would otherwise arise during the existence of the trust.

As we have already seen, an IIP is broadly treated as outright ownership for certain IHT purposes. Gifts to A&M trusts are treated similarly as 'potentially exempt transfers' since they will give rise to an IIP or to an outright transfer to an individual once the beneficiary reaches 25. For US aficionados, the A&M trust is similar to a Section 2503(c) gift tax exclusion discretionary trust for minors which must vest at 21.

d. 'Excluded property trusts'

Under current legislation, a trust which is fully settled *prior to the time when* the settlor becomes UK domiciled, either under general law principles or 'deemed domiciled' for IHT purposes, will be an 'excluded property trust' (EPT) for IHT purposes with respect to all of its non-UK sited property.[4] What that means is that the non-UK assets of an EPT are not subject to IHT, even though the settlor or an IIP holder later becomes domiciled in and dies in the UK. When combined with the favourable tax legislation noted in 5(d) below, with respect to capital gains taxation of non-UK resident trusts for the benefit of non-UK domiciled persons, such trusts offer significant UK tax protection and highly advantageous structuring for the non-UK domiciled UK resident. Such provisions are equally applicable to discretionary or interest in possession trusts.

This subject is addressed in detail in **Chapters 13** and **15**.

5. Other key concepts

a. 'Potentially exempt transfers' (PETs)

A potentially exempt transfer (PET) is the reason why most lifetime transfers are simply not subject to IHT. The UK transfer tax regime (though not the capital gains tax regime) is in most cases willing to forego taxing lifetime transfers as long as the transferor gives away his property, without retaining any benefit, more than seven years prior to his death. Therefore outright gifts, gifts into IIP trusts, to A&M trusts or to certain other favoured trusts (see **Chapter 6**) may qualify for such treatment. Transfers of value to companies or to discretionary trusts are always chargeable and do not qualify as potentially exempt.

---

[4] In addition, with respect to transfers on or after 16 October 2002, shares of a UK-authorised unit trust or an open-ended investment company will also be 'excluded property' if held by a trust settled by person who was not then UK IHT domiciled: IHTA 1984, s 48(3A).

Preface

b. 'Gift with reservation of benefit' rules

Where a donor makes a gift (whether immediately chargeable or a potentially exempt transfer) he cannot reserve any benefit (by way of legal or informal arrangement) from the transferred property at any time within seven years of his death. If he does, the value of the entire transferred asset will be clawed back into his estate even if he does survive by seven years. Unlike the UK equivalent of the 'grantor trust' rules which tax a settlor on trust income or gains if he *or his spouse* can benefit, the IHT reservation of benefit rules (like the US estate tax rules) only apply to an interest retained by the *settlor*.

A reserved benefit needs to be distinguished from an asset or interest which is separated from the gifted property and simply 'retained'. For example, retention of a life interest[5] by a donor is a 'retained' asset, whereas inclusion of a donor in a discretionary beneficial class is a 'reserved benefit'. Since a benefit is reserved even if the settlor is not a named beneficiary, but could be added as such, the settlor should specifically be excluded from potential discretionary benefit if the intention in settling the trust is to remove assets from the IHT charge.

The reservation of benefit rules apply to lifetime transfers to discretionary trusts, even though such transfers are taxable at a 20% rate, though provisions relieve potential double charges.

Under US estate tax rules, trust assets may be included in the settlor's taxable estate if he either retains certain interests as a beneficiary (eg a settlor retained life interest) or if he has power to control beneficial enjoyment of trust assets (even if he isn't a beneficiary). In contrast, the UK gifts with reservation rules focus on the settlor's ability to access the transferred assets, not his ability to determine benefits conferred on third parties.

c. Exempt spousal transfers

Gifts or bequests to a spouse are exempt from IHT, whether made outright or in an inter vivos or testamentary trust in which the spouse has an IIP – subject to one exception: a *transfer* by a UK domiciled spouse (for IHT purposes) to a spouse who is not UK domiciled (for IHT purposes) is subject to IHT if in excess of the decedent's unused nil rate band (currently £263,000 for 2004/05) plus an exemption of £55,000, subject to any greater estate tax treaty relief (see **chapter 7**); however, a *lifetime gift* by a UK domiciled spouse to a non-domiciled spouse, outright or in a spousal IIP trust, is a PET and under the general rules may be exempted if the donor survives seven years.

The gifts with reservation rules do not generally apply to exempt spousal transfers.

---

[5] Which remains included in his taxable estate for other reasons.

Preface

The UK regime has a significant advantage over the US spousal transfer rules, which only allow exempt transfers where the donee spouse is a US citizen. In the UK system, spouses can freely transfer assets between themselves as long as both are UK domiciled, both are non-UK domiciled or the donee spouse is UK domiciled.

d. 'Domicile' – am I there yet?

Domicile is a hugely important concept in the UK tax system. UK domicile, not nationality, is the basis for global IHT taxation and for global taxation of income and gains to UK domiciliaries who are also UK resident. Conversely, an individual who is not UK domiciled is generally only subject to IHT on UK sited assets such as real property and securities. Even more significantly, a non-domiciled UK resident is generally subject to UK tax on income and gains from UK sources but only on foreign income or gains remitted to the UK (ie brought to or in some cases indirectly enjoyed in the UK). Gains realised by a non-UK resident trust may be distributed tax-free to UK resident non-domiciliary beneficiaries, while income tax planning is also possible. To non-UK domiciliary residents with money, the UK is one of the world's most tax-favourable onshore jurisdictions.

The UK domicile and residence rules are currently under review, as periodically occurs. In 2002 the Labour Government announced its intention to review the rules and a White Paper was issued on 9 April 2003, though it does not appear that change is imminent. As on previous occasions the review has brought into focus the difficulties of modifying the present regime; not least because other countries also have their own favoured tax regimes and there is a need to maintain a level playing field for the UK as a location for global business activities, in what is generally a highly competitive environment.

Domicile normally refers to the place which is a person's permanent home – which may or may not be where he currently resides. If living there already, it may be the place he never intends to leave permanently or, if not currently living there, the place to which he always intends to return at some future time.

Domicile status can change. A person can acquire a new 'domicile of choice', generally by severing ties with one country or state and physically moving to another with the intent to remain there permanently. Domicile is a matter of fact, circumstance and intent, evidenced not so much by declarations as by one's lifestyle. The same factors, broadly speaking, define domicile for both US and UK tax purposes.

The UK, however, has a legal concept of a 'domicile of origin' totally lacking in the American legal system. In the UK system everyone has a domicile of origin, being the domicile of a person's father at the time of that person's birth. After age 16, a person can acquire an independent domicile, although most 16-year-olds would not have the requisite intention.

A domicile of origin is a very tenacious concept. Although it can be lost by acquisition of a domicile of choice, subsequent departure from that jurisdiction of

Preface

choice will cause a reversion to one's domicile of origin until a new domicile of choice is acquired. This is fundamentally different from the US, where the prior domicile of choice would continue.

The UK also has a concept of deemed domicile, which applies solely for IHT purposes. Such deemed IHT domicile is acquired by being UK income tax resident in all or part of 17 out of the prior 20 *UK* tax years (being from 6 April to the following 5 April). Hence a person who was an income tax resident of the UK from 1 April 1990 through to 30 March 2006 will be deemed domiciled in the UK for IHT purposes as of 6 April 2005. Do not confuse deemed IHT domicile with domicile for UK income and gains tax purposes, for which UK domicile under general law principles is relevant.

e. *'Residence' – am I there yet?*

The UK has two concepts of income tax residence. These two concepts, – 'residence' and 'ordinary residence' – derive from case law and Revenue Practice and are summarized in an Inland Revenue booklet, IR20. These concepts are variously used, with or without reference to domicile status, in defining the taxability of offshore income and gains.

An individual will be 'resident' in the UK in any tax year in which he is physically present in the UK for at least 183 days, not counting arrival and departure days. He will also be resident in the UK if his days of presence are 91 or more, taken over a four tax-year average period. 'Ordinary resident' status, which looks at habitual UK presence over a longer period, is relevant for certain taxes and is also achieved through a UK presence of 91 days or more, looking at the total days over four consecutive UK tax years. Depending on an individual's intentions as to length of stay when he first comes to the UK, he may in fact become resident (and ordinarily resident) from the outset. These concepts are considered in more detail in **Chapter 9**.

f. *Capital gains issues and 'connected party' transfers*

As a part of 'looking right' rather than 'left', American practitioners would do well to remember that the UK has entirely separate regimes for taxing income and capital gains. When a UK adviser uses the word 'income' he means 'income' and not capital gains, which are taxed under the Taxation of Chargeable Gains Act 1992. When a US practitioner says 'income' you know he's including capital gains. Even though differences in US taxation of income and capital gains abound, they are taxed under a single Code.

The UK system has a rather sensible rule that transfers between related ('connected') parties will never be arm's length in practice and therefore such transactions are generally deemed sales at market value as 'connected party' transfers. This rule *generally* extends to donative transfers by settlors to trustees, trustees to beneficiaries and family members to other family members. Although they are

Preface

connected parties, transfers to spouses are at no gain, no loss – in other words, the cost basis of the donor spouse carries over to the donee for capital gains tax (CGT) purposes.

6. Tax administration and enforcement

The body responsible for administering and enforcing UK taxes generally is the Commissioners of Inland Revenue. In practice and in this book, the Inland Revenue is commonly referred to as the *Revenue*. In particular, inheritance tax is managed by a specialist team at the Capital Taxes Office. Inspectors of Taxes deal with day-to-day matters and Collectors of Taxes deal with the collection of the tax. UK tax law is amended by legislation on an annual basis following a Budget issued by the Chancellor of the Exchequer (responsible for the Treasury), which generally occurs in March (or occasionally in early April). The Budget is followed by a Finance Bill, which is debated in Parliament and then passed into legislation as a 'Finance Act' each summer.

There are many relevant statutes, which have been consolidated from time to time, but the following Acts of Parliament are the key taxation statutes which represent legislation on the different taxes discussed in this book:

- the Inheritance Tax Act 1984 (IHTA 1984);
- the Income and Corporation Taxes Act 1988 (ICTA 1988);
- the Taxation of Chargeable Gains Act 1992 (TCGA 1992); and
- the Income Tax (Earnings and Pensions) Act 2003 (ITEPA 2003).

The last Act in the above list is part of a tax law rewrite to attempt to codify the legislation into plain English. The drafting of other such legislation is also in hand.

Various means are used to supplement the primary legislation and its interpretation.

Statutory Instruments. These are documents subordinate to, and authorised by, the legislation. For example, a Finance Act may authorise the Treasury to define detailed legislative provisions by issuing Regulations, which will be implemented through a Statutory Instrument. Such *Regulations* will supplement the principle taxing statutes and provide the detailed framework of a particular provision.

Extra Statutory Concessions. Certain situations may be treated on a favourable basis only by concession. Where they constitute normal Revenue practice, such concessions are generally published. For example, the tax legislation strictly applies on a full tax year basis but in some situations by concession the Revenue treat a person as resident only from the point when they arrive in or leave the UK. The Revenue will normally follow the position it sets out in a published Concession unless the specific circumstances are being used for tax avoidance, in which case the Concession can be withdrawn.

Statements of Practice and **Press Releases.** These are formal pronouncements which explain the Inland Revenue's interpretation of legislation and the way they apply the law in practice.

Preface

Inland Revenue Manuals and Tax Bulletins. The Manuals are the Revenue's published internal staff guidance on the application of tax law and can provide a useful insight into how the Revenue views certain legislation and approaches various tax issues. In addition, the Revenue provides a variety of explanatory publications for the taxpayer on various areas of the tax law as well as a regular *Tax Bulletin*. These all give general guidance, though they do not address particular taxpayer situations. Whilst they publicise the Revenue view of the law and indicate how they will apply it in a particular area, it is not always accepted as the correct interpretation and there is nothing to preclude a contrary position being taken by a taxpayer on appeal to the Commissioners (see below) or courts.

The UK has no general ability to call on the Revenue for a pre-transaction ruling (such as the US PLRs) and normally planning will need to be undertaken on the basis of the legislation as it is understood at the time by all of the parties, taking into account any views the Revenue may have made public in the above. There is, however, a Code of Practice under which a taxpayer may ask the Revenue for advice on its interpretation of the law if it falls into certain specified categories.[6] There are also certain specific legislative provisions which enable a taxpayer to make an application for prior clearance of the tax treatment of some transactions (eg where a share-for-share exchange is made on a takeover, and the taxpayer wishes to ensure no taxable gains accrue but his cost base carries over to the new shares).

If a dispute arises between the taxpayer and the Revenue an appeal can be made in a variety of circumstances either to the General or Special Appeal Commissioners. The General Commissioners are lay persons appointed on a voluntary basis whilst the Special Commissioners are specialist full-time civil servants (albeit independent of the Revenue and appointed by the Lord Chancellor). Appeals against a decision of the Appeal Commissioners can be made to the High Court and then on to the Court of Appeal and finally to the House of Lords.

Robert L Williams, Richard P Layman and Dawn Nicholson

---

[6] These are the interpretation of legislation passed in the last four Finance Acts; the application of double taxation agreements; the employment or self-employment status of an individual; Statements of Practice and Extra Statutory Concessions; areas of major public interest. They specifically state it must be an area of genuine uncertainty and that they will not assist with tax planning or transactions designed to reduce a charge which might otherwise arise.

Disclaimer

This publication is designed to provide accurate and authoritative information in regard to the subject matter covered. It is sold or distributed with the understanding that the Publisher is not engaged in rendering legal, accounting or other professional services. The reader is strongly advised that although the publication contains legal references and discussion of available planning scenarios, the authors are not providing legal, accounting, tax or other professional advice; that the views set forth herein are the personal views of the authors and do not necessarily reflect the views of the firm or company with which the authors are associated; that the planning may not be relevant for a particular reader or use; that the legal references or discussion of planning may not reflect all relevant laws applicable to the effectiveness of planning in any particular factual situation and/or at any particular time; and that the reader is solely responsible for determining whether any planning is appropriate and to consider all information that may affect the utility of the planning discussed in any situation. With respect to the entire publication, the reader must consider all applicable UK, foreign and US federal, state and local laws, and although diligent effort has been made to ensure the accuracy of these materials at the time of publication, the authors and publisher assume no responsibility for updating the same and no responsibility for any reader's reliance on any information or opinions expressed herein, and encourage all readers to verify all items by reviewing the original sources.

Acknowledgements

The authors acknowledge the tireless patience of various of their colleagues, including Philip Reynolds, Laura Kermally and Martin McGurn of Ernst & Young LLP (London), Ann Wylie and Paul Frith of Regent Tax Consultants Ltd (St Helier) and Jean Sheeley and Nancy Rocco of Jones Day LLP (Cleveland).

About the Authors

Robert L Williams is a US international tax attorney based in Jersey, Channel Islands. From 2000–04, he was a director of Regent Tax Consultants Ltd, an affiliate of the Royal Bank of Canada in St Helier, Jersey. Prior thereto, he joined Arthur Young in 1985 as the first member of its London-based international tax group. As an international tax partner with Ernst & Young Jersey from 1993 until 2000, he had a leading role in designing US tax focused offshore trust structures including variable annuity, life insurance, trust and company products. He was a founding member of Ernst & Young International's Private Wealth Group and editor of its 31 country internal reference book, *Private Wealth Taxation* (4th edn, 1998).

Prior to 1985, Lee practiced trade regulation, estate planning and international tax law for 16 years in Washington DC and Seattle. He was an adjunct professor of taxation at the University of Puget Sound (1981) and at Golden Gate University (1982–1983), where he taught courses in income taxation, estate and gift taxation and taxation of corporations and shareholders. He has been a speaker at various international tax conferences and courses since 1981 and has written articles and books on international tax issues.

Qualifications

BA (Hons) Amherst College, JD University of Washington, LLM (Taxation).
George Washington University.
Admitted to the Washington State and District of Columbia Bars.

Rick Layman is a partner in the international law firm Jones Day, currently resident in the firm's Cleveland, Ohio office. He joined Jones Day in 1980 and has practiced in the firm's personal tax area for more than 20 years, with special emphasis on US and international estate planning. Rick's US practice involves a full range of income and transfer tax planning for individuals and families. This includes related charitable planning as well as estate administration, audits, and related IRS disputes. He also has a strong international planning background, which he developed when he practiced in Jones Day's London Office from 1989–93. He advises US individuals resident in the United Kingdom and elsewhere in the world on traditional US estate planning, including special issues related to foreign transfer taxes, non-US spouses, and estate and gift tax treaties. Rick also advises on other aspects of international planning, including US investment and pre-immigration tax planning for non-US persons, and on expatriation and the use of foreign trusts by US taxpayers.

Qualifications

Ohio Northern University (BA with highest distinction, 1977).
University of Michigan (Law Review; Order of the Coif; JD magna cum laude; 1980).
Admitted to the Ohio bar.

About the authors

Dawn Nicholson is an English solicitor who, following qualification in 1981, has specialised exclusively in private client matters from within the UK legal and accounting professions. Dawn joined the firm of Arthur Young McCelland Moores in 1984 and in 1991 became a partner of the private client department of the UK firm of Ernst & Young LLP following the merger of Arthur Young and Ernst & Whinney.

Her areas of specialism have an emphasis on domestic and international trusts, estates and personal tax planning for high net worth clients and include a broad range of internationally focused individuals and trustees. She has also written and lectured extensively over the years on matters within her area of expertise.

Qualifications

LLB (Hons) University of Birmingham.
Solicitor – Member of the Law Society.
TEP – Member of the Society of Trust and Estate Practitioners.

Contents

	Page
Preface	v
Disclaimer	xxi
Acknowledgements	xxiii
About the Authors	xxv

	Para
Chapter 1 Types of Tax	1.1
A. United States	1.1
1. Introduction	1.1
2. Estate tax	1.2
3. Gift tax	1.13
4. Generation-skipping tax	1.26
5. Possible repeal	1.31
B. United Kingdom	1.34
1. Introduction	1.34
2. Transfers on death	1.38
3. Charge to income tax by reference to enjoyment of property previously owned	1.51
a. Excluded transactions	1.55
b. Exemptions from charge	1.56
c. Land	1.59
d. Chattels	1.60
e. Intangible assets	1.61
4. Lifetime transfers	1.67
Chapter 2 Who and What is Taxed	2.1
A. United States	2.1
1. Introduction	2.1
2. Citizens and domiciliaries	2.2
3. Non-domiciled aliens (NDAs)	2.8
a. Gift tax	2.9
b. Estate tax	2.13
c. Generation-skipping tax (GST)	2.19
4. Tax-motivated expatriates	2.21
B. United Kingdom	2.32
1. Introduction	2.32
2. UK domiciliaries	2.33
3. Non-UK domiciliaries	2.46
4. Liability for payment	2.51
Chapter 3 Deductions, Exclusions, Exemptions and Credits	3.1
A. United States	3.1
1. Introduction	3.1
2. Gift tax deductions, exclusions and credits	3.4
a. US citizens and domiciliaries	3.4

Contents

b. Non-domiciled aliens (NDAs)	3.13
c. Tax-motivated expatriates	3.16
3. Estate tax deductions and credits	3.18
a. US citizens and domiciliaries	3.18
b. NDAs	3.29
c. Tax-motivated expatriates	3.32
4. GST deductions, exclusions, exemptions and credits	3.34
a. US citizens and domiciliaries	3.35
b. NDAs	3.52
c. Tax-motivated expatriates	3.54
B. United Kingdom	3.56
1. Introduction	3.56
2. Main exemptions and reliefs in UK	3.57
3. Business property and agricultural property reliefs/other reliefs and exemptions	3.63
a. Business property relief	3.64
b. Agricultural property relief	3.71
c. Exemptions	3.74
4. Excluded property	3.82
5. Post death variations and disclaimers	3.83

Chapter 4 Transfers to Spouses — 4.1

A. United States	4.1
1. Introduction	4.1
2. History	4.2
3. Types of qualifying transfers – Outright gifts and marital trusts	4.6
a. General power of appointment trusts	4.7
b. Qualified terminable interest property (QTIP) trusts	4.9
c. Qualified domestic trusts (QDOTs)	4.16
d. Marital lead/charitable remainder trust	4.27
B. United Kingdom	4.28
1. Introduction	4.28
2. History	4.29
3. Types of qualifying transfers	4.33

Chapter 5 Tax Rates and Computation — 5.1

A. United States	5.1
1. Introduction	5.1
2. Estate and gift tax rate brackets	5.2
3. Equal application to citizens, domiciliaries and NDAs	5.6
4. Impact of prior taxable gifts	5.9
5. The 'tax-on-tax' effect of the US estate tax	5.15
6. Generation-skipping tax (GST)	5.17
B. United Kingdom	5.24
1. Introduction	5.24
2. Inheritance tax rate brackets	5.25
3. Impact of prior gifts	5.26
4. 'Tax on tax'	5.35
5. Liability and incidence of tax	5.38

Chapter 6 Transfer Taxes on Trustees — 6.1
A. United States — 6.1
   1. Introduction — 6.1
   2. QTIP marital trust — 6.2
   3. QDOT marital trust — 6.6
   4. GST imposed on taxable terminations — 6.8
   5. 'Statutory' executor — 6.10
   6. Transferee liability — 6.14
      a. Transferee liability for unpaid gift and estate taxes — 6.15
      b. Transferee liability under state law — 6.16
      c. Transferee liability with respect to life insurance or appointed property — 6.17
   7. Jurisdictional issues — 6.18
      a. Personal jurisdiction over trustee in US courts — 6.19
      b. Personal jurisdiction over a custodian of US assets — 6.23
      c. In rem jurisdiction over trust assets in US courts — 6.26
      d. Jurisdiction over the trustee in foreign courts and enforcement of tax judgments — 6.27
B. United Kingdom — 6.32
   1. Introduction — 6.32
   2. Discretionary trusts — 6.34
   3. Accumulation and maintenance trusts — 6.47
   4. Fixed interest trusts — 6.56
   5. Excluded property trusts — 6.62
   6. Lease for life — 6.67

Chapter 7 US and UK Estate Tax Treaties — 7.1
A. United States — 7.1
   1. Introduction — 7.1
   2. Older treaties — 7.3
   3. OECD treaties — 7.10
   4. US/Canadian treaty — 7.20
B. United Kingdom — 7.31
   1. Introduction — 7.31
   2. Double tax treaties — 7.34
      a. Older treaties — 7.37
         (i) France — 7.37
         (ii) India — 7.38
         (iii) Italy — 7.39
         (iv) Pakistan — 7.40
      b. Newer treaties — 7.41
         (i) Ireland — 7.42
         (ii) Netherlands — 7.43
         (iii) South Africa — 7.44
         (iv) Sweden — 7.45
         (v) Switzerland — 7.46
C. The US/UK estate and gift tax treaty — 7.47
   1. Introduction — 7.47
   2. Scope and taxes covered — 7.48
   3. Fiscal domicile — 7.51

4. Exception: immovable property (real estate) and permanent establishment property	7.54
5. Exception: taxation of nationals permitted	7.56
6. Taxing rights where transferor/decedent not domiciled in either country	7.57
7. Deductions and exemptions	7.58
8. Article 8(5) limits US tax exposure	7.63
9. Credits	7.68
10. A decedent's exposure to US/UK transfer tax	7.71

Chapter 8 Gains Tax on Gifts and Bequests — 8.1

A. United States	8.1
1. Introduction	8.1
2. Distributions from trusts and estates	8.4
a. Property in kind	8.5
b. Property sold to a beneficiary	8.6
3. Code § 684 – the basics	8.8
4. Code § 684 – nuances and enigmas	8.15
a. Release of powers	8.16
b. Loss of US beneficiary	8.17
c. Settlor's death – generally	8.18
d. Settlor's death – insurance	8.24
e. Grantor's departure from the US	8.34
f. Application of Code § 684 to pre-immigration trusts – a possible Code § 679(a)(4) tax trap?	8.44
g. Pre-immigration trusts – beyond Code § 679(a)(4)	8.51
5. Strategies for dealing with Code § 684 exposure	8.55
a. General strategies where appreciated property (or insurance) is held in a foreign grantor trust	8.55
b. Emigration strategies	8.62
c. Immigration strategies	8.66
B. United Kingdom	8.69
1. Introduction	8.69

Chapter 9 Capital Gains Taxation – Residents — 9.1

A. United States	9.1
1. Introduction	9.1
2. Individuals	9.2
a. Green card test	9.4
b. Substantial presence test	9.6
c. Capital gains 'trap'	9.10
3. Entities	9.14
B. United Kingdom	9.15
1. Introduction	9.15
2. Individuals	9.17
a. Residence	9.17
b. Ordinary residence	9.24
c. Domicile	9.27
d. Temporary non-residents	9.30
3. Personal representatives and trustees	9.33

Chapter 10 Capital Gains Deductions and Exclusions   10.1
A. United States   10.1
B. United Kingdom   10.4
   1. Introduction   10.4
   2. Exempt assets   10.5
   3. Exempt gains   10.6
   4. Exempt disposals   10.7
   5. Tax reliefs   10.8
      a. Taper relief and indexation relief   10.8
      b. Hold-over relief   10.15
         (i) Business assets   10.16
         (ii) Gifts subject to inheritance tax   10.18
         (iii) General   10.19
         (iv) Reinvestment relief   10.23

Chapter 11 Tax Basis Rules for Gifts and Bequests   11.1
A. United States   11.1
   1. Introduction   11.1
   2. Property acquired by gift   11.2
   3. Property acquired from a decedent   11.7
   4. GST transfers   11.15
B. United Kingdom   11.17
   1. Introduction   11.17
   2. General rules   11.19
      a. Market value rebasing   11.20
      b. Other deductions   11.22
      c. Matching rules   11.24
   3. Connected persons   11.28
      a. Property acquired by gift   11.30
      b. Property acquired from a decedent   11.33

Chapter 12 US Income Taxation of Trusts, Estates, Grantors and Beneficiaries   12.1
A. Summary   12.1
   1. Taxation of the 'grantor'   12.2
   2. Taxation of a non-grantor trust   12.3
   3. Taxation of beneficiaries   12.4
      a. US non-grantor trust/US beneficiary   12.5
      b. US Non-grantor trust/NRA beneficiary   12.6
      c. Foreign non-grantor trust/US beneficiaries   12.7
      d. Foreign non-grantor trust/NRA beneficiaries   12.8
B. Income tax residence of trusts   12.9
   1. The Court Test   12.12
   2. The Control Test   12.16
C. Taxation of the grantor   12.19
   1. General grantor trust rules   12.22
   2. Grantor and others taxed as the owner   12.32
   3. NRAs respected as owners only under limited circumstances   12.40
      a. Fixed or determinable annual or periodic income (FDAPI)   12.46
      b. Effectively connected income (ECI)   12.47
      c. Gains from the sale of US real estate interests   12.48

Contents

4. Foreign trusts and Code § 679	12.49
D. US taxation of domestic non-grantor trusts	12.55
1. Distribution deduction and DNI	12.57
2. Rates	12.65
E. US taxation of foreign non-grantor trusts	12.67
F. Taxation of the US beneficiaries on distributions from non-grantor trusts	12.71
1. Beneficiaries of simple trusts	12.74
2. Beneficiaries of complex trusts	12.79
3. Accumulation distributions, the throwback tax and UNI	12.85
a. General	12.85
b. Computation of the throwback tax	12.90
c. Application of throwback tax to immigrants	12.99
d. Special throwback rules related to foreign trusts	12.104
4. Loans from foreign trusts as distributions	12.118
5. Transfers through intermediaries	12.120
G. US taxation of foreign beneficiaries on distributions from non-grantor trusts	12.124
H. Taxation of estates and beneficiaries	12.132
I. Reporting requirements (and penalties) related to foreign trusts	12.137
1. Special reporting obligations	12.138
a. Reportable events	12.138
(i) Creation of/transfer to a foreign trust	12.139
(ii) Death of a US income tax or estate tax owner	12.140
(iii) Grantor trust ownership	12.141
(iv) Distributions from foreign trusts	12.142
(v) Gifts and bequests	12.143
b. Treatment of domestic trusts	12.144
c. Penalties	12.145
d. How, when and where to report	12.146
2. Treasury Form 90–22.1 reporting of foreign financial accounts	12.151
3. Income tax reporting and employer identification numbers (EINs)	12.153

Chapter 13 UK Income Taxation of Trusts, Settlors and Beneficiaries   **13.1**

A. Summary	13.1
B. Tax residence of trusts	13.10
1. Income tax residence of trust	13.10
2. Capital gains tax residence of trust	13.11
C. Taxation of trustees	13.13
1. Income taxation of discretionary trusts	13.13
2. Income taxation of fixed interest (interest in possession) trusts	13.18
3. Income taxation of bare trusts	13.20
4. Capital gains taxation of discretionary and fixed interest trusts	13.21
a. UK resident trusts	13.22
(i) Trustee taper relief	13.23
(ii) CGT on trust distribution or resettlement	13.27
(iii) Holdover relief for business property and assets subject to an IHT charge	13.29
(iv) Taxation of bare trusts	13.30
b. Exit charge on emigration of UK resident trust	13.32

D. Taxation of a UK resident settlor/grantor	13.39
1. Income tax	13.42
a. ICTA 1988, Pt XV – settlor interested trust income tax provisions	13.42
b. Transfer of assets abroad – ICTA 1988, ss 739 and 740	13.47
2. Capital gains tax	13.52
a. UK resident trusts	13.52
b. Non-UK resident trusts	13.55
E. Taxation of the beneficiaries	13.63
1. Income tax	13.63
2. Capital gains tax	13.70
F. Inland Revenue proposals for a modern income tax and capital gains tax system for trusts	13.82
1. The proposals	13.84
a. Definitions of trust/settlement, settlor and settlor-interested trust	13.84
b. Residence test for trusts	13.88
c. Basic rate band	13.89
d. Income streaming generally and capital gains of estates	13.93
e. Types of trust	13.98
f. Special trusts for disadvantaged groups and estates	13.99

Chapter 14 Non-domiciliary Planning to Remove Assets from US Estate Tax	**14.1**
A. Introduction and summary	14.1
B. Consider the scope of a UK person's exposure to US estate tax	14.10
C. Article 8(5) of the US/UK treaty	14.13
D. US/UK rate crossover point	14.15
E. US marital deduction planning	14.21
1. US gift tax considerations	14.22
2. US estate tax considerations.	14.26
3. UK IHT considerations	14.30
F. US estate tax reduction techniques	14.33
1. Gifts of US intangibles	14.34
2. Simple strategies for US-situated tangible property	14.36
3. Holding or acquiring US property in trust	14.39
4. Holding or acquiring US property in a corporation	14.50
a. Using a domestic US corporation	14.51
b. Using a foreign corporation	14.55
c. Foundations (Stiftungs) and Anstalts	14.56
d. Code §§ 2036 and 2038	14.58
e. Foreign hybrid entities	14.69
f. FIRPTA considerations	14.71
5. Holding or acquiring US property in a partnership	14.72
a. Aggregate theory	14.74
b. Entity theory	14.77
c. Limited precedent	14.78
d. Domestic attacks on FLPs – aggregation revisited	14.85
e. Conclusion	14.89
6. Joint Ownership	14.90

Contents

7. Estate freezes and split purchases	14.95
a. US corporate estate freeze	14.98
b. Split-interest purchase or formation of a US corporation	14.100
c. Split-interest purchase of US real estate	14.102
8. Non-recourse v recourse mortgages	14.106
9. Permanent establishment property	14.108
10. Life insurance	14.115
G. Alternative structures for holding US income-producing real estate	14.117
1. Summary of relevant income taxes	14.119
2. Summary of structures	14.120
a. Direct ownership	14.120
b. United States real property holding corporation (USRPHC)	14.121
c. Foreign holding company	14.125
d. Foreign company owing a US real property holding company	14.126
e. Foreign trust planning for US commercial real estate	14.127

Chapter 15 Non-domiciliary Planning to Remove Assets from UK Inheritance Tax   **15.1**

A. Introduction	15.1
B. Scope of UK tax exposure	15.2
1. US citizen domiciled in the UK	15.3
2. UK taxation of US domiciliary generally limited to article 6/7 property	15.4
C. US/UK rate crossover point	15.7
1. Crossover for US taxpayer with UK article 6/7 property	15.7
2. Crossover point for a US citizen who is domiciled in the UK	15.10
D. Spousal deduction planning	15.13
1. Non-UK domiciled individuals who do not intend to become UK domiciled	15.13
2. Married individuals who are both UK domiciled or deemed domiciled, one of whom is a US national or domiciliary	15.19
3. Married individuals where the spouse with assets is UK domiciled and the other spouse is not domiciled in the UK for IHT purposes	15.20
4. Individuals who are likely to become UK domiciled for IHT purposes	15.24
E. UK lifetime gifts to non-spouses – 'potentially exempt transfers'	15.25
F. Permanent establishment property	15.31
G. Excluded property trusts and offshore holding vehicles	15.32
H. Grantor trust and US transfer tax issues	15.48

Chapter 16 US Pre-Immigration Planning   **16.1**

A. Introduction and summary	16.1
B. Domicile – Am I there yet?	16.5
1. General principles	16.7
2. Domicile of UK emigrants	16.10
3. Summary	16.16
C. US income tax resident – Am I there yet?	16.19
D. Pre-immigration US income tax planning	16.26
1. Realize gains, income or deductions before or after becoming a US income tax resident	16.27

2. Bed and breakfasting	16.30
3. Avoiding onerous US 'Anti-avoidance' Rules (CFCs, FPHCs and PFICs)	16.32
4. Examine income tax implications of existing trusts	16.43
5. Income tax planning using variable insurance products	16.54
E. Pre-immigration gift planning	16.65
1. Avoid limits to US gift tax exemption	16.66
2. Avoid marital deduction restrictions on gifts to non-citizen spouses	16.67
3. Take advantage of the unlimited GST exemption	16.69
4. Transfer troublesome assets	16.70
5. Estate freeze	16.71
6. Estate planning	16.74
F. Pre-immigration gifts (to others) in trust	16.75
1. Completed gift	16.76
2. Excluded from US taxable estate	16.78
3. Grantor trust considerations	16.80
G. UK (and other foreign) tax considerations to pre-US immigration gift planning	16.85
H. Examine existing trusts for US estate tax exposure	16.98
1. Trusts funded by the settlor/immigrant	16.99
2. Trusts funded by others	16.102
I. Pre-immigration estate planning – drop off trusts	16.107
1. US asset protection trusts	16.117
2. Foreign asset protection trusts	16.121
J. UK tax implications for drop off trusts	16.123
K. Pre-immigration GST planning	16.130
1. Pre-immigration gifts	16.131
2. Trusts excluded from immigrant settlor/beneficiary's estate	16.132
L. Pre-immigration strategies for US real property	16.133
Chapter 17 US or Foreign Trust Providing for UK Beneficiary	**17.1**
A. Summary of relevant income and capital gains tax planning considerations	17.1
B. Planning income and capital gains distributions with respect to UK resident beneficiaries	17.5
C. UK tax consequences of US living trusts – a trap for unwary US expatriates	17.11
Chapter 18 UK or Foreign Trusts Providing for a US Beneficiary	**18.1**
A. Introduction	18.1
B. Foreign grantor trusts with foreign grantors	18.8
1. Existing 'grandfathered' grantor trusts.	18.10
2. Revocable trusts	18.13
3. Settlor and spouse only trusts	18.15
4. Planning for the post-grantor trust phase	18.17
C. Foreign non-grantor trusts with US beneficiaries	18.22
1. Domesticate the foreign trust	18.23
2. Rhythm method distributions of accumulated income	18.26
3. Distribution of all current trust income and net gains	18.27
4. UNI accumulations followed by DNI 'annuity' distributions	18.30

Contents

5. 'Capital First' trust distributions	18.34
6. Depleting a trust using the default distribution rule	18.35
7. Beneficiary's rent free use of trust owned property	18.36
8. Beneficiary's sale of assets to trust	18.37
9. Distribution of trust assets to settlor followed by a gift over	18.38
10. Distribution to other non-US beneficiaries followed by a gift over	18.42

Chapter 19 US Spouse Providing for a UK Spouse	**19.1**
A. Introduction	19.1
B. Lifetime gifts to the UK spouse by the US spouse	19.4
1. US gift tax implications to the US donor spouse	19.5
2. UK IHT implications to US donor spouse	19.8
3. US estate tax implications to the UK donee spouse	19.12
4. UK IHT implications to the UK donee spouse	19.14
C. Provisions for the UK surviving spouse at the US spouse's death	19.16
1. US estate tax implications to the US decedent spouse	19.18
2. UK IHT implications to the US decedent spouse	19.21
a. US decedent spouse not UK domiciled	19.21
b. US decedent spouse UK domiciled	19.27
3. US estate tax implications at UK surviving spouse's death	19.38
4. UK IHT implications at the UK surviving spouse's later death	19.42
a. IHT exposure depends on whether QDOT (or IIP by-pass trust) is an excluded property trust	19.42
b. Foreign tax credit issues	19.45
c. Excluded property planning: final thoughts	19.47

Chapter 20 A UK Spouse Providing for a US Spouse	**20.1**
A. Introduction	20.1
B. Lifetime gifts to the US spouse by the UK spouse	20.3
1. UK IHT implications to the UK donor spouse	20.4
2. US gift tax implications to the UK donor spouse	20.8
3. UK IHT implications to the US donee spouse	20.11
4. US estate tax implications to the US donee spouse	20.25
C. Provision for the US surviving spouse at the UK spouse's death3	20.31
1. UK IHT implications to the UK decedent spouse	20.31
a. General principles.	20.31
b. 'Nightmare on Planning Street' – a UK domiciled decedent and a US spouse who is not domiciled in the UK	20.40
2. US estate tax implications to the UK decedent spouse	20.46
3. UK IHT implications to the US surviving spouse	20.48
4. US estate tax implications to the US surviving spouse	20.50

	Page
Appendix I UK Tax Tables 2004/05	421
Appendix II US Tax Tables 2004	425
Appendix III 2001 United Kingdom-United States Income Tax Treaty	429
Appendix IV 1978 United Kingdom-United States Estate & Gift Tax Treaty	461
Appendix V 1995 Protocol to 1980 Canada-United States Income Tax Treaty	473
Appendix VI A Decedent's Exposure to UK/US Transfer Tax	491

Appendix VII UK Business Property Relief for Holdings of Unlisted Shares and Securities	497
Appendix VIII Illustrations	501
Appendix IX The American Jobs Creation Act of 2004	505
Index	509

Chapter 1

Types of Tax

A. United States

1. Introduction

1.1 The United States (US) transfer tax system consists of three taxes. The *estate tax*[1] and the *gift tax*[2] impose a tax on transfers made at death and during life. The *generation-skipping tax*[3] (or GST) imposes an additional transfer tax on certain transfers that 'skip' gift and estate tax in the intervening generation as property passes to persons two or more generations below the donor.

2. Estate tax

1.2 The US estate tax is imposed on property owned by a decedent at death.[4] This includes cash and bank accounts, real property (residential and investment), tangible personal property (such as jewelry, furniture, artwork, and automobiles) and intangible personal property (such as stock in public or private companies, partnership interests, notes and bonds).

1.3 A decedent's taxable estate also includes property transferred by the decedent during life (eg to a trust) where the decedent retained certain interests in, or control over, the transferred property. The decedent's retained right as beneficiary to receive trust income or to control benefits (eg through a retained power of appointment or power as trustee of a discretionary trust) brings the trust property into the decedent's taxable estate.[5] Also, a decedent's retained right to vote gifted

---

[1] § 2001 et seq of the US Internal Revenue Code (the 'Code').
[2] Code § 2501 et seq.
[3] Code § 2601 et seq.
[4] Code § 2031 for US citizens or residents; Code § 2103 for non-resident/non-US citizens, herein referred to as 'non domiciled aliens' or 'NDAs'.
[5] Code § 2036(a). The US Internal Revenue Service (IRS or 'the Service') took the position in Rev Rul 79–353, 1979–2 CB 325, that the decedent's retained right to remove and replace trustees of an irrevocable trust was a retained power to control the trust under Code § 2036. The Government lost this issue in *Wall v Comm'r 101 TC 300 (1993)*, a case where the decedent retained the right to replace independent trustees of three irrevocable trusts that she had created for her daughter and grandchildren. The Service acquiesced to *Wall* in Rev Rul 95–58, 1995–2 CB 191. That ruling limits the holding in *Wall* to a situation in which the settlor could remove and replace trustees who are not 'related and subordinate' to him (as that phrase is defined in Code § 672(c)).

1.4 *Types of Tax*

stock in a closely-held business (where the decedent and related parties owned at least 20% of the voting power of all classes of stock) will also cause that stock to be taxed his estate.[6]

1.4 Settlors will sometimes transfer assets to a revocable trust during life to facilitate asset management, probate avoidance and confidentiality. Revocable trusts also typically serve as testamentary devices, directing the disposition of trust property at the decedent's death in the same manner as a will. The decedent's retained right to revoke a trust causes the trust property to be included in her estate.[7] For US estate tax (and also income tax) purposes, the revocable trust is thus transparent.

1.5 If an individual had a right to an annuity or similar payment and that right passed to another upon his or her death, the annuity interest will be taxed in the decedent's estate.[8] This rule generally applies only to the portion of the annuity contract paid for by the decedent (or, in an employment context, by the decedent's employer).[9] This provision causes an employee's rights under a pension plan, as well as a decedent's interest in an individual retirement account (IRA), to be taxed in his estate. Note that the amount included in the taxpayer's estate is the value, not of the decedent's rights in the contract at the date of death, but of the present value of the beneficiary's rights under the contract. For example, if a retiree elects to take a full pension of $2,000 per month during his life but a half-pension for the surviving spouse, the amount included in the retiree's estate will be the present value of the survivor's rights to $1,000 per month for life.

1.6 The decedent's estate also includes the full value of all property held in a joint tenancy (with survivorship rights), unless the estate can prove the decedent's proportionate contribution.[10] For example, the full value of real property owned in joint tenancy by a brother and sister will be taxed in the first sibling's estate, unless the estate can show that the first sibling had contributed only a portion of the purchase price or that the siblings had inherited the property as joint tenants. Similarly, a bank account owned as joint tenants between a parent and child will be taxed in the estate of the first to die, unless the estate can prove disproportionate contributions. An exception is made for joint tenancies between spouses: if the surviving spouse is a US citizen, the first decedent is deemed to own one-half of the jointly-owned property, regardless of contribution.[11]

1.7 In contrast, the decedent's proportionate interest in property held as a tenant in common (without survivorship rights) is taxed in his estate.[12] For example, if a brother and sister (or husband and wife or a parent or child) each owned an undivided 50% interest in property as tenants in common, 50% of that property would be included in the decedent's estate at death.

---

[6] Code § 2036(b).
[7] Code § 2038.
[8] Code § 2039(a).
[9] Code § 2039(b).
[10] Code § 2040(a).
[11] Code § 2040(b) and see also Code § 2056(d)(1)(B) for disallowance of Code § 2040(b) exception for non-citizen spouses.
[12] Code § 2033.

1.8 The decedent's rights as a beneficiary of a trust created by another will generally not cause the trust property to be taxed in the decedent's estate, even if the decedent had been entitled to all trust income.[13] However, there are exceptions. The primary exception is where the decedent possessed a 'general power of appointment' which is defined as a power to appoint the trust to himself, his creditors, his estate, or creditors of his estate.[14] Limited or special powers of appointment do not cause similar problems.[15] A power in the decedent to invade the trust for his benefit will not be considered a general power of appointment, if that power is limited by an 'ascertainable standard relating to the health, education, support or maintenance of the decedent'.[16] Likewise, a power of appointment is not considered a general power of appointment if the decedent can only exercise that power in conjunction with either:

(a) the creator of the power; or

(b) a person having a substantial adverse interest in the trust.[17]

The decedent's estate also includes property held for the decedent's benefit in a so-called 'QTIP' marital deduction trust (qualified terminable interest property trusts – see **4.9** et seq) created by the decedent's spouse.[18] **CHAPTER 4** discusses the marital deduction and marital deduction trusts in more detail.

1.9 Insurance on the decedent's life is taxed in the decedent's estate if the proceeds are payable to the decedent's probate estate or if the decedent had an 'incident of ownership' in the policy.[19] This rule reaches not just policies in which the decedent had all ownership rights (including the right to the cash surrender value), but also a decedent's coverage under his or her employer's group term policy where the decedent's ownership rights are limited to the right to designate beneficiaries.

1.10 Prior to 1982, lifetime gifts made within three years of death were included in the decedent's estate,[20] with credit given for any prior gift tax.[21] This rule subjected post-gift appreciation to transfer tax. After the 1981 Tax Act, however, the three-year rule was restricted to transfers of only certain property.[22] For example, a

---

[13] See, for example, *Helvering v Estate of Rhodes* 117 F 2d 509 (8th Cir 1941), Rev Rul 66–86, 1966–1 CB 216.
[14] Code § 2041.
[15] Code § 2041(b); Treas Reg § 20.2041–1.
[16] Code § 2041(b)(1)(A). Based on the holding in Rev Rul 79–353, 1979–2 CB 325, the Service asserted that a beneficiary's power to replace trustees would essentially give the beneficiary the powers of the trustee, including the power to make discretionary distributions to the beneficiary. Unless those powers were limited by an ascertainable standard, the IRS took the position that the beneficiary would be considered to possess a general power of appointment. PLR 8916032 (21 April 1989)). After *Wall v Comm'r 101 TC 300 (1993)* and Rev Rul 95–58, 1995–2 CB 325, however, the beneficiary's power to remove and replace independent trustees would not cause the trust to be taxed in the beneficiary's estate. PLR 9735023 (30 May 1997).
[17] Code § 2041(b)(1)(C).
[18] Code § 2044.
[19] Code § 2042.
[20] Code § 2035(a).
[21] Code § 2012.
[22] Code § 2035(a).

1.11   *Types of Tax*

taxpayer cannot make a deathbed gift of a life insurance policy on his life and prevent the insurance proceeds from taxation in his estate.

1.11   Gift taxes paid within three years of death are also included in the decedent's taxable estate.[23] This rule effectively eliminates the advantage (discussed in more detail in **CHAPTER 5**) of computing the gift tax only on the property actually transferred to the beneficiary.

1.12   Although most lifetime gifts are not included in the decedent's taxable estate, they are nonetheless relevant in computing the estate tax. As described in more detail in **CHAPTER 5**, prior taxable gifts are taken into account in determining the tax rates that apply to the decedent's estate.[24]

3. Gift tax

1.13   The US gift tax supplements the estate tax and ensures that US transfer tax liability is not avoided by lifetime gifts.[25] Since 1976 the gift and estate tax have shared the same rate table.[26]

1.14   The gift tax is imposed on 'completed' gifts.[27] If the donor makes an outright gift to the beneficiary and retains no power or control over the gifted property, the gift is complete. If, for example, the transfer is made to a trust, and the donor retains a right to modify the trust, the gift is incomplete until a transfer is made to a beneficiary or until the donor's power of modification terminates or lapses.[28]

1.15   The gift tax applies to both direct and indirect transfers. For example, a parent's gratuitous transfer of property to a company owned by her children would be considered an indirect gift to the children. Also, a parent who pays a third party to render services to a child is considered to have made an indirect gift to the child.[29]

1.16   Transfers for 'less than adequate and full consideration in money or money's worth' are considered taxable gifts.[30] Thus, if a parent sells property to a child at a discount, the transaction would be characterized as partially both a sale and a gift.[31] If, however, the sale was for fair value, no gift would result.[32]

---

[23]   Code § 2035(b).
[24]   Code §§ 2001(b) and 2502(a). Taxable gifts are accumulated post-1932 for gift tax purposes and post-1976 for estate tax purposes.
[25]   Prior to 1976, the gift tax rates were substantially lower than the estate tax rates, thus encouraging lifetime gifts. Prior to the 1976 Tax Act, the highest marginal estate tax rate was 77% while the highest marginal gift tax was 'only' 57.75%.
[26]   Code §§ 2001(b) and 2502(a).
[27]   Treas Reg § 25.2511–2; Code §§ 2503 and 2511.
[28]   Treas Reg § 25.2511–2.
[29]   Treas Reg § 25.2511–1(h)(1) and (h)(2).
[30]   Code § 2512(b).
[31]   In a part-sale, part-gift, a proportionate share of the donor's income tax basis is allocated to the gift. The donee will take the donor's basis in the gift component, while the donor's gain on the sale component is measured against the portion of the basis allocated to the sale portion. Treas Reg § 1.1001–1(e).

1.17 A taxpayer's exercise or release of a general power of appointment is also considered a taxable gift.[33] For example, an individual who possesses a right to appoint trust property to anyone including himself will be treated as having made a taxable gift if he appoints trust property to others. Also, an individual who had a temporary power to withdraw trust property and allowed that power to lapse would also be considered to have made a taxable gift.[34]

1.18 A taxpayer with a right to trust income who appoints his interest in the trust principal to another is considered to have made a taxable gift of the discounted present value of his income interest.[35] In addition, a spouse with an interest in a so-called QTIP marital deduction trust is considered to have made a gift of the entire trust (not just the income interest) if she gives away any portion of her income rights.[36]

1.19 An individual's 'qualified disclaimer' of a gift or bequest is not considered a taxable gift.[37] To be qualified, the taxpayer's refusal to accept the gift or bequest must be irrevocable, unconditional, and in writing, delivered to transferor (or his legal representatives) within nine months of the date of the gift or, in the case of transfers at death, within nine months of the decedent's death.[38] In addition, the disclaimant cannot have accepted the transferred property (for example, by taking any benefits of it) and the disclaimed property must pass, without any direction or control by the disclaimant, to someone other than the disclaimant.[39]

1.20 The value of the donor's gift in trust can, under limited circumstances, be reduced by the value of the donor's retained interest. Congress enacted the so-called 'special valuation rules' in 1990[40] to limit this rule to arrangements where the value of the donor's retained interest is capable of somewhat accurate valuation and less susceptible to abuse. Under prior law, a donor's retained right to trust income for a period of years would be valued under IRS valuation tables, even though the assets transferred to a trust consisted of property that was expected to produce little or no

---

[32] Transfers pursuant to a written agreement between divorcing spouses that either:
  (a) settle property or marital rights; or
  (b) provide for the reasonable support of the spouse or the minor children of the marriage,
  are treated as made for adequate and full consideration. Code § 2515A.
[33] Code § 2514(b). Note that the gift tax definition of 'general power of appointment' is the same as the estate tax definition. Compare Code § 2514(c) and Code § 2041(b).
[34] However, lapses that, in any calendar year, do not exceed the greater of:
  • $5,000; or
  • 5% of the value of the property subject to the power (so-called '5 and 5 powers'),
  are not considered taxable gifts. Code § 2514(e).
[35] Rev Rul 79–327, 1979–2 CB 342.
[36] Code § 2519.
[37] Code § 2518.
[38] Code § 2518(b).
[39] Code § 2518(b)(3) and (4). The only exception is for the decedent's surviving spouse, who can receive a benefit in the disclaimed property, but cannot have any continuing control. Code § 2518(b)(4). For example, a surviving spouse might disclaim a portion of an outright bequest and allow that property to pass into trust for her benefit in order to take advantage of the first decedent's estate tax exemption. See **CHAPTER 4**.
[40] Revenue Reconciliation Act 1990 (PL 101–508), § 11602(a), codified at Code §§ 2701–2704.

1.21   Types of Tax

income.[41] Under those circumstances, the IRS tables would overvalue the retained income interest and thus undervalue the donor's remainder interest gift. If the donor survived the period of the retained income interest (and therefore escaped estate tax exposure), the property remaining in the trust could pass without any further gift tax to the remainder beneficiaries, the donor's gift of that remainder having been 'completed' at the time he funded the trust.

1.21   Under current law, the donor's retained rights are valued at zero unless they are 'qualified interests'.[42] Qualified interests include the value of the donor's retained right to a fixed annuity (in a so-called grantor retained annuity trust (GRAT)) or 'unitrust' interest (a fixed percentage of the annually revalued trust property, referred to a grantor retained unitrust (GRUT)).[43] A retained right to income is not a qualified interest. In addition, a donor's retained right to reside in a transferred residence for a period of years – although not defined as a qualified interest – is not subject to these special valuation rules.[44]

1.22   The special valuation rules also apply to transfers of certain corporate or partnership interests to members of the taxpayer's family.[45] These rules only apply if, immediately before the transfer, the transferor and 'applicable family members' controlled the entity.[46] For example, the special valuation rules would apply if the taxpayer and his spouse controlled a company prior to the taxpayer's transfer of an interest in that company to his child. In this context, a 'distribution right' and a 'liquidation right' (which include puts and calls) are generally valued at zero.[47] For instance, if the taxpayer retained preferred stock with a right to put that stock back

---

[41]   These trusts were referred to as grantor retained income trusts (GRITs). In contrast, a donor's retained right as a discretionary beneficiary was given no value. Rev Rul 77–378, 1977–2 CB 347.

[42]   Code § 2702(a)(2)(A).

[43]   Code § 2702(b)(1) and (2). If a retained interest is a qualified interest, the value of that interest is determined under Code § 7520 which sets out rules for determining the present value of certain trust interests. In the case of GRATs and GRUTs, the present value is based on a variety of factors, including the value of the trust, the size and frequency of the annuity or unitrust payments, the period of the donor's retained rights, the relevant discount rates (which are revised and published by the IRS on a monthly basis) and, in some situations, the donor's life expectancy. A donor does not retain an annuity or unitrust interest for life, otherwise the property would be included in his estate under Code § 2036. Instead, the donor's objective is to survive the period of retained interest. In that event, any property remaining in the trust passes to the decedent's beneficiaries free of any gift tax. If, during that period, the rate of return exceeds to the IRS discount rates, more property will be left in the GRAT or GRUT than had been projected by the IRS tables.

[44]   Code § 2702(a)(3)(i). There are two forms of qualifying residence trusts. A personal residence trust (PRT) is a trust that is prohibited by the trust agreement from holding any asset other than a residence or from selling or otherwise transferring the residence during the trust term. Treas Reg § 25.2702-5(b). In contrast, the terms of a qualified personal residence trust (QPRT) permit the sale of the residence as long as the proceeds are either reinvested in a new residence or set aside to provide the grantor with an annuity for the balance of the term. Treas Reg § 25.2702-5(c).

[45]   Code § 2701. Note that members of the transferor's family include only his spouse, his descendants, and spouses of his descendants. Code § 2518(e)(1).

[46]   Code § 2701(b). 'Control' is defined as having at least 50% of the vote or value of the corporate stock, or, in the case of a partnership, either:
- holding a 50% capital or profits interest; or
- serving as a general partner of a limited partnership. Code § 2701(b)(2).

The term 'applicable family members' means the transferor's spouse, ancestors of the transferor or his spouse, and spouses of any such ancestors. Code § 2701(e)(2).

[47]   Code § 2701(a)(2).

to the company at face value, this right would be ignored for purposes of determining the value of that stock. However, distribution rights in the form of dividends on preferred stock payable at a fixed rate and on a cumulative basis are respected.

1.23 To illustrate, assume a parent owned 100% of a company valued at $1.5m. After recapitalizing the company, the parent transferred all of the common stock to a child while retaining non-cumulative preferred stock with a $1m liquidation preference. Under prior law, the common would be valued at $500,000 after taking the preferred stock's liquidation preference into account. Under the special valuation rules, the non-cumulative preferred stock would be valued at zero. The value of the parent's common stock gift would therefore be $1.5m.[48]

1.24 Note that these rules apply even if the parent had sold the common stock to the child for $500,000. Absent the special valuation rules, the parent would have made no gift (since the sales price equaled the value of the common stock). The special valuation rules cause the parent's gift in this example to be $1m ($1.5m value of the business less $500,000 consideration).[49]

1.25 Even if the distribution rights of preferred stock are respected, the special valuation rules require that the 'junior equity interests' (e g the common stock) must equal at least 10% of the value of the total equity (plus any indebtedness to the transferor and applicable family member).[50]

4. Generation-skipping tax

1.26 The US generation-skipping tax (GST) was first introduced in 1976 to supplement the gift and estate tax and ensure that trusts could not be used to avoid transfer taxes in intervening generations. Prior to the GST, a wealthy individual could fund a substantial trust for his descendants and pay the initial gift or estate tax. If properly designed, the trust would not be subject to gift or estate tax in the intervening generations. Therefore, a child could receive all of the trust income for life, with the trust principal passing – tax-free – to the grandchildren at the child's death.

1.27 The original GST ensured that a transfer tax would be imposed when property passed from generation to generation. If, for example, a trust for the settlor's child passed to grandchildren at the child's death but was not subject to estate tax, the GST would be imposed. The rate of tax was determined as if, in this example, the trust property had been included in the child's estate. The original GST did not, however, reach all transfers that avoided tax in the intervening generations – most importantly, gifts directly from grandparents to grandchildren.

---

[48] Treas Reg § 25.2701–1(e) (Example 2).
[49] Treas Reg § 25.2701–1(b). These rules are also understood to apply to joint purchases. Thus, if a parent and child paid $1m for the business and the parent purchased non-cumulative preferred stock for $950,000 and the child paid $50,000 for the common stock, the parent would be treated as having made a $950,000 gift.
[50] Code § 2701(a)(4).

1.28   *Types of Tax*

1.28   In 1986, Congress completely revised the GST.[51] The GST is now imposed at a flat rate equal to the highest marginal estate tax rate (48% in 2004).[52] The revised GST applies to a 'generation-skipping transfer', which is further defined as a 'direct skip,' a 'taxable termination' and a 'taxable distribution'.[53]

1.29   The 1986 Act extended the GST to gifts and bequests to a person (referred to as a 'skip person') two or more generations below that of the 'transferor' (ie the person who made the relevant transfer subject to the US gift or estate tax). These taxable transfers – referred to as 'direct skips'[54] – also include transfers in trust where there is no person in the intervening generation with a current interest in the trust.[55] If property is held in trust for the intervening generation (eg in a child's trust), the GST is also imposed on a 'taxable distribution' or a 'taxable termination'. A taxable distribution is a distribution (other than a terminating distribution) from such a trust to a skip person. A taxable termination results when all members of the intervening generation ('non-skip persons') cease to be current trust beneficiaries of the trust (eg upon a child's death) and the trust continues for, or is distributed to, skip persons.[56] A distribution/termination that is itself subject to a gift or estate tax, however, will generally not be considered a taxable distribution or taxable termination.[57]

1.30   GST is imposed in addition to any gift or estate tax otherwise imposed on the original transfer. Thus, a direct gift from a grandparent to grandchild might first incur a 48% gift tax and then be subject to an additional 48% GST. In addition, the payment of GST on lifetime gifts is itself treated as a taxable gift, resulting in a gift tax being imposed on the GST.[58] A wealthy grandparent's $1m gift to grandchildren could, accordingly, result in as much as $1.2m of federal transfer taxes.

---

[51]   Tax Reform Act 1986 (PL 99–514), § 1431(a) et seq, codified at Code § 2600 et seq.
[52]   Code § 2602; see also Code §§ 2641 and 2642. Prior law had computed the GST on the basis of marginal tax brackets of certain persons in the intervening generation.
[53]   Code § 2611.
[54]   Code §§ 2611(a)(3), 2612(c) and 2613.
[55]   Code § 2613(a)(2).
[56]   Code §§ 2612, 2621 and 2622.
[57]   For example, if a grandparent had established a trust for a child and the child had a general power of appointment at death (which causes the trust to be included in the child's taxable estate), the termination of the child's trust and the distribution of trust funds to the grandchildren will not be subject to GST. For such a fundamental concept, one would expect to find an explicit exception in the Code. However, the exception is not easily 'found' but results from the GST's complex definitional maze and a clarification in the regulations. All generation-skipping transfers are measured against the 'transferor'. Direct skips are transfers to 'skip persons' who are defined as individuals two or more generations below that of the transferor. Taxable distributions involve distributions from trusts to skip persons and taxable terminations result when a trust terminates and either distributes to, or is held in trust for, skip persons. If an individual in the intervening generation is also subject to a gift or estate tax, that individual will also be considered a transferor. Thus, both the grandparent (who established the trust) and child (who had a general power of appointment at death) would be considered transferors. In that situation, the regulations provide that the generation-skipping transfer is measured against the transferor who most recently made the taxable gift or bequest. Treas Reg § 26.2652–1(a)(1). If, however, the child becomes the new transferor and the property skips the grandchildren's generation and passes instead to great-grandchildren, or in trust for their benefit, that transfer would be considered the child's direct skip and, therefore, subject to GST.
[58]   Code § 2515.

5. Possible repeal

1.31 The Economic Growth and Tax Relief Reconciliation Act 2001 (EGTRRA) provides for the gradual phase-out of the estate tax and GST. As discussed in **CHAPTER 3** and **CHAPTER 5**, EGTRRA provides for a staged increase in exemptions and a gradual reduction in rates through 2009. EGTRRA also repeals the estate tax for the estates of individuals dying in 2010 and the GST for GST transfers occurring that year.

1.32 EGTRRA does not, however, repeal the gift tax. The gift tax exemption was increased in 2002, but, unlike the estate tax and GST, no further increases are scheduled. The gift tax rates are, however, being reduced in parallel with the estate tax and GST.

1.33 The EGTRRA changes – including estate tax and GST repeal – all 'sunset' in 2011 and revert to the pre-EGTRRA rules. Repeal is therefore temporary. It is likely that the US Congress will revisit the issue of US transfer tax reform prior to 2010 and craft some 'permanent' reform. The balance of political power as well as budgetary considerations will, undoubtedly, influence whether repeal will be made permanent or some compromise – for example, high exemptions and low rates – will be enacted.

B. United Kingdom

1. Introduction

1.34 The United Kingdom (UK) tax on lifetime and testamentary transfers made by individuals operates under a single name – inheritance tax (IHT).[59] The tax is a donor-based tax[60] and applies to the person making the transfer (or to his personal representatives). Its effect is to impose a charge on occasions which result in a decrease in the value of the transferor's estate (a 'transfer of value'), whether by actual disposition of property[61] or by a deliberate omission to act resulting in loss[62] (eg failure to exercise voting rights over certain shares resulting in value passing out of one holding into another).

1.35 Various exemptions and reliefs apply, including provisions to prevent any exposure to tax where the loss occurs simply as the result of a bad bargain

---

[59] Finance Act 1986, s 100 (FA 1986).
[60] This is in common with the US but in contrast with civil law jurisdictions which often apply tax to the recipient of a gift.
[61] Inheritance Tax Act 1984, s 3(1) (IHTA 1984).
[62] IHTA 1984, s 3(3).

1.36 *Types of Tax*

(eg unintentional sale at an undervalue).[63] While generally this tax applies to individuals, a special regime exists which extends the principles to assets held in trust.[64] The tax is also extended to apply to transfers of value made by certain closely held companies, which are deemed to be transfers made by the company shareholders.[65]

1.36 In the context of trust taxation, the settlor's domicile status at time of settlement has enormous significance. If a settlor is UK domiciled at the time a trust is funded, as the law stands, the trust is attributed with the UK domicile of the settlor on a continuing basis, irrespective of a later change in his domicile.[66] For example, a trust settled by a UK domiciled settlor emigrating to the US, will be attributed with the settlor's UK domicile, even though the settlor and/or the holder of an interest in possession subsequently becomes solely US domiciled. Even though the settlor and the holder of an interest in possession may be treaty exempt from IHT (except with respect to a transfer of UK real estate or permanent establishment property comprised in their free estate) the trustees remain liable for IHT with respect to a chargeable distribution of any trust property, wherever situated.[67]

1.37 Conversely, if a settlor is not UK domiciled at the time of funding a settlement, the trust is an excluded property trust and remains exempt from UK IHT with respect to non-UK sited assets even though the settlor retains an interest in the trust and dies domiciled in the UK.[68] The same excluded property trust status applies with respect to the holder of an interest in possession who dies domiciled in the UK, though further complexities can arise where the settlor or his spouse have an initial interest in possession (see **CHAPTER 6**).

---

[63] IHTA 1984, s 10; *CIR v Spencer-Nairn [1991] STC 60.777.*
[64] IHTA 1984, Pt III, consisting of Ch I (ss 43–48, including definitions and terms), Ch II (ss 49–57A, taxation of interests in possession, reversionary interests and settlement powers, including termination of interests in possession), and Ch III (ss 58–85, taxation of discretionary trusts, including the decennial regime and exit charges)). Much of the complexity of the IHT regime is determining which chapter applies to a particular IHT event, eg termination of an interest in possession can be a non chargeable event due to the excluded property rule of s 53(1) (Ch II applicable to interests in possession) and yet be the creation of a UK domiciled discretionary trust with regard to the termination of an initial interest in possession of the settlor or his spouse under ss 80(1) and 82(3) (Ch III applicable to discretionary trusts).
[65] IHTA 1984, s 94. A 'close company' is defined in the Income and Corporation Taxes Act 1988, s 414 (ICTA 1988) and, broadly speaking, is a UK resident company which is under the control of five or fewer 'participators' or under the control of participators who are directors. A participator is a person having a share or interest in the capital or income of the company, including persons entitled to acquire any such interests and also including loan creditors. If 35% or more of the shares are publicly quoted, generally the provisions do not apply. It should be noted that notwithstanding that a close company is defined as a UK resident company, various tax anti avoidance provisions are applied to non-UK resident companies as if they were close companies.
[66] IHTA 1984, s 48(3).
[67] See IHTA 1984, ss 48(3) and 52 and **CHAPTER 7** and **CHAPTER 16**.
[68] IHTA 1984, ss 48(3) and 53(1).

2. Transfers on death

1.38 UK inheritance tax is imposed on the value of a decedent's estate calculated at the moment before his death.[69] He is deemed to have made a transfer of his entire estate at that time although adjustments are made to the value of property which increases or decreases in value by reason of the death, such as, life insurance policies which form part of the estate or assets which appreciate in consequence of perceived scarcity value.[70] A UK domiciled person[71] is taxed on his worldwide assets and a non-UK domiciled person is taxed on his UK sited assets. All real and personal property is included whether tangible or intangible and certain assets, outlined below, are also deemed to be included in the estate.

1.39 Liabilities (including outstanding tax liabilities of the deceased) can generally be deducted from the gross value of the estate if they were incurred in exchange for consideration given to the deceased by the creditor.[72] This is subject to a special anti-avoidance provision which disallows debts incurred to a person where the consideration given was property which was originally derived from the deceased (or, for example, where other property has been received from him and retained by the creditor).[73] A debt secured on a particular asset is deductible from the value of that asset.[74]

1.40 In the UK, jointly held property may take the form of a joint tenancy (with right of survivorship and with the decedent's interest passing directly to the survivor outside his probated estate) or a tenancy in common (where the decedent's proportionate interest passes as part of his estate and subject to the provisions of his will). In each case, the value of the deceased's share of the jointly-held asset is part of his estate for inheritance tax purposes. If the former, the first joint tenant to die is normally deemed to own one-half of the relevant asset. In the case of the latter, the value of the decedent's proportionate interest is taxed in his estate. Where spouses are concerned, property is valued as 'related property' and a proportionate share of the open market value of the whole will be relevant.[75] If the parties are not spouses then an appropriate open market value may involve the application of a discount.

1.41 In contrast with the US, the UK has less stringent criteria to judge whether insurance policy proceeds fall into the deceased's estate. Accordingly, the insured can transfer the policy to an irrevocable trust and retain, inter alia, the power to change beneficiaries. In such a case, the proceeds will not be taxed in his estate as

---

[69] IHTA 1984, s4; provision is also made in this section to cover simultaneous deaths. Where it cannot be shown which of two or more persons survived each other they are deemed for the purposes of IHT to have died at the same moment.
[70] IHTA 1984, ss 4 and 171. For example, the value of paintings or musical copyrights may appreciate in consequence of the death of the artist or musician, who will no longer be adding to the number of works available in the market.
[71] See CHAPTER 2 for the law of domicile.
[72] IHTA 1984, s 5(3) and (5).
[73] FA 1986, s 103.
[74] Since secured debts reduce the value of the asset on which they are secured, sensible planning will involve trying to secure debts against assets, which do not themselves attract favourable tax treatment. This is particularly important in the context of business assets which can benefit from reduced tax rates in some circumstances.
[75] IHTA 1984, s 161.

1.42 *Types of Tax*

long as neither he nor his estate can benefit from the trust. Actual or potential benefit,[76] rather than control, is the key factor for determining whether insurance proceeds are included in a decedent's UK taxable estate.

1.42 Subject to an exception for 'excluded property'[77] (discussed further in **CHAPTER 3** and **CHAPTER 6**) the deceased's taxable estate also includes the value of the assets in any trust fund of which he is a life tenant (with an absolute right to income).[78] Primary liability for such tax, however, falls upon the trustees rather than the deceased's estate. The corollary to this general principle of deemed ownership of the trust assets by the life tenant is that a reversionary interest in settled property is not generally taken into account as part of a decedent's estate for inheritance tax purposes.[79] There is a separate inheritance tax regime which applies to discretionary trusts (see **CHAPTER 6**).[80]

1.43 As discussed at **1.73**, 'potentially exempt transfers' made during lifetime by an individual are subject to inheritance tax at the donor's death if he dies within

---

[76] Generally, it will be assumed that a person may benefit if he is not irrevocably excluded from the trust. A power for the trustees to add a settlor to the beneficial class at some future time will be enough to cause him to be regarded as a potential beneficiary. In appropriate circumstances he may also be regarded as a potential beneficiary where the trusts are not exhaustive and, accordingly, a resulting trust for the settlor would arise in the event of the failure of all other trusts.

[77] IHTA 1984, s 48(3). Effectively the excluded property section provides 'exempt' status to non-UK sited property held in trusts created by persons at a time when they were neither UK domiciled nor deemed UK domiciled.

[78] IHTA 1984, s 49.

[79] IHTA 1984, s 48(1). Under UK tax law, the concept of a 'reversionary' interest means a vested or contingent future interest, including one that follows the life interest in an interest in possession (IIP) trust (IHTA 1984, s 47). The term is not limited to the settlor, but also applies to the future interest of other beneficiaries. Since the life tenant is considered the owner of the entire trust assets, the holder of the future interest would not normally be subject to IHT during the life tenant's life, either upon the holder's death or upon the holder's gift of that future interest.

Under US law, the term 'reversionary' interest generally refers only to a future interest held by the trust's settlor while future interests held by others are generally referred to as 'remainder' interests. The taxation of reversion and remainder interests under US law can be different from that in the UK. Under US law, a settlor's reversionary interest will cause the trust property to be included in the settlor's estate if:

(a) a person has an interest in the trust that can only be obtained by surviving the settlor; and

(b) the value of the settlor's reversionary interest immediately prior to death was greater than 5% of the value of the trust. Code § 2037.

This would apply even if a beneficiary had a life estate or interest in possession in the trust. The regulations include an example of a trust established by the decedent which provides his wife with a life estate, with a remainder to the decedent or, if he is not then living, to the decedent's daughter. Treas Reg § 20.2037–1(e) (Example 3). Since the daughter's right to the remainder is dependent on her surviving the decedent, the decedent's reversionary interest will cause the trust property to be included in his estate if it is valued at more than 5% at the date of his death. This applies even though his wife had a life estate.

A settlor's release or transfer of his reversionary interest within three years of death can result in the trust property being included in the settlor's US taxable estate. Code § 2035.

Under US tax law, the estate of a deceased beneficiary (other than the settlor) will not include the beneficiary's contingent remainder interest in a trust but will include a vested remainder interest.

[80] IHTA 1984, Pt III, Ch III.

seven years of the transfer. Thus, lifetime gifts made within seven years of death are cumulated with the decedent's estate to establish the tax rate applicable to the estate.[81]

1.44 Property over which the deceased has a general power of appointment, which is not settled property (ie property subject to the terms of a trust and held for persons in succession) will also be included in his estate.[82] Settled property remains unaffected, and is thus not taxable as part of a person's estate, merely by reason of the existence of such a power of appointment,[83] including a power of revocation.

1.45 The deceased's estate also includes any property which he has given away on or after 18 March 1986, but over which he reserves some actual or potential benefit – a 'gift with reservation of benefit'. The concept covers any de facto benefit whether directly over the property given or collateral to the gift (eg a facility for continued use of one asset in exchange for the gift of another) and whether or not obtained by reason of a binding or an informal arrangement.[84] To escape the application of this provision, the gifted property must be enjoyed to the entire, or virtually to the entire, exclusion of the donor. This de minimis provision has been given limited scope, although there is some concession to donors who unexpectedly fall on hard times. The Revenue has published its view of what might constitute an incidental benefit which can be ignored.[85]

1.46 The provisions are widely drawn and it is clear that a trust of which the settlor is a discretionary beneficiary would fall within these rules.[86] Prior to 18 March 1986, such trusts were widely used as estate planning vehicles for UK

---

[81] IHTA 1984, ss 3A and 9.

[82] For example, certain directly held US employer-provided death in service insurance, where the deceased has a right to designate the beneficiaries which is binding on the employer.

[83] IHTA 1984, ss 5, 47A and 272. Note that this was generally understood to be the law until the Court of Appeal decision in *Melville v IRC [2001] STC 1271*. Following the decision legislation was introduced with effect from 17 April 2002 to restore the position to that previously understood to apply.

[84] It also includes indirect benefits which are obtained by reason of 'associated operations'. This is a broadly framed provision which covers 'operations' affecting the same or different property, made by the same or different persons and whether or not they occur simultaneously. Associated operations contemplate a situation where a transfer of value arises in consequence of the combined effect of more than one transaction. IHTA 1984, s 268 and FA 1986, Sch 20, para 6(1)(c).

[85] Inland Revenue's *Tax Bulletin* Issue No 9 (November 1993). The Revenue takes the view that 'virtually to the entire exclusion' covers cases where the benefit to the donor 'is insignificant' in relation to the gifted property; it being a matter of fact and degree and each case turning on its own circumstances. For example, they cite staying at a residence given to the donee for no more than two weeks a year in his absence or staying for less than one month a year with him present, might be acceptable. Staying with the donee to recuperate after illness or to look after the donee while he is recuperating and for short social visits or to baby-sit, are also cited as acceptable parameters.

[86] FA 1986, s 102, Sch 20. Certain case law relating to the legislation existing prior to 1975 (Estate Duty) throws doubt on whether a discretionary beneficiary should be regarded as having a benefit reserved over the settled property under those rules. However, it is acknowledged that the terminology used in the 1986 legislation is framed broadly enough to include such interests. Certain trust planning strategies which exploited the interaction of the rules related to the exemption for gifts to a spouse and the reservation of benefit rules, involving the inclusion of the settlor in a discretionary class, subject to a prior interest in possession for a spouse, was curtailed by legislation taking effect from 20 June 2003. FA 2003, s 185.

1.47 *Types of Tax*

individuals. Whilst their use is now of limited benefit for UK persons, there remain benefits for non-UK domiciliary settlors.[87] However, a distinction needs to be made between a benefit reserved over the gifted property and circumstances where the donor has split his interest in the asset, giving away part and retaining part. For example, if the donor is either a life tenant of a trust or has an interest in remainder, this is not regarded as a reservation of benefit, but a retention of an interest which was not the subject of a gift.[88] This principle has been modified somewhat by statute to nullify specific planning strategies, particularly in the case of gifts of interests in land.[89]

1.47 The reservation of benefit provisions apply where actual or potential benefit exists at any time in the seven-year period immediately before the donor's death. Therefore, even where no reservation exists when the gift is made or when the donor dies, it is possible for the rule to apply and the gifted property to be included in the donor's estate if, during the relevant seven-year period prior to his date of death, the donor receives a benefit from the donee which is referable to the original gift.[90] Certain exemptions exist in respect of gifts of land which have been made to a relative, where the donor later falls on hard times[91] and further, the rules do not apply where the donor pays an arm's length consideration for any benefit received.[92] If all possible benefit has been relinquished more than seven years before the donor's death, the assets are not includible within his estate. If a person has made a gift which is subject to the reservation of benefit rules but later releases the benefit, he is deemed at that time to have made a potentially exempt transfer.[93]

1.48 Although assets subject to a reservation of benefit are taxed as part of the deceased's estate, the usual tax implications of the original gift remain. For example, if the original gift were made to a discretionary trust, that gift would have been subject to an immediate inheritance tax charge notwithstanding that the assets would still be deemed to be included in the taxable estate of the donor. This is in contrast with the US regime where generally such a transaction would give rise to an incomplete gift (such that no transfer would be deemed to have taken place). Potential double charges arising from the UK regime where assets are also later taxed as part of the deceased's estate, however, are relieved by Treasury Regulations.[94]

---

[87] The Inland Revenue verbally indicated in Autumn 2001 that it may change its long-held view on the interaction of these rules with the rules on excluded property trusts created by non-UK domiciled settlors. See **CHAPTER 6**. However, no formal announcement has been made and at the time of writing these trusts still offer viable planning for non-UK domiciliaries.
[88] An Inland Revenue letter dated 18 May 1987 states:
'In the case where a gift is made into trust, the retention by the settlor (donor) of a reversionary interest under the trust is not considered to constitute a reservation, whether the retained interest arises under the express terms of the trust or it arises by operation of general law, eg a resulting trust.'
See the detailed discussion in Section C4 of *Foster's Inheritance Tax*, Butterworths.
[89] See *Ingram v IRC [1999] STC 37* and FA 1986, ss 102A–102C.
[90] IHTA 1984, ss 102 and 102A.
[91] FA 1986, Sch 20, para 6(1)(b).
[92] FA 1986, Sch 20, para 6(1)(a).
[93] FA 1986, s 102(4). Accordingly, to escape IHT he must survive for a further seven years.
[94] Inheritance Tax (Double Charges Relief) Regulations 1987 (S1 1987/1130).

1.49 The gifts with reservation rules do not apply to dispositions which are exempt from inheritance tax (for example, gifts to spouses or to life interest trusts for the benefit of spouses).[95]

1.50 There have been a variety of tax planning strategies implemented over the years which have overcome the application of the reservation of benefit provisions and a number of specifically targeted legislative measures have been introduced to counter such strategies. However, in the Finance Act 2004 (FA 2004), the UK Inland Revenue has taken a broader approach in the introduction of an income tax charge designed to operate as a disincentive to certain planning, even in some circumstances where the reservation of benefit rules do not apply.[96]

3. Charge to income tax by reference to enjoyment of property previously owned

1.51 While not a transfer tax, this income tax charge depends on whether or not property is included in a person's estate for IHT purposes (including whether a person has elected for it to be so treated under the FA 2004 provisions[97]). From 6 April 2005, where a donor has previously owned an asset (either tangible or intangible) and no longer does so, but arrangements have been made to afford him continued enjoyment of such property, an income tax charge will be imposed on him broadly based on the value of the benefit he receives. The charge applies where there was previous ownership at any time since 17 March 1986 and, therefore, arrangements affecting assets, which have not been owned by the taxpayer since that date, escape the charge. In the representations made by professional bodies and in the Parliamentary debates on the Finance Bill, considerable pressure was put on the Government to bring this date forward to December 2003 (when the proposed legislative change was first announced) on the basis that this clearly amounted to retrospective legislation. However, the Government took a firm line that while they affected existing arrangements, the new charges were prospective and, in their view, not retrospective in their effect.[98]

---

[95] FA 1986, s 102(5). From 20 June 2003, the gifts with reservation of benefit rules may apply if the spouse's life interest is terminated in certain circumstances during the lifetime of the donor (FA 1986, s 102(5A)). This provision was introduced to counter the tax result of a specific planning strategy which involved a gift of a life interest to a spouse with the settlor remaining a beneficiary of the discretionary class potentially capable of benefiting from the trust fund at a future date.

[96] FA 2004, s 84 and Sch 15.

[97] FA 2004, s 84, 'charge to income tax by reference to enjoyment of property previously owned' and Sch 15, 'charge to income tax on benefits received by former owner of property'.

[98] In the Standing Committee debates, Dawn Primarolo stated:
'The hon. Gentleman seeks to make two points about his amendments. The first is about retrospection. He claims that inheritance tax arrangements made in 1986 should be completely immune from any change anywhere else in the tax system. As he well knows, no taxpayer is ever provided with such reassurance. Taxpayers make plans for the use of their income in the knowledge that the tax system may change. Retrospective measures in tax law seek to make a charge on benefits that have already accrued, but the schedule does no such thing. The bringing into charge occurs from the 2005/06 tax year. Therefore, the benefits that accrue in that tax year will fall within the charge. If the legislation were retrospective, it would backdate the charge to 1986 for accrued benefits over that entire period, but we do not seek to do that. I absolutely reject the hon. Gentleman's proposition

1.52 *Types of Tax*

1.52 The provisions apply to UK resident taxpayers[99] and to the extent of:

- the worldwide assets of a UK domiciled person;[100] or
- the UK sited assets of a non-UK domiciled person.[101]

1.53 However, for non-UK domiciled persons who subsequently become UK domiciled or deemed domiciled, overseas assets in an excluded property trust are exempt.[102]

The regime is broadly divided into three categories:

- that affecting the enjoyment of land;
- that affecting enjoyment of chattels; and
- that affecting enjoyment of intangible assets which are comprised in a settlement.

If one or more of the above categories apply, then the charge is imposed under whichever provision gives the higher tax result.[103] If the use of the property already gives rise to an income tax charge under the legislation which taxes remuneration and benefits in kind,[104] then the latter takes precedence.

1.54 Provisions exist to exempt the individual from the charge in various specified circumstances, which are either 'excluded transactions' or 'exemptions from charge'.[105]

a. Excluded transactions

1.55 Excluded transactions, which apply in the case of gifts of *land and chattels*, are as follows.

- It is property the whole interest in which has been sold on arm's length terms or on such terms as could be expected if it were an arm's length disposal.[106]

---

[99] that the proposals are retrospective. They start in 2005 and will assess the benefits at that point. If the taxpayer does not wish to pay the income tax charge at that time, they make an election. The inheritance tax rules will be deemed to operate, and the property is theirs and will be dealt with at the point at which the estate comes into charge.'

[99] FA 2004, Sch 15, para 12(1).

[100] See **CHAPTER 2** regarding the UK concept of domicile; it is the IHT concept of domicile, including deemed UK domicile under IHTA 1984, s 267 which is relevant.

[101] FA 2004, Sch 15, para 12(2).

[102] FA 2004, Sch 15, para 12(3) and IHTA 1984, s 48(3); and see **CHAPTER 6**. An excluded property trust is one which was created by a settlor neither UK domiciled nor deemed UK domiciled and which owns non-UK sited assets.

[103] FA 2004, Sch 15, para 18(1).

[104] Income Tax (Earnings and Pensions) Act 2003, Pt 3. For example, where a person may have the use of property owned by a company by which he is employed or by which he is deemed to be employed. FA 2004, Sch 15, para 19.

[105] FA 2004, Sch 15, paras 10, 11, 13, 16, 17.

[106] Provision is made for the express reservation of certain rights to be separated from, and excluded from, the property disposed of. Furthermore, the definition of 'connected persons' is for this purpose deemed to include uncles, aunts, nieces and nephews. FA 2004, Sch 15, para 2.

- It is property transferred to the settlor's spouse (or under a court order to a former spouse) or to a settlement in which the settlor's spouse (or under a court order a former spouse) has an interest in possession (and only for as long as that interest continues, unless it has ceased on the spouse's death).[107]
- It is a disposal which qualifies under the exemptions for dispositions for family maintenance, and in the case of outright gifts, the annual and small gifts exemptions.[108]
- It is an outright gift of cash (sterling or other currency) made at least seven years prior to the earliest time when the enjoyment of the property began.[109]

b. Exemptions from charge

1.56 Exemptions from charge[110] are applicable to land, chattels and settled intangibles. These state that the income tax charge will not apply where for the purposes of IHT a person's estate includes the 'relevant property'[111] or property which derives its value from the relevant property.[112] However, if the value of the latter is substantially less than that of the relevant property, the charge will apply but provision is made for a reasonable discount to avoid double counting. Provision is also made to counter any attempt to create liabilities which reduce the value of the relevant property ('excluded liabilities'). If this is done, then the exemption only applies to the extent the value of the property exceeds the excluded liability.

1.57 The relevant exemptions from charge also apply to the following circumstances where the reservation of benefit provisions are applicable:[113]

- the disposal falls within the gifts with reservation legislation, such that it remains within the transferor's UK taxable estate;[114]
- the disposal would have fallen within the gifts with reservation legislation if it had not been one of the specified exempt gifts;[115]
- where co-ownership exists following the donor giving away a share in property and either he uses it jointly with the donee (and any benefit to him is negligible) or he pays full consideration for his sole use;[116]

---

[107] FA 2004, Sch 15, para 10(3).
[108] IHTA 1984, ss 11, 19 and 20.
[109] FA 2004, Sch 15, para 10(2)(c).
[110] FA 2004, Sch 15, para 11.
[111] Eg if the settlor is the life tenant of the trust, IHTA 1984, s 49 will deem the value of the trust assets to be included in his estate.
[112] Eg a wholly owned company which holds the property.
[113] FA 2004, Sch 15, para 11(3).
[114] FA 1986, s 102.
[115] Ie to a charity, political party, housing association, employee trust, a gift for national purposes or to a maintenance fund for historic buildings (so long in the latter case as the fund continues to comply with the IHT statutory requirements) FA 1986, s 102(5) (d) – (i) and IHTA 1984, Sch 4, para 3(1).
[116] FA 1986, s 102B.

1.58 *Types of Tax*

- full consideration is paid for any enjoyment of property, or the donor of an interest in land later becomes frail and falls on hard times.[117]

1.58 Further exemptions apply as follows:

- where the aggregate benefits chargeable under the Schedule 15 provisions are within a £5,000 annual value de minimis or are incidental;[118]

- where the assets were originally inherited but the benefit was redirected under a deed of variation or disclaimer (or in certain other designated circumstances), with favoured status for inheritance tax;[119]

- the giving of certain guarantees is also excluded from the 'contribution condition' noted below.[120]

c. Land[121]

1.59 Subject to the applicability of any of the above exemptions, if a person physically occupies land which he owned at any time since 18 March 1986 (or if he owned other property which he had given away and which was sold by the donee and subsequently reinvested in the land), he is deemed to receive an annual income taxable benefit based on the rental value of the property (less any rent he actually pays under a binding legal obligation). This is referred to as the '*disposal condition*'.[122] The provision applies equally if he provided any funds (directly or indirectly) and the donee has applied them in buying such land or in buying other property, the disposal proceeds of which have ultimately been applied in buying such land. This is referred to as the '*contribution condition*'.[123] Provision is made for apportionment in situations where only part of the proceeds is so applied or where there has been a sale at less than market value.[124]

d. Chattels[125]

1.60 A charge also arises where a person is in possession of, or has the use of, a chattel which he previously owned since 18 March 1986, or the purchase of which he funded, or which represents other property which he originally gave away (in similar circumstances as described above in respect of land).[126] Here, a different formula applies in view of the generally low rental values attached to these types of

---

[117] FA 1986, s 102C.
[118] It should be noted that this is an all or nothing charge so that if the figure exceeds £5,000, the whole is brought into charge and not just the excess.
[119] IHTA 1984, s 17. For example, a person may redirect an outright bequest to a discretionary trust of which he is a beneficiary without invoking the reservation of benefit provisions. Section 17 also includes transfers in compliance with a testator's request. FA 2004, Sch 15, para 16.
[120] FA 2004, Sch 15, para 17.
[121] FA 2004, Sch 15, paras 3–5.
[122] FA 2004, Sch 15, para 3(2) and (4). It should be noted that this covers a part disposal, and also includes the granting of an interest out of an existing interest in land.
[123] FA 2004, Sch 15, para 3(3).
[124] FA 2004, Sch 15, para 4(2) and (4A).
[125] FA 2004, Sch 15, paras 6 and 7.
[126] FA 2004, Sch 15, para 6(2) and (3).

assets. Instead, the market value is deemed to be an interest free loan and a prescribed rate of interest is applied to the loan by Regulations. The former owner is taxable on that deemed interest sum less payments he makes for such use under a binding legal obligation.

e. Intangible assets[127]

1.61 The rules applicable to intangible property (defined as 'any property other than chattels or interests in land' – for example, cash, stock, shares, bonds, partnership interests, etc) are in point only if the property is comprised in a settlement from which the settlor can benefit.[128] The settlement must also have been created, or be one to which additions were made, at some time after 17 March 1986. To be 'relevant property' for the purposes of the charge, it must be intangible property which the chargeable person actually settled, or be property which represents such property. Broadly, the value of the relevant settled property is treated as an interest-free loan to the settlor and a prescribed interest rate applied, although there is a permitted deduction against the deemed interest received, for tax paid under certain other income tax and capital gains tax anti-avoidance legislation, which taxes a settlor on income and gains of trusts from which he or his spouse can benefit.[129]

1.62 In the case of the enjoyment of land, chattels or settled property which has invoked these provisions, an option exists for the donor to elect (by 31 January following the end of the tax year when they first become relevant to him) for the asset instead to be deemed to be included in his estate for UK inheritance tax purposes under the reservation of benefits legislation. If he does so elect, the income tax charge will not apply. Such an election can also be withdrawn by the taxpayer at any time during his life.[130]

1.63 In implementing lifetime planning for non-UK domiciliaries through the use of trusts and/or companies to hold UK sited assets, from 6 April 2005 it will be fundamental to have regard to the income tax charge imposed in these cases.[131] Accordingly, for the US taxpayer benefiting from any such assets it will be a relevant consideration.

---

[127] FA 2004, Sch 15, paras 8 and 9.
[128] The definition of settlor is imported from the income tax legislation and whether or not he has an interest is defined by reference to the income tax provisions in ICTA 1988, s 660A (see CHAPTER 13), as slightly modified (covering a settlement from which he is not excluded, as well as one where he is expressly included). However, unlike other income tax anti-avoidance rules, the provisions do not apply where a settlor's spouse can benefit. This is in line with the general scope of the IHT legislation, which does not normally apply anti-avoidance provisions where the spouse can benefit, only the transferor himself. The definition of 'settlement' and 'settled property' in para 1 is, however, taken from the IHT legislation.
[129] ICTA 1988, ss 547, 660A and 739; TCGA 1992, s 77 and s 86. Potentially, both sets of tax charges apply – the pre-owned assets charge and the aforementioned provisions. It should be noted that this is a *deduction* from the amount which is subject to tax under the pre-owned assets regime, and not a credit against the tax payable (FA 2004, Sch 15, para 9). This means that, effectively, the tax rate can be as high as 64%. For example, £100 gross rental value brought into charge less £40 tax paid under other legislation = £60 at 40% = £24. Thus, the total tax charge is £64.
[130] FA 2004, Sch 15, paras 20–22.
[131] FA 2004, Sch 15.

1.64 *Types of Tax*

1.64 As noted above, this charge does not apply in certain excepted cases including where the relevant property (or an asset which derives its value from the relevant property) is deemed to remain comprised in the estate of the donor for inheritance tax purposes under the IHT legislation. This clearly applies in the case of UK sited assets directly owned by trustees where the settlor has an interest in possession[132] or where he is a discretionary beneficiary and the trust therefore falls within the reservation of benefit regime.[133] The scope of the provisions was less clear where a non-UK company owned by an excluded property trust owns UK sited assets which previously belonged to the settlor. However, modifications were made to the draft legislation to clarify the position so that in all of the following examples the taxpayer should escape both the charge to inheritance tax and to income tax.

(a) Where a UK sited asset is directly owned by a trust with an interest in possession for the settlor the regime will not apply as he will be deemed to own the assets.[134]

(b) Where a UK sited asset is directly owned by a discretionary trust and the settlor is a beneficiary the regime will not apply as the assets will be deemed included in his estate.[135]

(c) Where a UK sited asset is held by a non-UK company owned by a trust with an interest in possession for the settlor, the regime will not apply as he will be deemed to own the assets which derive their value from the relevant property.[136]

(d) Where a UK sited asset is held by a non-UK company owned by a *discretionary* trust and the settlor is a beneficiary, he will be deemed to own the assets which derive their value from the relevant property.[137]

1.65 It should be noted that whether or not the income tax charge applies, or the assets fall within the reservation of benefit regime under the normal rules, or the taxpayer elects for this regime to apply under the above provision, this does not affect the legal position in so far as the donee continues to own the assets. Nor, despite the charge to tax on the donor in any of these circumstances, does it affect other tax consequences for the donor or donee. For example, there is no uplift in the cost basis of the asset for capital gains tax purposes at the donor's death as there would be had he owned the assets outright.[138]

---

[132] IHTA 1984, s 49.
[133] FA 1986, s 102.
[134] IHTA 1984, s 49; FA 2004, Sch 15, para 11(1)(a).
[135] FA 1986, s 102; FA 2004, Sch 15, para 11(3) and (5B).
[136] FA 2004, Sch 15 para 11 and (1). The company is deemed comprised within the estate under IHTA 1984, s 49 and it derives its value from the property. FA 2004, Sch 15, para 12(3). This provision preserves the benefit of excluded property status for previously created trusts, after the domicile of the settlor has changed to that of the UK.
[137] FA 2004, Sch 15, para 11(3) and (5B). The company is deemed comprised within the estate under the reservation of benefit provisions and it derives its value from the property. Paragraph 12(3) also preserves the benefit of excluded property status for previously created trusts, after the domicile of the settlor has changed to that of the UK.
[138] Despite some lengthy debate in the Standing Committee, it was considered that no extension of the capital gains tax uplift at the date of death was merited. Therefore, taxpayers need to be aware that planning may either give rise to a reservation of benefit charge or a pre-owned assets income

1.66 The legislative provisions contemplated that Regulations would be issued to address certain operational details relating to the pre-owned assets charge. On 16 August 2004 the Revenue published a further Consultation Document seeking the views of interested parties by 18 November 2004 to assist in the drafting of such Regulations. The issues covered principally relate to the appropriate valuation date for use in establishing the market value of assets, relevant to the computation of the charge, and the appropriate 'rates of return' for chattels and intangible assets.

4. Lifetime transfers

1.67 As in the US, the UK supplements the tax charge at death by imposing tax on certain lifetime gifts. However, there is considerable scope to make certain lifetime gifts free of transfer tax in the UK provided there is no retained benefit for the donor and provided he survives the gift by seven years. Furthermore, even in the case of chargeable lifetime gifts, the applicable rate of tax is one half of the death rate (20% instead of 40%). In other respects, the fundamentals of the tax regime applicable to lifetime gifts are the same as for transfers on death.

1.68 Again as in the US, gifts can be made directly or indirectly or by associated operations. Where funds are provided by one person to another for the purposes of an onward gift by the latter, the former may be regarded as the indirect settlor if there was never any intention that the latter had freedom of disposition.[139]

1.69 Sales at an undervalue are also regarded as partial gifts and potentially subject to tax to the extent that the proceeds of disposal fall below the open market value.[140]

1.70 Transfers between divorcing couples are normally exempt from tax either because they take place while the parties are still technically married and are hence exempt[141] or because they are dispositions for the maintenance of the family and exempt.[142]

1.71 Lifetime dispositions fall within three categories for inheritance tax purposes:

- exempt transfers;
- potentially exempt transfers; and
- chargeable transfers.

---

tax charge, negating the inheritance tax benefits of the planning, whilst still having the disadvantage for the donee of the cost basis at the time of the original gift.

[139] IHTA 1984, s 268. However, the Inland Revenue accepts that where unconditional transfers have been made between spouses, a gift by the donee out of the property transferred is not normally attacked under this provision. (See exchange of correspondence between the Institute of Chartered Accounts England and Wales (ICAEW) and the Inland Revenue dated 20 September 1985.)

[140] Unless this is as a result of a bad bargain in which case the exemption in IHTA 1984, s 10 will apply.

[141] IHTA 1984, s 18.

[142] IHTA 1984, s 11.

1.72 *Types of Tax*

Dispositions taking effect either on death or during lifetime have the benefit of certain exemptions and reliefs which may preclude chargeability. These are described in more detail in **CHAPTER 3**.

1.72 Additionally, certain lifetime dispositions may be free of inheritance tax if made more than seven years before death. Gifts which may qualify include outright gifts to individuals and include gifts on the following trusts:

- life interest trusts;
- trusts for disabled persons; and
- accumulation and maintenance trusts (a special type of discretionary trust for persons under the age of 25 when the trust is created and with restrictive vesting provisions (see **CHAPTER 6**).)

These gifts are described as 'potentially exempt transfers' or 'PETs'.[143]

1.73 PETs receive complete exemption from inheritance tax (although capital gains tax may remain relevant at the time of the gift) once the seven-year period has expired. However, if the donor dies within the seven-year period, the value of the property at the date of the original gift will effectively become chargeable to inheritance tax.[144] The tax attributable to a PET made within seven years of the donor's death may be reduced for such gifts depending on the period which elapses between the date of the gift and the donor's death (as outlined in **CHAPTER 5**). Even where death does occur within the seven-year period, there are valuable estate-freezing benefits to be secured, since only the original value of the asset at the time of the gift is subject to tax. Furthermore, where the rates of tax at the date of death are higher than those at the date of the gift, those prevailing at the earlier time will be used to compute the tax. In contrast, if the death rates are lower, those rates will be used to compute the tax.[145]

1.74 Since a life tenant of a trust is deemed to own the underlying assets of the trust in which his interest subsists,[146] it follows that if his interest is relinquished or prematurely terminated (eg through the exercise by the trustees of a power to divest him), he is deemed to have made a transfer of value. Whether this is a potentially exempt transfer or a chargeable transfer follows the general rules and depends upon its nature. For example, if the life tenant's interest were terminated in favour of a discretionary trust it would be a chargeable transfer but if it were terminated in favour of another beneficiary outright it would be a potentially exempt transfer.

1.75 A person who varies or disclaims a gift made to him on a death within a period of two years thereafter, is not treated as making a disposition for tax purposes.[147] The variation or disclaimer must be in writing and if a disclaimer, must

---

[143] IHTA 1984, s 3A.
[144] IHTA 1984, ss 3A(4) and s 7.
[145] IHTA 1984, Sch 2, paras 1 and 1A.
[146] IHTA 1984, s 49.
[147] IHTA 1984, ss 17 and 142. The document by which the variation or disclaimer is given effect must contain a statement by all relevant parties (being the person making the variation and the personal representatives, if further tax is due) that they intend the provision to apply and that the

be as to the whole of the gift[148] and prior to any implied acceptance. The legal criteria in regard to the disclaimer are broadly the same as those described above in the case of the US, save that in England and Wales there can be no partial disclaimer.

1.76 As noted at **1.47**, where there has been a gift with reservation of benefit and the transferor releases the reservation, he is deemed at that time to have made a potentially exempt transfer.[149]

1.77 Certain lifetime dispositions are immediately chargeable to inheritance tax (at one-half of the rates applicable on death, currently 20%). These are essentially gifts which do not pass into the estate of any person for tax purposes, for example, transfers to discretionary trusts or companies. As with potentially exempt transfers, chargeable lifetime transfers made within seven years of death are cumulated with the deceased's estate for the purposes of computing the inheritance tax rates applicable to the decedent's estate.[150] Once the seven-year period has elapsed, they too fall out of account. The retrospective application on death within the seven-year period of the tapered, but higher, rates of tax on death may also result in a higher tax charge attributable to the earlier chargeable gift and therefore additional tax to pay.[151]

---

gift should be treated as if it had been made by the deceased. A variation is susceptible to certain other tax anti-avoidance legislation, which a disclaimer is not and, therefore, in some cases the latter may be preferable, provided that those taking in default are the intended beneficiaries.

[148] The Inland Revenue accepts that in Scotland there are certain circumstances in which a partial disclaimer can be made: Inland Revenue Statement of Practice E18.
[149] IHTA 1984, s 102(4).
[150] IHTA 1984, s 7(1).
[151] IHTA 1984, s 7(4). See **CHAPTER 5**.

Chapter 2

Who and What is Taxed

A. United States

1. Introduction

2.1 The scope of the US transfer tax depends, in first instance, on the donor/decedent's domicile and citizenship. For a non-US domiciled alien (NDA), the scope of US taxation depends on the location of the transferred assets.

2. Citizens and domiciliaries

2.2 The US transfer tax has its broadest application to US citizens. A US citizen is subject to US transfer tax regardless of his residence or domicile and regardless of the location of the assets.[1] The US gift tax thus applies to gifts by a US citizen who is domiciled in Italy of her London flat, her stock in a German company and the diamonds she keeps in a Swiss vault.

2.3 Non-citizens who are US 'residents' are taxed in the same manner as US citizens, that is, without regard for the location of transferred assets.[2] Therefore, a US estate tax will be imposed on the value of a London flat, German stock and Swiss diamonds owned by an Italian national who is resident in the US at death.

2.4 For purposes of the US transfer tax rules, a US 'resident' is a person who is domiciled in the US.[3] This is a different test than is applied for determining US income tax residence. A non-citizen is considered a US income tax resident by reason of either the mathematical 'substantial presence' test (a 183-day rule) or the possession of a permanent residence visa (green card).[4] In contrast, a non-citizen is considered a US gift or estate tax resident (domiciliary) by residing in the US with an intention to make it his permanent home.[5]

---

[1] For estate tax purposes, this rule is found in Code § 2001(a). For gift tax purposes, Code § 2501 imposes the gift tax on all transfers by any individual, whether resident (domiciled) or non-resident, and Code § 2512(a) imposes the gift tax on transfers of all property, wherever located. However, in the context of a NDA, Code § 2512(a) provides that only property situated in the US is subject to tax. By implication, therefore, all property transferred by citizens (as well as residents/domiciliaries) are subject to gift tax.
[2] Code §§ 2001(a) and 2512(a).
[3] Treas Reg §§ 20.0–1(b)(1) and 25.2501–1(b). For purposes of these rules, the US includes the States and the District of Columbia.
[4] Code § 7701(b).
[5] Treas Reg §§ 20.0–1(b)(1) and 25.2501–1(b); see also *Estate of Paquette 46 TCM 1400 (1983)*. In Rev Rul 80–209, 1980–2 CB 248, the Service ruled that an illegal alien who resided in the US for

2.5 Who and What is Taxed

2.5 Under US law, a domicile once acquired is presumed to continue until it is shown to have changed.[6] For example, a Dutchman who lived in the US from 1940 until his death in 1946 was found not to have acquired a US domicile.[7] In contrast, another Dutchman who established a US domicile was found not to have abandoned that domicile even though he acquired a large home in Switzerland where he spent substantial periods each year.[8] Accordingly, a non-citizen who is domiciled in the US retains US domicile status upon his departure from the US, even if he has no intention of ever returning, unless and until he acquires a domicile in another country. This should be contrasted with the UK law, which considers a person to revert to his domicile of origin upon departure from a domicile of choice. See **2.34**.

2.6 The determination of a person's residence/domicile cannot be reduced to the simplified mathematical formula used for determining income tax residence. Instead, since domicile status depends on person's intent to make the US his permanent home, a variety of facts and circumstances might be considered to provide evidence of that subjective intent. Among the factors that might be considered are:

- the location of taxpayer's principal residence;
- the location of his immediate family;
- the location of his business activities;
- the location of personal items;
- the amount of time spent in each location;
- voter and driver's license registrations;
- declarations in estate planning documents;
- residence listed on State and local tax filings; and
- club, church or other organization membership resident or non-resident status.[9]

2.7 The US gift and estate tax rules specifically apply to both US citizens and residents/domiciliaries.[10] Similarly, the generation-skipping tax (GST) also applies where the 'transferor' is a US citizen or domiciliary, but the statutory provisions for this are less obvious. The GST depends, in part, on the relationship of the ultimate

---

19 years prior to his death could be considered domiciled in the US. Similarly, in *Estate of Jack v US* 2002–2 USTC ¶ 60,452 (Ct Cl 2002), the court held that a Canadian who held a temporary professional visa and lived and worked in the US could acquire the requisite intent to be considered domiciled in the US and thus subject to US estate tax.

[6] See *Mitchell v U.S.* 88 US (Wall) 350 (1874).
[7] *Estate of Nienhuys v Comm'r* 17 TC 1149 (1952), acq 1952–1 CB 3.
[8] *Estate of Fokker v Comm'r* 10 TC 1225 (1948), acq 1948–2 CB 2; see also *Fifth Avenue Bank of New York v Comm'r* 36 BTA 534 (1937) which involved a New York domiciliary who was found to have retained that domicile even though she lived in Paris from 1912 until her death in 1932.
[9] For a more detailed discussion of domicile, see **CHAPTER 16**.
[10] For estate tax purposes, this rule is *found* in Code § 2001(a). For gift tax purposes, Code § 2512(a) imposes the gift tax on transfers of all property, wherever located, but, in the context of a NDA, that section provides that only property situated in the US is subject to tax. By implication, therefore, all property transferred by citizens and domiciliaries are subject to gift tax.

transferees to the 'transferor'. Generation-skipping transfers (direct skips, taxable distributions and taxable terminations) all involve transfers to, or for, a 'skip person'. A skip person is defined as a person two or more generations below that of the 'transferor'. For purposes of the GST, a 'transferor' is a person who makes a gift subject to US gift tax or a decedent whose estate is subject to US estate tax.[11] Since US citizens and domiciliaries are subject to US gift and estate tax on their transfers regardless of the location of the transferred assets, they are similarly considered to be GST transferors. Therefore, a US citizen who is domiciled in France and who makes a one million euro gift to his Australian grandchild will be subject to both a US gift tax and a GST. Likewise, a non-citizen who is domiciled in the US and who transfers her Greek villa to her US or non-US grandchildren will also be subject to both US gift tax and GST.

3. Non-domiciled aliens (NDAs)

2.8 The application of the US transfer tax rules to a NDA depends solely on the nature of the transferred asset and whether or not it is considered situated in the US.[12]

a. Gift tax

2.9 With respect to a NDA, the US gift tax generally only applies to transfers of real estate and tangible personal property located in the US.[13] In contrast, intangible personal property (for example, stock) is not treated as a taxable transfer even though the evidence of that asset (the stock certificate) may be physically located in the US or the asset represents an interest in US property (eg stock in a US company).[14]

2.10 A NDA is technically subject to US gift tax on a gift of tangible personal property physically located in the US. Thus, a NDA, visiting the US with his wife, should wait to surprise her with the 20-carat bauble he picked up at Tiffany's until their flight has departed US airspace. These rules also apply to non-citizens who live in the US but are not domiciled here. Therefore, if a non-citizen temporarily resides in California and wishes to give her son the Renoir she has hanging in her San Francisco apartment, she should remove the painting from the US before presenting this gift.

2.11 US real estate obviously cannot be removed from the US. One option is to convert the real property into an intangible prior to the gift, for example, by first

---

[11] Code § 2652(a)(1).
[12] Code §§ 2511(a) and 2103.
[13] The US gift tax provisions begin by applying the US gift tax to all transfers of property by any person, resident or non-resident (Code § 2501(a)(1)). The rules provide that a NDA's gift of intangible property is not subject to gift tax (Code § 2501(a)(2)), making a NDA's gift of real estate and tangible personal property subject to US gift tax. Finally, Code § 2511(a) provides that, with respect to NDA's, the gift tax only applies to gifts of property situated in the US. These provisions, read together, result in the rule that a NDA is taxed on all gifts of real and tangible personal property situated in the US.
[14] Code § 2501(a)(2).

2.12 *Who and What is Taxed*

transferring that property to a US company. However, the IRS would likely treat such a transfer as a gift of US real estate.[15]

In one case, a NDA father owned US real estate in Hawaii and wished to transfer that property to his son. The father first made a gift to a newly opened British sterling account in the son's name. The account was established at the father's bank and the funds were immediately transferred back to the father as the down payment on the son's purchase of the property. The son also gave the father a promissory note, which he paid back from funds also later gifted to the son's UK account by his father. The IRS argued that the father made a taxable gift of US real estate. The father asserted that his gifts were only of non-US assets: the money he transferred to his son's UK account. The court reached a compromise decision. The father's initial cash gift was clearly a subterfuge for his intended gift of US real estate to his son. The measure of that gift was the difference between the US property's value and the amount of the son's promissory note. As to the annual gifts used by the son to service the debt, the court found that the son intended to pay his obligations from his own earnings and had not expected his father's continued generosity in later years. Thus the portion of the 'sale' represented by the promissory note was not considered a gift of US real estate.[16]

2.12   The gift tax situs of cash is less than clear. A NDA uncle's $20,000 gift of currency to his niece while in the US is considered to be a gift of US property.[17] But what if the uncle's gift was by means of a check? In an internal memorandum, the Service concluded that a check drawn on a US bank account is considered to be a transfer of US tangible personal property and therefore subject to US gift tax.[18]

---

[15]   In *De Goldschmidt-Rothschild v Comm'r 9 TC 325 (1947), aff'd 168 F 2d 975 (2d Cir 1948)*, the NDA taxpayer wanted to make a gift in trust for benefit of certain relatives. In order to avoid US gift tax, she converted US marketable securities into US Treasury notes and gifted the notes. At that time, a NDA's gift or US securities was subject to US gift tax, but a gift of US Treasury notes was exempt from US gift tax. The trust sold the notes soon after receipt and reinvested the proceeds in non-exempt property. The Tax Court concluded that:
   'the taxpayer's conversion of [non-exempt property] into [exempt property] under a pre-arranged program or understanding and solely for the purpose of making a tax exempt gift ... was ineffectual for tax purposes'.

[16]   *Davies v Comm'r 40 TC 525 (1963)*.

[17]   PLR 7737063 (17 June 1977), concluding that cash is a tangible asset and therefore does not qualify for the intangibles exception of Code § 2501(a)(2).

[18]   GCM 36860 (24 September 1976). Anomalously, NDA money deposited in a non-business US bank account is an intangible exempt from US estate tax, but money transferred from a US bank account in the US is a tangible US-sited asset subject to gift tax. US gift tax exposure can thus potentially apply to:
   (a)   a transfer by a donor's US dollar check drawn on a US bank account; or
   (b)   wiring of US dollar funds to the US bank account of the donee.
   Guidance is limited in this area, but advisers prudently advise the transfer of funds offshore, much as a remittance would be avoided for UK income tax purposes. One international tax practitioner uses a 'stoplight' approach in advising offshore donors with respect to gifts to US children:
   •   red – writing a dollar check on the donor's US bank account which is sent to and deposited in the donee's US bank account – this transfer should be subject to US gift tax, subject to the $11,000 per donee annual gift tax exclusion or estate and gift tax treaty relief;

United States **2.14**

b. Estate tax

2.13 The estate tax also applies to US-situated property owned by a NDA.[19] The estate tax reach is much more expansive than the gift tax rules. For example, stocks and bonds in US companies are considered to be situated in the US for estate tax purposes.[20] An Iraqi owning shares in Halliburton can gift those shares during life without US gift tax implications but, upon his death, those shares would technically be subject US estate tax.

2.14 The following list illustrates the US estate tax situs rules on various assets.

Type of property	*US property for US estate tax purposes*
Real estate in US	Yes[21]
Gold, jewelry, art and antiques:	
• physically located in US (other than in transit or loaned for exhibition)	Yes[22]
• physically located outside US	No[23]
Stock in US companies (even if the certificates are held outside the US	Yes[24]
Stock in foreign companies (even if the certificates are physically located in the US)	No[25]
American Depository Receipts (ADRs)	No[26]
Interest in partnership doing business in the US	Probably[27]
Currency in US safe deposit box	Yes[28]
Cash deposits with US brokers	Yes[29]

- amber – wiring US dollar funds from, say, a Swiss bank account to the donee's US dollar account – the issue here is where title to the currency passes; the risk is that until credited to the donee's account in the United States, the funds belong to the sender;
- green – the donor has a US dollar account with an foreign bank branch and asks his relationship manager to set up a US dollar account for his US resident son. US dollar funds are then transferred between the offshore branch accounts – it should not matter whether the offshore bank is a foreign branch of a US bank provided both the donor and donee accounts are at the offshore bank.

[19] Code § 2103.
[20] Code § 2104(a).
[21] Treas Reg § 20.2104–1(a)(1). A US real property holding company (Code § 897) is not considered US real estate for estate tax purposes, although stock in the US company would be considered situated in US unless exempted by treaty.
[22] Treas Reg § 20.2104–1(a)(2); Code § 2105(c); Treas Reg § 20.2105–1(b).
[23] Treas Reg § 20.2105–1(a)(2).
[24] Treas Reg § 20.2104–1(a)(5).
[25] Treas Reg § 20.2105–1(f).
[26] ADRs represent underlying foreign stock and thus are not situated in the US. PLR 200243031 (25 July 2002).
[27] The law is uncertain in this area, as discussed in detail at **CHAPTER 14 (14.72** et seq).
[28] Rev Rul 55–143, 1955–1 CB 465.

2.14 Who and What is Taxed

Type of property	US property for US estate tax purposes
Non-business cash deposits with US banks and savings & loan associations	
• Checking account	No[30]
• Savings account	No
• Time deposits	No
• CDs	No
Cash deposits with foreign commercial bank branches of US institutions	No[31]
Cash deposits with US commercial bank branches of foreign institutions	No[32]
Proceeds of US insurance on life of NDA	No[33]
Cash surrender value of US life insurance on life of another	Yes[34]
Cash held by US insurance companies at interest	No[35]
Annuity contract payable by US person or company	Yes[36]
'80/20 Company' debt obligations	No[37]
All US debt obligations issued before 18 July 1984	Yes[38]
All US debt obligations in bearer form and not part of foreign-targeted issue	Yes
US debt obligations issued after 18 July 1984 (if registered or if among targeted issued and not paying contingent interest):[39]	
• US Government T-bills (less than six months)	No

---

[29] *Estate of Ogarrio v Comm'r 337 F 2d 108*; Rev Rul 65–245, 1965–2 CB 379; see also *Rosenblum v Anglim 135 F.2d 512 (9th Cir 1943)*; Rev Rul 56–421, 1956–2 CB 602.

[30] Cash deposits with US banks and savings and loan associations are generally excluded, unless they are effectively connected 'with a US trading or business'. Code §§ 2105(b)(1) and 871(i).

[31] Code § 2105(b).

[32] Code §§ 2104(c), 2105(b), 871(i)(3), 861(a)(1) and 884(f)(1)(A).

[33] Code § 2105(a).

[34] Since the policy represents a debt of a US company, the decedent's interest in the insurance policy not on his own life would be considered situated in the US under Code § 2104(c). *Riccio v US 71–2 USTC ¶ 12,801 (D.P.R 1971)*.

[35] Code §§ 2105(b)(1) and 871(i)(3)(C), unless 'effectively connected' with the conduct of a US trade or business of the recipient of the interest.

[36] Code § 2104(c).

[37] Code §§ 2104(c) and 861(a)(1)(A).

[38] By implication – see reference to ADRs at footnote 26.

[39] Code §§ 2105(b)(3) and 871(h). Code § 871(h)(4) provides that contingent interest debt is not portfolio interest debt. Under Code § 2105(b)(4) such debt (to the extent allocable to its contingent interest) is not excluded from estate tax for post-1993 NDA estates. Prior to 5 August 1997, short-term OID was inadvertently not within the portfolio interest exception. Code §§ 871(h)(2), 871(a) and 871(g). The omission was corrected by Code § 2105(b)(4) which excludes short-term OID from estate tax exposure for decedents dying after 5 August 1997.

United States **2.16**

Type of property	US property for US estate tax purposes
• US Government T-notes	No
• US Government bonds	No
• Tax-exempt municipal bonds	Yes[40]
• Bonds issued by US corporations	No[41]
• Bonds issued by US partnerships	No[42]
• Euro/Yankee Bonds	No

2.15 Property held in a trust established by a NDA is subject to US estate tax if:

- the NDA retained a right to revoke the trust, a right to trust income or a right to control benefits in the trust; and
- the trust held US property at the NDA's death.[43]

Therefore, if a NDA's revocable trust owned US real estate at her death, that property would be subject to the US estate tax.

2.16 This rule also applies to a retained interest trust if the NDA initially transferred US property to such a trust, even if the trust is not invested in US property at the NDA's death. For example, if a NDA initially transferred US real estate to a revocable trust (a transfer that would not be considered a taxable gift) and, by the date of her death, the US property had been sold and the proceeds reinvested in non-US assets, a portion of the trust property would nonetheless be subject to US estate tax.[44] This result is a particular trap for the unwary. Moreover, to add even further complexity and confusion to this issue, the situs of property initially transferred to such a trust is based on the estate tax situs rules, not the gift tax rules.[45] The implication of this is illustrated by a gift of stock in a US company. Even though no US gift tax is imposed on gifts of US intangibles (such as stock in a US company), the US stock is, nonetheless, considered situated in the US for purposes of this rule.

---

[40] Interest on State and local bonds is exempt from US federal income tax by Code § 103. Other bonds and US resident portfolio debt, non-business US commercial bank accounts, savings accounts, foreign branch bank accounts and interest on an insurance policy are all exempt from US income tax withholding by Code § 871(h) and (i), but not municipal bonds, even though tax exempt. Since Code § 2105(b) only exempts from estate tax interest which is exempted under Code §§ 871(h) and (i), the inadvertent omission of municipal bonds exposes them to estate tax (as discussed in Glod, 'United States Estate and Gift Taxation of Nonresident Aliens: Troublesome Situs Issues', 51 The Tax Lawyer 109 (1997) at 133 *et seq*).

[41] However, if the NDA and the NDA's family together own 10% or more of the company or partnership, the bonds will be included in the NDA's estate. Code §§ 2105(b)(3) and 871(h).

[42] Ibid.

[43] Code §§ 2104(b) & 2038. See also Code § 2036.

[44] For example, assume a NDA funded a revocable trust with both US property (30%) and non-US property (70%). Even if there was no US property held in the trust at the donor's death, 30% of the trust would be taxed in the NDA's US estate. A NDA who initially funded a revocable with US property and wishes to avoid this trap would be advised to revoke the trust and form a new trust with non-US property.

[45] Treas Reg § 20.2104–1(b).

2.17   Who and What is Taxed

2.17   As suggested by the chart at **2.14**, a NDA whose estate would not otherwise be exempt from US estate tax by reason of a treaty might consider owning his US investments through a foreign holding company, since those shares would not be considered situated in the US.[46] There is some risk, however, that the rules discussed in **2.16** for retained interests in trust would also apply to corporations. The relevant Code provisions cause property transferred, *in trust or otherwise*, to be included in the donor's estate if the donor retained a right to revoke the trust or a beneficial interest in the transferred property.[47] While these provisions clearly apply to trusts, they might also apply with equal force to corporations.[48] For example, a NDA who owns 100% of a foreign holding company can liquidate the company, essentially revoking his earlier transfer. Similarly, a NDA shareholder might also be considered to have retained a beneficial interest in the company's underlying investments by reason of his right to declare and receive dividends. The risks are perhaps greatest in the context where the company holds US residential real estate used exclusively by the NDA.[49]

2.18   As an alternative to using a foreign corporation to hold US investments, the NDA might also use a trust, as long as he does not retain the power to revoke the trust, a right to trust income or the right to control benefits. It is also currently more income tax efficient to hold US real estate through an irrevocable foreign trust than through a foreign holding company. Gains from the sale of US real property by a non-US taxpayer are subject to US income tax.[50] The US long-term capital gains tax rate for individuals and trusts (including non-US individuals and trusts) is

---

[46]   Treas Reg § 20.2105–1(f).
[47]   Code §§ 2036 & 2038, discussed in detail at **CHAPTER 14** (**14.72** et seq).
[48]   Property held in a partnership, rather than the partnership interest itself, was recently included in a decedent's estate because of his retained right to indirectly benefit from the income of the underlying property and to control the distribution of partnership income to other partners. *Strangi v Comm'r TCM 2003–145, Doc 2003–12584 (47 original pages), 2003 TNT 98–16.* This case involved a US taxpayer and the primary implication of the decision was on how to value the property included in the decedent's estate. Had the partnership itself been found to be the asset taxable in the decedent's estate, substantial marketability discounts might have been available. However, because the court applied the principles of Code § 2036(a) to cause the transferred property (the underlying partnership assets) to be taxed in the decedent's estate, no valuation discounts were available. Many commentators have questioned the court's decision in *Strangi*. However, if the principles of that case were extended into this context, the underlying assets of a NDA's foreign holding company could be included in his estate to the extent US assets were initially transferred to the company or were held in the company at the NDA's death.
[49]   See Scheine and Kay, 'Transfer of US Vacation Property to a Canadian Corporation – A Viable Strategy to Avoid US Estate Tax?', 27 Tax Management International Journal 195 (April 1998). Most commentators had, at least prior to *Strangi*, considered this result to be unlikely given the relevant legislative history. See, for example, Lawrence, *International Tax and Estate Planning* (3rd edn, 1996) Practising Law Institute, § 3.2.1, § 3.2.3 and § 3.2.10[A]. However, two additional caveats apply. First, if corporate housekeeping rules are not followed, the corporation may be disregarded as a nominee. *Fillman v US 355 F 2d 632 (Ct Cl 1966).* Second, foundations risk trust/corporate classification issues and may be at the mercy of the IRS's choice of which attack yields the highest estate and income tax exposure. In particular, foundations with plenary retained founder controls are unlikely to shelter the NDA from US tax exposure. See, for example, *Estate of Swan v Comm'r 24 TC 829 (1955), rev'd 247 F 2d 144 (2d Cir 1957)* (founder retained powers to withdraw funds, amend and terminate a Liechtenstein foundation; *held*, the foundation's US sited property was subject to estate tax under Code § 2038).
[50]   Code § 897. In contrast, a non-US taxpayer is not taxed in the US on the gain from the sale of other US property, such as stock in a US company, unless that company is considered a US real property holding company under Code § 897(c)(2).

currently capped at 15%.[51] In contrast, corporations do not enjoy any rate break for capital gains. Instead, gains are taxed to a corporation along with its other income at rates as high as 35%.[52]

c. Generation-skipping tax (GST)

2.19 If a NDA's transfer is subject to US gift or estate tax, the NDA becomes a 'transferor' for GST purposes. The GST would, accordingly, be imposed if a generation-skipping transfer occurs that is related to the NDA's taxable transfer. For example, a NDA's gift to her grandchild of her Aspen ski home will be subject to both a US gift tax and GST. Similarly, a NDA's bequest of US stock to a grandchild will be subject to both a US estate tax and a GST.

2.20 Likewise, when a NDA's gift or bequest to a trust for the benefit of the intervening generation is subject to a US gift or estate tax, the US GST will be imposed on subsequent 'taxable distribution' or 'taxable termination.' For example, if a NDA decedent leaves US real estate in trust for the benefit of her children, the GST would be imposed at the child's later death when this property passes to (or is held in continuing trust for) the grandchildren. This is true without regard for the situs of the trust property at the child's subsequent death. Thus, if the trust in the prior example had sold the US real estate and, at the child's death, distributed only non-US assets to the grandchildren, the GST would still technically apply. Conversely, if a NDA decedent left foreign property to a trust for children (and therefore the transfer was not subject to US estate tax), no GST would be imposed on that trust at the child's later death, even if, at that time, part or all of that trust consisted of US property.

4. Tax-motivated expatriates

2.21 The US income tax and transfer tax system also includes special provisions for tax-motivated expatriates. A tax-motivated expatriate is generally an individual who has given up US citizenship with US tax avoidance being one of his or her primary motivations.[53] The Health Insurance Portability and Accountability Act 1996 (HIPAA) extended these rules to long-term green card holders who cease to be US income tax residents.[54]

2.22 In addition, HIPAA also deems an individual to have a tax motivation if either:

- his or her net worth exceeds $622,000; or

---

[51] Code § 1(h)(1)(C).
[52] Code § 11(b). The 35% rate applies to corporate income/gains in excess of $10m. A 34% rate applies to income/gains between $75,000 and $10m.
[53] Code § 877(a)(1).
[54] Code § 877(e). This rule extends to a green card holder:
- who gives up his green card and thus ceases to be US income tax residents; and
- who becomes resident in treaty countries and does not waive the benefits of the treaty.

A 'long-term resident' means an individual who has been a green card holder for at least eight of the previous 15 years.

2.23 Who and What is Taxed

- he or she had an average of US income tax liability for the prior five years of in excess of $124,000 per year.[55]

The anti-expatriation provisions generally apply for a ten-year period after expatriation.[56]

2.23 The anti-expatriation rules do not treat the tax-motivated expatriate as if he were still a US citizen.[57] Instead, the rules generally seek to tax the expatriate on US-source income and on the transfer of certain US property interests that would otherwise have been exempt from US tax.

2.24 NDAs are generally exempt from US gift tax on gifts of intangible personal property. However, gifts made by a tax-motivated expatriate within ten years of expatriation do not qualify for the intangibles exception.[58] This does not cause a tax-motivated expatriate to pay gift tax on gifts of all intangible personal property, just gifts of intangibles that are situated in the US.[59] Shares of stock in a US company and debt obligations of a US person or of the US, the District of Columbia, a State or a political subdivision of a State (eg a city or county) are all considered for this purpose as situated in the US.[60] Thus, during the ten-year period after expatriation, a tax-motivated expatriate's gifts of shares of a US company will be subject to the US gift tax.

2.25 US-situated intangibles owned by a NDA decedent are generally subject to US estate tax without regard to whether or not the NDA is a tax-motivated expatriate.[61] The gift tax anti-expatriation rule thus has little relevance to the estate tax. Instead, the estate tax anti-expatriation rules are designed to prevent expatriates from avoiding US estate taxes by investing in US property through certain foreign holding companies. As previously discussed, a NDA can (subject to certain caveats) generally avoid US estate tax by owning his US investments (real property, tangible personal property or intangibles) through a foreign company. If the individual:

- directly or indirectly (eg through trusts, partnerships or other companies) owns at least 10% of foreign company's voting power; and

- after applying certain attribution rules, owns more than 50% of the voting power or value of that company, then a proportionate share of the company's value attributed to the US assets will be subject to US estate tax.

---

[55] Code § 877(a)(2). Note that the amounts listed in the Code ($500,000 net worth and $100,000 average income tax liability) are adjusted for inflation. The amounts above reflect inflation adjustments for 2004. Rev Proc. 2003–85, 2003–49 IRB 1184.
[56] Code §§ 877(a)(1), 2107(a) and 2501(a)(3).
[57] However, in late 2003 and early 2004, the House Ways and Means Committee had proposed to tax such expatriates as US citizens during any year in the ten-year 'tail off' period in which the expatriate was present in the US more than 31 days per year. Further, the Senate Finance Committee had proposed to impose an 'exit tax' on such expatriates and to subject to US income tax, US donees of gifts or bequests from tax motivated expatriates.
[58] Code § 2501(a)(3).
[59] The anti-expatriation rules do not change the rule in Code § 2511(a) that restricts the US gift tax to only property situated in the US.
[60] Code § 2511(b).
[61] Code § 2104(b) and (c).

United States **2.29**

For example, if a tax-motivated expatriate owned a 60% interest in a foreign company worth $10m, and 20% of that company's assets were situated in the US under the estate tax rules, an amount equal to $1.2m ($10m × 60% × 20%) would be taxed in the individual's estate.[62]

2.26 There are no special anti-expatriation rules in the GST provisions, nor need there be. As previously discussed, the GST only applies if there was an initial transfer during life or at death that caused an individual (citizen, domiciliary, or NDA) to be considered the 'transferor.' If the anti-expatriation rules cause the NDA to be subject to US gift or estate tax, then the tax-motivated expatriate will be considered a 'transferor' for GST purposes. Thus, if a tax-motivated expatriate made a gift of US stock to his grandchildren within ten years of expatriation, the gift would be subject to both a gift tax and a GST. Likewise, if a tax-motivated expatriate dies within ten years of his expatriation and leaves his 100%-owned, US-invested foreign holding company in trust for a child, an estate tax will be imposed at the time of the decedent's death and the GST will be imposed on any later taxable distribution or taxable termination.

2.27 A tax-motivated expatriate wishing to avoid US gift tax, estate tax and GST need only transfer property that is not situated in the US (after applying the special gift and estate tax anti-expatriation rules). A tax-motivated expatriate's gift of non-US real estate, for example, would not be subject to any US transfer tax, even if that gift occurred within ten years of his expatriation.

2.28 As noted, HIPAA extended the anti-expatriation rules to departing long-term green card holders. The anti-expatriation income provisions direct that a departing long-term green card holder who is treated as a tax-motivated expatriate will also be treated as if he were a US citizen who had given up citizenship for purposes of the gift and estate tax provisions.[63] This can create some peculiar transfer tax results.

2.29 Consider the scenario of a foreign executive who moves to the US, acquires a green card, but always intends to return to his home country upon retirement. That individual might, accordingly, have never become a US domiciliary. As such, his exposure to US gift and estate tax would be limited. For example, even though the executive is a US income tax resident, he could presumably gift to his children an unlimited amount of US stock without US gift tax. If he retires, however, moves

---

[62] A tax-motivated expatriate who desires to reinvest in the US markets during the ten-year period after expatriation could do so by structuring his investments through a foreign holding company that did not meet the tests of Code § 2107(b). One way to do this would be to invest through a widely-held offshore mutual fund.

[63] Code § 877(e)(1). The gift and estate tax anti-expatriation Code provisions only refer to former citizens who have given up citizenship for tax avoidance purposes. Code §§ 2501(a)(3)(A) and 2107(a)(1). One would typically have expected Congress to amend these provisions at the same time they extended the anti-expatriation rules to departing green card holders. While the terms of revised Code § 877(e)(1) accomplish the same result, the failure to incorporate these changes specifically in the gift and estate tax provisions of the Code – or to even provide a cross-reference to Code § 877(e)(1) – makes the transfer tax analysis less than clear to the casual observer.

back to his home country, relinquishes his green card and then gifts the US stock, the anti-expatriation rules would impose a gift tax.[64]

2.30 In contrast, a long-term green card holder who would, because of the facts and circumstances, be considered domiciled in the US, could largely escape the US transfer tax net by retaining his green card but moving his domicile outside the US.[65] After becoming a non-domiciliary, the individual could make unlimited, tax-free gifts of US intangible property without US gift tax. The individual could also hold US investments through a non-US holding company and escape US estate taxes at death. To avoid the anti-expatriation rules, the individual need only retain the green card (albeit with the continuing and attendant US income tax exposure).

2.31 In the context of long-term green card holders, therefore, the anti-expatriation rules:

- impose a transfer tax on some expatriates who would not have been subject to the US gift or estate tax had they retained their permanent residence status; and

- fail to prevent a long-term green card holder from slipping the US transfer tax net by changing his domicile while retaining the green card.

B. United Kingdom

1. Introduction

2.32 UK inheritance tax exposure depends upon the transferor's or decedent's domicile status. Nationality/citizenship is of no tax consequence under UK domestic law. UK domiciliaries are subject to tax on their worldwide estate at death and on lifetime gifts; non-UK domiciliaries are exposed to tax only on their UK sited assets.[66]

---

[64] The presumption of tax avoidance in Code § 877(a)(2) can be overcome in certain situations described in Code § 877(c)(2). The Code provision deals with only a US citizen who is a dual national or who becomes a citizen of the county in which he, his spouse, his parents or his spouse's parents were born. A person so qualifying must, however, submit a ruling request to the IRS within one-year of expatriation for determination of whether tax avoidance was a primary motivating factor. Detailed financial information is required. Notice 98–34, 1998–2 CB 29, modifying Notice 97–19, 1997–1 CB 394. Until regulations are issued, this notice also authorises a long-term green card holder to file for this ruling request, but only if he is a citizen of the country in which he, his spouse, his parents or his spouse's parents were born, and he becomes a resident of that country within a reasonable period and becomes fully subject to tax in that country. A British executive who retires back to England could qualify for this exception, unless neither he, his spouse, his parents or his spouse's parents were born there. See, for example, PLR 200323030 (24 February 2003).

[65] For purposes of the US immigration rules, a green card holder who moves from the US, other than on a temporary basis, can lose his green card privileges. In contrast, a green card holder does not lose his status as a US income tax resident until the green card is 'rescinded or administratively or judicially determined to have been abandoned'. Treas Reg § 301.7701(b)-1(b)(1).

[66] IHTA 1984, s 6. The term 'UK domicile' is used for convenience. However, it should be noted that domicile is governed by reference to legal jurisdictions. Hence, technically a person will be domiciled in 'England and Wales' or 'Scotland' or 'Northern Ireland'.

2. UK domiciliaries

2.33 The meaning of domicile in the UK, as determined largely by case law, is similar to that in the US – being the place which an individual regards as his permanent home.[67] However, since the concept in the first instance relies on the application of legal principles to determine a person's 'domicile of origin', he can in some cases be regarded as having a domicile in a country in which he has no permanent home; and even in which he has never lived.[68] Furthermore, the fact that a person does not, for many years, live in the country he regards as his permanent home does not preclude him from being domiciled there under UK law, provided he has not formed an intention to make any other country his permanent home.[69]

2.34 Under UK law, a domicile of origin is acquired at birth, which is the domicile of the father at the date of a child's birth.[70] This is the most tenacious domicile concept, being difficult to displace and, unlike the position under US law, being capable of revival at any time when a domicile of choice is lost and no other has been acquired in its place. The domicile of an adopted child changes at the time of adoption and the legal principles are applied to establishing his domicile of origin, as if the child had been born to the adoptive parents.[71]

2.35 A minor under the age of 16 will normally follow any changes in domicile of his father (his 'domicile of dependency'). Technically, it is possible for a child to acquire an independent domicile from that age, however, the likelihood of a person, at that stage in his life, having the requisite intent to substantiate acquisition of a domicile of choice is remote. Where his parents separate he will normally take (as a domicile of dependency) the domicile of the parent with whom he continues to live. This domicile of dependency will then continue until a domicile of choice is acquired or his domicile of origin reverts.

2.36 A person may acquire a domicile of choice, which displaces his domicile of origin, by moving from one country of residence to another and living there with the intention to remain in the new location permanently.[72] As already stated in the case of the US, the determination of a particular country as his future permanent home involves the consideration of a variety of facts and circumstances to provide evidence of that subjective intent. Among such factors might be:

---

[67] *Whicker v Hume (1858) 7 HLC 124*; as to domicile generally, see Dicey & Morris, *The Conflict of Laws*, Vol 1 (13th edn) Sweet & Maxwell, at p 107 et seq.
[68] *Peal v Peal 46 TLR 645.*
[69] *CIR v Bullock [1976] 51 TC (CA).*
[70] *Udny v Udny (1869) LR 1 Sc & Div 441.* This applies to a legitimate child born during his father's lifetime. In the case of a child born after his father's death or an illegitimate child, the relevant domicile is that of the mother.
[71] Adoption Act 1976, s 39(1)(5).
[72] If a person intends to remain indefinitely but contemplates that he might move at some future date only in particular circumstances, these will be ignored if they are vague or indefinite (eg *Re Furse [1980] 3 All ER 838*, where the contingency was making a fortune, or *In the estate of Fuld (No 3) [1968] 674*, where the contingency was suffering ill health). Defined circumstances will, however, be taken into account in determining whether the requisite intent to remain exists; such as the death of a spouse in *CIR v Bullock [1976] 51 TC (CA)* or until the end of a child's education or the termination of employment.

2.37 Who and What is Taxed

- the location of taxpayer's principal residence;
- the location of his immediate family and education of children;
- the location of his business activities;
- the location of personal items;
- the amount of time spent in each location;
- voter and driver's license registrations;
- declarations in, and form and content of, estate planning documents;
- residence listed on tax filings;
- whether citizenship has been taken in the relevant country;
- affiliations with charitable organisations; and
- club, church or other organisation membership resident or non-resident status.[73]

2.37 The onus of proving a change of domicile is on the person asserting the change and the burden of proof where the assertion is the loss of a domicile of origin, in favour of acquisition of a domicile of choice, is onerous.[74] The loss of a domicile of choice may, however, be achieved by ceasing to reside in the relevant country and leaving it with the express intention not to return.[75] The domicile which replaces it will depend on whether the criteria are satisfied for the acquisition of an alternative domicile of choice and, if not, the domicile of origin will revive.

2.38 Since 1974, the UK has recognised that husbands and wives may have different domiciles,[76] but prior to that time a wife automatically took the domicile status of her husband on marriage. For those to whom the prior law applied, the spouse's domicile of dependency became a domicile of choice with effect from the change of law on 1 January 1974, capable of being changed independently of the husband's domicile thereafter.

2.39 Domicile is not necessarily defined by reference to a country but by reference to a jurisdiction which can be recognised as having a separate legal system. Thus, it is not strictly correct to speak of having a 'US domicile' because an individual's American's domicile is defined by reference to a particular state. This can cause difficulty in cases where a person may have moved from the UK to the US permanently and may have been there for many years, but where he has moved

---

[73] See, also, the discussion of domicile in **CHAPTER 17**. As to the matter of citizenship, whilst it is a relevant consideration, it should be noted it is not a decisive factor. 'It is not the law either that a change of domicile is a condition of naturalisation, or that naturalisation involves necessarily a change of domicile'. *Wahl v Attorney General (1932) 147 LT 382*. See, generally, the discussion in Dicey & Morris, *The Conflict of Laws*, Vol 1 (13th edn) Sweet & Maxwell, at p 120 et seq.
[74] *Civil Engineer v CIR [2002] STC SCD 72.*
[75] See *Zanelli v Zanelli (1948) 64 TLR 556* where the English court accepted jurisdiction to hear a divorce case on the basis that at the relevant time the husband was domiciled in England by choice. The domicile of choice was lost only when he had both made the decision to leave the UK permanently and had physically done so.
[76] Under the Domicile and Matrimonial Proceedings Act 1973, s 1(1).

between different states without having settled in any one in particular. Despite the intention to remain in the US and not return to the UK, he may have done insufficient to displace his domicile of origin as a matter of UK law.

2.40 It can be seen from the above that a person with a UK domicile of origin who has secured a US domicile of choice by moving permanently to a particular US state, but then changes his mind and moves, say, to New Zealand, with no definite intention to remain there, will be deemed under UK law to have reacquired his UK domicile of origin. In contrast, the US would be likely to treat him as having retained his US domicile of choice until a new domicile of choice is acquired.

2.41 A 'deemed domicile' in the UK can be acquired for IHT purposes following a long period of UK tax residence. If the individual has been resident in the UK in any part of 17 or more of the previous 20 UK tax years (6 April to the following 5 April), the provision will apply.[77] In reality, this may be less than 17 calendar years as the calculation is by reference to the number of tax years (or part) in which an individual has been UK resident for income tax purposes. For example, a person who had become UK tax resident on 31 March 1988 would become deemed UK domiciled as from 6 April 2003 (just over 15 calendar years – the first year being 1987/88 and the 17th year being 2003/04).

2.42 Generally, a person will acquire income tax residence by being present in the UK for 183 days or more during any tax year or if he visits on a regular basis and his average days of presence in the UK over a four-year period are 91 days or more per tax year.[78] See **CHAPTER 9** for a more detailed discussion of UK residence.

2.43 Deemed domicile is a concept only of relevance for inheritance tax purposes and not for the purposes of the general law or for any other taxes. An individual will also be regarded as a deemed domiciliary if he has been domiciled in the UK under UK general law principles within the preceding three calendar years. Accordingly, it will not be possible to lose a UK domicile for three full UK calendar years following a person's permanent departure.[79]

2.44 By way of example, assuming a person had lived in the UK over 20 years and left on 30 June 2004, under the rule first mentioned above, his deemed domicile would cease on 6 April 2008. The first year, during no part of which he will have been UK tax resident, will be 2005/06. Accordingly, at all times until 6 April 2008 he will have been resident in some part of 17 of the prior 20 tax years. From that date

---

[77] IHTA 1984, s 267(1)(b).
[78] The precise timing of the acquisition of residence status may depend on the intention of the taxpayer at the outset. If, when he first comes to the UK, it is clear that he intends to make visits of 91 days or more per annum on average over a four-year period, he may be treated as becoming resident at the outset. Where that intention does not exist, his residence status normally commences at the beginning of the fifth tax year of his stay. If his intention changes before the commencement of the fifth year of his stay, tax residence may commence in the tax year when he changes his intention. It should be noted that the rules governing residence are not set out in statutory form but are complex and are currently based on case law and Inland Revenue practice as outlined in its publication IR20.
[79] IHTA 1984, s 267(1)(a). In practice, this will be longer if the person has been tax resident throughout the prior 20-year period, since he will need to satisfy the test at subsection (1)(b) as well by reference to tax years.

2.45 Who and What is Taxed

he ceases to satisfy the test. Under the second rule mentioned above, assuming he left on 30 June 2004, his deemed domicile will cease on 1 July 2007.

2.45 In the April 2002 Budget, the UK Government announced its intention to review the rules on residence and domicile and a background paper[80] was published on 9 April 2003. The paper does not contain any specific or substantive proposals but a review of some aspects of the current rules in the UK and a number of other countries. It is possible that this review will give rise to changes to the way UK tax residence is established and lost and how non-UK domiciled individuals are taxed in the UK.

3. Non-UK domiciliaries

2.46 As noted, the exposure to IHT depends on the domicile of the transferor or deceased and the situs of the assets. UK domiciled persons are taxed on worldwide assets and non-UK domiciled persons are taxed on UK sited assets. The principles governing the situs of assets for IHT are found in the general law and are not set out in the IHT legislation. The following UK situs rules apply both to lifetime and testamentary dispositions.[81]

Kinds of property	Considered situated in the UK for UK IHT purposes
Real estate in the UK	Yes
Tangible movables located in the UK (eg gold, jewellery, art, antiques and including for example works of art in transit, although liability will by concession be waived if the assets are normally kept abroad but are in the UK for exhibition or restoration)[82]	Yes
Tangible movables located outside the UK	No
Shares/stock in UK registered companies	Yes[83]
Shares/stock in non-UK registered companies	No
Bearer shares in any companies:	
certificates located in the UK	Yes
certificates located outside the UK	No
Interest in a partnership whose principal business is in the UK	Yes[84]

---

[80] 'Reviewing the residence and domicile rules as they affect the taxation of individuals: a background paper – April 2003'.
[81] See, generally, Dicey & Morris (ibid).
[82] ESC F7.
[83] Where shares are dealt with on more than one register, they are sited in the country of the primary register – being the one on which they are normally dealt.

Kinds of property	Considered situated in the UK for UK IHT purposes
Cash deposits at a UK branch of a bank	Yes
Debts where debtor resides:	
in the UK	Yes
outside the UK	No
Specialty debts where the document is:	
in the UK	Yes
outside the UK	No
Rights under contract where the contract is enforceable:	
in the UK	Yes
outside the UK	No
Proceeds of UK insurance on the life of a non UK domiciliary	Yes[85]

2.47 Additionally there are exemptions from liability to UK inheritance tax for certain specific UK sited assets dependent on the status of the taxpayer as follows:

- certain designated UK government securities owned by persons not ordinarily resident in the UK (ie broadly persons who have not been present in the UK for an average of 91 days or more in four or more consecutive years);[86]

- certain designated UK government securities owned by trustees;

  - for persons with an interest in possession who are not UK ordinarily resident; or

  - for persons with discretionary interests provided all such potential beneficiaries are not UK ordinarily resident;[87]

---

[84] Provided the applicable partnership law is English law or is analogous to English law and, accordingly, that the partner's rights are represented by entitlement to a proportion of the net assets of the business. However, if the relevant law of the partnership is one which entitles the partners to a direct interest in the partnership assets themselves, the situs of each asset would appear to need to be determined on normal principles. As to the partnership goodwill, this would generally be determined by reference to the principal place of business. See *Lindley & Banks on Partnership* (18th edn) Sweet & Maxwell, at p 969.

[85] A contract under English law will give rise to a chose in action which, if enforceable in the UK, is UK sited. However, appropriate structuring of the policy itself, in particular, if it is written under trust to fall outside the estate of the life assured, can avoid the application of UK inheritance tax.

[86] IHTA 1984, s 6(2). Ordinary residence is a concept denoting habitual presence in the UK over a number of years and generally applies if a person is present in the UK for 91 days or more over any four tax-year period. As with residence the precise timing of acquisition of ordinary residence depends on the intention of the taxpayer (see the Inland Revenue's IR20).

[87] IHTA 1984, s 48(4). For the purposes of this exemption, domicile is now irrelevant. However, prior to 29 April 1996 it was, although the extended definition of domicile in IHTA 1984, s 267(1) did not apply (s 267(2)).

2.48 *Who and What is Taxed*

- holdings in authorised unit trusts or open ended investment companies if the person beneficially entitled is not domiciled in the UK;[88]

- lump sums payable to non-UK domiciliaries under certain overseas pension arrangements;[89]

- the interest of a beneficiary in a settlement created at a time when the settlor was not UK domiciled (irrespective of any later change in his domicile that may have occurred) provided that the trust assets are located outside the UK or comprise UK authorised unit trusts or open ended investment companies (so-called 'Excluded Property Trusts');[90]

- certain property situated in the UK belonging to members of visiting forces who are not British citizens or citizens of the dependent territories;[91]

- a foreign currency bank account owned by a non-UK domiciled deceased person who was neither resident nor ordinarily resident in the UK (or owned by the trustees of certain forms of trust in which such a person had an interest in possession).[92]

2.48 As in US planning, it is common for non-UK domiciliaries to use an offshore holding company as a means of converting the situs of a UK asset to that of an overseas company shareholding.[93] Care needs to be taken in the context of the new provisions affecting pre-owned assets.[94]

2.49 It may also be tax effective for such assets to be placed in a trust or settlement while the settlor is non-UK domiciled to secure the exemption referred to above for excluded property trusts.[95] Where a long period of UK residence is contemplated, careful planning can secure permanent IHT exempt status for offshore assets even if the individual later acquires UK domicile or deemed domicile status, since it is the domicile of the settlor at the time the trust is created (or is deemed to have been created) which is generally the key factor.[96]

---

[88] IHTA 1984, s 6(1A). Of interest is the fact that whilst deemed domicile in s 267(1) was specifically disapplied by s 267(2) in the case of government securities, it is not in the case of Authorised Unit Trusts and Open Ended Investment Companies.
[89] IHTA 1984, s 153.
[90] IHTA 1984, s 48(3) and (3A). See also **CHAPTER 6 (6.62** et seq) on excluded property trusts.
[91] IHTA 1984, ss 6(4) and 155(1).
[92] IHTA 1984, s 157.
[93] Care should be taken here for a variety of tax reasons to ensure that the management and control of the company properly takes place offshore from the UK. Otherwise the company itself may be liable to UK taxes. It should, however, be noted that for income tax purposes, certain anti avoidance legislation (ICTA 1988, ss 739 and 740) affecting offshore structures can apply equally to trusts and companies so giving rise to ongoing taxation of the transferor on income arising or other beneficiaries in receipt of benefits. In principle, this also applies to gains realised by the company but the relevant provisions are largely disapplied if the transferor is a non-UK domiciled person.
[94] FA 2004, s 84, Sch 15. See also **CHAPTER 1**.
[95] IHTA 1984, s 48(3). See also **CHAPTER 6 (6.62** et seq) on excluded property trusts.
[96] IHTA 1984, s 48(3). The Inland Revenue has indicated from time to time that it intends to review its interpretation of the application of these rules. Its current interpretation, widely agreed to be the correct one, is that the excluded property rules override the reservation of benefit rules such that even where the settlor's domicile subsequently changes to the UK any benefit reserved continues to be over excluded property.

2.50 Where the UK asset is a person's residence, there are other potential tax complications of holding the residence through an offshore company (whether or not that company is also held by a trust) and, accordingly, this strategy may best be avoided.[97]

4. Liability for payment

2.51 IHT is generally imposed on the donor of a lifetime gift or the personal representatives of the estate of a deceased and, in the case of settled property, on the trustees (or in some circumstances on the life tenant of an interest in possession trust, or on the settlor in the case of a non-UK resident settlement). It can also be recovered from any person whose estate has been increased by the transfer, any persons in whom the property has been legally vested and, in addition, from life tenants or other beneficiaries of donee settlements where funds have been applied for their benefit.

2.52 Where the donor dies within seven years of making a PET or a chargeable transfer and further tax accordingly becomes due, it is the latter categories of person and not the personal representatives who have primary liability for the additional tax.[98] The personal representatives may be called upon to pay the tax as a last resort or where it remains unpaid for more than a year after the death of the donor.

2.53 In each case the liability is, broadly speaking, limited to the extent of the property received.[99] However, where more than one person is potentially liable to pay the tax, the general principle is that each of them is liable for the whole of it.[100]

---

[97] The UK Inland Revenue take the position that an income tax liability arises on the 'benefit' of an individual occupying a home owned by a company in certain circumstances. In a recent criminal case before the House of Lords (*R v Allen [2001] STC 1537*) the Inland Revenue succeeded in establishing that the UK income tax legislation which taxes benefits received by employees (Income Tax (Earnings and Pensions) Act 2003, Pt 3, Ch 5 (ITEPA 2003)) covers the provision of living accommodation for 'deemed' directors of companies. The definition of director for this purpose is very wide and includes any person in accordance with whose instructions the named directors are accustomed to act. As result of a further court decision, the term may be even wider and include any person in accordance with whose advice the directors habitually act (*Secretary of State for Trade and Industry v Deverell and another [2000] 2All ER 365*). In theory, this could apply where the property is owned by a company which is in turn owned by a trust, however, the technical argument here is more difficult in a properly and independently managed structure. The value of the 'benefit' is calculated under a statutory formula and can be substantial in the case of larger properties.
[98] IHTA 1984, s 204(8).
[99] IHTA 1984, Pt VII.
[100] IHTA 1984, s 205.

Chapter 3

Deductions, Exclusions, Exemptions and Credits

A. United States

1. Introduction

3.1 The amount of the US transfer tax depends not just on the value of the transferred property, but on the availability of a variety of deductions, exclusions, exemptions and credits.

3.2 First, a note on the terminology. A 'deduction' is an amount subtracted from the value of the transferred property to determine the net upon which taxes are computed. An 'exclusion' is a non-taxable transfer. The term 'exemption' (used only in the GST provisions of the US Tax Code) exempts part or all of certain generation-skipping transfers from tax. Finally, 'credits' are dollar-for-dollar offsets of the taxes otherwise computed on the taxable transfer. These terms are often used interchangeably by taxpayers, advisors and even the authors. Items that are excluded from tax are also said to be exempt. The marital deduction and charitable deductions are said to exempt qualifying transfers to spouses and charity from transfer tax. The gift and estate tax credits effectively exclude a certain level of lifetime gifts and transfers at death from tax. Until recently, this 'applicable exclusion' credit was referred to as the 'unified credit' which was said to produce a 'unified credit exemption'. To add yet another term to the lexicon, deductions, exclusions, exemptions and credits are sometimes said to 'shelter' a transfer from tax.

3.3 Below is a list of the relevant US transfer tax deductions, exclusions, exemptions, and credits, followed by a more detailed discussion of these items in the context of US citizens and domiciliaries, non-domiciled aliens (NDAs) and tax-motivated expatriates.

- **Gift tax:**
    - marital deduction (unlimited tax-free gifts to spouses);
    - charitable deduction (unlimited tax-free gifts to qualified charities);
    - annual exclusion (limited tax-free annual gifts per beneficiary);
    - applicable credit (limited amount of additional tax-free gifts during life).
- **Estate tax:**
    - marital deduction (unlimited tax-free bequests to spouses);
    - charitable deduction (unlimited tax-free bequests to qualified charities);
    - exclusion for a qualified conservation easement;

3.4 *Deductions, Exclusions, Exemptions and Credits*

- deduction for debts, funeral expenses and administration expenses;
- applicable credit (limited amount of tax-fee bequests, effectively reduced by portion of applicable credit used on lifetime gifts);
- credit for state death taxes (replaced after 2004 with a deduction);
- credit for foreign death taxes;
- credit for gift taxes imposed on property re-included in the estate;
- credit for estate taxes imposed on recent inheritances.

- **GST**
  - annual exclusion;
  - orphan's exclusion (unlimited GST-free gifts/bequests to 'orphaned' grandchildren);
  - GST exemption (limited exemption to be used during life and/or at death to exempt 'direct skips' or trusts that eventually skip generations);
  - state GST exemption.

2. Gift tax deductions, exclusions and credits

a. US citizens and domiciliaries

3.4 The marital deduction[1] allows a US citizen or domiciliary to make unlimited lifetime gifts to a spouse, but only if the spouse is a US citizen. Gifts to a non-citizen spouse, even those who are domiciled in the US, generally do not qualify for the marital deduction.[2] Marital deduction gifts can be outright or in specially designed marital deduction trusts. **CHAPTER 4** explores this important topic in some detail.

3.5 The charitable deduction[3] allows a US citizen or domiciliary to make unlimited lifetime gifts to both domestic or foreign charities. In contrast, a taxpayer can receive a US income tax charitable deduction for gifts to only domestic charities, and that income tax deduction is subject to percentage limitations.[4]

3.6 A gift to charity of a partial interest in property does not qualify for the charitable deduction unless it meets certain exceptions. A gift that represents an undivided fractional interest in the donor's property (for example, a gift of a 50% interest in real estate) qualifies.[5] Also qualifying are gifts to charitable remainder trusts (which provide charity with a *remainder* interest after providing individuals receive annuity or unitrust payments for a period of years or life).[6] Also qualifying

---

[1] Code § 2523.
[2] Code § 2523(i).
[3] Code § 2522.
[4] Code § 170(b) and (c).
[5] Treas Reg.§ 25.2522(c)-3(c)(2)(i).
[6] Code § 2522(c)(2)(A). 'CRATs' and 'CRUTs' – as they are referred to – are also exempt from US income tax, but must meet a number of requirements. For example, the annuity must equal at least

United States 3.9

are charitable *lead* trusts (which provide the charity with an annuity or unitrust interest for a period of years, followed by a remainder to one or more individuals).[7] An individual can also make a tax-free gift to charity of a remainder interest in his personal residence.[8] In each case, the amount of the charitable deduction reflects only the value of the partial interest passing to charity.

3.7 The gift tax annual exclusion permits a US citizen or domiciliary to make gifts during the calendar year of a limited amount to an unlimited number of recipients. The annual exclusion is currently $11,000 and is indexed for inflation.[9] A donor who fails to take advantage of the annual exclusion privilege in any year or with respect to any beneficiary cannot carry that unused privilege over to the following year.

Example

A taxpayer with four children and ten grandchildren can give $11,000 to each such relative in 2004, for a total of $154,000 that year. If the taxpayer does not make a gift to one of the grandchildren in 2004, the taxpayer *cannot* double up and make a $22,000 annual exclusion gift to that grandchild in 2005.

3.8 Annual exclusion gifts must confer a 'present interest' on the beneficiary. Outright gifts obviously qualify, but gifts in most trusts would generally not, because the beneficiary's interest is typically delayed. Exceptions include gifts in trust:

- that entitle the beneficiary to all income;[10]

- for minors that distribute at or by age 21;[11] or

- that give beneficiaries a present right to withdraw the gifted property (even for a temporary time).[12]

3.9 As previously noted, gifts to spouses who are not US citizens will not qualify for the gift tax marital deduction. Instead, the US tax law permits a higher level of annual exclusion gifts to a non-citizen spouse: $114,000 in 2004 compared to $11,000 for gifts to others.[13] Outright gifts to a non-citizen spouse qualify for this expanded annual exclusion. Gifts in trust also qualify, but only if:

5% and no greater than 50% of the value of the property initially funding the CRAT and the CRUT unitrust percentage must also be at least 5% and no greater than 50%. The present value of the charitable remainder interest must equal at least 10% of the value of the gift to the trust. Code § 664.

[7] Code § 2522(c)(2)(B).
[8] Code §§ 2522(c)(2) and 170(f)(3)(B).
[9] Code § 2503(b). In 1981, the gift tax annual exclusion increased from $3,000 to $10,000 per donee, and was subsequently indexed for inflation. Rev Proc 2003–85, 2003–49 IRB 1.
[10] *Comm'r v Rubenstein* 124 F 2d 969 (8th Cir 1942).
[11] Code § 2503(c).
[12] *Crummey v Comm'r* 397 F 2d 82 (9th Cir 1968).
[13] Code §§ 2523(i)(2) and 2503. Note that the annual exclusion limit for gifts to non-citizen spouses was originally $100,000, but has been indexed for inflation since 1997. Rev Proc 2003–85, 2003–49 IRB 1.

3.10 Deductions, Exclusions, Exemptions and Credits

- the trust would have qualified for the marital deduction had the spouse been a US citizen; and
- the spouse has a 'present interest' in that trust as required by the annual exclusion rules.

3.10 The gift tax annual exclusion rules also permit tax-free gifts of medical and tuition expenses.[14] There are no limits on the size of these gifts, the relationship of the beneficiary to the donor, the number of beneficiaries, or where the medical services are provided or the school is located. Thus, a US citizen can, without any adverse gift tax implications, pay $200,000 of tuition expenses on behalf of a friend's son who attends college in Switzerland. The payments, however, must be made directly to the medical service provider or to the school. A taxpayer who reimburses a beneficiary for such expenses that the beneficiary has already paid (or intends to pay) will not qualify for this exclusion.

3.11 Married couples (both of whom are US citizens and/or domiciliaries) can also elect to 'split gifts,' which results in half of all gifts being attributed to each other regardless of the identity of the actual donor.[15] This election is made on gift tax returns filed by each spouse. Therefore, if a wife makes gifts from her funds of $22,000 to each of the couple's children and her husband elects to treat half of each gift as coming from him, the wife's gift will effectively be sheltered by both spouses' annual exclusions. If a couple makes the split-gift election, all gifts during that year (except for gifts to each other) are split. Thus, if in the same year the husband makes a $50,000 gift to his daughter from his prior marriage, his wife is treated as contributing $25,000 of that gift.

3.12 Finally, the gift tax applicable credit provides each US citizen and domiciliary with a tax credit that offsets an amount of otherwise taxable lifetime gifts. The amount effectively excluded by this credit is referred to as the 'applicable exclusion'. The Tax Code defines this credit as the amount of credit that will exempt $1m from gift tax.[16] Based on relevant tax rates, the credit is $345,800. Unlike the estate tax credit (which is currently $1.5m and scheduled to increase to as much as $3.5m), the gift tax applicable credit is frozen at the level of a $1m exclusion.[17] Because the applicable credit is a lifetime credit, unused amounts can be carried over and used in later years. Any applicable exclusion credit applied to lifetime gifts will effectively offset the amount of the taxpayer's applicable exclusion credit available to his estate.[18]

b. Non-domiciled aliens (NDAs)

3.13 As discussed in **CHAPTER 2**, the scope of the US gift tax on NDAs is generally limited to only gifts of US real estate and tangible personal property. The

---

[14] Code § 2503(e).
[15] Code § 2513(a).
[16] Code § 2505(a)(1).
[17] Until the 2001 Act, the gift and estate tax rules were unified in every way so that the relevant gift and estate tax credit was referred to as the 'unified credit'. Although the titles of the gift and estate tax code provisions still refer to it as the unified credit, the amounts exempted by the credit are no longer identical and, indeed, the text of the code provisions now use the term 'applicable credit amount'. Nonetheless, this credit is still commonly referred to as the unified credit.
[18] See the discussion in **CHAPTER 5**.

United States   **3.18**

scope of the gift tax deductions, exclusions and credits is also more limited. A NDA's gift of US property to charity qualifies for the charitable deduction under rules that are identical to US citizens and domiciliaries, with one important exception: the NDA's gift must be to a US charity.[19] Thus, a NDA who donates his Wyoming ranch to the Calcutta School for the Blind would be liable for US gift tax, unless that non-US charity has an affiliated US charity through which donations might be directed.

3.14   A NDA's gift of US property to a spouse qualifies for the marital deduction under rules that are identical to those of US citizens and domiciliaries. Gifts to US spouses can qualify for the marital deduction; gifts to non-citizens cannot. NDAs can also make annual exclusion gifts at the same levels and subject to the same rules and restrictions that apply to US citizens and domiciliaries. A NDA can also make expanded annual exclusion gifts ($114,000 in 2004) to a non-citizen spouse. A NDA *cannot*, however, elect to split gifts with a spouse.

3.15   Finally, NDAs are not entitled to any gift tax applicable credit.[20] Thus, while a US citizen and domiciliary can make lifetime tax-free gifts of up to $1m, a NDA's gift tax applicable exclusion is effectively zero.

c. Tax-motivated expatriates

3.16   A tax-motivated expatriate who remains a US domiciliary (by failing to establish a domicile outside the US) is subject to the same gift tax deductions, exemptions, exclusions and credits as a US citizen or domiciliary.

3.17   A tax-motivated expatriate who is no longer domiciled in the US is subject to gift tax on gifts of US intangibles for ten years after expatriation. The deductions, exclusions, exemption, and credit rules, however, are identical to those that apply to any other NDA. Importantly, a non-domiciled, tax-motivated expatriate who did not fully use his gift tax applicable exclusion credit on lifetime gifts while he was a US citizen cannot apply that unused balance to gifts of US property caught by the anti-expatriation rules.

3. *Estate tax deductions and credits*

a. US citizens and domiciliaries

3.18   The estate tax marital and charitable deductions operate identically to the gift tax marital and charitable deductions. There is, however, one important exception. Like the gift tax rules, the estate tax rules generally deny a marital deduction for bequests to a non-citizen spouse. However, bequests to certain testamentary trusts – known as 'qualified domestic trusts' (QDOTs) – will qualify for the marital deduction and thus permit tax deferral until the spouse's death. As discussed in

---

[19]   Code § 2522(b).
[20]   Code § 2505(a) provides this credit only to citizens and resident/domiciliaries.

3.19 Deductions, Exclusions, Exemptions and Credits

more detail in **CHAPTER 4**, a QDOT requires that there be at least one US trustee, and the related rules are designed to ensure the eventual collection of deferred US transfer taxes.

3.19 Conservation easements are legal restrictions placed by a landowner on the use or development of his land. Easements are granted to charitable organisations, such as The Land Conservancy, to enforce these restrictions. For estate tax purposes, easements can have two benefits. First, a conservation easement reduces the decedent's estate, either by reducing the value of the land (if the easement had been granted during life)[21] or by providing the decedent with an estate tax charitable deduction (for an easement granted at death).[22] Second, if the executor of the estate elects, the estate can exclude an additional amount up to the lesser of either:

- 40% of the value of the land (without the easement); or
- $500,000.[23]

3.20 The decedent's debts (including any unpaid income taxes and gift taxes) and funeral expenses are also deductible in computing his taxable estate.[24] For example, a decedent who owned a $1m residence subject to a $700,000 mortgage has a net equity of $300,000 in this property. For estate tax purposes, the $1m property is included in his taxable estate but the estate receives a $700,000 debt deduction, essentially leaving only $300,000 subject to tax.

3.21 Estate administration expenses (executor and attorney fees, probate costs, etc) are also deductible, but, at the option of the estate, can instead be taken as an income tax deduction.[25] For example, if a decedent's taxable estate were otherwise below the amount sheltered by the applicable credit, the administration expense deduction would be better used to reduce the amount of income taxes imposed on the estate.

3.22 The estate tax applicable credit serves the same function as the gift tax applicable credit, that is, to eliminate tax on a certain portion of the decedent's estate. In 2002 and 2003, the estate tax applicable credit offsets taxes otherwise computed on the first $1m of the decedent's estate. In 2004, the applicable exclusion increased to $1.5m (with a corresponding credit of $555,800). The applicable exclusion is scheduled to increase further:

---

[21] If the easement had been granted during life the donor will be entitled to an income tax deduction for this reduction in value. Code § 170(h). In addition, the gift of a conservation easement qualifies for the gift tax charitable deduction. Code § 2522(d).

[22] Code § 2055(f).

[23] Code § 2031(c). This exception only applies if the land is located in the US and has been owned by decedent or a member of his family for at least three years prior to the decedent's death. The 40% limit is scaled back if the easement does not sufficiently reduce the value of the property. For example, if the easement reduces the value of the property by less than 10%, no exclusion would be available. If the executor makes this election, the estate beneficiaries will take the decedent's income tax basis in the property and there will not be a basis adjustment to fair market value. Code § 1014(a)(4).

[24] Code § 2053.

[25] Treas Reg § 1.642(g)(1). Debts, funeral expenses and (after 2004) state estate taxes, in contrast, can only be taken as an estate tax deduction.

- to $2m (a $780,800 credit) for decedent's dying in 2006 through 2008; and
- to $3.5m (a $1,455,800 credit) for those dying in 2009.

After a scheduled one-year repeal of the estate tax for person's dying in 2010, the credit is scheduled to revert in 2011 to $1m (adjusted for inflation). Most believe that the repeal and 'sunset' will never become effective, replaced instead by a 'permanent' credit that excludes a relatively high amount of the decedent's estate.

3.23 The amount actually excluded by the estate tax applicable credit is effectively reduced by the amount of gift tax credit used on lifetime gifts. This is a consequence of the manner in which the estate taxes (and gift taxes) add prior taxable gifts into the computation of the transfer taxes imposed on the current transfers. This phenomenon is explained in **CHAPTER 5**, but can be illustrated by an example of a decedent who made the full $1m of applicable exclusion gifts during life. If she died in 2005, the estate tax credit ($1.5m that year) would effectively exempt only the first $500,000 of her estate.

3.24 Estate and inheritance taxes imposed by the states have historically been creditable against the decedent's federal estate tax. The state death tax credit is limited to the lesser of:

- an amount determined under a special table (capped at 16% for taxable estates of over $11m); or
- the amount actually paid to the states.

All states – even 'retirement states' like Arizona and Florida – have a so-called 'pick-up' tax. If the state estate taxes would otherwise be less than the state death tax credit allowable for federal purposes, the states have opted to pick up this difference. Their theory has been that this would cause no increase in the estate's total tax liability.

3.25 Beginning in 2002, the state death tax credit began to be scaled back. In 2004, the credit is only 25% of the prior levels. For example, if the credit had been $1m prior to 2002, the credit in 2004 would be only $250,000. The state death tax credit is eliminated beginning in 2005, replaced by a deduction for state death taxes.[26] These changes have resulted in a serious budget loss for many states that had previously enjoyed substantial economic benefit from the pick-up tax. Some have begun to 'decouple' their pick-up tax from the current federal rules, basing their tax not on the amount of scaled-back (or soon-to-be eliminated) state death tax credit but instead on credit that would have been available under prior law. As a result, the combined federal and state transfer tax rate imposed on the estate of a decedent who died a resident of a decoupled state or who owned taxable assets in such state could exceed 55%.

3.26 The foreign death tax credit provides a credit for death taxes paid to foreign countries. There are two limitations. The first limitation restricts the credit to only that portion of the foreign death taxes related to property actually located in that

---

[26] Code § 2058.

3.27   *Deductions, Exclusions, Exemptions and Credits*

country.[27] The second limitation restricts the credit to the proportion of the US estate taxes related to the foreign property.[28]

Example

For example, assume that the US citizen decedent's estate consisted of property located in Country A valued at $80X, property located in Country Y valued at $20X and US property valued at $100X. The decedent's US gross estate would thus be $200X. Assume Country A imposed a tax of $40X on property located in both Country A and Country B. The first limitation would thus be $36X ($40X × 80/100).

Assume also that the decedent's estate received a $40X US charitable deduction. The decedent's net taxable estate (after the charitable deduction) would thus be $160X. Assume the US estate tax (before the foreign death tax but after the estate tax applicable exclusion credit) was $50X. The ratio of property located in Country A ($80X) to the US net taxable estate ($160X) would be 50%, making the second limitation in this example $25X (50% of $50X). Since the foreign death tax credit cannot exceed either of these limits, the credit in this example would be limited to $25X.

3.27   To prevent gifted property that is re-included in the decedent's estate from being taxed twice, the decedent's estate also receives a credit for gift taxes.[29] Thus if a taxpayer made a gift to a grantor retained annuity trust (GRAT) and paid gift taxes on the value of the remainder gift, those gift taxes would be credited against the estate tax if the GRAT property were included in the taxpayer's estate by reason of his death before the end of the annuity term.

3.28   Finally, the credit for estate taxes on recent inheritances gives the decedent's estate a credit for the proportionate share of federal estate taxes imposed on property inherited from another person who died within ten years of the decedent's death.[30] The second decedent's estate is entitled to a full credit if he died within two years of the first decedent. Thereafter, the credit drops 20% every two years through year ten. Note that this credit is not given for any GST or gift tax imposed on the prior transfer.

b.   NDAs

3.29   A deceased NDA's estate is also entitled to a marital deduction and charitable deduction for the transfer of US-situated property to a surviving spouse and to charity.[31] Like US citizens and domiciliaries, a NDA who leaves US property to a non-citizen spouse must use a QDOT in order to qualify that bequest for the marital deduction. Unlike US citizens and domiciliaries, a NDA's estate will not receive a charitable deduction for property passing to a non-US charity or for

---

[27]   Code § 2014(a)(1).
[28]   Code § 2014(a)(2).
[29]   Code § 2011.
[30]   Code § 2013.
[31]   Code § 2106(a)(3) and (2).

non-US charitable purposes.³² A NDA's estate is also allowed a deduction for a proportionate share of all debts, funeral expenses and expenses of administration.³³ The portion is based on the ratio of the decedent's US estate to his worldwide estate.

3.30 If allowed by treaty, a NDA's estate will be entitled to credit equal to the applicable credit available to citizens, multiplied by the portion of the NDA's assets that are located in the US.³⁴ Otherwise, a NDA's estate is only entitled to a small estate tax credit of $13,000,³⁵ which offsets the tax on the first $60,000 of a NDA's taxable estate. If the NDA had previously benefited from the US gift tax credit (while a US citizen or domiciliary), the NDA's estate tax credit is appropriately reduced.³⁶

3.31 Finally, a NDA's estate is also entitled to a state death tax credit (until it is phased out after 2004), a credit for gift taxes on property re-included in the decedent's estate, and the credit for taxes imposed on recent inheritances.³⁷ A NDA is not entitled to a credit for foreign death taxes.

c. Tax-motivated expatriates

3.32 The estate tax imposed on the estate of a tax-motivated expatriate who is still a US domiciliary at death is determined on the same basis as US citizens and other domiciliaries. Such an estate would therefore be entitled to the same deductions, exclusions, exemptions and credits as are available to US citizens.

3.33 The estate of a tax-motivated expatriate who is not domiciled in the US at death is generally entitled to the same deductions, exemptions and credits as estates of other NDAs.³⁸ There a few meaningful exceptions. First, the $13,000 estate tax credit is inexplicably not reduced by any gift tax credit used by the tax-motivated expatriate while a US citizen.³⁹ Second, a tax-motivated expatriate is entitled to a credit for foreign death taxes paid with respect to certain foreign corporations that are included in the tax-motivated expatriate's US taxable estate by reason of the anti-expatriation rules.⁴⁰

4. GST deductions, exclusions, exemptions and credits

3.34 The GST applies to generation-skipping transfers attributed to a 'transferor' (a person who makes a transfer subject to US gift or estate tax) without any

---

32   Code § 2106(a)(2).
33   Code § 2106(a)(1).
34   See the discussion in CHAPTER 7.
35   Code § 2102(b)(1).
36   Code § 2102(c)(3)(B).
37   Code § 2102(a).
38   Code §§ 2107(a) provides for an estate tax to be imposed on the tax-motivated expatriate's taxable estate as determined in Code § 2106. That section, in turn, permits a NDA's estate to take deductions for debts, administration expenses, and payments to charity and spouses.
39   Code § 2107(c)(1)(A). Compare with Code § 2102(c)(3)(B).
40   Code § 2107(c)(2). A tax-motivated expatriate's estate must include a proportionate share of the company's US investments if the expatriate owned a sufficient interest in that company. Code § 2107(b).

3.35   Deductions, Exclusions, Exemptions and Credits

distinction between whether the transferor is a US citizen, domiciliary, NDA or tax-motivated expatriate. Except in the limited circumstances described below, the GST deductions, exclusions, exemptions and credits apply in an identical fashion to all transfers, regardless of the status of the transferor.

a. US citizens and domiciliaries

3.35   The GST rules include what is, in effect, an annual exclusion.[41] The gift tax annual exclusion treats annual gifts of $11,000 to an unlimited number of beneficiaries as if they were not taxable gifts. In addition, an unlimited amount of direct medical and tuition payments on behalf of others are also not treated as taxable gifts. For GST purposes, a grandparent's $11,000 gift to a grandchild or a $25,000 payment of the grandchild's tuition are not subject to GST. There are two refinements.

3.36   First, GST transfers in trust will only be excluded from the GST if a skip person is the only current beneficiary of that trust and all of the trust property would be included in that skip person's taxable estate if he or she were to die while property were still held in trust.[42] A grandparent's gift/GST annual exclusion trust for grandchildren would, therefore, typically grant the grandchild a general power of appointment or mandate a distribution to the grandchild's probate estate if the grandchild dies while property remains in the trust.

3.37   Second, a trust's direct payment of a skip person's medical expenses or tuition is not considered a 'taxable distribution'.[43] The theory behind this exclusion is that the member of the intervening generation (eg the child) could have made similar tax-exempt gifts; thus, no transfer taxes are avoided in the intervening generation. Thus, a trust established by a grandparent for the primary benefit of a child can make unlimited amounts of GST-excluded medical and tuition payments on behalf of grandchildren. The parallel to the gift tax annual exclusion is not absolute: the trust cannot make GST-free annual gifts of $11,000 per beneficiary.

3.38   The GST rules also include a so-called 'orphan's exclusion'. This rule elevates the generation assignment of an 'orphan' whose parent predeceased the initial gift or bequest by the GST transferor.[44]

Example

A grandparent's gift (regardless of the amount or purpose) to an 'orphaned' grandchild will not be subject to GST, because the grandchild will be assigned to the child's generation. The 'orphans'' exclusion does

---

[41]   Code § 2642(c). The GST rules do not label this as an annual exclusion, but instead give the gift an 'inclusion ratio' of zero. The concept of the inclusion ratio is discussed in more detail in the text at footnote 44. A direct skip with an inclusion ratio of zero is subject to no GST, because the amount of the GST equals the inclusion ratio (in this case zero), times the tax rate, times the value of the gift.
[42]   Code § 2642(c)(2).
[43]   Code § 2611(b)(1).
[44]   Code § 2651(e).

not apply to a taxable distribution or taxable termination of a trust if the grandchild's parent died after the initial gift or bequest to the trust. For example, a grandparent establishes a trust for the benefit of his children and grandchildren in 1999. One of the children dies in 2004. The grandchildren by that deceased child would not be considered orphaned for purposes of taxable distributions from, or the taxable termination of, this trust.

3.39 For this special rule to apply, both of the 'orphan's' parents need not have predeceased – only the parent who is in the relevant bloodline. Therefore, if a grandparent's son has died, the grandparent can make a GST-free gift or bequest to the deceased son's children, even though the grandchild's mother is still living.

3.40 The 'orphan's' exclusion originally applied to only descendants of the GST transferor (or his spouse or former spouse). The exclusion was extended in 1997 to collateral heirs – grandnieces and grandnephews (and their descendants) and similar relatives of the GST transferor's spouse or former spouse – but only if the GST transferor has no living descendants.

3.41 The GST exemption is probably the most important (and complex) feature of the GST rules. As its name suggests, this tax-saving device exempts certain transfers from the GST. When the new GST rules were enacted in 1986, the GST exemption was fixed at $1m and later made subject to inflation adjustments. (In contrast, the gift and estate tax exemption – sheltered by what was then called the unified credit – was only $600,000 in 1986.) The GST exemption increased to $1.5m in 2004 and will parallel the later increases in the estate tax applicable exclusion.[45] Also, similar to the gift tax and estate tax applicable exclusions, lifetime uses of the GST exemption will reduce the amount of GST exemption available for later gifts or at death.

3.42 The amount of the GST exemption applied to any transfer (direct or in trust) results in a so-called 'inclusion ratio'.[46] The inclusion ratio is essentially the portion of the transfer or trust that is not exempt from the GST. The eventual amount of the GST is computed by multiplying the inclusion ratio × the highest gift/estate tax rate × the value of the GST transfer.

3.43 The application of the GST exemption is best understood in the context of a direct skip.

Example

Assume a grandparent made a $100,000 gift to a grandchild in 2004. If the grandparent has sufficient GST exemption to fully exempt this gift, the gift will have an inclusion ratio of zero. The GST will thus be zero. If the grandparent's GST exemption only exempts 75% of the gift, the inclusion ratio will be 25% and the GST would equal $12,000 ($100,000 ×

---

[45] Note that the GST exemption, similar to the estate tax applicable credit amount, climbs to $2m in 2006 and $3.5m in 2009.
[46] Code § 2642.

3.44 Deductions, Exclusions, Exemptions and Credits

25% × 48%). If the grandparent had no GST exemption, the inclusion ratio would be 1 and the GST would be $48,000 ($100,000 × 1 × 48%).

3.44 When a taxpayer makes a taxable gift or bequest to a trust, the GST exemption can also exempt from the GST part or all of future taxable distributions from or the taxable termination of that trust.

Example

A grandparent transfers $1m to a trust for the benefit of children and grandchildren. If the grandparent applies $1m of his GST exemption to the trust, the trust will have an inclusion ratio of zero. Assuming no later contributions to this trust, there will be no GST exemption applied to later distributions from, or the termination of, that trust. This is true regardless of the amount distributed or the value of the trust at the time of termination.

If the grandparent applies enough GST exemption to only exempt 75% of the trust, the inclusion ratio will be 25%. Thus, essentially only 25% of all later distributions to grandchildren and 25% of the value of the trust at the time of termination will be subject to GST.

If the grandparent applies no GST exemption to the trust, a full GST will be imposed on all later taxable distributions from and the taxable termination of that trust.

3.45 The tax law automatically applies a taxpayer's GST exemption to gifts that are direct skips.[47] For lifetime transfers in trust that are not otherwise exempt, the taxpayer must generally file a gift tax return to affirmatively apply his available exemption.[48] If the donor applies the GST exemption on a timely-filed gift tax return, the exemption applies to the value of the property originally transferred to the trust. However, if the taxpayer files a late return, the exemption is generally applied against the value of the property on the date the late return is filed.

Example

For example, a grandparent with a GST exemption transferred $1.5m to a trust for a child in 2004, with the intention to exempt that trust for GST. If the grandparent files a timely gift tax return and applies his entire exemption to that gift, the entire trust will be exempt from GST, even if, by the date of filing, the trust had appreciated to $2m. If the grandparent

---

[47] Code § 2632(b).
[48] In an effort to 'protect' taxpayers from the consequences of failing to apply GST exemptions where they 'should', Congress enacted new rules that automatically apply the taxpayer's GST exemption in certain non-direct skip transfers in trust (Code § 2632(c)). These rules attempt to identify situations where taxpayers would have more than likely intended to apply their exemptions. While well intentioned, the artificial (and somewhat complicated and ambiguous) rules can just as readily 'waste' a taxpayer's GST exemption on transfers in trust that were never intended to be exempt. Taxpayers can, affirmatively elect for this rule not to apply, but must file a gift tax return to do so.

files a late return and the trust is again valued at $2m at that time, then only 75% (1.5/2) of that trust would be exempt and the trust would thus have an inclusion ratio of 25%.[49]

3.46 Wealthy grandparents will often use their GST exemptions to establish 'dynasty trusts' that will last for generation after generation without ever subjecting the principal to a transfer tax. The dynasty trust might leverage the GST exemption by acquiring a life insurance policy on the grandparent's life: the proceeds collected by the trust at the grandparent's death will remain exempt from the GST. Also, because it is possible to establish trusts in many US states that are not subject to the rule against perpetuities (and thus are not forced to terminate at an artificial date), these dynasty trusts could benefit an unlimited number of generations while perhaps being augmented by insurance proceeds of members of the intervening generations.

3.47 If the donor or decedent has transferred property to a split-interest charitable trust (a charitable remainder trust or a charitable lead trust), the calculation of the trust's inclusion ratio will be affected by the charitable deduction.

Example

For example, a decedent dies in 2004 and leaves $4m to a charitable remainder trust that provides a lead interest for his grandchildren. If the estate charitable deduction for the remainder interest were $1m (leaving a net of $3m) and the decedent's executor chose to apply the decedent's full $1.5m GST exemption to this trust, the resulting inclusion ratio would be 50% (Code § 2642(a)(2)(A)).[50]

3.48 The marital deduction has only a limited and indirect impact on the GST. A marital deduction trust for the beneficiary spouse will be included in the beneficiary spouse's taxable estate, thus making the beneficiary spouse (not the donor spouse) the eventual GST transferor. The GST rules, however, permit the donor spouse or the decedent spouse's estate to apply the GST exemption to a so-called 'QTIP' marital trust (qualified terminable interest property trusts – discussed in more detail at **4.9** et seq).[51] By so doing, the donor/decedent spouse (not the beneficiary spouse) will be considered the ultimate GST transferor.

3.49 There is also a state GST credit for any generation-skipping taxes paid to any state by reason of a taxable distribution or taxable termination occurring at the

---

[49] There is one exception to the late election rule, which applies in situations where the taxpayer intended for the trust to be exempt from GST, but failed to do so because of omissions by advisors or return preparers. The law now permits the taxpayer to seek IRS approval for a late GST allocation. If granted, the exception will apply against the value of the property at the date of the gift. Code § 2642(g).

[50] Special rules apply to a charitable lead annuity trust that require that the inclusion ratio not be computed until the termination of charity's lead interest. Code § 2642(e).

[51] Code § 2642(a)(2)(A). For gift and estate tax purposes the QTIP will qualify for the marital deduction and be included in the survivor's estate. If the GST election – sometimes referred to as a 'reverse QTIP' election – is made, the GST rules are applied as if there had been no QTIP marital deduction election and thus as if the property had not been included in the beneficiary spouse's estate.

3.50 Deductions, Exclusions, Exemptions and Credits

death of an individual.[52] This credit is limited to 5% of the amount of federal GST imposed on the relevant transfer and is eliminated for generation-skipping transfers after 2004.

3.50 In computing the GST imposed on a taxable termination, a debt and expense deduction – similar to the estate tax deduction – is allowed to the extent such debts or expenses are attributable to property held in the trust.[53]

3.51 Finally, there is no GST credit for inherited property recently subject to an estate tax. If a child tragically dies within one year of inheriting property outright from his parent, the child's estate is entitled to a full credit for the estate taxes imposed in the parent's estate on that inherited property. If the parents had instead left the child's inheritance in trust, no similar credit would be allowed in computing the GST imposed at the child's death when the trust passed to the next generation.

b. NDAs

3.52 The GST rules apply in an identical fashion to NDAs who make transfers that are subject to the US gift or estate tax. For example, a NDA's gift or bequest of US property to a grandchild will be exempt from GST to the extent the gift qualifies for the GST equivalent of the annual exclusion. Taxable gifts or bequests to orphaned grandchildren are also effectively exempt. NDAs are also entitled to a GST exemption, currently $1.5m.

3.53 Because US gift and estate tax is imposed only on certain US property transferred by a NDA, the application of the GST to transfers attributed to NDAs is similarly limited. A NDA's gift or bequest of non-US property is exempt from US gift and estate tax, and thus also exempt from GST. This effectively gives a NDA an unlimited GST exemption for gifts and bequests of non-US property. A NDA could therefore transfer non-US property valued at $10m (or billion) into a trust for his descendants and no GST would be imposed as that trust passes from generation to generation.

c. Tax-motivated expatriates

3.54 The GST rules apply to generation-skipping transfers that are attributed to a tax-motivated expatriate who is considered an estate or gift tax 'transferor'. The rules discussed above for the GST deductions, exclusions, exemptions and credits for US domiciliaries and NDAs apply in an identical fashion to a tax-motivated expatriate.

3.55 To determine whether or not the tax-motivated expatriate is considered the GST transferor, it is necessary to know:

---

[52] Code § 2604(a).
[53] Code § 2622(b).

- the taxpayer's citizenship or domicile status at the date of the relevant gift or bequest (not, in the case of a trust, at the time of any taxable distribution or taxable termination); and

- if he is not a US citizen or domiciliary at the time of the relevant gift or bequest, the application of the gift and estate tax situs rules discussed in CHAPTER 2 (including, if relevant, the anti-expatriation situs rules).

B. United Kingdom

1. Introduction

3.56 The amount of UK inheritance tax is dependent both on the transfer of value made (or deemed to be made) by the transferor or the deceased and any exemptions, exclusions and reliefs which may be available. These apply to UK domiciliary and non-UK domiciliary transferors alike.

Various exemptions exist which either exempt a specified monetary amount which is deductible from the value transferred, or exempt the asset itself as to the whole or part of its value, depending on the circumstances. There are additionally a number of reliefs which apply to reduce or eliminate the tax charge where certain conditions are fulfilled. Finally, certain dispositions are not considered to be transfers of value.

2. Main exemptions and reliefs in UK

3.57 The following list summarises the main exemptions and reliefs available in the UK:

a. Transfers during lifetime and on death:

- spouse exemption – transfers to a UK domiciled (or deemed domiciled) spouse or between two non-UK domiciled spouses.[54] This exemption also applies to a gift to a life interest trust for the spouse;

- non domiciled spouse exemption – £55,000 exemption for transfers to a non-UK domiciled spouse by a UK domiciled (or deemed domiciled) spouse.[55] As above, this exemption also applies to a gift to a life interest trust for the spouse;

- exempt gifts to, or on trust for, UK charities and housing associations;[56]

---

[54] IHTA 1984, s 18(1). Note that in the Special Commissioners decision of *Holland (executor of Holland deceased) v IRC [2003] STC SCD 43* it was expressly held that the spouse exemption is not available to co-habiting couples. They considered that the situation of married couples was different involving mutual rights and obligations of maintenance not applicable to co-habitees and which justified the different treatment.
[55] IHTA 1984, s 18(2).
[56] IHTA 1984, ss 23 and 24A.

3.57 Deductions, Exclusions, Exemptions and Credits

- exempt gifts to, or on trust for, designated bodies for national purposes;[57]
- exempt gifts to, or on trust for, political parties;[58]
- £263,000 nil-rate band (an amount subject to tax, but taxed at a nil rate);[59]
- 50/100% Business Property Relief;[60]
- 50/100% Agricultural Property Relief.[61]

b. Transfers during lifetime only:

- £250 per donee small gifts annual exemption;[62]
- £3,000 annual exemption;[63]
- exempt gifts between £1,000 and £5,000 on marriage (depending on identity of donor);[64]
- payments for certain family maintenance purposes to a spouse, or child (of either party) who is a minor or in full-time education, or to a dependent relative which are not regarded as transfers of value;[65]
- normal expenditure out of income exemption;[66]
- waivers of salary or dividends (in the case of the latter within 12 months prior to the time the legal entitlement arises) which are not regarded as transfers of value;[67]
- transactions where there was no intention to confer favourable terms on the other party (eg a bad bargain) which are not regarded as a transfer of value;[68]
- potentially exempt transfers to individuals and certain trusts which qualify for complete exemption on survival for seven years after the transfer.[69]

---

[57] IHTA 1984, s 25.
[58] IHTA 1984, s 24.
[59] IHTA 1984, s 7 and Sch 1. For 2004/05 £263,000.
[60] IHTA 1984, s 104.
[61] IHTA 1984, 116.
[62] IHTA 1984, s 20.
[63] IHTA 1984, s 19.
[64] IHTA 1984, s 22.
[65] IHTA 1984, s 11. This exemption covers dispositions made to a former spouse by way of financial provision on divorce. Any payments made to a person's widowed, separated or divorced mother are also covered, but payments to other dependent relatives are conditional on their being unable to maintain themselves through old age or infirmity.
[66] IHTA 1984, s 21. This exemption is particularly valuable for those with significant income surplus to requirements. It is important to ensure that taking one year with another the donor leaves himself with enough income to cover his day-to-day expenditure. Subject to this, any amount of surplus income can be given away. Provided gifts are made on a regular basis they need not be of the same amount nor made to the same persons. Care needs to be taken that it is income that is given away. For example, the proportion of the payments under an annuity, which comprise a return of capital, will not qualify.
[67] IHTA 1984, ss 14 and 15.
[68] IHTA 1984, s 10.
[69] IHTA 1984, s 3A. See **CHAPTER 2** for further details.

c. Transfers on death only:

- property situated in the UK belonging to members of visiting forces who are not British citizens or citizens of the dependent territories.[70]

- a foreign currency bank account in the UK owned by a non-UK domiciled deceased person who was neither resident nor ordinarily resident in the UK at death (or owned by the trustees of a non-UK resident trust, created by a non-UK domiciliary, in which such a person had an interest in possession).[71]

Transfers between spouses are covered in detail in **CHAPTER 4**.

3.58 Only gifts to UK registered charities qualify for the unlimited tax exemption although UK charities with overseas objects may qualify.[72] Nor does the gift attract the exemption if it is deferred (eg for a fixed period or is subject to someone's prior interest, such as a life interest), or it is conditional (unless the condition is satisfied within twelve months) or it is an interest which is defeasible. The gift can either be an outright gift to the charity or a gift to a trust provided its terms can only apply the funds to charitable purposes. If the value of the loss to the transferor's estate is greater than the value of the gift in the hands of the charity (eg the gift out of a majority shareholding which is a minority interest for the charity) the Inland Revenue accepts that the entire gift attracts the exemption.[73]

3.59 Similar provisions to the above are relevant in the case of gifts to political parties, gifts for national purposes, and so far as attributable to gifts of land in the UK to housing associations (now Registered Social Landlords).[74]

3.60 A gift to a political party qualifies for exemption under the relevant provision if at the last general election, the party had two members elected to the House of Commons or one member was elected and not less than 150,000 votes were given to candidates who were members of the party.

3.61 The £263,000 nil-rate band is effectively the equivalent of the US applicable credit. Technically, taxable gifts with a cumulative value of such sum are

---

[70] IHTA 1984, ss 6(4) and 155(1).
[71] IHTA 1984, s 157.
[72] *The Camille and Henry Dreyfus Foundation Inc v IRC 36 TC 126*. For a UK domiciled US citizen this can cause difficulty since the US will also deny relief on gifts to non-US charities. For those with significant wealth and charitable intent, suitable structuring can, however, achieve a dually tax-efficient two-tier charity structure. For those of lesser wealth levels, the Charities Aid Foundation has a similar vehicle to which tax-effective charitable donations can be made.
[73] Statement of Practice E13.
[74] The provisions defining a non-charitable body which is capable of qualifying as a Registered Social Landlord are set out in the Housing Act 1996. Under s 2(2) of that Act, the conditions are that the body is non-profit-making and is established for the purpose of, or has among its objects or powers, the provision, construction, improvement or management of:
  (a) houses to be kept available for letting;
  (b) houses for occupation by members of the body, where the rules of the body restrict membership to persons entitled or prospectively entitled (as tenants or otherwise) to occupy a house provided or managed by the body; or
  (c) hostels;
  (d) and that any additional purposes or objects are among those specified in S2 (4), which describes certain other ancillary objects.

3.62 *Deductions, Exclusions, Exemptions and Credits*

chargeable, but the charge is at a nil-rate.[75] The interaction of the nil-rate band and the seven-year rule in the UK can, under certain circumstances, result in a 'renewable' nil-rate band.

Example

Assume a UK donor (who has made no prior gifts) makes a £263,000 gift to a discretionary trust in June 2004. He makes no further gifts, and then later dies in the year 2014.

- The 2004 chargeable gift is free from tax because of the nil-rate band and, in the year 2014, the donor/decedent's taxable estate will not include his 2004 gift in the cumulative total of transfers (having survived the gift by more than seven years).

- The nil-rate band available to his estate will not be allocated to any prior lifetime gifts. Accordingly, the donor/decedent will have used this 'tax free' band, both for his 2004 gift and again against his 2014 estate.

3.62 Spouses are taxed independently of each other in the UK and, since both have an available nil-rate band, basic will planning should ensure that, at a minimum, each spouse uses this (and owns adequate assets at death to fund it). Passing the whole estate to the surviving spouse wastes the exemption in the estate of the first to die. This planning is often achieved by including in the will a nil-rate band discretionary trust of which the surviving spouse is one of the beneficiaries. This gives her facility to access the assets but without passing them into her estate for UK tax purposes so in emergencies the funds can be used for her benefit. The US equivalent planning refers to this as a 'by-pass trust'.

3. *Business property and agricultural property reliefs/other reliefs and exemptions*

3.63 The business property and agricultural property reliefs are significant. Dependent on meeting certain criteria (as to which see **3.64**), the value of specified assets is reduced by either 50% or 100% in computing the tax exposure on a gift or a decedent's estate. This can substantially reduce or even eliminate the inheritance tax charge where, for example, business assets are left to a chargeable beneficiary (eg a child or a trust) and the balance of the estate is left to a spouse.

a. Business property relief

3.64 Generally speaking, under IHTA 1984, s 106, business property relief will be relevant where assets have been held by the decedent for two or more years[76] and, by virtue of s 105, comprise:

---

[75] IHTA 1984, s 7 and Sch 1.
[76] IHTA 1984, s 107 makes provision for relief to apply in circumstances where the business assets have been reinvested in replacements and s 108 also provides for a person inheriting from his deceased spouse to inherit the ownership period of the spouse as well.

United Kingdom   **3.67**

- a business or an interest in a business (proprietorship or partnership);
- securities in an unquoted company which (alone or with other shares or securities) gave the transferor control of the company;
- a shareholding in an unquoted company;
- a controlling holding in a quoted company; or
- land, buildings, machinery or plant (equipment) used in such a business in respect of which the transferor was a partner or controlling shareholder.[77]

There are also provisions to cover the latter category of assets where the business is operated by a life tenant of a trust, but the assets are owed by the trustees.[78]

3.65   In the first three cases mentioned at **3.64**, the relief is 100% of the value effectively providing exemption from IHT. In other cases the business property relief is 50%.[79]

3.66   Business property relief does not apply to a business consisting of dealing in securities, stocks or shares (unless the business concerned is in the UK and wholly that of a market maker or discount house) nor dealing in land or buildings, nor the making or holding of investments. As to the latter, it can, however, apply to a holding company[80] provided that the business of its subsidiaries qualifies.[81] In so far as concerns companies with qualifying activities, however, the relief applies wherever the business is conducted and whether through UK or foreign companies.

3.67   The relief will not apply to the shares of a company in liquidation, save in limited circumstances.[82] Nor will it apply if the property concerned is subject to a binding contract of sale at the time of the transfer.[83] Shareholder and partnership agreements will often address the rights to sell or purchase a decedent's interest in the business. The Inland Revenue takes the position that business property relief is:

- denied if the agreement obligates the estate to sell the decedent's interest; *but*
- available if the agreement grants the estate an option to sell, or the other parties an option to buy, the decedent's interests.[84]

---

[77]   IHTA 1984, s 105.
[78]   IHTA 1984, s 105(1)(e).
[79]   IHTA 1984, s 104.
[80]   Section 736 of the Companies Act 1985 defines a holding company for this purpose as one which holds a majority of the voting rights in its subsidiary or, is a member of it and has the right to appoint or remove a majority of its board of directors or, is a member of it and controls alone, pursuant to an agreement with other shareholders or members, a majority of the voting rights in it.
[81]   IHTA 1984, s 105(3) and (4).
[82]   IHTA 1984, s 105(5).
[83]   IHTA 1984, s 113.
[84]   See the Inland Revenue Statement of Practice 12/80 and Memorandum TR557: CTT 'Buy and sell' agreements which publishes correspondence between the Inland Revenue and the ICAEW which outlines various examples when this might apply.

3.68 *Deductions, Exclusions, Exemptions and Credits*

3.68 In some circumstances, the value of the business capable of attracting the relief is abated as a result of 'excepted assets'.[85] Essentially, the legislation leaves out of account, assets which have not been used wholly or mainly for the purposes of the business concerned in the relevant period prior to the transfer and at that time, nor are they required for future business use.

3.69 For suitable assets which qualify as relevant business property, transfers can be made by will to persons who do not qualify for special exemptions without tax charge. This means, for example, that the strategy described earlier concerning the use of a nil-rate band discretionary trust for a class of beneficiaries, including the spouse, can be expanded to include such assets providing access for the survivor but without passing the assets into her taxable estate. This can be a tax-efficient strategy if the assets are to be sold at a later date by the trustees and reinvested in non-qualifying assets.[86] In US parlance, tax effective planning may involve funding a bypass trust with exempt business property which may be sold, in order to provide access to such asset value to the surviving spouse without leaving non exempt assets in her estate.

3.70 There are rules which confer certain beneficial tax treatment on lifetime disposals of business property for capital gains tax purposes. These rules are quite different from the inheritance tax rules and are set out in **CHAPTER 10**.

b. Agricultural property relief

3.71 Agricultural property relief is relevant where qualifying property (in the UK, Channel Islands or the Isle of Man) has been occupied by the transferor for the purposes of agriculture for two years prior to the transfer or was owned by him for seven years and during that period occupied by any person for agricultural purposes.[87] The property must comprise agricultural land or pasture and can include woodland and buildings ancillary to it which are used in connection with the intensive rearing of livestock or fish. It also includes cottages, farm buildings and farmland of a character appropriate to the agricultural land and occupied with it.[88] Where the transferor has the immediate right to vacant possession, or the right to it within twelve months, or the property is let on an agricultural tenancy which began after 31 August 1995, the relief is 100%; and in other cases the relief is 50%.[89] The relief is extended to situations where the land is occupied by a farming company which the transferor controls and also where certain agricultural property is owned

---

[85] IHTA 1984, s 112.
[86] Care needs to be taken that this will leave the spouse with an adequate free estate for her own needs. Caution is also required where a formula is used to make nil-rate band gifts (as is usually the case). Since the nil-rate sum taxed at the zero rate increases year on year, using a formula avoids the necessity for frequent revisions of the will. However, if the provision is widely drawn and if the estate contains a significant proportion of business assets, this can have the unintended effect of depriving the spouse of inheriting assets outright.
[87] IHTA 1984, s 117.
[88] IHTA 1984, s 115(2). In circumstances where substantial rural properties are purchased as country homes with an element of farmland attached, the question of what is a 'character appropriate' to the property can be very difficult. Where valuable properties are concerned, the Inland Revenue is likely to challenge vigorously any claim to the very favourable IHT reliefs.
[89] IHTA 1984, s 116(2).

by a company which the transferor controls.[90] Agricultural relief is limited to the use of the property for agricultural purposes (eg as restricted by an agricultural easement) and does not include higher use commercial use value or residential value.

3.72 Where a family has potential exposure to tax in both UK and US jurisdictions and where the above reliefs are in point, it is essential to compare the US and UK tax exposure carefully. Depending on the proportion of assets in the estate which attract 50/100% relief, the UK may well impose the lower overall tax even though the US may, on the face of it, be the more favourable tax regime for smaller estates (because of the higher exemptions and incremental rate, as opposed to flat rate). This may mean effective tax planning can be achieved by using gifts into trust which fully utilise the UK exemptions and preclude assets passing into the hands of a surviving US citizen spouse.[91]

3.73 It should be noted that where such business or agricultural property is the subject of a potentially exempt transfer, which becomes chargeable on the donor's death within seven years, or was the subject of a chargeable transfer within seven years of death there are additional criteria which the donee is required to satisfy at that time, before the original transfer qualifies for the relief. IHTA 1984, ss 113A and 124A require that:

(a) the assets (or replacement assets satisfying certain conditions) must be owned by the donee continuously from the transfer to the date of the donor's death (or the donee's own death if earlier); and

(b) must still be of a character capable of qualifying for the appropriate relief in the donee's hands either at the time of the donor's death or his own death, as relevant.

With respect to holdings of unquoted shares and to controlling holdings of unquoted securities or quoted shares, only the first of these conditions applies (provided in the case of unquoted companies the holdings must remain unquoted during the relevant period).

c. Exemptions

3.74 For those with high net income, the unlimited exemption for normal expenditure out of income can facilitate significant non-taxable 'transfers'. This exemption enables a donor to establish a pattern of regular gifts out of 'surplus' income without tax exposure, provided that his remaining income is sufficient to

---

[90] IHTA 1984, ss 119 and 122.
[91] A valuable planning tool exists in the difference in treatment in the US and UK of life interests. The UK will regard a gift to a spouse on life interest trusts as being capable of attracting the IHTA 1984, s 18 exemption since the spouse will be deemed to own the underlying assets. In the US, however, there will be no such deemed ownership so that the gift can be kept out of the US estate of the survivor whilst still attracting the UK spouse exemption.

3.75   *Deductions, Exclusions, Exemptions and Credits*

maintain his normal standard of living. The fact that the gifts must be regular does not mean that there is any requirement that they should be to the same persons or of similar amounts[92].

3.75   Unlike the US, the UK annual exemption of £3,000 can be carried forward for one year. Where this occurs, gifts will first be set against the current year's exemption of £3,000 and only the balance will be attributable to the portion of prior year's exemption that has been carried forward.

3.76   The £250 exemption is intended to cover the normal gifts of modest value made at Christmas or birthdays and cannot be used partly to offset gifts of greater sums. For example, it would not be possible to make a single tax-free gift of £3,250 by using the annual exemption plus the small gifts exemption. The £250 surplus would be potentially chargeable in that example. However, if a separate £250 gift were made to the donee, and later a £3,000 gift were made, it would appear at least arguable that both these gifts should escape UK tax.

3.77   Gifts in consideration of marriage,[93] made either outright to one of the parties or on trust for them, are exempt to the extent made by any one transferor, in respect of any one marriage, if they do not exceed specified amounts. The amounts are:

- £5,000 by a parent;
- £2,500 by a more remote ancestor or one party to the marriage to the other; and
- £1,000 in any other case.

For example, if the maximum gifts are made by all four parents, £20,000 could be given free of tax in respect of any one marriage.

3.78   Dispositions for family maintenance are not considered to be transfers of value for the purposes of IHT.

3.79   Dispositions which were not meant to confer gratuitous benefit are also not considered to be transfers of value, even if there is a reduction in the value of the transferor's estate inadvertently.[94] This provision applies if a transaction has been undertaken on arm's length terms between unconnected parties, or was on such terms as would be expected if they had been unconnected.

3.80   A waiver of a dividend is not a transfer of value if it is made within twelve months before the right to it has arisen.[95]

---

[92]   In particular, care needs to be taken where the character of the property is anticipated to change. For example, where a company is unquoted at the time of the gift but a Stock Exchange listing occurs at some time thereafter.
[93]   IHTA 1984, s 22.
[94]   IHTA 1984, s 10.
[95]   IHTA 1984, s 15.

3.81 The lifetime exemptions are now generally only relevant where the transfer is otherwise immediately chargeable to tax (that is, if it is not a potentially exempt transfer – a 'PET'). When a PET is made, it is assumed that the PET will prove to be exempt, and thus the lifetime exemptions can be allocated to other gifts.[96] If the PET subsequently proves to be chargeable (on death of the donor within seven years) it may be necessary retrospectively to reallocate exemptions which have been set against other chargeable transfers, for example, as illustrated in the table below.

	Gift	*Annual exemption*	*Taxable*	*Cumulative total*
	£	£	£	£
May 2000 PET	10,000	N/A	–	–
December 2001 chargeable	261,000	6,000	255,000	255,000
Death of transferor May 2003 – revised computations:				
May 2000 chargeable	10,000	(3,000)	7,000	7,000
December 2001 chargeable	261,000	(3,000)	258,000	265,000

The lifetime exemptions are not reallocated among gifts occurring with the same year (eg where the exemption has been allocated against a lifetime chargeable gift and a PET made earlier in the same year later proves to be chargeable).

4. Excluded property

3.82 Additionally there are exclusions from liability to UK inheritance tax for certain specific assets dependent on the status of the taxpayer as follows:

- certain designated UK government securities owned by persons not ordinarily resident in the UK (ie broadly persons who have not been present in the UK for an average of 91 days or more in four or more consecutive years);[97]

- certain designated UK government securities owned by trustees for persons:

    (a) with an interest in possession who are not UK ordinarily resident; or

    (b) with discretionary interests provided all such potential beneficiaries are not UK ordinarily resident;[98]

---

[96] IHTA 1984, s 3A(5).
[97] IHTA 1984, s 6(2). Ordinary residence is a concept denoting habitual presence in the UK over a number of years and generally applies if a person is present in the UK for 91 days or more over any four tax-year period. As with residence, the precise timing of acquisition of ordinary residence depends on the intention of the taxpayer – see the Inland Revenue's IR 20.
[98] IHTA 1984, s 48(4). For the purposes of this exemption, domicile is now irrelevant. However, prior to 29 April 1996 it was, although the extended definition of domicile in IHTA 1984, s 267(1) did not apply (s 267(2)).

3.83   *Deductions, Exclusions, Exemptions and Credits*

- holdings in authorised unit trusts or open ended investment companies if the person beneficially entitled is not domiciled in the UK;[99]
- lump sums payable to non-UK domiciliaries under certain overseas pension arrangements;[100]
- the interest of a beneficiary in a settlement created at a time when the settlor was not UK domiciled (irrespective of any later change in his domicile that may have occurred) provided that the trust assets are located outside the UK or comprise UK authorised unit trusts or open ended investment companies (so-called 'Excluded Property Trusts');[101]
- certain property situated in the UK belonging to members of visiting forces who are not British citizens or citizens of the dependent territories;[102]
- a foreign currency bank account in the UK owned by a non-UK domiciled deceased person who was neither resident nor ordinarily resident in the UK (or owned by the trustees of certain forms of trust in which such a person had an interest in possession).[103]

5. Post death variations and disclaimers

3.83   It is also worth noting that it is possible for the recipient of a gift which occurs at the time of someone's death, to make certain post mortem rearrangements without the usual inheritance tax consequences of a lifetime gift.[104] A similar provision exists for capital gains tax.[105]

3.84   Within two years of a person's death, the dispositions made by a will or under the laws of intestacy or otherwise (eg by a jointly-held asset accruing automatically to the survivor) of property comprised in his estate, can be varied. This is done by the original recipients, by a deed of variation or disclaimer and the substituted gifts are then treated for all inheritance tax purposes as if the deceased had made them. The provisions apply if the instrument effecting the variation or disclaimer makes an express statement to that effect.

3.85   This provides a practical planning opportunity where, as often happens, an adult child would rather his parents left their estate to his children, but where he is unwilling or they do not want him to interfere with their testamentary arrangements. It also provides a tax-efficient planning opportunity where the deceased is a non-UK domiciled person, but the original legatee is not. If the rearrangement is treated as made by the deceased, a settled legacy of non-UK sited assets may qualify as an

---

[99]   IHTA 1984, s 6(1A). Of interest is the fact that whilst deemed domicile in s 267(1) was specifically disapplied by s 267(2) in the case of government securities, it is not in the case of Authorised Unit Trusts and Open Ended Investment Companies.
[100]   IHTA 1984, s 153.
[101]   IHTA 1984, s 48(3) and (3A). See also **CHAPTER 6 (6.62** et seq).
[102]   IHTA 1984, ss 6(4) and 155(1).
[103]   IHTA 1984, s 157.
[104]   IHTA 1984, ss 142–144.
[105]   TGCA 1992, s 62(6).

excluded property settlement[106] and so be outside the scope of inheritance tax indefinitely going forward. This strategy also applies where the original legatee is included in the beneficial class and so, in effect, circumvents the application of the reservation of benefit provisions.[107] Furthermore, under the new rules relating to the income tax charge on pre-owned assets[108], property which has been the subject of a post-death rearrangement is not deemed to have been owned by the beneficiary redirecting it.

3.86 Similar provisions exist where a will requests a legatee to transfer property he receives to a third-party recipient. If done within two years of the death, no gift is deemed to have been made by the original legatee in complying with the testator's request.[109]

3.87 Finally, where a will settles property on discretionary trusts and the trustees powers are exercised within two years of death, no charges arise under the discretionary trust charging regime,[110] but the testator is deemed to have made the dispositions as they stand after the exercise of the discretionary powers.[111] This is an extremely practical provision to enable creation of flexible will trusts which can be modified as necessary to take into account changes in the family circumstances which occur between the execution of the will and the death, or within the two years after the death.

---

[106] See **CHAPTER 6**.
[107] FA 1986, s 102.
[108] See **CHAPTER 1** and FA 2004, s 84 and Sch 15.
[109] IHTA 1984, s 143.
[110] See **CHAPTER 6**.
[111] IHTA 1984, s 144.

Chapter 4

Transfers to Spouses

A. United States

1. Introduction

4.1 The marital deduction permits tax-free gifts or bequests to spouses. Unless the transferred property is consumed, the marital deduction property will generally be taxed in the spouse's estate or be subject to gift tax if gifted during her life. The marital deduction is thus said to only defer estate taxes, not avoid them altogether.

2. History

4.2 Prior to 1982, the US estate and gift tax marital deduction was subject to dollar and percentage limits.[1] A decedent with a large estate could generally leave only half of his estate tax-free to his widow. The marital deduction was also only available for transfers by US citizens and domiciliaries. Thus, an Italian countess could not leave her US property tax-free to her husband, even if he were a US citizen.

4.3 The Economic Recovery Tax Act 1981 (ERTA) made sweeping changes to the marital deduction rules.[2] ERTA removed the prior marital deduction limits, allowing US spouses to transfer an unlimited amount of property tax-free to each other. ERTA also introduced two new forms of marital deduction trusts – the qualified terminable interest property (QTIP) trust and the marital lead/charitable remainder trust – both of which are described in more detail at **4.9** et seq and **4.27**.

4.4 The final major change to the marital deduction rules came in 1988, when Congress closed a perceived loophole by substantially restricting the ability to make tax-free gifts and bequests to spouses who were not US citizens. Gifts or bequests to non-citizen spouses – even those who were domiciled in the US – would generally no longer qualify for the marital deduction or pass tax-free.[3] There were two exceptions. First, a US citizen or domiciliary could make tax-free annual gifts to a non-citizen spouse of up to $100,000 per year (indexed annually for inflation to

---

[1] See Treas Reg § 20.2056(c)(2). The deduction was generally limited to 50% of the value of the decedent's net taxable estate, or, for decedents dying between 1976 and 1982, the greater of $250,000 or 50% of the net taxable estate.
[2] PL 97–34, § 403.
[3] Code §§ 2056(d) (estate tax) and 2523(i) (gift tax). The estate tax restriction applied to estates of decedents dying after 10 November 1988, while the gift tax restrictions applied to gifts made after 14 July 1988.

4.5 *Transfers to Spouses*

$114,000 in 2004).[4] Second, bequests in specially designed testamentary trusts – called qualified domestic trusts (QDOTs) – would qualify for the estate tax marital deduction.[5] The QDOT is discussed in more detail at **4.16** et seq.

4.5 At the same time, Congress extended the marital deduction to transfers by NDAs.[6]

3. Types of qualifying transfers – outright gifts and marital trusts

4.6 Not every form of transfer to or for a spouse will qualify for the marital deduction. For example, a bequest to a discretionary trust for the surviving spouse and the children or to a trust in which the surviving spouse has only a remainder interest would not qualify for this deduction. Generally, the only forms of qualifying transfers to a spouse are either:

- an outright transfer; or
- a transfer to a special marital deduction trust.

An outright gift or bequest – in which the spouse receives title and complete control of the transferred property – is straightforward. The rules for marital deduction trusts are more complex.

a. General power of appointment trusts

4.7 For years, the primary form of marital deduction trust was the general power of appointment trust.[7] There are three basic requirements. First, the beneficiary spouse has to be the sole beneficiary of the trust during her life. Second, the trust has to give the spouse a right to all income, payable at least annually.[8] Finally, the spouse must have a general power to appoint the trust at death, that is, a power to direct the trustee to distribute the property remaining in the trust at the spouse's death to anyone, including the spouse's estate.

4.8 General power of appointment marital trusts can also:

- authorize the trustee to distribute principal to the beneficiary spouse;

---

[4] Code § 2523(i).
[5] Code §§ 2056(d)(2)(A) and 2056A.
[6] The marital deduction is available for transfers to surviving spouses by NDAs dying after 10 November 1988. Code § 2106(a)(3). The gift tax marital deduction is available for gifts of US property by NDAs after 14 July 1988. Code § 2523 and Treas Reg § 25.2523(a)-1(a).
[7] Code §§ 2056(b)(5) (estate tax) and 2523(e) (gift tax). Another seldom-used form of marital deduction trust is the so-called 'estate trust' in which income may be distributed to the spouse at the trustee's discretion or accumulated, as long as the balance of the trust is payable to the spouse's estate at her later death. Treas Reg § 20.2056(c)-2(b)(1)(iii); Rev Rul 72–333, 1972–2 CB 530.
[8] In order to satisfy the 'all-income' requirement, the terms of the trust or local law must require, or permit the beneficiary spouse to require, that the trustee make substantially unproductive assets (such as vacant land) productive or convert such property to productive property. Treas Reg §§ 20.2056(b)-5(f)(4) (estate tax) and 25.2523(e)-1(f)(4) (gift tax).

- grant the spouse a right during her life to withdraw part or all of the trust for herself; or
- confer a power on the spouse to appoint part or all of the trust to others.[9]

These provisions, though often included in general power of appointment marital trusts, are not required in order for the trust to qualify for the marital deduction. The beneficiary spouse's general power of appointment causes the trust property to be included in her US taxable estate at death.[10]

b. Qualified terminable interest property (QTIP) trusts

4.9 In the view of many taxpayers, the outright gift and general power of appointment trust suffer from the same infirmity: both give the beneficiary spouse an unlimited power to dispose of the marital deduction assets. This problem is particularly acute in the context of a second marriage where an individual might want to leave a portion of his estate to his surviving spouse (and defer estate taxes until her later death) but ensure that any of this property remaining at her later death passed to his children from his prior marriage(s). ERTA resolved this dilemma in 1981 by introducing a new form of marital deduction trust – the qualified terminable interest property (QTIP) trust.[11]

4.10 The beneficiary spouse must again be the sole beneficiary of the QTIP trust and must have a right to all trust income payable at least annually.[12] QTIP trusts also typically allow the trustee to make discretionary principal distributions to the spouse. The key difference is that the beneficiary spouse need not be given a general power to appoint the QTIP at death. The QTIP trust could give the spouse a limited power of appointment (for example, a power to appoint only among children) or might even give her no power of appointment. Thus, the decedent is able to use the QTIP to control or limit the ultimate disposition of the marital deduction property.

4.11 The donor/decedent spouse is automatically entitled to a marital deduction for transfers to a general power of appointment trust. In contrast, an affirmative election must be made to get a marital deduction for a transfer to a QTIP trust.[13] This QTIP election is made by the donor spouse on his gift tax return or by the executor of a decedent's estate on the estate tax return. The donor/executor can make a partial election and get a marital deduction for a fractional or percentage share of the QTIP trust.[14]

---

[9] Code §§ 2056(b)(5) and 2523(e) provide that there may be:
'no power in any *other* person [that is, any person other than the beneficiary spouse] to appoint any part of the [trust] to any person other than the [beneficiary] spouse'.
The beneficiary spouse's appointment of marital trust property to others during her life would be considered a taxable gift as a 'release' of her general power of appointment. Code § 2514(b).
[10] Code § 2041.
[11] Code §§ 2056(b)(7)(B) (estate tax) and 2523(e) (gift tax).
[12] This is generally referred to as a 'qualifying income interest for life'. Code §§ 2056(b)(7)(B)(ii) (estate tax) and 2523(e)(2) and (3).
[13] Code §§ 2056(b)(7)(B)(i)(III) and 2056(b)(7)(B)(v) (estate tax) and Code §§ 2523(f)(2)(C) and 2523(f)(2)(4) (gift tax).
[14] Treas Reg §§ 20.2056(b)-7(2) (estate tax) and 25.2523(f)-1(b)(3) (gift tax).

4.12   Transfers to Spouses

4.12   To the extent that a QTIP election is made, the donor/decedent's estate will be entitled to a marital deduction, and the property remaining in the QTIP trust at the beneficiary spouse's death will be taxed in her estate.[15] If a partial QTIP election is made, then only that portion will be taxed in the beneficiary spouse's estate. For example, if an election was made to receive a marital deduction for 75% of the QTIP trust, then 75% of the property remaining in the QTIP trust at the beneficiary spouse's death will be taxed in her estate.

4.13   The QTIP estate tax regulations had originally required that a QTIP trust must meet all of the requirements for qualification, whether or not a QTIP election was made. Thus, if the surviving spouse's income interest were conditioned upon the executor's QTIP election, the IRS took the position that the decedent's estate would not be entitled to the marital deduction, even if an affirmative election were made. After a series of lower court successes, the Government lost these cases on appeal.[16] The offending regulation was subsequently amended.[17] Now, if the decedent's executor elects not to qualify a portion of the QTIP trust for the marital deduction, the non-elected portion can be held on different terms For example, the trust agreement might provide for the income on the non-elected portion to accumulate or be distributed to the surviving spouse at the trustee's discretion. The trust agreement might even provide that the non-elected portion be held for the discretionary benefit of the spouse and children.

4.14   The beneficiary spouse cannot be given a power to appoint the QTIP trust property to others during her life.[18] This could be a disadvantage, for example, if the couple wants the beneficiary spouse to be able to use part of the QTIP trust property to make tax-advantaged gifts. If it is important that the beneficiary spouse be able to make gifts, the possible solutions are as follows:

- give the trustee broader discretion to make principal distributions to the beneficiary spouse; or
- use an outright gift or a general power of appointment trust for part or all of the marital deduction gift/bequest.

4.15   If the beneficiary spouse makes a lifetime gift of any part of her QTIP income interest, she is treated as having made a gift of the *entire* portion of the QTIP trust for which the donor spouse or decedent spouse's estate had received a marital deduction.[19] For example, if the decedent spouse's estate had received a full (100%) marital deduction for property funding the QTIP, the surviving spouse will be treated as having made a gift of 100% of the QTIP principal if she gives away the

---

[15]   Code § 2044.
[16]   See, for example, *Estate of Clayton v Comm'r 976 F 2d 1486 (5th Cir 1991)*, rev'g and rem'g 97 TC 327 (1991) and *Estate of Robertson v Comm'r 15 F 3d 779 (8th Cir 1994)*, rev'g 98 TC 678 (1992).
[17]   Treas Reg §§ 20.2056(b)-7(d)(3) and 25.2523(f)-1(c).
[18]   The QTIP rules (Code § 2056(b)(7)(B)(ii)(II)) require that:
   '... no person has a power to appoint any part of the property to any person other than the [beneficiary] spouse',
which is incorporated in the gift tax rules by Code § 2523(f)(3). Compare with the general power of appointment trust requirements cited at **4.7** and **4.8**.

right to any (eg 1%) of the QTIP income. This rule applies to the beneficiary spouse's gift of her *right* to QTIP income, not to the spouse's cash gifts funded from income distributions.

c. Qualified domestic trusts (QDOTs)

4.16 Transfers to qualified domestic trusts (QDOTs) are the only way to qualify bequests to a surviving non-citizen spouse for the estate tax marital deduction. For reasons that escape logic, the tax rules do not allow donors to use QDOTs for qualifying lifetime gifts to non-citizen spouses.

4.17 The QDOT must be either a QTIP trust or a general power of appointment trust, and thus must provide the survivor with all the income on an annual basis.[20] The trust must also be 'maintained under' US law and 'governed by' US law.[21] A trust created under a foreign will or trust agreement will only qualify as a QDOT if the relevant terms of that document designate that US law will govern the administration of the QDOT and if local law would respect that designation.

4.18 A series of security requirements are designed to ensure the eventual collection of the deferred US estate tax. Foremost are the requirements that:

- there be least one trustee who is a US citizen or a US corporation; and
- the US trustee has a right to withhold and pay any US estate taxes.[22]

The regulations also impose a 'bank, bond or letter of credit' requirement for certain large QDOTs.[23] If the aggregate amount held in one or more QDOTs for the spouse exceeds $2m, then the trust must either have a US bank as trustee or co-trustee or provide the US Government with a bond or letter of credit. For purposes of determining if the value of the trust exceeds $2m, the executor may elect to exclude up to $600,000 of value attributed to real property (and related tangibles) used by the surviving spouse as a personal residence (which is further defined to include the primary residence and one other residence).[24]

4.19 A smaller QDOT must either:

- meet the bank, bond or letter of credit requirement; or
- be prohibited by the terms of the trust instrument from owning non-US real property valued at over 35% of the value of the trust assets.[25]

---

[19] Code § 2519.
[20] The Code does not explicitly make this requirement. However, as originally enacted, Code § 2056A(a)(2) required that the spouse must be entitled to all the income from the trust. The 1989 Act eliminated this requirement, and the legislative history thereto indicates that this requirement was generally superfluous in light of the intended requirement that, independent of the QDOT rules, the trust must otherwise qualify for the marital deduction under Code § 2056(a). See HR No 247 101st Congress, 1st Session 1431 (1989).
[21] Treas Reg § 20.2056A-2(a). A trust is considered to be 'maintained under' US law if the records of the trust (or copies) are kept in the US.
[22] Code § 2056A(a)(1).
[23] Treas Reg § 20.2056A-2(d)(1)(i).
[24] Treas Reg § 20.2056A-2(d)(1)(iv).

4.20   Transfers to Spouses

The $600,000 personal residence exception does not apply for purposes of determining if 35% of the trust property consists of non-US real estate.

4.20   The executor of the decedent's estate must make an affirmative election for the estate to receive a marital deduction for a transfer to a QDOT.[26] If the QDOT is also a QTIP trust, both elections must be made. No partial QDOT election is permitted.[27]

4.21   The tax rules also permit a non-citizen spouse to transfer inherited property into a qualifying QDOT after the decedent's death.[28] For example, the surviving, non-citizen spouse could transfer insurance proceeds, survivorship property (such as bank accounts or jointly-owned real estate), or pension benefits that she has received (or is entitled to receive) into a QDOT (including one created by the surviving spouse) and qualify that property for the marital deduction (and thus tax deferral) just as if the decedent had funded the trust in his estate plan.

4.22   A non-citizen surviving spouse who becomes a US citizen after the decedent's death but before the decedent's estate tax return is filed will be treated as if the survivor were a US citizen at the decedent's death. In this event, a QDOT would not be required. This exception applies only if the survivor has been a US domiciliary at all times between the date of the decedent's death and the date of citizenship.[29]

4.23   An estate tax (referred to here as the 'QDOT estate tax') is imposed not just on the property remaining in the QDOT at the survivor's death[30] but also on distributions from a QDOT to a non-citizen spouse during her life.[31] There are a few exceptions as follows:

- income distributions to the survivor (which generally do not include capital gains or so-called 'income in respect of a decedent' such as deferred compensation) are not subject to the QDOT estate tax;[32]

- principal distributions on account of the survivor's 'hardship' are similarly exempt from this tax;[33]

- the payment of certain administrative expenses and income taxes (both on behalf of the trust and the spouse) are exempt from the QDOT estate tax;[34]

---

[25]   Treas Reg § 20.2056A-2(d)(1)(ii).
[26]   Code § 2056A(d).
[27]   Treas Reg § 20.2056A-3(b).
[28]   Code § 2056(d)(2)(B).
[29]   Code § 2056(d)(4); Treas Reg § 20.2056A-1(b).
[30]   Code § 2056A(b)(1)(B).
[31]   Code § 2056A(b)(1)(A).
[32]   Code § 2056A(b)(3)(A).
[33]   Code § 2056A(b)(3)(B). The regulations define hardship to mean 'an immediate and substantial financial need relating to the spouse's health, maintenance, education or support, or the health, maintenance, education or support of any person that the surviving spouse is legally obligated to support. Treas Reg § 20.2056A-5(c)(1).

United States   **4.25**

- finally, principal distributions are generally not taxed if the surviving spouse later becomes a US citizen and was a US domiciliary at all times after the decedent's death before becoming a US citizen.[35]

The QDOT estate tax is also imposed if the trust ceases to qualify as a QDOT (for example, if the trust ceases to have a US trustee or ceases to meet the other security requirements).[36]

4.24 The QDOT estate tax is computed as if the taxable property had been included and taxed in the *first spouse's* estate.[37] This rule subjects the QDOT property to tax in the marginal tax brackets of the decedent spouse's estate. If the QDOT estate tax is imposed by reason of the survivor's death, the amount of the QDOT estate tax will be computed after taking into account certain deductions (the marital deduction and charitable deduction) and credits (such as foreign death tax credit and, until 2005, the state death tax credit) that would otherwise have been available to the *survivor* had he or she been a US citizen.[38] For example, if the QDOT passes to the surviving spouse of the survivor, a second marital deduction is allowed in computing the QDOT estate tax. (If the survivor's surviving spouse is not a US citizen, a second QDOT would be required.)

4.25 In addition, the property remaining in a QDOT at the survivor's death might also be included in her US taxable estate and taxed along with her other taxable property. This could occur for a number of reasons. The survivor, though not a US citizen at the first spouse's death, might be domiciled in the US (or even a US citizen) at her later death. In that event, the survivor's US taxable estate would include the value of all property held in the QDOT/QTIP trust[39] or the QDOT/general power of appointment trust.[40] If the spouse is not domiciled in the US (and is not a US citizen) at her later death, any US property held in the QDOT would be taxed in her US estate because of the estate tax situs rules.[41] In addition, if the surviving spouse funded the post-death QDOT with US property and is not domiciled in the US at death, a portion of the QDOT related to that original contribution would be subject to US tax, even if there is no US property in the QDOT at the survivor's death.[42]

---

[34] Treas. Reg § 20.2056A-5(b)(3).
[35] Code § 2056A(b)(12). This rule only applies where the spouse becomes a US citizen after the estate tax return is filed: if she had become a US citizen beforehand, the spouse is treated as a US citizen and the marital trust need not meet the QDOT requirements (see **4.23**). This exception also requires that either:
   (a)   the survivor had received no prior taxable distributions from the QDOT; or
   (b)   she elect to treat any such prior taxable distributions as if those distributions *to* her had been gifts *by* her.
The second option could affect the amount of gift tax or estate tax on her later gifts or bequests.
[36] Code § 2056A(b)(4).
[37] Code § 2056A(b)(2).
[38] Code § 2056A(b)(10)(A).
[39] Code § 2044.
[40] Code § 2041.
[41] Code § 2106 subjects to a US estate tax all US property included in a NDA's 'gross estate'. The gross estate is determined as provided in Code § 2033 for US citizens (which in turn would cause QDOT/QTIP property and QDOT/general power of appointment property to be taxed in the surviving spouse's estate).

4.26 Transfers to Spouses

4.26 The QDOT estate tax is credited against any US estate tax imposed on the survivor's estate. A similar credit is given to the surviving spouse's estate for property passing to the non-citizen but not qualifying for the marital deduction.[43] The objective of these rules is to ensure one tax on this property in the couple's generation – not a double tax.

d. Marital lead/charitable remainder trust

4.27 Finally, a spouse's lead interest in a charitable remainder trust[44] will also qualify for the marital deduction if the spouse is the trust's sole non-charitable beneficiary.[45] Unlike QTIPs or general power of appointment trusts, the spouse's interest in a marital lead/charitable remainder trust need not last for life but can last only for a period of time. However, for a 'term-of-years' trust to qualify as a charitable remainder trust, it cannot last for more than 20 years.[46] The donor or decedent's estate will be entitled to both an estate tax marital deduction (for the present value of the spouse's lead interest) and an estate tax charitable deduction (for the present value of the charitable remainder interest).[47] Property remaining in a marital lead/charitable remainder trust at the survivor's death will not be taxed in her estate (although if it had, the estate would generally be entitled to an offsetting charitable deduction).

B. United Kingdom

1. Introduction

4.28 Transfers between spouses, outright or via an interest in possession (IIP) trust, are exempt from IHT unless the donee spouse is then non-UK IHT domiciled and the donor spouse is UK IHT domiciled. A testamentary transfer to a non-UK domiciled spouse may, therefore, be IHT taxable to the extent it exceeds £55,000 plus the transferor's unused nil-rate band. However, such a transfer during the donor's lifetime is a potentially exempt transfer (PET) which will escape IHT taxation if the donor spouse survives the gift by seven years. For couples where lifetime gifts are practicable therefore, lifetime PET transfers to a non-domiciled spouse may be desirable. To the extent that the spouse exemption applies, it will generally constitute only tax deferral as, absent planning, the transferred property will generally be taxable in the estate of the donee spouse.

---

[42] Code § 2104(b).
[43] Code § 2056(d)(3). The survivor's estate is entitled to a credit under Code § 2013 (the credit for prior tax on inherited property) without regard for when the first decedent died. The Code § 2013 credit is normally phased out over a ten-year period following the decedent's death, but, again, this phase-out does not apply to the credit allowed a non-citizen spouse.
[44] There are two forms of charitable remainder trusts, the charitable remainder annuity trust (CRAT) and the charitable remainder unitrust (CRUT). A CRAT gives one or more non-charitable persons a right to a fixed annuity for a period of years or the life of one or more individuals. A CRUT gives the non-charitable beneficiary(ies) a right to a fixed percentage of the value of the CRUT, as re-determined periodically. In both instances, the final remainder interest passes to charity.
[45] Code §§ 2056(b)(8) (estate tax) and 2523(g) (gift tax).
[46] Treas Reg § 20.2056(b)-8(a)(2).

United Kingdom **4.32**

2. History

4.29 A limited exemption for bequests to a spouse up to £15,000 was introduced in 1972 under the old UK estate duty provisions. Additionally, while a UK taxpayer's transfer of assets to a life interest trust for his spouse attracted full tax on the first death, it was exempt under the old rules from tax on the surviving spouse's later death.[48] Certain surviving spouse trusts, where the first decedent died prior to 13 November 1974, continue to have the residual benefits of this former exemption, but clearly they are becoming less common.[49]

4.30 In 1974, on the introduction of capital transfer tax,[50] which replaced estate duty, the limited exemption for outright transfers to a spouse was extended to a complete exemption and the position with respect to settled gifts was reversed. Transfers to trusts creating a life interest for a spouse are generally now tax free, but the property becomes chargeable upon the donee spouse's later death (or during lifetime when deemed transfers of value are made). This general scheme of taxation of gifts to spouses continued after the introduction of inheritance tax in 1986.[51]

4.31 Unlimited outright gifts, both during lifetime and on death, between UK domiciled spouses qualify for this exemption. The exemption is also unlimited where both spouses are non-UK domiciliaries, and where a non-UK domiciliary transferor gives UK situs property (such individuals having no UK liability on non-UK situs assets) to a UK domiciled spouse. However, where the transferor is a UK domiciliary (which may include a deemed UK domiciliary) but the transferee is non-UK domiciled, the marital exemption is limited to just £55,000.[52] This exemption is modified by certain tax treaties (see general discussion in CHAPTER 7).[53] Given the above parameters, it can be seen that the rationale of the limitation aims to prevent assets which otherwise would eventually be subject to UK inheritance tax in the estate of the surviving spouse, from flowing out of the UK tax net. However, it is unclear why the current level of this exemption, which was introduced in 1982, has now remained unchanged over some 20 years.

4.32 Prior to 1974, the limitation was unnecessary given that a spouse would have taken on the domicile status of her husband.[54]

---

[47] A trust that provides the surviving spouse with the right to all income for life and a remainder to charity will not qualify as a charitable remainder trust and thus will not qualify for the marital deduction under Code §§ 2056(b)(8) or 2523(g). However, such a trust could qualify as a QTIP and the donor/decedent's estate would be entitled to a marital deduction for the full value of the property transferred to this form of trust if so elected. At the spouse's death, the value of the property held in the QTIP/remainder trust will be included in the spouse's estate under Code § 2044, but the spouse's estate should be entitled to charitable deduction for the value of the charitable remainder.
[48] FA 1894, s 5(2); FA 1914, s 14.
[49] IHTA 1984, Sch 6, para 2.
[50] FA 1975.
[51] FA 1986, s 100; IHTA 1984, s 18.
[52] IHTA 1984, s 18(2). The previous figures were as follows: £15,000 from 27 March 1974 to 26 October 1977; £25,000 from 27 October 1977 to 25 March 1980; £50,000 from 26 March 1980 to 8 March 1982; £55,000 thereafter.
[53] Article 8 of the Estate and Gift Tax treaty between the US and the UK permits a 50% marital deduction in the UK for transfers from a UK domiciled person to their US domiciled spouse. By

4.33   *Transfers to Spouses*

3. *Types of qualifying transfers*

4.33   The exemption applies to outright gifts to the extent that the value transferred is attributable to property which becomes comprised in the estate of the donor's spouse[55] or which has the result of increasing the value of an asset in the donee spouse's estate.[56]

4.34   The UK exemption for gifts between spouses also applies to gifts made conditional on certain events, but only if the condition is satisfied within twelve months of the decedent's death. Similarly, it is permissible for the gift to be made subject to the spouse surviving the deceased for a specified period (usually between three and six months in UK wills), though the gift will not qualify if vesting is deferred for any other reason, for example, the gift is made conditional on the spouse obtaining a law degree within five years.[57]

4.35   Transfers into trusts giving a spouse an entitlement to income as of right[58] qualify for the UK spouse exemption. This is because the assets held within a life interest trust will generally be taxable on the same basis as if they had been comprised in the life tenant's UK estate, since the life tenant will be deemed to own them.[59] Unlike the US, the UK does not require that the marital trust give the spouse a general power of appointment; or be subject to the executor's special tax election.

A standard form of life interest trust where the spouse has no more than a right to income (including one which is defeasible prospectively at the discretion of the trustees) will suffice.[60]

4.36   A gift to any other form of trust, however, where the spouse does not have right to income (for example, a discretionary trust where she is comprised in the class of beneficiaries) will not attract the exemption, irrespective of any powers over the trust assets or other interests given to the spouse.

---

comparison, it is interesting to note that the wording of the treaty provides for relief against US tax for transferors who are nationals/domiciliaries of the UK to the same extent as would have been available had they been US domiciliaries. Where the donee spouse is not a US citizen, this, of course, provides no relief at all, save in cases where a QDOT can be used.

[54]   This was changed with effect from 1 January 1974 by the Domicile and Matrimonial Proceedings Act 1973, by virtue of which a wife can now acquire an independent domicile.

[55]   IHTA1984, s 18(1). Note that in the Special Commissioners decision of *Holland (executor of Holland deceased) v IRC [2003] STC SCD 43* it was expressly held that the spouse exemption is not available to co-habiting couples. They considered that the situation of married couples was different involving mutual rights and obligations of maintenance not applicable to co-habitees and which justified the different treatment for the purposes of the Human Rights Act 1998 (although, in fact, the Act did not apply in that case as the deceased died before it came into effect).

[56]   Eg payments in respect of a premium on a policy of insurance owned by the spouse or the cost of renovation work on a property owned by the spouse.

[57]   IHTA 1984, s 18(3).

[58]   *Pearson and others v CIR [1980] STC 318*. The spouse must be absolutely entitled to receive the income as it arises and once the income is in their hands, the trustees must have no discretion to determine who is to receive it or whether it is to be accumulated. It must be payable to the spouse.

[59]   IHTA 1984, s 49.

4.37 A 'deemed' transfer by a spouse who is himself entitled to a life interest in a trust, occurs when his life interest in trust property comes to an end. If this results in an outright gift of the trust assets to his surviving spouse or a sequential life interest for her, it is capable of qualifying for the spouse exemption. However, this would not be the case where a discretionary trust exists during the lifetime of the husband for the benefit of a class of persons which may include the husband, even though his surviving spouse is entitled under the terms of the trust to a life interest following his death. Although the assets are deemed to be included in his taxable estate by reason of the reservation of benefit provisions (assuming he is the settlor), the tax charge arising at his death is by reference to the IHT regime applicable to discretionary trusts.[61] Particular care needs to be taken in drafting trusts which are to have application in the US and/or the UK to ensure that a discretionary trust is not inadvertently created in these circumstances.

4.38 In contrast with the UK, and absent a QTIP election, the US tax regime will regard the life tenant of a trust (whose income interest is indefeasible) as being entitled to an asset which is valued on an actuarial basis (being the value of the right to receive the income over his anticipated life expectancy). A voluntary release by a life tenant would, therefore, normally trigger a US taxable gift by the beneficiary. However, the inter-relationship of the taxes and life interest rules in the US and UK regimes can have an advantageous effect.

For example, a life interest trust established by a UK domiciled person for the benefit of his US citizen spouse can attract the spouse exemption in the UK if she is also deemed UK domiciled.[62] If her life interest could not be revoked by the trustees and she released all or part of her life interest, there would be a taxable gift for US purposes of the actuarial value of the interest given up. However, if she were given a defeasible interest in possession under UK trust rules (which is all that is required for IHT deferral) and independent trustees exercised their power to defeat her interest in favour of others, there should be no US taxable gift since she made no voluntary disposition of her trust interest. Even if the spouse were considered to have somehow disposed of her interest, it arguably has no US gift tax value given its defeasible nature. For UK purposes, the transfer may constitute an exempt transfer, a potentially exempt transfer, or a chargeable transfer depending on the identity of the new beneficiary.

4.39 As noted, a spouse's defeasible life interest in a trust will be a sufficient interest to enable the gift into trust to qualify for the UK spouse exemption. Generally, this will also be a gift to which the reservation of benefit provisions cannot apply in view of the fact it is an exempt gift to a spouse.[63] However, a specific

---

[60] Provided the trustees cannot deprive the spouse of income once it has arisen, they can nevertheless exercise a power which changes the spouse's entitlement under the trust going forward, as to future income receipts.
[61] IHTA 1984, Pt III, Ch III, in particular s 65(1)(a): see also **CHAPTER 13**. The charge here would be an exit charge under s 65(1)(a), the maximum IHT being a proportion of the 6% decennial tax; a 40% charge would not apply to the decedent husband's estate, under the reservation of benefit provisions, in view of the exempt spousal transfer of the assets treated for the purposes of IHTA 1984 to be comprised in his estate.
[62] By reason of being income tax resident in the UK in at least 17 tax years out of the prior 20 year-period; IHTA 1984, s 267. See **CHAPTER 2**.

4.40 *Transfers to Spouses*

anti-avoidance provision is relevant in certain circumstances if, on or after 20 June 2003, the spouse's life interest in all or part of the trust fund comes to an end during the donor spouse's lifetime and the beneficiary spouse does not become beneficially entitled to the assets or to another life interest in those assets. In such a case the original donor/settlor spouse is treated as making a gift at that time for the purposes of the gifts with reservation provisions.[64] For example, if the spouse's life interest is brought to an end in favour of discretionary trusts of which the settlor is a potential beneficiary, he will be treated as having made a gift with reservation of benefit at that time (such that the assets will be deemed to be comprised in his taxable estate for the purposes of IHT). This is without prejudice to the normal application of the IHT provisions, which would impose a tax charge at that time as if the spouse whose interest had been terminated, had made a chargeable transfer of value.[65]

4.40 If instead, after the donor spouse's death, the trustees later exercise their power to deflect income away from his spouse, that event will be deemed to be a transfer of value by the surviving spouse of the property in which her life interest subsisted, in the usual way.[66]

4.41 The tax consequences of a termination of the spouse's life interest depend on a variety of factors. For example, if the trustees appoint the capital outright to a third party, the surviving spouse would be treated as if she had made a PET (with the consequences described in **CHAPTER 1**) or she would be deemed to have made a chargeable lifetime transfer if the appointment were to a discretionary trust. Whether a tax liability arose at that point may depend on the nature of the assets, the value of the transfer and whether the spouse's nil-rate band was available. The transfer will be deemed to have been made by the life tenant but the tax attributable to the trust assets will be payable by the trustees. See **CHAPTER 2** generally.

4.42 It should be noted that the general principles related to the taxation of IIP trusts will apply.[67] Under these principles, although the IIP holder is deemed to beneficially own the trust assets for IHT purposes, whether a transfer of non-UK sited trust assets will actually be chargeable depends on the IHT domicile of the settlor at the time of funding the trust. In effect, under the excluded property trust rule,[68] the trust is attributed with the IHT domicile status of the settlor at the time of transfer of assets to the settlement and its non-UK assets will be chargeable or not depending on that domicile, irrespective of the domicile of the interest in possession holder – even though such holder is deemed to be the 'transferor' for the purposes of UK IHT.

---

[63] FA 1986, s 102(5)(a).
[64] FA 1986, s 102(5A), (5B), and (5C).
[65] FA 1986, s 102(5C)(a).
[66] IHTA 1984, s 52(1).
[67] The principle outlined in IHTA 1984, s 6(1), which provides that property situated outside the UK is excluded property if beneficially owned by a person who is non-UK domiciled, will be overridden by IHTA 1984, s 48(3), which treats non-UK sited property as IHT exempt if owned by a trust settled by person who was non-UK IHT domiciled at the time of funding the trust, i e the settlor's domicile at the time of settlement will be the controlling factor, not that of the spouse who is deemed a beneficial owner of trust assets for IHT purposes. A transfer of non-excluded property assets, e g UK sited real property, is chargeable under IHTA 1984, s 52(1) regardless of the domicile of the settlor or the spouse.

4.43 This concept is particularly confusing to American practitioners because the UK system can subject a life interest holder to global taxation with regard to trust assets depending on the domicile of the settlor at the time of funding the settlement – even though neither the settlor nor the IIP holder may be domiciled at the time of a later taxable event, such as termination of her life interest.[69] Conversely, if the trust is an excluded property trust (ie, the settlor at the time of funding the settlement was non-UK IHT domiciled), non-UK sited assets[70] will not be subject to IHT on termination of an interest in possession whether or not the settlor or the IIP holder is UK IHT domiciled at the time of such termination.

4.44 In certain cases of a mismatched domicile between spouses, it may be preferable for the non-UK domiciled spouse to hold the greater part of the asset base for a number of reasons. One being that where the whole estate will be required to support the survivor during their lifetime, in the event of the prior death of the non-UK domiciled spouse, assets can then pass to an excluded property trust for the benefit of the UK domiciled spouse and descendants and be exempt from IHT at both deaths.

4.45 Transfers of property between the parties to a marriage (or former marriage) pursuant to a divorce settlement (or a variation of such a settlement) are also free of IHT.[71] For the purposes of the spouse exemption generally, the parties are regarded as married up to the time of their divorce, whether or not they are living together. This contrasts with the capital gains tax position,[72] where they cease to attract the favoured tax position for gifts between married persons from the beginning of the tax year following that in which they ceased to live together as husband and wife. Therefore, careful planning is needed where parties have separated or intend to do so, to avoid different treatment for the purposes of the two taxes, both of which may be relevant to a transfer of assets.

4.46 It should be noted that a husband and wife are regarded as 'connected parties' for IHT purposes and when transactions occur between them they are not automatically deemed to have taken place on arm's length terms.[73] For example, if a sale is made to a spouse rather than a gift, the consideration passing will be scrutinised and the open market price substituted, if it is thought to be different from the actual proceeds.

4.47 It should also be noted that where a husband and wife own property it is 'related property'.[74] This means that where, for example, on a disposal of an asset by one party to a marriage valuations are required, the relevant interests of both parties are taken into account. If the proportionate value of the aggregate of both interests

---

[68] IHTA 1984, s 48(3). Note that pursuant to s 48(3A), authorised unit trusts and open ended investment company shares held by a trust funded by a then non-UK IHT domiciled settlor are also 'excluded property'.
[69] Note that UK sited assets, not being within the excluded property trust rule, will remain taxable to the trust on a termination of her IIP interest, irrespective of her own or the settlor's domicile.
[70] As well as shares in an authorised unit trust or an open ended investment company. IHTA 1984, s 48(3A).
[71] IHTA 1984, s 11(6).
[72] TCGA 1992, s 58.
[73] IHTA 1984, s 270.

4.47   *Transfers to Spouses*

would be higher than the value of the interests, had they been valued separately, the higher value will be applied. For example, if each party owns two paintings and the four comprise a set that could be sold together at a premium, the higher valuation including a proportionate part of the premium will be used.

Chapter 5

Tax Rates and Computation

A. United States

1. Introduction

5.1 The US gift tax and estate tax share the same rate schedule set out below. The table shows that the larger the gift or estate, the higher the marginal tax rate. Also, as discussed in more detail at **5.9** et seq, the value of prior taxable gifts affects the rate of tax imposed on later gifts and imposed on the taxpayer's estate.

2. Estate and gift tax rate brackets

5.2 The 2001 Act[1] provides for a gradual reduction in the highest marginal tax rates. Below are the rates that currently apply to the cumulative transfers.

Value of cumulative transfers between		Tax on first amount	Tax rate on excess
($)	($)	($)	(%)
0	10,000	0	18
10,000	20,000	1,800	20
20,000	40,000	3,800	22
40,000	60,000	8,200	24
60,000	80,000	13,000	26
80,000	100,000	18,200	28
100,000	150,000	23,800	30
150,000	250,000	38,800	32
250,000	500,000	70,800	34
500,000	750,000	155,800	37
750,000	1,000,000	248,300	39
1,000,000	1,250,000	345,800	41
1,250,000	1,500,000	448,300	43

---

[1] The Economic Growth and Tax Relief Reconciliation Act 2001 (Pub L 107–16), sometimes referred to in this book as 'EGTRRA', the '2001 Act' or the '2001 Tax Act'.

5.3 Tax Rates and Computation

Value of cumulative transfers between		Tax on first amount	Tax rate on excess
($)	($)	($)	(%)
1,500,000	2,000,000	555,800	45–48%
			48% in 2004
			47% in 2005
2,000,000	and over	780,800	46% in 2006
			45% in 2007 through 2009

The 2001 Act also provides for the repeal of the estate tax for decedents dying in 2010 along with a further reduction in the top marginal rate of the gift tax (which is not repealed) to the then-highest marginal income tax rate (which, unless the law is changed, would be 35% for gifts in excess of $500,000).

5.3 The repeal and interim rate reductions are scheduled to *sunset* in 2011, reverting to the rate schedule in effect in 2001. Unless Congress changes the law, the marginal tax rate on cumulative transfers in excess of $2,000,000 for tax years 2011 and after will be as follows.

Value of cumulative transfers between		Tax on first amount	Tax rate on excess
($)	($)	($)	(%)
2,000,000	2,500,000	780,800	49
2,500,000	3,000,000	1,025,800	53
3,000,000	and over	1,290,800	55

5.4 Under prior law, certain larger estates (generally, above $10m and below $21m) were subject to an additional 5% excise tax.[2] This excise tax effectively recouped the tax benefits of the unified credit (now 'applicable exclusion credit') and of the lower tax brackets. The net effect was that taxable estates of over $21m paid a flat tax of 55%. This 5% excise tax would also be restored in 2011 by reason of the sunset provisions of the 2001 Act unless Congress provides legislative relief.

5.5 Congress will almost assuredly address estate and gift tax reform prior to 2010 or 2011. The alternative approaches at the two extremes would be to make the estate tax repeal (and the 35% gift tax rate) permanent or allow all the rules and rates to revert back to those in effect in 2001. One possible compromise would be to keep the estate tax, freeze the top rates at lower levels than in effect in 2001 (perhaps somewhere between 35% and 45%), while exempting transfers at some higher level

---

[2] Code § 2001(c)(3) (repealed 2001–2010).

than in 2001 (perhaps $2.5m or higher). In that event, the estate and gift tax would – like the UK – apply at one flat rate on transfers in excess of the exemption.

3. Equal application to citizens, domiciliaries and NDAs

5.6 This tax rate schedule applies equally to US citizens, domiciliaries, NDAs and tax-motivated expatriates. The only difference between these different categories of taxpayers is the marginal tax rate on which the first dollar of tax is actually imposed. This is a function of the applicable exclusion credit, not the rate tables.

5.7 For US citizens and domiciliaries (including tax-motivated expatriates who have not shed their US domicile), the applicable exclusion exempts the first $1m of cumulative gift. The marginal tax rate for the first dollar of cumulative gifts in excess of $1m is thus 41%. NDAs (including tax-motivated expatriates who are not US domiciliaries) receive no gift tax credit; thus the first dollar of taxable gifts are taxed at a rate of 18%.

5.8 The estate tax applicable exclusion in 2004 for citizens and domiciliaries (including tax-motivated expatriates) is $1.5m. The marginal estate tax rate for the first dollar of an estate in excess of that amount is therefore 45%. NDAs receive only a modest estate tax credit that exempts only the first $60,000. This causes a tax of at least 26% on the first taxable dollar of a NDA's estate.[3]

4. Impact of prior taxable gifts

5.9 Prior taxable gifts affect the amount and rate of tax imposed on later gifts and bequests. Later taxable transfers do not start over at the beginning of the rate brackets. Instead, the tax is effectively computed at the marginal bracket where prior transfers had stopped. This is accomplished by adding gifts in prior years to the current year's net taxable gifts or to the amount of the decedent's net taxable estate. The mechanics of computing the gift and estate tax are, however, slightly different.

5.10 For gift tax purposes, all taxable gifts for *all* prior years are taken into account.[4] A tentative gift tax is computed under the rate tables on this aggregate amount and then is reduced by a tentative tax computed under the same tables on prior taxable gifts. From this net amount is then subtracted the amount of the taxpayer's remaining, unused applicable exclusion credit.

Example
Assume a taxpayer makes $750,000 of taxable gifts (his first taxable gifts) in each of 2003 and 2004. The 2003 gift would have used $248,300 of applicable exclusion credit, leaving $97,500 of credit to apply against

---

[3] The first taxable dollar of a NDAs taxable estate could even be taxed at higher rates if the NDA had made US taxable gifts during life. For example, if a NDA had made $1m US taxable gifts during life, the first dollar of his taxable estate would effectively be taxed at the 41% tax bracket.
[4] Code § 2504.

5.11 *Tax Rates and Computation*

future gifts. In computing the 2004 gift tax, the 2003 gifts are added to the 2004 gifts, for an aggregate amount of $1.5m. The 2004 gift tax is computed as follows.

	$
Tentative tax on $1.5m total gifts	555,800
Less: tentative tax on $750,000 prior gifts	(248,300)
Gift Tax (before credits)	307,500
Less: remaining applicable exclusion credit	(97,500)
Gift Tax on 2004 Gift	210,000

5.11 For estate tax purposes, only gifts after 1976 are taken into account.[5] A tentative gift or estate tax is then computed on this total. If there were prior taxable gifts, a credit is essentially then given for the hypothetical gift tax (*after reduction for the applicable exclusion credit*) on the amount of the prior gifts. This hypothetical gift tax is computed under the then-current rate schedule – not the rate schedule in effect in the year the gifts were actually made – and again assumes application of the gift tax applicable exclusion credit to those gift.[6] The full estate tax applicable exclusion credit is then subtracted to determine the net tax liability.

Example

Assume a taxpayer made $750,000 of taxable gifts (his first taxable gifts ever) in each of 2003 and 2004, and then died in 2008 with an estate of $2m. The estate tax would be computed as follows.

	$
Tentative tax on $3.5m total	1,455,800
Less: tentative tax on $1.5m prior gifts	(210,000)
Estate Tax (before credits)	1,245,800
Less: applicable exclusion credit	(780,800)
2008 Estate Tax	465,000

5.12 Note the different way in which the gift tax applicable exclusion credit on prior gifts is taken into account in computing the gift and estate taxes. For gift tax purposes, only the net remaining applicable exclusion credit is used, while for estate tax purposes the full exclusion credit is available. This different approach is offset, however, by the different manner in which the tentative tax on prior gifts is computed.

---

[5] Code § 2001(b). For estate tax purposes, property that had been previously gifted will not be considered an 'adjusted taxable gift' if that property is re-included in the decedent's estate. This prevents the property from essentially being taxed twice.

[6] Therefore, if a taxpayer had made large taxable gifts in 2001 or earlier and paid gift taxes at a marginal rate of 55%, the effective credit for the hypothetical gift tax on adjusted taxable gifts would be capped at only 45% for gifts or bequests made in 2007/09.

5.13 For gift tax purposes, the tentative tax on prior gifts ignores the credit while the estate tax computes the tentative tax on prior gifts after taking into account the use of the credit. The gift tax computation therefore has:

- a smaller applicable exclusion credit; *but*
- a larger 'credit' for the tentative tax on prior gifts.

5.14 In contrast, the estate tax has:

- a larger applicable exclusion credit; *but*
- a smaller 'credit' for the tentative tax on prior gifts.

The net effect, however, is essentially the same: the prior use of the gift tax applicable exclusion credit reduces the amount of future gifts (or estate) that can pass free of tax, therefore, increasing the future gift and estate tax.

5. *The 'tax-on-tax' effect of the US estate tax*

5.15 There is an interesting anomaly in the manner in which the US gift and estate taxes are computed. The gift tax is computed on a *tax-exclusive* basis; that is, the tax is imposed only on the value of property actually passing to the donee. In contrast, the estate tax is computed on a *tax-inclusive* basis; that is, the tax is imposed on the decedent's entire estate, which includes not only the property that will eventually pass to the donees, but also the property that is used to pay estate taxes. The estate tax is thus said to impose a tax on a tax.

> To illustrate, assume a taxpayer in the 45% marginal tax bracket had $100,000 that he wished to give to his children and pay taxes. If he retained the $100,000 and made a bequest at death, the full $100,000 would be taxed in the 45% bracket, a $45,000 estate tax imposed, leaving $55,000 after taxes for the children. If the taxpayer instead makes a lifetime gift, he can give his children $68,966, and use the balance of the fund to pay the gift taxes of $31,034.[7] The tax savings from the lifetime gift is therefore $13,966.

5.16 As noted in **CHAPTER 1**, a decedent's estate includes gift taxes paid on gifts made within three years of the decedent's death. This rule effectively restores the overall taxes to those that would have been imposed had the entire amount passed under the estate. In the prior example, a 45% estate tax on the $31,034 of gift taxes paid on gifts made within three years would be $13,966 – the exact amount of the hypothetical tax savings from the gift.

6. *Generation-skipping tax (GST)*

5.17 The GST is imposed on three types of generation-skipping transfers: direct skips, taxable distributions and taxable terminations. The tax is computed by

---

[7] $100,000 = the amount of the gift (X) + the amount of the tax (.45X); $100,000 = 1.45X; $68,966 = X (the amount of the gift).

5.18   Tax Rates and Computation

multiplying the amount of the taxable transfer × the 'applicable rate'.[8] The applicable rate, in turn, is the product of the highest marginal estate tax rate (which, in 2004, is 48%) × the 'inclusion ratio'.[9] As discussed in **CHAPTER 3**, the inclusion ratio is the portion of the transfer subject to the GST after taking into account the taxpayer's GST exemption.

5.18   With respect to a *direct skip* (a gift or bequest directly to a person in a lower generation, skipping altogether an intervening generation), the taxable amount is the value of the property actually received by the donee.

Example

Assume a grandparent makes $2m of taxable gifts to a grandchild in 2004 and has previously used none of his GST exemption. The GST exemption in 2004 is $1.5m. The inclusion ratio with respect to this gift would be 25% ($(1 - \$1.5m/\$2m)$). The applicable rate would therefore be 12% (48% x 25%). The GST on this direct skip would therefore be $240,000 ($2m x 12%). Essentially, a GST of 48% is imposed on the $500,000 amount of this gift not exempted by the GST exemption. Note that the GST imposed on direct skips is *tax exclusive* in that no further GST is imposed on the funds used to pay the GST.

5.19   With respect to a *taxable distribution* (a transfer to a person in a lower generation from a trust held in for an intervening generation), the taxable amount is generally the amount received by the transferee.[10]

5.20   However, if the trust, rather than the transferee, pays the GST, the taxable amount also includes the amount of the GST imposed on that distribution.[11]

Example

Assume in 2004 a grandparent transfers $2m to a trust for his children and grandchildren and applies his $1.5m GST exemption to that trust. The trust would accordingly have an inclusion ratio of 25%. Assume later in 2004 the trust makes an actual distribution to a grandchild of $100,000. If the grandchild pays the GST, the GST is computed as $100,000 x 12% (25% x 48%) or $12,000, leaving the grandchild only $88,000 after taxes. If, instead, the trust pays the GST, the tax would be calculated algebraically as follows:

---

[8]   Code § 2602.
[9]   Code § 2641(a)(1). In prior years, when certain larger estates were subject to an additional 5% tax to recapture the benefits of the lower rate brackets and the estate tax credit, that 5% tax was not taken into account in determining the effective GST tax rate.
[10]   Code § 2621(a).
[11]   Code § 2621(b).

GST	=	($100,000 + GST) × 12%
GST	=	$12,000 + .12GST
.88GST	=	$12,000
GST	=	$12,000 ÷ .88
GST	=	$13,636

Under either approach, a GST is imposed (either on the grandchild or the trust) not only on the net amount ultimately received by the grandchild but also on the funds used to pay the GST. Thus, in this context, the GST is *tax-inclusive*.

5.21 With respect to a *taxable termination* (the termination of the intervening generation's interest in a trust resulting in the property passing to, or being held for, lower generations), the taxable amount is the value of the trust at the time of the termination. Again, in this context the GST is *tax-inclusive* in that the tax is computed on the gross value of trust, not the net amount passing to the next generation.

Example

Assume that the trust in the prior example terminates in 2004 and is distributed in full to the grandchild. If the value of the trust at the date of distribution is $2.2m, the GST would be $264,000 ($2.2m × 12%). The grandchild nets $1,936,000 after taxes.

5.22 The prior examples illustrate the computation of the GST on a taxable distribution from, or taxable termination, of a trust that is partially exempt from GST. If the trust is fully exempt, the 'inclusion ratio' would be zero and thus the 'applicable rate' would be zero. As a result, no GST would be imposed on an otherwise taxable distribution or termination. If, on the other hand, no part of the trust was exempt from GST, the inclusion ratio would be 1 and the applicable rate would accordingly be the then-highest estate tax rate.

5.23 Effective GST planning often involves segregating the exempt property into a separate trust. This offers the trustees flexibility to address investment and distribution strategies that take into account the exempt or non-exempt status of the respective trusts. For example, the trustee might invest the exempt trust for long-term growth, make current distributions to the next generation from the exempt trust, and limit distributions to the intervening generation from the non-exempt trust. The intent of this strategy is to maximize the value of the property eventually passing tax-free to the next generation via the exempt trust while minimizing the eventual size of the non-exempt trust.

B. United Kingdom

1. *Introduction*

5.24 A unified rate structure applies to UK inheritance tax on inter vivos and testamentary gifts, although the lifetime rate of charge is, in principle, one half the

5.25 Tax Rates and Computation

rate of charge applicable to transfers on death. The charging regime incorporated various bands of incremental rates in much the same way as the US until 14 March 1988, since which date inheritance tax has been applied at two rates only:

- a 'nil' rate, applied to a specified sum called the 'nil-rate band'; and
- a rate of 40% (20% in respect of lifetime transfers) applied to transfers of value above the specified sum.

Although the top rates of US tax are higher than those in the UK, in making a comparison between the way in which the two regimes affect any particular taxpayer and the planning opportunities which exist, it is fundamental to take into account the impact of both the graduated US tax rates (which are lower overall in the US on estates up to $1m), and the much more generous applicable exclusion credit available to US citizens and domiciliaries (which can be regarded as broadly equivalent to the UK nil-rate band and which is currently $1m on lifetime gifts and $1.5m on estates at death). Furthermore, the latter is due to increase substantially up to 2009, as noted at 3.22.

2. Inheritance tax rate brackets

5.25 After deduction of all relevant exemptions and reliefs, the first £263,000 of cumulative gifts (or estate) are taxed at a nil-rate; this being the current level of the nil-rate band.[12] Thereafter, tax is imposed at a flat rate of 40% for chargeable transfers on death[13] and 20% for chargeable lifetime transfers.[14] As mentioned in earlier chapters, gifts made during lifetime are aggregated to establish the applicable tax exposure, but the cumulation period is of limited duration and lifetime gifts fall out of account if the donor survives the gift for a period of seven years. This effectively makes the nil-rate band renewable and facilitates a cyclical pattern of making chargeable gifts every seven years. The rates of tax are applicable to UK and non-UK domiciliaries alike.

3. Impact of prior gifts

5.26 Where a donor dies within seven years of making any gift this may have an impact both on the level of tax applicable to his estate on death and on the level of tax applied retrospectively to the lifetime gift itself. When he dies within seven years of making a gift which was a PET at the time it was made, the potential exemption ceases to be applicable and the gift becomes a chargeable lifetime transfer, taxed as if it had been chargeable at the time it was originally made.[15] This may have a number of consequences as illustrated below.

---

[12] IHTA 1984, Sch 1. The rate bands are automatically indexed on an annual basis, unless provision is made to the contrary.
[13] IHTA 1984, Sch 1.
[14] IHTA 1984, s 7(2).
[15] IHTA 1984, 3A(4).

(a) To compute the tax on the original gift it will be necessary to have regard to the cumulation period relevant to that gift, ie the seven years prior to the gift. This can mean that effectively a cumulation period of up to 14 years may be relevant at death.

Example

Assume the following:

- 5 May 1989: gift on discretionary trusts being a lifetime chargeable gift;
- 1 April 1996: outright gift to son qualifying as a PET;
- 1 March 2003: death.

Death in March 2003 causes the 1996 PET to become chargeable and also to be cumulated with the estate at death. Furthermore, in computing the inheritance tax on the 1996 lifetime gift itself, the 1989 chargeable gift must be taken into account. If the latter had used the available nil-rate band then this would no longer be available to set against the 1996 gift. By comparison, if the 1989 gift had not used the nil-rate band, this may be available in whole or part to set against the 1996 gift.

(b) The allocation and past use of exemptions carried forward may need to be adjusted and set against the chargeable transfers previously treated as potentially exempt (refer to **CHAPTER 3**: Deductions, Exclusions, Exemptions and Credits).

Example

Assume the following:

- 10 April 1995: outright gift qualifying as a PET when made;
- 4 April 1997: chargeable gift to a trust – 1995/96 and 1996/97 annual exemptions allocated to this gift;
- 1 March 2000: death.

The 1995/96 annual exemption carried forward for use against the 1997 gift, would need to be reallocated and set against the gift made in 1995, which later became chargeable as a result of the death within the seven year period thereafter.

(c) As a gift retrospectively becomes chargeable at the original time when made, its value at that date is relevant for computing the tax. The rates of tax prevailing at that date will also apply unless there has been a reduction, in which case the lower rates prevailing at the date of the death will be relevant.

5.27 Tax Rates and Computation

5.27 Where a donor dies within seven years of a chargeable lifetime transfer, the tax referable to that gift will also be recomputed. The same principles apply as in the case of PETs.[16] Treasury Regulations provide credit for prior lifetime taxes paid in order to avoid a double tax charge.[17]

5.28 Where several different lifetime transfers are made by a person on the same day, they are treated as having been made in the order which gives rise to the lowest tax charge.[18]

5.29 The death tax rates applicable to prior gifts made within seven years of death (whether PETs or chargeable transfers) are discounted depending on the length of time between the gift and the date of death.[19] This discount, referred to as 'taper relief', is as follows:

Years between gift and death	Percentage of tax charged	Rate of tax charged
0–3	100%	40%
3–4	80%	32%
4–5	60%	24%
5–6	40%	16%
6–7	20%	8%

5.30 As can be seen, transfers within three years of death result in no tax savings (other than those which may have been achieved through the value-freezing effect of the transfer, the application of allowances and reliefs or rate reductions). Furthermore, since chargeable lifetime transfers will have already borne tax at 20%, there should be no further lifetime tax to pay once a period of five years has elapsed from the date of the original gift. However, where this discounting, by reason of the taper relief provisions, results in a lower tax exposure on a chargeable lifetime disposition than that originally assessed, no refund is payable.[20]

5.31 Additional tax assessed as a result of revised computations is primarily payable by the donee.[21] However, where the tax remains unpaid after 12 months or because the donee's exposure is limited, the Inland Revenue can have recourse to the personal representatives of the donor.

---

[16] IHTA 1984, s 7(4) and (5).
[17] Inheritance Tax (Double Charges Relief) Regulations 1987 (SI 1987/1130).
[18] IHTA 1984, s 266.
[19] IHTA 1984, s 7(4).
[20] IHTA 1984, s 7(5).
[21] The donee is any person in whom the gifted property is vested – whether legally (eg trustees) or beneficially. In the case of a gift by way of settlement, those liable also include a person who is beneficially entitled to an interest in possession in the trust or persons to whom the income or the settled property has been distributed or applied. In each case, limitations are applied to the extent to which the tax is recoverable, broadly being the value of the property received by each. IHTA 1984, ss 199(2) and 204.

5.32 Where death occurs within seven years of the gift and the market value of the property decreases between the date of the gift and the date of death of the donor, a further measure of relief exists. Provided the donee or his spouse still own the property or he has sold it to third parties on arm's length terms, the lower value can be substituted in computing the tax under the above provisions.[22]

5.33 A form of relief also exists where more than one tax charge arises in quick succession.[23] If a gift received by way of a chargeable transfer has increased the value of a person's estate within a period of five years before their death, tax on that later death is reduced by a percentage of the tax on the earlier transfer. The relevant percentage is applied to the following sum:

$$\frac{\text{First gross chargeable transfer less the tax payable on it}}{\text{First gross chargeable transfer}} \times \text{tax payable}$$

The percentages applied are as follows.

Period between transfers	Percentage of relevant sum
Less than 1 year	100%
1–2 years	80%
2–3 years	60%
3–4 years	40%
4–5 years	20%

5.34 The same principle applies to a charge arising in respect of settled property if the first transfer was a transfer into settlement of the same property now subject to tax, and the transferor in respect of the later transfer is entitled to an interest in possession.

Example

Assume a father bequeaths property worth £500,000 to a life interest trust for his son on 7 April 2001. The father's net estate subject to inheritance tax was valued at £1,000,000 and the nil-rate band was £242,000 at the time. The tax paid on his estate was £303,200. The son dies on 1 June 2004, between three and four years after the death of his father. The tax on the first death, which is deductible from the tax on the later death, is as follows:

$$\frac{£1,000,000 - £303,200}{1,000,000} \times £303,200 = £211,270$$

The son's death occurred between three and four years after that of the father and the quick succession relief in this case is 40%. Therefore, 40%

---

[22] IHTA 1984, s 131.
[23] IHTA 1984, s 141.

5.35 *Tax Rates and Computation*

of £211,270 is £84,508. As the son only inherited half of the estate, his entitlement would be to 50% (£42,254).

4. 'Tax on tax'

5.35 As IHT applies on a 'loss to the donor' principle, as with the US estate tax, in many circumstances there is a 'tax on tax' effect of IHT. The precise UK tax liability in the case of lifetime gifts depends on who bears the tax. If the donee agrees to bear the tax, the gift is the sum actually transferred to the donee.

> **Example**
>
> Having used his annual exemptions, a donor makes a gross lifetime gift of £273,000 to a discretionary trust. If the donee trustees agree to pay the tax, they would be liable for £2,000 of tax (£273,000 –£263,000 = £10,000 at 20% lifetime tax rate = £2,000).
>
> The sum of £273,000 would be set against the donor's cumulative total of transfers and aggregated with his estate in the event of his death within seven years.

In contrast, where the donor agrees to pay the tax, the tax itself is treated as part of the gift and so also becomes taxable, thereby increasing the total charge.

> **Example**
>
> If the donor made a net gift of £273,000 and he agreed to pay the taxes, the gift would cause a £2,500 tax liability. The gross gift would be £275,500 (£275,500 – £263,000 = £12,500 at 20% lifetime tax rate = £2,500 + £273,000 = £275,500). As a result of the 'grossing up' of the gift, the sum of £275,500 would be set against the donor's cumulative total of transfers and aggregated with his estate in the event of his death within seven years.

5.36 In the above examples, the amount of the tax exposure ultimately depends on who pays the tax.[24] In contrast, under the US rules noted at **5.15** et seq, if the donor pays the tax on a lifetime gift which he makes, there is no 'grossing up' for the purposes of computing his cumulative total of taxable gifts unless the gift taxes have been paid within the three years prior to his death.

5.37 In the case of the transfer of an estate which is deemed to occur immediately before death, the value transferred for UK IHT purposes is equal to the value of the net estate (ie assets *less* liabilities). As is the position with US estate tax, in this case it is the entire estate (subject only to any allowable exemptions and reliefs

---

[24] IHTA 1984, s 5(4). The loss to donor principle means that if the donor bears the IHT it also forms part of the value transferred and so is subject to tax itself. However, if the transferor pays any other tax related to the gift (eg capital gains tax) this does not form part of the value transferred on making the gift.

discussed in **CHAPTER 3**) which is subject to tax, including the assets which will ultimately need to be realised to pay the tax.

5. Liability and incidence of tax

5.38 The incidence of tax – ie who ultimately bears the cost of it and out of which assets it falls to be paid – is also fundamental to the overall computation. For example, the personal representatives may be the persons who are liable to make payment, but the tax will fall to be allocated amongst the beneficiaries of the estate depending on the terms of the will and also the general law.

5.39 Similarly, the identity of the recipient of specific legacies (and whether or not they are designated by the will as bearing their own tax) can impact the overall tax position. In particular, where there are tax-favoured assets or tax-exempt beneficiaries. For example, consider a situation where the estate at death comprises partly of exempt assets, such as business assets qualifying for 100% business property relief[25] and the legatees are the widow and son of the deceased.[26] If the tax-favoured assets are left to the exempt beneficiary, clearly, the overall tax exposure will be higher than if they are given to the chargeable beneficiary, with the non-favoured assets being given to the exempt beneficiary.

5.40 Under a testamentary instrument it is open to the testator to specify which gifts bear their own tax and which do not. For example, a specific cash legacy of a sum in excess of the unused nil-rate band, which is designated by a will as being 'free of tax' and where the residuary estate passes to the widow, essentially means that the widow's share of the estate bears the tax on the 'free of tax' legacy.

5.41 However, the inheritance tax legislation makes specific provision in the case of certain exempt gifts. There is an overriding general rule that a specific gift which is exempt (eg a legacy to charity) cannot be required to bear any tax attributable to the estate, and that where a gift of residue is partly exempt (eg part left to charity or a spouse and part to the testator's children) the whole of the tax must fall on the non-exempt part of residue.[27] For example, where a net estate of £1,000,000 is left to the widow and son equally, she will receive £500,000 and the son's share will bear the tax of £94,800 (£500,000 – £263,000 nil-rate band x 40% = £94,800).

5.42 Save as above, and in the event that the will is silent, certain general principles apply under English law. Subject to contrary indication in the will, where personal representatives are liable for tax on the deceased's estate at death, the tax is treated as a general testamentary and administration expense, provided it is attributable to property which is UK sited, vests in the personal representatives and was not settled property immediately before the death.[28] Where it is such a general

---

[25] IHTA 1984, Pt V, Ch I. See also **CHAPTER 3**.
[26] Note that IHTA 1984, s 18 provides for an unlimited exemption where the widow is UK domiciled.
[27] IHTA 1984, s 41.
[28] IHTA 1984, s 211(1). For example, assets comprising settled property, jointly held property, property given away in the seven years prior to death, or property which is subject to a reservation

5.42 *Tax Rates and Computation*

testamentary expense, the order against which the assets are applied is set out in the Administration of Estates Act 1925 and primarily falls on any property undisposed of by the will and then the residuary estate, before being set against other gifts.[29]

---

[29] of benefit, will fall outside the scope of the primary liability on the personal representatives even though tax may arise in consequence of the death. The beneficiaries of such assets bear the tax attributable to them.
This is broadly in the following order:
- (a) property of which the will has incompletely disposed (eg which is subject to the intestacy provisions);
- (b) residue of the estate;
- (c) property specifically left for payment of debts;
- (d) pecuniary legacies (rateably);
- (e) specific legacies (rateably); and
- (f) property appointed by will.

See, generally, on this subject Part K of *Foster's Inheritance Tax*, Butterworths.

Chapter 6

Transfer Taxes on Trustees

A. United States

1. Introduction

6.1 Liability to pay the US transfer tax is generally imposed on the donor of a taxable gift[1] or the executor (or other personal representative) of a decedent's taxable estate.[2] Trustees are generally not liable for such tax. However in a few situations, a trustee can be liable for US transfer tax.

2. QTIP marital trust

6.2 As discussed in **CHAPTER 4** at 4.9 et seq, a qualified terminable interest property (QTIP) trust is a form of trust that qualifies for the gift or estate tax marital deduction and thus the deferral of the US transfer tax. To receive this deduction, the donor (with respect to a taxable gift) or the executor of the decedent's estate (with respect to bequests at death) must make a so-called QTIP election. In the case of QTIP trusts established at death, the US Tax Code permits partial elections, resulting in only a portion of the trust qualifying for the marital deduction.

6.3 QTIP trusts are popular with donors and decedents who want to benefit the other spouse and defer transfer taxes, but do not want to give the spouse unlimited (or, in some cases, any) control over the eventual disposition of the trust property. A husband on his second or third wife might want to ensure that the property remaining in that trust after her later death will eventually pass to his children from earlier marriages. For example, a decedent with two children from a prior marriage and a daughter (Scarlett) from his marriage to his current wife might provide for the QTIP trust to be divided into three equal shares at her later death. One share would pass to Scarlett (subject perhaps to the widow's limited power of appointment) and the other two shares would pass to his children from the prior marriage (without any power in the survivor to modify the provisions for those children).

6.4 At the survivor's later death, the portion of the QTIP trust that qualified for the marital deduction is included in her taxable estate. If the spouse's independent

---

[1] Code § 2502(c). Note that a gift that, by its terms, obligates the beneficiary to pay the resulting gift tax is considered a 'net gift'. Rev Rul 75–72, 1975–1 CB 310 and Rev Rul 76–49, 1976–1 CB 294 (state and federal gift tax). In *Diedrich v Comm'r 457 US 191 (1982)*, it was held that gift tax paid by the donee in excess of the donor's basis resulted in income to the donor in the excess amount. This case was overruled by section 1026 of the 1984 Tax Act.

[2] Code § 2002.

estate were forced to pay the eventual tax on the QTIP trust, the relative allocation of the couple's estates among their respective families could be skewed. In the prior example, assume the surviving spouse had an independent estate of $2m (a vacation home – *Terra* – inherited from her parents) and the QTIP trust were valued at $6m at her death. If she died in 2009 under current law with a full applicable exclusion credit available, the estate tax on her $8m taxable estate would be $2m. Unless the QTIP trust were required to pay a portion of the tax burden, the survivor's estate would be forced to liquidate *Terra* to pay the tax bill. Scarlett would get her equal one-third share (valued at $2m) of the QTIP (and could perhaps use that inheritance to purchase *Terra* from her mother's estate), and the children from the prior marriage would each likewise receive $2m. Essentially, the children from the prior marriage would have received their share of their father's estate free of tax.

6.5 Fortunately (for Scarlett, at least), the tax laws give the spouse's estate a right to recover from the trustees of the QTIP trust the *incremental* portion of the estate tax imposed at the spouse's death by reason of the QTIP trust being taxed in her estate.[3] This is true regardless of whether the QTIP trust is considered a domestic trust (ie with US trustees) or a 'foreign' trust (with non-US trustees). The impact of this rule in the prior example is meaningful to all involved. Because the estate tax exemption in 2009 is $3.5m, the full value of *Terra* would be exempt from estate tax. The $2m estate tax could be charged against the QTIP trust, leaving only $4m after taxes to divide among the decedent's three children. The two children from the prior marriage would each get $1.33m, as would Scarlett. Scarlett thus inherits not only *Terra* but also some cash that will allow her to maintain that property for years to come.[4]

3. QDOT marital trust

6.6 The qualified domestic trust (QDOT) is the only way in which a decedent can qualify her bequest to a non-citizen spouse for the estate tax marital deduction. As discussed in some detail in **CHAPTER 4** at **4.16** et seq, one of the key tax requirements is that the QDOT trust must have at least one 'US trustee' – that is, a US citizen or a US corporation. This rule is designed to ensure collection of the US estate tax.

6.7 The Tax Code imposes a special estate tax (referred to here as the 'QDOT estate tax') not just on the value of the property remaining in the QDOT at the surviving spouse's death, but also on principal distributions from the QDOT during the survivor's life.[5] Further, for a QDOT trust to qualify for the marital deduction the trust instrument creating the QDOT must give the US trustee the right to

---

[3] Code § 2207A.
[4] This result also seems 'fair' to the decedent's children from his prior marriage. Had the decedent decided to give them their inheritance at his death rather than delaying their inheritance until their stepmother's death, their inheritance would have been depleted by estate taxes at his death.
[5] Code § 2056A(b)(1)(A) and (b)(1)(B).

withhold the QDOT estate tax.[6] The tax code imposes personal liability on all trustees (not just the US trustee) for this tax.[7]

4. *GST imposed on taxable terminations*

6.8 The GST is imposed on three types of transfers:

- direct skips (eg gifts from grandparents to grandchildren);
- taxable distributions (eg distributions to grandchildren from a trust established by a grandparent in which the child also has a benefit); and
- taxable terminations (eg the termination of a child's interest in a trust established by a grandparent, resulting in trust property passing to – or continuing in trust for the benefit of – the grandchildren).

Of these three types of generation-skipping transfers, a trustee is liable for only the GST imposed by reason of a taxable termination.[8] In most cases, a taxable termination will occur upon the death of a member of the intervening generation – for example, the child – for whom the trust is primarily held. The GST in that instance is a substitute for the estate taxes that would otherwise have been imposed had the trust property been included in the primary beneficiary's estate. In a sense, the trustee of a GST-taxable trust serves as a substitute for the beneficiary's executor.

6.9 It should be noted that this liability extends to both US and non-US trustees. If a US grandparent funded a Cook Islands asset protection trust to last in perpetuity for the benefit of himself and his family, the Cook Islands trustee would technically be liable for any US GST imposed on taxable terminations as this trust passed from generation to generation. An aware and cautious Cook Islands trustee, unwilling to face personal liability for this tax bill, might withhold funds from the trust to pay these taxes before distributing the entire trust to the grandchildren or before forwarding the trust funds to a replacement trustee.

5. *'Statutory' executor*

6.10 The US Tax Code obligates the 'executor' of a decedent's estate to pay the US estate taxes due by reason of his death.[9] If there is no executor or administrator 'appointed, qualified or acting within the United States, then any person in actual or constructive possession of any property of the decedent' is treated as if they were the executor of the decedent's estate and thus liable for the resultant estate tax.[10] The

---

[6] Code § 2056A(a)(1).
[7] Code § 2056A(b)(6).
[8] Code § 2603.
[9] Code § 2002.
[10] Code § 2203.

6.11 Transfer Taxes on Trustees

liability of the so-called 'statutory executor' is far reaching, and applies to custodians, joint owners, debtors, agents, brokers, bankers, safe deposit companies and, importantly, trustees.[11]

6.11 An executor (including a statutory executor) is generally liable for all of the decedent's estate taxes, not just those associated with the property within the executor's control.[12] If a trustee is treated as a statutory executor and assets within its control are insufficient to pay the full liability, the trustee will not be personally liable for the excess tax. However, the trustee will be personally liable to the extent it pays any inferior 'debt' (presumably including legacies and bequests to heirs) prior to paying such US taxes.[13] However, where the settlor is not himself a beneficiary of such a trust, there is precedent that this liability cannot apply because the trustee would have no legal authority to pay his debts, including federal taxes.[14]

6.12 The statutory executor rule technically applies to both domestic US and non-US trustees. Thus, a Bermuda-based trustee of a revocable Bermuda trust that holds direct investments in US real estate or US portfolio investments could be liable for any US estate taxes imposed at the settlor's death. A trustee could also be considered a statutory executor if a trust beneficiary held a power over the trust (for example, an unlimited withdrawal power, an unlimited power to appoint the trust at death, or an unlimited power to replace trustee) such as to cause the beneficiary to be treated as having a 'general power of appointment' under US tax law.

6.13 A trustee would not, however, be considered a statutory executor if there is an executor or other personal representative appointed and acting in the US. This would typically be the case for a US citizen or domiciliary, but often is not the case for a non-domiciled alien (NDA). Aware and cautious insurance companies, banks, brokers and trustees will often ask for proof of the appointment of a US executor before releasing funds to beneficiaries or next of kin. For example, a US broker holding securities in a US brokerage account owned by a NDA will often require either:

- proof of a US executor's appointment; or

- a 'transfer certificate' issued by the Internal Revenue Service attesting to the payment of US estate taxes.

Also, an aware and cautious trustee might seek similar assurances so that the institution will not face US tax liability, which it is unable to pay from the decedent's trust funds after distribution to the trust beneficiaries.

---

[11] Treas Reg § 20.2203–1.
[12] Treas Reg § 20.2203–1.
[13] Treas Reg § 20.2002–1 and 31 USC § 3713(b).
[14] In *Fitzgerald v Comm'r 4 TC 494 (1944), acq sub nom Arnett, 1945 CB 8*, the trustee of a trust created by a non-resident alien for the benefit of his divorced wife and their minor children was held not to be a 'fiduciary' under the federal priority statute and was not liable for any tax liability of the settlor. The rationale of the ruling is that the settlor was not entitled to either trust principal or income and thus could not be considered a person for whom the trustee was acting. Thus, the trustee of a trust, which excluded the settlor as a beneficiary (either specifically or because all US persons are excluded as beneficiaries), should literally not have liability as a fiduciary under the federal priority statute because the trustee could not legally make any distribution to the settlor or the settlor's creditors.

6. Transferee liability

6.14 A trustee may also become liable or subject to the transfer tax under the transferee liability provisions of the Code, under which unpaid estate or gift taxes result in personal liability of the trustees or other transferees of certain property. Trustees can have transferee liability for a US transferor's non-payment of US federal transfer tax in the following situations.

a. Transferee liability for unpaid gift and estate taxes

6.15 Trustees have *personal liability* as donees for the settlor's or estate's non-payment of US gift or estate tax. The liability is equal to the original value of transferred assets and generally lasts for ten years after the decedent's death.[15]

b. Transferee liability under state law

6.16 Under state fraudulent conveyance law, the IRS as a creditor for unpaid taxes (usually limited to those accrued at the time of transfer) could bring an action against the trustee to set aside a trust where it is shown that the transferor was already bankrupt, the transfer had that effect or the settlor had actual intent (shown by badges of fraud) to hinder or prevent the collection of taxes by transferring assets to the trust.

c. Transferee liability with respect to life insurance or appointed property

6.17 Unless the decedent's will provides otherwise, the US Tax Code gives the executor of a decedent's estate a right to recover a portion of the decedent's estate taxes attributed to life insurance proceeds taxable in the decedent's estate and payable to the trust as beneficiary.[16] A similar right of recovery is given with respect to trust property subject to the decedent's general power of appointment.[17]

7. Jurisdictional issues

6.18 As summarised above, a non-US trustee can face liability for US transfer tax under a variety of circumstances. The executor of a decedent spouse's estate could seek reimbursement from the non-US trustee for taxes related to a QTIP marital deduction trust and for taxable life insurance proceeds payable to a trust or for trust property subject to the decedent's general power of appointment. A non-US trustee could be liable for GST with respect to a taxable termination of a non-exempt trust. A non-US trustee might also be considered a statutory executor and thus liable for US estate taxes related to the US-taxable assets within its control

---

[15] Code § 6324(a)(2) and Treas Reg § 301.6324–1.
[16] Code § 2206.
[17] Code § 2207.

6.19 *Transfer Taxes on Trustees*

at the decedent's death. Finally, a non-US trustee could be liable for US tax under the transferee liability rules. The ability of the IRS (or the executor of the decedent's estate) to enforce that tax against the non-US trustee is, however, another matter.

a. Personal jurisdiction over trustee in US courts

6.19 To enforce a judgment against a defendant party, a US court must have *in personam* jurisdiction over the defendant. *In personam* jurisdiction is available against persons physically present within the jurisdiction, including resident individuals and entities, as well as non-resident persons who are transacting business through physical premises or agents within the jurisdiction. In addition, other non-residents, whose in-state business transactions or activities rise to a certain level, may be subject to the court's *in personam* jurisdiction through a state 'long arm' statute authorizing service by mail.[18]

6.20 In *US v Montreal Trust Co*,[19] the IRS filed suit in the federal district court in New York against the Montreal Trust Company, as executor of the estate of a deceased Canadian citizen and resident, to collect unpaid US income taxes assessed against the deceased. Service was made on the bank's New York correspondent bank with a copy of the summons and compliant delivered in Canada to a Canadian branch manager of the bank. Although the deceased himself was not engaged in US trade or business, his corporations were, and the appellate court held that the decedent had engaged in sufficient business activity in New York through his agents for service to be upheld against the estate under New York's 'long-arm' statute. In view of the refusal of foreign courts to assist in the collection of another country's taxes or to enforce a foreign tax judgment, discussed at **6.27**, the *in personam* jurisdiction of a US court under a long-arm statute may be limited to US reachable assets.

6.21 In the case *In re Portnoy*,[20] a US bankruptcy court applied New York law, under conflict of law principles, in determining that a debtor's transfer of assets to a Jersey, Channel Islands trust was fraudulent. But, since the court lacked *in personam* jurisdiction over the Jersey trustee to set aside the trust assets, its only available remedy was to refuse to grant a discharge in bankruptcy with regard to the transferred assets. Under Jersey law (which does not contain an 'asset protection' statute), relief would have been limited to the Jersey bankruptcy statute, which would not apply to a non-resident bankrupt where there were no Jersey sited assets.

6.22 If the IRS had *in personam* jurisdiction over the trustee, it could assert transferee liability under Code § 6901 by the same procedures it uses to collect taxes

---

[18] See, for example, *Hoffman Motors Corp v Alfa Romeo SpA*. 244 F Supp 70 (SDNY 1965).
[19] 235 F Supp 345 (SDNY 1964), rev'd, 358 F.2d 239 (2d Cir), cert denied, 384 US 919 (1966).
[20] 201 BR 685 (1996 Bankr SDNY). See also the June 2003 opinion of the Royal Court of Jersey in *Abacus v Esteem Settlement*, in which the Jersey Court *refused to set aside a Jersey trust holding assets settled prior to the settlor's defrauding of the Kuwait Investment Office's Grupo Torras, SA Spanish subsidiary (GT), for which GT subsequently obtained an £800 million UK judgment rendering the settlor insolvent. Although the trustees spent £6 million on the settlor's UK residence after the fraud commenced, the Jersey Court refused to set aside the trust on the grounds that the trust was a sham, that the settlor retained dominion and control, that the trust's veil should be pierced, that the trust violated public policy and/or that trust should be determined to be a remedial constructive trust for creditors.*

from the transferor, eg in a Tax Court proceeding where the transferor's tax is presumed to be due and the Government need only make a prima facie case of transferee or statutory liability for such tax. The IRS would not have to issue a notice of deficiency to or make an assessment against the transferor – before proceeding against the transferee.[21]

b. Personal jurisdiction over a custodian of US assets

6.23 In *Portnoy*, the court lacked *in personam* jurisdiction over any person holding the assets, as well as the assets themselves. Where a trustee holds assets through a US custodian or agent, such jurisdiction could be asserted. In *US v Omar SA et al*[22] a Uruguayan corporation held US-sited assets through a US national bank in New York and a US resident broker. When the IRS investigated Omar's tax liabilities, the corporation began to withdraw its assets from the US and the IRS issued a jeopardy assessment, served notice of lien and levy on the New York bank and broker and obtained an injunction enjoining the bank and broker from transferring Omar's assets from the US.

6.24 Although *in personam* jurisdiction had not been obtained over Omar SA, the Supreme Court reinstated the District Court's injunctions on the grounds that the court had personal jurisdiction over the US bank and broker and that while the bank's Montevideo branch might be beyond the jurisdiction of the US courts (to order the return of assets to the US), federal banking law required the national bank to exercise sufficient control over its branches to sue and be sued as a single entity and the court had jurisdiction to prevent the further removal of US sited assets.

6.25 *Omar* has been interpreted by the IRS and commentators as conferring US court jurisdiction over a US custodian to prevent the expatriation of US assets where the owner allegedly owes US tax. In addition, a national bank may be ordered to repatriate foreign branch assets removed from the US where there is a showing that the taxpayer has removed assets from the US to avoid liability for US tax or where there is a reasonable possibility of securing personal jurisdiction over the foreign owner.[23]

c. In rem jurisdiction over trust assets in US courts

6.26 If *in personam* jurisdiction could not be obtained over a foreign trustee or custodian under a long-arm statute. it would seem questionable that a US court could assert *in rem* jurisdiction over a US-sited asset, even US real property. Possibly, however, a Code § 6324 lien for unpaid gift or estate tax could be placed on US-sited property owned directly by a foreign trustee or custodian. Even though the IRS would presumably not be able to collect the underlying tax, the lien could effectively prevent disposition of US real property.

---

[21] *Gumm v Comm'r* 93 TC 475 (1989), aff'd 933 F 2d 1014 (9th Cir 1991).
[22] 64–1 USTC ¶9347 (SDNY 1962), rev'd sub nom *US v First National City Bank* 321 F 2d 14 (2d Cir 1963), rev'd 379 US 378 (1965).
[23] Treas Reg § 301.6332–1(a)(2); see also Zaritsky, BNA Tax Management Portfolio 911–2d, *US Taxation of Foreign Estates, Trusts & Beneficiaries*, at note 973.

6.27 Transfer Taxes on Trustees

d. Jurisdiction over the trustee in foreign courts and enforcement of tax judgments

6.27   A trustee can generally be sued in the courts of its own jurisdiction by any party who has standing to sue and who meets local procedural requirements and pre-requisites to suit, which can be formidable. Absent specific tax treaty relief, however, foreign courts will almost universally refuse to assist the collection of another country's taxes, and certainly not against its own residents. Relief will generally be denied even if the taxpayer appears in US court and the assessed taxes are reduced to judgment.[24]

6.28   This is an evolving area for multinational banks. The furthest reaches to date have involved documentary requests (not substantive tax liability) or abusive fraudulent transfers by US residents. The *Bank of Nova Scotia* case[25] involved an IRS subpoena to a US resident foreign bank to identify all US holders of bank accounts exceeding $10,000 with its Cayman affiliate bank. The US branch bank officials complied when faced with judicial imprisonment for contempt.

6.29   *Federal Trade Commission v Affordable Media Inc*[26] was an extreme fraudulent conveyance case in which US resident husband and wife promoters of a Ponzi (ie, pyramid sales) scheme were initial trustees of a Cook Islands trust to protect their allegedly ill-gotten gains and the court, disbelieving their assertion of lack of control over professional trustees, used its inherent contempt power to temporarily imprison the Andersons for failure to repatriate the trust funds.

6.30   The Andersons were eventually released from prison while the Cook Island trustees successfully thwarted the Federal Trade Commission's (FTC) efforts to gain control over the trust and trust funds. As a condition of their release, the Andersons appointed the FTC as Protector. The FTC attempted to exercise its authority and replace the Cook Islands trustee with – you guessed it – the FTC. However, the local Cook Island courts sided with the local trustee and denied the FTC's effort to appoint itself as Trustee. Ultimately the FTC and the Cook Islands trustee reached a negotiated settlement in which $1.2m – not an inconsequential amount but only a portion of funds held in the trust and sought by the FTC – was turned over to the US Government.

6.31   The limitations of US judicial jurisdiction should not be viewed, however, as an open invitation to avoid the collection of US transfer taxes by structuring one's holding through non-US trusts. Aware and cautious institutional trustees might be appropriately leery of facilitating any suspected US tax fraud of a transferor client.

---

[24]   *US v Harden 63–1 USTC ¶9217 (CA Brit Col 1962), aff'd 12 AFTR 5736 (Sup Ct Can 1963)*; see cases and treaties discussed in Zaritsky, BNA Tax Management Portfolio 911–2d, *US Taxation of Foreign Estates, Trusts & Beneficiaries*, at note 975 et seq. A principal exception is the enforcement provided in the current 1984 US income tax treaty with Canada.
[25]   *In Re Grand Jury Proceedings re Bank of Nova Scotia 740 F 2d 817 (11th Cir 1985), cert denied 469 US 1106 (1985).*
[26]   *179 F 3d 1228 (CA-9 1999).*

B. United Kingdom

1. Introduction

6.32 Under the UK transfer tax regime relevant to individuals, which is generally applicable at the time a gift is made to trustees, as noted in **CHAPTER 5** the trustees can be made liable as donees, for inheritance taxes attributable to gifts made to them. In addition, the trustees themselves may also be subject to inheritance tax in certain circumstances, under special provisions in the Inheritance Tax Act 1984 (IHTA 1984). These provisions apply to 'property comprised in a settlement', which is defined as any disposition of property (whether written, oral or taking effect by operation of law) as a consequence of which property is held for persons in succession or subject to a contingency, or where it is held by trustees with powers of accumulation and discretionary distribution, or where the property is charged with the payment of an annuity or other periodical payment for a defined period (including a person's life).[27]

6.33 Where the application of the legislation requires identification of a 'settlor' of the settlement (being any person by whom the settlement was made including someone who has provided funds directly or indirectly for the purposes of the settlement), where several persons have done so, the property is regarded as if it were comprised in separate settlements.[28] A person who has made a reciprocal arrangement with another to make the settlement is also regarded as a 'settlor' for this purpose. For example, where A settles a trust for B's children and B settles a trust for A's children, A may be deemed the settlor of the trust settled by B and vice versa. The liability of the trustees is generally categorised by reference to the type of trust – either discretionary or fixed interest. The main categories of trust created for family purposes are outlined below. However, special provisions apply to a number of other types of trust created for particular categories of beneficiary or funded with particular types of property.[29]

2. Discretionary trusts

6.34 From the UK point of view, discretionary trusts can be an effective means of transferring assets out of an individual's estate for inheritance tax purposes, since the trust assets are neither aggregated with the estate of the donor once the seven year period has elapsed[30] (subject to the operation of the reservation of benefit provisions discussed in **CHAPTER 1**) nor with the estate of any of the beneficiaries. Inclusion of the settlor's spouse as a beneficiary will not negate the inheritance tax benefits in the same manner as it does for income tax and capital gains tax, unless by

---

[27] IHTA 1984, s 43(2). This provision also extends to entities established under laws other than those of the UK which are equivalent in their effect (e g Foundations and Stiftungs) under civil law.
[28] IHTA 1984, s 44.
[29] IHTA 1984, s 70 (charitable trusts); ss 77 and s 78 et seq (maintenance funds and trusts of property held for national purposes); s 86 (employee trusts); s 87 (newspaper trusts); s 88 (protective trusts); s 89 (trusts for disabled persons).
[30] IHTA 1984, s 7(4).

6.35 *Transfer Taxes on Trustees*

reason of the spouse receiving a benefit, the settlor also receives some benefit. Where the reservation of benefit provisions do apply it should be noted that this does not affect the chargeability of the original gift on normal principles. Potential double charges arising are relieved by regulation.[31]

6.35 In this context excluded property settlements should be noted (see **6.62** et seq). The provisions conferring excluded property status are generally acknowledged to take precedence over those relating to gifts with reservation and, therefore, the favourable position for non-domiciliary settlors who are also beneficiaries of settlements they have created, is preserved.[32]

6.36 The UK has a separate inheritance tax regime which applies to discretionary trusts.[33] Tax is imposed on the value of the fund at the tenth anniversary of the commencement of the settlement[34] and at certain other times (an 'exit charge').

6.37 On ten yearly anniversaries of the commencement of the settlement, tax is imposed on the value of 'relevant property'.[35] This term is defined specifically to exclude property settled on trusts with tax-favoured status[36] and to exclude any property in which an individual has an interest in possession (or where a company has purchased such an interest for full consideration as part of its normal business activities).[37]

6.38 The tax rate imposed on these occasions is computed by reference to a statutory formula which cannot exceed 6% (at current rates).[38] The general scheme of the tax broadly aims to raise the same tax yield over the lifespan of the trust as would arise at the death of an individual had he owned the trust assets. The formula first computes a hypothetical tax at lifetime rates of charge (20%):

(1) on an amount representing:

- the value of the relevant property in the trust which is subject to the charge; *plus*

---

[31] The Inheritance tax (Double Charges Relief) Regulations 1987 (SI 1987/1130).
[32] IHTA 1984, ss 5 and 48(3). The Inland Revenue indicated informally in Autumn 2001 that it may be about to change its view on the interaction of these two sets of rules. However, no formal statement has ever been issued on this. The recent background paper on residence and domicile indicated that there has been no change in the Inland Revenue's stance on this ('Reviewing the residence and domicile rules as they affect the taxation of individuals; a background paper' April 2003).
[33] IHTA 1984, Ch III, Pt III.
[34] IHTA 1984, s 60. The charge arises on the anniversary of the date when any assets are first settled irrespective of further additions which may be made from time to time.
[35] IHTA 1984, s 58.
[36] IHTA 1984, s 58. Including accumulation and maintenance trusts and excluded property trusts (see **6.62**); charitable trusts; certain older trusts for the disabled and protective trusts; employee trusts; maintenance funds for historic buildings; certain pension schemes; trade and compensation funds: s 58.
[37] IHTA 1984, s 59.
[38] IHTA 1984, ss 64 and 65. The maximum charge is 30% of the lifetime rate of charge (20%).

United Kingdom 6.39

- the value immediately after it became comprised in the settlement of other trust property which was not and currently is not relevant property;[39] *plus*
- the value of any property in a related settlement[40] immediately after it commenced;

(2) made by a transferor with a prior cumulative total of:

- transfers of value in the seven years prior to creating the settlement, equal to those of the settlor;[41] *plus*
- transfers of a value equivalent to the value of the settled property on which tax has already been charged in the previous ten years (eg property which has ceased to be relevant property by being distributed and suffering an exit charge).

Once the hypothetical tax is computed, it is expressed as a percentage of the amount on which it is charged at (1) above. This is known as the 'effective rate', which is then multiplied by 30% to determine the tax rate applied to the relevant property in the trust at the ten year charge.

6.39 Where funds are added to or are distributed from the trust between ten-year anniversaries, the charge is reduced proportionately in line with the period since the previous, or remaining to the next, anniversary date as appropriate.[42] The charge is also reduced proportionately where property has not been held on discretionary trusts throughout that period.[43] The ten-year period is divided into forty quarters and, where relevant, the apportionment of the tax charge is done by reference to the number of quarters during which the property has been relevant property.

Example of decennial charge

Nicholas Carraway settled a discretionary trust on 6 April 1986. At 5 April 1996, the trust had assets valued at £150,000, none of which was excluded property. The decennial charge is £3,600, a rate of 2.4% on chargeable assets, computed as follows.

---

[39] It can be seen that property which is not itself subject to the tax charge, eg because it is overseas property in an excluded property settlement, can affect the rate of charge.
[40] Which is a settlement created by the same settlor on the same day, other than a charitable settlement. IHTA 1984, s 62.
[41] Where a settlor has made additions to a trust at a time when his cumulative total was higher, provision is made to substitute that higher figure in the computation. IHTA 1984, s 67.
[42] IHTA 1984, s 66.
[43] The charge can be mitigated by the use of several trusts instead of a single trust. The fragmentation does not affect the IHT charge which arises on creation of the trusts, only the ten-yearly and exit charges. A nominal sum is settled on several trusts created on different days, a larger sum being added to each trust on a single day thereafter. In computing the rate of decennial and exit charges, transfers on the same day are left out of account so that only the property comprised in the appropriate settlement itself is relevant and no aggregation occurs (IHTA 1984, s 67(3)(b)(i)). The Inland Revenue recently challenged this analysis in the Court of Appeal, but lost to the taxpayer, in *Rysaffe Trustee Co (CI) Ltd v CIR CA [2003] STC*.

6.39 *Transfer Taxes on Trustees*

	Gross	Tax using FA 1996 scale
	£	£
Ten yearly charge (using ½ the IHT lifetime rate at 6.4.96)		
Settlor's previous transfers within 7 years before commencement of settlement:	100,000	
Distributions subject to exit charges in previous 10 years (£4,000 + £6,000):	10,000	
	110,000	
Value of relevant property – 5 April 1996	150,000	12,000*
	260,000	12,000*

(* £260,000 – £200,000 nil rate band = £60,000 at 20%)

Actual rate is 30% of effective rate 12,000/150,000 × 100 × 30% = 2.4%

Tax payable by trustees is £150,000 × 2.4% = £3,600[44]

The 'exit charge' is imposed on other occasions, between the ten-yearly anniversaries, where the property ceases to be relevant property (though no such charge can arise within the first three months of either the commencement of the trust or after a ten-yearly charge has been imposed).[45] For example, the charge may apply where a trust is a discretionary trust but following the exercise of a power of appointment by the trustees, it has become an interest in possession trust. The exit charge also applies to any other case where the trustees have made a disposition, which results in a decrease in the value of the relevant property.[46] A specific exemption is provided to

---

[44] This example appears in *Tolley's Taxwise II: 2001–02*, LexisNexis, at para 60.3.
[45] IHTA 1984, s 65(4). An interesting issue arises with respect to property settled on discretionary trusts by will. IHTA 1984, s 144 makes provision for actions taken by the trustees within a period of two years of the date of death to be regarded as having been effected under the will, and hence without inheritance tax implication for the trustee. However, this applies only if, absent the relieving provision, there would have been a tax charge under the normal discretionary trust regime. Accordingly, precipitous action within the three-month period following death can cause the s 144 relief to be disapplied. In *Frankland v CIR [1997] STC 1450* assets left by will on discretionary trusts were transferred into trusts providing the surviving spouse with an interest in possession, with the objective of securing the spouse exemption under IHTA 1984, s 18 at death. As the rearrangement was effected within the first three months after the wife's death, the Court of Appeal disallowed the s 144 relief on the basis there would have been no tax charge under the discretionary trust regime.
[46] IHTA 1984, s 65(1). However, if the trustees have simply made a bad bargain in circumstances similar to those contemplated in the exemption in IHTA 1984, s 10, and had no intention to confer gratuitous benefit, or if they granted an agricultural tenancy over trust property, with a depreciatory effect on the trust assets, s 65(6) precludes the charge.

cover situations where simple reinvestment has caused the property to become excluded property and hence outside the tax charge.[47]

6.40 The computation of the exit charge is based on much the same principles as the ten-yearly charge. The rate of charge applied is generally that which was applicable at the date of the last ten-yearly charge, although adjustments are made where property has been added or has become relevant property since that time.[48]

6.41 However, where the exit charge applies before the first ten-year charge, the hypothetical transfer of value used to determine the effective rate, assumes the settlor's cumulative total to be that at the date of the commencement of the settlement, and assumes the value on which it is charged to be the aggregate value, immediately after it became comprised in the relevant settlement, of the initial trust property and any property subsequently added and of the property in any related settlement. Again, the rate of charge ultimately applied to the relevant property is 30% of the effective rate and the apportionment of the charge is by reference to quarters which have elapsed in the ten-year period.

6.42 Where tax is paid out of the property remaining in trust on the occasion of an exit charge then the transfer is 'grossed up' for the purposes of computing the tax.[49] See the discussion on 'tax on tax' at **5.35**.

Example of exit charge

On 27 May 2000, the Carraway Discretionary Trust distributed £20,000 to beneficiary C and the trustees paid thereon a (grossed up) exit charge of £84, computed as follows:

Exit charge on distribution to C

Actual rate at previous 10-year anniversary (revised using 2000/01 lifetime scale):

£260,000 − £234,000 nil rate band = £26,000 at 20% = £5,200

Actual rate is 30% of effective rate $^{5,200}/_{150,000}$ × 100 × 30% = 1.04%

Number of complete quarters between 6 April 1996 and 26 May 2000 = 16

Rate of exit charge applicable: 1.04% × $^{16}/_{40}$ = 0.416%

Distribution (net): £20,000

Gross equivalent thereof = £20,000 × 100/99.584 = £20,084

---

[47] A trust created by a non-UK domiciled person which invests outside the UK is not subject to the UK inheritance tax regime. Thus if UK investments (which would be relevant property subject to the charge) are sold and reinvested outside the UK the property ceases to be relevant property for this purpose.
[48] IHTA 1984, s 69.
[49] IHTA 1984, s 65(2)(b).

6.43 *Transfer Taxes on Trustees*

Exit charge payable by trustees = £20,084 × 0.416% = £84[50]

(had the beneficiary paid the tax, there would have been no gross up)

6.43 In determining when property becomes comprised in the settlement for the purposes of the tax charges which apply to discretionary trusts, a number of special rules apply. If the settlor or his spouse has an initial income interest in the trust, the property is not regarded as having become comprised in the settlement until that interest ceases and the settlement is deemed to be made at that later time by the person whose interest has ceased.[51] It does not, however, affect the relevant commencement date for the purposes of determining when the ten-yearly charges apply.[52] In addition, where property has been transferred between two trusts it is deemed to remain in the first trust for the purposes of these provisions.[53]

6.44 The advantage of using a discretionary trust is that a tax-favoured fund can be built up outside the taxable estate of the beneficiary. However, the disadvantage is that this is not a potentially exempt transfer on creation and there is an immediate inheritance tax charge at 20% on creation of the trust to the extent that the value of the gift exceeds the unused portion of the £263,000 nil-rate band of the settlor (or any other applicable allowances or reliefs).[54] Of significance is the fact that a gift to such a trust, being chargeable for inheritance tax purposes, facilitates the use of hold-over relief for capital gains tax purposes, which may also be a tax relevant at the time of transfer.[55]

6.45 TCGA 1992, s 260 applies to chargeable transfers, whether or not tax is actually paid, for example, where the transfer is within the nil-rate band. This can make the use of a discretionary trust attractive in the UK for assets – where capital gains tax holdover relief would not otherwise apply (see **CHAPTER 11**).

6.46 A discretionary trust can also be a useful way to hold assets that attract the 100% business property relief or agricultural property relief and where assets of

---

[50] This example appears in *Tolley's Taxwise II: 2001–02*, LexisNexis, at para 60.3.
[51] IHTA 1984, s 80. This provision also includes a widow or widower of the settlor.
[52] IHTA 1984, s 61(2). For this purpose the provisions of s 60 continue to apply, being the date when property first became comprised in the original settlement.
[53] IHTA 1984, s 81(1). Unless a beneficiary of the transferee trust becomes absolutely entitled to the property and not just to an interest in possession in it; either event would cause an exit charge to apply. This rule only applies to a transfer by a discretionary trust and does not apply to a transfer by an interest in possession trust (which is taxable under s 52 of Ch II).
[54] IHTA 1984, s 7(2).
[55] TCGA 1992, s 260. Unlike the US, the UK imposes deemed disposals for CGT on the making of certain gifts. This provision provides a form of relief which can achieve much the same result as the US regime – the cost base effectively carrying over to the trustees. The 'held-over' gain is deducted from the gain otherwise accruing to the transferor and from the consideration otherwise regarded as being given by the transferee. The relief is available in limited cases only, in particular, note that no hold-over relief is available where the donee is non-UK resident or is resident in more than one country and is not chargeable as a result of a double taxation convention (IHTA 1984, s 261). For disposals on or after 10 December 2003, the relief is also clawed back in specific circumstances where CGT principal private residence relief is being sought by trustees (Finance Act 2004, s117 and Sch 22) and it is denied in transfers to trusts where a settlor (being any person who has provided property for the trust) or his spouse are beneficiaries or where arrangements are made for them to be added later or to benefit indirectly (Finance Act 2004, s 116 and Sch 21).

more significant value can therefore be transferred without inheritance tax charge.[56] However, if such property is to be transferred in lifetime, regard must be had to the ongoing condition that applies to the donee following the gift, that the property must generally continue to be owned and to qualify as business or agricultural property in the donee's hands up to the transferor's death, if the transferor dies within seven years of the gift (see CHAPTER 3).[57] Furthermore, the formula applicable to determine the tax rate in the case of 'exit charges' prior to the first ten-year anniversary does not take into account these reliefs and, therefore, if such trusts are used they should contemplate a duration beyond ten years.[58]

3. Accumulation and maintenance trusts

6.47 A separate category of discretionary trust which attracts favoured tax treatment in a variety of ways is frequently used in tax planning for children or grandchildren – this is an accumulation and maintenance trust.[59] In order to qualify for the favoured status, it is essential that this hybrid trust is discretionary at the outset and subsequently either creates a life interest for the relevant beneficiaries, or distributes capital to them outright, on or before the beneficiaries reach a maximum age of 25 years.

6.48 The requirements on creation of the trust are as follows:

- the settlement is either limited in duration to 25 years or all potential beneficiaries must be grandchildren of a common grandparent (or children, widows or widowers of such persons who were potential beneficiaries); and

- one or more persons *will*, on or before attaining a specified age, not exceeding 25, become beneficially entitled to the settled property or an interest in possession[60] in it; and

- no interest in possession subsists in the settled property at the outset and the trust income is accumulated insofar as it is not applied for the maintenance, education or benefit of a beneficiary.

6.49 In effect, this means that all beneficiaries must be under the age of 25 when the trust is created and that their interests (in either income or capital) must vest by the age of 25 at the latest or they must before that age have been excluded from the beneficial class (eg at the discretion of the trustees).

---

[56] In particular, this strategy can be used to good effect in will planning where, in addition to assets to the value of the nil-rate band being left on discretionary trusts any property qualifying for business or agricultural property reliefs can be included without adverse tax effect.

[57] IHTA 1984, ss 113A and 124A. This means, for example, that the relief would be denied on a gift of a minority holding in qualifying unquoted shares, which were later listed on the Stock Exchange prior to the death of the donor, who died within seven years of making the gift.

[58] IHTA 1984, s 68(5). The value of the property taken into account is its value immediately after it became comprised in the settlement.

[59] IHTA 1984, s 71.

[60] Note that the term 'interest in possession' denotes a present right to present enjoyment of the income of the fund such that, once the income has arisen, the trustees have no discretion to apply it for any other purpose than to the beneficiary (see *Pearson and others v CIR [1980] STC 318*).

6.50   *Transfer Taxes on Trustees*

6.50 If these criteria are satisfied then the transfer into trust qualifies as potentially exempt from inheritance tax,[61] as opposed to being immediately chargeable, as in the case of other non favoured discretionary trusts. In addition, the normal discretionary trust regime does not apply, so that no charge arises when the beneficiary becomes entitled to the property or an interest in possession in it, or on the death of the beneficiary before he obtains his interest in possession, or on the decennial anniversaries.[62]

6.51 Although in contrast with other discretionary trusts, capital gains tax hold-over relief (see **CHAPTER 10**) is not available on creation of the trust unless the gifts are of certain business assets,[63] it is available to UK beneficiaries in some situations when property leaves the trust. This applies again if the assets are business assets or in the case of other assets, when the property passes absolutely to the beneficiary at the end of the discretionary period[64] provided that the beneficiary has not previously become entitled to an interest in possession.[65]

6.52 It is usual in drafting the trust to maintain the greatest flexibility as possible, within the confines of the legislation to ensure modifications can be made in the event of a change in circumstance or legislation. Therefore, the discretionary terms are generally allowed to continue[66] until the beneficiary is aged 25 if possible, with an interest in possession in the income being conferred thereafter and the trustees having the discretion to distribute all or part of the capital to the beneficiary in appropriate circumstances. The trustees are also generally given the power to modify the class of beneficiaries (within the permitted parameters) so long as they are under 25 years of age and are also often given the power to terminate a beneficiary's interest prematurely in favour of others after he or she has reached the age of 25 and become entitled to the income interest. As can be seen, despite the requirements of the legislation, a trust for children with reasonably flexible terms can be achieved, which will generally be desirable for practical non-tax related reasons. However, this structuring also means that while in principle capital gains tax hold over relief may apply on the distribution of assets, it will, in fact, rarely be applicable.

6.53 This type of settlement provides a tax-efficient estate reduction vehicle the trusts of which, even after the age of 25, can be refined by the use of sophisticated powers of appointment to achieve maximum flexibility in much the same way as other fixed interest trusts. They are particularly useful for settlors who are content to divest themselves completely of substantial assets which would trigger an inheritance tax charge on being given to a discretionary trust, but where the beneficiaries are too young to warrant a fixed income entitlement immediately.

---

[61] IHTA 1984, s 3A(1)(c).
[62] IHTA 1984, s 71(4).
[63] TCGA 1992, s 165.
[64] TCGA 1992, s 260(2)(d).
[65] Eg on majority under the provisions of Trustee Act 1925, s 31 where these have not been expressly excluded.
[66] Subject to complying with the relevant maximum legal period for accumulations under the Perpetuities and Accumulations Act 1964 or the Trustee Act 1925, s 31.

6.54 A further benefit of such trusts is that the settlor is allowed to retain an interest for himself or his spouse as a default beneficiary, without bringing into play the usual anti-avoidance rules for income tax or capital gains tax in circumstances where the benefit arises in the event of the death of his child whose interest had vested on or before attaining age 25 or where there are living beneficiaries under the age of 25, during whose lives neither he nor his spouse can benefit from the trust.[67]

6.55 Furthermore, where the settlor is a potential default beneficiary of a trust, the assets will not be regarded as remaining within his taxable estate by virtue of the provisions which relate to gifts with reservation. See **CHAPTER 1**.[68] Provided that the income tax criteria are satisfied, this should also preclude the settlor being within the 2004 provisions applicable to pre-owned assets, which impose an income tax charge on settlors who have an interest in trusts which fall outside the reservation of benefit provisions.[69]

Example

William Brewster III, a UK resident domiciliary, settles an A&M trust with £10m for his only son William Brewster IV, age 4. The terms of the trust are that William IV will become beneficially entitled to the property upon his 25th birthday. Should he die before such time, William IV's interest in trust assets reverts to William III, if he is then living, failing which to Harrow School. William III's default reversionary interest is not a retained interest under the gifts with reservation rules and will not cause trust assets to be included within his estate if he dies. Moreover, William III is not taxable on trust income accumulated during William IV's minority or on gains at any time prior to William IV's death.

4. Fixed interest trusts

6.56 Where a beneficiary has the right to income as it arises from a fund (an interest in possession[70]), he is deemed for inheritance tax purposes to own the underlying assets of the fund.[71] They are aggregated with his free estate to quantify the inheritance tax consequences of his death or of any lifetime disposition (eg a release by the life tenant of his interest or an appointment away from him by the trustees exercising overriding powers in favour of other beneficiaries). If the settlor was not UK domiciled and the trust is an excluded property trust (see **6.62** et seq)

---

[67] ICTA 1988, s 660A(4)(d) and (5) and TCGA 1992, s 77(4)(d) and (5).
[68] FA 1986, s 102. See also Inland Revenue letter dated 18 May 1987 which states:
'In the case where a gift is made into trust, the retention by the settlor (donor) of a reversionary interest under the trust is not considered to constitute a reservation, whether the retained interest arises under the express terms of the trust or it arises by operation of general law, eg a resulting trust.'
[69] ICTA 1988, s 660A; FA 2004, Sch 15, para 8(1)(a).
[70] *Pearson and others v CIR[1980] STC 318.*
[71] IHTA 1984, s 49. Note that this is in contrast with the US position where it is the actuarial value of the interest which is generally relevant. This difference in treatment can provide useful cross-border opportunities: for example, a gift into trust for a US spouse can, in appropriate cases, be made without UK IHT implication and without creating an interest which becomes taxable at her death in the US.

6.57   *Transfer Taxes on Trustees*

where the assets are non-UK sited, there will be no inheritance tax charge on such assets whatever the life tenant's UK tax status. In contrast, if the life tenant is not UK domiciled, but the settlor was UK domiciled when he created the trust, the worldwide assets will potentially be subject to inheritance tax irrespective of the tax status of the life tenant.[72] Although the tax is computed as if the beneficiary owned the fund, the liabilities are apportioned between the free estate and the trust and those attributable to the latter are payable out of the trust assets (in the case of non UK resident trusts there is a right to recover unpaid tax from the settlor, if he is still alive).[73]

6.57 Tax on termination of the interest in possession by the trustees or simply under the terms of the settlement itself is governed by the general principles set out in CHAPTER 1. This is computed as if the life tenant owned the assets, and the deemed disposition may constitute an exempt, potentially exempt or chargeable transfer depending on the identity of those receiving subsequent benefits.[74] The same principle applies if the life tenant himself disposes of his interest in the settlement.[75] However, if the life tenant becomes entitled to the assets outright (or to another interest in possession in them, should the transfer be to another trust) at that time, no charge arises. Nor does any charge arise if the property reverts to the settlor during his lifetime.[76]

6.58 The corollary of the life tenant being deemed to own the whole of the underlying property is that the person entitled to the reversionary (or remainder) interest is deemed to own 'excluded property' which is generally outside the charge to tax.[77] This offers certain planning opportunities if the remainderman is in a position to give away his reversionary interest before it vests in possession.[78]

6.59 A simpler form of fixed interest trust, known as a 'bare trust' is commonly used where the intended recipient of an outright gift is under some legal disability (e g he is a minor) or where a third party is holding assets effectively in a nominee capacity for another. However, the usual administrative responsibilities will attach to the office of bare trustee in contrast with a mere nomineeship.

6.60 The essential characteristic of such a trust is that the beneficiary is absolutely entitled as against the trustees and (save for being a minor or under some other legal disability) has the exclusive right to call for the asset to be transferred to him or to direct how it is to be dealt with, subject only to the trustees lien for taxes

---

[72]   IHTA 1984, s 48(3) but see other specific exclusions in that section.
[73]   IHTA 1984, s 201(1).
[74]   IHTA 1984, ss 3A(7) and 52.
[75]   IHTA 1984, s 51.
[76]   IHTA 1984, ss 53 and 54. This exemption also extends to the settlor's spouse if she is UK domiciled, including to his widow, provided he died no more than two years previously.
[77]   IHTA 1984, s 48(1). This applies save in circumstances where it has been purchased at any time, or is one to which the settlor or his spouse is or has been beneficially entitled or is an interest expectant on the determination of a lease for life (which is deemed to be a settlement).
[78]   Care needs to be taken where interests in non-UK resident settlements are concerned, and UK resident settlements which have at some time previously been non UK resident, since the exemption from CGT on the disposal of interests in settled property will not generally apply. TCGA 1992, ss 76 and 85.

or expenses.[79] Once a child has reached the age of eighteen the trustees will be obliged to pay over the funds at his request and, therefore, such trusts are generally suitable only for smaller cash sums where that requirement is unlikely to be an issue. For those wishing to settle larger sums on a child or grandchild, the Accumulation and Maintenance Trust is likely to be the more suitable option.

6.61 Where a bare trust exists, the beneficiary is treated as if he owned the assets outright for tax purposes. Therefore, a gift to a bare trustee for another individual will be treated as if it were a gift to that individual himself and will be subject to the general principles outlined in earlier chapters.

5. Excluded property trusts[80]

6.62 Where a settlor creates a trust at a time when he is neither UK domiciled nor deemed UK domiciled, provided that the trust assets are not UK sited, they will be outside the scope of inheritance tax altogether. This will be the case irrespective of the type of trust and irrespective of whether the settlor is a beneficiary.

6.63 Such a trust can be a useful means of protecting non-UK sited assets from UK inheritance tax where a non-UK domiciliary is about to acquire deemed domicile status after a prolonged period of UK residence.[81] Under current rules the non-UK sited assets remain outside the inheritance tax net even after the settlor has become UK domiciled or deemed domiciled. Furthermore, the provisions relating to the income tax charge on a donor's continued benefit from assets he previously owned do not apply to non-UK sited property in so far as the gifts were made into trusts prior to becoming UK domiciled or deemed domiciled.[82] Such trusts are also useful where it is intended to benefit a UK domiciled person. A gift on trust from a non UK domiciled benefactor, rather than an outright gift, can result in significant longer term inheritance tax savings.

6.64 In the case of discretionary trusts where the special rules, described at **6.34** et seq, apply (that is, to cases where the settlor or his spouse have an initial income interest in the fund or where trusts have been funded by transfers from other trusts), a further condition is imposed before the excluded property rules apply. The condition is that both the actual settlor of any of the trusts under consideration, and additionally the person who is deemed to be the settlor for the purposes of those sections, must have been non-UK domiciled at the time the settlement was made or was deemed to have been made.[83] For example, in the case of a trust where the settlor and his wife (who survives him) sequentially have an interest in possession, the later death of the wife is deemed, for the purposes of the *discretionary trust IHT regime*, to be the creation of a trust by her.[84] If the original settlement was an

---

[79] TCGA 1992, s 60.
[80] IHTA 1984, s 48(3).
[81] This will be relevant where a person has been UK tax resident in some part of 17 or more UK tax years out of the prior 20 years. IHTA 1984, s 267.
[82] FA 2004, Sch 15, para 12.
[83] IHTA 1984, s 82.
[84] IHTA 1984, s 80(1).

6.65 *Transfer Taxes on Trustees*

excluded property trust, because the husband had not been UK domiciled when he created it, any discretionary trust created after the wife's death will only continue to be an excluded property trust if, in addition, she was non-UK domiciled at her death.[85] This will apply even where the husband remained non-UK domiciled throughout.

6.65 For trusts settled by a UK domiciliary, this rule will not have any impact, since the UK domicile status of the original settlor will also be attributed to any discretionary trust created by termination of such life interest, irrespective of the domicile of the spouse whose interest in possession has last terminated. However, for an excluded property trust, this rule can result in loss of that status if, by the time of death, either a settlor's domicile (where he is the last life tenant) or that of his spouse (where she is the last life tenant) has changed to the UK. Whilst this is a trap for the unwary, it can be overcome in appropriate cases by creating a short initial period where the trust is discretionary, prior to converting it to an interest in possession, or by giving the residuary beneficiaries interests in possession thereby ensuring that no discretionary trusts arise.

6.66 The future of excluded property trusts is uncertain as a result of the review of the Domicile and Residence rules which is currently being undertaken by the Inland Revenue.[86]

6. Lease for life[87]

6.67 It should be noted that in some circumstances a lease of property which has not been granted at a full open market consideration, may be treated as a settlement for inheritance tax purposes. This will be the case where the duration of the lease is defined by reference to one or more lives or for a period ascertainable only by reference to a death. In such a case, the inheritance tax provisions apply as if the lease constituted a settlement and the property was settled property.

---

[85] IHTA 1984, s 82.
[86] IHTA 1984, ss 5 and 48(3). The Inland Revenue indicated informally in Autumn 2001 that it may be about to change its view on the interaction of these two sets of rules. However, no formal statement has ever been issued on this. The recent background paper on residence and domicile indicated that there has been no change in the Revenue stance on this (see 'Reviewing the residence and domicile rules as they affect the taxation of individuals: a background paper' April 2003).
[87] IHTA 1984, s 43(3).

Chapter 7

US and UK Estate Tax Treaties

A. United States

1. Introduction

7.1 The United States has bilateral tax treaties in force with 17 countries that affect some aspect of the US estate tax, gift tax or generation-skipping transfer tax.[1] With the exception of the Canadian treaty, none of the treaties apply to transfer taxes imposed by any of the 50 States or the District of Columbia.

7.2 The following sections briefly summarize the older pre-1970 treaties, the newer Organisation for Economic Co-operation and Development (OECD) model treaties, and the special provisions of the US/Canadian treaty. A more detailed summary of the Estate and Gift Tax treaty between the US and the UK is provided at Section C (**7.47** et seq). Each of these treaties have similarities to one or more of the other treaties, but there are also substantial differences in their terms, conditions and reliefs. Reference to the detailed provisions of the particular treaty or treaties should be made in each planning situation.

2. Older treaties

7.3 The first group of treaties (all entered into prior to 1970) are with the following nine countries: Australia, Finland, Greece, Ireland, Italy, Japan, Norway, South Africa and Switzerland. Australia has separate gift and estate tax treaties, while the US/Japan treaty applies to both gifts and bequests. All of the rest deal only with the US estate tax. None of the nine apply to the US generation-skipping transfer (GST) tax.

7.4 These treaties all include detailed rules that address the situs (and thus primary taxing authority) of various assets, including corporate stock, bank deposits, real estate, tangible personal property, government debt, corporate debt, negotiable notes, judgement debt, tort claims, life insurance, annuities, pensions, partnership interests, business goodwill, patents, trademarks and copyrights.[2] A separate provision in these treaties governs the situs of all other property. Treaties with Greece, Ireland, Italy and Norway fix the decedent's domicile as the situs of 'other' property.

---

[1] Note that a number of reference services provide US Tax Treaties. All references herein are to *CCH US Tax Treaties* (2004), CCH Incorporated, 4025 W Peterson Avenue, Chicago, IL 60646–6085, Tel: 1 800 344 3734: website: www.cch.com.

[2] These situs rules are found in article 4 of the Greek treaty and article 4 of the six other pre-70 treaties.

7.5 US and UK Estate Tax Treaties

The remaining treaties allow local law to determine the situs of property not otherwise covered by the specific situs provisions of those treaties.

7.5 Seven of these treaties (excluding only Ireland and South Africa) grant a resident (ie a domiciliary) of the treaty country a portion of the 'specific exemption' that would otherwise have been allowed had the resident been a US citizen or domiciliary. The relevant portion is based on a ratio of the decedent's US situated property to his worldwide estate.

7.6 Prior to 1978, US domestic law provided US citizens and domiciliaries a $30,000 'specific exemption.' Beginning in 1978, the specific exemption was replaced by an estate and gift tax credit that exempts a certain level of gifts and bequests. In 2004, for example, the estate tax applicable exclusion credit effectively exempts $1.5m of a decedent's estate.[3]

7.7 Subsequent to the changes in the US tax laws, two cases concluded that the treaty references to the 'specific exemption' should be interpreted to mean the estate tax unified credit.[4] Congress codified these holdings in the 1988 Tax Act.[5] It is, therefore, clear that residents of these seven treaty countries will be entitled to a pro rata share of the estate tax applicable exclusion credit.

7.8 This treaty benefit can be substantial. Non-domiciled aliens (NDAs) are generally entitled to only a $13,000 estate tax credit, which in turn exempts only $60,000 of US property from estate tax. By contrast, a resident of one of these seven treaty countries will be entitled to a pro-rata share of the estate tax credit. If, for example, one-third of a Greek decedent's worldwide estate consisted of US situated property, the pro-rata credit (and equivalent exemption) available to his estate would be computed as follows.

Year of death	US estate tax credit	Pro rata credit	Exemption equivalent
2004	$555,800	$185,267	$580,000
2006	$780,800	$260,267	$780,000
2009	$1,455,800	$485,267	$1,335,000
2011	$345,800	$155,267	$500,000

Again, this should be compared with the $13,000 credit and $60,000 exemption generally available to a NDA's estate.

---

[3] Code §§ 2010, 2502 and former § 2521.
[4] *Estate of Burghardt v Comm'r 80 TC 705 (1983), aff'd 734 F2d 3 (3d Cir 1984)* (Italian treaty) and *Mudry v US 86–2 USTC ¶13,706 (Ct Cl 1986)* (Swiss treaty).
[5] Code § 2101(c)(3); Treas Reg § 20.2102–1(c)(2) (conferring pro rata $600,000 exemption); see Bissell, '1988 US Estate and Gift Tax Changes: Tax Rates on Foreign Investors Can Reach 55 Per Cent', Tax Planning International Review 5 (1989) and Williams, *International Estate and Gift Tax Planning* (1990/3) Intertax, at 159.

7.9   If, because of the relative size of the decedent's US estate, the proportionate credit would be less than the $13,000 credit otherwise available under the US Tax Code, the decedent's estate can opt for the Code credit rather than the proportionate treaty credit.

3. OECD treaties

7.10   The second group of treaties (all entered into after 1979) are with the following seven countries: Austria, Denmark, France, Germany, The Netherlands, Sweden and the UK. The Dutch treaty is limited to estate taxation while the others apply to estate, gift and generation-skipping transfer taxes.

7.11   The hallmark of these newer, OECD-influenced[6] treaties is the allocation of taxing rights between the source country (where the transferred property is located) and the domiciliary country (where the donor or decedent is domiciled). These treaties generally grant the source country the primary right to tax only real estate and permanent establishment property located in the source country.[7] The US can thus tax a Swedish resident on his US real estate investments, but not his US stock portfolio. The domiciliary country is given primary taxing rights to all other property. Therefore, Sweden can tax a Swedish domiciliary on all other property, including his US stock portfolio.

7.12   These newer treaties also generally obligate the domiciliary country to give a tax credit for transfer taxes paid by the donor or decedent's estate to the source country.[8]

7.13   Many of the newer treaties also include special US marital deduction rules. Two of the seven new treaties – those with Denmark and the UK – allow domiciliaries of the treaty partner a US estate or gift tax marital deduction to the same extent that deduction would have been allowed had the decedent or donor been a US domiciliary.[9] This provision was more important under prior law where the US estate and gift tax marital deduction was only available for bequests or gifts by a US citizen or domiciliary.

---

[6]   These treaties are based, in part, on the 1966 OECD model estate tax convention and on the 1977 and 1980 US model estate and gift tax convention.

[7]   Contained in articles 5 and 6 of all but the Dutch and UK treaties). The French treaty also allows taxation of source country sited tangible movable property, except personal use property (article 7). The Germany treaty permits source country taxation of partnerships if, and to the extent, attributable to article 5 and 6 property (article 8). Further, the US/German treaty does not prevent Germany from taxing an heir, donee or beneficiary domiciled in Germany when the gift was made (article 9).

[8]   In contrast, the earlier treaties typically provided for a split credit mechanism where each country would allow, as a foreign tax credit, a percentage of the lower of the taxes otherwise payable to the two countries before credit. For example, if the US tax would have been 40X and the foreign tax would have been 60X, the US would offer credit of 16X (40% of 40X) and the foreign country would offer a credit of 24X (60% of 40X).

[9]   Denmark, article 9(2); UK, article 8(2).

7.14 US and UK Estate Tax Treaties

7.14 The US treaty with France provides a French domiciliary the same marital deduction as was available to US domiciliaries on 24 November 1978.[10] At that time, the US gift tax martial deduction was available for the first $100,000 of lifetime gifts to a spouse, none of the next $100,000 and 50% of the cumulative gifts over $200,000. The estate tax marital deduction was generally the greater of $250,000 or 50% of the decedent's estate. These limits – no longer part of the US domestic tax rules since 1981 – effectively remain for gifts or bequests of US property by a French domiciliary to his or her spouse. Further, the special QTIP marital deduction rules that came into effect in 1981 would not be available to a French domiciliary seeking benefits under the treaty.

7.15 The US/German treaty provides that US property (other than community property) passing to a spouse from a decedent or donor who was domiciled in, or a national of, Germany will only be subject to US estate or gift tax to the extent the value of that property exceeds 50% of the value of the decedent's or donor's US taxable property.[11] Effectively, up to 50% of a German decedent's or donor's US property can be given to his spouse free of US tax. Although not couched in those terms, this provision effectively grants the decedent's estate a US estate and gift tax marital deduction. The US/Swedish treaty has a similar provision that applies to transfers by Swedish domiciliaries (but not nationals).[12]

7.16 In 1988, Congress substantially restricted the availability of the marital deduction for gifts or bequests to non citizen spouses. Congress indicated at the time that it believed that these provisions did not violate or affect the provisions of any treaty. For example, the provisions in the Danish and UK treaties are not impacted by the 1988 Tax Act, because the changes in the US tax law applied equally to transfers by domiciliaries of the US and those two treaty countries. Thus, a bequest of US real property by a domiciliary of Denmark or the UK to a non-citizen spouse can only qualify for the US marital deduction if the property is placed in a QDOT (qualified domestic trust) marital deduction trust – the same rule that applies to bequests by US citizens (or domiciliaries) to a non-citizen spouse.

7.17 The French, German and Swedish treaties confer marital deduction (or marital deduction-like) benefits on domiciliaries (and, in the case of the German treaty, a national) of those countries. Unlike the treaties with Denmark and the UK, the benefits are not made available on the same basis as the marital deduction otherwise allowed to US domiciliaries or citizens. Further, there is no restriction in French, German or Swedish treaties regarding the citizenship of the recipient spouse. As a general rule, when the provisions of the US Tax Code and an earlier treaty conflict, the Code will prevail even without express Congressional intent. However, in this context, Congress specifically stated that the changes in the 1988 Tax Act would not supersede marital deduction provisions of certain treaties.[13] The legislative history extensively discussed this rule in the context of the French and German treaty, but it would appear that this rule has equal application to the Swedish treaty.

---

[10] Article 11(4).
[11] Article 10(4).
[12] Article 8(8).
[13] Section 7815(d)(14) of the Omnibus Budget Reconciliation Act 1989 (OBRA), PL 101–239.

7.18 As a result, domiciliaries of France, German and Sweden (as well as German nationals) would appear to have an advantage over other NDAs – and, for that matter, over US citizens – in their ability to qualify some portion of their US gifts and bequests to non-citizens for the US marital deduction. A French domiciliary would be entitled to the US marital deduction to the extent of the pre-1978 limitations summarised above, even if the recipient spouse is not a US citizen. A German and Swedish domiciliary (and a German national) would similarly be entitled to a marital-deduction like exclusion for up to half of the transferred US property, even if the spouse is not a US citizen.

7.19 The US tax regulations provide that a decedent's estate can choose to either:

- exempt a portion of a spousal transfer from US tax by reason of the marital deduction treaty provisions, or

- qualify a transfer to a surviving spouse for the marital deduction by using a QDOT marital trust, but cannot avail itself of both provisions.[14]

Therefore, a German national cannot pass half of his US property to his wife free of tax under the treaty and defer US estate taxes on the balance of his US property by using a QDOT. He could, however, defer the entire US tax by placing all of his US property in a QDOT.

4. US/Canadian treaty

7.20 Since 1971, Canada – the United States' largest trading partner – has imposed neither a gift nor estate/inheritance tax. Instead, under Canadian income tax law, property held at death is deemed to have been disposed of for its fair market value with resulting income tax on the decedent's final return. An exception applies for property bequeathed by a Canadian resident to a Canadian resident spouse, outright or in a spousal life interest trust.[15] For non-residents of Canada, this Canadian tax is generally imposed only on the decedent's interests in Canadian real estate, shares in Canadian private companies, and large shareholdings in certain Canadian public companies.

7.21 The very different methods by which each country taxes transfers at death created a mismatch in the tax laws, particularly with respect to the foreign tax credits. Prior to the 1995 Third Protocol to the US/Canadian income tax treaty summarised below, neither country's tax laws granted a tax credit for taxes imposed by the other country at a decedent's death. Thus, for example, the US would not grant an estate tax credit for Canadian federal or provincial taxes imposed by reason of the US decedent's death on the decedent's appreciated Canadian summer home. Similarly, Canada would not grant an income tax credit for US estate taxes imposed on a Canadian's winter home in the US.

---

[14] Treas Reg § 26.2056A-1(c).
[15] Canadian Income Tax Act (ITA) § 70(5) and 70(6).

7.22 US and UK Estate Tax Treaties

7.22 In the mid 1990s, the US and Canada sought to address this problem by amending their tax treaties. However, since the prior estate tax treaty between these two countries had expired many years earlier, the two countries inserted these special treaty provisions in new article XXIX B of the 1984 US/Canada income tax treaty. The 17th US 'estate' tax treaty is, therefore, buried in the middle of the US/Canadian income tax treaty – just where you'd expect to find it.

7.23 Like many of the older US transfer tax treaties, the Third Protocol to the US/Canadian income tax treaty grants the estate of a Canadian resident decedent a proportionate estate tax credit based on the ratio of the value of the decedent's US property to his worldwide estate.[16] For example, assume a Canadian died in 2004 with a worldwide estate of US $4m and US property valued at US $1m. The Canadian would be entitled to 25% of the 2004 estate tax credit otherwise available to US decedents, or $138,950 (25% × $555,800). That credit will effectively exempt $450,000 of the US property from estate tax.

7.24 The estate of a Canadian resident (as well as a US citizen or resident) can also elect a unique *spousal credit* in lieu of the US marital deduction for a qualifying transfer of property to a surviving spouse. The surviving spouse must be a resident of either country and if both spouses are US residents, at least one must be a Canadian citizen. This optional spousal credit equals the lesser of the US estate tax credit (adjusted as provided in the prior paragraph) and the US estate tax attributable to the qualifying spousal transfer.[17] If, for example, a Canadian decedent's estate would have otherwise been entitled to a proportionate US estate tax credit of $138,950, the optional spousal credit could be as high as $138,950. Both credits can be taken. In this example, the combined credit of $277,900 would exempt approximately $825,000 of the Canadian decedent's estate from US estate tax.

7.25 Bequests of Canadian property by a US resident decedent to his spouse will qualify for Canadian 'roll over relief' and, therefore, deferral from Canadian income tax until the spouse dies or the Canadian property is sold.[18] Under Canadian domestic tax law, this relief is generally only available if both spouses are Canadian residents. At the discretion of CCRA, this relief might extend to property left in a QDOT marital trust for a non-citizen spouse. Normally, only Canadian resident trusts will so qualify.

7.26 Canadian residents are permitted a US estate tax deduction for US-situated property bequeathed to a Canadian tax-exempt charity.[19] Under general US tax laws, a NDA is only entitled to a charitable deduction for bequests to US charities.

7.27 For purposes of computing the US estate tax, the treaty importantly extends the US foreign death tax credit to include Canadian and provincial income tax imposed by reason of the death of a US citizen or domiciliary.[20] The foreign

---

[16] Para 2 of article XXIX B.
[17] Paras 3 and 4 of article XXIX B.
[18] Para 5 of article XXIX B.
[19] Para 1 of article XXIX B.
[20] Para 7 of article XXIX B. Note that the Canadian tax must be paid or claimed as a credit within four years of filing the US estate tax return. Code § 2014.

death tax credit is also available for Canadian tax imposed by reason of a surviving spouse's death upon property held in a QDOT martial trust. The US credit would not, however, be available for Canadian taxes imposed during the spouse's life on the sale of the Canadian property. To get full benefit of the tax credits, the spouse (or the QDOT marital trust) will, therefore, need to retain the inherited Canadian property until the spouse's death.

7.28 Conversely, for purposes of computing the Canadian income tax on a deceased's assets, the treaty grants a Canadian tax credit for US federal and state estate and inheritance taxes imposed on his or her US situated property.[21] A Canadian tax credit is also available for US federal or state estate or inheritance taxes imposed upon the death of a surviving spouse with respect to certain property held in a spousal trust.

7.29 Finally, if the value of the Canadian resident decedent's worldwide estate (determined under US rules) does not exceed US $1.2m, the US estate tax will effectively only apply to the Canadian decedent's investment in US real property and US permanent establishment (business) property.[22] This small estate exception was relevant in the mid-90s when the estate tax credit exemption was only $600,000. However, as illustrated by the following table, this small estate exception has been rendered effectively irrelevant by:

- the increase in the US estate tax credit exemption to $1.5m; and
- the treaty provisions that otherwise grant a Canadian resident decedent a proportionate estate tax credit.

Value of Canadian's worldwide estate: $1,200,000				
Percentage of estate in US	25%	50%	75%	100%
US estate	$300,000	$600,000	$900,000	$1,200,000
US tax before credit	$87,800	$192,800	$306,800	$427,800
Proportionate credit				
2004	$138,950	$227,900	$416,850	$555,800
2006	$195,200	$390,400	$585,600	$780,800
2009	$363,950	$727,900	$1,091,850	$1,455,800

7.30 At all levels, the proportionate credit exceeds the US tax (before credits) on the Canadian's US property. Simply put, if the Canadian decedent's worldwide estate is less than the US estate tax exemption, all of his US property (including US real estate investments) will be exempt from US tax by reason of the proportionate

---

[21] Para 6 of article XXIX B. For smaller estates (under US $1.2m), this benefit is generally limited to US-sited property which produces income that, in the hands of a Canadian resident, would generally have been subject to US income taxes under the treaty (e g US real estate and US-sited assets which produce income subject to US withholding tax under the treaty).

[22] Para 8 of article XXIX B.

B. United Kingdom

1. Introduction

7.31 The United Kingdom gives relief against double taxation by way of unilateral relief where no international convention exists with the relevant country.[23] Credit is given for overseas taxes paid which have a character similar to IHT or which are chargeable with respect to death or lifetime gifts if IHT becomes due on the same property.[24] Where the property is located in the overseas jurisdiction concerned, full credit is given. However, only a proportion of the overseas tax is credited with respect to property regarded as being located in both countries (ie if each regards it as sited in its own jurisdiction), or in a third country, based on a formula.[25] If the relief given unilaterally exceeds the measure of relief under the relevant double tax treaty, the taxpayer can claim the unilateral relief instead.

7.32 In addition to the above, the UK has also entered into bilateral inheritance tax treaties with various countries.[26] As in the case of the US, there are certain older treaties and certain newer treaties which each, as a group, have some differences.[27]

7.33 It should be noted that while, in principle, credit should be given only in circumstances where the tax payable is an estate or gift tax and is paid on the same event, the Inland Revenue generally makes allowance for taxes arising on the same assets and at the same point in time. For example, relief may be given by concession for gains taxes arising by reference to death, where no estate taxes are charged (for example, Canada),[28] or where the tax triggers on one death but is imposed by reference to the estate of an earlier deceased person (eg in the case of a US QDOT where the tax is deferred to the later death of a surviving spouse, but arises with respect to the estate of the first deceased).[29] Credit is also generally given where the taxpayers are different, for example in the case of the UK the tax is a donor based tax, whereas in other jurisdictions (particularly those governed by civil law), it is the donee who bears the tax.

---

[23] IHTA 1984, s 159(1).
[24] Note that where the taxes are not of a similar character, this may not apply. For example, in the case of Canada, which imposes a deemed income tax on gains immediately before death, relief is given by an Inland Revenue Concession (Extra Statutory Concession (ESC) F18) through deduction as a liability against the estate. The tax is first treated as reducing the value of the assets outside the UK, with any excess being set against UK assets.
[25] IHTA 1984, s 159(3). The formula expresses the IHT as a fraction of the total IHT and overseas tax. It is that fraction of the IHT or the overseas tax (whichever is the lesser) which is given by way of credit.
[26] IHTA 1984, s 158.
[27] For a full discussion and analysis see *Simons Direct Tax Service*, Butterworths, Volume J at Division 4: Locality (Situs) of Assets and Division 5: Double Taxation Relief.
[28] ESC F18 makes provision for the Canadian tax to be treated as deductible liability of the estate.
[29] In a letter dated 7 September 1990 from DJ Ferley of the Capital Taxes Office (CTO) to Paul Knox of Ernst & Young it was indicated that while the treaty did not make any specific provision the CTO would consider any application for relief sympathetically.

2. Double tax treaties

7.34 There are currently ten double tax treaties relevant to inheritance tax. The treaties with France, India, Italy and Pakistan date back to estate duty (which was replaced by capital transfer tax in 1975) and relate only to transfers on death and not to lifetime transfers.[30] Those with Ireland, South Africa, Sweden and the USA date to the days of capital transfer tax (the predecessor to IHT and which was replaced in 1986) and apply to transfers on death and in lifetime. The treaties with the Netherlands and Switzerland have been concluded since the introduction of IHT, although the scope of the latter remains limited to transfers on death.

7.35 Pursuant to many, but not all, of these treaties, UK taxation of non-UK domiciliary donors or deceased persons is generally limited to UK real estate and permanent establishment property[31] and double tax credit relief is provided for such UK tax against domiciliary country taxes. Summarised below are some of the common features of the current treaties. However, each varies and reference should be made to the relevant treaties for further detail.

7.36 The old estate duty treaties are of some interest as they do not incorporate the deemed domicile rules where the individual is a general law domiciliary of one of those countries. Accordingly, no IHT is chargeable on non-UK situs property even where the deceased is deemed UK domiciled.[32] This offers planning opportunities for long-term (but not permanent) UK residents. These treaties apply if a person is domiciled in one of the countries which is a party to the agreement, as determined under local law, and, generally speaking, incorporate situs rules to determine the locality of assets. If having applied the terms of the treaty to determine the situs of the assets and the general liability of the deceased, there is tax in both countries, credit is then given for tax which is paid in the country where the assets are located. However, of the four countries with such treaties, three have now abolished estate tax.

a. Older treaties

(i) France

7.37 The French treaty, which is limited to tax at death, covers UK inheritance tax and French succession duties. It relies on a combination of a situs code and on determining domicile through a process which tries to tie together the very different approaches of the UK and France to this concept. It establishes a single treaty domicile in cases of dual domicile by reference to centre of vital interests and habitual abode, which more closely reflect the French domestic factors determining exposure to succession duties. The domiciliary country has worldwide taxing rights.

---

[30] IHTA 1984, s 158(6).
[31] Eg in the treaty with Ireland, treaty domicile determines the country with primary, rather than exclusive, taxing rights.
[32] See IHTA 1984, s 267 with respect to 'deemed UK domicile' for persons either:
  - resident in the UK in all or part of 17 tax years out of a prior 20-year period; or
  - for persons who have been domiciled in the UK as a matter of general law at some time within the last three calendar years.

(ii) India

7.38 The Indian treaty is again limited to tax on death and precludes the UK from taxation of non-UK sited assets (which do not devolve by reason of a UK testamentary document) of persons domiciled in India as a matter of general law. It precludes operation of the rules relating to deemed UK domiciliaries as noted above. The treaty applies notwithstanding the repeal of Indian estate tax in 1985.

(iii) Italy

7.39 Italian inheritance tax also has been repealed and the position would appear to be similar to that of India in so far as a UK deemed domiciliary, who is domiciled in Italy as a matter of Italian general law, is not subject to UK tax on non-UK sited assets. As with India, this leaves open the possibility of estate taxation in neither country.

(iv) Pakistan

7.40 The Pakistan treaty has broadly the same effect as the Indian treaty, again notwithstanding the repeal of estate tax in Pakistan as long ago as 1979.

b. Newer treaties

7.41 The newer treaties, which apply to transfers in lifetime and on death, are in line with the OECD Model and do not contain a detailed situs code but look to determine a treaty domicile of the transferor, to which country the principal taxing right is given. In general, where dual domicile arises a treaty domicile will be determined by the taxpayer's: (i) location of permanent home, and if one exists in both or neither; (ii) the centre of vital interests; failing which (iii) the country of habitual abode; failing which (iv) the country of nationality. In all cases, land and business assets of a permanent establishment, and ships and aircraft, may also be taxed on a situs basis (with the country of domicile giving credit for situs based tax), but, generally speaking, other assets are taxed in the country of treaty domicile.

(i) Ireland

7.42 This treaty specifically includes deemed UK domiciliaries within its scope and once treaty domicile is determined in line with the above factors, the relevant country is given primary taxing rights (as opposed to sole taxing rights). That country's tax is then permitted as a credit against tax arising in the other. Accordingly, in appropriate cases, the treaty still permits both countries to tax on a worldwide basis, albeit with credits to avoid double tax arising.

(*ii*)   *Netherlands*

7.43   This treaty has similar features to the US treaty summarised at Section C (7.47 et seq). Again, the concept of deemed domicile is expressly included and this treaty also relates to tax on lifetime gifts and at death. Where dual domicile occurs, the UK is given primary taxing rights for UK nationals (who are not also Dutch), who do not intend to remain in the Netherlands indefinitely, and who were not resident there in seven or more of the preceding ten years. A similar test is applied to UK resident Dutch nationals. Where the position is not resolved, there are further provisions in line with the OECD tests noted above. The treaty also includes the other main feature of the OECD treaty, giving situs country taxing rights for real and business assets. However, if property is sited in a country of which the individual was a national, and in which he had been domiciled within the previous ten years, it can be taxed by such country (subject to giving credit for tax in the primary taxing jurisdiction of the treaty domicile). Again, in parallel with the US treaty, the 50% relief for gifts to a spouse can apply in certain circumstances.

(*iii*)   *South Africa*

7.44   Application of the rule relating to deemed domiciliaries is specifically included, but in resolving matters of dual domicile, this is limited to the first limb of the test,[33] being three *calendar* years from leaving the UK and ceasing to be UK domiciled as a matter of general law. The relevant South African test is ordinary residence. The seven out of ten-year test linked to nationality, and noted above in the context of the Netherlands, is also applied in this treaty, as is the fallback OECD test, where the former does not resolve the issue. However, there is a further extension of taxing rights where the individual is treaty domiciled in one country but had been domiciled in the other country within the previous ten years. In this case, the former domiciliary country may tax, giving credit for tax arising in the country of current treaty domicile. Shares, debentures and unit trust holdings are included in the situs based taxation provisions, in addition to the standard OECD provisions.

(*iv*)   *Sweden*

7.45   Deemed UK domiciliaries are included and the relevant Swedish criteria applied are residence or nationality. The OECD tests noted above are applied to determine treaty domicile in cases of dual domicile, as are the OECD provisions relating to situs based taxation of land and business assets of a permanent establishment, along with a fixed base for the performance of professional services, and ships and aircraft. Again, where the individual is treaty domiciled in one country, but he had been treaty domiciled in the other country within the previous ten years, such other country may still tax its nationals. Furthermore, a dual-domiciled person who is a national of one country, and treaty domiciled in the other, is not taxable in the

---

[33]   IHTA 1984, s 267(1)(a).

country of treaty domicile if he had not been domiciled there in seven or more of the prior ten years. The Swedish treaty also provides for a 50% spouse relief where this is greater than would otherwise apply.

(v) Switzerland

7.46 This treaty (which came into force after the introduction of IHT) does not cover lifetime transfers, only transfers on death. Deemed UK domicile is specifically included and the treaty will apply to Swiss domiciliaries, residents or nationals if Swiss law governs succession to the assets. A specific exclusion applies in the case of a person who is a national and domiciliary of one country, temporarily resident in the other for employment, provided they have no intention to remain permanently. The OECD provisions noted above apply both to the determination of treaty domicile in a case of dual domicile and to the situs based taxation of real and business assets along with a fixed base for the performance of professional services, and of ships and aircraft. Where Switzerland has primary taxing rights, the UK may nevertheless also tax the shares of a UK incorporated company. Additionally, if a person is domiciled in both countries under local domestic laws (and hence potentially taxable on worldwide assets in both), each country has sole taxing rights over other property sited in their respective jurisdictions. This is subject to the proviso that if the UK is the country of treaty domicile, the UK has secondary taxing rights over Swiss-sited property. Furthermore, if the individual was Swiss treaty domiciled, but had been UK domiciled within the prior five years and was a UK national, the UK also has secondary taxing rights over Swiss and third-country property. The Swiss treaty also provides for a 50% spouse relief where this is greater than would otherwise apply.

C. The US/UK estate and gift tax treaty

1. Introduction

7.47 The US/UK estate and gift tax treaty (hereafter, the 'US/UK treaty') is broadly representative of the newer OECD-influenced treaties discussed at **7.10** et seq. As summarised below, this treaty:

(a) generally grants exclusive taxing rights to the country of domicile; *but*

(b) gives primary taxing rights to the situs country with respect to real estate and permanent establishment property (article 6/7 property);

(c) permits the non-domiciliary country to tax its citizens according to its domestic laws; *and*

(d) mandates credits to prevent double taxation in most cases.[34]

The Convention was signed in 1978 and the US/UK treaty entered into force on 11 November 1979.

---

[34] Eg, no provision is made for a person domiciled in neither country, but a citizen of both countries.

2. Scope and taxes covered

7.48 The US/UK treaty covers:

(a) the US federal gift tax;

(b) the US federal estate tax;

(c) the US tax on generation-skipping transfers; and

(d) the UK inheritance tax.[35]

The US/UK treaty also applies to 'any identical or substantially similar taxes' later imposed by either country.[36]

7.49 By its terms, the treaty specifically applies to generation-skipping transfers. The treaty even includes a special provision that prohibits the US from applying the GST if, at the time of the relevant transfer, the 'deemed transferor' was domiciled in the UK.[37] Nonetheless, the application of the US/UK treaty to the US generation-skipping tax is somewhat uncertain, given the radical changes in the basic structure and terminology of the GST since 1979. For example, the current GST provisions do not include the concept of 'deemed transferor,' although generation-skipping transfers are measured against an actual 'transferor'. Despite these changes, the US Tax Code and the US/UK treaty are very likely in harmony. For example, the US Tax Code and regulations would generally only impose a GST on a generation-skipping transfer that was attributed to a UK domiciled transferor who was subject to a US gift or estate tax on the transfer of US real estate or permanent establishment property. Similarly, the treaty would appear to allow the US to impose a GST only on transfers of such article 6/7 property attributed to a 'deemed transferor' who was a UK domiciliary.

7.50 It should be noted that the US/UK treaty, like other US treaties (with the exception of the US/Canadian treaty[38]), does not apply to state transfer taxes, which can be significant. Further, consistent with the US practice of treating its possessions as foreign countries for tax purposes, the treaty does not apply to those persons acquiring US citizenship by birth, residence or citizenship within such possessions. In contrast, British nationals include Commonwealth and other citizens possessing the right of UK abode at the time of death or transfer.

3. Fiscal domicile

7.51 Article 4 of the US/UK treaty provides rules for determining an individual's domicile for the purposes of the treaty, including tie-breaker rules for resolving cases of dual domicile. Article 4's determination of a single treaty domicile is

---

[35] Under article 2(1) and (2) of the US/UK treaty (inheritance tax replaced 'capital transfer tax', to which the treaty refers, in 1986).
[36] Article 2(2).
[37] Article 5(3). The treaty would appear to allow the US to tax a generation-skipping transfer attributed to a UK domiciliary of US-situated real estate and permanent establishment property.
[38] See the discussion at **7.20** et seq on the estate tax provisions of article XXIX B of that tax treaty.

important, since (except as noted below, and notwithstanding local law) the country of treaty domicile will generally have *sole* taxing rights with respect to its domiciliaries. Under article 4, domicile is initially determined under local law. Under general law principles, domicile is similar in the US and the UK (see **CHAPTER 2**). In addition, the UK has two deemed IHT domicile rules. These are met by any person who has been:

- domiciled under the general UK law at some time in the prior three calendar years; or
- an income tax resident of the UK in all or any part of 17 of the prior 20 UK tax years, including the tax year of the transfer.[39]

7.52 For treaty purposes, US domicile status is retained for tax purposes for a period of three years after a change of domicile is actually made. Thus, the US will *not* retain primary taxing rights with respect to its citizens who have been domiciled outside the US for at least three years.

7.53 For persons who are domiciliaries of both countries under their domestic rules as defined above, the following treaty tie-breaker rules apply.

1. A UK national is deemed to be domiciled in the UK if not resident in the US for income tax purposes in seven out of the ten US tax years ending with the year of the transfer.
2. A US national is similarly deemed to be domiciled in the US if not resident in the UK in seven out of the ten UK tax years ending with the year of the transfer (determined without reference to a UK place of accommodation).[40]
3. If a single treaty domicile is not deemed under (1) and/or (2) above, an individual is deemed to be domiciled in the country in which he or she maintained a permanent home.
4. If there is a permanent home in neither or both countries, domicile is attributed to the country with which the person's personal and economic relations were the closest (the centre of vital interests).
5. If this determination cannot be made for either country, domicile is in the country in which the individual had an habitual abode.
6. If an habitual abode is maintained in both or neither country, domicile is deemed to be in the country of which he or she is a national.
7. If the individual was a national of neither or both countries, the competent authorities will decide the issue by mutual agreement.

4. *Exception: immovable property (real estate) and permanent establishment property*

7.54 Notwithstanding the general rule that extends exclusive taxing rights to the domiciliary country and notwithstanding the nationality of the transferor, the treaty

---

[39] IHTA 1984, s 267(1).
[40] Note that the existence of available accommodation used to be relevant to determination of UK residence but no longer is so.

gives primary taxing rights to the country in which article 6 property (immovable property – real estate) and article 7 property (permanent establishment property) is located. Thus, the US has primary rights to tax the US real estate transferred by a UK domiciliary, and the UK has primary taxing rights with respect to a US domiciliary's transfer of UK real estate. The domiciliary country can still tax the transfer, but must give credit for taxes imposed by the situs country.

7.55 For the purposes of article 6, the concept of 'immovable property' is defined by local law, but debts secured by a mortgage are not considered immovable. Ships, boats and aircraft are not considered immovable. The term does include property accessory to immovables, such as, livestock and equipment used in agriculture and forestry, as well as mineral deposits and natural resources. On the other hand, assuming the real estate or other immovable property were held in a holding company (whether in the country where the transferor/decedent is domiciled or where the property is situated), and assuming that company were respected by the situs country, the transferor/decedent's interest in the holding company should not be considered an immovable.

5. Exception: taxation of nationals permitted

7.56 The treaty preserves the right of both countries to tax their nationals as though the treaty had not come into effect.[41] Thus, a UK national who is domiciled in the US can still be taxed on UK situated property (such as stock in a UK company or a UK bank account) that would not have been taxable under the article 6/7 source country rules. Similarly, the US can tax its citizens (even those domiciled in the UK) on worldwide transfers, although the UK may have first taxing rights (as the domiciliary country) on all property other than article 6/7 property situated in the US.

6. Taxing rights where transferor/decedent not domiciled in either country

7.57 If the transferor/decedent were not domiciled in either the US or the UK but was a national of one (but not both) of the countries, the US/UK treaty can still limit taxing rights. Article 5(2) provides that (except for article 6/7 property which the situs country can always tax) a treaty country cannot tax property of that transferor/decedent that is taxable by the country of which he is a national. Since only the US taxes by reason of nationality, this presumably only limits the UK's ability to tax a US national's transfer of UK property (other than article 6/7 property).

Example

Ralph Retiree, a US citizen, is domiciled in the Cayman Islands at the time of his death. Among his investments was stock in a UK company,

---

[41] Article 5(1)(b).

7.58   *US and UK Estate Tax Treaties*

which would (but for the treaty) be subject to IHT. However, because the US will tax Ralph on this property by reason of Ralph's US citizenship, article 5(2) precludes the UK from taxing this investment. If Ralph also owned a London pied-a-terre, the UK could tax that property, as could the US, giving credit for the UK tax paid.

Example

Ralph's neighbour, Nigel Pensioner, a UK national, is also domiciled in the Cayman Islands at the date of death. Nigel owned stock in US companies. Since the UK will not tax Nigel's US stock investments, the US/UK treaty will not prevent the US from taxing that property. If Nigel owned a New York pied-a-terre, the US could also tax that property.

7. Deductions and exemptions

7.58   Deductions from the estate tax base are dealt with in article 8.[42]

7.59   The US/UK treaty purports to extend the US marital deduction to transfers of US property by a UK national or domiciliary.[43] This was more important under prior law (in effect in 1979, but not currently), whereby the US marital deduction was generally only available for transfers by US citizens and domiciliaries. The treaty treats the UK decedent or transferor as if he were a US domiciliary. This treatment will not, however, give a UK transferor or decedent a US marital deduction if the recipient spouse is not a US citizen. Under current US law, gifts or bequests to non-citizen spouses (even by US citizen/domiciliary transferors or decedents) will not qualify for the marital deduction. The only exception is a transfer, at death, to a QDOT marital deduction trust.

7.60   Under UK domestic law, an unlimited marital deduction is provided for inter-spousal transfers in all cases *except* where a UK domiciliary donor transfers property to a non-UK domiciliary spouse.[44] In such event, UK domestic law provides a lifetime exemption of £55,000. Treaty article 8(3) provides a greater exception to the extent of 50% of the value of property passing to a non-UK domiciled spouse from a spouse who is a US national (but UK domiciled).[45] The £55,000 UK domestic exemption and the treaty UK deduction for 50% of the

---

[42]   With respect to the deductibility of estate debts, UK inheritance tax law provides that a liability secured by a particular property is deductible, as far as possible, from the value of that property. A liability to a non-resident of the UK which is neither re-payable in the UK nor an encumbrance on UK property is deductible, as far as possible, from property outside the UK. In either case, if the debt exceeds the value of the property, it may be deducted from the rest of the decedent's or transferor's property.
[43]   Article 8(2).
[44]   IHTA 1984, s 18.
[45]   The treaty literally provides the 50% deduction only with respect to US national or domiciliary donors. However, a US domiciliary donor would be entitled to 100% marital deduction relief with respect to property left to a non-UK domiciliary spouse, so that the 50% treaty relief can only apply to US nationals who are UK domiciliaries.

property left by a UK domiciliary to a non-UK domiciliary spouse are only applicable to outright gifts or gifts in trust of which the spouse is a present life tenant.

7.61 With respect to trusts, however, the 50% treaty deduction is only available under article 8(4), by election, if the donee spouse was domiciled in or a national of the United States. Further, the 50% deduction for interest in possession trusts only provides for deferral if the donee spouse subsequently becomes absolutely entitled to the trust property, since in that event article 8(4)(b) deems the election never to have been made and the UK retains full rights to tax the donee spouse on 100% of the vested property.

7.62 In contrast, with respect to outright gifts, the treaty 50% deduction requires that the donor spouse be a US national and UK domiciliary without reference to the US nationality or domicile of the donee spouse (compare article 8(3) with article 8(4)). The difference appears attributable to the UK rule deeming a life tenant to own trust principal for IHT purposes (just the opposite of the US rule). The rationale may be that while the trust will retain the settlor's UK domicile for UK tax purposes, limiting the treaty relief to the US national or domiciled donee spouses could provide greater treaty information exchange rights to the UK with respect to the spouse's involvement in the trust.

8. Article 8(5) limits US tax exposure

7.63 At first blush, article 8(5) seems oddly placed in article 8, the deductions and exemptions article. Article 8(5) generally limits the amount of US tax that can be imposed on the death of a UK national who is not a US domiciliary or citizen. There is no requirement that the UK national be domiciled in the UK. Thus, this rule would appear to apply to a UK national domiciled in another treaty country with less favourable treaty rules, or even to a UK national domiciled in a tax haven.

7.64 Under article 8(5), the amount of US tax imposed on the death of a UK national (again, who was not a US citizen or domiciliary) is limited to no more than the amount of US tax to which he would have been subject had he become domiciled in the US immediately before his death. The relevance of this exception, and thus its placement in article 8, must be the expanded credit available to the estate of a US domiciliary. Estates of decedents who are not US citizens or domiciliaries are generally allowed a credit of only $13,000, which exempts only $60,000 of transfers. In contrast, US domiciliaries (as well as citizens) are entitled to a much larger credit that exempts $1.5m of transfers from US tax.

7.65 The trade-off for this expanded credit is expanded exposure to US estate tax, because a US domiciliary is subject to US estate tax on his worldwide estate.

7.66 If a UK national's estate exceeds the US estate tax exemption, the election might still save some US estate taxes, depending on the size of the worldwide estate and the value of the US property. For example, if the decedent's worldwide estate were valued at $5m and included a $2m US residence, article 8(5) would reduce the US estate taxes by about $100,000. If the decedent's worldwide estate were instead valued at $10m (including a $2m US residence), the US estate tax might actually increase by over $2.2m had the UK national been a US domiciliary and, therefore, the article 8(5) claim should not be made. Finally, reducing a UK national's US estate tax might have little impact on his worldwide tax liability, because of the corresponding reduction in the available foreign tax credit.

7.67 This exception does not technically require an election by the decedent's executor. The estate will simply avail itself of the benefits of a claim under this provision by providing appropriate information on the decedent's US estate tax return.[46]

9. Credits

7.68 Article 9 of the US/UK treaty requires each country to credit taxes imposed by the other country on a domiciliary basis or on the basis of the situs of article 6/7 property. The US must accordingly give credit for UK taxes imposed in the following scenarios:

(a) where a US citizen or domiciliary is subject to primary taxing rights in the UK on UK-situated article 6/7 property; and

(b) save for tax on US-situated article 6/7 property, where a US citizen is subject to UK tax on his worldwide transfers by reason of the individual's UK domicile status.

Similarly, the UK must give credit for US taxes imposed:

(i) where a UK domiciliary is subject to primary taxing rights in the US on US-situated article 6/7 property; and

(ii) save for tax on UK-situated article 6/7 property, where a UK national is subject to US tax on his worldwide transfers by reason of the individual's US domicile status.

Examples

- *The UK has first taxing rights to UK-situated real property.* The US estate tax imposed on a US citizen's UK-situated real estate is credited with the UK tax imposed on that property.

- *A US citizen is domiciled in the UK.* The UK has first taxing rights to his worldwide estate (except for US-situated article 6/7 property). The US can still tax its citizens on this same property, but must give credit for the UK taxes.

- *A UK domiciliary owns US real property subject to US estate tax.* Both countries can tax this property, but the US has first taxing rights and the UK must give a credit for the US taxes so imposed.

---

[46] Article 8 of the Technical Explanation of the Convention Between the Government of United States of America and the Government of the United Kingdom of Great Britain and Northern Ireland for the Avoidance of Double Taxation and the Prevention of Fiscal Evasion with Respect to Taxes on Estates of Deceased Persons and on Gifts.

- *A UK citizen is domiciled in the US and subject to US estate tax on his worldwide estate.* The UK retains rights to tax its citizens on all UK-situated property (not just article 6/7 property). Thus, the UK can impose IHT on a UK national's shares in a UK registered company owned by a US-domiciled decedent, but must give credit for US estate taxes imposed on that property.

7.69   The US/UK treaty does not require a full dollar-for-dollar, pound-for-pound credit – only that the relevant country grant a credit under the provisions of its domestic law for the taxes first imposed by the other country. Thus, if US estate taxes are imposed at a 48% marginal tax rate, the UK IHT (which is capped at 40%) will not credit the excess US tax.

7.70   Finally, both the US and the UK retain the right under local law to tax *trust-owned* property with respect to article 6/7 source country property, but are prohibited from other taxing rights if, at the time of the transfer into the trust, the settlor (or deemed transferor in the case of the GST tax) was domiciled in the other country and also not a national of the first country (article 5(3) and (4)). With respect to credits, however, a country taxing a trust on the basis of the nationality of the settlor must generally credit against its tax the tax imposed by the other country on the basis of domicile. Thus, article 9(3) provides that where both countries impose tax on the same event with respect to trust property:

(a)   the article 6/7 source country has primary taxing rights as to such property and the other country must credit against its tax the source country's article 6/7 tax;

(b)   the UK gives credit against its tax for the US tax imposed on the trust property by reference to the US domiciliary status of the settlor, the holder of a power of appointment or the deemed transferor for purposes of the GST tax, in each case limited to such domiciliary status at the time of the taxable event;

(c)   where neither (a) or (b) apply, the US gives credit against its tax for the UK tax with respect to such property.[47]

10. A decedent's exposure to US/UK transfer tax

7.71   APPENDIX VI summarises a decedent's exposure to US estate tax and UK IHT at death, depending on the decedent's nationality and domicile. This table reflects the applicable domestic tax laws of the two countries, as impacted by the US/UK treaty.

---

[47] The country of nationality may thus tax the estate or transfers of its nationals, but must credit the tax paid to the other state on a domiciliary or article 6/7 situs basis.

Chapter 8

Gains Tax on Gifts and Bequests

A. United States

1. Introduction

8.1 As a general rule, the US does not impose a capital gains tax when a US taxpayer transfers appreciated property by gift or bequest. Instead, a taxpayer is only subject to capital gains tax upon the sale or exchange of appreciated assets.[1] Therefore, if a father gives appreciated securities to his children or a mother leaves appreciated real estate to her grandchildren, the US capital gains tax will be deferred until the donee later sells or exchanges that property.

8.2 There are a few minor exceptions. A US taxpayer can be taxed on the gift of appreciated and encumbered property (such as mortgaged real estate) if the donee assumes the liability and the amount of the liability exceeds the donor's tax basis.[2] The same principle can apply in the context of a so-called 'net gift' (where the donee agrees to pay the donor's gift tax as a condition of the gift). If the amount of the gift tax liability exceeds the donor's basis in the gifted property, the donor must recognize taxable gain.[3] A US taxpayer's gift of a tax-deferred installment note or an annuity also will result in taxable gain on the difference between the taxpayer's basis in the obligation and the fair market value of the obligation on the date of the gift.[4] A tax-motivated expatriate who removes appreciated tangible personal property (eg the *Picasso*, an exotic car collection, the Hope Diamond) from the US within ten years of his expatriation (even for personal use) will be taxed as if that property had been sold at fair market value even though the transfer is neither a sale nor a gratuitous transfer.[5] Finally, a US taxpayer's gift of stock in a passive foreign investment company (PFIC) to a non-US person is considered, under 1991 proposed regulations, a disposition that triggers tax as if that stock had been sold at fair market value.[6]

---

[1] Code § 1001.
[2] Treas Reg §§ 1.1001–1(e), 1.1001–2(a)(1), 1.1001(c) (Example 6).
[3] *Diedrich v. Comm'r* 457 US 191 (1982).
[4] Code § 453B; Rev Rul 79–371, 1979–2 CB 294; Code § 72(e)(4)(C) (limited to excess of annuity cash surrender value over investment in the contract).
[5] Code § 877(d)(2)(E).
[6] Prop Treas Reg § 1.1291–6 provides that certain non recognition provisions, including rules that provide that gifts do not result in the realisation of income, will not apply with respect to disposition of PFIC shares. An exception is made for gifts to US persons. Prop Treas Reg § 1.1291–6(c)(2). A PFIC is generally a non-US company where either:
- 75% or more of the company's income is from passive sources (such as dividends, interests, rents, royalties, and annuities); or
- 50% or more of the company's assets are held for the production of passive income Code § 1297(a).

8.3   *Gains Tax on Gifts and Bequests*

8.3   The following US sections discuss:

- the US tax implications of distributions from trusts and estates; and
- Code § 684 imposition of a capital gains tax on transfers to foreign, non-grantor trusts.

2. *Distributions from trusts and estates*

8.4   Under US tax law, gain is generally *not* realized on a distributions of appreciated property from trusts and estates. There are two exceptions.

a. Property in kind

8.5   First, gain or loss is realized by a trust or estate upon a distribution of property *in kind* if the distribution is in satisfaction of a beneficiary's right to receive a distribution of:

- a fixed amount (a pecuniary obligation);
- other property; or
- a right to income.[7]

Example

The terms of a trust provide for its beneficiary, Tommy Ecks, to receive all trust income annually and, upon his attaining the age of 40, an amount of $100,000 plus 100 shares of stock of the family business, Ecks Why Zee Inc. In the year Tommy reaches age 40, the trust earns $21,254 of income. Rather than distributing $121,254 of cash to Tommy, the trustee transfers appreciated real estate to him valued at the same amount. The trust is deemed to realize a gain as if it had sold that property. No gain would be realized if the trust distributed 100 shares of Ecks Why Zee Inc (as required by the terms of the trust instrument). However, if the trustee distributed (and Tommy agreed to receive) depreciated shares of Ay Bee See Inc, the trust would realize a loss.

Most non-US mutual or unit investment funds would be considered PFICs. Unless the company is subject to other special anti-avoidance rules or the US taxpayer makes a special election that causes him to be currently taxed on his share of the company's current earnings or annual change in listed net asset value, a US taxpayer is generally adversely taxed on so-called 'excess distributions' from the company, which also can include gain from the sale of PFIC shares. The PFIC gain is generally spread back over the taxpayer's holding period. Any such gain carried back to prior years is taxed at the highest marginal ordinary income tax rate (not capital gains rate) in effect during that year. The PFIC tax attributed to prior years is also subject to an interest charge.

[7]   Treas Reg § 1.661(a)-2(f); *Kenan v Comm'r* 114 F 2d 217 (2d Cir 1940); *Suisman v Eaton* 15 F Supp 113 (D Conn 1935), aff'd per curiam 83 F2d 1019 (2d Cir 1936), cert denied 299 US 573 (1936).

b. Property sold to a beneficiary

8.6 Second, a trust or estate can elect to recognize gain or loss on a distribution as if the distributed property had been sold to a beneficiary for fair market value.[8] The trustee of a domestic US trust might make this election to offset gains or losses that it has otherwise realized.

Example

A domestic US trust had realized $20,000 of capital gains on transactions earlier in the year of its termination. Among the assets otherwise distributable to the trust's beneficiary are shares in Loser Inc, valued at $35,000 in which the trust has a tax basis of $22,000. If the trust elects to treat the distribution of the Loser shares as a sale, the resulting $13,000 loss can offset a portion of the trust's realized gains. As discussed in **CHAPTER 12**, the trust's net gain in the year of distribution is taxable to the beneficiary. Accordingly, because of this election the beneficiary will only be taxed on a net capital gains of only $7,000. Note that the beneficiary could have achieved this same result if no trust election had been made; the beneficiary would take the trust's $22,000 basis in the distributed property and could immediately sell the property and realize the $13,000 loss, which in turn would offset a portion of the trust's $20,000 gain that is taxable to the beneficiary by reason of the distribution.

8.7 The trustee of a foreign trust might make this election to avoid mismatches between the US tax laws and the foreign tax laws with respect to distributions to beneficiaries. For example, the UK treats transfers to a 'connected party' (including to and from trusts) as market value sales.[9] This results in a foreign tax that (absent a Code § 643(e) election) might not be creditable by the US beneficiary.[10]

---

[8] Code § 643(e).

[9] Similarly, under Canadian tax law, a distribution from a Canadian trust to a Canadian resident is tax free, while a distribution to a non resident is a taxable event.

[10] Code § 904 generally limits a US taxpayer's foreign income tax credit to a proportionate share of the US tax liability based on the ratio of taxpayer's foreign source income to his worldwide income. Thus, if 10% of the taxpayer's world-wide income is foreign-sourced income, then the foreign tax credit can, at most, offset only 10% of the taxpayer's US tax liability before credit. In the extreme example where the only income under local law earned by a UK or Canadian trust is from the deemed sale of appreciated property upon a distribution to the US beneficiary, the trust would generally have no taxable income (let alone foreign source income) under US principles. Accordingly, the numerator of the US taxpayer's fraction defining the foreign tax credit limitation would be zero, and thus none of the resulting foreign taxes would be creditable. In addition, while the later sale of the appreciated asset by the US taxpayer would result in a taxable US gain, that gain would generally not be considered foreign source.

Moreover, the foreign tax credit deemed to be distributed to the US beneficiary in Example 2 above could be characterised as a 'general limitation' credit that can only offset foreign-sourced general limitation income (such as foreign-sourced compensation). The US foreign tax credit rules generally treat foreign source income as falling within various 'baskets', allowing only the foreign tax credits attributed to that basket to offset the US taxes that apply to that basket. Gain from the sale of portfolio investments would generally fall within the 'passive income' basket. However, the so-called 'high tax kick-out' will re-characterise the foreign tax on passive income as a general limitation income tax if foreign tax paid on the income exceeds the highest rate of US tax that could be applied to that income. If the distribution of appreciated property is considered a taxable event under foreign law, the resulting foreign tax on that deemed gain will, by definition,

8.8 *Gains Tax on Gifts and Bequests*

3. Code § 684 – the basics

8.8 In the context of international estate and trust planning, Code § 684 presents the most important exception to the general rule that no gain is realized by the transferor upon a gratuitous transfer of appreciated property. This provision became effective 5 August 1997 and replaced Code § 1491. The latter section had applied a 35% excise tax on the unrealized appreciation in property transferred to a foreign trust, corporation or partnership. The taxpayer could alternatively elect to have the gain taxed as if the transfer were a sale.

8.9 New section 684 instead treats a US taxpayer who transfers property to a foreign trust or a foreign estate[11] as if he sold that property for fair market value. The US transferor is then required to recognize any resulting gain. The regulations make clear that the taxpayer will not be able to recognize any resulting losses (even to offset section 684 gains) on the transfer of *depreciated* property to a foreign trust or estate.[12]

8.10 Section 684(b) provides that no gain is realized on a transfer to a foreign trust if *any* person (not just the transferor) is considered the 'owner' of the trust under the so-called grantor trust rules. The grantor trust rules, described in more detail in **CHAPTER 12**, define situations where a person (typically an individual) is subject to income tax as if he still owned the underlying trust property. The grantor – not the trust or the beneficiaries – is taxed on the income and gains within the trust.

---

exceed the US tax on that same transaction since, under general US rules, the distribution would not be a taxable event. The consequence, again, would be that the relevant foreign tax credit would only be available to the US beneficiary to offset foreign-sourced general limitation income (such as compensation income). He could not offset US taxes later imposed on foreign source passive income.

By making a Code § 643(e) election, the UK or Canadian trustee in this example will cause the inherent gain to be realised for US tax purposes too. Depending on the relevant local taxes that apply, the resulting local tax may well be less than the highest marginal US tax rate. The high tax kick-out would thus not apply, and the income and credit would still be considered passive. Moreover, the gain from the deemed sale would be characterised as foreign source income, thus providing the US taxpayer with a numerator in the computation of his foreign tax credit ratio.

[11] As discussed in some detail at **12.9** et seq, the US Tax Code (and regulations) now provide detailed rules defining when a trust is considered a 'foreign trust'. The term 'foreign estate' is simply defined as an estate that is not a domestic estate, and there is no guidance in the Code or regulations and limited ruling precedent for determining when an estate is domestic or foreign. See the discussion at **12.135** et seq. Unlike Code § 1491, new Code § 684 does not apply to transfers to foreign partnerships or corporations.

[12] Treas Reg § 1.684–1(a)(2). Even though losses are not 'recognized' under Code § 684, there remains some question as to what tax basis the foreign non-grantor trust would take in such loss property. As discussed in **CHAPTER 11**, Code § 1012 generally gives a purchaser a cost basis in acquired property, while Code § 1015 gives the donee of a gift of loss property a fair market value for purposes of determining losses on the donee's later sale. So is a foreign non-grantor trust a purchaser or donee? Code § 684 would appear to make the trust a purchaser, since the transferor is deemed by Code § 684 to have sold all transferred property (not just appreciated property) to the trust. That section requires that only gains be recognized, and therefore is implicitly a non-recognition provision with respect to losses. In other contexts where the Tax Code prohibits the recognition of gains or losses, the Code also includes special rules for determining the recipient's basis. Examples include Code §§ 1031(d), 1033(b)(1), 1091(d), 1058(c) and 453B(b). The problem in Code § 684 is that Congress created a non-recognition provision for losses but apparently neglected to include a special basis rule that, in fairness, should have at least allowed the trust to use the transferor's basis for purposes of determining future gains.

8.11 Congress arguably did not need to include a specific grantor trust exception in Code § 684. If the transfer by the trust's grantor/owner is treated as a sale, the grantor would, in effect, be both buyer and seller. Prior law was fairly well established that gain or loss cannot be realized on a taxpayer's transaction with his own grantor trust.[13] Code § 684(b) thus effectively codifies that principle (at least in this context).[14] The logic behind the statute's exempting transfers to foreign trusts deemed owned by persons *other than* the transferor is that, for income tax purposes, the transfer should properly be characterized as one from the US transferor directly to the third party grantor/owner of the foreign trust and should not be taxable since donative transfers between individuals are not subject to income tax.[15]

8.12 Section 684 also applies to so-called 'outbound migrations', that is, where a 'domestic trust' becomes a 'foreign trust'.[16] The regulations offer an example of a domestic, non-grantor trust with a US trustee for the benefit of the settlor's non-US mother. The US trustee resigns and is replaced by a foreign trustee. The trust remains a non-grantor trust but, in the process, becomes a foreign trust and is taxed on any inherent gain.[17]

8.13 The 2001 Tax Act made two changes to Code § 684, *both of which apply only to transfers at death after 2009*. First, section 684(a)'s deemed sale treatment will extend to *testamentary* transfers to non-resident alien (NRA) *individuals*.[18] Second, the grantor trust exception will only apply if a US taxpayer is considered the trust's grantor/owner and will thus not apply if a NRA is considered the trust's owner.[19] This makes sense, since a transfer to a grantor trust is essentially considered to be a transfer to the grantor/owner. The effective date of these changes coincides with US estate tax repeal and corresponding rules that generally provide for a donee to take the decedent's tax basis in inherited property. Estate tax repeal, carry-over basis, and these 2001 Tax Act changes to Code § 684 are all scheduled to *sunset* in 2011 unless Congress were to enact permanent changes. As discussed at **1.31** et seq and elsewhere, it is anticipated that Congress will revisit the issue of estate tax repeal

---

[13] Rev Rul 85–13, 1985–1 CB 184; but see *Rothstein v US 735 F. 2d 704 (2d Cir 1984)* (in which the Second Circuit Court of Appeals held that a grantor who purchases assets from his grantor trust should be entitled to a basis in those assets equal to his purchase price). Shortly thereafter, the IRS repudiated that position in Rev Rul 85–13 and has consistently maintained ever since that transactions between the grantor and the grantor trust should be ignored for US income tax purposes.

[14] The IRS had reached a similar conclusion under the prior rule in Code § 1491. Rev Rul 87–61, 1987–2, CB 219, concluded that no excise tax would be imposed on the transfer of appreciated property to a foreign trust deemed owned by the transferor under the grantor trust rules.

[15] Treas Reg § 1.684–3(a).

[16] Code § 684(c). The regulation includes an exception for 'inadvertent migrations' that are corrected within a certain period. Treas Reg § 1.684–1(c). The distribution of assets from a US trust to a foreign non-grantor trust pursuant to exercise of a donee's special power of appointment is considered a taxable transfer by the US trust. However, assets may be distributed or appointed from a US or foreign trust to a foreign individual beneficiary without tax under Code § 684.

[17] Treas Reg § 1.684–4(d) (Example 2) In contrast, if the trust were held for the US settlor's US (rather than foreign) mother, and the settlor were still living, Code § 679 would cause the trust to become a grantor trust at the same time it becomes a foreign trust. In that event, the 'transfer' would be excepted by Code § 684 until such time as the trust's grantor trust status terminated. Treas Reg § 1.684–4(d) (Example 1).

[18] Code § 684(b)(2).

[19] Code § 684(b)(1).

8.14 *Gains Tax on Gifts and Bequests*

prior to 2009. The future of this extension of section 684 to bequests to NRAs or foreign trusts deemed owned by NRAs under the grantor trust rules is, therefore, presumably tied to the future of estate tax repeal.

8.14 Finally, the regulations provide that gain is realized immediately under Code § 684 even though, under traditional US tax principles, the gain would be deferred until some later payment. Thus, a sale to a foreign non-grantor trust in return for a private annuity or an installment note will cause the US taxpayer to be taxed currently on any inherent gain.[20]

4. *Code § 684 – nuances and enigmas*

8.15 As noted, Code § 684 provides that no gain is realized upon the transfer of appreciated property to a foreign trust that is deemed owned by any person under the grantor trust rules. But is the inherent gain realized when the grantor trust status terminates? The new regulations say 'yes': the grantor/owner is deemed to have transferred the property immediately before (but on the same date) as the event causing the grantor trust status to terminate.[21] This result is consistent with an IRS ruling under prior section 1491[22] and similar precedent dealing with transfers of encumbered property to grantor trusts, all of which addressed the tax consequences of trusts ceasing to be grantor trusts *during the grantor's lifetime*.[23] There are a number of ways grantor trust status might terminate.

a. Release of powers

8.16 A foreign trust created by a US taxpayer for the benefit of only *non-US* persons could be considered a grantor trust because of certain powers retained by the settlor or held by others. For example, the settlor's retained power to substitute property for trust assets of equal value causes the settlor to be taxed as the owner of the trust. Similarly, the trustee's power to add to the class beneficiaries will similarly make the trust a grantor trust. If these powers were released or otherwise terminated, the trust will cease to be a grantor trust and the settlor would be taxed on any inherent gain.[24]

Example

Walter Bigbucks, a US citizen, funds a foreign trust for the benefit of his wife's parents, who are UK citizens and residents. Walter retains the right to substitute trust assets, thus remaining taxable on the trust

---

[20] Treas Reg § 1.684–1(d) (Examples 4 and 5).
[21] Treas Reg § 1.684–2(e).
[22] Rev Rul 87–61, 87–2 CB 219.
[23] See *Madorin v Comm'r 84 TC 667 (1985)*, where the court ruled that the termination of an irrevocable trust's grantor trust status by reason of the trustee's release of certain powers causes the grantor to be taxed to the extent his release from certain partnership liabilities exceeded his basis in the underlying partnership held in the trust. See also Rev Rul 77–402, 1977–2 CB 222 and Treas Reg § 1.1001–2(c) (Example 5).
[24] Treas Reg 1.684–2(e) (Example 3).

income under the grantor trust rules. If Walter releases his power to substitute assets in order to rid himself of continuing US tax exposure, he would be immediately taxed on all inherent gain within the trust.

b. Loss of US beneficiary

8.17 A foreign trust created by a US taxpayer is considered a grantor trust if the trust is for the current (or future) benefit of US beneficiaries. The foreign trust can thus cease to be a grantor trust (resulting in the imposition of tax under Code § 684) if the trust ceases to have US beneficiaries.[25]

Example

Same as the previous example at **8.16**, but:

- Walter has no power to substitute assets; and
- the trust is also held for the benefit of Walter's mother (who is a US citizen).

Walter's mother dies and the trust ceases to be a grantor trust. Walter is taxed on all inherent gain in the underlying trust property.

c. Settlor's death – generally

8.18 The settlor's deemed ownership can also terminate upon the settlor's death. Commentators have debated for years:

- whether the termination of a trust's status as a grantor trust by reason of the grantor's death could be an income tax recognition event under Code § 684 and its predecessor (Code § 1491); and
- if so, who should be taxed (the grantor or the grantor's estate); and
- whether these issues are moot if the property held in the foreign non-grantor trust is included in the decedent's estate.

8.19 Let's tackle the easy issue first. As discussed more fully in **CHAPTER 11**, appreciated property included in the decedent's estate receives a basis step-up.[26] Would this prevent the inherent appreciation from being taxed when a foreign trust's grantor trust status terminated by reason of the grantor's death? Under prior law, the IRS never indicated which would come first – the chicken (35% excise tax under Code § 1491 when the foreign trust's grantor trust status terminated at the settlor's death) or the egg (the basis step-up for the foreign trust property included in the settlor's estate). Fortunately, the new regulations offer a clear (and favorable) resolution – the egg. If the basis of the trust property is determined under Code §

---

[25] Treas Reg 1.684–2(e) (Example 1).
[26] Code §§ 1014(a). For example, where the settlor has made an incomplete gift to a trust (eg by retaining a right to revoke or appoint the trust), the trust property will be included in the decedent's taxable estate and receive a basis adjustment to fair market value.

1014(a) at the transferor's death, the regulations provide that no tax will be imposed under Code § 684, rendering moot the question of whether death should be considered a capital gains event.[27]

Example

Walter Bigbucks creates an asset protection trust in the Cayman Islands. Walter retains the power to add or remove persons from the class of beneficiaries with the consent of the trustees, making his transfer to the trust incomplete for gift tax purposes, and causing the trust property to be included in his taxable estate at death. At Walter's death, the income tax basis of the trust property is adjusted to fair market value. No tax is imposed on the unrealized gain that existed just prior to Walter's death.

8.20   The issue of whether death should be a capital gains event is not moot in all circumstances. If the foreign trust property is *not* included in the grantor's taxable estate (and thus the property keeps its historical basis), we are still left with the fundamental question: should the grantor's death cause the grantor to be taxed on any inherent gain in the trust property? The new regulations answer this question in the affirmative: the grantor/decedent is taxed under Code § 684 as if he had sold the appreciated property to the trust on the date of (but immediately before) his death.[28] In so providing, the regulations are of questionable legality for a number of reasons.

- First, in order to address the issue of who should be taxed (the grantor or the grantor's estate), the regulations treat the grantor as having sold the property to the trust immediately prior to his death. However, by taking this approach the regulations contradict Code § 684(b), which exempts a transfer to a grantor trust from tax. Since the foreign trust is a grantor trust immediately prior to the grantor's death, any deemed sale to that trust by the grantor prior to death should arguably be excepted from tax.

- Second, there is no precedent for imposing an income tax by reason of the grantor's death. The courts have held that a settlor can be taxed if encumbered, low-basis property is held in a trust that ceases to be a grantor trust *during the settlor's life*.[29] The authors are aware of no cases or rulings extending this principle to a situation where the trust ceases to be a grantor trust by reason of the settlor's death On the contrary, there is Supreme Court

---

[27] Treas Reg § 1.684–3(c). Code § 1014(a) provides a date of death market value rebasing for property 'acquired' from a decedent. Code § 1014(b) defines specific categories of property 'acquired' from a decedent, including property held in certain revocable or settler retained powers trusts, incomplete gift trusts and varying date of death basis rules, including carry-over basis rules applicable to foreign personal holding companies. Since property held by incomplete gift trusts is treated as bequeathed at death (Treas Reg § 25.2511–2), technically such carry-over basis property held in an incomplete gift trust is exempt from taxation at the settlor's death.

[28] The issue only arises if the trust ceases to be a grantor trust with respect to any person. Treas Reg § 1.684–2(e) (Example 2). If, upon the settlor's death, another person became the owner of the foreign trust under the grantor trust rules, no tax would be imposed under Code § 684.

[29] *Madorin v Comm'r* 84 TC 667 (1985), Rev Rul 77–402, 1977–2 CB 222 and Treas Reg § 1.1001–2(c) (Example 5).

precedent that a decedent's transfer of encumbered property at death (albeit encumbered property included in the decedent's taxable estate) is not taxable as a sale.[30]

- Third, some commentators believe that the 'no gain at death' rule has constitutional dimensions, from which any exceptions require a clearly expressed legislative mandate.[31] Since no such explicit exception is found in the text of Code § 684, the regulation would appear open to challenge on constitutional grounds.

- Fourth, nothing in the legislative history of Code § 684 suggests that Congress intended to create a general exception to the long established 'no gain at death' rule. Contrast this with the specific changes to Code § 684 in the 2001 Tax Act that tax inherent gain on property left at death to a NRA *individual*.[32]

8.21 Despite these arguments, there is a certain logic to the regulations. The purpose of Code § 684 is clearly to impose a US tax on the inherent appreciation in property transferred to a foreign non-grantor trust. This tax reaches direct transfers to foreign non-grantor trusts during the US taxpayer's life, as well as outbound migrations and distributions from domestic to foreign non-grantor trusts, which could occur after death. It would seem too 'easy' for a US taxpayer to avoid this tax by merely ensuring that the appreciated property was held in the foreign grantor trust at death.

8.22 Further, as noted earlier, there is ample precedent in the law to disregard transactions between the grantor and a grantor trust. Thus, a grantor's contribution of property to a foreign grantor trust might not be considered a completed 'transfer' for purposes of Code § 684, since the grantor is treated as still owning the trust property for US income tax purposes. When that ownership terminates – even by death – the grantor's 'transfer' is arguably complete and tax on the inherent gain should arguably then be imposed.

8.23 However, the logic, as well as the legal basis, of taxing gains to a living settlor is distinguishable from taxing gains at the settlor's death. There are constitutional impediments to treating death as an income tax event and legal infirmities in the regulations' deemed disposition while the trust is still a grantor trust. As stated in *Citizen's National Bank of Waco v United States*:

---

[30] *Crane v Comm'r 331 US 1 35 (1947)*, Rev Rul 73–183, 1973–1 CB 364.

[31] See authorities cited in Blattmachr, Gans and Jacobson, 'Income Tax Effects of Termination of Grantor Trust Status by Reason of the Grantor's Death', Journal of Taxation (September 2002) at footnote 11 of that article: see also, Mulligan, 'Sale to an Intentionally Defective Irrevocable Trust for a Balloon Note – An End Run Around Chapter 14?', 32 University of Miami Philip E Heckerling Institute on Estate Planning, Chapter 14 (1998) at p 14–38 ('... it would appear that the sale at death analysis produces too many incongruities to be correct. The best result conceptually appears to be that the seller's death has no income tax consequences').

[32] Code § 684 (a)(2). Also, in addressing provisions of the 2001 Tax Act dealing with the basis of property acquired from a decedent in 2010, the Conference Committee explicitly noted 'that gain is not recognized at the time of death when the estate or heir acquires from the decedent property subject to a liability that is greater than the decedent's basis in the property'. House Report No 107–84, 107th Cong, 1st Sess 113 (2001).

8.24   *Gains Tax on Gifts and Bequests*

'regulations must by their terms and application, be in harmony with the statute. A regulation which is in conflict or restrictive of the statute, is to the extent of the conflict or restriction invalid (*Scofield v Lewis 5 Cir 1958 [58-1 USTC ¶9212], 251 F 2d 128, 132)*'.[33]

Further as a matter of tax policy, the penal accumulation distribution rules of Code §§ 665–668 are generally viewed as a more than adequate deterrent to realizing gains through a post mortem non-grantor trust.

d.   Settlor's death – insurance

8.24   Code § 101 generally exempts the proceeds of life insurance from US income tax. Does this change if the policy is held in a foreign trust at the insured/grantor's death? If so, this would produce an anomalous, severe, and arguably inappropriate result in the context of a foreign, irrevocable life insurance trust. Consider the following example.

Example

Walter Bigbucks (as US taxpayer) creates an irrevocable discretionary trust with Jersey (Channel Islands, that is, not *New Jersey*) trustees for the benefit of his descendants (all of whom are US persons) and funds it with a $1m cash gift. The trust is considered a grantor trust. The Trustees use this cash to acquire a $4m face value variable universal life insurance policy. Walter's objective is to leverage his $1m gift and exclude the $4m proceeds from estate tax at his death. The trust will have a tax basis in the policy of $1m – the premiums paid to date. Assume that at Walter's death the policy has a cash surrender value (and fair market value) of $1.75m. What are the income tax consequences under Code §§ 684 and 101?

8.25   If Code § 684 indeed applied to a foreign irrevocable insurance trust at the insured's death, then there could be two adverse results:

- First, any inherent gain in the policy (the difference between basis and cash surrender value) would be subject to tax. Under normal rules, the sale of a life insurance policy can result in both ordinary income and capital gains. The difference between the seller's basis and the policy's cash surrender value (representing essentially accumulated tax-deferred earnings within the policy) is taxed as ordinary income. In the prior example, Walter would thus have $750,000 of ordinary income. The excess of value, if any, over cash surrender (or, if greater, the seller's cost basis) is taxed as a capital gain.

- Second, the deemed Code § 684 sale might also trigger the so-called 'transfer for value' exception to Code § 101.[34] That exception applies where the policy owner has acquired the policy by a 'transfer for valuable consideration' and permits the transferee to exclude from tax only the amount paid for the policy (including future premium payments). If, because of Walter's deemed sale,

---

[33]   *417 F 2d 675 (5th Cir 1969)*.
[34]   Code § 101(a)(2).

Walter's Jersey trust were treated as having acquired the policy for value, then the proceeds ($4m) in excess of the trust's deemed acquisition cost ($1.75m) would be subject to US income tax.

8.26   If this interpretation holds, then Walter's death would cause:

- Walter to realise $750,000 of taxable income; and

- the Jersey trust to realise an additional $2.25m ($4m − $1.75m) of taxable income under the transfer for value rules.

This despite the general principles of Code § 101 that would generally have exempted the entire $4m of proceeds from US income tax. Ouch! Talk about a trap for the unwary.[35]

8.27   There are a number of reasons why these results should arguably not apply. First, is a simple matter of tax policy. Code § 684 is designed to prevent US tax avoidance that would occur if appreciated assets could be transferred to a foreign non-grantor trust where the gain, once realized, would escape at least immediate US tax. No such avoidance occurs in the context of life insurance, since the receipt of the life insurance proceeds is made exempt by specific provisions of the US Tax Code (Code § 101), not by the insurance beneficiary's status as domestic or foreign. The fact that no tax avoidance occurs can be simply illustrated by considering a domestic life insurance policy which becomes foreign resident after the settlor's death.

Example

Walter creates a domestic, irrevocable insurance trust for the benefit of his wife and children. The trust is considered a grantor trust for US income tax purposes during Walter's life. The insurance proceeds are still excluded from estate tax at Walter's death and are exempt from income tax by reason of Code § 101. If the domestic trust were to transfer the cash proceeds to a foreign trust (*or to migrate offshore*) after Walter's death, no tax would be imposed under Code § 684.

8.28   That being said, Code § 684 also does not carve out an exception for the transfer of appreciated US real property interests to a foreign non-grantor trust, even though (under the FIRPTA rules[36]) the foreign trust would remain liable for US tax on the later sale of that property.

8.29   Second, this result is again contrary to Code § 684(b), which precludes tax on transfers to foreign grantor trusts. Immediately prior to the grantor/insured's death (when the taxable transfer is deemed to have occurred), the trust would still be a grantor trust. There simply cannot be a taxable transfer to this trust while the grantor/insured is still living.

---

[35]   This trap is acknowledged in Basset, 'New Regs On The Tax Effects of Funding Outbound Foreign Trusts', 29 Estate Planning 113 (March 2002).

[36]   Foreign Investment in Real Property Tax Act, codified in Code §§ 897 & 1445, and discussed further at **14.119**.

8.30 *Gains Tax on Gifts and Bequests*

8.30 Third, there is no precedent for subjecting life insurance proceeds to income tax at the insured's death *when the insured owns the policy*. Indeed, the 'transfer for value' rule does not apply where the policy is purchased by the insured.[37] At the grantor/insured's death, the grantor trust rules treats the grantor as the owner of the trust assets; thus, if the grantor/insured were deemed to have sold the policy to the trust immediately prior to death, he would have sold the policy to himself (an excepted purchaser under the transfer for value rules). (Despite this argument, some commentators had expressed caution under the predecessor to Code § 684 (ie Code § 1491) that life insurance held in a foreign trust at the grantor's death might be subject to tax under that provision.[38]

8.31 The Code § 684 regulations were floated for comment prior to becoming final, and some had questioned the principle in the regulations that extended the application of that section to foreign trusts – including those holding life insurance on the settlor's life – that ceased to be grantor trusts at the settlor's death. In the preamble to the final regulations, the Treasury responded to the public's comments and justified the final regulations by a strained analysis that identified Congressional intent, not in Code § 684, but in other marginally related provisions of the Code dealing with foreign insurance or foreign trusts.[39] In reading and rereading the preamble, one question comes to mind: '*Is this the best they can do?*' One would have thought that if Congress had intended to override long-standing statutory principles and case law it would have offered a clearer indication of that intent. Instead, there is nothing in the text of Code § 684 or the legislative history that suggests Congress intended these results.

8.32 In the authors' view, it is unlikely that Congress ever considered that new Code § 684 could subject insurance proceeds to income tax. If it had, it is probable – given the purpose of that section, the general exemption of life insurance proceeds from tax by Code § 101, and the lack of tax avoidance – that Congress would have excepted that deemed transfer from taxation. That is, unless Congress was just so paranoid about tax abuse that it would choose to penalize an arrangement in which a foreign trust held a life insurance policy for no other reason than the fact that the trust is foreign.

---

[37] Code § 101(a)(2)(B).
[38] See the following web articles, Rosen, 'Foreign Irrevocable Life Insurance Trusts Can Save Estate and Income Tax' (www.protectyou.com/ILIT-fr.HTML), a version of which was published in the *Journal of Taxation of Investments* (Autumn 1992) Warren, Gorham & Lamont (although Rev Rul 87–61 'did not specifically address the death termination situation ... and no authority exists on this point', putative tax could be avoided by using a domestic trust which migrated post mortem); 'Planning Opportunities for US Citizens Utilizing Foreign Situs Trusts' (www.spectrumcap.com/AlanDocs/FORSITUS.html).
[39] TD 8956, IRB 2001–32, 112 (19 July 2001). On the general principle as to whether termination of grantor trust status at death could be considered a taxable event, the Treasury cited Code § 679(a)(2)(A) (transfers to a foreign trust by reason of death do not cause the transferor to become the grantor/owner) and Code § 6048(a)(3)(A)(ii) (the death of a US grantor of a foreign trust is a reportable event). Code § 679(a)(2)(A) does show that Congress knows how to carve out an exception for transfers at death: in that context the result is that transfers to a foreign trust at death do not make the transferor the grantor/owner of the foreign trust. That section does not evidence some Congressional intent to recognise death as a gains event. In the context of life insurance, the Treasury denied a request to create an exception for life insurance held in a foreign non-grantor trust, referencing the 1997 amendment of Code § 1035(c), which prohibited the tax free exchange of a US policy for a foreign life insurance policy (as if that section somehow has any direct or indirect relevance to the transfer of a domestic (or foreign) policy to a foreign trust.

8.33   Despite these arguments, taxpayers (and their planners) should consider that, because of these final regulations, there could be onerous tax consequences if life insurance is held in a foreign trust at the grantor/insured's death. Further, they should consider that courts will generally (though not always) give deference to regulations, even though they are not 'law'.[40] At 8.55 et seq, the authors offer a number of planning ideas to avoid various intended or unintended applications of these regulations.

e. Grantor's departure from the US

8.34   A foreign trust can also cease to be a grantor trust when the grantor ceases to be a US citizen or income tax resident. This is a result of special rules – discussed in more detail in **CHAPTER 12** – which substantially limit when a non-US person is respected as the trust's grantor/owner.[41] Thus, a trust that was considered a grantor trust while the settlor was still a US taxpayer could cease to be a grantor trust when the settlor ceases to be a US taxpayer.

> **Example**
>
> Walter Bigbucks has created an irrevocable foreign asset protection trust for the benefit of himself, his wife and children. Walter renounces his US citizenship and becomes an income tax resident in another country. Because Walter does not have an absolute right to revoke the trust and because the trust is not held for the sole benefit of himself and/or his wife, Walter ceases to be respected as the grantor/owner after he expatriates.

8.35   The same rule would apply if Walter were not a US citizen but was a US income tax resident. **CHAPTER 9** discusses the income tax residence rules that cause a non-citizen to be subject to US income tax on the same basis as US citizens (as a 'resident alien'). When a resident alien becomes a non resident alien (NRA), his deemed ownership of a trust could terminate and, if the trust were a foreign trust, an immediate US tax could be imposed on the unrealized gain.

> **Example**
>
> Wallace Many-Sterling is a UK national who has lived in the US for a number of years, where he has headed a large a multinational corporation. Wallace had an immigrant visa – a green card – making him taxable in the US as a resident alien. Fearing the pandemic risk in the US of frivolous class action litigation against not only the company but also its directors, Wallace had established a foreign trust for the current benefit of himself and his family. While Walter is a US tax resident, he is taxed as the grantor/owner of the foreign trust. Upon retirement, Wallace gives

---

[40] See Gans, 'Deference and the End of Tax Practice', Real Property Probbate and Trust Journal 731 (2002); Schee and Seado, 'Deference Issues in the Tax Law: Mead Clarified the Chevron Rule – Or Does It?', 96 Journal of Taxation 366 (June 2002).
[41] A non US person will generally only be respected as the trust's owner if he has a power to revoke the trust or, during the settlor's life, the trust is held for his and/or his spouse's sole benefit. Code § 672(f)(2)(A).

8.36 *Gains Tax on Gifts and Bequests*

up his green card and moves back to the UK, where he intends to spend the rest of his days tending his Cotswolds garden. However, when Wallace relinquishes his green card, the trust loses its grantor trust status and Wallace is immediately taxed on any inherent gain.

8.36   The application of Code § 684 to an expatriating citizen or a departing resident alien seems inappropriate. Congress specifically considered imposing an *exit tax* (similar to the tax imposed in Germany, Canada and other countries on departing residents) but rejected that idea in the mid-1990s. Could they have intended Code § 684 to indirectly achieve this result? That seems unlikely. Why, as matter of sound tax policy, impose an exit tax on the inherent gain of foreign trust assets, while not subjecting to tax the inherent gain of assets owned directly by the exiting taxpayer? The answer has to be that there is no sound policy for this result.

8.37   We have already (at **8.20**) commented upon the conflict between the regulations (which treat the US taxpayer has having made a taxable transfer to the trust immediately *prior to* the trust ceasing to be a grantor trust) and Code § 684(b) (which makes a transfer to a grantor trust exempt from tax under this section). It would seem that Code § 684(b) would exempt from tax any transfer that is deemed to be made to this trust while it is still a grantor trust (in this case, while the individual is still a US citizen or income tax resident). On the other hand, if the expatriating citizen or departing resident alien were instead treated as having transferred the appreciated property to the foreign trust immediately *after* departure, then the US tax would arguably be restricted by the limited scope of the anti-expatriation rules.

8.38   The anti-expatriation rules subject an expatriating citizen (Walter) to US tax on the sale of US property for a period of ten years after expatriation.[42] The expatriate is not taxed, however, on the sale of appreciated foreign property. These rules apply to actual sales and exchanges, as well as to other transactions identified by the regulations as transforming the gain from US-sourced to foreign-sourced.[43] Although the Treasury has not yet issued regulations, they have issued Notice 97–19, which provides an example of an expatriate who transferred appreciated US property to a foreign non-grantor trust.[44] That notice concludes that such a transfer would subject the expatriate to tax on the pre-contribution gains.

8.39   Notice 97–19 predated the enactment of Code § 684, yet that Notice arguably continues to have affect in instances not specifically governed by Code § 684. By its terms, Code § 684 applies only to transfers by US taxpayers, and there is nothing in the text of that section or the legislative history that would extend its application to tax-motivated expatriates, even during the ten-year period after expatriation. However, if the principles of Notice 97–19 are valid, a post-expatriation transfer of appreciated *US property* to a foreign non-grantor trust will cause an expatriate to be subject to US tax, not under Code § 684 but under the anti-expatriation rules.

---

[42]   Code § 877(1)(a).
[43]   Code § 877(d)(2)(E).
[44]   1997–10 IRB 1 (Example 8).

8.40 Which brings us back to appreciated property held in a foreign grantor trust upon a US citizen's expatriation. The effect of expatriation is to cause the trust to be converted to a non-grantor trust immediately after expatriation. Thus, the expatriate's transfer arguably occurs the moment *after* he expatriates, not the moment before. If that is the proper analysis, then the expatriate's US tax exposure would be governed by the anti-expatriation rules and Notice 97–19, not the provisions of Code § 684. Accordingly, the expatriate would be subject to US tax only on the gain from appreciated *US property* held in the foreign trust, *but not on the inherent gain on the trust's appreciated foreign property.*

8.41 The anti-expatriation rules also apply to certain long-term green card holders (individuals who have been green card holders for eight of the prior 15 years) who cease to be US income tax residents.[45] Thus, if Wallace were subject to these rules, there is an argument that the anti-expatriation rules – not Code § 684 – would apply to tax him on the inherent gain in US situated property (including stock in US companies) held in the foreign trust, but not the inherent gain on foreign situated property.

8.42 The anti-expatriation rules do not apply to the following three categories of departing resident aliens:

- individuals who had non-immigrant visas;

- individuals who held a green card for less than eight of the prior 15 years; and

- long-term green card holders who qualify for the exception to the anti-expatriation rules and receive a ruling from the IRS that their 'expatriation' was not tax motivated (Wallace might qualify in this category).

8.43 For these departing resident aliens, there is a reasoned argument that they should not be taxed on any inherent appreciation of property held in a foreign grantor trust. Code § 684 should not apply, because any deemed transfer occurring immediately:

(a) *before* departure is exempted by Code § 684(b); and

(b) *after* departure is made when the individual is not a US taxpayer.

Further, since the individual is not subject to the anti-expatriation rules, the principles of Notice 97–19 would not subject him to tax, even on the inherent gain of US property held in the foreign trust.

f. Application of Code § 684 to pre-immigration trusts – a possible Code § 679(a)(4) tax trap?

8.44 The application of Code § 684 to all trusts that cease to be grantor trusts could be particularly harsh for a non-citizen who had set up a foreign trust prior to moving to the US. To understand this issue, we first need to take a quick side tour to the grantor trust rules and Code § 679.

---

[45] Code § 877(e).

8.45   Gains Tax on Gifts and Bequests

8.45   As noted, the grantor trust rules define the many circumstances in which the grantor is taxed as if he were the owner of the underlying trust assets. In this context, the key provision is Code § 679, which generally causes a US taxpayer who transfers property to a foreign trust to be taxed as the trust's owner if the trust has (or could have) US beneficiaries. Historically, this section had only applied to transfers by US taxpayers, and thus, by implication, did not apply to trusts created by non-US persons, even if the trust were funded as the last step in pre-immigration planning. That changed in 1996, when Congress enacted Code § 679(a)(4). This new section is designed to cause a non-US person who creates a foreign trust within five years of becoming a US taxpayer to be taxed as the grantor/owner of that trust if the other requirements of Code § 679 are met. To accomplish this, Code § 679(a)(4) treats the immigrant has having:

> 'transferred to such trust on the residency start date an amount equal to the portion of the trust attributable to the property transferred by such individual to such trust [within five years of the residency start date]'.

There's that pesky 'transfer' concept again. Where did we last hear about transfers and deemed transfers? Oh yeah – Code § 684 and its regulations.

8.46   With that background, now consider the following example.

Example

Two years prior to moving to the US – and without any US tax planning in mind – Wallace formed a UK accumulation and maintenance trust (in English tax and trust parlance, an 'A&M Trust') for the benefit of his four children. Wallace moves to the US with his family. Under Code § 679(a)(4), Wallace is taxed as the grantor/owner of this foreign trust once he becomes a US income tax resident. Does this expose Wallace to tax under Code § 684 when the trust ceases to be a grantor trust (for example, upon his death, his ceasing to be a US resident, or even the trust ceasing to have US beneficiaries)?

8.47   For Code § 684 to apply to this fact pattern, there must first be a *transfer* by a US taxpayer to a foreign trust. Wallace's only *actual* transfer to this foreign trust occurred prior to his becoming a US taxpayer, and clearly Code § 684 would not have applied at that time. But Code § 679(a) also *deems* Wallace to have made a transfer to that trust on his residency start date, that is, the day he becomes a US income tax resident. Could that deemed transfer expose Wallace to the Code § 684 tax when the trust ceases to be a grantor trust? The answer is debatable, and indeed the authors have debated this issue among themselves and with peers (without satisfactory resolution) for months before submitting this chapter to the publishers.

8.48   The argument against the application of Code § 684 in this context is the limited scope of Code § 679(a)(4). By its specific terms, Code § 679(a)(4) only applies for purposes of the grantor trust rules of Code § 679 and the reporting requirements of Code § 6048. At the time Congress extended Code § 679 to certain pre-immigration trusts, the predecessor to Code § 684 (ie Code § 1491) subjected a US taxpayer to a 35% excise tax (or an optional capital gains tax) on transfers to foreign trusts. Yet, Congress did not include Code § 1491 among the limited list of Code provisions to which the Code § 679(a)(4) would apply. A year later when Congress replaced Code § 1491 with Code § 684, Congress had another opportunity to explicitly expand Code § 679(a)(4)'s scope. If Congress had intended for Code § 679(a)(4) to apply for purposes of new Code § 684, it could have crafted Code § 684 – or amended Code § 679(a)(4) – to so provide. Neither happened.

8.49 The argument for application of Code § 684 in this context is the expansive reach of the grantor trust rules. As noted, Code § 679(a)(4) specifically applies for purposes of Code § 679 – that is, for purposes of determining if a foreign trust is considered a grantor trust. If a foreign trust is considered a grantor trust, then the grantor/owner is treated by Code § 671 (and the relevant regulations) as if he owned the underlying trust assets. This treatment has broad and expansive application well beyond the grantor trust rules. For example, the US tax laws exempt from capital gains tax the first $250,000 of gain on the sale of an individual's primary residence.[46] The section 121 regulations make clear that this exemption also applies to a primary residence held in trust that is deemed to be owned by the grantor under the grantor trust rules.[47] The authors believe that the sale of a primary residence held in a foreign trust considered to be a grantor trust by reason of Code § 679(a)(4) would qualify for the Code § 121 exemption, despite the fact that Code § 121 was not among the specific Code sections to which Code § 679(a)(4) specifically applied. Think of the grantor trust rules as a virus, spreading the 'disease' of Code § 679(a)(4) throughout the Code, even to Code § 684. The argument might thus go that, if the immigrant's deemed transfer under Code § 679(a)(4) causes the immigrant to be considered the foreign trust's grantor/owner, then the later termination of the trust's grantor trust status would subject the immigrant to US tax.

8.50 The authors have learned through informal inquiries that the IRS intends to make this second interpretation, however unintended this result might have been when Congress drafted Code §§ 684 and 679(a)(4). This obviously is an issue that warrants monitoring for future legislative, regulatory and judicial attention.

g. Pre-immigration trusts – beyond Code § 679(a)(4)

8.51 There are two other contexts in Code § 684 might apply to certain pre-immigration trusts. The first is the pre-immigration trust established within five years of immigration, but that would not be considered a grantor trust.

> **Example**
>
> Prior to moving to the US, Wallace formed a UK-based trust for the benefit of his UK parents. Wallace moves to the US within five years, but the trust is not considered a grantor trust because it has no US beneficiaries.

8.52 If the trust is not considered a grantor trust because there are no US beneficiaries, is Wallace immediately taxed on any inherent gain when he becomes a US resident? Code § 679(a)(4) does, after all, treat Wallace as if he had transferred

---

[46] Code § 121.
[47] Treas Reg § 1.121–1(c)(3)(i).

8.53 Gains Tax on Gifts and Bequests

the property to the foreign trust upon his residency start date – that is, the first day he becomes a US resident. This just cannot be. To expand Code § 679(a)(4) in this manner would effectively create a highly unusual (and surely inappropriate) *entrance tax*. The authors believe that, if the deemed transfer under Code § 679(a)(4) does not cause the immigrant to be considered the grantor/owner of the foreign trust, the grantor trust rules should not provide a backdoor to the application of Code § 684.

8.53   Second, is the example of a foreign trust created more than five years before the grantor became a US taxpayer, but which is, nonetheless, considered to be a grantor trust under other provisions of the Code.

Example

Ten years before moving to the US, Wallace funded a UK-based irrevocable trust for the benefit of wife and children. Wallace is not respected as the grantor/owner of the trust while he is a non-US person, but is considered the grantor/owner of the trust once he moves to the US (because of his wife's beneficial interest in the trust). Can Code § 684 apply if the trust ceases to be a grantor trust (for example, upon the death of Wallace's wife)?

8.54   The application of Code § 684 to this fact pattern is also problematic. Because this trust was not funded within five years of immigration, there is no deemed 'transfer' to this trust upon Wallace's US residency start date. Without an actual or deemed transfer to this trust while a US taxpayer, it's hard for the authors to see how Code § 684 could apply upon the later termination of the trust's grantor trust status.

5.   Strategies for dealing with Code § 684 exposure

a.   General strategies where appreciated property (or insurance) is held in a foreign grantor trust

8.55   The previous sections discussed a number of ways in which the US grantor/owner of a foreign trust will be taxed on the inherent gain within that trust when the trust's grantor trust status terminates. There are a number of strategies that one might employ to avoid this tax. The strategies would need to be implemented prior to the trust's ceasing to be a grantor trust (including the grantor's death).

(i)   Distribute the appreciated assets to the beneficiaries

8.56   If the taxpayer is concerned about the possible application of Code § 684 upon the termination of a foreign trust's grantor trust status, the trust could always distribute the appreciated assets to any US beneficiary or foreign individual beneficiaries prior to that event. No gain would be realized to the trust on that distribution (and thus no gain attributed to the grantor/owner under the grantor trust rules). If the grantor/owner is also a beneficiary, distribution of appreciated assets to him will also avoid Code § 684. The trick, of course, is timing the distribution, since grantor trust status can terminate for a number of reasons, including the death of the settlor or of the trust's lone US beneficiary.

(ii)   *Sell appreciated assets to the grantor*

8.57   The US grantor/owner might also periodically 'purchase' the appreciated assets from the foreign trust for cash. No tax should be imposed on the grantor or the trustee by reason of that transaction. If the trust only holds cash when grantor trust status terminates, no tax should be imposed under Code § 684.[48] Again, timing is important to ensure that the sale occurs prior to the termination of the foreign trust's grantor trust status.

(iii)   *In the case of irrevocable insurance trust, migrate trust to the US prior to insured's death*

8.58   If possible without affecting other aspects of the planning, the foreign trust might migrate to the US prior to the insured's death. The insurance proceeds could then be collected without any tax exposure under Code § 101. The domestic trust could then migrated back offshore (with cash) without any tax exposure under Code § 684.

(iv)   *Create a US trust with a right to withdraw the insurance proceeds*

8.59   The US grantor/owner could also create a US trust that:

- has a temporary right to withdraw the insurance proceeds from the foreign trust upon the insured's death; and

- folds into the foreign trust after a limited period of time.

8.60   The termination of a foreign irrevocable insurance trust's status as grantor trust will not trigger tax under Code § 684 if the transfer is to a trust deemed owned by any person under the grantor trust rules. A US trust might be formed with the same beneficiaries as the foreign trust (except for the insured). The terms of the foreign trust might be modified to grant the US trust a temporary power to withdraw the insurance proceeds upon the insured's death. This would cause the US trust to be considered the grantor/owner of the insurance proceeds under Code § 678. This would appear to prevent the application of the general rule of Code § 684, since that rule does not apply to a transfer to a foreign trust that is deemed to be owned by any person (which can also include another trust). In addition, this would also appear to avoid the application of the transfer for value rule of Code § 101(a)(2). If the general rule of Code § 684 does not apply, there is no deemed transfer. If there is no deemed transfer, there should be no transfer for value. After a period of time expires (eg 60 days after the insured's death), the terms of the US trust might provide for its assets (including any insurance proceeds withdrawn from the foreign

---

[48]   The only exception would be for currency gains under Code § 988 if the cash is held in non-functional currency.

8.61   *Gains Tax on Gifts and Bequests*

trust and not otherwise distributed to the other trust beneficiaries) to fold back into the foreign trust. The US trust's grantor trust status then terminates, but so what? The only section 684 transfer is of cash, so not tax would be imposed.[49]

(*v*)   *Make the foreign irrevocable insurance trust a partner with the insured*

8.61   Making the foreign trust a partner with the insured in a partnership will not avoid tax under Code § 684 upon the settlor's death. This might not be much of a concern, however, if the value of the policy prior to the settlor's death is lower than the trust's basis in the policy – for example, if the trust holds a group term policy. The real problem, in many instances, will be the possible application of the transfer for value exception to Code § 101(a)(2). Even if the deemed transfer under Code § 684 occasioning the insured's death were considered a transfer for value for purposes of Code § 101(a)(2), it should be relatively easy to structure the foreign trust to fit within an exception to the transfer for value exception. Code § 102(a)(2) does not apply where the transfer for value was to 'the insured, to a partner of the insured, to a partnership in which the insured is a partner, or to a corporation in which the insured is a shareholder or officer'. The only one of these exceptions that would apply in this context is if the trust were a partner of the insured. So, in addition to the irrevocable insurance trust holding the insurance policy, it might be structured to hold, say, a 1% limited partnership interest in a partnership in which the insured is also a partner.

b.   Emigration strategies

8.62   The following strategies might be considered by a US citizen planning to expatriate or a resident alien planning to cease to be a US taxpayer, if that individual is considered the grantor/owner of a foreign trust with appreciated assets.

(*i*)   *Confer power on the settlor (or settlor's spouse) to revoke the trust prior to expatriation*

8.63   A US citizen's expatriation or a resident alien's departure from the US can cause a foreign trust to become a non grantor trust if the departing taxpayer ceases to be respected as the grantor/owner of the trust. One way to avoid that result is if the settlor or the settlor's spouse were to have (or be conferred) a power to revoke the trust prior to the settlor's departure from the US. If that occurred, the trust would continue to be a grantor trust after departure,[50] and no tax should be imposed under Code § 684. Of course, the other tax implications of this strategy (including the US estate tax implications) would need to be considered.

---

[49]   Some advisers take the view that the withdrawal power cannot be timely exercised if coterminous with the settlor's death and hence that it must be a power always in existence. Given the fact that the IRS's deemed transfer 'on death' rule actually occurs before death while the trust is still grantor trust and that the trust automatically continues under § 678 to be a 'Crummey Power' grantor trust at death by virtue of the settlor's death, it would seem sufficient to use the coterminous power.

[50]   Code § 672(f)(2)(A)(i).

(ii) Purchase the appreciated assets

8.64 If Code § 684 were deemed to apply to an expatriating citizen or departing resident alien, then the irony is that this *exit tax* could be easily avoided if the individual – rather than the trust – owned the appreciated assets prior to departure. To do this, the individual could purchase the appreciated assets from the foreign trust prior to departure. No tax would be imposed on this sale (the grantor being treated as having purchased the assets from himself). The trust could later buy back the assets.

(iii) Distribute the trust assets prior to emigration

8.65 There are a number of distribution options to avoid Code § 684 upon the settlor's emigration. The trust assets can be distributed the day before departure to the trust beneficiaries (including the settlor or the settlor's spouse, if either is a beneficiary). If the trustee of the foreign trust has appropriate authority, the trustee might resettle the trust property on another foreign trust in which the settlor would be respected as the grantor/owner after the settlor's departure for the US. For example, if the settlor (or the settlor's wife) were given the power to revoke the trust or were named as the sole beneficiaries of the trust during the settlor's life, the trust would remain a grantor trust after the grantor's departure and thus avoid the immediate application of Code § 684.

c. **Immigration strategies**

8.66 A NRA who had established a foreign trust prior to becoming a US resident should consider the following strategies to avoid Code § 684.

(i) Distribute trust assets prior to immigration

8.67 Appreciated trust property could be distributed to the trust beneficiaries (including the settlor or the settlor's spouse, if beneficiaries) prior to the settlor becoming a US resident. This would avoid any argument about the settlor's being subject to a Code § 684 *entrance tax* (pre-immigration trust created within five years but not otherwise a grantor trust under Code § 684) on entry or a Code § 684 tax applying if and when the trust ceases to be a grantor trust. If the appreciated assets are held by the settlor, at least he can control the realization event and can even depart the US without subjecting those appreciated assets to tax.

(ii) Realize the inherent gain

8.68 The possible impact of Code § 684 to pre-immigration trusts can also be minimized if the foreign trust were to realize any inherent gain in the trust assets prior to the settlor's immigration.

8.69 *Gains Tax on Gifts and Bequests*

B. United Kingdom

1. Introduction

8.69 A UK taxpayer is subject to a capital gains tax (CGT) liability for gains realised on a 'disposal' of assets. Disposals not only occur on open market sales, but also on gifts of assets and on certain other specified occasions. This includes the case where the gift is made to a trust in respect of which the settlor/grantor remains the taxable person under anti-avoidance legislation.[51]

8.70 Special rules apply to gains made by trustees which, depending on the circumstances may be taxable to the trustees, the beneficiaries or the settlor and these are covered separately in **CHAPTER 13**. A detailed consideration of this complex tax is beyond the scope of this book but the following chapters provide an overview of some of the key concepts relevant to gift and succession planning.

8.71 The time of the disposal in the case of a sale is when a binding contract is concluded between the parties. Accordingly, where the contract provides for a later completion of the transaction, it is the date of the contract which is the point of the disposal for CGT.[52] As to the time of a gift, this will have been made on general principles, when the donor has done all that he can as a matter of the relevant local law applicable to the asset, to pass title to it. For example, providing the donee with a stock certificate and a signed stock transfer form in his favour where the gift is of stock in a listed company.[53] Equally, if the donor of a gift makes a binding declaration that he holds as bare trustee for the intended donee, this can be adequate evidence of the title having passed at the date of such declaration.[54]

8.72 It is also possible for there to be a part disposal of an asset and for an asset to be deemed to have been disposed of, for example, in situations when it is destroyed[55] or where assets have become of negligible value.[56]

---

[51] Taxation of Chargeable Gains Act 1992 (TCGA 1992), s 70. This long-standing principle is currently under review. The Inland Revenue discussion paper of 17 December 2003, 'Modernising the Tax System for Trusts', suggested adopting a system closer to that of the US in cases where the settlor or his spouse can benefit under the terms of the trust. However in the further consultation paper issued on 13 August 2004 this possibility appears now to have been rejected in favour of retaining the existing rule.
[52] Unless the contract is one which subject to a condition precedent, where the fulfilment of the condition marks the disposal point. TCGA 1992, s 28.
[53] As to the general principle, see *Re Rose [1952] 1 All ER 1217* where the settlor transferred shares to trustees by voluntary deed, the registration of the transfer being effected some time later. The date of the deed was held to be the effective date of transfer as the settlor had done everything necessary at that stage. Providing a stock certificate and the completed transfer form is normally acceptable in the UK as evidencing gifts of shares. However, note that in the US it is generally registration of the shares in the donee's name which denotes the time of irrevocable transfer.
[54] This can be an effective way of achieving a timely disposal of assets, where this is important, since the gift is complete at the moment of the declaration of trust. The trustee (being the donor) will already have title to the intended trust assets and, therefore, the trust will be completely constituted at that time, only the capacity in which he holds the assets having changed. Care needs to be taken in formulating the trust to ensure that the intentions are clear. *Richards v Delbridge (1874) LR 18 Eq 11.*
[55] TCGA 1992, s 24(1).
[56] TCGA 1992, s 24(2).

8.73 Special provisions exist to preclude gains arising in some circumstances. For example, this can apply to shareholders in certain cases where companies undertake a reorganisation of their share capital (eg a bonus or rights issue or reduction of share capital) in the normal course of their business or, for example, where companies are subject to a take-over and new shares or securities are issued in exchange for the original holding.[57] Where this occurs, provided the transactions are being undertaken made for bona fide commercial reasons (without a main tax avoidance motive) the new holding is normally treated as if it were the original holding for the purposes of computing the gains or losses on a later disposal.

8.74 Equally, special provisions exist to deem gains to arise in some situations where disposals are made by others. For example, a UK domiciled individual who is also UK resident or ordinarily resident, and is a shareholder in a non-UK resident company, may be attributed with a proportion of the gains made by that company. This applies in the case of a company which would have been regarded as a 'close company', if it had been UK resident.[58] It also applies whether or not the shareholder receives a distribution out of its assets (eg by way of dividend or on liquidation), but if he does so then the tax can be credited against such a distribution if it occurs within a specified period.[59]

8.75 A person is also taxed in some circumstances where gains are made by the trustees of UK resident or non-UK resident trusts which he has created.[60] See **CHAPTER 13**.

8.76 No filing requirement now exists for individuals, personal representatives or trustees where the proceeds of disposal do not exceed four times the individual annual exemption (ie £32,800 for 2004/05) provided that the gain made does not exceed the annual exemption (£8,200 for individuals and up to £4,100 for trustees for 2004/05) or no claim is being made for relief for losses against gains and there is no liability after the application of taper relief (see **CHAPTER 10**). For individual taxpayers who ultimately have chargeable gains and whose income exceeds the lower and basic rate bands (£31,400 for 2004/05), the top rate is, in principle, 40%,

---

[57] An acceptable exchange for this purpose must result in the new company holding more than 25% of the ordinary shares, or more than 50% of the voting rights, of the original company. Alternatively, it must have been pursuant to a general offer intended to secure control of the original company and made to all of its shareholders (or a specific class). TCGA 1992, s 135.

[58] TCGA 1992, s 13. A close company is one in the control of five or fewer participators or participators who are directors. It should be noted that provisions exist to apportion through holding companies to the ultimate shareholder/participators, including apportionment up to trustees of a non-UK resident trust and onwards to settlors or beneficiaries under the relevant anti avoidance legislation. See **CHAPTER 13**.

[59] The specified period is the *earlier* of:
 (a) three years from the end of the period of account when the gain arose; *or*
 (b) four years from the date when the gain was realised.
 If distribution does not occur in this timeframe, then the tax paid by the participator is allowable expenditure against the proceeds on disposal of his interest in the company.

[60] TCGA 1992, s 77 as regards UK resident trusts from which he or his spouse may benefit and s 86 as regards UK domiciled settlors of non-UK resident trusts from which he, his spouse, his children or grandchildren, and certain family-controlled companies can benefit.

8.77 *Gains Tax on Gifts and Bequests*

although the overall effective rate is reduced by the application of a variety of exemptions and reliefs. Trustees also pay CGT at 40%.[61]

8.77 To calculate the gain on an asset disposal, the following may be set against the proceeds (actual or deemed) of disposal:

- the cost basis – being the acquisition cost or the deemed market value at acquisition, depending on the circumstances (see **CHAPTER 11**);
- incidental costs of acquisition;
- expenditure incurred to enhance the value of the asset;
- expenditure incurred to establish or defend title to the asset; and
- costs incurred in making the disposal.

Such costs include agent's/surveyor's/valuer's fees, auctioneer's fees, accountancy/legal fees, costs of transfer or conveyance, stamp duty, advertising costs, etc. Capital costs of repairing an asset (such as re-roofing a house or rebuilding a wall, though not the regular costs of annual maintenance and repair) and making improvements (such as building an extension) are allowable deductions.

8.78 Losses may also be available to further offset any potential gains, as well as special deductions, exclusions and reliefs (see **CHAPTER 10**). Losses are normally available to offset current gains and may also be carried forward to offset future gains, provided they have been claimed by filing a return with the Inland Revenue.[62] Allowable losses which arise on an asset disposal, can be deducted from gains on the disposal of other assets, and are generally computed in the same way as chargeable gains, although indexation relief (applicable to enhance the cost basis of assets to 5 April 1998 in order to offset inflationary gains – see **CHAPTER 10**) cannot be used to create a loss. If indexing the costs attributable to assets, of itself turns a gain into a loss, the indexation is limited to the amount necessary to eliminate the gain.[63] Losses computed in the normal way, which are not offset against gains made in the same year, can be carried forward indefinitely and offset against future gains on other assets.[64]

---

[61] Various differential rates have applied to discretionary trusts and interest in possession trusts, although in recent years these have been aligned. From 6 April 2004 the CGT rate applicable to all trusts is 40%. Finance Act 2004, s 29.

[62] TCGA 1992, s 2(2). The claim must be notified within five years of the 31 January filing deadline applicable to the tax year in which the losses arose. For example, losses which arose on 31 August 2004 (tax year 2004/05) would need to be notified within five years of the filing deadline for that year (31 January 2006), which is 31 January 2011. Although the claim must be made within this timeframe, the losses do not have to be used within it.

[63] This rule applies from 30 November 1993, prior to which time it was possible to index losses.

[64] In certain, very limited, circumstances capital losses can be carried back. For example, certain losses realised prior to death, but in the same tax year, can be carried back and set against gains in the three tax years preceding that in which the death occurred. Also, where an asset is disposed of and an element of unascertainable deferred consideration depends on certain future events, the deferred consideration is an asset which has to be valued. If this valuation proves to have been too high, a loss may arise when the deferred consideration is ultimately paid. From 10 April 2003 an election may be made on such disposals to carry back the loss to chargeable gains made in the earlier year. Furthermore, a loss made on the disposal of *newly issued* shares for which the taxpayer

8.79 When computing chargeable gains, losses are deducted before taper relief is applied, which effectively results in tapering the losses as well, although they are applied in an order that otherwise gives the donor the greatest benefit from taper relief.[65] The application of losses against gains is nevertheless restricted, to ensure that the annual exemption can be used in full.

8.80 However, any loss on a disposal to a 'connected' person is deductible only from chargeable gains arising on other disposals to the same person (while he is still connected).[66] An individual is considered connected with his spouse and all of his own relatives (and their spouses) and with those of his spouse.[67] These provisions also apply to business partners and to certain companies. A trustee of a settlement is deemed connected with the settlor and any person connected with the settlor.[68]

8.81 As can be seen, in most instances of estate planning the CGT disposal will be between connected parties.

8.82 As noted above, the gain realised on making a gift is the gain which would have arisen on a deemed disposal of the asset at its open market value.[69] The gain is computed as the difference between the deemed proceeds and the tax-cost basis, subject to an uplift of the cost basis to account for inflationary gains (indexation relief) for periods of ownership up to 5 April 1998. With effect from that date, the amount of gain chargeable to CGT is reduced by 'taper relief'.[70] The amount of this relief depends on the nature of the asset (ie whether it is a business asset or not) and how long (in complete years) the asset has been held between 6 April 1998 (or the date of acquisition if later) and the date of the gift.[71]

8.83 It is, therefore, possible that both IHT and CGT can arise in relation to the same gift. For example, a gift may give rise to a chargeable gain and if it is a potentially exempt transfer, it may also later become subject to IHT on the death of the donor within seven years. In making any lifetime gift with a view to saving IHT, it is essential to consider any offsetting exposure that may arise to CGT, since an asset received instead as a bequest on a death, will normally benefit from a tax-free uplift in cost basis.[72] Where a gift has been made and the donor fails to pay the tax within 12 months of the due date, within a further period of 12 months thereafter,

---

had subscribed, can be offset against income taxes for the year of disposal or the preceding year, if the appropriate election is made to claim the relief.

[65] TCGA 1992, s 2A(1) and (6).
[66] TCGA 1992, s 18(3).
[67] TCGA 1992, s 286.
[68] See Inland Revenue Interpretation RI 38, which confirms the Inland Revenue's view that the trustees are considered to be connected with the settlor at the time of the initial transfer into trust and also that once the settlor is dead, the connection between the beneficiaries and the trustees ceases. Since the link between all of the connected parties in this case is the settlor, the connection ceases after his death.
[69] TCGA 1992, s 17.
[70] TCGA 1992, s 2A.
[71] For assets already held at 17 March 1998, the period is enhanced by a further 'bonus' year. However, this ceased to apply to the more generous business asset taper relief with effect from 6 April 2000. See **CHAPTER 10**.
[72] TCGA 1992, s 62. See also **CHAPTER 11**.

8.83 *Gains Tax on Gifts and Bequests*

the donee (who then has a statutory right of recovery against the donor or his personal representatives) can be assessed to the tax in the name of the donor.[73]

---

[73] TCGA 1992, s 282.

Chapter 9

Capital Gains Taxation – Residents

A. United States

1. Introduction

9.1 US citizens wherever resident and foreign nationals (aliens) who are US income tax residents are subject to US income tax on their worldwide income and gains. By its terms, Code § 684 (analyzed in CHAPTER 8) applies only to deemed gains resulting from transfers by 'US persons', which is generally defined in the US Tax Code as (i) US citizens, (ii) non citizens (aliens) who are considered to be US income tax residents, and (iii) US entities. Thus, § 684 would not apply to transfers by non-resident aliens (NRAs) and foreign entities.

2. Individuals

9.2 Since 1985, the US has determined a person's income tax residence based on two objective tests:

- a 'green card' test; and
- a 'substantial presence' test.[1]

Residence results if either test is met. Special rules apply in the first and last year of residence.[2]

9.3 Before examining the above two tests, it is important to note that the determination of an individual's income tax residence is wholly independent of the individual's transfer tax residence. As previously discussed in CHAPTER 2, the latter is based on the individual's domicile. (The different use of the term 'resident' for income and transfer tax purposes is unfortunate – and explains the authors' attempt to distinguish between NRAs and non-domiciled aliens (NDAs).) It is entirely possible for a person to be temporarily resident in the US for income tax purposes, while maintaining his domicile in some other country. Conversely, it is also possible (although much less likely) that a person will have retained his US domicile status (under the US rule in which a domicile of choice is retained until a new domicile of choice is established) even after relinquishing his income tax residency status (eg his US 'green card').

---

[1] Code § 7701(b).
[2] Code § 7701(b)(2).

9.4 *Capital Gains Taxation – Residents*

a. Green card test

9.4 The green card test is absolute: an individual is considered a US income tax resident if he holds an immigrant visa (the so-called 'green card'). The 'price' a person pays for the *right* to permanently reside in the US is the exposure to US taxation on the individual's worldwide income.

9.5 Once the individual acquires a green card, he will remain a US income tax resident even if he technically loses his rights under the immigration laws to permanent residence (for example, by moving from the US for many years without taking steps to retain green card privileges). Under relevant regulations, resident status continues until the green card 'is rescinded or administratively or judicially determined to have been abandoned'.[3] To terminate income tax residence, a green cardholder should affirmatively relinquish the green card. The authors have seen numerous cases in which a green card holder leaves the US, never intending to return, but fails to formally relinquish the green card.[4] In those instances, the individual will continue to have US income tax exposure, including exposure to tax under Code § 684.[5] The only exception would be if the individual becomes a resident of an OECD treaty country and, under the relevant tie-breaker provisions, would be treated as a resident of that other country.

b. Substantial presence test

9.6 The 'substantial presence' test uses a mathematical formula based on the number of days an individual is physically present in the US during the calendar year. The magic number is 183. An individual will be considered an income tax resident if he or she is physically present in the US for 183 days during the year – determined however under a three-year weighted average test of US presence days. Under this test, if the individual is present in the US *at least 31 days during the current year*, he or she will be considered a US resident if the three-year total is at least 183 days, counting each day of US presence in the current year in full, each day of the preceding year as one-third of a day, and each day of the second preceding year as one-sixth of day.[6]

> **Example**
> Anthony Blare, a UK national, spends 90 days in the US during 2004 after having spent 150 days vacationing in the US during both 2003 and

---

[3] Treas Reg § 301.7701(b)-1(b)(1).
[4] Note that under current State Department practice, the green card can be relinquished by a NRA by mailing it to the US Embassy, Grosvenor Square, London W1A 1AE together with Form I-407.
[5] If a non-resident green card holder uses it to return to the US, INS (now a part of Homeland Security) may request the individual to relinquish his green card; however, legally, the authors understand that the Government's only remedy to recover the card is to commence deportation proceedings.
[6] Code § 7701(b)(3)(A). For this purpose, any portion of a day spent in the US counts as a whole day. However, in computing the three-year total, one must add the fractional portions of days resulting from multiplying the days spent in the US during the prior two years by one-third and one-sixth. For example, 100 days spent in the US during each of the prior two years counts as 33.333 days and 16.667 days towards the 183-day limit.

United States **9.10**

2002. Tony would not be considered a US income tax resident for 2004, because his three-year adjusted total is only 165, computed as follows:

Year	Actual days	Adjusted days
2004	90	90
2003	150	50
2002	150	25
	Total:	**165**

9.7 An alien who is, on average, present in the US for 122 days or more during each year of a three-year period will be considered a resident for US income tax purposes in the third year. Unlike the UK rules, part days of US presence count as a full day (unless in continuous transit from and to a foreign country).

9.8 An individual who is US resident under the 183-day, three-year weighted average test, can nonetheless be considered non-resident if he is not present in the US for more than 182 actual days of US presence during the current year *and* he can establish that he has a 'tax home' with a 'closer connection' to one or more foreign countries.[7]

9.9 There are also a number of exemptions by which certain individuals will not be considered physically present in the US for purposes of the substantial presence test. For example, certain students or scholars (F or J visa holders), persons who come to the US for medical treatment, as well as diplomatic staff and employees of certain international organizations such as the World Bank or the United Nations (A visa holders) will not have their US days counted against the 183-day test.[8]

c. **Capital gains 'trap'**

9.10 A capital gains 'trap for the unwary' lurks for NRAs who spend substantial time in the US. As noted at **9.9**, many persons (including a number of wealthy foreign nationals) who spend considerable time in the US might still be considered NRAs for income tax purposes because of the statutory exemptions. NRAs who are physically present in the US for at least 183 actual days during the calendar year are

---

[7] Code § 7701(b)(3)(B). Taxpayers must file a timely return (Form 8840) with the IRS's Philadelphia office to claim this exception. However, see Bissell, BNA Tax Management Portfolio 907–1st, *US Income Taxation of Non-Resident Aliens*, at footnote 21:
   'There is no basis whatsoever in Section 7701(b) for classifying an alien as either resident or non-resident simply because he has or has not filed a particular form with the IRS'.
The exception is not available if during the year the person has applied for a green card (Code § 7701(b)(3)(C)). However, a green card holder who is resident in a country with which the US has an OECD-patterned bilateral income tax treaty may claim to be a foreign resident under the tie-breaker provisions of the treaty (Article 4). Treas Reg § 301.7701–7 again predicates this claim on the timely filing of a form (8833). Bissell's comment is relevant for those wishing to undertake the risk of litigating with the IRS.

[8] Code § 7701(b)(5).

9.11 Capital Gains Taxation – Residents

nonetheless subject to a 30% tax on gains derived from US sources.[9] Under the sourcing rules, gains from the sale of personal property are sourced in or outside the US depending on the residence of the taxpayer.[10] However (now here is the trap), the sourcing rules include a special definition to determine if the taxpayer is a US resident for the purposes of taxing him or her on capital gains. Under this special definition, an individual who is otherwise considered a NRA for US income tax purposes can be considered a US resident for purposes of the capital gains sourcing rule if the individual has a 'tax home' (principal place of residence) in the US.[11]

9.11 Many individuals who are considered NRAs because of the statutory exemptions will be considered to have a tax home in the US. As a result, if they are physically present in the US for at least 183 days during the calendar year, they will be subject to a 30% tax on gains derived from US sources. This will include gains from the sale of all personal property (including tangible personal property such as works of art and intangible personal property such stocks and bonds). This includes personal property that one would typically consider as situated outside the US.

Example

Debbie Diplomat, a NRA working at the UN, is physically present in the US for at least 183 days during 2004. During that year, she sells at a gain:

(a) a Picasso and some family jewels given to her years ago by her mother and held by Debbie outside the US;

(b) stock in Diplomat Investments GmbH, a non-US company; and

(c) a beach house in Bermuda.

If Debbie has a tax home in the US, her gain from the sale of the art, jewelry and stock (but not the foreign real estate) would be subject to a 30% US tax.

This trap is easily avoided through an offshore holding structure – if the taxpayer and her advisors are aware of it in advance.

9.12 What, then, are the implications of this tax trap to Code § 684? Will a NRA who is physically present in the US for more than 183 days and who has a tax home in the US be subject to US tax on the transfer of appreciated personal property to a foreign non-grantor trust? As discussed in more detail in **CHAPTER 12**, NRAs are respected as the grantor/owner of trusts (domestic or foreign) in much more limited circumstances than US citizens and residents. Therefore, there is a greater likelihood that a foreign trust created by a NRA will be considered a non-grantor trust. Again, if that is the case, will tax be imposed under Code § 684 when the NRA with a US tax home transfers appreciated personal property to such a trust? From a logical perspective, it would seem like this particular NRA should be taxed under Code § 684, since a direct sale by this NRA would be taxed. However, Code § 684 on its face only applies to transfers by US persons – meaning citizens and residents.

---

[9] Code § 871(a)(2).
[10] Code § 865(a).
[11] Code § 865(g)(1)(A)(i)(II).

Importantly, Code § 684 does not incorporate or include the special 183-day, tax-home residence rules that create the tax trap for direct sales. Thus, Code § 684 would not apply.

9.13 Stated another way, a transfer to a foreign non-grantor trust would generally not be a capital gains realisation event, but for Code § 684. That section only applies to transfers by US persons (citizens and residents) and thus does not apply to transfers by NRAs. There is no exception in Code § 684 for NRAs that are physically present in the US for at least 183 days and who have a tax home in the US. Thus, because a NRA who transfers appreciated personal property to a foreign non-grantor trust will not be treated by Code § 684 as having sold that property, the general rule – that a gift of appreciated property to a trust is not a gain realization event – would apply. As a result, since there is no gain realized on the gift, the special sourcing rules discussed at **9.10** should never apply to subject that transfer to a 30% US tax.

3. Entities

9.14 Code § 684 also applies to entities that are included in the general definition of 'US persons' including domestic partnerships, corporations, estates and trusts.[12] **CHAPTER 12** at **12.9** et seq provides a detailed discussion of rules for determining whether a trust is considered domestic or foreign.

B. United Kingdom

1. Introduction

9.15 Like in the US, there is a significant difference in the rules that determine a person's potential exposure to UK IHT and CGT. In the UK, an individual's domicile generally determines the scope of his exposure to IHT while his potential exposure to CGT is fundamentally linked to residence.[13]

9.16 The liability of an individual to capital gains tax is governed by their UK resident or ordinarily resident status[14] although, as regards non-UK sited assets, their domicile status can be relevant as well.[15] The residence rules are not generally found in the tax code itself but have been developed over the years through Inland Revenue practice and case law. These are summarised in the Inland Revenue publication IR20, however, the rules on residence and domicile are currently under

---

[12] Code § 7701(a)(30).
[13] TCGA 1992, s 10. As an exception to the general rule, non-UK residents can also be subject to capital gains tax, however, on UK sited trading activities conducted through a UK branch or agency.
[14] TCGA. 1992, s 2.
[15] See **CHAPTER 2**.

9.17 *Capital Gains Taxation – Residents*

review with a view to creating a statutory code.[16] Special capital gains tax rules exist in the case of certain persons who are temporarily non-UK resident.[17]

2. Individuals

a. Residence

9.17 UK residence is determined by reference to two alternative tests; a mathematical 183-day test of UK presence or a habitual presence (broadly, 91 days or more per year on average over four years). The Inland Revenue divides taxpayers into two categories of person. Those who are short-term visitors to the UK, present for limited periods and who do not have an intention to remain for an extended period, and those who come on a longer-term basis who intend to stay indefinitely or over a period of several years.

9.18 A person physically present in the UK for 183 days or more in the tax year (6 April to the following 5 April) will always be regarded as UK tax resident. Additionally, a person visiting the UK regularly over a number of tax years, for an average of 91 days or more taken over a four-year period, will also be regarded as tax resident in the UK. In the latter case, the taxpayer's intention has an impact on when he becomes UK tax resident. If on arrival in the UK it is his intention to spend 91 days or more in the UK over the next four years, he will be regarded as UK tax resident from 6 April of the year in which he arrives. However, if he has no such intention but, in fact, after four years he does satisfy this test, then he is UK tax resident from the beginning of his fifth tax year of UK presence. If, having come with no such intention, he changes his mind during the four-year period, he becomes UK tax resident from the beginning of the tax year in which he makes that decision.[18]

9.19 In addition to the 183-day rule, persons who come to the UK intending to be present for two years or more for a particular purpose (eg employment in the UK), are treated as longer-term visitors and are resident here from the outset. The same applies to persons who, on arrival already own UK accommodation (or have a lease of three or more years), or buy (or lease over three or more years) accommodation during the year of arrival.

9.20 Non-UK residents are not subject to UK capital gains tax on the disposal of any assets, with only two exceptions:

- trading assets held by a UK branch or agency; and
- certain gains realised by temporary non-UK residents, discussed at **9.30**.

---

[16] 'Reviewing the residence and domicile rules as they affect the taxation of individuals: a background paper' – April 2003.
[17] TCGA 1992, s 10A.
[18] Prior to 6 April 1993, a person with available accommodation in the UK was regarded as UK tax resident if he came to the UK, irrespective of the length of the visit, however, this rule no longer applies.

Thus, unlike many countries, the UK does not tax gains of non-residents from the disposition of UK real property, unless that property is used in a UK trade conducted through a UK branch or agency. Accordingly, a non-UK resident individual's sale of a UK residential property will not be taxable and, similarly, a non-UK resident trust's sale of such property will not be taxable to the trustees (nor to the settlor even if he is UK resident, provided that he is also not UK domiciled).

9.21 The residence rules apply for a whole tax year, so that arrival mid-year means a person is technically resident from the previous 6 April. However, by Extra Statutory Concession, the Inland Revenue splits the tax year in certain cases.[19] Where a person comes to the UK permanently or for two or more years, he is treated as resident from the date of his arrival and when a person having been resident longer term in the UK leaves the UK permanently or for three or more years, he is treated as non-UK resident from the day following the date of his departure. In neither case is the person ordinarily resident (see **9.24**) in the UK either before his arrival or after his departure.

9.22 The concession is also extended to situations where a person leaves the UK to take up full time employment[20] abroad in circumstances where both his absence and the employment cover a complete tax year and provided he neither breaches the 183-day rule nor the 91-day rule.

9.23 In counting the number of days for the above purposes, days of arrival and departure are ignored so, for example, a person arriving on a Monday morning and leaving on a Friday evening will have spent three days in the UK. Days of presence in the UK which are beyond a person's control (eg through illness) are also ignored for this purpose.

b. Ordinary residence

9.24 Ordinary residence is a concept denoting habitual presence and hence greater permanence than mere residence. The rules applicable to ordinarily resident status are the same as those which apply to the 91-day test noted above in the case of short-term visitors.

9.25 For longer-term visitors, ordinary residence begins on the date of arrival if it is clear that a person intends to spend three years or more in the UK or if he does not at the outset, but later changes his mind in that tax year. The same applies to persons who, on arrival already own UK accommodation (or have a lease of three or more years), or buy (or lease over three or more years) accommodation during the

---

[19] ESC A11, although it should be noted that the split year concession can never apply to trustees in determining the residence status of a trust. See **CHAPTER 13**.
[20] See IR20, para 2.5. The Inland Revenue generally expects to see the same number of standard hours worked as in a typical UK working week depending on the nature of the job and local conditions and practices. Several part-time jobs can qualify if in aggregate they are equivalent to a full time job.

year of arrival. If he changes his mind at a later date he is ordinarily resident from the beginning of the tax year in which he changes his mind or acquires such accommodation.[21]

9.26 In addition to being resident and ordinarily resident, a person can be resident but not ordinarily resident (for example, if he is in the UK for 183 days in a single tax year) or ordinarily resident but not resident (for example, where a person is normally resident in the UK but has a prolonged absence from the UK, for example on holiday, and he does not come to the UK at any time during a complete tax year).

c. Domicile

9.27 UK residents, or persons who are ordinarily resident in the UK, are subject to capital gains tax on worldwide gains realised in the UK tax year on an arising basis, if they are also UK domiciled. No concept of 'deemed' domicile exists for the purposes of this tax as it does for inheritance tax and, therefore, it is the general legal principles of domicile which will apply.

9.28 Non-UK domiciliaries who are UK resident or ordinarily resident, are exposed to capital gains tax on gains from the disposal of foreign situs assets, only if and when they are received in the UK.[22] This is a broadly framed provision, however, which taxes amounts 'paid, used or enjoyed in or in any manner or form transmitted or brought to the UK'. Even where the proceeds of disposal may not have been remitted to the UK, care therefore needs to be taken to avoid indirect enjoyment of such gains.

9.29 The situs rules for inheritance tax and capital gains tax differ somewhat, the former being derived from the general common law and the latter set out in statute.[23] The following list outlines the capital gains tax position on situs of assets.

Kinds of Property	Considered situated in the UK for capital gains tax purposes
Rights and interests in real estate located:	
• in the UK	Yes
• outside the UK	No
Rights and interests in tangible movables physically located:	
• in the UK	Yes

---

[21] If a person has such accommodation but, in fact, gives it up and leaves within the three-year period, the taxpayer can retrospectively be treated as not ordinarily resident, if it is to his advantage.
[22] TCGA 1992, s 12.
[23] TCGA 1992, s 275.

United Kingdom **9.29**

Kinds of Property	Considered situated in the UK for capital gains tax purposes
• outside the UK	No
Debts (whether secured or unsecured) the creditors of which are resident in the UK	Yes
Shares/securities issued by a UK municipal/government authority	Yes
Shares/securities issued by an overseas municipal/government authority	No
Registered shares (other than above) registered[24]	
• in the UK	Yes
• outside the UK	No
Ships/aircraft (or rights over such assets) located in the UK	
• owned by a UK resident	Yes
• owned by a non-UK resident	No
Goodwill of a business:	
• carried on in the UK	Yes
• carried on outside the UK	No
Patents, trademarks, registered designs:	
• registered in the UK	Yes
• registered outside the UK	No
Rights/licences to use patents, etc:	
• exercisable in the UK	Yes
• exercisable outside the UK	No
Judgement debts:	
• recorded in the UK	Yes
• recorded outside the UK	No
Non-sterling balances at UK sited branches of bank standing to the credit of a non-UK domiciliary:	
• who is a UK resident	Yes
• who is not a UK resident	No

---

[24] TCGA 1992, s 275(e) (shares registered on more than one register are deemed situated where the principal register is located).

9.30 *Capital Gains Taxation – Residents*

d. Temporary non-residents

9.30 Special rules apply to certain individuals who are temporarily non-UK resident.[25] Individuals who were UK resident or ordinarily resident in any part of at least four out of the seven tax years preceding their year of departure from the UK, will be taxable on certain gains realised during their period of absence unless this period (throughout the whole of which they must be neither UK resident nor ordinarily resident) lasts five or more complete UK tax years.

> **Example**
>
> Assume a person leaves the UK on 30 April 2003 and arrives back on 30 May 2008. The years of absence throughout which he has not been UK resident and which therefore qualify are 2004/05, 2005/06, 2006/07 and 2007/08. Therefore, despite the fact he has been absent for five *calendar* years he has only been absent throughout four *tax* years. All relevant disposals of property in that period will therefore be taxable in the UK. To avoid the problem he would have to remain out of the UK until 6 April 2009.

9.31 Gains are only caught by these rules on disposals of assets which were owned at the time of departure, but not those which were acquired during the period of absence.[26] The latter is subject to certain caveats which seek to counter avoidance strategies.[27]

9.32 The tax charge is imposed as if any gains (or, if appropriate, losses) had accrued in the tax year of return to the UK.[28] Gains and losses made in the year of departure and return are also caught under the general rules and the concession mentioned above as to the split year of residence is disapplied in these cases.

3. *Personal representatives and trustees*

9.33 A lifetime disposal of assets (whether by sale or gift) may give rise to a chargeable gain or allowable loss as noted in **CHAPTER 8**. However, unrealised appreciation in assets owned outright at the date of death (or by a trust of which the

---

[25] The rules took effect from 17 March 1998.
[26] TCGA 1992, s 10A.
[27] Property acquired after departure will still be caught unless:
- it was not received from a person in a transaction treated as giving rise to neither a gain, nor a loss (e g a gift between husband and wife);
- the asset is not an interest in or arising under a settlement; and
- there was no roll over of cost basis on acquisition pursuant to various roll over and hold over reliefs. TCGA 1992, s 10A(3).

[28] TCGA 1992, s 10A(2). This provision does not, however, override any relevant treaty relief (s 10A(10)). Therefore, residence in a country with which the UK has a suitable treaty that taxes gains only in the country of residence and that has no remittance limitation (e g Switzerland) can, to a large extent, avoid the application of this provision to non-trust gains. In the case of trust gains taxed under the anti avoidance provisions, difficulties lie in the fact that the non-resident taxpayer is generally not the 'alienator' for treaty purposes.

United Kingdom **9.38**

decedent was life tenant) are generally not subject to capital gains tax because of the cost basis adjustment that occurs upon death.[29]

9.34 The personal representatives of a deceased and trustees of a settlement are also subject to capital gains tax. The capital gains tax treatment of trusts is highly complex and an overview is provided separately in **CHAPTER 13**.

9.35 As to personal representatives, they will be deemed to acquire the deceased's assets at their market value at the date of death without tax charge or allowable loss arising.[30]

9.36 If the estate is also liable to inheritance tax the same value as is used for that tax will be used for capital gains tax purposes.[31] Nor is there any capital gains tax charge if the personal representatives later transfer the asset in specie to the relevant legatee (including any trustees of testamentary trusts who take in their capacity as legatees). The latter takes the asset at its market value at the date of death.[32]

9.37 If the personal representatives sell an asset in the course of administering the estate, the usual capital gains tax consequences follow from the disposal but they are given the same annual exemption as would have been available to the deceased in the tax year of death and for the two tax years following.[33] They are also able to dispose, free of capital gains tax, of any property previously used as the deceased's principal private residence, where it was previously and continued thereafter to be occupied by persons either entitled to the proceeds absolutely, or for life under a trust.[34] Subject to this, the tax rate applicable with effect from 6 April 2004 is 40%.[35]

9.38 A specific provision allows certain post mortem rearrangements to be made by the original legatees without the usual capital gains tax consequences of a lifetime gift.[36] This is similar to the relevant provision for inheritance tax.[37] Within two years of a person's death, the dispositions made by a will or under the laws of intestacy or otherwise (eg by a jointly held asset accruing automatically to the survivor) can be varied by the original recipients (by a deed of variation) or disclaimed and the substituted gifts are treated as if the deceased had made them so that the substituted

---

[29] TCGA 1992, s 62. However, see TCGA 1992, s 74 which excludes from the tax-free uplift any gains which had previously been held over under TCGA 1992, s 165 or s 260 on the transfer into settlement.
[30] Where substantial losses exist and pre-death planning is a practical option, it may be worth making a sale prior to the date of death to crystallise such losses. Losses arising in the year of death which cannot be set against gains arising in the same year can be set against gains realised in the three tax years prior to that in which the death occurs. TCGA 1992, s 62(2). Certain deemed gains arising under specified anti-avoidance legislation cannot, however, be offset.
[31] TCGA 1992, s 274.
[32] No CGT charge arises on gifts made by the deceased prior to, but in contemplation of, his imminent death (*donatio mortis causa*). TCGA 1992, s 62(5). The donee is treated as if he were a legatee on death.
[33] £7,900 for 2003/04 and £8,200 for 2004/05.
[34] ESC D5 and TCGA 1992, s 225A as amended by FA 2004, s 117 and Sch 22.
[35] TCGA 1992, s 4(1AA) and FA 2004, s 29.
[36] TGCA 1992, s 62(6).
[37] IHTA 1984, s 142.

9.39 beneficiary will then take the assets at their date of death value. The provisions apply if the instrument effecting the variation or disclaimer makes an express statement to that effect.

9.39 For all other purposes the varying or disclaiming beneficiary will be treated as the person making the gift. So, for example, if the gift is redirected by a parent onto trusts for his children he will be regarded as the settlor for the purposes of the income tax and capital gains tax legislation applicable to the settlement itself and, in particular, any relevant anti-avoidance provisions.[38] Even so, the ability to redirect unwanted inheritances is a useful opportunity for tax-effective giving for inheritance tax purposes, without capital gains tax implication on making the gift. The 'look back' provision is not mandatory in either the case of inheritance tax or capital gains tax and it may be that a decision is taken to apply that treatment for one tax but not the other.

9.40 As in the case of trustees, changes in the identity of individual personal representatives are ignored as they are treated as a single and continuing body of persons. For the purposes of establishing their exposure to capital gains tax, they are also treated as having the same domicile, residence and ordinary residence status as the deceased, at the date of his death.[39]

---

[38] *Marshall v Kerr [1994] STC 638*. Whilst this is true for capital gains tax, it is not true for inheritance tax and the deceased is treated as the donor for all inheritance tax purposes. This is useful in the case of a non-UK domiciled settlor where use of this strategy can retrospectively achieve excluded property status for a settlement. See **CHAPTER 6**.

[39] TCGA 1992, s 62(3). This is in contrast with the position for income tax purposes which is governed by FA 1989, s 111.

Chapter 10

Capital Gains Deductions and Exclusions

A. United States

10.1 As discussed in **CHAPTER 8** and **CHAPTER 11**, taxable gains are generally limited to sales and exchanges for value. Except for limited exceptions (most notably, the section 684 tax for transfers to foreign, non-grantor trusts), there is no taxation of gains on a gratuitous transfer, including contributions to, or distributions from, trusts. See **CHAPTER 11** for tax basis rules and adjustments to basis.

10.2 On the sale of a principal residence (used as such by the taxpayer for two out of the previous five years), $250,000 of the gain is exempt from taxation ($500,000 for married couples filing joint returns).[1] Thus, in the (presumably) rare circumstance where a US taxpayer transfers his principal residence to a foreign non-grantor trust, a portion of the deemed gain would be excluded from tax under Code § 684.

10.3 Individual taxpayers are currently subject to a maximum tax of 15% on net capital gains (net 'long-term' gains from sale of capital assets held more than one year offset by net short-term losses) from dispositions after 5 May 2003 and before 1 January 2009.[2] In the context of Code § 684, note again that short-term and long-term losses related to depreciated property transferred to a foreign non-grantor trust will not be recognized, and thus cannot offset the deemed gain from the transfer of appreciated property to that trust. However, a US taxpayer would be able to offset other capital losses against the Code § 684 gain.

Example

Harlan Hidethebucks, a US taxpayer, transfers his stock in ABC Inc (tax basis $10,000; fair market value $100,000) and XYZ Limited (tax basis $100,000, fair market value $10,000) to a foreign non-grantor trust. Under Code § 684, Harlan must realize the $90,000 gain on the deemed sale of ABC, but cannot offset that gain by the inherent loss in XYZ.

If, however, Harlan were to actually sell his shares in XYZ Limited (at a $90,000 loss) and transfer the $10,000 proceeds to the foreign non-grantor trust, he would be able to use that actual loss to offset the $90,000 deemed gain under Code § 684 on the transfer of the appreciated ABC shares to this trust.

---

[1] Code § 121.
[2] Code §§ 1(h), 1223(11), 6013(a).

10.4   *Capital Gains Deductions and Exclusions*

B. United Kingdom

1. Introduction

10.4   Various exemptions, reliefs and exclusions are available to offset a capital gains tax liability occasioned on a gift or sale. They fall into four categories:

- exempt assets;
- exempt gains;
- exempt disposals; and
- tax reliefs.

The following discussion outlines some of the main exemptions by way of example, although a wide variety exists.

2. Exempt assets

10.5   Gains arising on disposals of the following exempt assets are not chargeable and neither are losses allowable:

- a dwelling house (with grounds up to half a hectare, or more, in certain appropriate cases) which has been the only or main residence during the period of ownership of the person in occupation.[3] Spouses living together as husband and wife must have the same principal residence for the purpose of this relief. Various periods of absence are permitted without causing restriction of the relief, including the last three years of ownership and any other period of up to three years. Additionally absences are permitted for periods where the owner's employment requires him to work elsewhere (for up to four years in the UK and for an unlimited period abroad). Where two or more properties are owned, an election can be made (within two years of the acquisition of the second property) as to which is to qualify for the relief and where part of the property is used for business purposes, the relief is apportioned. To claim the relief in these cases the owner must have lived in the property both before and after the period of absence and not have any other property which qualifies for the relief;

- a dwelling house (as above) owned by a trust, which has been the only or main residence of a beneficiary entitled to occupy under the terms of the trust. This exemption can apply equally to a person who has an interest in possession in the trust assets or where the trustees have exercised their discretion to allow a

---

[3]   Taxation of Chargeable Gains Act 1992 (TCGA 1992), s 222–224. If the property is let out for a period, such that it does not qualify as to part of the gain, the relief is apportioned and a further exemption of up to £40,000 is permitted against the non-exempt portion of the proceeds.

beneficiary to occupy the property. In the latter case, the Inland Revenue may, in certain circumstances, take the view that an interest in possession has been created;[4]

- a dwelling house (as above) owned by personal representatives of a deceased person, which has been the only or main residence before and after the death, of a legatee (of either an outright bequest or on interest in possession trusts);[5]

- debts, where the subject of a disposal by the person to whom they were incurred (other than a debt on a security, i e a loan stock or similar issued by a government or public authority or by a company);[6]

- certain specified UK government securities, national savings certificates and certain corporate bonds;[7]

- life or deferred annuity insurance policies unless acquired for consideration (which does not include the payment of premiums under the policy);[8]

- Motor cars used as private vehicles;[9]

- an interest under a settlement with UK resident trustees (provided it has not been acquired by purchase at any time, that the trustees have never been non-UK resident and no settled property is derived from another trust which has been non-UK resident);[10]

- tangible movable property with disposal proceeds under £6,000 (note that sets of assets are valued together for determining whether the limit is exceeded).[11]

3. Exempt gains

10.6 The following gains are not chargeable:

- gains arising before 31 March 1982;[12]

- annual exemption for aggregate gains under £8,200 (for 2004/05) for individuals and for personal representatives in the year of death and the two years following death and £4,100 (for 2004/05) for trustees;[13]

---

[4] TCGA 1992, s 225; *Sansom v Peay 1976 52 TC 1*; see Statement of Practice 10/79 (15 August 1979). See also Finance Act 2004 (FA 2004), s 117, Sch 22, para 6, which denies the relief on a disposal made by the donees of a gift in certain circumstances where gains were originally 'held over' at the time of making the gift. See **10.15**.
[5] FA 2004, s 117, Sch 22, para 5.
[6] TCGA 1992, ss 251 and 132. Note in the case of bank deposits that this will not exempt currency gains.
[7] TCGA 1992, ss 115(1) and 121(1). Qualifying corporate bonds include most, but not all, securities issued by public or local authorities or by a company. The status of any particular holding should always be clarified.
[8] TCGA 1992, s 210 as amended by FA 2003, s 157.
[9] TCGA 1992, s 263.
[10] TCGA 1992, s 76.
[11] TCGA 1992, s 262.
[12] TCGA 1992, s 35(2).
[13] TCGA 1992, s 3. This exemption is available to husband, wife and children separately. Furthermore, a child's annual exemption can be used effectively by the trustees in respect of the assets of a bare trust (taxed as if they belonged to the child), which has been created by the parents

10.7 Capital Gains Deductions and Exclusions

- gains on qualifying shares held in an enterprise investment scheme;[14]
- gains on qualifying disposals of ordinary shares in a venture capital trust;[15]
- trees where managed as a commercial woodland with a view to the realization of profit;[16]
- gains made within a Personal Equity Plan (taken out before 6 April 1999)[17] or an Individual Savings Account.[18]

4. Exempt disposals

10.7 Exempt disposals taking effect at a value which gives rise to neither gain nor loss for the donor (thus taking account of any indexation allowance and allowable expenditure due to the donor) include the following:

- gifts of certain property for national purposes or to housing associations;[19]
- gifts to UK charities;[20]
- outright transfers between spouses living together. The criterion is that the spouses must be living together as husband and wife and, therefore, care needs to be taken to ensure that transfers of assets between separating spouses occurs before the relieving provision ceases to apply. Transfers after a marriage has broken down, but at any time in the tax year in which separation occurs, will qualify for the relief;[21] For taper relief purposes (see below) the donee spouse takes over the holding period of the donor, so that it is the aggregate of the two ownership periods which are relevant at the time of eventual disposal.
- transfers to settlements for the benefit of employees.[22]

5. Tax reliefs

a. Taper relief and indexation relief

10.8 Prior to 6 April 1998, an indexation allowance applied at the time of an asset disposal, being a deduction to offset inflationary gains, which worked by

---

of the beneficiary, without invoking any of the anti-avoidance provisions which usually apply to parental settlements. This position may change when the proposals on modernising the tax system for trusts are implemented. See **CHAPTER 13**.

[14] TCGA 1992, s 150A(2) and (3).
[15] TCGA 1992, s 151A.
[16] TCGA 1992, s 250.
[17] TCGA 1992, s 151.
[18] s 151 and Individual Savings Account Regulations 1998 (SI 1998/1870).
[19] TCGA 1992, s 257(1)(b).
[20] TCGA 1992, 257(1)(a) (provided the charity is a UK-registered charity and satisfies certain criteria as to the application of its funds for bona fide charitable purposes, its disposal of the asset will be exempt).
[21] TCGA 1992, ss 58 and 288(3). This provision contrasts with the inheritance tax exemption in IHTA 1984, s 18 which applies whether or not the spouses are separated, as long as they are not divorced. Furthermore, there is no requirement as to the spouses' domicile or their residence status.
[22] TCGA 1992, s 239.

enhancing the cost basis of the asset. The indexation factor applied to the cost basis was related to the increase in the Retail Prices Index[23] between the time when the expenditure was incurred and the date of disposal. Taper relief was introduced to replace the indexation allowance for chargeable gains accruing to individuals, trustees and personal representatives from 6 April 1998, however, indexation relief remains relevant up to that date.

10.9 Taper relief reduces the taxable proportion of the capital gain, arising on the disposal of an asset by way of sale or gift, according to how long (in complete calendar years) the asset has been held since 6 April 1998 (or the date of acquisition, if later). For example, if an asset was acquired in November 2003 and sold in September 2006, it will have been held for a two-year qualifying period. The longer the asset is held, the less of the gain on sale is taxable.[24] Although for assets acquired before 6 April 1998, only the period from 6 April 1998 is counted,[25] any asset held on 17 March 1998 will be entitled to a 'bonus' year if, at that date, it was regarded as a non-business asset.

10.10 Taper relief is available to reduce gains on disposals of both business and non-business assets. The relief given for business assets, however, is considerably more generous. The current percentages of the gain that remain taxable in either case is set out in the following table.

Gains on disposals of business assets		*Gains on disposals of non-business assets*	
Number of whole years in qualifying holding period	*Percentage of gain chargeable*	*Number of whole years in qualifying holding period*	*Percentage of gain chargeable*
1	50	1	100
2 or more	25	2	100
		3	95
		4	90
		5	85
		6	80
		7	75
		8	70
		9	65
		10 or more	60

10.11 The definition of business assets has been changed on more than one occasion since 1998 and it is possible that the status of an asset may have changed between non-business and business during the period of ownership. In these circumstances, the gain is time-apportioned over the relevant period, and the

---

[23] Published by the Inland Revenue.
[24] TCGA 1992, s 2A.
[25] TCGA 1992, s 2A(8).

10.12 *Capital Gains Deductions and Exclusions*

appropriate rate of taper relief applied accordingly. For example, the gain on an asset acquired in June 2002, which was used for business purposes until December 2006, then for non-business purposes until its sale in June 2012, would be apportioned as to 45% of the gain business asset taper relief and 55% of the gain non-business asset taper relief. As the asset had been owned for ten complete years (for the purposes of business and non-business taper relief), the respective percentages of the gain which would be chargeable would be 25% and 60%, ie a 10% business taper relief CGT rate would apply to 45% of the gain and a 24% non-business taper relief CGT rate would apply to 55% of the gain.

10.12 The definition of 'business assets'[26] for the purposes of taper relief is currently as follows.

Shares:

- all unquoted shares in trading companies or the holding company of a trading group;
- all shareholdings held by outside investors in quoted companies providing their holding in that company represents at least 5% of the share capital;
- all shareholdings held by employees in their employing company provided it is:
    (a) a trading company; or
    (b) it is a non-trading company and the employee (and connected persons, either together or separately) effectively holds less than 10% of the company.

Other assets:

- used for the purposes of a trade carried on by an individual either alone or in partnership or by an individual's qualifying company; or
- used for the purposes of an office or employment held by that individual with a person carrying on a trade.[27]

10.13 From 6 April 2004, with effect for subsequent periods of ownership and for disposals from that date, the definition applicable to 'other assets' is relaxed to remove the requirement that the owner of the asset be involved in carrying on the trade concerned. Providing the asset is used wholly or partly for the purposes of a trade carried on by individuals, trustees or certain partnerships, the asset will qualify as a business asset for taper relief purposes.[28] If a share or other asset is not a business asset, it is a non-business asset for taper relief purposes and attracts the less generous taper provisions noted above.

10.14 In this book, we discuss three business property tax reliefs for UK tax purposes:

---

[26] TCGA 1992, Sch A1, paras 4 and 6.
[27] TCGA 1992, Sch A1, para 5.
[28] FA 2003, s 160.

- business property relief for the purposes of IHT (see CHAPTER 3);
- business asset taper relief for the purposes of CGT; and
- hold-over relief for gifts of business assets (see 10.16 et seq).

While the definitions of qualifying business property or assets differ for each of these three reliefs, there are certain broad similarities of application. We set out in the comparative table in APPENDIX VII a summary of the criteria as they apply to unlisted shareholdings.

b. Hold-over relief

10.15 Capital gains tax can also be deferred on gifts of business assets and certain gifts that are subject to inheritance tax. 'Hold-over relief' is of particular importance since a lifetime gift can attract both inheritance tax and capital gains tax.

(i) Business assets

10.16 Hold-over relief applies to gifts of 'business assets' broadly defined as follows:

- assets (or an interest in assets) used for the purposes of a trade, profession or vocation carried on by the transferor or a company in which he has an interest of 5% or more (or in the case of a trading group, in its holding company); or
- unlisted trading company shares; or
- shares of a listed company in which the transferor has an interest of 5% or more (or, in the case of a trading group, such shares in the holding company).

10.17 The relief does not apply in circumstances where a gift of shares is made to a company.[29] However, the above categories are further extended to agricultural property which does not satisfy the trading requirement, but does qualify for inheritance tax agricultural property relief (see CHAPTER 3). The relief also applies to transfers of business assets out of a settlement.[30] In this case, the above criteria are modified such that

- use of the assets as stipulated above by either the trustees or beneficiaries with an interest in possession will qualify; and
- the ownership requirement for listed shares is increased to 25%.

(ii) Gifts subject to inheritance tax

10.18 Hold-over relief is available where an individual or trustee makes an immediately chargeable gift for inheritance tax that is not a potentially exempt transfer (eg a gift to a discretionary trust). The relief is also extended to gifts made

---

[29] TCGA 1992, s 165(3) as amended by FA 2004; this provision was accidentally repealed with effect from 5 April 2003 but is restored from 21 October 2003.
[30] TCGA 1992, s 165(5) and Sch 7.

10.19 *Capital Gains Deductions and Exclusions*

to certain tax-favoured bodies (eg heritage organisations) and to gifts out of an accumulation and maintenance trust (see **CHAPTER 6**) where the beneficiary's interest vests absolutely, provided he has not previously become entitled to an income interest.[31]

(iii) General

10.19 If hold-over relief applies, the donee takes the donor's base cost and effectively assumes responsibility for the tax on subsequent disposal. For taper relief purposes only the holding period of the donee[32] is relevant on that subsequent disposal and care therefore needs to be taken that the tax exposure has not been significantly increased by making the transfer. This facility to defer CGT by hold-over relief is only available where the donee is a UK resident such that the gain remains subject to UK taxation. If the donee is not UK resident or ordinarily resident, the gain cannot be held over and a charge arises. Furthermore, the possibility of tax avoidance by leaving the UK is countered by the imposition of a clawback charge on emigration of the donee within specified time limits.[33]

10.20 Where the gift is not a business asset, as described above, and the transfer bears no immediate charge to inheritance tax, CGT deferral is not possible and the deemed gain is immediately subject to tax at the donor's marginal income tax rate.

10.21 Hold-over relief has been modified extensively over the years and, in particular, to counter various planning strategies which have been developed using this relief. The most recent of such modifications were introduced in FA 2004 and take effect from 10 December 2003 as follows.

- Hold-over relief is no longer available where a gift is made to a settlor-interested trust[34] and can be clawed back, where a trust is not settlor interested at the outset, but within a six year period becomes settlor-interested. Such a trust is one from which any of the property (or any 'derived' property) can be paid to or applied for the benefit of the settlor or his spouse, in any circumstance whatsoever, or where, as a matter of fact, he or his spouse directly or indirectly enjoy it.

---

[31] TCGA 1992, s 260. Illogically, if the beneficiary has received an income entitlement but has had his capital entitlement deferred for a longer period, this relief does not apply. Technically, in this case when his capital rights mature, the trust is no longer within the situation contemplated by IHTA1984, s 71(4) which is the hold-over relief requirement, but is within s 52(1).

[32] Save where the gift is to a spouse.

[33] TCGA 1992, s 168 (six years from the end of the tax year of the gift. However, exceptionally, absence for employment purposes of no more than three years will not trigger the gain if the asset has not been disposed of).

[34] TCGA 1992, s 169B, as amended by FA 2004. For example, hold-over relief might have been used in certain circumstances where trustees had allowable losses available to offset the gains at the time of disposal. The usual caveat applies to the new legislation, that former and separated spouses are excluded from its application, as are widows/widowers. Similarly, an exclusion applies in certain circumstances where the settlor or spouse are default beneficiaries in the event of the death of the main beneficiaries to a marriage settlement or the death of a child whose interest has vested at the age of 25.

- Exemption for trustees from CGT on disposal of a principal private residence occupied by a beneficiary under the terms of a settlement is unavailable where the exempt amount has, in effect, been enhanced by the previous use of hold-over relief.[35]

10.22 Anti-avoidance legislation taxes a UK resident or ordinarily resident settlor on gains of a UK trust from which he or his spouse may benefit[36] and a UK domiciled and resident (or ordinarily resident) settlor on the gains of a non-UK resident trust from which he or members of his immediate family and certain connected companies can benefit[37] (see **CHAPTER 13**). Even so, a transfer into such a settlement will, nevertheless, constitute a chargeable CGT disposal unless one of the above reliefs apply.[38]

(iv) Reinvestment relief

10.23 UK resident or ordinarily resident individuals (or trustees) may claim to roll over gains which arise on the disposal of any assets where they invest all or part of the proceeds of that disposal (and not just the gain element of the proceeds) in a cash subscription for new ordinary shares issued by a company operating a qualifying trade under the Enterprise Investment Scheme (EIS).[39] The relief applies to an unlimited amount and subject to the investment occurring within one year prior to the date of realisation of the gain or three years afterwards. Limits apply to the level of permitted gross assets of the company and, effectively, the relief is aimed at providing funding for smaller unlisted companies carrying on certain acceptable trading activities.[40]

10.24 Disposal of the EIS investment (other than by way of a gift to a spouse) is itself exempt from capital gains tax, but this will trigger tax on the deferred gain, which is not exempt. It also triggers if the investor becomes non-UK resident within three years of making the investment, although there is an exception for persons going to work abroad if they return within the three years without having disposed

---

[35] TCGA 1992, s 226A as amended by FA 2004 (intended to preclude an exemption for the gain on a principal private residence at the trustee level, where the property would not have so qualified prior to its transfer into trust). In circumstances where the relief does apply, the trustees are now also required to make a claim to that effect.
[36] TCGA 1992, s 77.
[37] TCGA 1992, s 86.
[38] TCGA 1992, s 70.
[39] The rules relating to reinvestment relief were recast into the EIS for shares issued with effect from 6 April 1998. TCGA 1992, ss 150A–150D and Sch 5B.
[40] The list of unacceptable activities is lengthy:
- dealing in land/shares/financial instruments;
- dealing in goods (other than in a normal trading capacity);
- banking/insurance /finance;
- certain activities in the oil industry;
- leasing/letting/licensing activities;
- legal/accounting services;
- property development;
- farming/operating woodlands;
- hotel/nursing home management.

10.24 *Capital Gains Deductions and Exclusions*

of the asset. The gain triggers in similar circumstances to the spouse. There are also provisions which trigger the gains if the shares cease to comply with the requirements of the EIS regime.

Chapter 11

Tax Basis Rules for Gifts and Bequests

A. United States

1. Introduction

11.1 For US tax purposes, gain or loss is measured by reference to the taxpayer's basis. A taxpayer's basis is generally his cost.[1] Special rules, summarized below, determine the basis of property received as a gift, or from a decedent, or as a distribution from a trust. The basis can be adjusted up or down for items such as depreciation, expenses attributable to the property which are not currently deductible, and other items.[2] Unlike the pre-1998 UK rules, the US taxpayer's cost basis is not adjusted for inflation.

2. Property acquired by gift

11.2 The donee's basis of property received by gift is generally the same basis that the donor had in the gifted property.[3] This applies whether the donee is an individual or a trust. The donor's basis is thus said to 'carry over' to the donee.

11.3 The Code includes a special provision designed to prevent shifting loss property to donees (who might be in a better tax position to effectively use the realized losses). In those instances, the donee's basis for the purposes of determining losses is the fair market value of the property at the time of the gift.[4] For the purposes of determining gain, the donee takes a carry over basis.

Example

Tom Riske had invested $100,000 in stock of ThroughtheRoof.com Inc. Three years later, after the company changed its name to Bubblebust-.com Inc, the value of Tom's stock was only $10,000. Tom gives those shares to his son, Junior. For the purposes of determining gain, Junior's basis will be $100,000. Thus, if the stock later comes back and Junior is able to sell for $120,000, Junior's gain will be $20,000. For the purposes of determining losses, Junior's basis will be limited to $10,000. Thus, if the stock continues to plummet and Junior sells for $1,000, Junior will

---

[1] Code § 1012.
[2] Code § 1016.
[3] Code § 1015.
[4] Code § 1015(a).

11.4 Tax Basis Rules for Gifts and Bequests

realize only $9,000 of loss. The inherent loss in Tom's hands ($90,000) therefore disappears. If Junior sells between $10,000 and $100,000, he will realize no gain or loss.

This rule applies regardless of the donee's relationship to the donor.

11.4 If US gift or generation-skipping taxes were payable with respect to the gift, the donee's basis is increased to the extent of such transfer taxes attributable to the appreciation on the gifted property.[5]

Example

Daddy Bigbucks gives his daughter, Annie, stock in his company, Tomorrow Enterprises. Daddy's basis in the stock is $100,000 and the fair market value is $1m. Daddy, who had previously used all of his gift tax applicable exclusion credit on prior gifts to Annie, pays $480,000 of gift taxes. 90% ($900,000/$1,000,000) of the gift taxes (or $432,000) is attributable to the appreciation. Accordingly, Annie's basis in the stock will be $532,000 ($100,000 carry-over basis plus $432,000).

11.5 As discussed in **CHAPTER 8**, if a US person transfers property to a foreign non-grantor trust, the transfer is treated as a sale or exchange for fair market value and the US transferor is required to realise gain (but cannot take a loss) on the transfer. Thus, if the transferred property has appreciated, the foreign non-grantor trust should clearly receive a fair market value basis, otherwise, the inherent gain is potentially subject to double tax.[6]

11.6 A beneficiary's basis in property distributed *in kind* from a trust or estate is the trust's or estate's basis in the property, adjusted for any gain or loss realized on

---

[5] Code §§ 1015(d) and 2654(a)(1).
[6] If, however, the contributed property is in a loss position and the US transferor is precluded from realising a loss, it would only seem fair that, for purposes of determining later gains, the foreign trust's basis should be the US transferor's higher basis. However, this does not appear to be the case. Section 684 arguably has two rules:
- first, it treats all transfers to foreign non-grantor trusts as sales (not gifts) and
- second, it requires the US transferor to realise gains (but not losses).

The first rule does not appear to be limited by the second (that is, the transfer is considered a sale regardless of whether or not the US transferor is required to realise a gain), although the second rule is clearly dependent on the first (the US transferor will be required to realise gain only if the transfer to the foreign trust is treated as a sale).

If, as appears to be the case, section 684 treats all transfers to foreign non-grantor trusts as sales regardless of the inherent gain or loss in the transferred property, the foreign trust should receive a 'cost' basis, not a basis determined under the gift rules described above. This would cause not only inherent losses to disappear but also cause the foreign trust to measure all future gains against the lower cost basis (rather than the donor's higher basis). The regulations under section 684 appear to endorse this interpretation by specifically prohibiting the US transferor from offsetting any gain under that section by any 'loss realised on the transfer of a depreciated asset to the foreign trust'. Treas. Reg § 684–1(a)(2). If, as the regulations suggest, the US taxpayer realises (but cannot take) such a loss, the foreign trust would presumably have a basis in the property equal to its deemed cost.

The problem of disappearing losses described in 11.3 would seem easy enough to avoid. The US transferor could actually sell the loss property, realise a real (not deemed) loss and give the cash proceeds to the foreign trust. That real loss could then be used to offset the gain that the US transferor would be deemed to have realised upon the transfer of appreciated property to the foreign trust.

that distribution.[7] Thus, if the trust or estate makes an election under Code § 643(e)(3) to realize a gain or loss on the distribution of property to a US beneficiary, the beneficiary's basis should equal the fair market value of that property.

3. Property acquired from a decedent

11.7 Property 'acquired from a decedent' generally receives a new basis equal to its value for estate tax purposes.[8] Generally, this is either the date of death value or, if the estate makes an appropriate election on a US estate tax return, the value on the alternate value date (six months after the decedent's death). As a result, appreciated property is said to receive a 'step up' in basis (eliminating all inherent gains) while depreciated property receives a 'step down' in basis (thus losing the benefit of any inherent losses).

11.8 Property is considered to have been acquired from a decedent if it is acquired by bequest, devise or inheritance.[9] Property received by the decedent's probate estate is also considered to have been acquired from the decedent. For the purposes of this rule, it is not necessary that the property be subject to US estate tax. Therefore, if a deceased NDA's will leaves appreciated non-US property to her US children, the children will take a fair market value in that property.[10]

11.9 Property held in a revocable or an incomplete gift irrevocable trust at the settlor's death will receive a basis adjustment to market value as property acquired from the decedent. Where the settlor has retained dominion and control over assets transferred in trust (eg a revocable trust or an irrevocable trust in which the settler has retained the right to change the enjoyment of income),[11] the gift becomes complete at death and is taxed as a bequest, not a gift.[12] Accordingly, assets in an incomplete gift trust receive a fair market value basis at death[13] (whether or not such assets are subject to US estate tax).[14]

11.10 Property acquired from a decedent by reason of death, form of ownership, or other conditions (including the non-exercise of a power of appointment) will also receive a new tax basis if the property is included in the decedent's US taxable gross estate.[15] This rule applies equally to property inherited from a deceased citizen, domiciliary or NDA (although, in the case of a NDA, will apply only to US situs property).

---

[7] Code § 643(e)(1).
[8] Code § 1014(a).
[9] Code § 1014(b)(1).
[10] Rev Rul 84–139, 1984–2 CB 1.
[11] See the discussion of complete and incomplete gifts at **16.76**.
[12] Treas Reg § 25.2511–2; *Estate of DiMarco 87 TC 653 (1986)*.
[13] Code § 1014(a). Because revocable trusts are incomplete gift trusts, reliance on IRC § 1014(b)(2) is unnecessary to achieve a rebasing of trust assets at the settlor's death. That section applies to trusts in which the settler had retained at all times the right to revoke the trust and that income is paid to him or at his direction.
[14] Because assets held by an irrevocable trust which is an incomplete gift trust are rebased under IRC § 1014(b)(1), reliance on IRC § 1014(b)(3) is unnecessary.
[15] Code § 1014(b)(9).

11.11   Tax Basis Rules for Gifts and Bequests

11.11 There are a number of exceptions. A person who inherits the decedent's interest in an entity considered to be a foreign personal holding company (FPHC) will take a basis in that property equal to the lower of the decedent's basis or fair market value.[16] A foreign company is considered to be an FPHC if (through attribution rules) it has five or fewer US owners who own more than 50% of the company's stock (by vote or value) and if at least 60% of the income from the company is from generally passive sources. The FPHC provisions include detailed attribution rules that attribute stock owned by individuals, trusts, corporations and partnerships to family members, beneficiaries, shareholders and partners. Stock owned by a non-resident alien (NRA) will generally not be attributed to US family member, unless:

- the US family member also owns stock; or
- the US family member is the individual's spouse.[17]

The 'spouse' exception can cause a surprising consequence.

Example

Samuel Ross, a NDA, is married to Betsy Ross, a US citizen. Samuel owns 100% of the stock in Flags Ltd, a foreign company that holds portfolio investments. Flags Ltd is considered a foreign personal holding company because Samuel's shareholdings are attributed to Betsy. Samuel dies and leaves his shares of Flags Ltd to Betsy, to the couple's children, or to a trust for their benefit. The recipient's basis will be the lesser of Samuel's basis or fair market value.[18]

11.12 Property representing 'income in respect of a decedent' does not receive a basis adjustment at death.[19] For example, the decedent's rights under a pension plan, a deferred compensation plan, an annuity, and an installment sale note (in which gain is deferred until payment is received) will *not* be adjusted to fair market value. Therefore, the heir's receipt of pension or annuity payments, deferred compensation payments, and payments on the installment note will remain taxable to them in the same manner those payments would have been taxed to the decedent.

11.13 If (i) appreciated property is acquired *by* the decedent by gift within one year of death and (ii) such property is left by the decedent *to* the donor (or the donor's spouse), then the basis taken by the donor (or donor's spouse) in that inherited property will be the same basis that the decedent had in that property.[20] Under rules described above, the decedent/donee's basis in appreciated property will be the donor's basis in the gifted property. This special rule prevents the original donor from 'using' a dying person as a way to step-up the basis on appreciated property which returns to the original donor from the decedent's estate at little or no extra estate tax cost (because, for example, of the decedent's estate tax credit or marital deduction).

---

[16] Code § 1014(b)(5).
[17] Code § 554(c)(1).
[18] PLR 9110019 (5 December 1990).
[19] Code § 1014(c).
[20] Code § 1014(e).

Example

Carol owns stock in Microhard Corp with a basis of $100,000 and a fair market value of $1m. Carol's husband is diagnosed with inoperable lung cancer. In an effort to step up the basis in this stock, Carol gives the stock to her husband. If her husband dies within one year of the gift and leaves the stock back to Carol, she will take a $100,000 basis. If he instead leaves the stock to the couple's children, the children will take a new basis in the stock, regardless of when he dies. If he survives the gift by a year and leaves the stock to Carol, she will get a new basis in the stock.

11.14 Pursuant to the 2001 Tax Act, the estate tax is repealed for one year in 2010. As a trade-off for the temporary repeal of the estate tax, property 'acquired from a decedent' will have a basis determined under an entirely new set of complex rules. Under this rule, assets transferred at death acquire a tax basis equal to the lower of date of death market value or the decedent's tax basis in such assets.[21] Inherent gains will therefore remain and inherent losses will disappear. However, this basis is increased by:

- $3m for property acquired by a surviving spouse; and
- $1.3m for property acquired by other persons (limited to $60,000 for property received from a NDA decedent), and
- the decedent's (other than a NDA decedent's) disappearing built in losses and any unused carryover losses at death.

Under the sunset provisions of the 2001 Tax Act, these changes are repealed in 2011 and the rules for determining the basis of property acquired from a decedent revert back to current law.

4. GST transfers

11.15 The basis of property acquired in a generation-skipping transfer is increased by the portion of any GST imposed with respect to the inherent gain in transferred property.[22] This rule is applied after any adjustments for gift taxes paid on the inherent gain.

Example

Daddy Bigbucks gives his grandson, Andy, stock in his company, Tomorrow Enterprises. Daddy's basis in the stock is $100,000 and the fair market value is $1m. Assume Daddy pays $480,000 of gift tax and $200,000 of GST. 90% ($900,000/$1,000,000) of the gift tax (or $432,000) is attributable to the inherent appreciation. Accordingly, Andy's basis in the stock after adjustment for the gift tax will be $532,000 ($100,000 carry-over basis plus $432,000). After that adjustment, the inherent gain represents 46.8% of the property's value ($468,000/$1,000,000). Andy is

---

[21] Code § 1022.
[22] Code § 2654(a)(1).

therefore able to increase his basis by another $93,600 ($200,000 × 46.8%) on account of the GST. Andy's final basis is therefore $635,600.

11.16 In the case of a generation-skipping transfer that is characterized as a taxable termination and occurs by reason of a person's death (eg the death of the transferor's child who is a beneficiary of the trust), the GST rules provide for the tax basis to be adjusted in a manner similar to those in Code § 1014 (basis generally adjusted to fair market value).[23] (Since the GST is scheduled to be repealed for generation-skipping transfers occurring in 2010, there would be no basis adjustment for taxable terminations occurring in that year.) If, however, the 'inclusion ratio' of the relevant trust was less than 1 (and, therefore, less than a 'full' GST is imposed on the taxable termination), the increase or decrease in basis is limited by multiplying that basis adjustment by the inclusion ratio.

Example

Property with a basis of $200,000 and a fair market value of $500,000 is held in trust for Daddy Bigbuck's daughter, Annie. The trust has a GST inclusion ratio of 50%. Annie dies and the trust property passes to her son, Andy, in a GST taxable termination. Andy will be entitled to adjust the $200,000 basis by only 50% of the inherent gain. Therefore, Andy will take a new basis in this property of $350,000 ($200,000 + $150,000). If the trust was exempt from GST (and thus had and inclusion ratio of zero), Andy's basis would instead be limited to $200,000.

B. United Kingdom

1. Introduction

11.17 For UK tax purposes, as in the US, gain or loss is measured by reference to the taxpayer's cost basis. Special rules, determine the cost basis of property received as a gift, or from a decedent, or as a distribution from a trust. Similarly, the cost basis can be adjusted up or down for items such as capital expenses attributable to the property.

11.18 The US has no equivalent of the pre-1998 UK rules that result in an enhancement to the cost basis of an asset to offset inflationary gains up to that date. Nor does the US have any equivalent of the reduction in the taxable gain by reference to the holding period, nor the favourable 10% rate for gains on business assets. Against all of this is the fact that the long-term US gains tax rate is currently 15% and the principles are relatively straightforward, whereas the UK capital gains tax regime is highly complex and rates applicable to non-business assets range from 24% to 40% (depending on the ownership period).

---

[23] Code § 2654(a)(2).

2. General rules

11.19 Where a gain has to be computed, subject to the comments made below, the same general principles apply to determine the cost basis and relevant deductions, exclusions and reliefs whether the transaction is an actual disposal by way of sale (where consideration is received), a disposal by way of gift (where no consideration is received), or it is a deemed disposal (where no disposal actually occurs at all). The starting point is the actual sum paid for the asset (or the open market value of other consideration given) or in the case of a gift, the open market value of the asset at the time of the gift. In the case of such consideration (for the acquisition or disposal) being in a foreign currency it is converted into sterling for the purposes of computing the UK capital gains tax exposure. Accordingly, exchange rate fluctuations can themselves have a considerable impact on the liability.

a. Market value rebasing

11.20 With effect for disposals after 5 April 1988, assets held on 31 March 1982 are (subject to certain exceptions) rebased by reference to their market value on the latter date such that gains attributable to the prior period are no longer taxed.[24] An election was required for this new cost base to apply, with respect to all assets held on 31 March 1982, at the time of the first relevant disposal after 5 April 1988. However, where no election was made, the cost base at this date is still deductible where it creates either a smaller gain or a smaller loss than would be the case using the actual cost basis. If there would be a gain by reference to the original cost but a loss by reference to the March 1982 value (or vice versa) the disposal is treated as giving rise to neither a gain nor a loss. Hence no tax is payable but losses are not allowable. A similar rebasing took place for assets held in 1965 which in theory can be, though rarely is, relevant for the purposes of computing tax.

11.21 Acquisitions since March 1982 carry a cost basis which represents the taxpayer's cost, ie the consideration paid plus incidental expenditure such as professional fees.[25]

b. Other deductions

11.22 Expenditure wholly and exclusively incurred for enhancing the value of the asset or defending title to it is also added to the base cost[26] as are incidental costs of disposal.[27] Additionally, a measure of further relief is given for inflationary gains for periods of ownership up to 5 April 1998[28] by way of an 'indexation allowance' applied to these costs and the cost basis.

11.23 Generally, the cost base and certain other allowable expenditure is increased by a figure which represents the percentage increase in the Retail Prices

---

[24] TCGA 1992, s 35.
[25] TCGA 1992, s 38(1)(a).
[26] TCGA 1992, s 38(1)(b).
[27] TCGA 1992, s 38(1)(c).
[28] TCGA 1992, s 53.

11.24   *Tax Basis Rules for Gifts and Bequests*

Index from the time the expenditure was incurred (or on 31 March 1982 if later) to the earlier of 5 April 1998 or the date of gift/sale. For holding periods after 5 April 1998, indexation allowance is not available but 'taper relief' may reduce the chargeable gain depending on the nature of the asset and the period of ownership (see CHAPTER 10).[29] Indexation relief continues to apply to companies, both UK resident and non resident.

c. Matching rules

11.24 Where shares and securities are concerned the rules which establish the cost basis can become extremely complex, particularly where they have been acquired piecemeal over a period of time or, for example, where there have been bonus issues or reinvestment through scrip dividends. Where the taxpayer disposes of only part of his share holdings, the UK rules (unlike those in the US) do not permit the taxpayer to choose which shares (with which cost base) are disposed of. Instead, the Inland Revenue has specific rules (which have been modified many times over recent years and are hence quite complicated) to determine which shares or securities are the subject of disposal.

11.25 Acquisitions of shares and securities of the same class prior to 6 April 1998 (when taper relief was introduced) are 'pooled'. The cost basis of shares and securities in this pool is, in effect, averaged and indexed for the purposes of computing the gain on later disposal.

11.26 The introduction of 'taper relief' (see CHAPTER 10) for shares and securities acquired after 6 April 1998 means that the date of each separate acquisition is relevant to determine the proportion of the gain that will be chargeable. Working out the cost base and the chargeable gain on a disposal, on or after 6 April 1998, of part of a single holding of shares and securities can be a tortuous matter. Such disposals are matched with acquisitions in the following order:

- acquisitions which may have been made on the same day;
- acquisitions which may be made in the following 30 days;
- acquisitions made prior to the disposal, but after 5 April 1998, on a last in first out basis;
- shares in the pool held at 5 April 1998;
- shares held at 5 April 1982;
- shares acquired prior to 6 April 1965.

11.27 The requirement to match disposals with re-acquisition of assets made in the subsequent 30-day period essentially removes the ability for an individual to 'bed and breakfast' by sale and reacquisition on sequential days (to determine the timing of realisation of gains or losses[30]) without significant exposure to market volatility. However, it should be noted that this rule does not preclude a spouse from acquiring

---

[29]   TCGA 1992, s 53(1A).
[30]   Eg to use annual allowances prior to the end of a tax year where they would not otherwise be used.

on the Stock Market an equivalent asset as may have been disposed of by her husband, nor trustees of a settlement of which he may be the settlor from taking such action.

3. Connected persons

11.28 Disposals made between 'connected persons'[31] are regarded as having been made other than on arm's length terms. Therefore, in determining the cost basis of the donee and any gain or loss[32] made by the donor, the open market value of the asset is substituted for the consideration (if any) that was actually paid.[33] Most disposals made as part of a succession planning exercise will be to connected persons.

11.29 The persons with whom an individual is connected include the following:

- his spouse and her 'relatives'[34] (including spouses of those relatives);
- his own relatives (and their spouses);
- his business partners[35] and their spouses and relatives;
- trustees of a settlement of which he is a settlor. The trustees are connected with all persons connected with him as long as he is alive[36] and any close company of which they are a participator.[37]

a. Property acquired by gift

11.30 Where someone disposes of an asset he owns by making a gift to another,[38] or where someone acquires an asset on other than arm's length terms (including transfers into and, in many cases, distributions out of trusts), the recipient's cost basis (and the donor's deemed disposal proceeds) is considered to be the market value of the asset at that date.[39]

---

[31] See Inland Revenue Interpretation RI 38 which confirms the Inland Revenue's view that the trustees are considered to be connected with the settlor at the time of the initial transfer into trust and also that once the settlor is dead, the connection between the beneficiaries and the trustees ceases. Since the link between all of the connected parties in this case is the settlor, the connection ceases after his death.

[32] See also **CHAPTER 8**. Any loss on a disposal to a 'connected' person is deductible only from chargeable gains arising on other disposals to the same person (while his is still connected).

[33] TCGA 1992, s 18.

[34] TCGA 1992, s 286(8). Note that 'relative' means brother, sister, ancestor, lineal descendant.

[35] With the exception of certain bona fide commercial transactions.

[36] See the Inland Revenue's *Tax Bulletin*, February 1993.

[37] Including any non-UK resident company which would be a close company if it were UK resident and also including a company which is controlled by such a company. This provision applies if more than 10% of the gain is attributable to the participator and persons connected with him/them. TCGA 1992, s 13(4). A close company is one in the control of five or fewer participators or of participators who are directors. ICTA 1988, s 414(1).

[38] This pre-supposes there is an existing asset that is the subject of a disposal or a part disposal. However, in some cases where an asset arises in a situation where there is no corresponding disposal, it may have no attributable cost basis.

[39] TCGA 1992, s 17(1).

11.31 This general rule does not apply in the limited circumstances where hold over relief is available.[40] In that event the donee takes over the donor's base cost, indexed (where applicable) to 5 April 1998. However, for purposes of taper relief, the holding period for the donee (other than a donee spouse) commences on the date of the gift. (The donee spouse's holding period carries over from the donor spouse.) Care needs to be taken that a hold-over transfer does not increase the overall level of tax.

11.32 Where hold over relief is claimed for a disposal that is also a chargeable transfer for IHT purposes, the IHT paid may be treated as a deduction against the donee's subsequent proceeds of sale (but not a credit against the tax due).[41] In contrast with hold-over relief, where a claim is necessary to defer the tax, in certain transactions the donee automatically takes the donor's indexed cost basis (see **CHAPTER 10**). Examples include transfers between:

- spouses living together as husband and wife;[42]
- a person and a UK charity, or a body established for national purposes, or a housing association;[43] and
- personal representatives transferring to a legatee.[44]

b. Property acquired from a decedent

11.33 As in the US, upon death property included in the decedent's UK taxable estate (including in the UK any trust property in which he has an interest in possession) receives a new cost basis equal to its market value for estate tax purposes but without a charge to capital gains tax.[45] Therefore, on death it is usual for there to be an inheritance tax charge but no capital gains tax charge.[46]

11.34 This contrasts with lifetime gifts in the UK where there may well be a capital gains tax charge but there will generally be no inheritance tax charge where the gift is structured appropriately as a potentially exempt transfer, if the donor survives for a period of seven years.[47] In any lifetime planning this means that a careful comparison needs to be made of the trade off between one tax and the other. For example, it may be preferable to retain an asset qualifying for inheritance tax business property relief until death rather than making a lifetime gift, since this may

---

[40] TCGA 1992, ss 165 and 260. From 10 December 2003, hold-over relief is denied for all transfers into settlor-interested trusts. FA 2004, s 116 and Sch 21. See **CHAPTER 10**.
[41] TCGA 1992, s 260(7).
[42] TCGA 1992, s 58.
[43] TCGA 1992, ss 257–259.
[44] TCGA 1992, s 62.
[45] TCGA 1992, s 62 as to the free estate, under which provision the personal representatives acquire the assets without any corresponding disposal having been made, and s 72 as to assets in which the deceased has an interest in possession, where the trustees are deemed to make a disposal and reacquisition at the then market value of the assets.
[46] This rebasing principle applies to assets 'of which the deceased was competent to dispose', effectively being his free estate and any co-owned assets (including assets subject to a joint tenancy).
[47] IHTA 1984, s 3A.

avoid both inheritance tax and capital gains tax. A lifetime gift on the other hand may result in a current or postponed (where hold-over relief is used) capital gains tax exposure.

11.35 The uplift in cost basis without tax charge on the death of a beneficiary with an interest in possession does not extend to any gains held over on the transfer of assets into a UK trust. These gains will crystallise at the beneficiary's death.[48]

11.36 Just as no capital gains are realised by reason of an individual's death, no losses arise by reason of death. Since the decedent's heirs take a new market value basis, the inherent losses will be lost. In contrast, if the deceased had himself made disposals in the year of death which resulted in losses that cannot be set against current year's gains, those losses can generally be carried back and set against chargeable gains made by him (but excluding gains which are deemed taxable to him under certain anti-avoidance rules) in the three prior tax years. It may, therefore, make sense in appropriate cases for the individual to make asset disposals to realise losses prior to death.

11.37 Losses realised by the personal representatives in the course of administration are not passed on to the legatees. However, where a legatee acquires an asset as part of his entitlement under an estate, and which had either been comprised in the deceased's estate itself, or was acquired at a later date by the personal representatives, he is effectively placed in their position and takes as if their acquisition date and cost basis had been his.[49] Accordingly, where assets are standing at a loss to their acquisition or date of death value, it may be desirable to consider appropriating these to the beneficiaries and allowing them to make the relevant disposals. If the personal representatives make disposals at a gain they are liable to tax on the normal basis (see **CHAPTER 9**).

11.38 As in the case of the inheritance tax legislation, a person benefiting from an estate (whether under a will, on an intestacy or by reason of automatic succession to the deceased's share of jointly-held assets) may enter into a deed of variation or disclaimer which is treated favourably for capital gains tax purposes.[50] Such variation or disclaimer must occur within two years of a person's death and must relate to the dispositions of property comprised in his estate. The substituted gifts are then treated for all inheritance tax and certain capital gains tax purposes (including the cost basis) as if the deceased had made them.[51]

---

[48] TCGA 1992, s 74. For example, if the assets had been business assets, hold-over relief under TCGA 1992, s 165 may have been applicable or, if the trust was initially a discretionary trust, relief may have been available under TCGA 1992, s 260.
[49] TCGA 1992, s 62.
[50] TGCA 1992, s 62(6); as to inheritance tax, see **CHAPTER 3**.
[51] Despite the fact that the provisions of the deed are deemed to have been effected by the deceased and thus the disposition by the beneficiary of itself gives rise to no taxable event, for the purposes of the anti avoidance settlement legislation (ICTA 1988, Pt XV and TCGA 1992, s 77; see **CHAPTER 13**) it is deemed to be a settlement by the varying beneficiary (*Marshall v Kerr (1994) 67 TC 56*). This is in contrast with the position taken for inheritance tax purposes.

11.39   *Tax Basis Rules for Gifts and Bequests*

11.39   The provisions apply as a matter of course if the instrument effecting the variation or disclaimer makes an express statement to that effect.[52] This provides a practical planning opportunity where, as often happens, an adult child would rather his parents left their estate to his children, but where he is unwilling or they do not want him to interfere with their testamentary arrangements.

---

[52]   From 31 July 2002. Prior to that time an election was required to be made within six months of the date of the deed.

Chapter 12

US Income Taxation of Trusts, Estates, Grantors and Beneficiaries

A. Summary

12.1 Under US law, income and gains earned by the trust can be taxed to the grantor (settlor), the trust itself, or to the trust beneficiaries depending on the relevant facts. These facts include the residence of the trust (as domestic or foreign), the source of the income, the terms of the trust deed, the status of the grantor (as a US citizen, resident alien, or non-resident alien), the tax status of the beneficiaries, and the trust's history of distributions and accumulations. These rules are briefly summarized below.

1. Taxation of the 'grantor'

12.2 If the trust is considered a 'grantor' trust, the trust is not separately taxed on its income and gains. Instead, it is essentially considered transparent and the person considered the trust's grantor (typically the settlor) is taxed as if he owned the underlying trust assets. The grantor will be liable for US tax as follows:

(a) if the grantor is a US citizen or resident alien, the grantor is subject to US tax on the trust's net income and gains, regardless of source;

(b) if the grantor is a non-resident alien (NRA) and is respected as the grantor/owner, the NRA grantor is generally only subject to US tax on:

  (i) US-sourced 'fixed or determinable annual or periodic income' (FDAPI) – such as interest, dividends, and rents – which is taxed at a flat 30% rate by withholding at the source by the payor;

  (ii) income effectively connected income with a US trade or business (ECI), which is taxed at marginal rates up to 35%; and

  (iii) gains from the sale of US real estate interests, which are taxed as if ECI, but, in the case of individuals, the tax rate on long-term gains is capped at 15% through 2008.

2. Taxation of a non-grantor trust

12.3 If the trust is not a grantor trust, it is considered a separate taxpayer (a non-grantor trust). Subject to deductions for certain distributions to beneficiaries, the trust will be subject to US tax as follows:

12.4   US Income Taxation of Trusts, Estates, Grantors and Beneficiaries

(a) if the non-grantor trust is considered to be a *'domestic' trust*, the trust will be subject to US tax on net income and gains, regardless of the source. Ordinary income is taxed to the trust at compressed marginal tax rates, reaching the top rate of 35% on income over $9,350. Net long-term capital gains and qualifying dividends are taxed at a maximum 15% rate from 5 May 2003 through 2008;

(b) if the non-grantor trust is considered to be a *'foreign' trust*, US tax is generally limited to:

   (i) a flat 30% withholding tax on US-sourced FDAPI;

   (ii) US tax – at compressed rate brackets up to 35% – on ECI; and

   (iii) US tax on gains from the sale of US real estate interests, capped at 15% for long-term gains.

3. Taxation of beneficiaries

12.4   If the trust is a grantor trust, beneficiaries will not be taxed on current trust distributions. Instead, the trust income and gains will be attributed and taxed to the grantor/owner to the extent he is subject to US tax. If the trust is a non-grantor trust, then distributions to the beneficiary can cause the beneficiary to be subject to US tax.

a. US non-grantor trust/US beneficiary

12.5   A US beneficiary who receives distributions from a US non-grantor trust will generally be subject to US tax on part or all of the trust's current income. In some instances, capital gains realized in the trust will also be taxed to a US beneficiary on distribution. The trust, in turn, is entitled to a deduction for any such distributions taxed to the beneficiary. As a result, the income is only taxed once – to the trust (if accumulated) or to the beneficiary (if distributed). A distributing non-grantor trust is considered a 'conduit' such that income flows through the trust is ultimately taxed to the recipient beneficiary. If US or foreign taxes have been withheld on the trust income, the distribution is 'grossed up' to include those taxes, but those taxes are creditable by the beneficiary.

b. US Non-grantor trust/NRA beneficiary

12.6   The same 'conduit' principles apply where the beneficiary is a NRA, except that the NRA beneficiary will generally only be subject to US tax on:

- US-sourced FDAPI;
- US-sourced ECI income; and
- gains from the sale of US property interests.

c. Foreign non-grantor trust/US beneficiaries

12.7 A US beneficiary who receives a distribution from a foreign non-grantor trust will be subject to US tax (regardless of the source of the trust's earnings) on the following:

- first to the extent of the foreign trust's current net income (including net gains); and
- then to the extent of the foreign trust's accumulated income (including net gains).

The US tax imposed on distributions of accumulated income is computed at ordinary income rates (even if the accumulation represents capital gains) and is determined under complex 'throwback' rules. The 'throwback' tax is then subject to an interest charge based on the weighted age of the accumulations. 'Gross-up' principles described at **12.5** apply to US and foreign taxes paid by the foreign trust on income distributed to US beneficiaries.

d. Foreign non-grantor trust/NRA beneficiaries

12.8 NRA beneficiaries of foreign trusts are technically taxed on current or accumulation distributions attributed to FDAPI and ECI (including gain from the sale of US real estate).

B. Income tax residence of trusts

12.9 The classification of a trust as a domestic or foreign trust is important for several reasons as follows.

- **Grantor trust rules – Code § 679** – Under Code § 679, a foreign trust funded by a US settlor will automatically be a grantor trust (and the settlor taxed as the grantor/owner) if any US person is a current or future trust beneficiary. The same rule applies to a foreign trust funded by a NRA within five years of becoming a US resident. Section 679 only applies to foreign trusts. In contrast, a domestic trust with US beneficiaries will not automatically be a grantor trust; instead, a domestic trust's status as a grantor trust will depend on other factors.

- **Special reporting obligations** – US settlors and beneficiaries must file special US tax information returns to report transfers to, the ownership of, and distributions from foreign trusts. Foreign trusts with US grantor/owners must file special US tax information returns to report the income and gains which are taxable to the US grantor/owner. US grantor/owners of foreign trusts must similarly file special US tax information returns to report the income and gains of a foreign trust taxable to them. Severe penalties – for example, 35% of the amount transferred to or received from a foreign trust – are imposed for failure to report, regardless of the tax consequences. Similar reporting requirements (and penalties for failure to report) do not apply if the trust is a domestic trust.

- **Taxation of non-grantor trusts** – Domestic non-grantor trusts are taxed on all income, regardless of source (subject to deductions for distributions to beneficiaries). Foreign trusts, on the other hand, are subject to US tax only on certain US-sourced income.

- **Application of 'throwback tax'** – The throwback tax is imposed on distributions of accumulated income from trusts and previously applied to both domestic and foreign trusts. Since 1997 the throwback tax has generally only applied to distributions from foreign trusts.

- **Loans treated as distributions** – Certain loans from foreign trusts can be taxed as if they were distributions.

- **Transfers through intermediaries** – A US taxpayer can be treated as having received a distribution from a foreign trust if the US person receives a payment from an intermediary. There are no similar rules for distributions from domestic trusts.

- **Subchapter S rules** – A foreign trust cannot be a 'qualified shareholder' of a 'subchapter S' corporation (a US corporation the income of which is taxed to its US shareholders), even if the trust would be considered a grantor trust.[1]

12.10   Prior to 1996, the residence of a trust as domestic or foreign was – much like transfer tax rules for determining US domicile – based on an unscientific set of facts and circumstances. Would it be based on the residency of the settlor? The proper law of the trust? The location of the trust assets? The residency of the trustees? The place of administration? Some weighted combination of factors? Courts were ultimately able (or forced) to make these determinations, but no clear rules were in place for planners wishing to achieve (or avoid) foreign trust status. All that changed in 1996. Concerned about a number of perceived abuses involving foreign trusts, Congress changed many tax rules related to foreign trusts, implemented special reporting obligations with respect to foreign trusts (see **12.137** et seq) and imposed substantial penalties on US taxpayers who fail to comply with the reporting requirements. If Congress was going to crack down on foreign trusts, it desperately needed to define the beast. Fortunately, Congress did just that.

12.11   The Small Business Jobs Protection Act 1996 (SPJPA) established a two–part objective test for determining whether a trust is a foreign trust or a domestic trust. A trust will be considered a domestic trust (resident in the US for US income tax purposes) where *both* of the following criteria are satisfied:

(a)   a court within the US is able to exercise primary supervision over the administration of the trust (the 'Court Test'); and

(b)   one or more US persons have the authority to control all substantial decisions of the trust (the 'Control Test').[2]

A foreign trust is any trust that is not a domestic trust, that is, any trust that fails *either* the Court Test or the Control Test.[3]

---

[1]   Code § 1361(c)(2)(A).
[2]   Code § 7701(a)(30)(E).
[3]   Code § 7701(a)(31).

Income tax residence of trusts **12.16**

1. The Court Test

12.12 A trust satisfies the Court Test if a court within the US is able to exercise primary supervision over the administration of the trust.[4] The term 'primary supervision' means that a court has authority to determine substantially all issues regarding the administration of the trust.[5] Simply having jurisdiction over the trustee, a beneficiary, or trust property is not always equal to having primary supervision, and one court may have primary supervision over the trust even though another court has jurisdiction over a trustee, a beneficiary, or property of the trust. Exclusive primary jurisdiction is not required. If, for example, both a US court and a UK court were able to exercise primary supervision over the administration of a trust, the trust would meet the Court Test.[6]

12.13 The term 'administration of the trust' means the carrying out of the duties imposed by the terms of the trust instrument and applicable law, including maintaining the books and records of the trust, filing tax returns, managing and investing the assets of the trust, defending the trust from suits by creditors, and determining the amount and timing of distributions.[7]

12.14 The regulations provide that a trust will fail the control test if it includes an automatic migration provision that purports to shift jurisdiction and administration of the trust to a foreign jurisdiction if a US court attempts to assert jurisdiction over a trust or to supervise the administration of a trust.[8] In an apparent acknowledgement to the military might and imperial intentions of Fidel Castro, a flight clause (sometimes referred to as a 'Cuba Clause') will not cause a trust to fail the control test if it is triggered by a foreign invasion or by widespread confiscation or nationalization of US property.

12.15 The regulations also include a safe harbor. A trust will satisfy the court test if:

- the trust deed does not direct administration outside the US;
- the trust is in fact administered exclusively in the US; and
- the trust does not include an automatic migration clause.[9]

2. The Control Test

12.16 The Control Test is satisfied if one or more US persons (whether or not fiduciaries) control all substantial decisions related to the trust.[10] The term 'substantial decisions' means all decisions (other than ministerial decisions) that persons are authorized or required to make under the terms of the trust instrument and

---

[4] Code § 7701(a)(30)(E)(i).
[5] Treas Reg § 301.7701–7(c)(3)(iv).
[6] Treas Reg § 301.7701–7(c)(4)(i)(D).
[7] Treas Reg § 301.7701–7(c)(3)(v).
[8] Treas Reg § 301.7701–7(c)(4)(ii).
[9] Treas Reg § 301.7701–7(c)(iv)(ii).
[10] Code § 7701(a)(30)(E)(ii).

12.17 *US Income Taxation of Trusts, Estates, Grantors and Beneficiaries*

applicable law. Ministerial (and thus non substantial) decisions include bookkeeping, collecting rents, and executing investment transactions directed by others.[11]

12.17 The regulations give the following (non-exclusive) examples of substantial trust decisions:

- whether and when to distribute the trust's income or capital;
- the amount of any distributions;
- the selection of a beneficiary;
- whether to terminate the trust;
- whether to compromise, arbitrate, or abandon claims of the trust;
- whether to remove, add, or replace a trustee; and
- investment decisions.[12]

The term 'control' means having the power, by vote or otherwise, to make the substantial decision, with no other person having power to veto that decision.[13]

Example

A trust has three fiduciaries, A, B, and C. A and B are US citizens and C is a NRA. The trust instrument provides that no substantial decisions of the trust can be made unless there is unanimity among the fiduciaries. The trust is considered a foreign trust, since C (a NRA) has effective veto power over substantial decisions. If, however, trustee decisions could be made by *majority* vote, the Control Test would be met since the two US trustees (A and B) acting by majority could control decisions. This is true even though C (the NRA) could join with either A or B to control the actions of the trust.[14]

12.18 The IRS initially had proposed that the control test could be satisfied even if a NRA beneficiary controlled a particular substantial decision with respect to his own trust. However, the final regulations dropped this exception and determine control without regard to whether the holder of the power is a beneficiary or even a fiduciary.

Example

A Mexican national and resident settlor funds an irrevocable, discretionary trust with non-US assets for the benefit of his children. The trust is formed under the laws of the State of Texas and the trustee is a US bank. One of the settlor's children – also a Mexican national and resident – is given the power, as protector, to remove and replace the trustee. The trust is a foreign trust, which is not subject to US income tax (except on

---

[11] Treas Reg § 301.7701–7(d)(1)(ii).
[12] Treas Reg § 301.7701–7(d)(1)(ii). A foreign discretionary investment adviser can be hired if a US trustee can remove such person. Treas Reg § 301.7701–7(d)(1)(ii)(J).
[13] Treas Reg § 301.7701–7(d)(1)(iii).
[14] Treas Reg § 301.7701–7(d)(1)(v) (Example 2).

certain US-source income). If the settlor retained the right to revoke the trust, then the trust would still be a foreign trust but would also be considered a grantor trust, under special rules discussed at **12.40** et seq.

C. Taxation of the grantor

12.19 The grantor trust rules of the US Tax Code are found in sections 671–679 of the Code. These provisions determine the circumstances in which the 'grantor' (the person who funds the trust) – or in limited circumstances another person taxed as if he were the grantor – is taxed as the 'owner' of the trust. The income, gains, deductions, and credits of a grantor trust are taxed to the owner as if the trust did not exist, that is, as if the taxpayer were the direct owner of the underlying trust assets.[15]

12.20 If the grantor is taxed as the trust owner, then there are two related consequences: First, the trust will not be taxed on the income or gains it earns. Second, a trust beneficiary (even one entitled to all trust income) is not taxed on trust distributions. In Rev Rul 69–70,[16] for example, a NRA created a foreign grantor trust for the benefit of US beneficiaries. The IRS ruled that distributions to the US beneficiaries would not be subject to tax, since the NRA grantor was currently taxable as the grantor/owner of the trust. Although as discussed at **12.40** et seq, the foreign grantor in that ruling would not, presumably, be respected as grantor/owner under current law, the principle of that ruling – that beneficiaries of grantor trusts are not taxable on trust distributions – remains in force.

12.21 We will first summarize the general rules that define when a person is taxed as the grantor/owner of the trust. We will then follow with a discussion of changes to the tax laws during the 1990s that limited the circumstances in which a NRA will be respected as the grantor/owner of a trust.

1. General grantor trust rules

12.22 The grantor trust provisions of the US Tax Code encompass a complex maze of general rules, exceptions, and exceptions to exceptions. Generally, a grantor will be treated as the owner of the trust under any of the following circumstances:

---

[15] Prop. Treas Reg § 1.671–2(f). The grantor trust rules apply only for US income tax purposes. They do not define when trust property will be included in the grantor's estate for US estate tax purposes, although there is some overlap. For example, a grantor's retained right to revoke the trust will cause him to be treated for income tax purposes as the trust's owner and will cause the trust property to be included in his estate at death. In many other circumstances, however, grantor trust property will not be included in the grantor's estate at death. An example would be an irrevocable life insurance trust: the mere fact that trust income is used to pay premiums on life insurance on the grantor's life will make the trust a grantor trust for income tax purposes, yet the insurance proceeds should be excluded from tax in the grantor/insured's estate as long as he has not retained any economic benefit from or control over the trust.

[16] 1969–1 CB 182.

12.23   *US Income Taxation of Trusts, Estates, Grantors and Beneficiaries*

- the grantor or the grantor's spouse has a current or future interest (even as a discretionary beneficiary) to the trust income;[17]
- the grantor (or a non-adverse party) in fact uses trust income to discharge the grantor's legal obligation;[18]
- the grantor (or a non-adverse party) uses trust income to pay life insurance premiums on the life of the grantor or grantor's spouse;[19]
- the grantor has a reversionary interest valued at 5% or more of the value of the trust assets;[20]
- the grantor (or a non-adverse party) has a power to control the beneficial enjoyment over the trust;[21]
- the grantor (or a non-adverse party) has the power to revoke the trust and return trust assets to the grantor;[22]
- the grantor (or a non-adverse party) holds certain administrative powers in a non-fiduciary capacity;[23]
- a US grantor creates a foreign trust for the current or future benefit of US beneficiaries;[24]
- a NRA creates a foreign trust for the current or future benefit of US beneficiaries and then moves to the US within five years of settling the trust.[25]

12.23   Powers and interests held by the person who was the grantor's spouse at the creation of the power are attributed to the grantor for the purposes of these rules.[26] The grantor is also attributed powers and interests of a person who becomes the grantor's spouse after the powers or interests are created, but this attribution applies only after the individual becomes the grantor's spouse.

12.24   Many of these rules are subject to an 'adverse party' exception. In Code § 677, for example, a grantor will not be treated as the owner if distributions of income to the grantor are subject to the consent of an adverse party. As the name implies, an adverse party is a person having a substantial beneficial interest in the trust that would be adversely affected by the exercise of the particular power.[27] For example, a grantor, whose spouse is a beneficiary of a trust, would not be taxed as the owner if distributions to the spouse were subject to the consent of the couple's daughter, who had a remainder interest in the trust.

---

[17]   Code § 677(a)(1) and (2).
[18]   Code § 677(b).
[19]   Code § 677(a)(3). This is true – according to the IRS – even though the trust deed directs that premiums be paid out of trust principal and not income. PLR 8839008 (23 June 1988).
[20]   Code § 673.
[21]   Code § 674.
[22]   Code § 676.
[23]   Code § 675.
[24]   Code § 679.
[25]   Code § 679(a)(4).
[26]   Code § 672(e).
[27]   Code § 672(b) and Treas Reg § 1.672(b)(1). A trustee – even one entitled to substantial fees based on net underlying asset value – is not considered to have an adverse interest in the trust. Treas Reg § 1.672(a)-1(a).

12.25 Code § 673 treats the grantor as the owner where the grantor (or the grantor's spouse) has a reversionary interest valued at more than 5% of the value of the trust assets. For this purpose, the trustee is assumed to exercise its maximum authority in favor of the grantor.[28] Unlike most other grantor trust provisions, the reversionary interest rule does not have an 'adverse party' exception.[29] Many had thus believed that the 'maximum exercise' rule would cause the settlor to be treated as owner in all discretionary trusts where the trustee could exercise immediate discretion to terminate the trust and distribute all trust assets to the grantor (or grantor's spouse). However, the IRS has not apparently agreed with that interpretation, ruling in two instances that section 673 would not apply.[30] The authors understand from counsel who were responsible for at least one of these rulings that the IRS does not consider a settlor's discretionary beneficial interest to be a 'reversionary interest' in the sense that term is used in section 673, therefore, limiting the application of this section to situations where the trust property reverts to the settlor (or settlor's spouse) at the termination of a prior interest.

12.26 There is a certain intrinsic logic to taxing a settlor as owner if the settlor has retained a personal economic interest (Code §§ 673 and 677), a right to revoke the trust (Code § 676), or the power to control trust distributions (Code § 674). However, under some circumstances, the grantor need not have any interest or control to trigger personal taxation. For example, Code § 677 taxes the grantor as the owner if trust income is used to pay the premiums on life insurance on the life of the grantor or the grantor's spouse.

12.27 Another example where the grantor's powers and interests are irrelevant is Code § 674. The general rule of that section – stated in a mere three lines of the Code – causes the grantor to be taxed as the trust's owner if a non-adverse party (or the grantor) has the power to control beneficial enjoyment – that is, the power to decide on the timing of distributions and the identity of the recipients. The exceptions to this general rule then cover a few pages of the Code and numerous pages of the regulations.

12.28 Certain Code § 674 exceptions apply regardless of the identity of the power holder, that is, even if the grantor holds the excepted power. These exceptions include the power to:

- appoint by Will;[31]

- allocate among charitable beneficiaries;[32]

---

[28] Code § 673(c).
[29] Compare Code § 673(c) with Code §§ 674(a), 675, 677(a), but see PLR 9016079 (25 January 1990) where Code § 673 was ruled not to apply where the grantor, as co-trustee with other trust beneficiaries, had the power to distribute principal to himself; the ruling did not focus on Code § 673(c) or on a possible implicit adverse party exception to Code § 673.
[30] PLR 9106079 (25 January 1990), PLR 200148028 (27 August 2001).
[31] Code § 674(b)(3). This exception does not apply to the grantor's power to appoint accumulated income.
[32] Code § 674(b)(4).

12.29 *US Income Taxation of Trusts, Estates, Grantors and Beneficiaries*

- distribute principal according to an 'ascertainable standard' or to the income beneficiary as a charge against his share;[33]

- accumulate income if the accumulated income is eventually payable:

    (a) to the beneficiary, his estate, his appointees or takers in default of the beneficiary's appointment; or

    (b) upon termination of the trust, to the current income beneficiaries according to irrevocably specified shares;[34]

- accumulate income during the beneficiary's minority or disability.[35]

12.29 Another section 674 exception applies where an independent trustee has the power to 'sprinkle' income or principal to, or among, named beneficiaries or members of a defined class.[36] The trustees are considered independent if 'none of [them] are the grantor and no more than half of whom are related and subordinate parties who are subservient to the wishes of the grantor'. Parties are 'related and subordinate' to the grantor if they are:

- the grantor's spouse (but only if she is living with the grantor);

- the grantor's parents;

- the grantor's issue;

- the grantor's brother or sister;

- an employee of the grantor; or

- an employee of a corporation in which the grantor's or trust's shareholdings are significant from a standpoint of control.[37]

Related and subordinate parties are assumed to be 'subservient' to the wishes of the grantor unless the contrary can be proven by a preponderance of the evidence.[38]

12.30 The final exception to the general rule of Code § 674 applies where trustees (other than the grantor and the grantor's spouse) have a power to apply income to or among named beneficiaries or members of a defined class if such power is limited by an ascertainable standard.[39]

12.31 To further complicate matters, many of the section 674 exceptions listed above do not apply if a person has the power to add to the class of the beneficiaries, other than by inclusion of after-born or after-adopted children.[40] (If you are keeping score, an exception to the exception to the general rule means the general rule

---

[33] Code § 674(b)(5). An 'ascertainable standard' means distributions for the beneficiary's health, maintenance, support, and education, but not for his pleasure, desire or happiness. See Treas Reg § 1.674(b)-1(b)(5).
[34] Code § 674(b)(6).
[35] Code § 674(b)(7).
[36] Code § 674(c).
[37] Code § 672(c).
[38] Code § 672(c).
[39] Code § 674(d).
[40] Code § 674(b)(5)–(7), (c) and (d).

applies – that is, that powers to control beneficial enjoyment cause the grantor to be taxed as the owner.) And, what exception to an exception would be complete without a couple of exceptions of its own: powers to add to the class of beneficiaries do not cause grantor trust status if exercisable (i) by an adverse party or (ii) by Will.[41] (If these rules were a game of 'tag', *non-grantor* trust status would now be 'it'.)

2. Grantor and others taxed as the owner

12.32 The grantor trust rules require the proper identification of the grantor. Generally, this is the person who contributed property to the trust. Therefore, a nominal settlor (the person whose name is on the trust as settlor or who contributed a nominal amount to the trust) will be ignored for purposes of the grantor trust rules.[42]

12.33 In 2000, the IRS issued new regulations that define the grantor as the person who 'either creates a trust, or directly or indirectly makes a gratuitous transfer ... of property to the trust'.[43] A person who funds a trust on behalf of another or is reimbursed within a reasonable period of time for funding a trust is not considered the grantor. A transfer is said to be 'gratuitous' if it is not made for fair market value, for example, if property is gifted to the trust or sold for less than fair market value.

12.34 It is possible to have multiple grantors of a trust; in that event, each will be taxed as the owner of the portion of the trust contributed by them.[44]

Example

George and Martha Washington each contribute $10,000 to a trust. Each is considered grantor as to half of the trust.

Example

George contributes $10,000 to a trust. Later, Martha sells $20,000 of stock in Flags-R-Us Inc to the trust for $10,000. Martha has made a gratuitous transfer of $10,000 and as is considered an equal grantor with George.

---

[41] Treas Reg § 1.674(d)–2(b).
[42] See, generally, Bittker & Lokken, *Federal Taxation of Income, Estate and Gifts* (3rd edn, 2003), Warren, Gorham & Lamont, at ¶ 80.1.2; see *Stern v Comm'r 77 TC 614 (1981), rev'd on other grounds 747 F2d 555 (9th Cir 1984)*, and *Bixby v Comm'r 58 TC 757 (1972)*. A nominal grantor will not be ignored for purposes of reporting the settlement of a trust on Form 3520 under Treas Reg § 1.671–2(e)(6) (Example 3) (attorney required to report even though he is reimbursed $100 for setting up a trust; however, the 35% excise tax penalty would be nominal). Note that under these regulations, the grantor of a trust is deemed (but only for income tax purposes) to also be the grantor of any trust created or funded by the first trust, even after the settlor's death. Treas. Reg § 1.67–2(e)(6) (Example 8).
[43] Treas Reg § 1.671–2(e)(1).
[44] Treas Reg §§ 1.671–2(e)(6) (Example 7) and 1.671–3(a)(3).

12.35   *US Income Taxation of Trusts, Estates, Grantors and Beneficiaries*

12.35 The Revenue Reconciliation Act 1990 limits the applicability of this foreign grantor trust rule in potentially abusive situations where a US person has made direct or indirect gifts to the foreign grantor.[45] Under this rule (affectionately referred to as the 'give and go' rule), a US person will be considered the grantor/owner of a trust (domestic or foreign) if he has at any time made a gift to a foreign person who, but for this special rule, would be considered the grantor/owner of a trust that has as one of its beneficiaries the US donor.

Example

Nigel Branson makes a £1m gift to his brother, Rick, prior to Nigel's move to the US. Without overt pre-arrangement, brother Rick subsequently funds a £1m trust for the benefit of Nigel and his family. If, but for this special rule, Rick would have been considered the grantor/owner of the trust, then the US tax laws will instead tax Nigel as the trust's grantor/owner.

12.36 Gifts by US beneficiaries within the gift tax annual exclusion are ignored. This rule only applies with respect to trusts settled by foreign settlors after 9 November 1990, but there is no similar limit for when the US beneficiary's gift to the foreign settlor was made. No proof of pre-arrangement is required. Note that this special rule only applies if, but for the rule, the foreign donee/grantor would be considered the owner of the trust. Given the limited circumstances under which a NRA will be respected as a trust's owner after the SPJPA, the give and go rule has considerably less importance than it had when first enacted.

12.37 Finally, Code § 678 treats certain persons (other than the grantor) as if they were the trust owners. Derived from the *Mallinckrodt* case,[46] a third person will be taxed as the owner if:

- he currently has a power to distribute trust income or principal to himself; or

- he previously released such a power but has retained an interest or power in the trust that would have caused a grantor to be taxed as the trust owner under sections 671 through 677

12.38 The most common example of this is a so-called 'Crummey' withdrawal power conferred on beneficiaries to qualify gifts to the trust for the gift tax annual exclusion. A beneficiary's right to withdraw funds from the trust, or his continued beneficial interest in a trust in which such withdrawal rights have lapsed, can cause the beneficiary to be taxed as the trust owner. The beneficiary is not taxed as owner, however, if the trust's 'real' grantor is taxed as the owner.[47]

12.39 As can be seen, maneuvering through the complex maze of the grantor trust rules offers many challenges. In some ways, these rules provide a trap for the unwary, including the unaware non-US tax planner who has prepared the tax plan

---

[45] Originally enacted as Code § 672(f), this provision is now found in Code § 672(f)(5). See also Layman, 'New US Tax Act Affects Taxation of Foreign Grantor Trusts with US Beneficiaries', 18 Tax Planning International Review 13 (February 1991).
[46] *Mallinckrodt v Nunan 146 F2d 1 (8th Cir 1945), cert denied 324 US 871 (1945).*
[47] Code § 678(b).

for her non US client which satisfies the tax objects in the client's current jurisdiction of residence, but may fall foul of the US grantor trust rules if the client is, or becomes, a US taxpayer.

3. *NRAs respected as owners only under limited circumstances*

12.40 Prior to 20 August 1996, the grantor trust rules generally applied with equal force to US citizens, resident aliens, and NRAs. This provided some interesting planning opportunities. As previously noted, if a person is treated as the grantor/owner of the trust, distributions could be made to US beneficiaries free of US tax. This rule was specifically blessed in the context of a trust created by a foreign settlor for the benefit of US beneficiaries.[48] Further, as noted above, a settlor need not have any interest or powers over a trust to be considered its grantor/owner. Grantor trust status could be achieved by something as simple as a trustee having discretion to distribute among a class of beneficiaries – coupled with an exception-beating exception of a non-adverse party's power to add to the class of beneficiaries (a common provision in many offshore trusts). If such a trust were created in an offshore tax haven, it was possible that no one would be taxed on the trust income:

- not the foreign grantor whose home-country tax laws are different than those in the US;

- not the foreign trust formed in a tax haven that imposes no tax on local trusts; and

- not the US beneficiary who can receive tax-free distributions from the foreign trust.

Some even suggested using a foreign corporation to fund the trust, so that grantor trust status was not dependent on a settlor's life. All of this was a tax-planner's dream.

12.41 Ah, but leave it to the US Congress – like Freddy in *Nightmare on Elm Street* fame – to spoil a good dream. The SPJPA substantially limited the situations in which a NRA will be respected as the grantor/owner of a trust. Effective 20 August 1996, the grantor trust rules apply only to the extent those rules cause a US taxpayer to be treated as the trust's owner.[49] The rule applies without regard to whether the trust is a domestic trust or a foreign trust.

12.42 There are three important exceptions in which a NRA will be respected as a trust's owner:

- a trust which is revocable by the settlor, either acting alone or with the consent of the infamous 'related or subordinate party' who is 'subservient' to the grantor's wishes;[50] or

---

[48] Rev Rul 69–70, 1969–1 CB 182.
[49] Code § 672(f)(1).
[50] Code § 672(f)(2)(A)(i).

12.43 *US Income Taxation of Trusts, Estates, Grantors and Beneficiaries*

- a trust which, during the grantor's life, can only make distributions of income or principal to the grantor or the grantor's spouse;[51] or

- a trust to the extent funded prior to 19 September 1995, but only if the foreign settlor would be taxed as the grantor/owner under Code § 676 (revocable trusts) or Code § 677 (trusts whose income could be distributed or accumulated for the settlor and/or the settlor's spouse).[52]

12.43   Compensatory trusts (that is, trusts the distributions from which are taxable as compensation income to the settlor) are not subject to this rule.[53] Pursuant to relevant regulations, this exception is generally limited to:

- non-exempt employee's trusts under Code § 402(b); and

- certain deferred compensation trusts subject to the employer's right to revoke or the employer's creditors in bankruptcy – so-called 'rabbi trusts'.[54]

12.44   Finally, a foreign corporation that is a so-called 'controlled foreign corporations' (CFCs) can be respected as the grantor-owner of a trust.[55] Certain US shareholders are taxed currently on their share of certain types of the CFC's income. If the grantor trust rules prohibited CFCs from being respected as grantor/owners of foreign trusts, US taxpayers (and their clever tax planners) could shelter passive income in foreign trusts created by CFCs.

12.45   If a NRA is respected as the grantor/owner of a trust, the NRA's US tax exposure is generally limited to the following three types of income:

---

[51] Code § 672(f)(2)(A)(ii).
[52] This effective date rule is found in the SPJPA itself. If contributions are made to an otherwise qualifying trust after the effective date, the trust must be accounted for as a grantor trust (with respect to pre-effective date contributions) and non-grantor trusts (with respect to post-effective date contributions). Treas Reg § 1.672(f)-3(d). If not separately accounted for in this fashion, the foreign settlor will not be respected as the grantor/owner.
[53] Code § 672(f)(2)(B).
[54] Treas Reg § 1.672(f)-3(c).
[55] Code § 672(f)(1); Treas Reg § 1.672(f)-2(a). Similar rules apply to trusts settled by foreign personal holding companies (FPHCs) and passive foreign investment companies (PFICs).

Taxation of the grantor **12.49**

a. Fixed or determinable annual or periodic income (FDAPI)[56]

12.46 FDAPI includes such items as US-sourced dividend, rents and interest. Income on the termination of a US-based insurance policy is also considered FDAPI.[57] This income is generally taxed at a flat 30% rate, collected by withholding at the source.[58]

b. Effectively connected income (ECI)[59]

12.47 Income effectively connected with a US trade or business is also subject to US tax. This income is taxed on the same graduated rate scale that applies to citizens and resident aliens. A NRA who earns ECI will be required to file a US tax return to report this income.

c. Gains from the sale of US real estate interests[60]

12.48 The so-called FIRPTA rules (Foreign Investment in Real Property Tax Act) impose a tax on a non-US taxpayer's gain from the sale of certain US real property interests. These interests include both US real estate directly owned by the foreign investor and US property owned through certain US holding companies. Gain from the sale of US property interests are taxed as ECI. If the gains are long term, the US tax rate is currently capped at 15%. The purchaser of US real estate interest from a foreign seller is generally required to withhold 10% of the sales price,[61] requiring the foreign seller – in this case, the NRA – to file a US tax return to collect any refund (or pay any additional US tax liability).

4. Foreign trusts and Code § 679

12.49 Under Code § 679, a US taxpayer who transfers property to a foreign trust for the current or future benefit of US beneficiaries will be taxed as the trust's owner. Regulations interpret the trust as capable of benefiting a US person unless:

- the trust deed precludes US persons from benefiting from the trust; or
- no US persons are named as beneficiaries under the deed and there is no power to add a US person as a beneficiary.[62]

The fact that a named beneficiary might one day become a US resident does not cause the trust to be treated as having US beneficiaries.[63]

---

[56] Code § 871(a)(1)(A).
[57] Rev Rul 64–51, 1964–1 CB 322.
[58] Code §§ 871(a)(1) and 1441(a).
[59] Code § 871(b).
[60] Code § 897(a).
[61] Code § 1445(a).
[62] Treas Reg § 1.679–2(a). This determination is made on an annual basis.
[63] Treas Reg § 1.679–2(a)(3)(i).

12.50 *US Income Taxation of Trusts, Estates, Grantors and Beneficiaries*

12.50   Code § 679 has been part of the US Tax Code since 1976 but, historically, had applied only to transfers by US persons. An immigrant could easily avoid the reaches of this provision by transferring property to a foreign trust prior to his US residency start date.[64] The original provision also included a 'sale or exchange' exception for a transfer to a foreign trust for fair market value in which the transferor realizes gain on the transfer, either at the time of the sale or over time under the installment sale rules. Finally, if a foreign trust had not been a grantor trust in prior years and later acquires a US beneficiary (for example, by a named beneficiary becoming a US tax resident) thus causing the US settlor to become the grantor/owner, the US settlor is immediately subject to US tax on *all undistributed income* of the trust from prior years.[65]

12.51   The SPJPA made a number of significant changes that affect Code § 679. First, the SPJPA (and related regulations) introduced an objective test for determining the residency of a trust as domestic or foreign. Second, the SPJPA made a number of changes to the sale and exchange exception, primarily related to sales in which the US seller takes back debt. Under prior law, the sale and exchange exception applied even if the seller took back debt and realized gain under the installment basis. Under the SPJPA, debt will not be considered fair value in an exchange unless:

(a)   the foreign trust is not a related party to the settlor;[66] or

(b)   if the trust and settlor are related, the debt is considered a 'qualified obligation'.

12.52   In relation to (b) above, a 'qualified obligation' must be:

- in writing;
- for no longer than five years;
- denominated in US dollars;
- the interest rate must be between 100% and 130% of the applicable federal interest rates; and
- the seller reports the loan on multi-purpose Form 3520.[67]

As a consequence of these rules, a demand note and private annuity cannot be considered a 'qualified obligation'.[68]

12.53   Third, the SPJPA offers some relief to the rule where a foreign trust's later acquisition of a US beneficiary causes the US settlor to be taxed on all prior trust

---

[64] See the discussion of an immigrant's residency start date at **16.21**.
[65] Code § 679(b).
[66] Treas Reg §§ 1.679–1(c)(5) and 1.679–4(c) provide that a trust and US seller are related if the seller is (i) a grantor of the trust, (ii) the owner of the trust under other grantor trust rules, (iii) a beneficiary of the trust, or a person who is 'related' to the trust's grantor, owner or beneficiaries under the rules of Code § 643(i)(2)(B). See also Treas Reg § 1.679–4(d)(7) (Example 3) (loan to unrelated foreign trust not considered a 'transfer' even though not a 'qualified obligation').
[67] Treas Reg § 1.679–4(d)(1).
[68] Treas Reg § 1.679–4(d)(7) (Examples 1 and 2).

accumulations. That general rule remains, but the SPJPA added an exception whereby a person who moves to the US more than five years after the US person's transfer to the foreign trust will not be considered a US beneficiary.[69]

Example

Benjamin Frank Lynn, a US resident, forms a foreign non-grantor trust for the benefit of the children of his French 'friend', Madame Versailles. Six years after forming the trust, one of the children moves to the US and becomes a US income tax resident. The trust remains a foreign non-grantor trust and Ben is not taxed on the trust's accumulations. If the child had moved to the US within five years of funding, then Ben would be considered the grantor/owner and would be taxed on interim trust accumulations.

12.54 Finally, the SPJPA extended section 679 to certain immigrants who funded the foreign trust within five years of becoming a US resident.[70] This extension targeted the practice of forming pre-immigration trusts just prior to immigration to avoid the reaches of section 679. This change applies to immigrants who made transfers after 6 February 1995. The SPJPA achieves this result by treating the immigrant as having waited to transfer the relevant property to the trust until immediately after becoming a US resident. This deemed transfer applies for purposes of both section 679 (and thus the grantor trust rules) and the reporting rules of Code § 6048. As discussed in **CHAPTER 8** (see 8.49), it is also possible that the Code § 679 'deemed transfer' rule affects the 'deemed sale' rule of Code § 684. The latter section treats a US taxpayer who transfers property to a foreign non-grantor trust to be taxed as if that property had been sold and to realize gain (but not losses) on any inherent appreciation.

D. US taxation of domestic non-grantor trusts

12.55 Grantor trusts are transparent for US tax purposes, with the trust's income, gains, deductions and credits flowing directly through to the grantor/owner. Non-grantor trusts, on the other hand, are separate taxpayers, subject to being taxed on any income and gains realized in the trust.

12.56 A domestic non-grantor trust is taxed on its net income and gains. Like US citizens and resident aliens, a domestic trust is taxed on its worldwide income and gains, regardless of the source. Among the deductions allowed to a domestic non-grantor trust, perhaps the most important is the 'distribution deduction' for certain distributions to beneficiaries.[71]

---

[69] Code § 679(c)(3).
[70] Code § 679(a)(4).
[71] Code §§ 651 and 661(a) provide for the trust's deduction.

1. Distribution deduction and DNI

12.57 The distribution deduction effectively shifts the tax on certain income and gains from the trust to the beneficiary.[72] The amount of the distribution deduction is limited by the trust's distributable net income (DNI).[73] DNI generally consists of all of the trust's ordinary income, with some adjustments.[74]

12.58 Historically, DNI has *not* included capital gains. There were limited exceptions. Gains that were required by local law or the terms of the trust to be distributed to trust beneficiaries would be included in DNI.[75]

> **Example**
>
> The terms of a Georgia trust deed provide for real property – called *Terra* – to be held for Scarlett's benefit. If *Terra* is sold, the trust deed directs that the proceeds be distributed to Scarlett. In the event of a sale, the *Terra* gains are included in DNI and taxed to Scarlett with the distribution.

12.59 Also, gains realized during the trust's final tax year are included in DNI and thus become taxable to the beneficiaries upon the termination of the trust.[76]

12.60 Recently the IRS has issued new regulations that significantly expand the circumstances under which capital gains can become part of DNI. Under these regulations, capital gains can be included in DNI if:

- pursuant to the terms of the trust deed and applicable local law; or

- pursuant to the trustee's reasonable and impartial exercise of discretion (in accordance with authority granted under the trust deed and not prohibited by local law,

those gains are allocated to fiduciary income.[77]

12.61 This change was, in part, in response to advances in modern portfolio theory emphasizing 'total return' (that is, a total increase in portfolio value from both gains and ordinary income). If a trustee is investing for total return, the concern is that traditional fiduciary income might be short-changed. Many states in the US have enacted statutes specifically authorizing trustees to adopt a 'total return unitrust' approach (treating as fiduciary income an amount of ordinary income and additional net gains up to a percentage of trust asset value) or to otherwise adjust as between income and principal.

---

[72] Code §§ 652 and 662 provide for the inclusion in the beneficiary's gross income.
[73] Code § 643(a).
[74] Code § 643(a).
[75] Code § 643(a)(3).
[76] Treas Reg § 1.643(a)-3(d) (Example 4).
[77] Treas Reg § 1.643(a)-3(b). This rule also applies if (i) capital gains are allocated to corpus but consistently treated by the trustee on the trust books as allocable to a beneficiary, or (ii) capital gains are allocated to corpus but actually distributed to a beneficiary or used by the trustee to determine the amount to distribute to a beneficiary.

12.62 The following examples illustrate these principles.

Example

A US non-grantor trust earns $20,000 of interest and dividend income and realizes $15,000 of capital gains. None of the special rules apply to cause any of the gains to be included in DNI. Accordingly, the trust's DNI is $20,000.

- If the trust distributed (or was required to distribute) $15,000 to the beneficiaries, the distribution deduction would be limited $15,000 (the amount distributed). The trust would be taxed on the remaining $5,000 of ordinary income not deemed distributed to the beneficiary and the $15,000 of capital gains that were not a part of DNI.

- If the trust distributed $30,000 to the beneficiary, the DNI deduction would be limited to $20,000 (the amount of DNI). The beneficiaries would be taxed on the $20,000 of distributed DNI and would receive the remaining $10,000 free of tax. The trust would be taxed on the $15,000 of gains that were not part of DNI and thus were not deemed distributed to the beneficiaries.

Example

Same facts as above, but assume that, under local law and the terms of the trust deed, the trustee allocates $5,000 of the capital gains to income. DNI in that case is $25,000, comprised of $20,000 of ordinary income and $5,000 of capital gains.

- A $15,000 distribution to beneficiaries will have the effect of carrying out $15,000 of DNI, consisting of a proportionate amount of ordinary income (80% or $12,000) and capital gains (20% or $3,000). The undistributed DNI and the portion of the gains that were not part of DNI would be taxed to the trust.

- A $30,000 distribution would carry out all of the $25,000 of ordinary income and capital gains that were a part of DNI. The portion of the capital gains that were not part of DNI ($10,000 in this example) would be taxed to the trust.

Example

Same facts as above, but the trust terminates during the year and distributes all assets equally to its two beneficiaries, A and B. The trust's DNI includes both the ordinary income ($20,000) and all of the capital gains ($15,000). The distributions to A and B provide the trust with a $35,000 distribution deduction: the trust pays no taxes on its income or gains for the year.

12.63 Most, but not all, distributions carry out the DNI of a non-grantor trust to its beneficiaries. A non-grantor trust is generally entitled to a distribution deduction for the following:

- discretionary or mandated distributions of trust income (and, in the case of mandated distributions, whether or not the distribution is actually made);

- discretionary distributions of trust principal;
- mandatory distributions of trust principal (except as noted below);
- final distributions to trust beneficiaries on the termination of the trust.

12.64 Trusts do not receive a distribution deduction for certain gifts or bequests mandated by the terms of the governing instrument.[78] The corollary is that beneficiaries are not taxed on these mandated distributions. This rule applies to (i) gifts or bequests of (ii) a fixed sum or of specific property (iii) mandated by the terms of the governing instrument and (iv) payable in three or fewer installments. Amounts payable only out of income do not qualify for this exception.

Example

An irrevocable trust deed provides for A to receive a distribution of $25,000 upon reaching the age of 25. This is a specific gift of a fixed amount, so the trust does not receive a distribution deduction and A is not taxed on this distribution.

Example

The terms of a Georgia trust deed provide for real property – *Terra* – to be held for Scarlett's benefit and distributed to her on her 40th birthday. The distribution to Scarlett of the deed to *Terra* on her 40th birthday will not be a taxable event: the trust will not receive a DNI deduction and Scarlett will not be deemed to have received any taxable income.

Example

An irrevocable trust deed provides for A to receive one-third of the trust principal upon reaching age 30. Since the amount is not fixed at the trust's inception but dependent on values at A's 30th birthday, this gift does not qualify for the exception. At the time of distribution, the trust will receive a DNI distribution deduction and A would be taxed on part, or all, of the trust's DNI in that year.

Example

An irrevocable trust provides for A to receive an annual annuity of $50,000 for the rest of his life. Although the amount is fixed, the number of installments could exceed three and, therefore, none of the installments qualify for this exception. The trust receives a DNI deduction each year and A is taxed on a portion of the trust's DNI in each year.

---

[78] Code § 663(a)(1).

2. Rates

12.65 Prior to 1987, non-grantor US trusts shared the same rate tables as married individuals who filed separate returns.[79] These trusts were sometimes used as a way to shift income from a high tax-rate donor to a lower-rate trust, or at least provide another 'run up the rate brackets'. However, the Tax Act 1986 subjected trusts to a new compressed rate structure that largely eliminates these benefits. Trusts are now subject to tax under the following schedule:

Taxable Income $		Tax on Base ($)	Rate on Excess
From	To		
0	1,950	0	15%
1,950	4,600	292.50	25%
4,600	7,000	955.00	28%
7,000	9,550	1,627.00	33%
Over 9,550		2,468.50	35%

12.66 The tax rate applied to a trust's long-term capital gains and qualifying dividends is currently capped at 15% through 2008. These rates should be compared with the 2004 rates on married-filing-separate individuals, where the 28% bracket begins at $58,625 of income and the 35% bracket begins at $159,550. The current rates for long-term gains and qualifying dividends are capped at 15%.

E. US taxation of foreign non-grantor trusts

12.67 Foreign non-grantor trusts are subject to US taxation only on certain US source income. These include:

- fixed or determinable annual or periodic income (FDAPI);[80]

- effectively connected income (ECI),[81] taxed on the same compressed rate scale that applies to domestic trusts;

- gains from the sale of US real estate interests.[82]

12.68 A foreign non-grantor trust is not subject to US tax on foreign-sourced income. However, the foreign income – as well as US income not taxable under the rules set out above – do become part of a foreign trust's DNI. This is important because it can affect the tax imposed on distributions to US taxpayers from the trust.

---

[79] Code § 1(e) prior to Section 101(a) of the 1986 Tax Act.
[80] Code § 871(a)(1)(A).
[81] Code § 871(b).
[82] Code § 897(a).

12.69 Also, importantly, the DNI of a foreign trust automatically includes all of the trust's capital gains (net of capital losses)[83] without regard for whether the net capital gains are considered to be part of accounting income under local law, the terms of the trust or the trustee's reasonable and impartial exercise of discretion. As discussed at **12.77** and **12.81**, this can impact the amount and character of income deemed taxed to a US beneficiary on distributions from a foreign trust's current and accumulated income.

12.70 Like domestic trusts, a foreign trust is entitled to a DNI deduction for distributions to beneficiaries, whether or not the beneficiaries are US taxpayers. The distribution deduction rules have the same impact on foreign trusts that they do for domestic trusts by causing the DNI to be carried out to the beneficiaries.

F. Taxation of the US beneficiaries on distributions from non-grantor trusts

12.71 This section discusses the taxation of US beneficiaries on distributions (or deemed distributions) from non-grantor trusts. As previously discussed, beneficiaries are not taxed on distributions from grantor trusts, since the income and gains of a grantor trust are attributed and taxed to the grantor/owner. This is true even if:

- the trust is a foreign trust;
- the grantor is not a US taxpayer; and
- the US beneficiary has a life estate or interest in possession.

12.72 If a person is considered the owner of only a portion of the trust, then the US beneficiary can be taxed with respect to distributions from the non-grantor trust portion.[84]

12.73 The taxation of US beneficiaries on distributions from non-grantor trusts depends on whether:

- the trust is a 'simple' or 'complex' trust;
- the distribution is deemed to include 'accumulated' income; and
- the trust is a domestic or foreign trust.

1. Beneficiaries of simple trusts

12.74 The terms 'simple trust' and 'complex trust' are not found in the US Tax Code. The terms refer not to how easy the trust deed was to draft or understand,

---

[83] Code § 643(a)(6)(C).
[84] Treas Reg § 1.671–3(a)(2). Under some circumstances, a grantor might be considered the owner of only a portion of the trust. For example, the grantor might have contributed only half of the property to the trust and would, accordingly, be considered the grantor only as to half. In other instances, the grantor might be considered only the owner of the income or of the principal (and thus the capital gains on the principal). Treas Reg § 1.671–3(a).

how much the lawyers charged to prepare the deed, the length (or weight) of the trust deed, or whether the trust is written in American or British English; instead, these shorthand terms are used in the regulations and by practitioners to describe two distinct taxing regimes.

12.75 A simple trust is one which, with respect to the taxable year:

- is required to distribute all of its income currently to one or more beneficiaries;

- makes no other distributions; and

- has no amounts which are paid, set aside or used for charitable purposes.[85]

12.76 A US life tenant or interest in possession holder in a simple trust is taxable on the lesser of the trust's DNI (discussed at **12.57** et seq) or the trust fiduciary income (determined by the trustees under the local law and the terms of the trust deed).[86] The US beneficiary is taxed on the income of a simple trust whether or not the trustee actually makes the required distributions during the tax year. The beneficiary's income inclusion offsets the trust's distribution deduction.[87]

12.77 DNI distributed currently from a simple trust retains its character (for example, as dividend, interest, and, where relevant, capital gains) in the hands of the beneficiary.[88] This can be important because of the tax rate differences available to certain types of income, such as long-term capital gains and qualified dividends.

12.78 If US taxes or foreign taxes have been withheld on the income of a simple trust, a beneficiary should be entitled to a proportionate share of the corresponding tax credit.[89] Similarly, if a simple trust has made estimated US tax payments, the trustee can elect to treat some portion of those tax payments as attributed to the beneficiaries.[90]

2. *Beneficiaries of complex trusts*

12.79 A 'complex' trust is any trust that is not a simple trust. A trust that is not obligated to distribute all of its fiduciary income to beneficiaries is thus a complex trust. A trust that authorizes (or directs) the trustee to make principal distributions is also considered a complex trust. A trust that has some simple trust features (for

---

[85] Code § 651(a).
[86] Code § 652(a).
[87] Code § 651(a).
[88] Code § 652(b).
[89] Code § 643(d) allocates the credit for US taxes withheld on a domestic trust among the beneficiaries. If foreign taxes are withheld on income earned by a domestic or foreign trust, those taxes should similarly be allocated to the beneficiary of a simple trust. Code § 642(a) provides that a trust is entitled to a foreign tax credit to the extent that credit is not allocated to a beneficiary (see, also, Treas Reg § 1.642(a)(2)-1). Similarly, Code § 901(b)(4) provides for foreign tax credits to be allocated to beneficiaries of the trust. Finally, a US beneficiary of a foreign simple trust should considered the beneficial owner of US-sourced income, and. Therefore, no withholding should be required under Code § 1441. Treas Reg § 1.1441-1(c)(6)(ii)(C).
[90] Code § 643(g).

example, mandating distribution of all trust income) but also complex trust features (authorizes distributions of trust principal) will be considered a complex trust.

12.80 A US beneficiary of a complex trust is first taxed on any income mandated by the trust deed to be distributed to the beneficiary.[91] The trust, in turn, gets a DNI deduction for the income mandated to be distributed from a complex trust.[92] US beneficiaries are next taxed on all other amounts that are paid, credited or required to be paid to the beneficiary, but only to the extent of their share of the trust's remaining DNI.[93]

Example

A trust has $40,000 of DNI. The trust deed requires $10,000 of income be distributed to A. The trust also authorizes the trustee to make principal distributions, and the trustee exercises his discretion and distributes $20,000 each to A and B. A is taxed on $25,000, consisting of $10,000 of income required to be distributed to him from income and one-half of the trust's remaining $30,000 of DNI. B is taxed on $15,000, consisting of one-half of the DNI remaining after the $10,000 mandated income distribution to A.

12.81 As with simple trusts, DNI currently distributed to a US beneficiary retains the same character in the beneficiary's hands.[94] Beneficiaries are not required to recognize income on certain gifts or bequests from a trust mandated by the terms of the governing instrument.[95] This rule is discussed at **12.64**.

12.82 Just like with simple trusts, if US taxes or foreign taxes have been withheld on a complex trust's current income, then the beneficiary should be entitled to a portion of that tax credit attributed to DNI distributed to that beneficiary. The distribution to the beneficiary should need to be 'grossed up' on account of the beneficiary's share of the withheld taxes, so that the US tax can be computed on the gross amount. In addition, if a complex trust has made estimated US tax payments, then the trust can elect to allocate a portion of those withheld taxes to the beneficiary. In that event the withheld taxes are treated as an additional distribution, thus grossing up the beneficiary's distribution.[96]

12.83 At the trustee's election, distributions made within 65 days after the close of the trust's tax year can be treated as made at the end of the trust's prior year.[97]

---

[91] Code § 662(a)(1).
[92] Code § 661(a)(1).
[93] Code § 662(a)(2).
[94] Code § 662(b).
[95] Code § 663(a)(1).
[96] Code § 643(g).
[97] Code § 663(b). The election deems such distribution to have been made on the last day of the previous year, but only to the extent to the trust's undistributed accounting income or DNI. Treas Reg § 1.663(b)-1(a)(2). The 65-day election *cannot*, therefore, cause a distribution to be treated as an accumulation distribution and subject to throwback tax.

12.84 Finally, if distributions from a complex trust exceed DNI, then the excess can be treated as an 'accumulation distribution' and subject to the 'throwback' tax on 'UNI'. These terms and rules are summarized in the following section.

3. Accumulation distributions, the 'throwback tax' and UNI

a. General

12.85 An accumulation distribution occurs when the amounts distributed (or required to be distributed) from a complex trust exceeds the trust's DNI for the year.[98] There is no accumulation distribution, however, if the amount distributed is less than the trust's fiduciary accounting income.[99] Differences between DNI and fiduciary income can result for many reasons, including the fact that all fiduciary fees are deductible for determining DNI while only a portion (usually half) will be allocated to fiduciary income.

12.86 If the 'accumulation distribution' to a US beneficiary exceeds accounting income, then the US beneficiary could be subject to a special tax – referred to as the 'throwback' tax – on the trust's undistributed net income (UNI). UNI is the excess of the trust's DNI over the sum of:

(a) the trust's distributions for the tax year; and

(b) the taxes paid by the trust with respect to that accumulated DNI.[100]

12.87 In the context of a domestic trust, UNI is computed by subtracting only US taxes paid on DNI.[101] By contrast, UNI of a foreign trust is computed by subtracting both US and foreign taxes.[102] As discussed below, taxes that are subtracted out in computing UNI are added back into the equation when computing the throwback tax on accumulation distributions. It is possible for a trust to accumulate DNI in more than one year and thus have UNI attributed to multiple years.

12.88 The throwback tax is computed – under complex rules discussed at **12.90** et seq – as if the accumulated income had been distributed and taxed to a US beneficiary in certain prior years. The purpose of the throwback tax is, in large part, to prevent using trusts to accumulate income and pay taxes at lower rates in one year and then distribute that accumulate income in a later year to a US beneficiary who is taxed in a higher tax bracket.

---

[98] Code § 665(b).
[99] Code § 665(b).
[100] Code § 665(a) and (d).
[101] Code § 665(d)(1).
[102] Code § 665(d)(1) and (2). Also, since a foreign trust will include capital gains in DNI, any taxes paid on a foreign trust's capital gains will be subtracted in computing UNI. Taxes paid on the capital gains of a domestic trust that are not included in the trust's DNI do not affect the calculation of UNI and the throwback tax.

12.89 Beginning in 1987, the tax rates for trusts were substantially compressed, thus reducing the potential benefits of accumulating income in domestic trusts. It took ten years, but Congress eventually came to its senses, realizing that the complexities of the throwback tax did not warrant the relatively small (if any) extra taxes collected in taxing accumulation distributions from domestic trusts. In 1997, Congress accordingly repealed the throwback tax for most domestic trusts.[103] The throwback tax still applies to:

- foreign trusts;
- domestic trusts that had once been foreign trusts; and
- certain other domestic trusts created before 1 March 1984.

b. Computation of the throwback tax

12.90 With that introduction, now the rules. We warn you, these rules are not pretty. But as you review these rules, consider this: these rules are sometimes referred to as the 'short cut' method, providing a much simplified calculation of the tax on an accumulation distribution – simplified, that is, in comparison to prior law.

12.91 To compute the US taxpayer's throwback tax, it is first necessary to determine the number of years to which the distributed UNI is attributed.[104] For this purpose, distributed UNI is attributed on a first-in, last-out (FIFO) basis. However, if the amount of UNI attributed to an accumulation year is less than 25% of the average accumulation in the relevant accumulation year, that year is ignored for purposes of this first step.

Example

A trust makes a 2004 accumulation distribution of $40,000. The trust has $62,000 of UNI accumulated in the following years:

1997	$10,000
1998	$ 1,000
1999	$ 1,000
2002	$50,000

The $40,000 accumulation distribution is attributed to all four years, making the average $10,000 per year. Since the amount attributed to 1998 and 1999 is less than 25% of this average, the UNI for those years is ignored for purposes of this first step. The $40,000 distribution is accordingly treated as coming from only two years.

12.92 The average annual accumulation is then computed by dividing the amount of UNI distributed by the number of accumulation years to which that

---

[103] Code § 665(c); Taxpayer Relief Act 1997.
[104] Code § 667(b)(1)(A).

F. Taxation of US beneficiaries **12.95**

income is attributed.[105] In the prior example, the average accumulations would be $20,000 ($40,000 divided by two). This average annual accumulation is then added to the taxpayer's other taxable income from three of the taxpayer's previous five years.[106] The taxpayer's years with the highest and lowest incomes are discarded for this purpose (sort of like Olympic figure skating, but without the French judge).

Example

Lyon Woods, a US taxpayer and the leading money winner on the professional putt-putt tour, receives a $40,000 accumulation distribution from a foreign trust in 2004. Under rules outlined above, the average annual accumulation is determined to be $20,000. That amount is added to Lyon's income in three of the prior five years. Lyon's earnings in 1999 through 2003 were as follows:

1999	$100,000
2000	$120,000
2001	$ 75,000
2002	$180,000
2003	$140,000

In this example, 2001 and 2002 are discarded, and Lyon adds the $20,000 of average accumulation to his income for 1999, 2000 and 2003.

12.93 Note that the test years need not have any relationship to the years in which the UNI had been accumulated. In the prior example, 1999, 2000 and 2003 would still be the test years even if the distributed UNI had been attributed to the 1980s.

12.94 Next, the US beneficiary computes the increase in his taxes that would have occurred had the average annual accumulation been included in his income for the three test years.[107] The UNI is taxed as if it were generic ordinary income, thus losing any special tax rate benefits that might have been attributed to dividend or capital gains income.[108] The total increase for those three years is then divided by three to determine the average tax increase. If the total tax increase in the three test years was $18,600, the average would be $6,200.

12.95 The average increase ($6,200 in this example) is next multiplied by the number of accumulation years (two in this example) to determine the throwback tax.[109] In this example, the throwback tax would thus be $12,400.

---

[105] Code § 667(b). Note that if accumulations are attributed to more than one year, two average calculations are required: first to determine whether to ignore an accumulation year (because that year's accumulation is less than 25% of the average) and, second, to determine the final average accumulation used for computing the throwback tax.
[106] Code § 667(b)(1)(B).
[107] Code § 667(b)(1)(D).
[108] Code § 667(a). The only exception is for tax exempt interest income.
[109] Code § 667(b)(1)(D).

12.96 To add further complexity to the mix, taxes paid on a trust's accumulated income can also factor into the computation of the throwback tax, but in different ways. Accumulation distributions are first grossed up for certain taxes paid by the trust on the UNI.[110] The amount of the hypothetical tax increase in each of the three test years will be computed with reference to this grossed up income and credit given for the taxes paid by the trust in different years. These rules apply in different ways for domestic and foreign trusts.

12.97 In the context of a domestic trust, UNI is computed by subtracting only US taxes related to the accumulated income.[111] Accordingly, only US taxes related to the UNI will be grossed back up for purposes of computing the throwback tax. In our running example, assume that the trust had paid $10,000 of US taxes with respect to the $40,000 of UNI. The accumulation distribution would accordingly be grossed up to $50,000, making the average income attributed to the two accumulation years $25,000 (instead of $20,000). The average increase in taxes for the test years is, accordingly, computed by adding the $25,000 average annual accumulation (adjusted for taxes paid by the trust) to Lyon's income in each of the three test years. In doing so, assume that Lyon's total tax increase for those three years increases to $24,000, or an average of $8,000 per year. The $8,000 average tax increase is multiplied by the accumulation years (two) for a throwback tax (before credits for US taxes) of $16,000. The US taxes of $10,000 are then subtracted from that amount leaving a net throwback tax of $6,000. The same result would apply if the trust had paid $5,000 of foreign taxes on its accumulated income.

12.98 With respect to a foreign trust, UNI is computed by subtracting both domestic and foreign taxes.[112] Assume that in our running example, Lyon was a beneficiary of a foreign trust that had the same $40,000 of UNI (which is net of $10,000 of US taxes withheld on US source income and $5,000 of foreign taxes). The $40,000 accumulation distribution is grossed up for both the US and foreign taxes, causing the throwback tax to be computed as if Lyon had received $55,000 of income (or, $27,500 average for the two accumulation years). Now here's the wrinkle: Lyon uses the foreign tax credit (an average of $2,500) to compute the hypothetical tax increase for each of the three test years.[113] Once the average increase is computed (again, net of foreign tax credit), that amount is multiplied again by the number of accumulation years, and the US taxes then subtracted. So, foreign tax credits are applied to compute the test year tax increase while US taxes are applied against the throwback tax. It is that simple.

c. Application of throwback tax to immigrants

12.99 The first sentence of Code § 667(a) provides that the throwback tax only applies:

---

[110] Code § 666(b) and (c).
[111] Code § 665(d)(1).
[112] Code § 665(d)(1) and (2).
[113] Code § 667(d)(1)(A).

F. Taxation of US beneficiaries   **12.102**

'*to the extent* that such [accumulated income] would have been included in the income of such beneficiary ... if such [accumulated income] had been paid to such beneficiary on the last day of such preceding taxable year [in which the accumulated income had been earned]'[114]

Does this clause limit an immigrant's exposure to the throwback tax with respect to pre-immigration UNI? Prior to immigration, a NRA would have been subject to US tax only with respect to US-sourced FDAPI and ECI (including gains from the sale of US real estate) distributed from the foreign trust. Does this mean that only that portion of pre-immigration UNI attributed to FDAPI and ECI should be taxable with respect to a post-immigration accumulation distribution? There is not only a certain logic to that conclusion, but it is one unqualifiedly accepted by one of the most respected commentators on US taxation of trusts and estates.[115]

12.100 That favorable result in this admittedly limited context would depend on being able to trace (and respect) the character of the foreign trust's UNI. As a general rule, however, Code § 667(a) causes accumulated income to lose its character when distributed as part of an accumulation distribution.[116] Therefore, it would seem inconsistent with the loss of character rule for an immigrant to be able to limit the scope of Code § 667(a) to only UNI attributed to pre-immigration FDAPI and ECI.

12.101 In an analogous setting, UNI accumulated in a foreign trust prior to a taxpayer's birth can be taxed to a taxpayer as part of an accumulation distribution. Despite the repeal of the throwback tax for domestic trust, the Code still provides that income accumulated in a domestic trust prior to a beneficiary reaching age 21 and prior to birth would not be subject to the throwback tax.[117] This exception does not apply to foreign trusts (and to certain multiple domestic trusts). If this exception does not apply to foreign trusts, the general (but unstated) rule must be that income that accumulates prior to a beneficiary's death can be subject to the throwback tax.

Example

A foreign non-grantor trust is established in 1985 for the benefit of a decedent's current and future grandchildren. UNI accumulates in years 1985 through 1990. A US citizen grandchild is born in 1991 and later receives an accumulation distribution from that trust that is attributed to UNI accumulated in 1985. That distribution presumably is subject to the throwback tax.

12.102 But how can that be? The 1985 UNI would not have been taxed to the grandchild if distributed in the year earned – the poor chap was not even born yet. The US tax system is said to tax from cradle to grave – but to reach back to when the taxpayer was but a twinkle in his father's eyes ... Despite the 'to the extent' clause in section 667(a), income accumulated in a foreign trust prior to a beneficiary's birth

---

[114] Code § 667(a).
[115] Lane & Zaritsky, *Federal Income Taxation of Estates and Trusts* (3rd edn, 2003) Warren, Gorham & Lamont, at ¶ 6.06[6][b]. See the planning discussion at footnote 49 of **Chapter 16**.
[116] Code § 667(a) makes an exception only for tax-exempt interest income.
[117] Code § 665(b).

would, it seems, be subject to the throwback upon distribution. If pre-birth UNI could be taxed to a beneficiary, it would seem equally possible (although unfair) to tax an immigrant on all income (not just US-sourced income) accumulated in a trust prior to immigration.

12.103 An immigrant does have one advantage with respect to UNI distributions: as discussed at **12.109** et seq, the *interest charge* imposed on accumulation distributions from foreign trusts is computed by disregarding UNI accumulated prior to the individual becoming a US resident.[118]

d. Special throwback rules related to foreign trusts

12.104 Accumulation distributions from foreign trusts are, in many ways, treated differently than accumulation distributions from domestic trusts.

12.105 First, as noted at **12.89**, accumulation distributions from most domestic trusts are no longer subject to the throwback tax. Accumulation distributions from foreign trusts (and from domestic trusts that were once foreign trusts) remain subject to this special tax.

12.106 The second significant difference relates to accumulated capital gains and dividend income. Capital gains are typically not treated as part of the DNI of domestic trusts; even if they were, accumulation distributions from domestic trusts are generally no longer subject to the throwback tax. As a result, accumulated gains of domestic trusts are generally taxed once – to the trust – at relevant capital gains tax rates in the year of accumulation. In contrast, the DNI of a foreign trust will always include net capital gains. If those gains are accumulated and then later deemed distributed as a part of an accumulation distribution to US beneficiaries, the capital gains effectively lose their character as such and are taxed under the throwback rules as if they were generic ordinary income.[119] Similarly, dividends that accumulate in a foreign trust and that are distributed as part of an accumulation distribution also lose their character.

12.107 This can have significant (and adverse) implications given the current US tax rate differences between long-term capital gains and qualified dividends (currently capped at 15%) and ordinary income (with the highest marginal tax rate on individuals at 35%). Accumulating qualified dividend and capital gains income in a foreign trust for just one year can increase the effective tax rate on that income by a whopping 20%. So much for the benefits of deferral.

12.108 The third difference between the computation of the throwback tax for domestic and foreign trusts is that a beneficiary of a foreign trust must take into account UNI accumulated prior to attaining age 21.[120] To the extent still relevant to

---

[118] Code § 668(a)(4).
[119] Code § 667(a). The character of accumulated income is retained for distributions to NRAs. Code § 667(e).
[120] Code § 665(b).

F. Taxation of US beneficiaries **12.113**

domestic trusts, UNI accumulated in a domestic trust prior to a beneficiary attaining age 21 will not be taxed as part of an accumulation distribution.

12.109   The fourth significant difference is that the throwback tax computed on an accumulation distribution from a foreign trust is subject to an interest charge based on the *weighted age of the trust's entire UNI* – not just the weighted age of the UNI deemed distributed as part of the accumulation distribution. In our running example, the average age of the trust's UNI with respect to a 2004 accumulation distribution would be computed as follows.

Accumulation Year	*UNI*	*Age (2004 Year)*	*Product*
1997	10,000	7	70,000
1998	1,000	6	6,000
1999	1,000	5	5,000
2002	50,000	2	100,000
Total	62,000		181,000
Product Divided by Total UNI			÷62,000
Weighted Age of UNI			2.9 years

12.110   In our running example, the throwback tax of $12,400 (or $11,000 after foreign and US tax credits) would, therefore, be subject to an interest charge on the assumption that the age of the accumulated income was 2.9 years. The interest rates are computed based on the compounded interest rates for tax underpayments for the relevant period.[121] The interest rate for accumulations prior to 1996 is fixed at 6% (and thus is not based on the underpayment rate).

12.111   In computing the interest charge on an accumulation distribution from a foreign trust, UNI accumulated in a year when the beneficiary was a NRA is ignored. If, for example, the beneficiary became a US tax resident in 1998, the weighted interest calculations would exclude 1997, making the weighted age 2.1 ($111,000/52,000). From this weighted average, the accumulated interest can be obtained from the interest rate tables found on Form 3520 instructions.

12.112   It should be clear to the casual observer that the throwback tax and interest rate regime were the creation of tax writers with too much time on their hands, too much paranoia, and probably too much caffeine. 'Short cut' indeed. Put these guys in charge of simplifying the tax system and writing a 'flat tax' rule and we would probably end up with a structure that is about as flat as the newest roller coaster at Euro Disney.

12.113   To make matters even more complicated, in order for the US beneficiary taxpayer to compute his US tax liability on an accumulation distribution, the trustee

---

[121]   Code §§ 668(a)(1) and 6621(a)(2).

12.114 must keep two sets of UNI books: one for computing the throwback tax and one for the purpose of computing the interest charge. For the purpose of determining the average accumulations, prior UNI distributions are charged to prior years on a FIFO basis. In our running example, the $40,000 UNI distribution would be charged as follows:

1997	$10,000
1998	$1,000
1999	$1,000
2002	$28,000

The remaining $22,000 of UNI ($62,000 – $40,000) would be attributed to 2002 for the purpose of computing the throwback tax on future accumulation distributions.

12.114 For the purpose of computing the interest charge, however, the UNI is applied to the accumulation years in proportion to the UNI in each such year on a weighted average basis.[122] For example, as illustrated in the table below.

Accumulation year	UNI ($)	Percentage of total	Allocation ($)	Net UNI ($)
1997	10,000	16.13%	6,450	3,550
1998	1,000	1.63%	645	355
1999	1,000	1.63%	645	355
2002	50,000	80.65%	32,260	17,740
Total	62,000		40,000	22,000

12.115 Oh, and don't think you can avoid the throwback tax and interest charge by migrating the foreign trust to the US prior to the accumulation distribution. First, the throwback tax specifically applies to domestic trusts that were once foreign trusts.[123] Second, the IRS ruled that the interest charge continues to apply to accumulation distributions attributed to UNI accumulated while a US trust used to be a foreign trust.[124]

12.116 Finally, one should not lose track of the fact that party responsible for keeping track of all of the information necessary to assist the US taxpayer in computing the throwback tax – the trustee of the foreign trust – is (with a few exceptions) often ill equipped for the task.

12.117 The sometimes brutal combination of:

- continued exposure to the throwback tax and its complexities;

---

[122] Code § 668(a)(2).
[123] Code § 665(c)(2)(A).
[124] Rev Rul 91–6, 1991–1 CB 89.

F. Taxation of US beneficiaries **12.119**

- the interest charge on accumulation distributions from foreign non-grantor trusts; and

- the conversion of potentially tax-favored income (eg capital gains and qualified dividends) into generic ordinary income when distributed as part of an accumulation distribution,

should lead a US beneficiary to think twice before leaving income to accumulate in a foreign trust or, for that matter, to leave a trust offshore at all. Current distribution of all foreign trust income to US beneficiaries would avoid these problems, as would the current migration of the foreign trust to the US. The trade off, however, is making the trust of all of its income subject to current US tax. That being said, foreign non-grantor trusts for US beneficiaries can offer interesting planning opportunities to defer, reduce or not incur the accumulation distribution tax, which are discussed in **CHAPTER 19**.

4. *Loans from foreign trusts as distributions*

12.118 As discussed at **12.104** et seq, a distribution from a foreign trust can cause a US beneficiary to be subject to substantial tax and interest penalties. To skirt these rules, US beneficiaries in the past could borrow funds from the trust and claim the loans were not taxable distributions. To eliminate this perceived abuse, new rules implemented by SBJPA treat certain loans from foreign trusts as if they were distributions.[125]

12.119 The loans must be of cash or marketable securities. The loan must also be made directly or indirectly to the US grantor or US beneficiary, or to any other US person who is related to the US grantor or US beneficiary. For this purpose, 'related parties' generally include:

- the person's spouse, siblings, ancestors, and lineal descendants;

- a corporation in which the person owns more than 50% of the value; and

- a qualified charity controlled by the individual and members of his family.

If this rule applies, subsequent transactions with respect to the loan principal (including repayment and cancellation) are ignored for purposes of the US income tax rules.[126]

Example

John Carry is a beneficiary of an offshore trust established for his benefit by his French grandparents. John borrows $500,000 from the trust to pay for his Yale student council campaign. The loan is taxed as if it were a distribution. If John later repays the loan (from his 'winnings' in

---

[125] Code § 643(i).
[126] Code § 643(i)(3).

231

the spousal lottery), he will not be treated as having made a contribution to a foreign trust. If the loan is instead later forgiven, it will not be treated as a distribution.

5. Transfers through intermediaries

12.120 The SPJPA also provides that amounts paid to a US person and directly or indirectly derived from a foreign trust will be treated as distributions from the foreign trust to the US person in the year of payment.[127] Distributions through the 'grantor' of the foreign trust are not subject to this rule.

Example

Maggie T Hatcher, a UK national and resident, creates a funded irrevocable trust in the UK. Maggie receives a distribution from the trust and later makes a gift to Ray 'Gipper' Rongun, a US citizen. Ray is not considered to have received a distribution from the foreign trust.

12.121 The regulations clarify that this rule applies if the intermediary had received the initial trust distribution as part of a plan to avoid US taxes.[128] Tax avoidance will be assumed if the US person is related to the trust's grantor[129] and the intermediary transfers the property to the US person within 24 months before or after receiving a distribution from a foreign trust.[130]

Example

A wealthy lady forms a foreign non-grantor trust for the benefit of her descendants. One of her grandchildren, Nigel Nuworld, is a US income tax resident. Rather than Nigel receiving a direct distribution from the foreign trust, Nigel suggests to the trustee that a distribution be made to Nigel's brother – Sunny – who currently resides in a Caribbean tax haven. Sunny pays no local taxes on the trust distribution and is not subject to any transfer taxes on his gifts, including gifts to his dear brother Nigel. The new rule can tax Nigel as if he received the distribution directly from the trust.

12.122 Note that this rule applies even if the US person is not a named beneficiary of the foreign trust. Thus, Nigel would not escape this principle by convincing his grandmother to exclude him as a named beneficiary of the trust, with the understanding that Nigel would be funded by distributions funneled through Sunny. If this rule applies, the foreign trust is deemed to have made the distribution to the US beneficiary in the year the US beneficiary received the payment from the intermediary. The deemed distribution can carry out both DNI and UNI in the same manner as any direct distribution.

---

[127] Code § 643(h).
[128] Treas Reg § 1.643(h)-1(a)(1).
[129] Treas Reg § 1.643(h)-1(a)(2). The US person is deemed to be related to the grantor under rules set out in Code § 643(i)(2)(B), with some modifications.
[130] Treas Reg § 1.643(h)-1(a)(2)(ii).

12.123 The intermediary rule effectively shifts the burden of proof back to the taxpayer to prove the absence of a tax avoidance scheme. Under prior law, the IRS could attempt to tax the US person by arguing that the intermediary was serving as the US person's agent or by applying the 'step-transaction' doctrine, but the IRS had the burden of proof. Now, it is the US taxpayer who needs to prove that the intermediary was acting independently of the grantor and trustee and was not the US person's agent.[131]

G. US taxation of foreign beneficiaries on distributions from non-grantor trusts

12.124 Foreign beneficiaries of non-grantor trusts can also be subject to US tax on distributions of US-sourced current or accumulated income. Again, this will generally be limited to FDAPI, ECI and gains from the sale of US real property interests (taxed as ECI).

12.125 Distribution to foreign beneficiaries from US non-grantor trusts do not provide any special reporting complexities. The US trust will generally be obligated to withhold the 30% US tax on FDAPI distributed to a foreign beneficiary.[132] Note that any foreign source income deemed distributed to a foreign beneficiary from a US non-grantor trust will effectively escape US tax. Had that foreign income accumulated in the US non-grantor trust, the US trust would pay tax on that income.

12.126 Distributions to foreign beneficiaries from foreign non-grantor trusts are more complex (and, in some instances, problematic). If a foreign trust had ECI or gain from the sale of US real property interests taxed as ECI, then it should file a US tax return to report this income and pay relevant US taxes. If the foreign trust makes distributions to beneficiaries – US or foreign – during the year, the foreign trust should claim a distribution deduction. The trust would also provide the IRS and the beneficiary with a 'K-1,' that identifies the beneficiary to whom the distribution is made and the amount (and character) of the trust's income taxable to him. A foreign beneficiary who thus receives a K-1 from a foreign trust would himself then have an obligation to file a US tax return to report that distributable income and pay US taxes on any ECI (including gains from the sale of US real estate) deemed distributed to him.

12.127 If, as is more common, the foreign trust only earned FDAPI, then the US tax picture begins to blur. Typically, the US payor of FDAPI will withhold US taxes – at a flat 30% rate – and distribute the net amount to the foreign payee. If the foreign payee trust is a complex trust (by far the most common form), then the US withholding rules treat the trust itself as the beneficial owner of the income.[133] If the foreign payee trust is a simple trust or a grantor trust, then it is viewed as a pass-through entity and the income beneficiary (in the case of the simple trust) or

---

[131] Treas Reg § 1.643(h)-1(a)(2)(iii).
[132] Treas Reg § 1.1441–5(b)(2)(ii) and (iii).
[133] Treas Reg § 1.1441–1(c)(6)(ii)(D).

12.128 *US Income Taxation of Trusts, Estates, Grantors and Beneficiaries*

grantor (in the case of the grantor trust) is treated as the beneficial owner of the FDAPI.[134] Under the relevant withholding requirements, the foreign simple or grantor trusts should file certificates and statements that identify the income beneficiary or grantor and provide relevant withholding statements for the beneficiary/grantor.

12.128 Assume the US tax has been withheld on the payment of FDAPI to a foreign non-grantor complex trust and that the trust makes a further distribution of that FDAPI to a foreign beneficiary. What would be gained (to anyone) for the foreign trust to essentially 'K-1' that income to the foreign beneficiary? The distribution would be 'grossed up' for the withheld US taxes and then credited to the foreign beneficiary. Aside from strict compliance with the US tax laws, the only situations where it would seem to make any difference is if either:

- the US payor had not withheld on the payment of US FDAPI to the foreign trust; or

- the beneficiary might be entitled to treaty relief on certain kinds of US source income.

12.129 The absurd extra-territorial extension of the complexities of the US tax law reaches its zenith in the context of an accumulation distribution from a foreign non-grantor trust to a foreign beneficiary. If a foreign non-grantor trust makes an accumulation distribution in later years, the FDAPI and ECI associated with the distributed UNI would, technically, be taxable to the foreign beneficiary and subject to a throwback tax computed as set out at **12.85** et seq. The throwback tax would be limited to FDAPI and ECI – accumulated foreign income would thus not be taxed on distribution to a foreign beneficiary – and the foreign beneficiary would receive appropriate credits for US taxes paid by the trust (or withheld at the source) when that income was originally earned. In order to make this all work, the tax rules provide for accumulated income to retain its character when distributed from a foreign trust to a foreign beneficiary.[135] But to what end? The foreign beneficiary will receive a credit for the US tax originally imposed on the ECI (at essentially the highest marginal rate of 35%) and on FDAPI (at a flat withholding rate of 30%). Unless the effective US tax rate that applies to the foreign beneficiary exceeds those rates, no additional US tax will be due or collected.

12.130 In practice, it is likely that few (if any) foreign trustees are aware of these rules or inform their foreign beneficiaries of their potential exposure to US 'throwback' tax on something called an 'accumulation distribution' out of the trust's UNI related to FDAPI or ECI. A foreign beneficiary so-informed would likely throw the note back in the trustee's face. Even if the foreign beneficiary went to the trouble of computing the throwback tax, it is likely – given the flat rate that applies to FDAPI and the compressed rates that apply to ECI – that the US taxes already paid by that foreign trust on that income and creditable against the throwback tax will approximate, if not exceed, the throwback taxes before these credits. So much complexity for so little real purpose. But that, my friend, is the throwback tax in all its shining glory.

---

[134] Treas Reg § 1.1441–1(c)(6)(ii)(C).
[135] Code § 667(e).

12.131   Even if a foreign beneficiary of a foreign trust is not subject to US tax by reason of a distribution out of current income (for example, because the distributed income is not FDAPI or ECI), the distribution nonetheless reduces the trust's DNI and thus its UNI that might be taxed to US beneficiaries in a later accumulation distribution. Similarly, a non-taxable accumulation distribution to a NRA reduces the trust's UNI that could later be taxed to US beneficiaries.

H.   Taxation of estates and beneficiaries

12.132   Estates are generally taxed in the same manner as complex trusts.[136] Likewise, beneficiaries who receive distributions from estates are taxed in the same manner as beneficiaries receiving distributions from complex trusts.[137]

12.133   There are two important differences. First, the throwback rule does not apply to distributions from estates. The definition of 'accumulation distribution' refers only to distributions from trusts and the definition of UNI refers only to the accumulated DNI of a trust.[138]

12.134   Second, a foreign estate DNI is limited to US source taxable income.[139] Accordingly, foreign source income earned within a foreign trust will not be taxed upon distribution to a US beneficiary.

12.135   Although Congress provided clear guidance for defining the residence of foreign trusts (see Section B at **12.9** et seq), the income tax residence of an estate is not defined in the Code or regulations.[140] The determination is, therefore, left to relevant facts and circumstances as discussed in rulings and case law.[141]

12.136   Limited guidance is provided in the few rulings in this area.[142] The three principal factors seem to be:

- the nationality and residency of the domiciliary personal representative;
- the country of the estate's domiciliary administration; and
- the location of the estate assets.

The nationality of the decedent and of the beneficiaries is of little relevance.[143]

---

[136]   Code § 661.
[137]   Code § 662.
[138]   Code § 665(b) and (a); Treas Reg § 1.665(a)-OA(d) confirms that the throwback rules do not apply to any estate.
[139]   Code § 643(a)(6), which adds back foreign source income for trusts, but not estates. Therefore, foreign source income is never included in a foreign estate's DNI. Lane & Zaritsky, *Federal Income Taxation of Estates and Trusts* (3rd edn, 2003) Warren, Gorham & Lamont, at ¶ 18.06[3].
[140]   See Code § 7701(a)(31)(A).
[141]   Compare Rev Rul 57-245, 1957-1, CB 286; Rev Rul 58-232, 1958-1 CB 261; Rev Rul 62-154, 1962-2 CB 148; Rev Rul 81-112, 1981-1 CB 598.
[142]   See, for example, Rev Rul 81-112, 1981-1 CB 598 (estate of deceased US citizen who resided abroad for 20 years was foreign resident); Rev Rul 62-154, 1962-2 CB 148.
[143]   Zaritsky, BNA Tax Management Portfolio 854-2d, *US Taxation of Foreign Estates, Trusts and Beneficiaries*, discusses the applicable precedent at his portfolio article note 907.

I. Reporting requirements (and penalties) related to foreign trusts

12.137 The SPJPA instituted a strict reporting regime for US taxpayer's dealings with foreign trusts and also for gifts received by US persons from foreign sources. And if you think the reporting is harsh, wait until you get a load of the penalties!

1. Special reporting obligations

a. Reportable events

12.138 The SPJPA imposed the following reporting requirements.

(i) Creation of/transfer to a foreign trust

12.139 A US taxpayer is required to report the creation of, or direct or indirect transfer of property to, a foreign trust.[144] Recall from our discussion of the grantor trust rules and Code § 679 that an immigrant who has established a foreign trust for the benefit of US persons and moves to the US within five years of funding will be treated as if he transferred property to the trust immediately upon becoming a US taxpayer for purposes of both the grantor trust rules and these reporting rules.[145]

(ii) Death of a US income tax or estate tax 'owner'

12.140 The executor of a decedent's estate is obligated to report the death of a US taxpayer who was taxed as the owner of the foreign trust under the grantor trust rules or if any portion of the property of the foreign trust is included in the US decedent's estate.[146]

(iii) Grantor trust ownership

12.141 If a US taxpayer is treated as the owner of a foreign trust under the grantor trust rules, the US taxpayer must ensure that the foreign trust files an informational return with the IRS that provides a full and complete accounting of the trust's activities.[147] The US owner must also ensure that the foreign trust appoints a US agent from whom the IRS can seek information regarding the trust's activities.[148]

---

[144] Code § 6048(a)(3)(i) and (ii).
[145] Code § 679(a)(4).
[146] Code § 6048(a)(3)(iii).
[147] Code § 6048(b)(1).
[148] Code § 6048(b)(2).

(iv) Distributions from foreign trusts

12.142 A US beneficiary who directly or indirectly receives a distribution from a foreign trust must file a special report with information required by the IRS regarding the trust's activities.[149] A beneficiary is obligated to report distributions even if another person is considered to be the owner of the trust under the grantor trust rules.[150]

(v) Gifts and bequests

12.143 A US taxpayer must also report gifts or bequests received from foreign persons.[151] Gifts or bequests reported under the prior rule as a distribution from a foreign trust do not need to be reported as gifts. The Code provides that foreign gifts and bequests only need to be reported if the aggregate during the year exceeds $10,000. The IRS has increased this threshold to $100,000 for gifts and bequests from any individual; gifts from certain related parties are aggregated for this purpose.[152] The $10,000 threshold – inflation adjusted to $12,907 for 2004[153] – still applies for gifts from foreign entities (other than foreign trusts).

b. Treatment of domestic trusts

12.144 For the purposes of these reporting requirements, a domestic trust can be treated as a foreign trust if the trust has 'substantial activities' or holds 'substantial property' outside the US if, and to the extent, provided by regulations.[154] No such regulations have been issued to date and the IRS has indicated that, until they issue further guidance on this subject, domestic trusts will not be considered foreign trusts under this rule.[155]

c. Penalties

12.145 Hold on to your hats. The penalties for failing to comply with these reporting requirements are summarized as follows.

- **Failure to report creation of or transfers to foreign trusts** – The penalty for failure to report creation of, or transfers to, foreign trusts is 35% of the amount transferred to the trust. The penalty applies without regard to whether the transfer was a taxable event. Thus, the penalty for failing to report a $1m transfer to a revocable foreign trust – an incomplete gift for gift tax purposes and a non-event for purposes of the Code § 684 – results in a $350,000 penalty.[156]

---

[149] Code § 6048(c).
[150] Code § 6048(d)(1).
[151] Code § 6039F.
[152] Notice 97–34, 1977–2 CB 422.
[153] Rev Proc 2003–85, 2003–49 IRB 1.
[154] Code § 6048(d)(2).
[155] Notice 97–34, 1977–2 CB 422.
[156] Code § 6677(a)(1) and (c)(1).

- **Failure to have foreign trust provide information related to US person's ownership** – This *annual* penalty is 5% of the value of the trust at the end of the year.[157]

- **Failure to have foreign grantor trust appoint a US agent** – If a foreign grantor trust does not appoint a US agent, the IRS is essentially authorized to fabricate the amount of income and gains to tax to the US owner.[158]

- **Failure to report distributions from foreign trusts** – The penalty for a US beneficiary's failure to report a distribution from a foreign trust is 35% of the amount received.[159] Again, this is even though the US beneficiary is not otherwise subject to income tax on the distribution from the trust – for example, if the trust is a grantor trust. Further, if the US beneficiary does not provide sufficient records and information, the distribution will be treated as an 'accumulation distribution' and taxed under the throwback rules described at **12.85** et seq.[160]

- **Failure to report gifts from foreign persons** – The penalty for a US donee's failure to report gifts from a foreign person totaling more than $100,000 annually (applying family attribution rules) is 5% of the gift received for each month not reported up to a maximum penalty of 25% of the gifts.[161]

d. How, when and where to report

12.146 Revised Form 3520 is a multi-purpose form used to report the following events and items:

- a US person's creation of a foreign trust;
- a US person's ownership of a foreign trust under the grantor trust rules;
- the death of a US person if:
    (a) the decedent had been the owner of the foreign trust under the grantor trust rules; or
    (b) any of the property of the foreign trust is included in the decedent's estate;
- a distribution to a US person from a foreign trust;
- the calculations related to UNI distributions from foreign trusts, including the computation of the interest charge on 'accumulation distributions';
- the receipt of a large gift or bequest by a US person from a non US person.

12.147 The form must be filed with the Internal Revenue Service's Philadelphia Service Center. The form is generally due on the date the taxpayer's income tax return is due (generally, 15 April of the following year), including extensions.

---

[157] Code § 6677(b) and (c)(2).
[158] Code § 6048(b)(2)(A).
[159] Code § 6677(a)(1) and (c)(3).
[160] Code § 6048(c)(2).
[161] Code § 6039F(c).

12.148 The US grantor of a foreign trust must also ensure that the foreign trust files Form 3520-A with the IRS's Philadelphia Service. The due date for this form is the 15th day of the third month following the termination of the trust's tax year. Since trusts generally have a calendar year, this means by 15 March. Note that the US grantor's extension of time to file his or her own income tax returns does not extend the time for a foreign grantor trust to file Form 3520-A. A foreign trust wishing to extend the time to file Form 3520-A must apply for an extension of time using Form 2758.

12.149 A foreign trust with a US grantor/owner is also obligated to provide the US grantor/owner with a so-called 'Foreign Grantor Trust Owner Statement' and a 'Foreign Grantor Trust Beneficiary Statement'. Samples of these statements are part of Form 3520-A. A foreign trust with a US grantor/owner is also required to name a US agent from whom the IRS can request trust records and against whom the IRS can issue a summons. The IRS provided a sample of this appointment form in Notice 97–34.[162]

12.150 If a foreign non-grantor trust makes a distribution to a US beneficiary, the US beneficiary is obligated to report – using Form 3520 – relevant information regarding the operation of the trust. In order to comply with this requirement, the US beneficiary will need certain information to be maintained and provided by the trustee. Notice 97–34 sets out the details required in that so-called 'Foreign Nongrantor Trust Beneficiary Statement', but the IRS has issued no sample forms for this purpose. Generally, the information required on that form will be similar to that provided by a US beneficiary on a 'K-1' issued by a domestic trust.

2. Treasury Form 90–22.1 reporting of foreign financial accounts

12.151 In addition to the special reporting rules discussed above, every US resident is required to report if he or she had a financial interest in or signatory authority over a foreign bank, securities or financial account exceeding $10,000 on any one day during the prior tax year. Treasury Department Form TD F 90–22.1, Report of Foreign Bank and Financial Accounts, including Trust Accounts, is to be used for this purpose. That Form must be filed by 30 June of the succeeding year with the Department of the Treasury, PO Box 32621, Detroit, Michigan 48232–0621 (or hand carried to a local IRS office). Failure to report an interest in a foreign financial account can be punishable by civil and criminal penalties of up to five years in prison and $500,000 of fines.

12.152 Trust-held foreign financial accounts must be reported *by any US person* who has a 'present beneficial interest' in more than 50% of the trust's assets or who receives more than 50% of its current income.

---

[162] 1997–1 CB 422.

3. Income tax reporting and employer identification numbers (*EINs*)

12.153 The trustee of a foreign trust does *not* have to file a US income tax return unless the trust is a non-grantor trust that:

- has ECI income;

- has FDAPI income on which US withholding tax has not been collected at source (eg, original issue discount income); or

- is seeking a refund on taxes that have been over collected at source.

In such cases, the foreign trust must file Form 1040NR (the form typically used by NRA individuals) rather than Form 1041 (which is used by domestic trusts). Inexplicably there is no comparable Form 1041NR.

12.154 Code § 641 is the substantive income taxing provision with regard to trusts. It states that the taxable income of every trust shall be computed in the same manner as an individual and the income tax paid by the trustee. This only applies to a non-grantor trust since grantor trusts by definition do not have any taxable income and are not taxpayers. Code § 641(b) states that a foreign (non-grantor) trust 'shall be treated as a non-resident alien individual who is not present in the United States at any time'.

12.155 Code § 6012 specifies who must file income tax returns. Pursuant to Code § 6012(a)(4), a trust (ie non-grantor) is only required to file a return if it has gross income exceeding $600.[163] Section 1.6012–1(b)(2) of the regulations specifically exempts NRAs (including non-grantor trusts) from filing a return if all US income tax liability is satisfied by withholding at source and the taxpayer is not engaged in a US trade or business.[164] As a result, the trustees of a foreign trust have no US

---

[163] Code § 6012(a)(5) also requires a income tax return by every trust or estate which has a non resident alien beneficiary. However, Treas Reg § 1.6012–3(b)(2) limits such reporting to *domestic* fiduciaries 'charged with the care of the person or property of a non resident alien individual' and *only if the NRA fails to make a return of his or her own income and to pay the tax thereon.*

[164] Treas Reg § 1.6012–3(a)(9), with respect to any trust which is a grantor trust under Code §§ 671–678, refers to Treas Reg § 1.671–4. Note that Treas Reg § 1.671–4(a) provides that items of income, deduction and credit which are treated as owned by the grantor (or a US beneficiary in the case of a Crummey Power) are not reported by the trust on Form 1041, but are instead reported in a separate statement attached to Form 1041. Treas Reg § 1.671–4(b) provides an exception for single owner grantor trusts whereby, if the trustee provides the grantor's social security number to all US payers, and provides the grantor with a statement of his trust taxable income, the trustee 'is not required to file any type of return with the Internal Revenue Service', Treas Reg § 1.671–4(b)(ii)(B). This alternative filing procedure does not apply to various trusts, including any trust that has a foreign grantor, situs or assets, Treas Reg §§ 1.671–4(b)(6)(ii) and (v).

The inference, however, is not that foreign grantor trusts with a US or foreign settlor have to file Form 1041, with an attached statement of taxable income. Form 1041 is a form which is only used by domestic trusts, not by foreign trusts. Further, Code §§ 671–678 are not filing sections. They simply define which trusts are grantor trusts. Code § 6012 specifies which trusts, domestic or foreign, have to file an income tax return. As stated at **12.153**, Code § 6012 only requires an income tax return (Form 1040NR, not 1041) by foreign non-grantor trusts which have US ECI

income tax return filing obligations if all US tax has been properly withheld on FDAPI and the trust has no ECI (including from disposition of US real estate).

12.156 Code § 6109 and its underlying regulations set out the requirements for a taxpayer to obtain a taxpayer identification number (TIN). Section 301.6109–1(a)(1) of the regulations requires an individual to use his social security number (SSN), or, if an SSN cannot be issued, an individual taxpayer identification number (ITIN). Trusts, corporations and employers *who are US taxpayers* must obtain and use an employer identification number (EIN).[165]

12.157 Treas Reg § 301.6109–1(b)(1) provides that every 'US person' who makes a return, statement or other document must furnish his own TIN 'as required by the forms and the accompanying instructions'. However, Treas Reg § 301.6109–1(b)(2) states this requirement shall apply only to the following *foreign* persons:

- a foreign person that has ECI;
- a foreign person that has a US office or fiscal or paying agent at any time during the year;
- a NRA treated as a resident alien because of a taxpayer election;
- a foreign person that makes a return of income, gift or estate tax, or a refund claim;
- a foreign person that makes a 'check the box' election;
- a foreign person that furnishes a withholding certificate under Treas Reg § 1.41–1(e)(4)(vii).

Accordingly, there is no statutory or regulatory requirement for a foreign trust to obtain an EIN if it does not have ECI or is not described in any of the other provisions above.

12.158 Forms 3520 and 3520-A both have a box for a trust EIN. However, the regulations only require 'US persons' to obtain and use an EIN if required by the relevant tax form. With respect to *foreign* persons, an EIN number is only required if the trust is filing an income, gift or estate tax return. Form 3520-A (required to be filed by the trustee of a foreign trust with a US grantor/owner) is an informational return, not an income tax return.

12.159 Further, a foreign trust does not have to file an income tax return, except in the limited circumstances set out at **12.153**. Trustees of foreign trusts that are not required to file a US income tax return may, therefore, fill in the Form 3520-A EIN box with the words 'Not Applicable', or could use a US settlor's SSN since the trust is a grantor trust. Similarly, a US taxpayer required to file Form 3520 to report a transfer to a foreign trust, ownership of the foreign trust or a distribution from the

---

income or FDAPI on which US withholding tax is not fully satisfied at source. Therefore, foreign trusts do not have to file Form 1041 with the attached statement.

[165] Treas Reg § 301.6109–1(a)(2) requires a trustee of a grantor trust that is required by Treas Reg § 1.671–4(a) to file Form 1041 with attached income statement to obtain an EIN for the trustee. However, as explained at **12.153**, a foreign trust is required to file Form 1040NR, not Form 1041.

12.159 *US Income Taxation of Trusts, Estates, Grantors and Beneficiaries*

foreign trust could insert 'Not Applicable' in the trust EIN box or use the SSN of the trust's US grantor/owner (if known).[166]

---

[166] Notwithstanding the lack of a legal EIN requirement, advisers in at least one 'big four' accounting firm appear to follow a practice of obtaining an EIN number for each foreign trust and using it on all Form 3520 filings, in order to prevent any possibility of an excise tax penalty for failure to file an 'accurate' return. For at least two reasons, this would seem to be unnecessary and costly for a foreign trustee without US-based advisers. First, the penalty cannot be imposed if there is reasonable cause not to supply an EIN. The failure of any statute or regulation to require an EIN is obviously 'reasonable cause'. Second, it is much harder and more costly for foreign based trustees to obtain EIN numbers for every US-connected trust they administer. The costs can amount to several hundreds of dollars per EIN and foreign trustees generally cannot recover these unnecessary costs from their clients.

Chapter 13

UK Income Taxation of Trusts, Settlors and Beneficiaries

A. Summary

13.1 This chapter addresses the UK law as it stands at the time of writing. However following the issue of a number of consultative papers, the most recent of which was issued on 13 August 2004, there are likely to be certain changes to the taxation regime for trusts with effect from 5 April 2005. These changes are summarised in Section F (**13.82** et seq).

13.2 As in the US, the UK has rules defining the tax residence of a trust, although the rules for UK residence are currently different for capital gains and income tax purposes. These may be harmonised following the proposed changes in the regime (see Section F at **13.82** et seq). In addition, a trust's UK income tax residence can depend on the settlor's residence or domicile at the time of settlement.

13.3 In contrast with the US position, it is common for trustees to be subject to UK taxes in their own right even where distributions of current income and gains are made to beneficiaries (albeit the distribution may carry with it a tax credit for the beneficiary). The manner in which trustees are taxed depends on whether the trust is an interest in possession or a discretionary trust, although that is not a fundamental factor in the application of many of the anti avoidance provisions. Furthermore, the residence of a trust is also of relevance for UK income tax and CGT purposes to determine the tax exposure of the grantor/settlor or trustees (as opposed to the beneficiaries under the trust). Non-UK resident trustees are only subject to UK income tax on UK source income and are only subject to UK CGT on gains from a UK trade conducted through a UK branch or agency. All other UK source gains (significantly including non-trading UK real estate gains) are not taxed to the trustees (although they may be taxed to the beneficiaries or the settlor).

13.4 Like the US, the UK has wide-ranging anti-avoidance provisions, called here 'settlor interested trust' provisions[1] which are broadly similar in effect to some of the US 'grantor trust' rules, but which are also substantially different. Where they apply, these settlor interested trust rules tax a grantor/settlor, rather than the trustees, or in some cases the beneficiaries, on trust income and/or gains.

---

[1] The term is not a consistently applied statutory term of art, although commonly used by practitioners to describe four or five anti-avoidance provisions which tax the settlor on trust income or gains if he or his spouse (and others in the case of non-UK resident trusts) can benefit. These definitions may be harmonised to some degree under the current Revenue proposals. See Section F (**13.82** et seq).

13.5 The substantial differences relate first to the fact that these settlor-interested trust rules apply differently to UK domiciled and non-domiciled settlors of a non-UK resident trust. A UK resident and domiciled settlor is generally taxed on worldwide trust income and gains. However, a UK resident but non-domiciled settlor is generally taxed only on UK source income of a non-resident trust, assuming appropriate planning is also undertaken to avoid remitting non-UK source income. Such planning may differ according to whether the trust is an interest in possession or discretionary trust. Furthermore, he is not taxed at all on capital and capital gain distributions, including UK source trust gains.[2]

13.6 A second major difference is that the income tax rules generally tax a settlor on a totally transparent basis while the capital gains rules generally tax the settlor on gains 'equal in amount' to the gains realised by the trustee. Since the CGT rules do not 'transparently' tax a settlor on trust gains, they can cause a non-domiciled but UK resident settlor of a UK resident trust to be taxed on worldwide gains (as the terminology of the taxing provisions denies remittance basis taxation).

13.7 A third major difference is that undistributed trust income and gains of a non-resident trust which are not taxable to a UK resident but non-domiciled settlor, can be taxable to UK resident beneficiaries who receive distributions of such income or who receive a capital payment or benefit, such as the use of trust assets. While both income and gains can be taxed at rates of up to 40%, trust gains undistributed for up to six years can also invoke 'supplementary charges' (broadly equivalent to penalty interest charges) of up to 24%.

13.8 Again, the taxing provisions substantially distinguish between UK resident beneficiaries who are UK domiciled and those who are not. UK domiciled and resident beneficiaries of a non UK resident trust can be taxable on the distribution of previously undistributed trust income, and then stockpiled gains, to the extent of a trust distribution or the value of a capital benefit enjoyed anywhere. The value of a capital benefit in excess of such income or gains is carried forward and allocated to future trust income, and then realised gains, which are taxable to a UK domiciled beneficiary to the extent of the prior years' excess benefit enjoyed. In contrast, UK resident but non-domiciled beneficiaries of a non UK resident trust can be distributed trust gains which may be remitted to the UK without UK capital gains tax. Further, such beneficiaries are only subject to income tax with respect to an actual distribution of trust income (if remitted to the UK in the case of non UK source income) or a benefit enjoyed within the UK (such as occupation of a trust-owned UK residence).

13.9 In December 2003, the Inland Revenue published a paper entitled 'Modernising the tax system for trusts' and a further consultation paper was issued on 13 August 2004. These papers propose a wide-ranging review of the income and gains taxation of UK resident trusts with a view to simplifying the complex code which has developed, somewhat ad hoc, over many years. They are currently the subject of consultation but, when implemented (anticipated by 5 April 2005), are

---

[2] Such gains are CGT exempt in the hands of a non-UK resident trust if not connected with a UK trade conducted by the trust through a UK branch or agency.

likely to impact significantly on the current regime and bring it closer to the current US regime in some respects. A summary of the key issues under discussion is provided at Section F (at **13.82** et seq).

B. Tax residence of trusts

1. Income tax residence of trust

13.10 For *income* tax purposes, the trust will clearly be UK resident if all of the trustees are UK resident. Additionally, if at least one trustee is UK resident and one is not, the trust will be UK resident if the settlor was UK resident, or ordinarily resident or domiciled in the UK either:

- at the settlor's death (in the case of a will trust or trust created on intestacy); or

- at the date the settlor contributed funds to the trust (in the case of an inter vivos trust).[3]

Subject to what is said below on the anti avoidance legislation, where the trust is UK resident the trustees' tax exposure is generally on worldwide income, whereas if the trust is not UK resident, the trustees are only taxed on UK source income.

2. Capital gains tax residence of trust

13.11 For CGT purposes, a trust will be non-resident if:

- the majority of the trustees are non-UK resident and not ordinarily resident; and

- the general administration of the trust is carried on outside the UK.[4]

A trust will also be considered non-resident if:

- the trustee is a professional UK resident trustee; and

- the settlor was not domiciled, resident or ordinarily resident in the UK at death (with respect to a trust created at death) or at the date the settlor transferred property to the trust (with respect to an inter vivos trust).[5]

13.12 Where a trust is not UK resident for CGT purposes, the trustees have no exposure to CGT (save potentially in the context of a UK trade) but see **13.55** et seq and **13.71** concerning the exposure of the settlor and the beneficiaries.[6] UK resident

---

[3] FA 1989, s 110.
[4] Taxation of Chargeable Gains Act 1992, s 69(1) (TCGA 1992).
[5] TCGA 1992, s 69(2). The Inland Revenue discussion paper proposes adopting a single residence test for income and CGT purposes, based on the current income tax test. See **13.88** and footnote 3 above. Under these proposals the exemption for professional trustees would be removed.
[6] TCGA 1992, ss 86 and 87.

trustees are exposed to CGT on worldwide gains. However, if the settlor or his spouse can benefit from the trust, the settlor is subject to tax on the trustees' gains under the anti-avoidance provisions.[7]

C. Taxation of trustees

1. Income taxation of discretionary trusts

13.13 A discretionary trust is one which gives the trustees the power to choose the persons to whom distributions of both income and capital are to be made. No beneficiary can have the right to trust income as it arises (or to call for that income to be paid to him). The trustees must have the power to withhold income and distribute it as they see fit to one or more beneficiaries.[8]

13.14 The discretionary trust may take a variety of forms. For example, permitting accumulation of all or part of the income during the period permitted by UK law, or requiring distribution of all income but allowing the trustees the discretion to select among a class of beneficiaries. Accordingly, such a trust can offer total flexibility. In most modern trusts, whether discretionary or fixed interest, the trustees are given wide discretionary powers over distribution of capital. However, it is the extent of their powers over income which determines the tax status of the trust.

13.15 The UK resident trustees of discretionary trusts are subject to tax on worldwide income (other than Schedule F income – see below) which is not taxable on the settlor at the 'rate applicable to trusts' (40% from 6 April 2004).[9] Trust income chargeable under Schedule F, such as dividends and distributions from companies, is taxed on the trustees from 6 April 2004 at 32.5%. No personal allowances are available. Trustee expenses properly chargeable to income are deductible against income in calculating taxable income in the following order:

1. Schedule F income;
2. foreign dividends;
3. savings income;
4. other income.

A beneficiary receiving a trust distribution is treated as receiving a distribution from which tax at the rate applicable to trusts (currently 40%) has been deducted. The beneficiary is therefore treated as having paid tax at 40%.

---

[7] TCGA 1992, s 77.
[8] *Pearson v IRC [1980] 2 All ER 479.* A fundamental distinction was made between administrative and dispositive powers vested in the trustees. Dispositive powers (eg a power of accumulation) would be fatal to the existence of an interest in possession since it would deprive the life tenant of *the right* to call for the income to be paid to him. It should be noted that a trust can still be discretionary in nature even if it currently has only one potential beneficiary provided the trustees are able to exercise their powers of accumulation for the ultimate discretionary class.
[9] Income and Corporation Taxes Act 1988, s 686 (ICTA 1988).

Taxation of trustees **13.16**

13.16 The trustees are assessable to tax on all income at either the rate applicable to trusts (40%) or the trust Schedule F rate (32.5%). However, because the Schedule F dividend income has a 10% tax credit attached which is not refundable, a distribution made to a beneficiary which consists of such dividend income will result in further tax liability as illustrated in the following example.

Example

Tax on receipt of dividend	(£)	
Dividend	900	
Non-repayable tax credit	100	
Gross trust income	1000	
Less: Tax on trustees at 32.5%	(325)	
Trustees income after tax	675	
Tax due from trustees	325	
Less: Tax credit	(100)	
Additional tax due	225	(25% of the cash dividend)
On distribution to beneficiary of 540 (*so as not to distribute more than the dividend*)		
Distribution	540	
Plus: Tax deemed deducted (40%)	360	
Gross Payment	900	
Trustees further tax due		
On Dividend	325	
Less: Non-refundable tax credit	(100)	
Tax available to set against distribution	225	
Additional tax due from trustees	135	
Tax credit available for beneficiary	360	
Beneficiary's gross receipt	£900	(comprising £540 cash and £360 Trustee withheld tax, such tax being equal to 40% of the £900 cash dividend received by the trustee)

13.17 *UK Income Taxation of Trusts, Settlors and Beneficiaries*

13.17 As can be seen from the above example, the income tax position in such a case is unfavourable when compared with receipt of a dividend by an individual directly or through an interest in possession trust, where the highest tax rate will be 32.5%.[10] Where the only trust income is Schedule F income, trustees of discretionary trusts need to take care not to over distribute income so as to ensure they have sufficient funds to pay the additional tax due on distribution.

2. Income taxation of fixed interest (interest in possession) trusts

13.18 If a beneficiary has a vested interest in the income as it arises (whether or not that interest may be defeasible at the instance of the trustees) the UK rules 'look through' the trustees and regard the beneficiary's source of income as being the underlying trust assets.[11] Such trusts are referred to as 'interest in possession trusts',[12] the beneficiary having an interest in the income which is vested in possession. This is in contrast with a discretionary trust where the source of the income originates in the exercise of the trustees' discretion, and the source is thus considered to be the trust itself, rather than the underlying trust assets.

13.19 The income beneficiary of an interest in possession trust is therefore taxed as if he had received the income from the underlying source. It is usual for the trustees of such a trust to authorise that income on trust assets be paid directly to the beneficiary.[13] However, where UK trustees themselves receive the income, they will nevertheless remain liable to tax on the income, and the distribution will carry with it the appropriate tax credit for the beneficiary. Whether the higher rate of tax is payable (ie 32.5% for Schedule F income or 40% for other income[14]) will depend on the beneficiary's personal circumstances, the gross trust distribution being aggregated with the beneficiary's other income.

3. Income taxation of bare trusts

13.20 For income tax purposes, property held as nominee or bare trustee for another person who would be absolutely entitled but for being under a disability (eg a minor or a person who is mentally incapacitated) is taxed as if the income were received directly by the person entitled.

4. Capital gains taxation of discretionary and fixed interest trusts

13.21 The capital gains taxation of trusts has been subject to considerable legislative changes in recent years. However, there are a number of key situations which dictate *substantially different treatment*:

---

[10] Except in the case where a person is taxed on the remittance basis of taxation in which case his highest rate may be 40% – ICTA 1988, s 1A(4).
[11] *Baker v Archer-Shee [1927] AC 844.*
[12] *Pearson and others v CIR [1980] STC 318.*
[13] The Taxes Management Act 1970, s 76 provides that the trustees are relieved from the necessity to make returns of income in such a case if they advise the Inland Revenue of the name, address and profits of the relevant person.
[14] The trustees will pay tax at the basic rate.

Taxation of trustees **13.23**

- **UK resident trusts:**

    (a) where the settlor and/or his spouse may benefit and where an equivalent sum to the worldwide gains realised by the trustees annually is taxable to the UK resident settlor, and not the trustees, under anti-avoidance provisions;[15]

    (b) where neither the settlor nor his spouse can benefit, the trustees themselves are liable to CGT on worldwide trust asset disposals or other events of charge.[16]

- **Non-UK resident trusts:**

    (a) where created by a UK domiciled and resident settlor, broadly speaking, for his family (being any one or more of himself, his spouse, his children, his grandchildren, companies controlled by any of the foregoing), the UK resident settlor will be taxable on all gains realised by the offshore trustees as they arise;[17]

    (b) where created by a non-UK domiciled settlor (either UK resident or non-UK resident *but who remains non-UK domiciled*) trust gains are *only* taxed to UK domiciled and resident beneficiaries receiving capital payments (whether directly or indirectly and whether in cash or by way of benefit in kind).[18]

a. UK resident trusts

13.22 UK resident trusts from which neither the settlor nor his spouse can benefit, and therefore to which the anti-avoidance provisions do not apply, are subject to CGT on the disposal (or 'deemed' disposal) of capital assets in so far as the proceeds (or deemed proceeds) exceed the base cost deductible.[19] The latter will generally be the trustees' acquisition cost or the market value of the asset at its date of transfer to them. The general CGT principles discussed in **CHAPTER 8** and **CHAPTER 11** will apply.

(i) *Trustee taper relief*

13.23 For periods of ownership prior to 6 April 1998, there is a measure of relief for the trustees attributable to inflationary gains, by way of indexation of the base cost in line with the Retail Prices Index. For disposals after 5 April 1998, taper relief is available to reduce the chargeable gain on assets which qualify for such relief.[20] As with individuals, taper relief is available to trustees with eligible gains if their total

---

[15] TCGA 1992, s 77; see **13.39**. The remittance basis of taxation will not benefit a UK resident but a non-domiciled settlor of a UK resident trust because the s 77 'settlor interested trust' rule does not look through the trust, like the US grantor trust rules, but rather deems the settlor taxable on 'chargeable gains of an amount equal to' the gains of the trust (s 77(1)(c)).
[16] TCGA 1992, s 2; see **13.22**.
[17] TCGA 1992, s 86; see **13.39**.
[18] TCGA 1992, s 87; see **13.63**.
[19] TCGA 1992, s 65.
[20] TCGA 1992, s 2A(1); see **CHAPTER 10**.

13.24 *UK Income Taxation of Trusts, Settlors and Beneficiaries*

chargeable gains for the year exceed their allowable losses for that year and those brought forward from prior years. The rate of taper relief which is available to trustees (again as for individuals) depends on whether or not the asset is a business asset and how long it has been held (see **CHAPTER 10** for general principles).

13.24 For trust-owned shares in a company to qualify for the more generous business asset taper relief, the company must be a 'qualifying company' in the hands of the trustees.[21] If the company is a trading company (or a holding company of a trading group) then:

- the company must be unlisted; *or*
- an eligible beneficiary must be an officer or employee of the company or a connected company; *or*
- not less than 5% of the voting rights must be exercisable by the trustees.

For a non-trading company (or a holding company of a non-trading group) to qualify:

- an eligible beneficiary must be an officer or employee of the company or a connected company; *and*
- the trustees must not have a material interest in the company or any controlling company.

13.25 For purposes of taper relief, the term 'eligible beneficiary' means a beneficiary with an interest in possession in trust assets which include those shares.[22] The term 'material interest' means ownership of more than 10% of the issued shares, voting rights, income rights or rights to capital on a winding up. The trustees are considered to have a material interest if either they and/or persons connected with them have such an interest.

13.26 A trust asset, other than shares, may also qualify as a business asset if it is used wholly or partly for the purposes of a trade carried on by one or more of the following:

- the trustees or a partnership whose members include the trustees;
- an eligible beneficiary or a partnership whose members include that beneficiary;
- a company which is a qualifying company[23] for the trustees or an eligible beneficiary;
- certain holding companies; or
- for the purposes of any office or employment held by an eligible beneficiary with a person carrying on a trade.[24]

---

[21] TCGA 1992, Sch A1, para 6(2).
[22] TCGA 1992, Sch A1, para 7(1).
[23] TCGA 1992, Sch A1, para 6.
[24] TCGA 1992, Sch A1, para 5(3).

Taxation of trustees **13.29**

The charge on the amount of the tapered gain (either business asset taper or non-business asset taper relief dependent on the above criteria) arises at the trustee's rate of 40%. There is also an annual exemption available (£4,100 for 2004/05), which is one-half of that available to individuals regardless of the type of trust (although certain special exemptions exist, for example, in the case of trusts for the disabled and also provisions to prevent exploitation of the exemption by fragmentation).[25]

(ii)   CGT on trust distribution or resettlement

13.27   A CGT charge may arise on the trustees making disposals of assets in the normal course of administering the trust.[26] A charge may also arise where a beneficiary becomes absolutely entitled to all or part of the settled property or where the trustees of a separate trust become so entitled.[27] In these events, the trustees are deemed to make a disposal of the relevant assets and a re-acquisition at their then market value – CGT arising as appropriate. Whether or not the exercise of a power has caused a separate settlement to be created for CGT purposes is not always a simple matter and there is considerable case law on the subject. However, this will typically be the case where the assets become subjected to completely new trusts without the necessity in any foreseeable circumstance for further reference to any of the former provisions.[28]

13.28   A deemed disposal also occurs on the death of a beneficiary with an interest in possession in the fund although the trustees' base cost is uplifted to the market value of the assets at the date of death without any tax charge arising.[29] However, where hold-over relief was used on creation of the trust or on any addition of property thereafter, the death of the beneficiary will crystallise the tax charge on the held-over gain, which will not be removed by reason of the general exclusion on death.[30]

(iii)   Holdover relief for business property and assets subject to an IHT charge

13.29   Where a deemed disposal occurs on transfer to a UK resident beneficiary, it is possible in certain circumstances to defer the tax charge which would otherwise arise to the trustees. The same criteria apply here as for the hold-over relief available to individuals.[31] If a beneficiary receives an asset subject to a hold-over relief claim,

---

[25]   TCGA 1992, Sch 1, para 1.
[26]   TCGA 1992, s 65.
[27]   TCGA 1992, s 71.
[28]   *Bond v Pickford [1983] STC 517; Roome v Edwards [1981] ALL ER 736*; Inland Revenue Statement of Practice SP7/84 sets out the circumstances where they will consider a deemed disposal to have occurred. Since the removal of the general hold-over relief for gifts in 1989, these cases have become significant in planning situations where it is desired to modify trusts for IHT planning purposes but without giving rise to a deemed transfer into a new trust and hence a CGT disposal.
[29]   TCGA 1992, ss 72 and 73.
[30]   TCGA 1992, s 74.
[31]   TCGA 1992, ss 165 and 260.

if he subsequently ceases to be UK tax resident within any of the following six tax years, the held over gain crystallises and falls into charge in the year when he ceases to be UK resident.[32]

(iv) Taxation of bare trusts

13.30 Where the trustees hold assets as bare trustees or nominees for a beneficiary who is absolutely entitled as against them (either from the outset or by reason of an earlier trust interest, for example having matured), or would be entitled but for being a minor or under some other legal disability, the trustees are ignored and the beneficiary is subject to CGT as if he owned the assets outright.[33]

13.31 Losses realised by the trustees on the deemed disposal when a beneficiary becomes absolutely entitled to trust assets, and which cannot be offset against gains made by the trustees in that year, can be treated as losses accruing to the beneficiary. This loss can be used by the beneficiary to offset future gains on the disposal of the same asset.[34]

b. Exit charge on emigration of UK resident trust

13.32 Following a fundamental review of the CGT provisions relevant to offshore trusts, the Finance Act 1991 introduced a number of anti-avoidance measures which tax a UK resident and domiciled settlor or beneficiaries on offshore trust gains. These measures were substantially widened by provisions contained in the Finance Act 1998. Since that time, various further amendments have been introduced, largely to counter specific planning strategies which had been developed and which the Inland Revenue considered were not within the spirit of the original legislation.

13.33 Under this legislation, taxation of the gains of non-UK resident trusts is limited to UK resident and domiciled settlors or beneficiaries. Trustees who are neither UK resident nor ordinarily resident will not have any liability to UK CGT (unless they are conducting business in the UK through a branch or agency). One of the measures introduced in 1991 imposed an 'exit charge' where a UK resident trust became:

(a)   non-UK resident on or after 19 March 1991; or

(b)   dually tax resident and, in consequence, tax protected by reason of a double taxation convention.[35]

---

[32] TCGA 1992, s 168. An exemption applies for persons going to work abroad, provided that they resume residence without having disposed of the asset, within three years of leaving. Provision is made to recoup tax still unpaid 12 months after the due date from the transferors (ie the trustees), subject to a right for them to reclaim it from the beneficiary (s 168(7)).

[33] TCGA 1992, s 60. Complexities arise in the case of certain assets, for example UK land, where beneficiaries' interests vest under a trust at different times. In *Crowe v Appleby 1976 [STC] 301* it was held that, for this purpose, a beneficiary did not become 'absolutely entitled' within the meaning of this legislation, to a share in real property as against the trustees.

[34] TCGA 1992, s 71(2).

[35] TCGA 1992, s 80.

13.34 Relief is provided if a trust ceases to be a UK resident upon the death of a UK trustee (that is, where the death of a UK resident trustee leaves the trust with a majority of non-UK resident trustees), provided that the trust becomes UK resident again within six months beginning with the date of death.[36]

13.35 For UK CGT purposes, trustees are normally regarded as a single and continuing body of persons and (subject to the comment above on the cessation of UK residence) changes in trustee do not trigger any taxable events.[37]

13.36 Where the trustees of a settlement become neither resident nor ordinarily resident in the UK, they are deemed to dispose of, and immediately reacquire, all assets constituting the settled property for a consideration equal to their market value immediately before the date of migration. Certain exceptions exist where the assets would remain in charge despite the non-resident status of the owners (eg UK assets used for the purposes of a trade carried on in the UK through a branch or agency) and certain measures are introduced to avoid exploitation of other reliefs. The rate of charge is the flat 40% rate which is now applicable to all trusts from 5 April 2004.

13.37 The liability to tax is on the former UK trustee in office immediately prior to the time of migration. However, it should be noted that where tax is not paid within six months of the due date, the Inland Revenue is able to seek recovery from a past trustee (being a person who has occupied that office within the 12 months prior to migration of the trust, unless he can show that at the date of his retirement there was no proposal that the trust would migrate).[38] Accordingly, although a past trustee is given a statutory right of recovery from current trustees, the former will need to give serious consideration to any indemnities (and their enforceability if against offshore trustees) or retentions which he may feel to be appropriate.

13.38 Where the settlor is the taxable person under the CGT anti-avoidance provisions relating to a UK resident trust (see **13.39**) the effect of the deemed disposal is that an amount equal to the deemed chargeable gain will be treated as accruing to the settlor in the relevant year.[39]

D. Taxation of a UK resident settlor/grantor

13.39 Broadly speaking, any trust from which a UK resident settlor or his spouse (excluding a former or separated spouse or a widower/widow) may benefit in any circumstances whatsoever will be ignored for income tax and in many instances for CGT purposes. Instead, the trust income and, in many cases, gains realised by the trustees will remain taxable to the settlor even though the settlor may have been subject to CGT on the creation of the settlement.[40]

---

[36] TCGA 1992, s 81.
[37] TCGA 1992, s 69(1).
[38] TCGA 1992, s 82.
[39] TCGA 1992, s 77.
[40] TCGA 1992, s 70.

13.40 The legislation is broadly framed and (subject to certain express exclusions[41]) any possibility of benefit, however remote, is sufficient.[42] The benefit must, however, arise under the terms of the trust (or, for example, where a resulting trust may arise on failure to dispose of the whole fund) and not through extraneous means, for example through inheriting the estate of one of the beneficiaries on an intestacy.

13.41 Under the Finance Act 2004 provisions on pre-owned assets, with effect from 6 April 2005 the settlor may also be subject to an income tax charge with respect to his use of certain trust assets which he previously owned or which were acquired with funds or property he provided, if such assets are not already regarded as part of his estate for UK inheritance tax purposes. With respect to UK resident but non-domiciled settlors, this charge is generally limited to UK assets, as discussed in further detail in **CHAPTER 1**. Provision is made to avoid any double charges arising under both sets of rules.

1. Income tax

a. ICTA 1988, Pt XV – settlor interested trust income tax provisions

13.42 The income tax provisions of Pt XV[43] transparently tax a UK resident settlor, rather than the trustees, on income of a 'settlor interested' trust. A settlor interested trust is one from which the settlor and his spouse are not excluded from benefit or where income has been paid to or for the benefit of the settlor's unmarried minor child.[44] This also applies to income retained by the trustees in circumstances where it would be treated as income of the child, for example, in the case of a bare trust (s 660B(1)(b)). Where income has been retained or accumulated in other trusts and a payment is later made to or for the benefit of the settlor's unmarried minor child, the settlor will be subject to income tax on that payment to the extent of the accumulated income.[45] The above provisions apply to all trusts, domestic or offshore and apply regardless of whether the settlor was UK resident or domiciled when the trust was settled. They apply only during the lifetime of the settlor, who has the right to reclaim the tax paid from the trustees.[46]

---

[41] Applicable where the only possible circumstances in which he can benefit are:
- the bankruptcy of the beneficiary;
- the assignment or charge of his interest by the beneficiary;
- in the case of a marriage settlement, the death of both parties to the marriage and all of the children;
- the death of certain specified beneficiaries whose interests are, or were, contingent on attaining 25 years of age.

[42] The likelihood of the occurrence is irrelevant since the legislation looks at possibilities, not probabilities. In *Unmarried Settlor v IRC [2003] WTLR 915* it was held to apply to the situation where a future spouse could be added to the class of beneficiaries of a trust settled by a 60-year-old homosexual man.

[43] ICTA 1988, Pt XV, s 660A et seq.
[44] ICTA 1988, Pt XV, s 660B(1).
[45] ICTA 1988, Pt XV, s 660B(2).
[46] ICTA 1988, Pt XV, s 660D.

13.43 However, since Part XV of ICTA 1988 'looks through' the trust to tax the settlor directly on trust income as though the trust did not exist, a non-UK domiciled settlor will retain the ability to take advantage in appropriate circumstances of the relevant remittance legislation.[47] The trustees will need to segregate overseas income from capital in the same manner that the settlor might have done had the assets remained in his ownership. (Assuming the settlor is not taxable under s 740, discussed at **13.49**, planning is thus possible as remittances to the UK from capital will not trigger income tax exposure.)

13.44 Planning for a non-domiciled UK resident settlor should also take into account ICTA 1988, s 677. That provision generally provides that, where a capital sum (which includes a loan or other payment otherwise than out of income) is made available to the settlor or his spouse by the trustees, the payment will be taxed as income to the extent of the available income of that year or subsequent years (up to a maximum of ten years).[48] Planning should therefore consider the removal from the trust of 'income available' to be distributed to the settlor as part of a loan or payment of capital.

13.45 For a non-UK resident trust settled by a non-UK domiciled settlor, such planning may differ depending on whether the trust is an interest in possession trust or a discretionary trust. Such planning might involve:

- maintaining separate income and capital accounts within the trust;

- distributions to the UK, in appropriate circumstances, only from capital accounts; and

- 'sweeping' the trust annually of non-UK source income.[49]

In the latter case this might be done by either:

- paying out all such income to non-UK resident beneficiaries or making payment offshore for the account of UK resident but non-UK domiciled beneficiaries; or

- granting the UK resident non-domiciled settlor an interest in possession in the trust (which would require annual income distribution – which should also occur offshore).[50]

---

[47] ICTA 1988, Pt XV, ss 660G(4) and 682A.
[48] ICTA 1988, Pt XV, s 677. 'Available income' covers both income of the current year and any undistributed income accumulated in the trust from previous years, less sums already taxed under a variety of other provisions. The manner in which this provision applies can be particularly penal. A separate provision, s 678, taxes capital sums paid to a settlor by companies connected with the trust.
[49] UK source income realised by the trust or an underlying company will be taxable to the settlor under s 739 without reference to the remittance basis of taxation.
[50] Provided a non-UK domiciled settlor initially creates a discretionary trust and is not granted an immediate interest in possession, this should avoid the 'either/or' domicile trap of IHTA 1984, s 80(1) which could result in loss of excluded property trust status. See the discussion in **CHAPTER 6** on excluded property trusts at **6.62** et seq.

13.46 The above provisions apply not only to trusts, but also to 'settlements'; a broadly defined term that 'includes any disposition, trust, covenant, agreement, arrangement or transfer of assets'.[51]

b. Transfer of assets abroad – ICTA 1988, ss 739 and 740

13.47 In addition, two further income tax provisions are directed specifically towards attempted tax avoidance by the use of offshore structures (eg foreign trusts or companies).[52] Where it is possible to show that the offshore structure is created for bona fide commercial reasons unrelated to UK tax avoidance (which may include creation for the purposes of some foreign tax), the sections do not apply.[53] These sections are, however, extremely wide in their scope and, despite the chapter heading in the legislation 'Transfers of Assets Abroad', they are not limited to transfers of assets from the UK. Furthermore, the provisions are not directed towards any particular structure so that companies, settlements and any other 'arrangement' might be the subject of attack. Section 739 is directed towards taxation of transferors who are ordinarily resident in the UK in respect of income arising to offshore structures from which they or their spouses have (or may have) power to enjoy income or capital. Section 740 is directed towards taxation of persons who are not transferors but actually receive benefits from such a structure.

13.48 Until 25 November 1996, the transferor had to be ordinarily resident in the UK at the time of the transfer of assets to be caught by Section 739.[54] However, in respect of income arising after 25 November 1996, the status of the transferor at the transfer date is irrelevant.[55]

13.49 The broad effect of s 739 is to disregard the alienation of the property so that the transferor's income tax position is unaffected. This means, as mentioned above, that the facility is preserved for a non-UK domiciled transferor to benefit from the remittance basis of assessment for overseas income by the segregation of foreign source income for retention offshore.[56] This provision differs somewhat from the wording of s 740 which taxes offshore income on a 'benefits received' basis. This will mean that in addition to applying to distributions of income, income tax exposure can trigger where a capital sum is received or a benefit in kind is conferred. Accordingly, segregation of foreign source income and remittance of capital only, will not avoid exposure under this provision. The capital sum, or value of the benefit, is 'attributed' to any available accumulated income within the fund (ie which has not been spent or paid away to others, which is a means of avoiding this issue). In the event of the taxable amounts exceeding the available income, the excess is carried forward and set against future income.[57]

---

[51] ICTA 1988, s 660G.
[52] ICTA 1988, ss 739 and 740.
[53] ICTA 1988, s 741.
[54] *IRC v Willoughby [1997] STC 995, HL.*
[55] ICTA 1988, s 739(1A).
[56] ICTA 1988, s 743(2) and (3).
[57] However, if TCGA 1992, s 87 applies to the trust (see **13.71** et seq) this may instead trigger a CGT charge for the recipient beneficiary.

13.50   Section 740 taxes an individual 'who is not liable to tax under s 739'.[58] It is a matter of academic debate whether a settlor/beneficiary potentially liable under s 739, but enjoying only the benefit of tax-free remittances of capital (which are not taxable under s 739), can be taxed as a beneficiary under s 740 (which would give rise to an income charge by reference to that capital). Opinions are split, but the better view is that the sections are mutually exclusive such that a settlor potentially liable under s 739 cannot be liable under s 740.[59]

13.51   Given the above, in appropriate cases, full annual distribution of the income of both a non-UK resident trust and any of its underlying companies, either to non-UK residents or non-UK domiciliaries (if retained offshore), may avoid the application of these sections.

> **Example**
>
> A Kenyan settlor, with no prior UK connections, sets up a Jersey resident irrevocable discretionary trust for the benefit of his niece, who is UK resident but not UK domiciled. There were UK tax motives in the manner of structuring the trust. It owns a UK residence and a Jersey investment holding company and the Jersey company and the trustees themselves both own investment portfolios. The trust and the company earn investment income from the portfolios. The settlor's niece is allowed to live rent free in the UK property. Unless the income of both the company and the trust are fully distributed, these may be regarded as 'relevant income' and potentially available to attribute to the annual value of the niece's enjoyment of the UK trust property.[60]

2. Capital gains tax

a. UK resident trusts

13.52   The anti-avoidance provisions relevant to trusts of which the trustees are UK resident and ordinarily resident apply where the settlor or his spouse can benefit directly or indirectly from the trust property in any circumstances whatsoever.[61]

13.53   Under these provisions, where the trustees make chargeable gains (although not losses), an equivalent amount is deemed to represent chargeable gains

---

[58]   ICTA 1988, s 740(1)(b).
[59]   The issue turns on whether in s 740(1)(b) the word 'liable' includes potential liability where no actual charge arises because income is retained outside the UK. The Inland Revenue appears to accept the mutual exclusivity of the two provisions. See Inland Revenue Interpretation 201 (April 1999).
[60]   The income of both the company and the trust will be susceptible to attack under s 740 unless distributed in such manner that it is no longer 'relevant income' for the purposes of that section. Care also needs to be taken in any initial structuring to ensure no doubling up of income occurs. For example, in extracting funds from the company it may be preferable to have established it with loan finance to enable loan repayments instead of dividends, which might themselves be regarded as income.
[61]   TCGA 1992, s 77. The extended definition of 'settlement' found in the income tax provisions, does not apply for this purpose.

accruing to the settlor. Since the legislation does not deem the trustees' gains to arise to the settlor for all the purposes of the relevant legislation (as it does in the case of the income tax anti-avoidance provisions),[62] but instead treats chargeable gains of an equivalent amount as accruing to the settlor in these circumstances, there is no ability for a non-UK domiciled settlor to benefit from the remittance basis of assessment where the trust itself is UK resident.[63] Tax paid can be reclaimed from the trustees.[64]

13.54 In computing the chargeable gain the trustees' losses are deductible. The settlor is also able to use personal realised losses (if they exceed his personal gains) to offset the trust gains ultimately attributed to him.[65] The provision only applies to a settlement if the settlor and the trustees are either resident in the UK during any part of the year, or ordinarily resident in the UK during the year.[66] Despite the above provisions, a transfer into such trust will remain a disposal for CGT in the usual manner.[67]

b. Non-UK resident trusts

13.55 Anti-avoidance measures introduced in 1991 and expanded in 1998 apply the basic principle of the provisions described above to non-UK resident trusts. However, their scope is considerably wider.[68] In order for these provisions to apply, the trustees must be neither resident nor ordinarily resident in the UK for any part of the year, or dually resident and taxed as a non-resident under the terms of a double taxation convention.

13.56 To be taxable on worldwide trust gains on an arising basis, a settlor must also be domiciled in the UK at some time in the year the gains arose to the trustees and either resident during any part of the year or ordinarily resident during the year.[69] However, if the settlor is UK-domiciled and is caught by the temporary non-residence rules (ie he is non-resident for less than five years) he may be liable in the year of return to the UK for worldwide trust gains which arose whilst he was non-resident.[70]

13.57 Further, the trust must be a 'qualifying settlement'. A qualifying settlement is one that is (i) created on or after 19 March 1991, or (ii) with effect from

---

[62] ICTA 1988, ss 660A et seq.
[63] For potential new residents to the UK, care needs to be taken to ensure that they are not both trustee and potential beneficiary of family trusts which they have created. In such cases, if the trust becomes a UK resident trust, the settlor's qualification for the remittance basis of assessment may be lost as to gains realised on overseas assets, where he would have so qualified had they simply been held personally. US Probate avoidance trusts often cause such difficulties.
[64] TCGA 1992, s 78.
[65] TCGA 1992, s 77. A specific anti-avoidance provision does, however, preclude the trustees from using certain realised losses against held-over gains, where the person who settled the assets subject to the hold-over claim acquired his interest in the trust by purchase from a third party. s 79A.
[66] TCGA 1992, s 77(7).
[67] TCGA 1992, s 70.
[68] TCGA 1992, ss 86 and 86A.
[69] TCGA 1992, s 86(1).
[70] TCGA 1992, s 86A. See the discussion of these rules in **CHAPTER 9**.

6 April 1999, is any trust created before 19 March 1991 that is not a 'protected settlement'.[71] The circumstances in which protected settlements exist are extremely restrictive and unlikely to be widely applicable.[72]

13.58 The provisions impose the tax charge on a settlor where he has an 'interest' in the trust, as defined in the legislation.[73] Such an interest will exist if any of the following 'defined persons' actually do enjoy a benefit from the settlement income or capital (whether directly or indirectly), or if they will or might do so in any circumstances whatever.

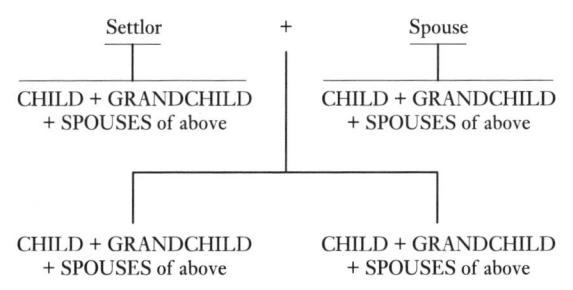

```
         Settlor            +              Spouse
            |                                 |
   ─────────────────           ─────────────────
   CHILD + GRANDCHILD          CHILD + GRANDCHILD
    + SPOUSES of above          + SPOUSES of above
            |
   ─────────────────           ─────────────────
   CHILD + GRANDCHILD          CHILD + GRANDCHILD
    + SPOUSES of above          + SPOUSES of above
```

13.59 For the purposes of this legislation the definition of a child includes a stepchild. In addition, the provisions will apply if the settlement can benefit any company controlled by any of the above persons or a company associated with such a company (ie one has control of the other or both are under the control of the same persons).[74] As can be seen the categories of beneficiaries that cause the settlor to be taxed on gains of non-UK resident trusts as they arise are very broad.

---

[71] TCGA 1992, Sch 5, para 9(1), (1A) and (1B).
[72] Under TCGA 1992, Sch 5, para 9(10A) to (10D) (inserted by FA 1998, s 132) a 'protected settlement' is a trust, the beneficiaries of which are confined to:
- children of the settlor or spouse who are under 18;
- unborn children of the settlor and his/her spouse or future spouse;
- future spouses of any of these children;
- a future spouse of the settlor;
- persons outside the 'defined persons' mentioned above in 13.58.

The settlor is not taxed on gains of a protected settlement as they arise, unless and until one or more of certain specified conditions is fulfilled (ie the settlement is 'tainted'). TCGA 1992, Sch 5, para 2A. The five conditions are as follows:
(a) property or income is added to the trust (other than pursuant to an arm's length transaction or pursuant to an obligation incurred before 19 March 1991). However, it is permissible to add funds to the settlement to defray the settlement's administration or taxation expenses provided that the funds added do not exceed the difference between the expenses and the amount of income of the settlement;
(b) the trustees become neither resident nor ordinarily resident on or after 19 March 1991, or they become dually resident and taxed as non-UK resident persons by reason of a double taxation convention;
(c) the terms of the trust are varied so that any of the 'defined persons' becomes for the first time capable of benefiting under the trust;
(d) one of the 'defined persons' actually enjoys a benefit even though this would not appear to be possible on looking at the provisions of the settlement;
(e) the settlement ceases to be a protected settlement on or after 6 April 1998.

Given the limited nature of the 'protected settlement' rules these are unlikely to be widely applicable.

[73] TCGA 1992, Sch 5, para 2 subject, however, to the same categories of exceptions described previously. Sch 5, para 2(4) and (5).
[74] TCGA 1992, Sch 5, para 2(3) and (7).

13.60 If the settlement falls within the scope of these provisions and the settlor is (i) UK domiciled and (ii) either UK resident during any part of the year or ordinarily resident during the year, an amount equal to the chargeable gains realised by the trustees for the year will accrue to the settlor. In computing those gains, the trustees are treated as if they were UK resident, although no annual exemption is available. (However, see **13.56** in relation to settlors who are out of the UK for less than five years.[75])

13.61 Significantly, gains arising to certain companies owned by the trustees are deemed to be realised by the trustees and thus can flow through and become taxable to the settlor under these provisions – see **13.81**.[76] Such attributed gains of underlying companies (which would have been closely held companies had they been UK resident) are not entitled to taper relief, although they do qualify for indexation relief.

13.62 The proviso as to the settlor's UK domicile is of considerable importance since the provisions will not apply to non-UK resident settlements created by non-UK domiciliaries (who remain so). These consequently remain effective tax planning vehicles for such persons and their UK resident families. (see **13.63**).

E. Taxation of the beneficiaries

1. Income tax

13.63 A beneficiary of a discretionary trust will receive income distributions from the trustees which carry with them a credit for tax borne by the trustees, who are liable to account to the Inland Revenue for tax when such payments are made.[77] In this instance the source of the income will be deemed to be the exercise of the trustee's discretion. The current position may be modified under certain Inland Revenue proposals. See Section F (**13.82** et seq).

13.64 The trustees of an interest in possession trust may, by agreement with the UK Inland Revenue, arrange for the beneficiary to declare the income on his return (in which case it is unnecessary for the trustees to declare it) and will often arrange for the income to be paid directly to the beneficiary. The source of income in the case of an interest in possession trust, where the beneficiary has the absolute right to receive it, is deemed to be the underlying trust assets.[78]

---

[75] TCGA 1992, s 10A.
[76] TCGA 1992, s 13.
[77] The trustees are taxed on an annual basis under ICTA 1988, s 686 in respect of income which they receive. However, they are also obliged to deduct tax on a distribution made to a beneficiary under s 687, credit being given for tax they have paid and certain other payments. This can result in additional tax having to be paid by the trustees at the time of the distribution. The Inland Revenue discussion papers issued on 17 December 2003 and 13 August 2004 suggest a possible modification of the existing rules such that income distributions made during the year (and by 31 December following the end of the year) may be taxed on a look-through basis to the beneficiary, in much the same manner as an interest in possession trust.
[78] *Williams v Singer (1921) 7 TC 387; Archer-Shee v Baker (1927) 11TC 749.*

13.65 Certain distributions out of trust capital can be taxed as income of the beneficiary, for example, where the purpose of the power exercised is to maintain a particular level of income in the beneficiary's hands.[79]

13.66 In one case, that of a bare trust, the Inland Revenue will generally look through the trustees for both income tax and capital gains tax purposes[80] and will tax the income and the asset disposals as if the underlying fund is in the direct ownership of the beneficiary. A bare trust is, in effect, little more than a nomineeship and commonly occurs where assets are being held for a minor unconditionally, but pending the attainment of the age of majority. Certain UK trust legislation provides the facility to accumulate income and make distributions for maintenance in the usual manner, notwithstanding the basic form of the trust and the tax treatment of the beneficiary.[81] However, if the bare trust is created by the minor's parent, the income will be regarded as the income of (and taxed to) the parent whilst the minor is unmarried and under the age of 18.[82] This does not currently apply to capital gains made, but may be extended under the Inland Revenue proposals. See **13.86**.

13.67 A UK resident and domiciled beneficiary will be taxable on all income distributions from a UK resident trust or from a non-UK resident trust. A UK resident but non-UK domiciled beneficiary is taxed generally on the remittance basis so that non-UK source income will be taxed only if it is received (or in some cases, indirectly enjoyed) in the UK. If the trust is UK resident but the beneficiary is not, then he will be taxed on trust income which has a UK source.

13.68 In each of the above cases, in respect of an interest in possession trust, the source of the income will be determined by the situs of the underlying trust assets, but in the case of a discretionary trust, the source of the income will be determined by the residence of the trustees, since it will arise in consequence of the exercise of the discretion of the trustee.

13.69 Income taxation of a beneficiary of an offshore trust may also arise under the anti-avoidance provisions of ICTA 1988, s 740 (see **13.10**). Again the remittance basis rules are relevant for non-UK domiciliaries.

2. Capital gains tax

13.70 With respect to UK resident trusts (except for settlor-interested trusts and bare trusts), the UK resident trustees (not the beneficiaries) will be subject to CGT (see **13.22**).

13.71 However, as noted earlier, non-resident trustees have no exposure to UK capital gains tax (save as relates to a UK trade). Therefore, unless the settlor is taxed

---

[79] *Brodie v IRC (1933) 17 TC 432*; but see also *Stevenson v Wishart [1987] STC 266* where exceptional payments to supplement income pursuant to a power over capital were not considered taxable as income.
[80] TCGA 1992, s 60.
[81] Trustees Act 1925, s 31.
[82] ICTA 1988, s 660B.

13.72 UK Income Taxation of Trusts, Settlors and Beneficiaries

under TCGA 1992, s 86 (see **13.55**), the UK seeks to bring the gains of such trusts into charge by taxing beneficiaries who receive 'capital payments'.[83] For gains realised and capital payments made, on or after 17 March 1998, the capital payments regime applies irrespective of the settlor's non-UK domicile status.[84]

13.72 A running computation is made of 's 87 trust gains' in each year of assessment (6 April to 5 April) as if the trustees had been UK resident. This pool of gains is carried forward from year to year and is reduced by capital payments. A beneficiary who receives a 'capital payment' will be regarded as receiving gain in so far as it does not exceed the total pool of 'trust gains'. The beneficiary will be personally liable to UK CGT at his marginal income tax rate.

13.73 'Capital payments' are also carried forward to set against future gains where no current 'trust gains' exist.[85] The term 'capital payment' is broadly defined to include any 'benefit' whether in cash or kind and including, for example, the annual value of the benefit of an outstanding interest-free loan or the rent-free use of trust-owned property.[86]

13.74 Although trust gains are attributed to any beneficiary receiving a capital payment, only a beneficiary who is UK resident and domiciled will be taxable on that payment. Generally, s 87 gains can, therefore, be attributed to non-UK domiciled or non-UK resident beneficiaries without a UK tax charge, thereby reducing the pool which remains to be offset against other distributions and giving rise to planning opportunities by judicious distribution policies.

13.75 Where more than one distribution is made in a tax year, however, the trust gains are rateably apportioned. If the distribution is not to an individual, but to another trust, subject to certain anti-avoidance provisions (see **13.77**), part of the pool of trust gains will be transferred with the distribution, in proportion with the fraction of the fund which the latter represents.[87]

13.76 The rules of s 740, discussed above, can also apply where a benefit is received by a beneficiary out of capital (if there is also undistributed income in the trust structure) and, therefore in theory, a double charge might arise under both income and gains legislation. However, if relevant, the s 740 charge is applied in priority to the CGT 'capital payments' rule under TCGA 1992, s 87. In either case, if the value of the benefit enjoyed is less than accumulated income or stockpiled gains (depending on the relevant legislation), both rules can apply with respect to benefits conferred in the future. In addition, where the value of the benefit is in excess, such excess can be attributed to future income or gains.

13.77 The position regarding the taxation of trust gains has been made more complex as a result of anti-avoidance legislation introduced in recent years specifically to nullify certain CGT planning strategies. Certain of these measures apply

---

[83] ICTA 1988, s 87.
[84] FA 1998, s 130. Prior to that time the regime only applied where the settlor was UK resident and domiciled in the UK either when the settlement was created or when the gains accrued.
[85] TCGA 1992, s 87(4).
[86] *Cooper v Billingham [2001] STC 1177*.
[87] TCGA 1992, s 90.

Taxation of the beneficiaries **13.81**

where trustees have outstanding borrowings at a time when they make a transfer of assets (or a loan) to any person, including the trustees of another trust, and cause a deemed disposal of the trust assets on the occasion of such transfer, at fair market value. The resulting gain is taxable on the settlor or beneficiaries receiving capital payments as described above.[88]

13.78 The original provision introduced did not close all planning routes and therefore the anti-avoidance measures were subsequently extended such that these s 87 gains must be kept in a separate gains pool for attribution only to UK resident and domiciled beneficiaries of either the transferor or the transferee settlement who receive a capital payment. The gains are not removed from the pool unless there is a tax charge and hence the planning strategy mentioned above for distributions to non-resident or non-domiciled beneficiaries will not apply in this case.[89]

13.79 The ability to defer UK tax by realisation of gains offshore is also eroded by the supplementary tax charge imposed at the time when the benefit is conferred on the beneficiary. This 10% per annum additional charge is levied on the s 87 tax payable by the beneficiary and is computed by reference to the period which has elapsed between realisation of the gain and the conferring of the benefit on the beneficiary. Complex matching provisions apply on a 'first in, first out' basis, although no supplementary charge applies to payments matched with gains in the same or the immediately preceding fiscal year. These are penal provisions which can give rise to an effective tax charge of up to 64%.[90]

13.80 The taper relief rules (and pre-1998 indexation) apply to the trustees in determining the amount of the gain that is stockpiled and potentially chargeable. The penal interest rules then apply to the beneficiary's marginal rate of tax on the gains deemed to have been distributed.

13.81 One further provision, TCGA 1992, s 13, should be noted in the context of capital gains tax.[91] This affects offshore companies controlled by five or fewer persons (directly or indirectly) and generally applies to investment holding companies wholly owned by overseas trust structures. Chargeable gains of such a company are allocated to the ultimate participators (including through each company, where there are a series of holding companies) proportionately to their participation in the company (as long as the gain attributable to that participation would exceed 10% of the total gain).[92] Where such a company is owned directly or indirectly by non-resident trustees the gains will be apportioned to those trustees.[93] Whether or not the apportioned gain is currently, or subsequently becomes, chargeable will depend on whether the 'trust gains' are taxable to a UK domiciled and resident settlor or are only taxable to a UK resident and domiciled beneficiary

---

[88] TCGA 1992, Sch 4B.
[89] FA 2003, s 163. Where the deemed disposal triggers a charge on the settlor, it should also be noted that he is now denied the ability to offset personal losses. TCGA 1992, Sch 4C, para 6(2).
[90] TCGA 1992, s 91.
[91] TCGA 1992, s 13. It should also be noted that under s 13(10A) gains attributed under this provision do not qualify for taper relief. However, indexation relief still applies to companies, and thus would reduce the gain attributed to the trust.
[92] TCGA 1992, s 13(4).
[93] TCGA 1992, s 13(10).

receiving capital payments. It should be noted that where shares of such non-resident companies are directly owned by non-UK domiciliaries, s 13 will not apply.[94]

F. Inland Revenue proposals for a modern income tax and capital gains tax system for trusts

13.82 In the light of its piecemeal development over many decades, the UK tax system applicable to trusts has become highly complex, as is apparent from the outline discussion above. In particular, there has been no uniformity in the way that the exemptions, definitions and anti-avoidance provisions have been developed, or apply. The Inland Revenue also freely admits that the tax rates (which have in the past borne little relation to the rates applicable to individuals) have been a compromise to reflect the likely mix of different tax rates that would have been applicable to the underlying beneficiaries.

13.83 In recognition of a need for reform, in December 2003, four papers were produced which sought representations from interested parties and contained discussion of a number of proposals under consideration for modernising and rationalising the way in which UK resident trusts are taxed. The intention was to have formulated the proposals for introduction from 6 April 2005 and to publish draft legislation in Autumn 2004. A further Consultation Document was issued on 13 August 2004 in respect of which the consultation period ran to 5 November 2004.

The broad areas covered by the latter paper and its revised proposals are as follows.

1. *The proposals*

a. Definitions of trust/settlement, settlor and settlor-interested trust

13.84 It is proposed to harmonise the various definitions which exist for the purposes of the different taxes at present.

13.85 While the broad definitions of 'settlement' for the purposes of various anti-avoidance provisions will be retained, the starting point for the new definition of 'trust' applicable to all taxes will be that which is used for IHT in IHTA 1984, s 43. The CGT rule, which treats the trustees as a single and continuing body of persons distinct from the individuals who occupy the role, is also to be adopted for income tax.

13.86 The definition of 'settlor interested trust' is intended to be harmonised for income and gains tax purposes insofar as it relates to UK trusts, and the current income tax definition used as the basis for the new provision. This would mean that

---

[94] TCGA 1992, s 13(2).

F. Inland Revenue proposals   **13.93**

a UK trust would be subject to the anti avoidance rules where the settlor or his spouse could benefit and additionally the current income tax rules applicable to trusts which benefit the minor children of the settlor would be extended to CGT. The broader definition applicable to the capital gains tax regime for non UK resident trusts would be retained.

13.87 Income which is taxable to the settlor is currently taxed as a special category of income but the proposal is that going forward it should simply be taxed in the same way as if the actual income had arisen to him directly.

The Budget 2004 announced that this harmonisation would be implemented from April 2005.

b. Residence test for trusts

13.88 As noted above there are currently different residence criteria for capital gains tax and income tax, and development of a single definition is suggested, which would be based on the existing test for income tax purposes Trusts affected by the proposals would have a transitional period of 12 months to resolve any prospective changes in their residence status under the new rules.

c. Basic rate band

13.89 Currently trusts are taxed at a fixed rate (40% for most income and gains save for dividend income, which is taxed at 32.5%). Whilst trustees have an exemption for capital gains taxes (normally one-half of that available to individuals) there has been no personal allowance or lower and basic rate tax bands in the same way as for individuals, in the case of income tax.

13.90 It is proposed that from 6 April 2005, trustees who are liable to tax at the rate applicable to trusts will be given a basic rate band of £500 and that where the level of taxable income remains within this band, taxes deducted at source (whatever the rate) would satisfy the trustees' liability in full. Income over this tax band will be taxed to the trustees as normal. For trusts where the income is habitually below the £500 figure, tax returns would only be issued periodically (once every five years is proposed), though the trustees would need to notify the Inland Revenue if they had a tax liability in any particular year.

13.91 The Inland Revenue view is that this will simplify the administrative burden for smaller trusts removing the filing obligation entirely for many of them.

13.92 The above principles will be applied to income to which the rate applicable to trusts is relevant; that is after deduction of trust management expenses and after the deduction of income to which **13.93** applies.

d. Income streaming generally and capital gains of estates

13.93 From 6 April 2005 the Inland Revenue intends to introduce a system similar to that of the US where trust income received and distributed by the trustees annually would be taxed on a flow-through basis to the beneficiaries and not to the UK resident trustees at the rate applicable to trusts, as at present in the case of certain types of trust.

13.94 The proposal is that the trustees would still pay tax at the lower, basic and dividend rates (as at present) and where this was deducted at source it would satisfy the liability of the trustees in full. This tax would also be available as a tax credit to the beneficiary in receipt of the distribution.

13.95 The flow-through principle would apply to income paid to a beneficiary by 31 December following the end of the tax year in which the income arose to the trustees. From the beneficiary's perspective the proposal is to treat the income as income of the year in which it is paid over. It is suggested that the distribution would be treated as a proportionate part of each type of income that had arisen to the trustees in the relevant year and that a 'last in first out' basis would be applied to track income flowing through the trust. In cases where a beneficiary is entitled to an income stream from a particular source he would be treated as receiving that income.

13.96 Various transitional provisions (proposed to extend to 5 April 2008) would be necessary, in particular related to the ability to use tax credits which the trustees may have built up under existing rules.

13.97 While the original proposals suggested streaming of gains, this appears to have been rejected, since lower tax rates applicable to distributed capital gains could create a conflict with the trustees' desire to retain assets in the longer term interests of the beneficiaries.

e. Types of trust

13.98 Three categories of trust would exist:

1. **Settlor interested trust**
    - *Income* would be taxed as income of the settlor and retain its underlying character for the purposes of computing taxes. The UK resident trustees would deduct tax at 40% (the rate applicable to trusts) and the settlor would reclaim overpaid tax. Payments of income to other beneficiaries would be treated as gifts by the settlor to the beneficiary and reliefs, normally due to an individual in such a case, would be applicable to the settlor (eg gifts to a UK charity).
    - *Gains but not losses* would be treated as if they were the settlor's and as currently, settling assets would be treated as a disposal by the settlor and an acquisition by the trustees.

2. **Bare trust**
    - *Income* would be taxed to the beneficiary as if the trust did not exist and the trustees would not be obliged to deduct tax (although there may be a facility to permit this for administrative purposes).

- *Gains* would be taxed to the beneficiary as if the trust did not exist and the trustees would not pay tax. Transfers out of the trust to the absolute beneficiary would not restart the taper clock nor be treated as a disposal

3. **General trust (corresponding to US 'non-grantor' trusts)**

All other trusts would be regarded as general trusts whether or not discretionary or with an interest in possession.

- *Income* would be taxed at source in the normal way but if it were payable to a beneficiary as of right or paid out at the trustees discretion by the tax year end (or by 31 December thereafter) it would be taxed as a flow through to the beneficiary and not taxed to the trustees. Income not paid out of discretionary trusts in excess of the £500 basic rate band would be accumulated and taxed to the trustees at the rate applicable to trusts (40%) or the 32.5% dividend rate. Payments of trust income thereafter would carry a tax credit of 40% but if this exceeded the beneficiary's liability, it would not be repayable.

- *Actual and deemed capital gains* would be taxed to the trustees in the normal way at 40%. Disposals into and out of such trusts would be taxed in the normal way and appropriate reliefs (eg taper relief or hold-over relief, if relevant) would be available. A separate CGT allowance (one-half of the individual allowance) would be available as would the principal residence exemption on normal principles, where a beneficiary occupies under the terms of the trust.

f. Special trusts for disadvantaged groups and estates

13.99 The Inland Revenue suggested that some special trusts – trusts for the disabled (as defined in IHTA 1984) and trusts created for minors at the death of a parent (either by will or under the intestacy rules or under certain pension arrangements) – should be able to elect for 'look-through' treatment for income and gains tax purposes. The election would be irrevocable and would need to be made jointly by the trustees and the beneficiary (or their parent, guardian or legal representative) within two years from the end of the tax year in which the trust was created or in which a decision was made to opt into the regime, if later. The proposal is that, when introduced, the regime will be backdated to 6 April 2004 and for existing trusts, who wish to elect for this status from the outset, the election can therefore be made up to 5 April 2006.

13.100 Trusts for minors will only qualify if the terms are such that the trust capital vests unconditionally no later than the age of 18.

13.101 If applicable the trust will be taxed to the trustees as if it were a bare trust and the beneficiary would reclaim any tax deducted, in excess of that due.

13.102 There was also a suggestion that the taxation of estates of deceased persons in the course of administration should be harmonised and taxed as if they were general trusts though this appears to have been rejected. Various proposals were considered to simplify the position of personal representatives and also to encourage them to wind up estates promptly. In consequence it is proposed that for

13.102 *UK Income Taxation of Trusts, Settlors and Beneficiaries*

the year of death and the following two years they would be liable to CGT at the lower rate (20%) as opposed to the current 40% rate and continue to benefit from the full annual exempt amount available to an individual.

Chapter 14

Non-domiciliary Planning to Remove Assets from US Estate Tax

A. Introduction and summary

14.1 A significant amount of the world's private wealth is invested in US portfolio assets and real estate. For investors who are not US citizens or domiciliaries (Non-Domiciled Aliens or NDAs),[1] techniques are readily available to hold and transfer this wealth to US or foreign family members without US gift, estate or generation skipping transfer (GST) taxes. For individuals who choose not to take appropriate measures there can be a high cost, including estate taxation at rates of up to 48% (2004). Further, bank custodians and trust fiduciaries are personally liable for ten years for any unpaid US gift and estate taxes of their clients.[2]

14.2 In this chapter we discuss planning techniques whereby NDAs, wherever resident, can remove assets from US transfer taxes (gift, estate and GST). In addition, we focus on planning for UK domiciled clients – where the primary objective is either to mitigate US estate tax or match US estate tax exposure with creditable UK inheritance tax. For the well advised, US and UK gift taxes can be easily avoided.

14.3 UK domiciliaries are generally, under the 1979 US/UK Estate and Gift Tax treaty (the 'US/UK treaty'), only subject to US transfer taxes with respect to US real estate and business property. In addition, the US/UK treaty caps the US estate tax imposed on a UK national (whether or not UK domiciled) at no more than would have been imposed on a US domiciliary; this can be of particular benefit to

---

[1] Regrettably, the Code and the Regulations refer to domicile as 'residence', a use of the term which is very confusing in the transfer tax area since 'residence' for income tax purposes has two objective tests (green card and substantial presence) and is not at all determinative of domicile. In this book we attempt to minimize this confusion by referring to estate and gift tax 'residence' as domicile, and to non-'resident' foreign nationals as 'non-domiciled aliens' or NDAs – to distinguish them from income tax non-residents, whom the Code calls 'non-resident aliens' or NRAs. See Treas Reg § 20.0–1(b) (estate tax), which states:
  'A "resident" decedent is a decedent who, at the time of his death, had his domicile in the U.S. ... A person acquires a domicile in a place by living there, for even a brief period of time, with no definite present intention of later removing therefrom. Residence without the requisite intention to remain indefinitely will not suffice to constitute domicile, nor will intention to change domicile effect such a change unless accompanied by actual removal'.
The same definition applies for gift tax. Treas Reg § 25.2501–1(b). See, generally, Troxell, BNA Tax Management Portfolio 837–1st, *Aliens – Estate, Gift and Generation-Skipping Taxation*. An intention to leave the US in the near to medium term could suffice. *Fara Forni v Comm'r* 22 TC 975 (1954). See, also, the discussion of US domicile in **CHAPTER 16**.

[2] See **CHAPTER 6**.

14.4 *Non-domiciliary Planning to Remove Assets from US Estate Tax*

smaller estates by effectively exempting the first $1.5m of assets ($3.5m as of 2009) from US estate tax. UK resident but non-domiciled clients are generally subject to US estate tax on all US sited assets, including US real estate, equity securities, tax exempt bonds and mutual funds.

14.4 Married clients can defer or avoid US estate tax by bequeathing US sited assets outright or in a qualified life interest marital trust to a surviving spouse. This is limited in the case of a non-US citizen donee spouse to an indexed $114,000 annual gift tax exclusion for lifetime gifts and to testamentary Qualified Domestic Trust transfers. Lifetime and testamentary transfers to US citizen spouses are exempt from gift and estate tax. Greater relief is available in the UK to spouses subject to UK Inheritance tax (IHT) as all spousal transfers are exempt, except if made by a UK IHT domiciled spouse in favour of a non-UK IHT domiciled spouse. Even in the excepted case, a lifetime outright transfer or a transfer to an interest in possession trust for such a spouse is potentially exempt from IHT (and fully exempted if the donor spouse survives the transfer by seven years).

14.5 The basic structuring to mitigate US estate tax involves holding US assets through an appropriate foreign trust or foreign company. For larger estates and income tax planning for family members, a trust is usually preferable. A trust may be also be preferable for holding US real estate in that FIRPTA gains are currently taxable to the trustees at only 15% as opposed to corporate tax of 34% to 35%. In the case of a trust there are a variety of UK anti-avoidance provisions which may be relevant to trigger taxes on a settlor or beneficiary of a trust, depending on whether he is UK resident and domiciled, or just UK domiciled, or just UK resident.[3]

14.6 In the case of using a company alone, there are also UK issues to consider in that the UK Inland Revenue takes the view that enjoyment of company-owned assets gives rise to a an income tax charge on the shareholder in certain circumstances, whether or not he is also a director of the company.[4] There are also issues to consider in the context of the tax residence of the company itself and whether or not

---

[3] See the discussion in **CHAPTER 13**. Gains taxes can arise in principle to the settlor on disposal of the property or to a beneficiary by reference to the value of the benefit of occupation (Taxation of Chargeable Gains Act 1992 (TCGA 1992), ss 86 and 87); income taxes can arise to a beneficiary where there is accumulated income in the trust, by reference to the value of the benefit of occupation (ICTA 1988, s 740); and depending on the nature of the trust and its funding, an income tax charge may arise to the settlor by reference to the pre-owned assets legislation to be introduced with effect from 6 April 2005. FA 2004, s 84, Sch 15; see also **CHAPTER 1**.

[4] Note that the UK Inland Revenue takes the position that an income tax liability arises on the 'benefit' of an individual enjoying assets owned by a company in certain circumstances. In a recent criminal case before the House of Lords (*R v Allen [2001] STC 1537*), the Inland Revenue succeeded in establishing that the UK income tax legislation which taxes benefits received by employees (Pt 3, Ch 5 of the Income Tax (Earnings and Pensions) Act 2003 (ITEPA 2003) covers the provision of living accommodation for 'deemed' directors of companies. The definition of director for this purpose is very wide and includes any person in accordance with whose instructions the named directors are accustomed to act. As result of a further court decision, the term may be even wider and include any person in accordance with whose advice the directors habitually act (*Secretary of State for Trade and Industry v Deverell and another [2000] 2All ER 365*). In theory, this could apply where the property is owned by a company which is in turn owned by a trust, although the technical argument here is more difficult in a properly managed structure. The value of the 'benefit' is calculated under a statutory formula and can be substantial in the case of larger properties.

management and control can properly be said to be conducted outside the UK. If not, the company may, in principle, be taxable in the UK as well as the US.

14.7 For an individual who is UK resident but non-UK domiciled, rent free use of an offshore company owned US residence may not have UK imputed income tax exposure nor US constructive dividend consequences (as long as the company has no realized profits). For such clients, the higher FIRPTA corporate tax cost of selling the residence may be small in comparison to the estate tax savings. However, in appropriate cases the UK Inland Revenue may still seek to argue that income tax applies in that the deemed employment to which the taxable benefit of occupying the property attaches, is being exercised in the UK.[5] Furthermore, the same issues arise as to management and control of the company itself and whether or not it might be argued to be UK resident (and hence UK taxable).

14.8 For portfolio assets, a properly managed offshore company works well from a US tax perspective as the only US tax is the 30% withholding tax on dividends. The investor would suffer this tax anyway if he held the assets as an individual, subject to treaty relief; but if the investor is subject to foreign income tax, there will be no credit for the US withholding tax suffered by the offshore company. Some US international tax advisers are proactively using foreign partnerships not engaged in a US trade or business as a holding vehicle for avoiding US estate tax, as well as achieving a date of death market value re-basing of partnership assets under a partnership election available on death of a partner. This is an evolving area involving whether an entity or aggregate ('look through') approach should apply to partnerships for estate and gift tax purposes. Although the IRS refuses to rule in the area, the limited historical precedent evidences a 50-year-old IRS 'entity' approach and any rationalization of the law in this area may well be prospective only in application.

14.9 Where income producing US real estate is involved, the estate plan should take into account US and UK income/gains tax exposure. At Section G (**14.117** et seq) there is a discussion on the alternatives for holding such real estate. Relevant issues include a potential trade off between estate and capital gains taxation (FIRPTA), differences in corporate, grantor and non-grantor trust income tax rates, second-tier withholding and branch profits taxes and foreign tax credit relief.

B. Consider the scope of a UK person's exposure to US estate tax

14.10 The first step in the planning process is to determine the scope of the UK individual's US transfer tax exposure. UK individuals (and their exposure to US tax) come in many shapes and sizes: some are UK nationals only; some are domiciled in the UK for purposes of the UK IHT; some are merely residents in the UK; Some are both UK nationals and domiciliaries; some might also be US citizens and/or

---

[5] If the only company asset is the property and if the taxpayer himself has a hand in managing it (for example, in organizing day-to-day maintenance and repairs from the UK) then this remains a real issue.

14.11 *Non-domiciliary Planning to Remove Assets from US Estate Tax*

domiciliaries; and some might be dual nationals and/or considered domiciled in both countries. Sorting out this mishmash of combinations and the US tax implications also requires familiarity with the provisions of the US/UK treaty (examined in **CHAPTER 7**), particularly as those provisions affect the determination of an individual's transfer tax domicile.

14.11 In **APPENDIX VI** we provide a table that shows the possible combinations. A few patterns emerge. For example, a UK person who is a US citizen or (after application of treaty tie-breaker provisions) a US domiciliary will be subject to US tax on his worldwide estate. Traditional US estate and transfer tax planning is required – and will generally not be discussed in this chapter or this book. Instead, the focus of this chapter will be on a UK person (national, domiciliary, or resident) whose exposure to US tax is limited to:

(a) all US-situated property (a UK person who is not a US citizen and who is domiciled in neither the US nor the UK); or

(b) only US-situated real estate (article 6) and US-situated permanent establishment property[6] (article 7) (a UK domiciliary who is not a US citizen or, after the tie-breaker rules, a US domiciliary).

14.12 The planning for these folks is to eliminate, minimize or delay this US tax exposure. Section C (**14.13** et seq) touches on how article 8(5) of the US/UK treaty can limit the US estate tax imposed on a UK *national* who is not a US citizen or domiciliary. The 'crossover' point at which the US estate taxes become more expensive than the UK IHT is examined at Section D (**14.15** et seq); a UK taxpayer with US assets valued at less than that level might not need overly complicated or sophisticated US planning since the UK will provide a full foreign tax credit for the US taxes so imposed. There then follows at Section E (**14.21** et seq) a brief discussion of marital deduction planning to defer US tax exposure. The various planning techniques to minimize or eliminate the US tax exposure with respect to US-taxable property are considered at Section F (**14.33** et seq). Finally, the income, gains and transfer tax consequences of different holding structures for US income producing real estate are discussed at Section G (**14.117** et seq).

---

[6] A 'permanent establishment' is defined in the US/UK treaty in exactly the same manner as in the newer OECD-patterned income tax treaties. It means an 'enterprise' (industrial or commercial undertaking) conducted through:
- a US office or other fixed base or place of business; or
- a dependent agent (including a partner) resident in the US with habitual authority regularly exercised to contractually bind the deceased (or donor) to matters affecting his business in the US.

Article 7 also includes 'assets pertaining to a [US] fixed base used for the performance of independent personal services' – although it is now commonly accepted that a 'fixed base' is synonymous with the term 'permanent establishment'.

If the term 'permanent establishment' is applied on an annual basis, as it is in income tax treaties, this taxing right should apply only if, in the year of death or gift, the donor had a US permanent establishment with which gifted property is effectively connected. In the income tax treaties a 'permanent establishment' implies the *continuous* use of a fixed place of business (of the principal or his dependent agent). Continuous use is a standard defined in US cases and rulings as being at least a full year's presence or at least six months' presence in each of two consecutive tax years. However, it is sufficient if such continuous use existed 'at any time' during the taxable year.

C. Article 8(5) of the US/UK treaty

14.13 Before diving too deeply into the tax planning, we should first note that article 8(5) of the US/UK treaty effectively caps the US estate tax that applies to a UK national decedent who was not a US citizen or domiciliary at death. That provision limits the US estate tax to no more than would have applied had the UK national been a US domiciliary at death. The key benefit of this rule is the ability of the UK national to take a full estate tax applicable exclusion credit rather than the measly $13,000 credit (which exempts only $60,000 of US property from tax) otherwise available to the estate of a NDA. In contrast to the $60,000 exemption, the applicable exclusion credit currently exempts $1.5m and is scheduled to increase to $2m (2006) and to $3.5m (2009).

14.14 As a result, a UK national who dies in 2009 with a worldwide estate (computed under the US rules) of less than $3.5m should have no liability for US estate tax regardless of the value of his US-situated property subject to US estate tax. Even if the decedent's worldwide estate exceeds the US applicable exclusion, article 8(5) could reduce the decedent's US tax exposure. For example, a UK national who dies in 2009 with a $3.9m estate – $1m of which includes real estate in Florida – will pay a smaller amount of US tax by reason of article 8(5) than would have applied if decedent had been entitled to only a $13,000 credit. Note that this rule applies to all UK nationals (except those who are US citizens or domiciliaries). The rule does not apply to a national of another country who is domiciled in the UK, but does apply to a UK national who is domiciled outside the UK (for example, in France or in a tax haven like Bermuda).

D. US/UK rate crossover point

14.15 A UK domiciliary (assuming he is not a US citizen) will only be subject to US estate tax on US-situated article 6/7 property. The UK domiciliary is subject to IHT on his worldwide estate (including his US article 6/7 property), but the UK gives a credit for the US taxes imposed on that US property. The UK will not, however, always give a UK domiciliary *full* credit for US taxes. As discussed in **CHAPTER 3**, the UK foreign tax credit is limited to a fractional share of the UK taxes (before credit), the numerator of which is the value of the foreign property and the denominator of which is the value of the domiciliary's worldwide estate. In many instances, the actual foreign taxes will be higher than the UK foreign tax credit limitation. Thus, a UK domiciliary could pay a higher US estate tax on his US article 6/7 property than his estate will receive as a credit against his IHT.

14.16 At some level (what we refer to here as the 'crossover point'), the amount of the US estate tax on US-situated article 6/7 property will be credited in full against the UK IHT. The threshold will depend on the size of the US estate and the ratio of the decedent's US estate to his worldwide estate, as illustrated by the following table.

14.17 *Non-domiciliary Planning to Remove Assets from US Estate Tax*

Size of US estate	$500,000		$1,000,000		$2,000,000	
US estate tax	$142,800		$332,800		$767,800	
Exchange rate	Worldwide Estate Crossover	US/WW Ratio	Worldwide Estate Crossover	US/WW Ratio	Worldwide Estate Crossover	US/WW Ratio
$1.50 = £1	$1,380,000 (£920,000)	36.23%	$2,348,000 (£1,565,500)	42.58%	$9,801,000 (£6,534,000)	20.41%
$1.75 = £1	$1,610,000 (£920,000)	31.06%	$2,740,000 (£1,565,500)	36.5%	$11,435,000 (£6,534,000)	17.49%
$2.00 = £1	$1,840,000 (£920,000)	27.17%	$3,131,000 (£1,565,500)	31.94%	$13,068,000 £6,534,000)	15.3%

Example

Assume a UK domiciliary owns US real estate valued at $1m. The US estate tax on that property would be $332,800. At an exchange rate of $1.75 = £1, if the decedent's worldwide estate was $2.74m, the UK would give the UK decedent's estate full credit for the US estate tax.[7] If the decedent's worldwide estate were higher, the credit limit would be higher and thus a full credit would be provided.[8] If the decedent's worldwide estate were less than $2.74m, the UK would *not* give a full credit for the US taxes.[9] Conversely, if the decedent's worldwide estate were $2.74m, the UK would give a full credit for US estate taxes if the US estate were valued at $1m or less, but would *not* give a full credit if the US estate were valued at more than $1m.

14.17   The table above should be compared with the one found at **15.8**, which identifies the crossover point for a US citizen/domiciliary with UK article 6/7 property. Notice how in the table at **14.16** the crossover point *when expressed in UK pounds sterling* is unaffected by the exchange rates. By comparison, the crossover point in **CHAPTER 15** *when expressed in US dollars* is unaffected by rate changes. At **15.11** is another table that shows the global crossover point, which is relevant to a US citizen who is domiciled in the UK and thus subject to worldwide tax in both jurisdictions. Since US citizens will always be subject to US estate tax by reason of citizenship, the planning techniques described at Section F (**14.33** et seq) will be of no relevance.

14.18   The table above assumes a UK nil-rate band of £263,000 (the 2004/05 figure). A higher nil-rate band will increase the crossover point at which the UK will give full credit for US taxes.

---

[7]   UK IHT of 40% ($2,740,000 – $460,250 (dollar equivalent £263,000 nil-rate band) = $911,900 × 36.5% US assets portion = $332,800 credit limitation against US tax of $332,800 (assuming $60,000 NDA lifetime exclusion. These calculations were done on a test-value basis to determine the relevant crossover point and are dependent, in addition to the above stated variables, on the assumption that no UK reliefs are available other than the nil-rate band.

[8]   This result follows empirically because UK tax is increasing while US tax is static. The decrease in the limitation ratio will always be more than offset by the increase in total UK tax.

[9]   This result follows empirically because while the US tax is static, the credit limitation ratio is increasing while the worldwide tax base is decreasing faster. Basically the delta change in the tax base is 40% per dollar of additional or less taxable value, there is no way the credit limitation offsetting change is going to be of that magnitude.

14.19 Note that if the decedent is a UK national (who is neither a US citizen nor a US domiciliary), article 8(5) of the treaty will cap the US estate tax at an amount no higher than the tax that would have been determined had the UK national been a US domiciliary. As discussed, at Section C (**14.13** et seq), this provision benefits smaller estates by effectively giving them the higher US estate tax credit available to US citizens and domiciliaries. As a result, in 2004 and 2005, a UK national with a worldwide estate of $1.5m or less will not be liable for any US estate tax. This factor will skew the crossover point. For example, the prior chart places the crossover point at $1.61m for a UK domiciliary with US assets of $500,000 and an exchange rate of $1.75/£1. This assumes, however, that the US estate tax on the US assets was $142,800. Because of article 8(5), however, the US estate tax would actually be limited to $49,500 (which would be fully creditable at this level). When one factors in the implications of article 8(5), the crossover point – assuming $500,000 of US assets and an exchange rate of $1.75/£1 – increases to approximately $1.817m. At that level, the US estate taxes – computed under article 8(5) – are just under $142,800 and are fully credited against the UK taxes. Because of the scheduled increases in the US estate tax applicable exclusion credit in coming years, article 8(5) will have the effect of causing the crossover point to increase as well.

14.20 If the UK domiciliary's estate is *under* the crossover point, then in effect he is paying a higher tax in the US than he would have paid had the US property been subject to only a UK tax. A UK domiciliary finding himself under the crossover should accordingly consider the planning techniques discussed at Section F (**14.33** et seq) to reduce his US tax exposure.

E. US marital deduction planning

14.21 Okay. Say you're a married UK person (national, resident, domiciliary) who owns US property. The question in this section is the extent to which you can give or leave US property to your spouse without any US gift or estate tax.

1. US gift tax considerations

14.22 The ability of a UK person to make lifetime gifts of US property to his spouse without US gift tax exposure will depend on the nature of the US property gifted, the citizenship of the spouse, and the size of the gift.

14.23 First, the UK donor who is not a US citizen or domiciliary should keep in mind the limited scope of the US gift tax that applies to NDAs. Generally, the US gift tax will be limited to US-situated real estate and, if the US/UK treaty does not apply, US-situated tangible personal property. Thus, such a UK donor could give an unlimited amount of US intangibles (such as US portfolio investments) to his spouse free of US gift tax. This is true regardless of whether the spouse is a US citizen. (This is also true regardless of the marital status of the donor and donee: a UK donor's gift of US intangibles to his mistress would be exempt from US gift tax, although he must, of course, consider the UK tax implications of this gift.)

14.24 Second, if the gifted property is within the scope of the US gift tax (such as a gift of US real estate), a UK donor can give an unlimited amount of this property to a US citizen spouse free of US gift tax. An outright gift to a US citizen spouse (or a gift into a qualifying marital deduction trust) will qualify for the US gift tax marital deduction. The US transfer taxes are thus postponed until the US citizen spouse either gifts that property to others or dies.

14.25 Third, if the gifted property is within the scope of the US gift tax and the spouse is *not* a US citizen, the UK donor's only tax-free option is the gift tax annual exclusion, which is currently $114,000 for gifts to non-citizen spouses occurring in 2004.[10]

2. US estate tax considerations

14.26 Similarly, the ability of a UK person to leave US property to his spouse at his death without US estate tax exposure will depend on the nature of the US property gifted and the citizenship of the spouse.

14.27 First, the UK decedent who is not a US citizen or domiciliary should keep in mind the scope of the US estate tax that applies to NDAs. Importantly, US-situated intangibles (including stock in US companies) owned by a NDA are generally subject to US estate tax. However, if the donor is a UK domiciliary (and, again, not a US citizen), the treaty will generally limit US estate tax to US-situated real estate and permanent establishment property. As a result, a UK-domiciled decedent could leave an unlimited amount of US intangibles (such as US portfolio investments) to his spouse (regardless of her citizenship), or indeed to any other person, free of US estate tax.

14.28 Second, if the property is within the scope of the US estate tax (such as a bequest by a UK domiciliary of US real estate), the UK decedent can leave an unlimited amount of this property to a US citizen spouse free of US estate tax. An outright gift to a US citizen spouse (or a gift into a qualifying marital deduction trust) will qualify for the US estate tax marital deduction. Again, the US transfer taxes are thus postponed until the US citizen spouse either gifts that property to others or dies.

14.29 Third, if the property is within the scope of the US estate tax and the spouse is *not* a US citizen, the UK donor's bequest of this property to a non-citizen spouse will qualify for the US estate tax marital deduction (and thus US tax deferral) only if the property is transferred to a qualified domestic trust (QDOT). A more detailed summary of the QDOT rules is found in **CHAPTER 4**.

3. UK IHT considerations

14.30 A person who is domiciled in the UK for the purposes of UK IHT must also be aware of the UK tax implications of transferring US property to a spouse.

---

[10] Note that, as discussed in **CHAPTER 3**, this exclusion is indexed for inflation.

US marital deduction planning **14.32**

This is because UK domiciliaries are subject to UK inheritance tax on their gifts or bequests of property, wherever located. As summarised previously in this Section, a UK domiciliary's gift or bequest of US-situated property to a spouse might not be subject to US gift or estate tax because:

(a) the property is not within the scope of the US gift or estate tax by reason of the US tax laws or the provisions of the US/UK treaty;

(b) the property passes to (or in trust for) a US citizen spouse in a manner qualifying for the gift or estate tax marital deduction;

(c) the property passes (at death) to a QDOT for the benefit of a non-citizen spouse, qualifying for the US estate tax marital deduction; or

(d) the value of the gifted property is within the gift tax annual exclusion.

The fact that the gift or bequest of such property is not subject to US gift or estate tax does not mean that the gift or bequest is exempt from UK IHT.

14.31 With one exception a donor/decedent can give or leave an unlimited amount of property to his spouse free of IHT (as well as capital gains tax). Such a gift or bequest qualifies for the UK spousal exemption whether made outright or to a trust in which the donee spouse has an interest in possession.[11] The *one exception* is a gift or bequest by a UK IHT domiciled spouse to a spouse who is not UK IHT domiciled.[12] In this case a limited exemption is available of only £55,000 by way of marital exclusion for gifts or bequests to a non-UK domiciled spouse (or a life interest trust for her benefit).[13] However, if the surviving spouse is a US citizen or domiciliary, article 8(4) of the US/UK treaty expands this marital exemption relief *at death* to 50% of the amount of a bequest, provided it is made to a trust in which the spouse has an immediate interest in possession.[14]

14.32 Other than the above, the UK spouse must rely on the usual exemptions and reliefs (as to which see **CHAPTER 3**). The main opportunities, where the gift is made in lifetime, arise from the potentially exempt transfer regime and the opportunity to make gifts qualifying as normal expenditure out of income. In the former case, an outright gift or a gift into a trust in which the spouse has an interest in possession would be potentially exempt, and would be free of tax if the donor survived for a period of seven years thereafter.[15] As to gifts out of income, for donors with a significant level of annual income surplus to day-to-day expenditure, gifts out

---

[11] IHTA 1984, s 18.
[12] IHTA 1984, s 18(2). In the UK, a wife no longer takes the domicile of her husband (for post-1973 marriages) and typically an American of any means residing in the UK would take pains to preserve her American domicile in order to continue to claim the benefit of UK-remittance basis income taxation, as well as to avoid IHT on non-UK assets.
[13] IHTA 1984, s 18(2).
[14] This relief must be elected by the personal representative and the trustees of every trust in which the decedent had an interest in possession and only applies to exempt 50% of an otherwise taxable transfer at the death of the UK domiciled spouse. When and if the surviving spouse later becomes indefeasibly entitled to the assets in question (e g by distribution to her), the election is treated as having never been made and the UK has the full statutory right to tax the distribution or vested amount as though made to her absolutely on the death of the UK domiciled spouse.
[15] IHTA 1984, s 3A.

14.33 *Non-domiciliary Planning to Remove Assets from US Estate Tax*

of such income are exempt if they are habitual and leave the donor with enough income to maintain his normal standard of living.[16]

F. US estate tax reduction techniques

14.33 There are a number of estate reduction techniques available to reduce the higher of applicable US and UK transfer taxes to the lower. These techniques involve trusts, companies or partnerships and are summarized at the beginning of this chapter. They are discussed further in the following paragraphs.

1. Gifts of US intangibles

14.34 A UK person who is subject to US estate tax on US-situated intangibles (such as stock in a US company) can take advantage of the radically different manner in which the US taxes this property for gift and estate tax purposes. Simply put, US intangibles can be gifted tax-free but, if held at death, will be included in the NDA decedent's US taxable estate. With that in mind, a UK person might consider gifting that property during life.

> **Example**
>
> Jimmy Bond, a UK national retired from government service and now domiciled in Tahiti, has a US stock portfolio. Jimmy could gift these US assets during his life without US gift tax. If he retained these US investments until his death, they would be included in his US taxable estate.

14.35 This strategy would not be necessary for a UK domiciliary. This is because the US/UK treaty limits the US tax to article 6/7 property. Thus, a UK domiciliary will not be subject to US estate tax on his US portfolio investments, and thus need not gift those assets during life to avoid US estate tax. However, if he wishes to make such gifts as part of a UK estate planning strategy, this can be done without US tax disadvantage.

> **Example**
>
> Similar to above, but here Jimmy is still employed in her Majesty's service, and remains domiciled in the UK (although he travels extensively on business). Since Jimmy is a UK domiciliary, the US will not tax his gifts of these US assets during his life and will not tax any US portfolio investments that he owns were he to meet an untimely death.

---

[16] IHTA 1984, s 21.

2. Simple strategies for US-situated tangible property

14.36   A UK person who is subject to US estate tax on all US-situated property (which would exclude a UK domiciliary) might consider removing US-situated tangible personal property (such as art, boats, planes or libraries) from the US prior to death. If that property remains in the US at death, it will be subject to US estate tax. If held outside at death, it will not.

> **Example**
>
> Jimmy Bond – retired and domiciled in Tahiti – has stored the world's largest lipstick collection at a warehouse in Miami. Jimmy should consider moving this collection outside the US before his death.

14.37   A UK domiciliary might also consider gifting that property prior to death. Although that property would be considered situated in the US for gift tax purposes, the US/UK treaty generally limits the US to imposing a tax on a UK domiciliary's interest in article 6/7 property. Unless the tangibles were connected with a US trade or business, the UK domiciliary will not be taxed on the lifetime gift of that property.

> **Example**
>
> Jimmy Bond – employed and still domiciled in the UK – could make a lifetime gift of his US-stored lipstick collection without US gift tax. (This assumes, however, that the collection is not article 7, permanent establishment property used in his trade or business.)

14.38   A UK person who is not considered domiciled in the UK will be taxed on all US-situated property (not just article 6/7 property), and thus could not make a tax-free gift of that property during life – at least while the property remained in the US. The UK person could, however, remove the tangibles from the US and then gift that property without US gift tax.

> **Example**
>
> Jimmy Bond – retired and domiciled in Tahiti – would be subject to US gift tax if he made a lifetime gift of his lipstick collection while that property remained in the US. Jimmy could ship the collection to Tahiti and make the gift there, thus avoiding US transfer tax.

3. Holding or acquiring US property in trust

14.39   A properly structured trust can also hold or acquire US property and not subject the UK settlor or UK beneficiaries to US transfer tax. With respect to the UK settlor of the trust, it is first important that he does not make a gift of US-situated property to the trust if this would subject him to a US gift tax. A UK person (who is not a US citizen or domiciliary) could give his US intangibles to a

14.40 *Non-domiciliary Planning to Remove Assets from US Estate Tax*

trust without US gift tax. A UK domiciliary (who is not a US citizen) could also give US-situated tangibles to a trust without US gift tax. However, a UK person's gift of US real estate would be taxed.

14.40 The UK settlor also needs to be sure that he does not retain any 'strings' over the trust that would cause the trust property to be included in his US estate under the US Internal Revenue Code ('the Code') §§ 2104(b) and 2036 to 2038. Retained strings include:

- the possession or enjoyment of trust property or the right to income from that property;[17]
- the right (as trustee or otherwise) to control who benefits from the trust property or its income;[18]
- the right to vote shares of a controlled corporation;[19]
- the right, under local law, for the settlor's creditors to reach the trust assets;[20]
- a reversionary right valued at more than 5%;[21] and
- a right to modify or revoke the trust.[22]

To be effective, the trust must thus be irrevocable. In addition, the UK settlor must not retain power to remove and replace trustees, unless the settlor could only appoint independent trustees who are not 'related and subordinate' to him.[23]

14.41 Code § 2104(b) includes a notorious 'trap for the unwary.' If a NDA settlor retains 'strings' over the trust and either:

(a) he transferred US property to the trust; or

(b) the trust included US property at the date of death,

then the relevant portion of the trust will be included in his US taxable estate. The trap is that the *estate tax situs* rules apply for determining the situs of property gifted to the trust. Thus, if a NDA gifted US intangibles to a trust and retained the power to revoke the trust, the relevant portion of the trust would technically be included in his estate even if the US property had been sold prior to death.[24]

---

[17] Code § 2036(a)(1).
[18] Code § 2036(a)(2).
[19] Code § 2036(b) (a controlled corporation is one in which the decedent, during the prior three years, owned (after applying certain attribution rules) or had the right to vote stock with at least 20% of the combined voting power of all classes).
[20] See Rev Rul 76–103, 1976–1 CB 293; *Comm'r v Vander Weele* 254 F 2d 895 (6th Cir 1958); *Paxton v Comm'r* 86 TC 785 (1986) (applying Washington law); *Outwin v Comm'r* 76 TC 153 (1981), acq 1981–2 CB 2 (applying Massachusetts law); and *Paolozzi v Comm'r* 23 TC 182 (1954).
[21] Code § 2037.
[22] Code § 2038.
[23] Rev Rul 95–58, 1995–1 CB 191.
[24] See PLR 9507044 (31 May 1994), strictly interpreting the statute, even though as a policy matter it creates inconsistent treatment with respect to directly held US stock, which if sold before death is not subject to estate tax. See also Cassell, Karlin, McCaffrey and Streng, 'Estate Planning for Non-resident Aliens Who Own Partnership Interests', Tax Notes (16 June 2003), at pp 1683 and 1686. Code § 2104(b) requires inclusion of such assets with respect to a 'string' interest in the

14.42 To protect the UK beneficiaries from exposure to US transfer tax, the trust must also not confer a 'general power of appointment' on the beneficiary.[25] The beneficiary should accordingly not have the right to withdraw the trust assets or a right to appoint the property (during life or at death) to himself, his estate, his creditors or creditors of his estate. Limited powers held by a beneficiary (other than the settlor) are not a problem. Also, a UK beneficiary's right to trust income will not, however, expose the beneficiary to US tax on the underlying trust assets (unless the beneficiary was also the settlor). Finally, the UK beneficiary should not have the power to remove or replace trustees, unless only independent trustees who are not 'related and subordinate' to the beneficiary can be appointed.[26] Alternatively, the UK beneficiary could have the power to remove and replace any trustees (and, for that matter, could even serve as trustee, subject to any non-US considerations) if the trustee's discretionary power to distribute to the beneficiary were limited by an ascertainable standard.[27] Note that the use of a fully discretionary trust (as that term is understood for UK purposes) would not be suitable for use by a UK domiciliary since this would be regarded as a gift subject to UK IHT.

14.43 CHAPTER 16 discusses in more detail the use of these trusts – referred to as 'drop off trusts' – in the pre-immigration context. A UK person migrating to the US can drop his assets off in a properly structured irrevocable trust and avoid US estate tax exposure even if he is domiciled in the US at death. In a similar fashion, a UK settlor not planning to migrate to the US but wishing to invest in US property that would be subject to US estate tax at death (such as US real property) could use a similarly structured trust to accomplish the same objectives.

14.44 Holding US investments a through properly structured foreign trust can also offer the following benefits:

- a 15% tax rate on US real estate and business gains (compared to a 35% corporate tax rate);

- avoiding 30% second-tier US withholding and branch profits taxes (compared with structures, discussed at Section G (**14.117** et seq), in which US business assets are held in a US or foreign company);

- avoiding foreign law tax rules which may impose an income tax on rent-free use of corporate-owned (but not trust-owned) property;[28]

- preservation of family assets from speculative litigation and some family member claims, including those arising from marital break-up;

- professional asset management;

---

trust held or relinquished within three years of death. See Stephens, Maxfield, Lind & Calfee, *Federal Estate and Gift Taxation* (7th edn, 1997) Warren, Gorham & Lamont, at pp 6–12.

[25] Code § 2041, made applicable to NDAs by Code § 2103.

[26] PLR 9735023 (30 May 1997) citing Rev Rul 95–58, 1995–1 CB 191; in which the settlor's power to remove and replace trustees who are not related and subordinate to the settlor will not cause trust to be included in settlor's estate).

[27] See, eg PLR 9310012 (10 December 1992), citing Code § 2041(b)(1) and Treas Reg § 20.2041–1(c)(2).

[28] Care must be taken that the use of property owned by a trust does not inadvertently fall within the income tax charges relating to pre-owned assets. Properly structured, this should not be a concern.

14.45 *Non-domiciliary Planning to Remove Assets from US Estate Tax*

- co-ordinated implementation of an estate plan and inter-generational transmission of wealth consistent with family management objectives;
- avoidance of probate, executor and legal administration fees and preservation of financial privacy (wills are publicly available in most common law jurisdictions).

14.45 Note that a revocable trust will not, in and of itself, protect the UK settlor (or the UK beneficiary with a power to withdraw trust assets) from US estate tax. In such instances, the trust will need to employ some other strategy – such as acquiring and holding US tax-exposed property in a holding company – to protect the UK settlor or beneficiary from US estate tax exposure. This may give rise to UK tax considerations.[29] A revocable trust holding its US assets through an offshore holding company is a structure commonly used to avoid US estate tax by Latin American NDAs. It offers the additional benefits that it is a grantor trust, allowing income tax-free distributions to US family members, and due to its revocability, offers the potential of a market value re-basing of assets in the structure on death of the settlor.

14.46 For this revocable trust/holding company structure to work for US gift and estate tax purposes, it is essential that no US sited assets have ever been transferred to the trust or held by the trust at the settlor's death (although such property could be acquired by and held in the holding company).[30] If US property were transferred to the revocable trust during life or held in that trust at the settlor's death, the relevant portion of the trust would technically be subject to US estate tax under the tax trap of Code § 2104(b).

14.47 The shares of the non-US holding company owned by the revocable trust will be re-based to market value on the settlor's death.[31] Accordingly, the company's underlying assets can also acquire a date of death value by liquidation of the company, either in fact or for US tax purposes, by making a 'check the box' liquidation to treat it as a disregarded foreign single owner entity.[32]

14.48 The post-mortem timing of this election can be crucial if the remainder trust beneficiaries are US residents. If, for example, US resident children have equal shares in more than half of the trust assets, the company will be a controlled foreign company (CFC)[33] if it is allowed to exist for more than 30 days after the date of death. In such event, the liquidation would cause the company's unrealized gains,

---

[29] The UK Inland Revenue takes the position that an income tax liability arises on the 'benefit' of an individual occupying a home owned by a company in certain circumstances (see **14.7**). In theory, this could apply where the property is owned by a company which is in turn owned by a trust, although the technical argument here is more difficult in a properly managed structure where there is no possible inference of the settlor's control. In cases where it does apply, the value of the 'benefit' is calculated under a statutory formula and can be substantial in the case of larger properties.

[30] Unlike the 'drop off trust' discussed in **CHAPTER 16**, the revocable trust cannot be used as a US pre-immigration trust. Making the trust irrevocable just prior to immigration would expose the immigrant to US estate tax if he died within three years. Code § 2035(a)(2). Instead, an immigrant wishing to protect trust property from US estate tax on immigration should withdraw the assets from the revocable trust and contribute them to a new drop off trust.

[31] Code § 1014(b)(2).

[32] Treas Reg § 301.7701–3. See the discussion of this election in **CHAPTER 16** at **16.40** et seq.

[33] Code § 951 et seq.

realized on liquidation (or 'check the box' deemed liquidation), to be taxed to the children as a 'Subpart F deemed dividend'.

14.49 This taxation of unrealized earnings at the settlor's date of death can be avoided by liquidating the company (or making the 'check the box' election effective) within 30 days of the settlor's death – as Subpart F exposure cannot exist.[34] As a planning point, the 'check the box' election can be filed with the IRS Philadelphia office as late as 105 days after the settlor's death since the election can be made retroactive in effect up to 75 days.[35]

4. Holding or acquiring US property in a corporation

14.50 Corporations have historically been used by NDAs to protect their US investments from US transfer tax. This section briefly examines this technique.

a. Using a domestic US corporation

14.51 Holding US property in a US corporation will generally not exempt the NDA from US estate tax. The US Tax Code treats shares of stock issued by a domestic company as situated in the US for purposes of the US estate tax.[36] However, since a NDA, who is a UK domiciliary, is generally only subject to US transfer tax on article 6/7 property, the UK domiciliary could escape US estate tax by, for example, holding his US real estate investments in a properly structured US corporation. So doing would effectively transform that property from taxable real estate to a non-taxable intangible. Under the US/UK treaty (and similar 'domicile-styled' treaties), a real property holding company is generally *not* considered 'real property' within the meaning of article 6.[37]

14.52 A NDA should also be able to gift the shares of a US company that holds US real estate without being exposed to US gift tax, since a NDA's gift of stock of US companies is generally not taxed. However, the gift might be considered a gift of

---

[34] Code § 951(a)(1)(A).
[35] The effective date should not be made on, or prior to, the date of death since the election would then expose US sited assets held by the company to US estate tax – see Treas Reg § 301.7701–3(c)(2)(ii). It is also uncertain whether a *post-mortem* effective election would eliminate any potential foreign personal holding company income taxation which might arise under the FPHC rules (Code § 551 et seq). These rules do not have a 30-day grace period and could apply even if the CFC rules did not, e g because the FPHC rules attribute ownership of foreign siblings to US siblings who otherwise own, or are deemed to, own shares of their own (e g by attribution of a proportionate interest in trust assets) (Code § 554(c)(1)). Because of this uncertainty, some advisers have considered using a revocable trust-owned partnership not engaged in a US trade or business in reliance on Rev Rul 55–701, 1955–2 CB 836, (see the discussion at **14.81** et seq), which arguably could avoid the US CFC, FPHC and PFIC rules while offering a step-up of partnership assets on death through a Code § 754 election. As discussed at **14.72** et seq, guidance is limited in the area of using partnerships as entities to shield NDAs from US estate and gift tax and thus carries potential risk that eventual reform may not come prospectively only.
[36] Code § 2104(a).
[37] However the transfer of the US real property to a US company would be a capital gains taxable event for a UK domiciled and resident transferor. See **14.8** as regards potential UK income tax issues related to property which is used by the UK transferor.

14.53   the underlying US property if the NDA transferred his shares of the US holding company soon after funding it with the US real estate.[38]

14.53   It should also be noted that a NDA's transfer of US real estate to a domestic company is not considered a taxable event under the Foreign Investment in Real Property Tax Act (FIRPTA).[39] FIRPTA taxes a foreign investor's disposition of US real property as US trade or business gains.[40]

14.54   Limited Liability Companies (LLCs) are special companies formed under the law of any US state. In many regards, LLCs operate like partnerships, but shield all owners ('members') – not just limited partners – from liability. Unless a special election is made,[41] LLCs are either treated for US tax purposes as a disregarded entity (if there is only one member) or a partnership (if there are two or more members)[42] resulting in all income flowing through to the LLC's member(s). If the LLC has one owner (and thus is considered a disregarded entity), it would not provide the NDA owners with effective protection from US estate tax. If the LLC is treated as a partnership (with two more owners), the uncertain situs of a US-formed partnership (discussed below) would make the LLC a questionable choice.

b.   Using a foreign corporation

14.55   It is much more common for a NDA to own his US investments through a non-US corporation. Indeed, a non-US corporation would be needed unless the NDA were domiciled in a treaty country (such as the UK) that only permits the US to tax article 6/7 property. While 'offshore' companies in tax havens (such as the British Virgin Islands (BVI) or the Bahamas) are often used, it is only necessary that the company not be incorporated under the laws of a US state or under federal law.[43] Thus, a UK company could be used to shelter a NDA's US property from US estate tax. If the NDA is not domiciled in the UK, however, the use of a UK company would expose the NDA to UK IHT.

c.   Foundations (Stiftungs) and Anstalts

14.56   Foundations (Stiftungs) and Anstalts should be avoided as offshore holding vehicles since the classification of such entities is uncertain under the meager US tax law precedent which exists. In particular, substantive retained founder's powers and the absence of shares can result in the IRS or a court treating the entity as a revocable trust, a nominee, or as an entity in which the founder retained an interest in the underlying assets, exposing the underlying US assets to US estate tax.

---

[38]   *De Goldschmidt-Rothschild v Comm'r* 9 TC 325 (1947), aff'd 168 F 2d 975 (2d Cir 1948). See **2.11**.
[39]   Code §§ 897 and 1445; Treas Reg § 1.897–6T.
[40]   Gifts are not FIRPTA taxable because no money or other property is received for such a transfer and thus no taxable gain is realized. Treas Reg §§ 1.897–1(h) and 1.1001–1(a). See also, the discussion of this planning at **16.133** et seq.
[41]   Members can make a so-called 'check the box' election to treat the LLC as a corporation for US tax purposes. Treas Reg § 301.7701–3(b)(1). Note that the tax transparency of this vehicle, which is otherwise adopted for US purposes, is not necessarily accepted in other countries, e g the UK.
[42]   Treas. Reg § 301.7701–3.
[43]   Code § 7701(a)(4).

14.57 In the *Swan* case[44] the Dutch decedent was the founder of a Liechtenstein and Swiss Stiftungs in which he retained the power to amend the articles of the Stiftungs, to revoke the Stiftungs and to reacquire the Stiftungs' assets. The Tax Court treated the Stiftungs as revocable trusts, since they were intended to benefit the founder's family and had no business purpose. The estate had argued that the Stiftungs should be treated as corporations, but the Tax Court concluded that, 'regardless of the precise nature of the Stiftung, transfers such as involved in the instant case' result in estate tax inclusion.[45] In the Tax Court's view, the key was the ability of the decedent to alter, amend and revoke the transfer.

d. Code §§ 2036 and 2038

14.58 For years practitioners have recommended NDAs to use a foreign holding company as effective protection against US estate tax. There has been some concern, however, about the possible application of the principles of Code §§ 2036 and 2038 (made applicable to a NDA via Code § 2104(b)) to foreign corporations owned by NDAs. Code § 2104(b) causes property transferred 'in trust or otherwise' to be taxed in the NDA's estate if the NDA retains certain powers over or interests in the property, including the powers or interests found in Code §§ 2036 and 2038. Code § 2104(b) applies if the transferred property was situated in the US either at the time of transfer or at the time of the decedent's death.

14.59 Code § 2038 applies to revocable transfers. Thus, a decedent who transfers property to a revocable trust will have that property taxed in his estate just as if he continued to own the underlying trust property. Code § 2036 applies to transfers where the decedent retained either:

- the possession or enjoyment of, or the right to income from, the transferred property; or

- the power (alone or with others) to designate the person who will possess or enjoy the transferred property or its income.

14.60 Code §§ 2104(b), 2038 and 2036 apply to transfers 'in trust or otherwise'. A corporation is obviously not a trust, but is it an 'or otherwise'? In the *Swan* case, discussed at **14.57**, the Tax Court (and, on appeal, the Second Circuit) were willing to apply the predecessor to Code § 2038 where the deceased founder retained the power to alter, amend and revoke his transfers to two Stiftungs, regardless of whether the Stiftungs were considered to be trusts or corporations. The recent *Strangi* case (discussed at **14.86** et seq) similarly extended the reach of Code § 2036 to cause property held in a partnership (rather than the partnership interest) to be taxed in the decedent's estate.

14.61 Code §§ 2036 and 2038 – and, by implication, Code § 2104(b) – include exceptions for transfers 'for adequate and full consideration'. These sections would not apply, for example, if a NDA decedent sold US residential property to her

---

[44] *Estate of Swan v Comm'r* 24 TC 829 (1955), aff'd in part, rev'd in part, 247 F 2d 144 (2d Cir 1957).
[45] See *Estate of Swan v Comm'r* 24 TC 829, 856 (1955).

children for fair value, but 'retained' the right to use that property rent-free. The sale for adequate consideration prevents estate tax inclusion, despite the retained right of use. A gratuitous transfer to the children (or in trust for their benefit) with a retained right of use, however, results in estate tax inclusion.

14.62 Practitioners have argued that a NDA's transfer to a foreign corporation should be excepted from these sections, because the NDA receives adequate consideration for his transfer – namely, the stock issued by the foreign corporation. The *Swan* case did not directly address the adequate consideration argument, since a Stiftung does not issue shares to its founder. A different result arguably should apply where the foreign corporation issues shares to the NDA in return for his transfer. By analogy, recent cases (cited at footnote 68 in **14.88**) have applied the adequate and full consideration exception to partnerships despite the adverse result in the *Strangi* case.

14.63 Further, the legislative history to Code § 2107 – a provision that taxes US property held in a foreign corporation owned by a tax-motivated expatriate who dies within ten years of expatriation – strongly suggests that Congress' belief that US property held in a foreign corporation would not otherwise have been taxed in the expatriate's estate.[46] If US property held in a foreign corporation would be taxed in a NDA's estate under Code § 2104(b), then presumably Code § 2107 would not be necessary.

14.64 On balance, the adequate and full consideration exception – coupled with the implications of Code § 2107 – would seem to strongly support the continued viability of a foreign corporation as effective protection from a NDA's US estate tax exposure. A few additional thoughts are warranted.

14.65 First, some commentators have suggested that a NDA could avoid the reach of Code § 2104(b) by not transferring any US property to the foreign corporation, even if that company were to hold US property at the NDA's death.[47] Thus, it is recommended that the NDA fund the foreign corporation with cash, and that the foreign corporation then directly purchase the US property investments. True, Code § 2104(b) applies if US property is the subject of the initial transfer and the decedent retained the tainted rights or powers. However, this exposure would seem to also exist if US property were held in the entity at the date of death. Code § 2104(b) specifically applies to transferred property if that property is situated in the US 'either at the time of transfer or at the time of the decedent's death.' For example, if a NDA funds a revocable trust with cash that is later used to purchase US real estate, the US real estate would be subject to US estate tax at the NDA's death. It would thus seem that funding a foreign corporation with cash that is later used to acquire US assets would not – solely by reason of the steps employed – avoid the application of Code § 2104(b).

---

[46] S Rep No 1701, 89th Cong 2d Sess 54 (1966).
[47] See Lawrence, *International Tax and Estate Planning* (3rd edn, 1996) Practising Law Institute, at § 3.2.1, § 3.2.3 and § 3.2.10[A]; Bissell, BNA Tax Management Portfolio 94, *Aliens Who Invest in the United States Through a Low-Tax Jurisdiction*, at A-15.

US estate tax reduction techniques **14.69**

14.66 Second, some have also suggested that a NDA should form a foreign corporation with a third party, thereby better shielding the corporation's underlying US assets from US estate tax.[48] Note, however, that Code §§ 2036 and 2038 apply if the decedent's retained powers can be exercised either alone *or in conjunction with others*. Thus, the fact that the NDA decedent could 'revoke' the foreign corporation by joining with other shareholders in a liquidation vote would not – in and of itself – seem to avoid Code §§ 2036 and 2038. The existence of third-party, minority shareholders does give the corporation some additional 'substance' and, arguably, imposes fiduciary obligations on the NDA majority owner.

14.67 Third, the substance of a foreign corporation and thus its efficacy in protecting against US estate tax is tested where the foreign corporation owns US-situated residential real estate and/or tangible personal property (furniture, works of art, automobiles) used by the decedent. To minimize this risk, the foreign corporation could rent the property for a fair rental price, but this would create US-source taxable income that is potentially subject to *two* US taxes (the regular US tax and a 'branch profits' tax[49]).

14.68 Finally, for the foreign corporation to provide effective protection from US tax, it is important that the NDA decedent respects the existence of, and asset ownership by, the company as well as the corporate formalities. Otherwise, the IRS (and, more importantly, the courts) might consider the corporation a 'sham' or otherwise disregard it. Maintaining proper corporate books and records, appointing officers and directors, and holding regular corporate meetings are all important. These are the same steps that would be recommended to prevent creditors from piercing the 'corporate veil' and imposing corporate liabilities on the corporation's shareholders. The corporation should also not be treated as a mere nominee or custodian for the NDA/shareholder's assets.[50]

e. Foreign hybrid entities

14.69 In some jurisdictions, it is understood that residents are advised that they can remove US real property or securities from US estate tax by acquiring and holding such property through a foreign entity which is treated as a corporation under US tax rules, but which is transparent under local law (eg a 'partnership' entity with no unlimited liability member) – called in US tax parlance 'a foreign reverse hybrid' company. An arguable advantage of this entity might be that local corporate level tax is avoided and dividends and gains are taxed under local rules as though directly received by the shareholder with credit for any US withholding tax. With respect to income tax treaty relief, under US 'anti-hybrid' regulations, it would

---

[48] In the second edition of *International Tax and Estate Planning* at § 3.02(c), Lawrence stated: 'The problem [of exposure to Code § 2036 and 2038, via Code § 2104] is substantially minimized if one or more additional unrelated shareholders of the foreign corporation contribute property to it for stock.' This recommendation is not found, however, in the 1996 third edition of this book (cited in footnote 47).
[49] Code § 884(a).
[50] See *Fillman v US 355 F 2d 632 (Ct Cl 1966)* where the Swiss shareholder was represented as the beneficial owner of assets owned by his Argentine corporations in statements made to the US Office of Alien Property and the corporations were referred to as a 'depositor' or 'custodian' for the decedent.

appear the shareholders might claim treaty reduction of US withholding taxes on the company's portfolio income because they are taxed on such income under local law and the company is not.[51]

14.70 Dutch partnerships (CVs), for example, might be used as vehicles to remove assets from US estate tax, either as a 'reverse hybrid' (making a 'check the box' election to treat the entity, which has a general partner, as a corporation) or without the election, in which case it could have a default characterization as a foreign partnership (two or more owners).[52] A reverse hybrid (or any foreign corporation) can be disadvantageous if used to hold US real estate since the US will impose FIRPTA tax on its real estate gains at corporate rates of up to 34%, whereas a trust would only have a 15% FIRPTA tax. FIRPTA taxation is allowed by all US income tax treaties and should be imposed on a reverse hybrid because the company is a corporate taxpayer under US domestic tax rules and the US can define who is the taxpayer under its own law for the purpose of applying its own tax. In contrast, in the case of US portfolio withholding taxes, the same 30% statutory rate applies to individual shareholders and corporations and the US anti-hybrid regulations do grant treaty relief to the shareholders because under local law the company would not be able to claim treaty relief (because it is not subject to local tax) while its shareholders are and can.[53]

f. FIRPTA considerations

14.71 The transfer of US real property to a corporation in exchange for its shares is not subject to US gift tax, due to the exception for bona fide consideration (implicit in the value of the shares). However, the transfer of a US real property interest, including the shares of a US Real Property Holding Corporation (USRPHC),[54] to a foreign corporation is subject to US income tax under FIRPTA. Moreover, the gift of such an interest could be subject to gift tax if the foreign corporate transferee were owned by a trust. Gift tax can be avoided by a sale of such US real property interest to an offshore company – which may be an acceptable option if the property has little built in gain or in view of the current low 15% tax rate on gains from the disposition of assets held more than one year.

5. *Holding or acquiring US property in a partnership*

14.72 The situs of a NDA's interest in a partnership is not specifically addressed by the US Tax Code or relevant regulations. As summarized below, the cases and rulings are few and far between (and somewhat dated), and various theories abound.

---

[51] Treas Reg § 1.894–1(d).
[52] Treas Reg § 301.7701–3. Planning, using partnership status, would require that the entity is not engaged in a US trade or business, and would have to rely on Rev Rul 55–701, discussed at **14.81** et seq.
[53] Treas Reg § 1.894–1(d). It should be noted that although a UK unlimited company is a regular hybrid company (transparently taxable under US rules), the US authors are unaware of any UK entities that qualify as US reverse hybrids.
[54] Code § 897(c), defined as a US incorporated company, whose US real property interests equalled or exceeded 50% of its assets by fair market value on any day in the preceding five-year period.

US transfer tax situs of partnerships (and thus the ability to use a partnership to shelter a NDA's ownership of US property from US transfer tax) is therefore uncertain.[55]

14.73 At one level is the fundamental question of whether the partnership should be viewed as a mere aggregate of its underlying assets (the 'aggregate' theory) or as a distinct entity (the 'entity' theory).

a. Aggregate theory

14.74 If the aggregate theory were adopted, the situs would depend on the location of the partnership's underlying assets. Presumably, only US-situated property held in the partnership would be subject to US transfer tax.

14.75 The IRS applied the aggregate theory in the transfer tax context in only one internal ruling, which has since been revoked.[56] In its only published ruling on this subject, the IRS specifically considered and rejected the situs of the underlying assets as relevant.[57] In the 1955 Revenue Ruling, the IRS specifically concluded that locating a partnership at the place of its underlying assets was not supported by the weight of authority.

14.76 Over 35 years later, the IRS did apply a form of the aggregate theory in the *income* tax context, when it concluded in 1991 that the gain on a NRA's sale of a partnership interest would be considered effectively connected income (ECI) subject to US income tax, but only to the extent the sale of the partnership's underlying assets would give rise to US-taxable ECI.[58] To date, however, the IRS has not sought to extend the theory of this 1991 income tax ruling to the transfer tax context.

---

[55] See Glod, 'United States Estate and Gift Taxation of Non-resident Aliens: Troublesome Situs Issues', 51 The Tax Lawyer 109 (1997) (hereafter, 'Glod') an excellent and comprehensive article by an estate tax attorney at the IRS national office, which despite its disclaimer contains some revealing insights about the IRS' position in this area), Troxell, BNA Tax Management Portfolio 871-1st, *Aliens, Estate, Gift and Generation-Skipping Taxation*, Cassell, Karlin, McCaffrey and Streng, 'US Estate Planning for Non-resident Aliens Who Own Partnership Interests', Tax Notes (16 June 2003) at p 1683; Hudson, 'Current Techniques for Investing in the United States', 22 Tax Planning International Review 3 (1995); Lawrence, *International Tax and Estate Planning* (3rd edn, 1996) Practising Law Institute, at § 3.2.6, Goldberg, 'Critical Tax Concepts in International Estate Planning', *International Estate Planning Principles and Strategies* 19 (Kozusko and Shoenblum, eds 1991).

[56] GCM 16164 (look through approach applied to a French partnership's interest in a US partnership), revoked by GCM 18178, 1937-2 CB 476 (holding on similar facts there was no inclusion in the US estate). The latter ruling was in turn declared 'obsolete' for unknown reasons by Rev Rul 70-59, 1970-1 CB 280.

[57] Rev Rul 55-701, 1955-2 CB 836.

[58] Rev Rul 91-32, 1991-1 CB 107. This *income* tax ruling, applying the aggregate approach to gain on disposition of a partnership interest, has no application in the estate and gift tax area. Nor should its logic necessarily apply. At least four income tax provisions in the US Tax Code apply an aggregate theory to tax a non-resident partner's sale of a partnership interest with respect to underlying realizable US real property and ECI gains of a partnership. Code § 897(g) (taxing gain from a non-resident partner's disposition of his partnership interest to the extent attributable to the partnership's US real property interests); Code § 875(1) (attributing US trade or business status of a partnership to its non-resident partners); Code § 864(c)(5) (attributing the office or fixed place of business of a dependent agent, including a general partner, to its non-resident partners); and Code § 865(e)(2) and (3) (deeming US source treatment for personal property gains

b. Entity theory

14.77 Respecting a partnership as a separate entity (distinct from its underlying assets) only leads to the next unanswerable question – where is the entity situated? Here are a few of the alternatives.

- Like an interest in a corporation, the NDA's interest in a partnership could be situated in the jurisdiction under whose laws it is formed.

- The partner's interest in the partnership is akin to debt, which under the Code is situated in the US only if the partnership is a US person.[59]

- Under the Latin doctrine *mobilia sequuntur personam* (movables are attributed to the domicile of the decedent owner), a partnership owned by a NDA would be considered situated outside the US.

- The partnership is situated where it is doing business.

c. Limited precedent

14.78 The principal authority in the area consists of two old court cases and the 1955 IRS ruling. Interpretation of this precedent over the years by commentators has given them urban legend status, standing for propositions not fully supported by their facts or rulings.[60]

(i) *Blodgett v Silberman*[61]

14.79 This 1928 Supreme Court decision is often cited (mistakenly) for the proposition that a partnership interest, as intangible property, is situated in the domicile of a decedent partner under the Latin doctrine of *mobilia sequuntur personam*.[62]

The court merely upheld Connecticut's constitutional right to tax its deceased domiciliaries on their interests in intangible property wherever located. Once the court determined the decedent's New York partnership interest was an intangible asset and not foreign-situated realty – even though the partnership owned New York

---

attributable to a US office, including an deemed office under § 864(c)(5), except for inventory sold for use abroad through a foreign office). See also *Donroy Ltd v US 301 F 2d 200 (9th Cir 1962)* (attributing under the US/Canada income tax treaty the permanent establishment of partnership engaged in a US trade or business to its non-resident limited partner) and *Unger v Comm'r TC Memo 1990–15, 58 TCM 1157,1159* ('the office or permanent establishment of a partnership is the office of each of its partners, whether general or limited').

[59] Code § 2104(c) treats debt obligations of a US person as situated in the US.
[60] See Glod (at footnote 55) for a full discussion of these cases and their factual/legal disparities. See, generally, Martin, 'Why 2104 Must Address When Partnerships Are (and Are Not) Subject to US Estate Tax', Tax Notes (15 May 2003).
[61] *Blodgett v Silberman 277 US 1 (1928)*.
[62] As stated by Glod (at footnote 55), at p 113:
'In fact, no US court has every applied *mobilia sequuntur personam* in a situs determination. Additionally, the common law maxim has not been adopted by Congress [citing *Burnett v Brooks, 288 US 378, 389 (1933)*]'.

realty – Connecticut had the right to tax that property interest. What *is* informative about *Blodgett v Silberman*, is that the court treated the partnership *as an entity*, not as an aggregate of its underlying assets.

(*ii*)   *Sanchez v Bowers*[63]

14.80   This 1934 Appellate Court decision is cited for applying an aggregate theory where the partnership terminates on death of a partner. In fact, the deceased was a Cuban domiciliary whose New York ancillary estate consisted of portfolio assets titled in the name of a Cuban *sociedad de garanciales*, which was actually not a partnership but a form of community property ownership which terminated on his death. Interestingly, Judge Learned Hand suggested in dictum that an alternative basis for taxation might arise out of sufficient business activity of the foreign entity in the United States, which is the position subsequently adopted by the IRS.[64]

(*iii*)   *Rev Rul 55–701*[65]

14.81   In this 1955 public ruling, the IRS found that a deceased British domiciliary's interest in a partnership, organised and doing business in New York, was sited in the US for US estate tax purposes. The IRS considered (but rejected) treating the decedent's partnership interest as a debt, which, under the relevant treaty in effect at that time, would have situated the partnership in the UK where the decedent was domiciled. As previously noted, the IRS also considered (but rejected) siting the partnership interest at the location of the underlying assets.

14.82   Instead, the IRS determined the situs of the partnership to be where the partnership business is carried on. And what was the support for this position? The IRS cited, of all precedents, a British case that determined that New South Wales could properly tax a British domiciliary on his investment in a partnership doing business in that jurisdiction.

14.83   Although the ruling was decided under a now-revoked treaty, the treaty contained no provisions which would distinguish the principles of that ruling outside the context of that treaty. The only caveat might be the willingness of the IRS to embrace a non-US case as support for its conclusion that a partnership is deemed to be situated where it is doing business. Had the ruling been addressing the situs of a partnership under the US/Denmark estate tax treaty – or had no treaty applied – it is doubtful that the IRS would have so readily embraced (or even been aware of) an obscure case involving a UK person's investment in an Australian sheep farming partnership.

14.84   Even if a partnership is considered situated in the jurisdiction where it is doing business, it is unclear from Rev Rul 55–701 (and from the commentators) whether the entire partnership would be considered sited in the US if any of its assets are engaged in a US trade or business. What if the partnership owned both

---

[63]   *70 F 2d 715 (2d Cir 1934)*; see also *Vandenhoeck v Comm'r 4 TC 125 (1944)*.
[64]   Discussed in Glod (at footnote 55), at pp 111–112.
[65]   1955–2 CB 836.

14.85 *Non-domiciliary Planning to Remove Assets from US Estate Tax*

US rental property and foreign-situated portfolio investments? What if the partnership owned both US and foreign real estate? Will the existence of any US trade or business taint the entire partnership, or will some form of aggregate allocation apply? Suffice to say that these questions – like so many in this context – are open to debate.[66]

d. Domestic attacks on FLPs – aggregation revisited

14.85 Family limited partnerships (FLPs) have long been used by US estate planners. In addition to consolidating ownership and control of certain property within an entity, FLPs offer substantial valuation discounts, that can reduce the value of a US transferor's FLP interest by reason of the lack of marketability and control represented by that interest. Discounts of 30% or more (from net asset value) are common.

14.86 The IRS has, over the years, challenged FLPs on a variety of grounds and, in recent years, has enjoyed some surprising success. *Strangi v Comm'r*[67] involved

---

[66] It would appear that some practitioners view the ruling as taking an 'all-or-none' approach with regard to underlying partnership assets, i e treating an interest in a partnership engaged in a US trade or business as 100% US sited, similar to US estate taxation of shares in a US incorporated corporation, such that non-ECI assets are arguably subject to US estate tax if owned by a partnership which is engaged in a US trade or business. Conversely, it would follow that a NDA's interest in a partnership which is not engaged in a US trade or business is a foreign sited asset which is not subject to US estate tax, even though the partnership owns US real property and US securities. The IRS took this entity approach in a gift tax ruling which treated the gift of a partnership interest as the gift of an intangible. PLR 7737063 (17 June 1977).
In this regard, planners might turn to Code § 864(b)(2), which provides that a non-resident alien can actively trade US securities and commodities on his own account without being considered to be 'engaged in a US trade or business'. This is true whether such trading is done individually, through a dependent agent, or through a partnership provided that (Treas Reg § 1.864–2(c)(ii) and (iii)):
(a) the trader is not a 'dealer'; and
(b) the trading is not done through a US office of the enterprise *unless* the trader is a partnership controlled by five or fewer partners or the partnership satisfies the ten foreign office fund administration tests of the regulations.
Otherwise, the key concept of a 'US trade or business' is only vaguely defined in a few cases and rulings, the essence of which is that trading activity must be regular, active and continuous (see Huston and Williams, *Permanent Establishments – A Planning Primer* (1993) Kluwer, at pp 48 and 118.
The mere rental of one or two residential real properties (*Herbert v Comm'r 30 TC 26 (1958)*; *de Amodio v Comm'r 34 TC 894 (1960), aff'd 299 2d 623 (3rd Cir 1962)*), triple net leases (Rev Rul 73–522), one, two or perhaps a few sales or loans, even though large in size, one, two or sporadic meetings in the US even though a part of process of effecting a substantial transaction (*Comm'r v Spermacet Whaling & Shipping 281 F 2d 646 (6th Cir 1960)*) or the periodic or regular presence of a local representative or office for mere investment monitoring, administrative or listening post acitivites (*Scottish American Investment Co Ltd v Comm'r 12 TC 49 (1949)*), will not generally rise to the level of a US trade or business. See also *InverWorld, et al v Comm'r 71 TCM 3231 (1996)* (a 100-page plus decision which contains a comprehensive discussion of the concept together with the Code §§ 863–864 related concepts of a 'US office or fixed place of business', dependent agencies and the income tax treaty 'permanent establishment' concept).

[67] TCM 2003–145, Doc 2003–12584 (47 original pages), 2003 TNT 98–16. See Korpics, 'The Practical Implications of *Strangi II* for FLPs – A Detailed Look,' 99 Journal of Taxation 270 (2003); see also Gans and Blattmachr, '*Strangi*: A Critical Analysis and Planning Suggestions' Tax Notes (1 September 2003).

the question of how to tax a US decedent's interest in an FLP established just prior to death. Had the partnership itself been found to be the asset taxable in the decedent's estate (as argued by the estate), substantial marketability discounts would have been available. However, the courts accepted the IRS argument and applied the principles of Code § 2036 to cause the transferred property (the underlying partnership assets) to be taxed in the decedent's estate. As a result, no valuation discounts were available.

14.87 If the *Strangi* principles were extended into this context, the underlying assets of a NDA's partnership could be included in his estate to the extent US assets were initially transferred to the partnership or were held in the partnership at the NDA's death. The aggregate theory – introduced through the backdoor of Code §§ 2036 and 2104(b) – would find renewed application.

14.88 Many commentators have questioned the court's decision in *Strangi* and its broader application to more benign facts. (The decedent in *Strangi* transferred virtually all of his assets to the FLP, including his personal residence. Should this be a warning to holding a personal residence through a foreign corporation or partnership?) A few recent cases have alternatively embraced the 'adequate and full consideration' exception and thus rejected the application of Code § 2036 to tax a partner's shares of underlying partnership assets.[68]

e. Conclusion

14.89 Guidance in this area is desperately needed, but the IRS refuses to rule on where a partnership interest is considered situated for US transfer tax purposes. The uncertain status of the law on the situs of partnerships, coupled with the open animosity of the IRS to FLPs in the domestic setting, makes the partnership a less than satisfactory alternative for a NDA's ownership of US property.

6. Joint ownership

14.90 Joint ownership of property can affect the amount included in a US estate. Property held in a spousal joint tenancy (created on or after 14 July 1988) with a surviving non-US citizen spouse is assumed to be included in its entirety in the first decedent's taxable estate, unless and to the extent contribution by the other spouse can be proven. However, property held in joint tenancy with a surviving US citizen spouse is treated as half-owned by the decedent, regardless of contribution.[69]

14.91 In contrast, only the decedent's undivided interest in property held as a tenant in common is taxed in his estate. Thus, a client who is married to a non-US citizen might consider purchasing US property as a tenant in common rather than in joint tenant. However, unless the non-US citizen spouse contributes toward the

---

[68] See *Estate of Stone* 86 TCM (CCH) 551 (2003) and *Kimbell v US* 2004–1 USTC ¶ 60,486 (5th Cir 2004). See Korpics, 'Mining *Stone* for Material Direction Regarding the Bona Fide Sale Exception (and More) as Applied to FLPs', Tax Notes (2 March 2004).
[69] See CHAPTER 1.

14.92 *Non-domiciliary Planning to Remove Assets from US Estate Tax*

purchase, taking title to the property in this fashion could be considered a current taxable gift, subject to the indexed gift tax annual exclusion ($114,000 for 2004). Gift tax might be avoided if the NDA spouse were to first gift one half of the purchase consideration to the non-US citizen spouse – which is not subject to US gift tax provided the funds do not come from a US bank account.

14.92 If the property has already been acquired in joint names with the NDA spouse furnishing the consideration, the joint tenancy might be unwound without gift tax by titling the property solely in the NDA spouse, followed by annual gifts to the non-US citizen spouse of an undivided interest equal to the indexed gift tax annual exclusion.[70] When the spousal interests are approximately equal in value a new joint tenancy can be created.

14.93 It should be noted that in both the US and the UK, tenant in common ownership is subject to probate, whereas a joint ownership interest is not.

14.94 In domestic US estate planning, family limited partnerships (FLPs) are often used as holding vehicles for family wealth – due to taxpayer-favorable court decisions which have allowed discounted values for estate and gift tax purposes for minority limited partnership interests owned by senior generation family members. Discounts of 45% or more have been upheld for minority undivided interests and non-publicly traded properties owned by the FLP (even though 100% of the FLP is controlled by the immediate family and even though, in some cases, the property was transferred on the parent's deathbed).[71]

Generally these vehicles do not achieve the same benefits for a NDA who is a UK taxpayer and, additionally, the discounts normally applied by the UK Inland Revenue are less generous that in the US.

7. *Estate freezes and split purchases*

14.95 Estate freezing techniques are a classic method of reducing estate value by transferring to younger generation beneficiaries future growth rights in certain property a present low gift tax cost. Freezes had traditionally been attractive in the family-owned business setting, where the parent would retain a voting, preferred interest (with a current value approximating the value of the business as a whole) while gifting (or selling) to the lower generation the low-value common stock that would essentially enjoy all future growth.

---

[70] If annual exclusion gifts were made in a life interest trust, Code § 7815(d)(1)(B) of the Omnibus Budget Reconciliation Act 1989 (OBRA 1989) requires that the trust additionally qualifies under the marital trust provisions applicable to US citizen donee spouses. Why the gift should also meet the present interest requirement of § 2503(b) is therefore an anomaly – perhaps this requirement only applies to the first $11,000. (See Plaine and Siegler of Sutherland Asbill & Brennan, Washington DC, 'The Federal Gift and Estate Tax Marital Deduction for Non-United States Citizen Recipient Spouses' at p 203 (ALI-ABA Video Law Review Advanced Tax Issues in Estate Planning, 11 October 1990).

[71] *Estate of Harrison v Comm'r 52 TCM 1306 (1987)*; *Estate of McClendon v US 96–1 USTC* ¶ *60,220 (5th Cir 1996)*, and other cases discussed in Bray, 'Was Strangi II a Setup?', Tax Notes (9 February 2004).

14.96 Split purchases were also used to limit a decedent's exposure to US estate tax. In the context of a business investment, the younger generation would purchase the growth stock while the senior generation would purchase the high-value preferred interests. In the context of real estate investments, the younger generation would acquire the remainder interest and the senior generation the life estate. The key to this planning is that, for purposes of US estate tax, property in which a decedent had a legal life estate would generally not be included in the decedent's US taxable estate as long as the decedent had not made a gift of the property and retained that interest.

14.97 The special valuation rules – found in Chapter 14 of the US Tax Code and effective in 1990 – substantially limit various estate freeze techniques and all but eliminate split-interest purchases. In the context of estate freezes, these rules apply for purposes of determining the value of a taxpayer's gift, and operate by assigning a value of zero to retained property interests and rights unless they satisfy certain strict rules. Split-interest purchases are treated as if the member of the senior generation had acquired the entire property and then sold an interest in that property to the younger family members.[72] If the senior member's retained interest is valued by the Chapter 14 rules at zero, the interest sold to the younger family members would be valued at the full value of the property. The senior member would be treated as having made a gift measured by the difference between the value of the property as a whole and the amount paid by the younger family members for their interest. Despite these rules, there might be limited opportunity for certain NDAs investing in the US to utilize these planning techniques. From the UK tax perspective, these types of strategies have generally become unnecessary since 1986 in view of the ability to make lifetime gifts of unlimited value for IHT purposes under the potentially exempt transfer regime.

a. US corporate estate freeze

14.98 A NDA who is a UK domiciliary and who has invested in a US corporation will generally not be concerned about US estate tax exposure with respect to this investment. This is because the US/UK treaty generally limits the US scope of the US tax to only US real estate and business property. For this purpose, a UK domiciliary's investment in a US corporation would not be considered a US business interest, and thus would not be exposed to US estate tax. Accordingly, US transfer tax planning for such a person is unnecessary.

14.99 However, for a non-UK domiciliary (or a UK domiciliary contemplating emigration to the US), then a traditional US estate freeze could be effective.[73] Special valuation rules determine the value of a taxpayer's gift by assigning a value of zero to his retained interest unless that interest meets strict annuity payout requirements. Assume that those requirements are not met and the individual's retained preferred interest is valued at zero for purposes of computing his US

---

[72] Code § 2702(c)(2). The special valuation rules are discussed in **CHAPTER 1** at **1.20** et seq.
[73] In this case if the gift is to be made to a trust rather than to an individual, care needs to be taken that this does not cause the trust to be fixed with the settlor's then UK domicile status (and consequently ongoing potential UK inheritance tax exposure). It may, in such a case, be better to wait until UK domicile is lost before effecting any such planning.

taxable gift of common stock in a US corporation. So what? A NDA's gift of stock in a US company is not subject to US gift tax.[74] Thus, even if the NDA's retained preferred shares were valued at zero, he would presumably not be subject to US gift tax on the transfer of the common.

b. Split-interest purchase or formation of a US corporation

14.100 The same principles would apply to a split-interest purchase or formation of a US corporation by a NDA and members of his family. If the NDA parent were to purchase (or, upon formation, receive) the high-value preferred and the children purchased (or received) the low-value common, the parent would not be subject to US gift tax. This result does not turn on the applicability or inapplicability of the special valuation rules: it turns instead on the limited scope of the US gift tax that generally does not reach gifts of US intangibles by NDAs.

14.101 Due to the UK hold-over relief as it relates to gifts of business assets[75] (including closely held trading stock – see APPENDIX VII) and the inheritance tax exemption for gifts survived by seven years, such planning is no longer necessary in the UK.

c. Split-interest purchase of US real estate

14.102 In contrast, a NDA is subject to US gift tax on gifts of US real property. Thus, a traditional split-interest purchase of US real estate – where the parent buys the life estate and the children the remainder interest – would no longer be effective. Again, the NDA parent would be treated as having acquired the entire property and then sold the remainder interest to the children. Since the NDA parent's retained life estate would be valued at zero, the NDA parent would be treated as having made a taxable gift, measured by the difference between:

(a) the property's value; and

(b) the price the children paid for the remainder interest.

14.103 The special valuation rules include one exception that might be relevant in this context. The value of a taxpayer's retained interest in a qualified personal residence trust (QPRT) will be respected.[76] Thus, if a taxpayer transfers a personal residence to a trust and retains the right to live in the property rent-free for a period of years, the value of this right (measured under IRS tables) can be subtracted from the value of the property to determine the value of the taxpayer's remainder interest gift.[77] If the taxpayer survived the period of retained interest, the property passes to

---

[74] Code § 2501(a)(2). The only exception would be for a NDA who is considered a tax-motivated expatriate who gifts US intangibles (including stock in a US company) within ten years of expatriation. Code § 2501(a)(3).
[75] Note that this relief only applies where the settlor or his spouse can no longer benefit from the property. Finance Act 2004 (FA 2004), s 116 and Sch 21.
[76] Code § 2702(a)(3).
[77] In this situation, there is a lifetime taxable gift by the donor in the US, albeit at a discounted rate. For a UK domiciliary, there is likely to be no transfer of value at this point but there would be a chargeable, or potentially chargeable, event when his interest in possession terminated (although

the remainder beneficiaries without further gift/estate tax. If the taxpayer died within the period, the property would be included in his taxable estate (but credit given for the prior remainder interest gift to prevent double taxation).[78]

14.104 Some commentators have suggested combining a split-interest purchase with a QPRT.[79] The QPRT would be used to acquire the legal life estate and the younger generations would acquire the remainder interest. Since the taxpayer's interest in the QPRT is a qualified interest, the value of that interest would be respected. Assuming the younger generation paid full value for their remainder interest, no taxable gift would result. Moreover, the QPRT could be designed to give the decedent a right to reside in the residence for life, not just a term of years. Since the decedent would have made no initial gift, the retained life estate would not cause the property to be included in his taxable estate.

14.105 This idea would seem to have promise for not only US taxpayers, but also some NDAs who are investing in US residential property (subject to any local domiciliary law considerations). Complexities could arise for a UK taxpayer given the UK rules which deem a person entitled to a life interest (including a lease for life, not granted for full consideration, treated as a settlement by the legislation[80]) to be entitled to the property in which his interest subsists for the purposes of inheritance tax. Care is also required in implementing any such planning to ensure that tax is not exacerbated by the UK income tax legislation relating to continued enjoyment of pre-owned assets, although this should be avoided if the property is, in fact, still deemed to be within the taxpayer's inheritance taxable estate, whether as life tenant or by reason of the reservation of benefit legislation.[81]

8. Non-recourse v recourse mortgages

14.106 A recourse mortgage[82] on taxable US property does not reduce its value *pro tanto* for US estate tax purposes (although for gift tax purposes the value of the taxable gift is reduced by the amount of debt assumed by the donee). Instead, the mortgage and other debts of the decedent are allocated to US taxable property in the ratio of US taxable to worldwide property of the decedent. Direct debt offset relief may apply in some older treaties for mortgages taken on at the outset to fund the purchase.

---

the tax liability would be that of the trustees). Care needs to be taken for a UK domiciliary considering this US planning that double taxation does not occur in view of the tax charge arising on different events, at different times and on different persons.

[78] Note that the above UK analysis may be slightly different in this case, depending on the circumstances.

[79] See Blattmachr and Painter, 'When Should Planners Consider Using Split Interest Transfers?', 21 Estate Planning 20 (January/February 1994).

[80] IHTA 1984, s 43(3) and see CHAPTER 13.

[81] FA 2004, s 84 and Sch 15 as to pre-owned assets and FA 1986, s 102 as to reservation of benefit. Note also the need to avoid falling foul of various anti-avoidance provisions designed to negate particular IHT planning with real estate. See also CHAPTER 1.

[82] Where the lender has access to the borrower's general assets for payment, in contrast with a non-recourse mortgage where the lender has recourse only to the mortgaged property.

14.107 In contrast, a non-recourse mortgage on US taxable property will reduce the taxable US estate by the amount of the mortgage.[83] Clients who are able to secure such financing should therefore consider placing a non-recourse mortgage on US taxable property to reduce US estate tax *pro tanto*. A mortgage secured on UK taxable property will reduce the taxable estate by the full amount of the mortgage.

9. Permanent establishment property

14.108 Under article 7 of the US/UK Estate and Gift Tax treaty, the US can tax the transfer of the business property of a 'US permanent establishment' of a UK domiciliary. A *permanent establishment* is defined in the estate tax treaty in exactly the same manner as in the newer OECD patterned income tax treaties. It means an 'enterprise' (industrial or commercial undertaking) conducted through:

(a) a US office or other fixed base or place of business; or

(b) a dependent agent (including a partner) resident in the US with habitual authority regularly exercised to contractually bind the deceased (or donor) to matters affecting his business in the US.

14.109 Article 7 also includes 'assets pertaining to a [US] fixed base used for the performance of independent personal services' – although it is now commonly accepted that a 'fixed base' is synonymous with the term 'permanent establishment'.[84]

14.110 If the term 'permanent establishment' is applied on an annual basis, as it is in income tax treaties, this taxing right should apply only if, *in the year of death or gift*, the donor had a US permanent establishment with which gifted property is effectively connected. In the income tax treaties a 'permanent establishment' implies the *continuous* use of a fixed place of business (of the principal or his dependent agent). Continuous use is a standard defined in US cases and rulings as being at least a full year's presence or at least six months' presence in each of two consecutive tax years. However, it is sufficient if such continuous use existed 'at any time' during the taxable year.[85]

14.111 What US authority exists suggests that an employee will not be attributed the permanent establishment of his employer.[86]

---

[83] Treas Reg § 20.2053–7.

[84] Huston, 'The Case against Fixed Base', Intertax (October 1988). The equivalence is accepted in the US technical explanation of the US/UK estate tax treaty and the 24 July 2001 US/UK income tax treaty (which was ratified 31 March 2003).

[85] Williams, 'Permanent Establishments in the US', *Income Tax Treaties* (Bishel, ed, 1978) Practising Law Institute, at Chapter 4.

[86] Robert and Warren, *US Income Taxation of Foreign Corporations and Non-Resident Aliens* (1966) Practising Law Institute, at IX/12, n 161 (citing Rev Rul 55–508, treaty legislative history and regulations). In this seminal work in the area, the authors state:

'The obverse question, when does the fixed place of business of the principal qualify as a permanent establishment of his agent, arises commonly where an employee regularly works at the office of his employer. It has generally been assumed that the employer's fixed place of business does not constitute a permanent establishment of the employee'.

14.112 However, it is possible that *partnership* pension, retirement and deferred compensation plans could be permanent establishment property. For US income tax purposes, income is 'effectively connected' with a US trade or business if either:

(a) derived from assets used or held for use in the business; or

(b) materially generated by the activities of the business.

In determining whether an asset was so used or whether business activities were a material factor in generating such income, § 864(c) (2) gives due regard to whether the asset or income is shown on the accounting records of such business.

14.113 If these income tax principles applied to estate tax, pension and other deferred compensation rights derived directly from partnership business profits (as opposed to a personal investment by a partner from his distributed share of partnership profits), could be considered effectively connected permanent establishment property. If on the other hand, such assets are subject to third-party administration, segregated from the partnership's assets and not reflected on its books, such assets should be exempt personal assets rather than business property of the permanent establishment subject to tax under the treaty.

14.114 If exposure exists with respect to pension rights and other deferred compensation, US estate tax could be reduced by removing the funds from the US, to the extent that such plans can be cashed out (e g on retirement, separation from service or reaching a prescribed age), often with effective income tax planning. For example, a technique used with returning British expatriates has been to cash out US pensions and deferred compensation plans qualifying under US 'pension' rulings. Upon resuming residence in the UK, arguably distributions from non-qualified plans might still be paid out free of US tax, under article 17 of the 2001 US/UK Income Tax treaty. UK tax will often not apply (by concession) as a matter of domestic law to the extent of earnings associated with a certain periods of non-UK residence.[87]

---

[87] Articles 17(1)(a) and 17(4) of the 2001 US/UK treaty continue the old treaty rule under which (1) lump sum *and* periodic *non-tax qualified* pensions and annuities as well as (2) periodic *qualified* pension plan distributions are exempt from source country tax – such pensions or annuities are taxable only in the state of the recipient, subject to US savings clause with regard to US citizens. (Note that UK Extra Statutory Concession A10 generally only exempts lump sum distributions). With respect to *lump sum qualified* pension distributions, Article 17(2), which the UK asked for without considering the impact of the US savings clause of Article 1(5), allows only source country tax subject to the US savings clause. As a result, the new treaty will allow the US (but not the UK) to tax *lump sum* US *qualified* plan distributions, whereas both countries can tax UK qualified plan distributions (the UK as the source country and the US under its savings clause ability to tax its residents).

Exceptions to the above rule apply with regard to *certain* distributions from *tax exempt* pension plans. Article 17(1)(b) provides that a pension distribution from a 'pension scheme' which could have been received tax free had the recipient been resident in the distributing state, shall also be exempt in the other state (this would only appear to apply to the non taxable lump sum portion of UK qualified pension plans). Article 17(3) provides that social security and similar payments can only be taxed in the state of residence, including US citizen distributees (under Article 1(5), the savings clause does not apply).

In order for US withholding tax relief under the treaty article on pensions and annuities, the deferred payment plan distribution must qualify under as a 'pensions' under various rulings which establish a 3 fold test: (1) the Participant must have been employed by the Employer for 5

10. Life insurance

14.115 Group term and other life insurance policies held by a NDA on his *own* life are statutorily exempt in the US.[88] Proceeds can be received or policies transferred without US estate or gift tax. Policies held on the life of another are subject to US estate tax if the insurer is incorporated in the US.[89] For a UK domiciled person planning for UK inheritance tax effective receipt of life insurance proceeds, this is generally achieved by writing the policy on trust for the benefit of others such that neither the insured nor his estate has any prospective interest in the proceeds.

14.116 US provision of employee death benefits is often dealt with by group term insurance, as noted above, directly held and under which the employee has rights to designate beneficiaries from time to time. Such designations are normally binding on the insurers. In contrast, the usual manner of providing death in service benefits in the UK is for the policy to be written under discretionary trusts where the employee does not own the policy though he may *nominate* beneficiaries. Such nominations are not normally binding on the trustees. In the former case, problems can arise as such powers, over property which is not settled, can cause the US policy proceeds to be includible in a UK domiciled employee's estate for UK inheritance tax purposes.[90] The corollary is that where the trust route is used for a UK death in service benefit due to a US domiciliary, the employee's ability to add to, or modify the, beneficial class of the trust can cause US estate tax inclusion. Accordingly, care needs to be taken in crafting the suitable recipient trusts in either of these cases to ensure that these potential pitfalls are avoided.

G. Alternative structures for holding US income-producing real estate

14.117 US income tax planning should always be considered in connection with estate planning for income producing US real estate, particularly if that income is considered effectively connected with a US trade or business (ECI). This section considers five alternative holding structures for US income producing real estate: (1) direct ownership, (2) US real property holding company, (3) foreign holding company, (4) US real property holding company owned by a foreign company and (5) non-grantor and grantor trust holding structures for commercial real estate.

---

years, or if for fewer years he must have first been employed by the Employer on or after his age 60; *and* (2) the distribution must be made on account of his death or disability *or* as an annuity for his life or for the joint lives of the Participant and his beneficiary *or* be paid upon his retirement after attaining age 55 *and* (3) all distributions must be made after the Participant has separated from service or attained age 70½. PLR 9041041 (13 July 1990). IRAs which do not qualify as pensions (ie as a rollover from a qualified pension) can qualify for treaty exemption under the 'other income' article (PLR 9253049). Lump sum payments qualify as 'periodic' payments under treaties exempting such payments as consideration for past services. PLR 8901053 (13 October 1988), PLR 8904035 (31 October 1988).

[88] Code § 2105(a).
[89] See **CHAPTER 2**.
[90] IHTA 1984, s 5(2).

14.118 Each structure is analysed according to:

- US income tax on rental/business income;
- US branch profits/dividend tax;
- US capital gains tax on sale of property/entity; and
- US gift/estate tax exposure.

1. Summary of relevant income taxes

14.119 In addition to US transfer taxes, ownership of income-producing US real estate may be subject to one or more of the following income taxes, depending on whether the form of ownership is individual, trust or corporate, as listed below.[91]

- **Individual income tax** – at rates of 10% to 35%, applies to ECI rental or business income. The mere rental of one or two properties may not rise to the level of a US trade or business, in which case such rental income is subject to a gross basis 30% withholding tax. In such case, an election may be made to treat such rental income as ECI, allowing deduction of interest, depreciation, commissions, utilities, maintenance expenses and state and local taxes.[92]

- **Top individual rates and net capital gains** – for non-resident alien (NRA) individuals, including settlors of grantor trusts,[93] the top 35% rate is reached at about $160,000 on net rental income. For non-grantor trusts, the top 35% rate is reached at net rental income of $9,550 for 2004. Individuals and non-grantor trusts are entitled to a maximum rate of 15% on 'net capital gain' (property held more than one year).[94]

- **Corporate income tax** – at rates of 15% to 35%, applies to ECI rental or business income. The mere rental of one or two properties may not rise to the level of a US trade or business, in which case such rental income is subject to a gross basis 30% withholding tax. In such case, an election may be made to treat such rental income as ECI, allowing deduction of interest, depreciation, commissions, utilities, maintenance expenses and state and local taxes.[95]

- **Maximum corporate rate** – the maximum corporate rate is 35%, with a rate of 34% applying to net rental income and capital gains in excess of $75,000. There is no maximum rate on net capital gain.

- **Withholding tax on US corporate dividends** – a 30% withholding tax applies to dividends paid by a US corporation to a foreign shareholder. By treaty, this statutory rate is reduced to 5% for qualified corporate residents of the UK which own at least 10% of the voting power of the company paying the dividend, 0% for certain qualified corporate residents of the UK which

---

[91] This discussion is generally limited to federal income taxes. In addition US real property will be subject to state income, property and sales taxes, which can be substantial.
[92] Code § 871(d). See **14.84** (footnote 66) on what constitutes a US trade or business.
[93] See CHAPTER 12.
[94] Code § 1(h). Net capital gain is the excess of net long-term gains over net short-term losses (Code § 1222(11)). In 2009, the maximum rate reverts to 20%.
[95] Code § 882(c).

14.119 *Non-domiciliary Planning to Remove Assets from US Estate Tax*

own 80% or more of the shares of the dividend paying company[96] and 15% for other UK qualified resident shareholders, including individual residents of the UK.[97]

- **Branch profits taxes on foreign corporations engaged in a US trade or business** – A 30% branch profits tax (BPT) applies to the after-tax ECI earnings of a foreign corporation which are retained but not reinvested in the business, creating a total US tax burden of up to 54% of pre-tax profits.[98] The 30% BPT is treaty reduced to 5% for qualified corporate residents of the UK and to 0% for certain qualified corporate residents[99] of the UK.[100]

  A 30% US withholding tax also applies to interest allocable to, or payable by, the US branch of a foreign company with ECI income. Such interest will be treaty exempt from the 30% US BPT provided the interest payee is a qualified UK treaty resident[101] or if the interest is statutorily exempt from withholding (such as portfolio interest).[102] A US deduction for interest may be granted subject to the US earnings stripping limitation and other limitations.[103]

  A foreign holding company which is not a qualified UK treaty resident (eg a non-UK resident BVI company owned by a non-domiciliary UK resident) could be subject to the BPT if it merely owned a seasonally rented Florida residence *and* made a Code § 882(d) election to treat the rental income as ECI (to obtain a deduction for taxes, interest, depreciation and property maintenance expenses to avoid a 30% withholding tax on the gross rental income).[104] However, given current costs of owning and maintaining a Florida rental home, such a property is unlikely to generate net rental income subject to either corporate income tax or the BPT.

- **Foreign Investment in Real Property Tax Act (FIRPTA)** – the disposition of a 'US real property interest' (USRPI) by a NRA or a foreign

---

[96] Note that the 0% rate extends to holdings owned by UK corporate shareholders amounting to 80% or more and which were in existence as of 1 October 1998 *or* where the shareholders are treaty 'qualified residents' under articles 23(2)(c), 3 & 6 (publicly traded companies, derivative benefit EU shareholder companies, and competent authority approved companies). Article 10(3) of the 2001 US/UK treaty. Other UK corporate shareholders which are qualified residents and own at least 10% of the voting shares of the company paying the dividend, are subject to a 5% withholding tax rate.

[97] For non-UK domiciled residents, the dividend must be remitted to the UK (ie UK taxable) to qualify for treaty relief. Article 1(7) of the 2001 US/UK income tax treaty.

[98] Assuming a 34% federal corporate tax and a 30% branch profits tax on the 64% after-tax profit. Code § 884.

[99] Note that the 0% rate extends to companies so engaged prior to 1 October 1998, or which would be entitled to the 0% rate on dividends had the US branch activities instead been conducted through an 80% or more owned US subsidiary (see footnote 96). A 5% BPT tax applies to other qualified corporate residents of the UK. Article 10(7), (8) of the US/UK treaty.

[100] A qualified UK treaty resident company is treaty exempt as well as from the US statutory withholding tax on dividends paid by a foreign corporation 25% or more whose income is connected with the US trade or business (article 10(7); Code §§ 884(e) and 861(a)(2)(B)).

[101] Article 11.

[102] Code §§ 871(h) and 881(c).

[103] Code §§ 163(j) and 267(a)(3) and Treas Reg § 1.882–5.

[104] Code § 884(d)(1) Blessing, BNA Tax Management Portfolio 909–2d, *Branch Profits Tax*, at n 39.

corporation is subject to US income tax under FIRPTA.[105] A USRPI includes a 'US real property holding corporation' (USRPHC), defined as a US incorporated corporation the value of whose USRPI assets amounted to 50% or more of the value of its total real property and business assets on any day in the preceding five-year period.[106] Gain is treated as effectively connected with a US trade or business. However, if the property is investment property, rather than inventory, the gain will be taxable as capital gain, which if 'net capital gain', can qualify for the maximum 15% rate applicable to individuals and trusts.

FIRPTA income taxation does not apply to a gift of US real property (except to the extent the donee assumes a mortgage exceeding the donor's tax basis) or to a transfer of US real property on death.[107] Further, if an NRA owns US real property, his heirs or legatees will receive a market value date of death basis in such property.[108] They will thereby avoid FIRPTA tax on pre-death appreciation.

2. *Summary of structures*

a. Direct ownership

14.120 The tax consequences of direct ownership are as follows.

- **US income tax on rental/business income** – up to 35% on net rental income with the top rate applying to income in excess of about $160,000.

- **US branch profits/dividend tax** – none.

- **US capital gains tax on sale of property** – 15% on net capital gain.

- **US gift/estate tax exposure**[109] – subject to both gift and estate tax.

b. United States real property holding corporation (USRPHC)

14.121

The tax consequences of using a US holding company are as follows:

- **US corporate tax on rental/business income** – up to 35% on net rental income with a 34% rate applying to income in excess of $75,000.

- **US branch profits/dividend tax** – 30% withholding tax on dividends, reduced to 15% for NRAs who are UK residents.

---

[105] Code §§ 897 and 1445.
[106] Code § 897(c)(2).
[107] Gifts and bequests of US real property are not FIRPTA taxable because no money or other property is received for such transfer and thus no taxable gain is realized. See Treas Reg § 1.897–1(h) and § 1.1001–1(a). See also the discussion of related planning in CHAPTER 16.
[108] Code § 1014(a)(1); market value rebasing would also apply for UK CGT purposes. See CHAPTER 11.
[109] GST exposure will also potentially exist if a transfer by a NDA is subject to US gift or estate tax. See CHAPTER 1.

14.122 *Non-domiciliary Planning to Remove Assets from US Estate Tax*

- **US capital gains tax on sale of property** – taxed as ordinary income at corporate rates of up to 35%; if instead, the shares are sold by an NRA shareholder, a 15% maximum rate could apply (although a purchaser might discount the price by the latent US corporate tax exposure). Liquidation of the USRPHC results in a deemed sale of its USRPI with no further tax on the foreign shareholder.[110]
- **US gift and estate tax exposure** – no NDA gift tax exposure exists since the shares are classed as an intangible asset not subject to US gift tax. The shares of any US incorporated corporation are subject to US estate tax, unless the holder is a UK domiciliary under the US/UK 1979 estate and gift tax treaty.

14.122 Assuming a combined US federal and state corporate tax rate of 40%, the total US distributed tax burden on a UK resident individual shareholder would be 49%. As only the US withholding tax would be creditable against UK income tax, a residual UK tax equal to 10.5% of pre tax profits – 32.5% of 60% = 19.5% UK tax less a credit for US withholding tax of 9% (15% of 60% = 9%) – results in a total tax burden of 59.5% for a UK domiciled shareholder. For a non-UK domiciled shareholder the tax burden is higher, since on remittance he will be taxed at 40% (rather than 32.5%) making the additional tax 15% and the overall burden 64%.

14.123 In contrast, leveraging the US holding company will shift profits from the US to the UK to the extent the US 'earnings stripping' limitation does not apply.[111] This limitation generally limits the deduction for interest paid to a treaty-exempt related party lender to 50% of the US borrower's cash flow income (assuming its debt equity ratio is greater than 1.5:1).[112] To the extent US rental profits are paid as interest to a UK shareholder, the distributed rate drops to 40% on such profits. Under the income tax treaty, no withholding tax applies to interest paid to a UK resident lender.

14.124 In view of taper relief (albeit at the lower non business rate) applicable to a sale of shares for UK CGT purposes (and the lack of tax credit to an individual UK resident shareholder for the underlying US corporate tax paid), the sale of shares at the UK CGT rates may be the best alternative.

c. Foreign holding company

14.125 The tax consequences of using a foreign holding company are as follows.

- **US corporate tax on rental/business income** – up to 35% on net rental income with a 34% rate applying to income in excess of $75,000. If the company were a UK corporate resident, a 30% UK corporate tax would apply with a credit for US corporate tax.[113]

---

[110] Code § 897(c)(1)(B).
[111] Code § 163(j).
[112] Limitations have been proposed on the earnings stripping rules, e g Chairman Thomas' HR 2698 bill.
[113] Note that tax base differences may affect the credit.

G. Alternative structures **14.126**

- **US branch profits/dividend tax** – 30% BPT applies to unreinvested US trade or business earnings and a 30% withholding tax applies to interest paid by or allocable to the US branch. The BPT on after tax earnings will generally be reduced to 5% and on interest to 0% for qualified UK resident companies.[114]

- **US capital gains tax on sale of property** – taxed as ordinary income at corporate rates of up to 35%; in contrast, the sale of the foreign holding company shares by any NRA is exempt from US tax (although a purchaser might discount the price by the latent US corporate tax exposure). Liquidation of the foreign holding company results in a deemed sale of its USRPI.[115] Gains on a sale of property or liquidation may be taxed in the country of residence of the company (eg the UK) with credit for US tax. Care also needs to be taken that local law anti-avoidance rules do not apply to attribute gains of non-resident holding companies to resident shareholders (eg in the case of the UK, TCGA 1992, s 13).

- **US gift and estate tax exposure** – no NDA gift or estate tax exposure exists since the shares are an intangible asset not subject to US gift tax and are foreign sited assets not subject to US estate tax.

d. Foreign company owing a US real property holding company

14.126 The tax consequences of using a foreign company owing a US real property holding company are as follows:

- **US income tax on rental/business income** – a 35% US rate applies to the USRPHC (see **14.121**).

- **US branch/profits/dividend tax** – a 30% dividend withholding tax applies to dividends paid by the USRPHC, subject to treaty relief (generally 5% for a qualified UK corporate resident shareholder).

- **US capital gains tax on sale of property/entity** – the USRPHC is taxable on a sale of its property at rates of up to 35%. If then liquidated, no further FIRPTA tax applies. The foreign holding company's sale of the USRPHC shares is taxable under FIRPTA at rates of up to 35%. If the foreign holding company is also UK resident, it is subject to UK 30% corporate tax with credit for the US FIRPTA tax on the sale of the USRPHC shares. Following a sale of the property by the US company, a dividend payment out of the proceeds would be subject to UK corporation tax, but carry a tax credit for the US tax on the distributed gains. Upon liquidation of a UK company, UK CGT (at a maximum rate of 40%, subject to taper relief which would reduce the tax to 24% after ten years) would be imposed on a UK resident individual shareholder (UK CGT would apply to liquidation of any company by a UK resident and domiciled shareholder).

---

[114] Certain qualified UK resident companies may qualify for a 0% rate.
[115] BPT will not apply provided the proceeds of the liquidation are not reinvested in the US in the following three-year period. FIRPTA rollover treatment is provided for liquidation of a foreign holding company into an 80% foreign holding company or for transfer of its USRPI by a tax-free merger.

14.127   *Non-domiciliary Planning to Remove Assets from US Estate Tax*

- **US gift and estate tax exposure** – no NDA gift or estate tax exposure exists since the shares are an intangible asset not subject to US gift tax and are foreign sited assets not subject to US estate tax.

e. Foreign trust planning for US commercial real estate

14.127   In this section we discuss structures for investment by a NDA in commercial income producing US real property through an offshore trust, which will remove trust held assets from estate and gift tax and also be income tax efficient. We consider both a leveraged non-grantor trust for direct investment and a grantor trust structure for private equity investment.

(i) Leveraged non-grantor trust structure for direct investment

14.128   A leveraged non-grantor trust might be used to make a direct investment in US income-producing property, with the objective of reducing the income tax cost and removing the assets from US estate tax. With regard to removing assets from estate tax, a drop off (irrevocable) trust is recommended as it can hold US real property directly without estate tax exposure[116] and be subject to a single level of income tax. Use of a revocable trust would be undesirable as it would require a holding company for the US real estate investment, thereby introducing undesirable secondary level withholding and branch profits tax exposure and a higher corporate rate on capital gains. An income tax transparent LLC (either under US state law, or foreign incorporated with a 'check the box' election being made[117]) could be used to provide the trustees with a limited liability investment vehicle.

14.129   This trust would be a *non-grantor* trust for income tax purposes (unless its beneficiaries are limited to the settlor and spouse during the settlor's lifetime)[118] with the result that it would be subject to compressed rate bracket taxation such that its ECI income in excess of $9,550 would be taxed at 35%.[119] However, it might be possible to substantially pay out the trust's rental income by deductible interest payments resulting from leveraging the trust (or the LLC) with debt capital provided by the settlor or another offshore entity of the settlor which is not otherwise engaged in a US trade or business.[120]

14.130   It is assumed that the rental activity would not rise to the level of a US trade or business[121] but that the trustee would make the Code § 871(d) election to treat the rental income as ECI – in order to get a deduction for taxes, interest, insurance and operating expenses. However, the lender would not be engaged in a US trade or business with respect to a single loan.

---

[116] See **Chapter 16** at **16.107** et seq for a full discussion of drop off trusts.
[117] Treas Reg § 301.7701–3.
[118] Code § 672(f)(2).
[119] See the discussion in **Chapter 12**.
[120] Care needs to be taken, in the case of a UK settlor, with respect to the possible denial of relief for interest which might be regarded as having been incurred solely for the purposes of obtaining relief. ICTA 1988, s787.
[121] See **14.84**.

G. *Alternative structures*   **14.134**

14.131   Since the borrower is neither a corporation nor a partnership in which the lender has a 10% or greater profits or capital interest, the interest paid is 'portfolio' interest[122] which is neither subject to US withholding tax nor the 'earnings stripping' limitation[123] on the deductibility of interest by a corporate borrower. If the debt is held by a NDA it will be 'portfolio' debt not subject to estate tax.[124] With respect to the drop off trust's equity investment, the US real property would not be subject to US estate tax.[125] This leveraged trust structure might therefore be used to remove US rental real property from US estate tax and substantially eliminate US income tax on its rental income.

14.132   The tax effect is as follows.

- **US income tax on rental/business income** – while the US income tax would apply at 35% on rental income, the base might be substantially eroded by interest payments which are not subject to US income tax.

- **US branch profits/dividend tax** – none.

- **US capital gains tax on sale of property** – a 15% maximum capital gains tax rate would apply to the trust's sale of property held more than one year (applicable until 2009, when a 20% maximum rate applies).

- **US gift/estate tax exposure** – none.

(*ii*)   *Grantor trust structure for private equity investment*

14.133   This structure might be used for an investment in a private equity partnership investing in US commercial real estate, such as a US shopping center, office building or golf course gated-community development project. Such projects usually have a developmental phase, a sale or rental phase, and a target exit strategy whereby the development is sold off after, say, five years. A NDA investor would generally want a structure which avoids:

(a)   US estate tax exposure;

(b)   two-tier income taxation (income, withholding/branch profits),

and minimises US income taxation of US effectively connected trade or business income (ECI).

14.134   For such an investment, generating substantial ECI, the tax cost of which may not be mitigated by debt, it might make sense to use a *grantor* trust, to access the higher tax brackets applicable to a married filing separate settlor[126] (which is the tax status of a NDA investor). For transfer tax purposes, the investor will want a drop off trust, to remove the investment from US transfer taxes. If the drop off trust

---

[122]   Code § 871(h).
[123]   Code § 163(j).
[124]   Code § 2105(b).
[125]   See **CHAPTER 16** at **16.107** et seq.
[126]   All married NRAs are required to file US trade or business returns at the 'married filing separate' rates. These rates apply according to rate bracket amounts which are half the amount of those applicable to married filing joint taxpayers (who must be US residents), but 15 times higher than the compressed rate brackets applicable to non-grantor trusts.

14.135 *Non-domiciliary Planning to Remove Assets from US Estate Tax*

is drafted so that it can only benefit the settlor and his or her spouse during the settlor's lifetime, it will be a 'grantor' trust which is transparent for US income tax purposes. The effect is that the 35% income tax rate only applies on income in excess of $159,550 (the married filing separate top bracket amount). Capital gains from assets held more than one year (the sell-off phase of the project) qualify for the 15% maximum rate (regardless of whether the trust is a grantor trust or a non-grantor trust).

14.135 The effect of this strategy is, therefore, to reduce the average US income tax on ECI income to about 26% on the first $160,000 of ECI while capital gains (ie upon the venture's exit sale of the project assets) are taxed at 15% (as with a non-grantor trust) and trust held assets are removed from US estate and gift tax.

14.136 The tax effect is as follows.

- **US income tax on rental/business income** – while the US income tax would apply at rates of up to 35% on rental income, the larger rate bracket amounts available to a grantor trust settlor mean that only a 26% average tax cost applies to the first $160,000 of ECI income annually, with the excess taxable at 35%. Subsequent distributions of retained ECI as UNI (undistributed net income) are effectively not taxable as they would effectively carry tax credits equal to those applicable to the accumulation distribution.

- **US branch profits/dividend tax** – none.

- **US capital gains tax on sale of property** – a 15% maximum capital gains tax rate would apply to the trust's sale of property held more than one year (applicable until 2009).

- **US gift/estate tax exposure** – none.

14.137 A possible issue in inbound trust planning is whether the trust might be viewed as sufficiently engaged itself in a US trade or business as to be taxed as a corporation at the 35% rate.[127] Generally a trust, all of whose assets are contributed by one or more donors without receiving certificates of beneficial ownership in exchange, should be respected as a private trust and not as a corporate fund whose trust managers have the power to vary the investment interest of the certificate holder contributors.[128]

14.138 From a UK perspective, a non-UK resident trust created by a UK resident *UK domiciliary* is likely to invoke anti-avoidance legislation designed to tax the settlor on income and gains arising to the overseas resident trustees. While the inclusion as a beneficiary of virtually any family member (and certain companies) will invoke the CGT anti-avoidance provisions,[129] the income tax provisions will only tax the settlor of an irrevocable trust on *income* on an 'arising basis' where he

---

[127] Treas Reg § 301.7701–4(b).
[128] Treas Reg § 301.7701–4(c); *Comm'r v North American Bond Trust 122 F 2d 545 (2d Cir 1941)*, cert denied, *324 US 701 (1942)*, Rev Rul 75–192, 1975–1 CB 384. Under this principle, US tax rules classify unit investment trusts as foreign corporations.
[129] TCGA 1992, s 86.

G. Alternative structures **14.140**

and/or his spouse may benefit.[130] If that is not the case, then other UK resident beneficiaries may be income taxable when assets or income are distributed or are enjoyed by them.[131] Broadly speaking, the same result applies where the trust is UK resident and the settlor and/or his spouse can benefit since the legislation is similar in scope.[132]

14.139 As to UK inheritance taxation, the trust fund will remain includible with respect to a UK domiciled settlor if he has a life interest or, under the reservation of benefit rule),[133] he has reserved a benefit as a discretionary beneficiary or receives de facto benefit from the trust assets through some other arrangement.

14.140 If the settlor is *not* UK domiciled for general law purposes and not IHT deemed domiciled when the trust is settled, an offshore 'excluded property trust' may be set up which can be structured and administered not only to mitigate US transfer taxes, but also which potentially escapes UK taxation of gains and which will also be outside the scope of inheritance tax with respect to non-UK sited assets.[134]

---

[130] ICTA 1988, Pt XV and s 739.
[131] ICTA 1988, s 740.
[132] TCGA 1992, s 77 (which is more limited in its scope than the equivalent offshore provision) and ICTA 1988, Pt XV.
[133] FA 1986, s 102.
[134] See **CHAPTER 15**.

Chapter 15

Non-domiciliary Planning to Remove Assets from UK Inheritance Tax

A. Introduction

15.1 Here the emphasis is primarily on reducing any UK inheritance tax (over and above the US estate tax) down to the point where it has no effect. The planning considered looks at the tax exposure of US taxable persons (citizens or domiciliaries) who own UK sited assets and also those who, through long-term UK residence, become subject to worldwide inheritance taxation in the UK.

B. Scope of UK tax exposure

15.2 The first step in the planning process is to determine the scope of the US individual's UK transfer tax exposure. At **APPENDIX VI** we provide a chart that shows the possible combinations of US/UK citizenship and domiciliary status and the effect which this can have.

1. US citizen domiciled in the UK

15.3 A US citizen who is deemed UK domiciled by reason of long-term UK tax residence[1] will be subject to global estate taxation in both the US and the UK (subject to tax credit relief). The estate tax treaty, however, does not override the statutory right of the United States to tax its citizens on a worldwide basis. Rather, if a US citizen is deemed to be a UK domiciliary under the treaty, the treaty merely requires the US to give credit for UK tax on all property other than US real and permanent establishment property. The credit is limited to the lower of the US and UK tax on such property and therefore the UK-deemed domiciled US citizen will always pay the higher tax under the two regimes.

2. UK taxation of US domiciliary generally limited to article 6/7 property

15.4 On the other hand, a US domiciliary (who is not deemed UK domiciled or as determined after application of the treaty tie breaker rules) is subject to UK

---

[1] Inheritance Tax Act 1984 (IHTA 1984), s 267.

15.5 Non-domiciliary Planning to Remove Assets from UK Inheritance Tax

inheritance tax (IHT) only with respect to UK real estate and permanent establishment property. Under the treaty, a US domiciliary (under US domestic rules) cannot acquire a UK treaty domicile prior to his seventh year of UK income tax residence in the ten-year period including the year of transfer or gift under consideration.[2] A US citizen, with no intention to remain in the UK permanently, will usually not thereafter acquire a UK domicile under general UK law prior to acquiring deemed domicile status for IHT purposes by UK residence in 17 years out of the previous 20-year period.[3]

15.5 Wealthy US citizens who are approaching this deemed IHT domiciliary status may consider a voluntary absence from the UK for the ensuing four complete UK fiscal years. Temporary stays in the UK during this four-year period are possible provided that in no one tax year does UK presence exceed 182 days and in no tax year does the average yearly presence in the UK exceed 90 days, when taken over a four-consecutive-year period.[4] Such absence from the UK will, in principle, break IHT-deemed domicile for another 17 years and may, in appropriate circumstances, be supportive of his lack of intention to make the UK his permanent home and hence general law country of domicile.

15.6 The UK does reserve a residual right under the treaty to tax its nationals on UK-situated property – not just article 6/7 property.[5] Thus, a UK national who is domiciled in the US will also be subject to UK IHT on UK registered stocks and bonds. If the UK tax exceeds the US tax on such property, the UK will retain the residual tax on such property after giving credit for the US tax.[6]

C. US/UK rate crossover point

1. Crossover for US taxpayer with UK article 6/7 property

15.7 A US taxpayer (assuming he is not a UK domiciliary) will only be subject to UK IHT on UK-situated article 6/7 property. The US citizen/domiciliary is also subject to US estate tax on his worldwide estate (including his UK article 6/7 property), but the US gives a credit for the UK taxes imposed on that UK property. The US will not, however, always give a US taxpayer a *full* credit for UK taxes. As discussed in **CHAPTER 3**, the US foreign tax credit is limited to a fractional share of the US taxes (before credit), the numerator of which is the value of the foreign property and the denominator of which is the value of the domiciliary's worldwide estate. In many instances, the actual foreign taxes will be higher than the US foreign tax credit limitation. Thus, a US domiciliary could pay a higher UK estate tax on his UK article 6/7 property than his estate will receive as a credit against his US estate tax.

---

[2] Article 4(3) of the US/UK treaty.
[3] IHTA 1984, s 267(1).
[4] Inland Revenue IR 20 and see **CHAPTER 9**.
[5] Article 5(1) of the US/UK treaty.
[6] Article 9(2)(b).

15.8 At some level (what is again referred to as the 'crossover point'), the amount of the UK IHT on UK-situated article 6/7 property will be credited in full against the US estate tax. The threshold will depend on the size of the UK estate, the relevant exchange rate and the ratio of the decedent's UK estate to his worldwide estate, as illustrated by the table below.[7]

Size of UK estate	£500,000		£1,000,000		£2,000,000	
UK IHT	£94,800		£294,800		£694,800	
Exchange Rate	Worldwide estate crossover	UK/WW ratio	Worldwide estate crossover	UK/WW ratio	Worldwide estate crossover	UK/WW ratio
$1.50 = £1	$2,530,000 (£1,687,000)	29.64%	$3,970,000 (£2,647,000)	37.78%	$5,545,000 (£3,697,000)	54.10%
$1.75 = £1	$2,530,000 (£1,446,000)	34.58%	$3,970,000 (£2,269,000)	44.08%	$5,545,000 (£3,169,000)	63.12%
$2.00 = £1	$2,530,000 (£1,265,000)	39.53%	$3,970,000 (£1,985,000)	50.38%	$5,545,000 (£2,773,000)	72.14%

This table should be compared with the table at **14.16**, which identifies the crossover point for a UK domiciliary with US article 6/7 property. Notice how in this table the crossover point *when expressed in US dollars* is unaffected by the exchange rates. By comparison, the crossover point in the table at **14.16** *when expressed in UK pound sterling* is unaffected by rate changes.

15.9 The crossover point at which the US taxes become the higher of the two will increase in later years as the US estate tax applicable exclusion credit increases and the US estate tax rates drop. Further, the US foreign death tax limitation (and thus the crossover point) is also subject to a number of adjustments and refinements. For example, the amount of debts and estate expenses will reduce the amount of US estate tax, but not the denominator of the fraction defining the limit of the foreign death tax credit. If a US citizen with UK article 6/7 property valued at £500,000 had $200,000 of deductible debts and expenses, the crossover point (assuming an exchange rate of $1.75 = £1) would increase from $3,305,000 to $3,636,000. Accordingly, it is important to emphasise that the above table is only illustrative and that the figures need to be considered on their own merits in each individual situation.

---

[7] For example, if a US citizen owned UK property valued at £1m, the UK taxes would be £294,800. The crossover point is fixed at a worldwide estate of $3.970m. The US estate tax (before foreign death tax credit) on a $3.97m estate would be $1.170m. At an exchange rate of $1.75 to £1, the ratio of UK property ($1.75) to worldwide property ($3.97m) is 44.08%. The foreign death tax credit limit in that example would thus be about $516,000 ($1.17m × 44.08%), which approximates the amount of UK taxes converted to dollars (£294,800 × 1.75 = $515,900).

15.10 *Non-domiciliary Planning to Remove Assets from UK Inheritance Tax*

2. Crossover point for a US citizen who is domiciled in the UK

15.10 A US citizen who is domiciled in the UK is subject to both US and UK tax on his worldwide estate. For this US citizen, the crossover is the point at which the US tax (computed at US higher rates but with the higher US exemptions) and UK taxes (computed at the lower, flat 40% rate but with a smaller exemption) are identical. At levels of estate below the crossover point, the US citizen will be paying a higher UK tax than US tax. At levels above the crossover point, the US citizen will be paying a higher US tax than UK tax. Since the US citizen will always be subject to US estate tax by reason of citizenship, the planning techniques described at Section G (**15.32** et seq) will be of no benefit.

15.11 The following table identifies the hypothetical crossover point for years 2004 to 2009. During this period, the US rates are dropping and the exemptions are increasing, thus causing a gradual increase in the crossover point. The crossover point is also sensitive to exchange rates. For the purposes of this table, a UK nil-rate band of £263,000 throughout the period has been assumed, although the likely increase in the nil-rate band in later UK Finance Acts would cause the crossover point to drop.

		Exchange Rate	
Year	$1.50 = £1.00	$1.75 = £1.00	$2.00 = £1.00
2004	$7,215,000[8] (£4,810,000)	$6,885,000[9] (£3,934,000)	$6,555,000 (£3,278,000)

---

[8] The 2004 US estate tax, before the applicable exclusion credit, on an estate of $7,215,000 would be $3,284,000. After the applicable exclusion credit of $555,800, the net US estate tax would be $2,728,200. At an exchange rate of $1.50 = £ 1.00, the value of the UK estate would be £4,810,000. After reducing that amount by the nil-rate band of £263,000, the UK tax (at a flat rate of 40%) would be £1,818,800. Converted to US dollars, the UK tax would also be $2,728,200.

[9] The logic behind this math is to find the point at which (i) the higher US tax rates will offset (ii) the UK taxes imposed on the amount exempt from US estate taxes. For example, in 2004 (when the US estate tax exemption is $1.5m), the UK taxes on that amount would be $415,900 (assuming an exchange rate of $1.75 to £1) computed as follows:

$1.5m divided by 1.75	=	£857,143
£857,143 – £263,000	=	£594,143
£594,143 × 40%	=	£237,657
£237,657 × 1.75	=	$415,900

The UK tax rates for estates in excess of $1.5m is fixed at 40%, while the US rates (in 2004) are 45% for the next $500,000 and 48% thereafter. The higher US rates on the next $500,000 thus recapture $25,000 (5% × $500,000) of the higher UK taxes on the first $1.5m. The gap is thus narrowed to $390,900. The balance of that gap is then offset by the additional 8% tax (48% US tax less 40% UK tax) imposed on the next $4,886,250 ($390,900/8% = $4,886,250). The exact crossover point is accordingly $6,886,250 ($1,5000,000 plus $500,0000 plus $4,886,250), rounded in this table to $6.885m.

The 'proof' is as follows:

2005	$7,960,000	$7,585,000	$7,210,000
	(£5,307,000)	(£4,334,000)	(£3,605,000)
2006	$12,705,000	$12,265,000	$11,825,000
	(£8,470,000)	(£7,009,000)	(£5,913,000)
2007/08	$14,845,000	$14,320,000	$13,790,000
	(£9,897,000)	(£8,183,000)	(£6,895,000)
2009	$28,345,000	$27,820,000	$27,290,000
	(£18,897,000)	(£15,897,000)	(£13,645,000)

15.12 The actual crossover point for a US citizen domiciled in the UK is further subject to a number of variables that are impossible to quantify. Differences in the composition of the US and UK taxable estates, availability of special tax reliefs under the UK rules,[10] the US and UK implications of potentially exempt transfers (PETs), the effective use of part of the US citizen's gift/estate tax exemption on lifetime gifts, and (as noted above) later changes to the UK nil rate band will all affect the exact crossover point for a particular individual in a particular tax year. Again, use the above table as a starting point, not as gospel.

D. Spousal deduction planning

1. Non-UK domiciled individuals who do not intend to become UK domiciled

15.13 For individuals who are not UK domiciled and do not intend to become deemed domiciled, an excluded property trust will generally be unnecessary for IHT planning purposes. The principal exposure to UK IHT will usually be UK residential property (a main or second home). For such individuals who have a non-UK domiciled spouse, generally the easiest and least expensive way to avoid/

UK Taxes:	$6,886,250 divided by 1.75	=	£3.935m
	£3.935m – £263,000	=	£3,672,000
	£3.672m × 40%	=	£1,468,800
	£1,468,800 × 1.7	=	$2,570,400
US Taxes:	US tax on $1.5m	=	$0
	US tax on $500,000	=	$225,000
	US tax on $4,886,250	=	$2,345,400
Total US tax:	$2,570,400 ($225,000 + $2,345,400)		

[10] See **CHAPTER 3**. These reliefs include a generous 50% or 100% deduction (dependent on certain criteria being satisfied) for agricultural or business property. The relief also covers all shares in UK private trading companies and a controlling interest in a UK public company, although (except in the case of a US domiciled UK national mentioned at **15.10**) such assets would normally be covered by the treaty relief if owned by a US domiciliary who was not UK deemed domiciled. Business or agricultural property relief can result in an effective UK IHT rate of 20% or even zero.

15.14 *Non-domiciliary Planning to Remove Assets from UK Inheritance Tax*

defer UK IHT on UK sited assets is to make a testamentary disposition of the property to the spouse, or to hold the property in joint tenancy with the spouse, such that she takes automatically by right of survivorship. Either planning will avoid UK inheritance tax in the husband's estate under the exemption for transfers between spouses.[11]

15.14 IHT exposure remains on the death of the surviving spouse with respect to the UK property if still owned by her or a testamentary trust of which she is the life tenant. This exposure may be avoided if, following the husband's death and during the wife's lifetime:

- the property is sold to a third party and the proceeds of sale are invested offshore;[12] *or*

- if the property is transferred to an offshore holding company (if it is real estate in which she is not going to reside); *or possibly*

- if she is planning to reside there, loan finance is raised on arm's length terms, secured against the property and the proceeds reinvested outside the UK. The latter would also be a planning option for the original spouse in respect of directly owned property (and could be the simplest way to plan for IHT in a common death situation).[13]

15.15 To qualify for the UK exemption for gifts between spouses, the transfer must be outright or convey a life interest to her (an 'interest in possession' trust[14]). A life estate, by comparison, will not normally qualify for the US marital deduction but such a strategy could be effective if covered by a US settlor spouse's $1.5m applicable US estate tax exclusion (increasing to $3.5m by 2009) as the property will then not be subject to US tax in either estate. However, this planning may not prove the most effective use of the US exclusion if the property is still owned at the date of death of the second spouse. In such a case, the UK tax will trigger by reference to the second death, whilst the US tax would have triggered by reference to the first death (albeit using the applicable credit to avoid tax at that time). Triggering both tax charges on the second death should allow the UK tax to offset any US tax charge on the same assets without having to make use of the applicable US exclusion.

15.16 An outright testamentary gift will qualify for the *US* spousal deduction if the surviving spouse is a US citizen. Otherwise, a deferral of US estate tax may be obtained only if the property is placed in a qualifying marital trust (QTIP) for which the qualified domestic trust (QDOT) election is made. Alternatively, deferral is possible for an outright gift to the surviving non-US citizen spouse provided she settles a QDOT trust with the inherited assets within the time for filing the US

---

[11] IHTA 1984, s 18.
[12] The trust's sale, as a non-resident, is not subject to UK CGT. Furthermore, where there is a risk of a charge under s 87 of the Taxation and Chargeable Gains Act 1992 (TCGA 1992) arising on a UK domiciled beneficiary (see **CHAPTER 13**) it may still be possible to claim the principal private residence exemption to exempt the gain on disposal. However, stamp duty is not insignificant, particularly on higher value transfers.
[13] If lifetime trusts are to be created by a settlor and the home settled it will be necessary for the settlor to take account of the income tax regime related to pre-owned assets. See **CHAPTER 1** and also FA 2004, s 84, Sch 15.
[14] See *Pearson and others v CIR [1980] STC 318*.

Spousal deduction planning **15.19**

estate tax return on his death,[15] this is generally 15 months after the date of death, provided a six-month extension is timely obtained. Such a trust will be a grantor trust for US income tax purposes.

15.17 In summary, for non-UK domiciled individuals who are married, IHT exposure on UK residential property can be:

- deferred by holding the property as joint tenants with right of survivorship, in which case the property will automatically pass to the surviving spouse without probate;[16]

- deferred by testamentary disposition to a surviving spouse outright or via a testamentary life interest trust;[17]

- avoided by sale of the property (and reinvestment of the proceeds outside the UK) before the death of the surviving spouse, without UK CGT if the property is either the main residence or the owner is then non-UK resident;

- mitigated by securing loan finance secured on the property, the proceeds of which are invested offshore (protecting against IHT exposure in a simultaneous death scenario).

15.18 Non-UK domiciled individuals who:

(a) have or may in the future have substantial non-UK sited assets; and

(b) are married to a UK domiciled spouse or have UK domiciled beneficiaries,

should consider the settlement of a trust during lifetime or at death. Such a trust will be an excluded property trust with respect to non-UK assets and can hold such assets without UK IHT exposure for the benefit of the UK domiciled spouse or beneficiaries, who would otherwise be exposed to IHT either at the time of an outright gift or bequest or subsequently, with respect to their own estates at death.

2. *Married individuals who are both UK domiciled or deemed domiciled, one of whom is a US national or domiciliary*

15.19 For married individuals, both of whom are UK domiciled or deemed domiciled and one of whom is a US citizen or domiciliary, specific integrated US/UK planning is discussed in detail in **CHAPTER 19** (US spouse providing for a UK spouse) and **CHAPTER 20** (UK spouse providing for a US spouse).

---

[15] Code § 2056(d)(2)(B).
[16] If the property purchase price were provided by a US citizen or domiciled joint tenant, it will be included in full in his estate. The surviving spouse, if a non-US citizen, could achieve US estate tax deferral by timely settling the jointly held property in a QDOT trust.
[17] Such a trust will be an excluded property trust as to non-UK sited assets and certain UK unit trusts. IHTA 1984, 48(3A). See **CHAPTER 6**.

3. Married individuals where the spouse with assets is UK domiciled and the other spouse is not domiciled in the UK for IHT purposes

15.20 The one situation where UK spousal deduction planning is problematic is during any period where the donor spouse is UK domiciled and the donee spouse is not UK domiciled (for IHT purposes). In this case, complete UK IHT deferral will not be possible for testamentary transfers from the UK domiciled spouse to a non-UK domiciled spouse. There may, however, be 50% treaty relief for outright bequests to the surviving spouse by a US national or domiciliary or 50% deferral for a testamentary interest in possession trust for the surviving spouse where she is a US national or domiciliary.

15.21 Of course, lifetime transfers between such spouses can make use of the UK potentially exempt transfer regime, which will exempt outright gifts and the creation of interest in possession trusts by a UK domiciled spouse to, or for, a non-domiciled spouse, subject to survival of the donor for seven years thereafter. The UK capital gains tax consequences of such planning differ from testamentary transfers. A testamentary transfer will result in a market value re-basing of the transferred assets, while the creation of such a lifetime trust is a CGT chargeable event.[18] An outright gift to a spouse (even a non-domiciled spouse) is also a potentially exempt transfer for IHT purposes, but is a no-gain, no-loss transaction for CGT purposes, such that no taxable gain arises at that time.[19] On the death of the surviving spouse, the transferred assets held by her outright or in a spousal interest in possession trust will be re-based to market value.

15.22 A trust will be attributed with the UK domicile or deemed UK domicile status of the settlor at the time of settlement. Accordingly, if the husband is UK domiciled, even if the surviving spouse is non-UK domiciled at her death, the underlying trust assets in which her interest in possession subsists would be aggregated with her UK taxable estate (for the purposes of computing the inheritance tax[20] at the second death).[21] A similar aggregation would apply to the extent the trust held UK sited assets at the time of her death, regardless of her domicile or that of the settlor.

---

[18] There were certain limited forms of deferral into all trusts through hold-over relief, although these have been restricted with respect to transfers on or after 10 December 2003. TCGA 1992, ss 165 and 260 as amended by FA 2004, s 116, Sch 21 amend CGT hold-over relief for transfers to discretionary trusts or transfers of business assets to trusts, where any such trusts are settlor interested trusts. The usual provision applies that former and separated spouses are excluded, as are widows/widowers. Similarly, an exclusion applies in certain circumstances where the settlor or spouse are default beneficiaries in the event of the death of the main beneficiaries to a marriage settlement or the death of a child whose interest has vested at the age of 25.

[19] TCGA 1992, s 58. See also **CHAPTER 10**.

[20] Although the tax would be payable by the trustees.

[21] If the trust were settled when the settlor was UK domiciled for IHT purposes, the trust assets would be taxable as a result of the UK domicile of the settlor at that time, independently of the spouse's domicile at her death. If, however, the settlor were not UK domiciled at the time of settlement, the trust would be an excluded property trust (see **15.32**) as to non-UK sited assets, under IHTA 1984, s 48(3), and only UK sited assets would be exposed to IHT.

15.23 Trust assets[22] will be re-based for capital gains tax purposes to market value on *her* death, as if she had owned the property outright since the trustees are deemed to make a disposal and immediate reacquisition of the trust property. Whether the trust is UK resident or not, the trustees are exempt from any CGT charge at that time, with the exception of any gains which were the subject of a hold-over relief claim when the assets were settled.[23]

4. Individuals who are likely to become UK domiciled for IHT purposes

15.24 Individuals who are likely to become domiciled in the UK for IHT purposes should consider whether it would be tax effective to settle non-UK sited assets in an excluded property trust. Deemed domicile status for IHT purposes will be acquired by persons who have been UK income tax resident for all or any part of 17 out of the 20-year period ending with the year of an IHT chargeable transfer. Such planning is discussed at Section G (**15.32** et seq) and, since part-year residence counts to the same extent as a whole year of residence, should be considered well in advance. For example, arrival in the UK on 31 March 1990 would cause deemed UK domicile to arise on 6 April 2005 (just over 15 years later).

E. UK lifetime gifts to non-spouses – 'potentially exempt transfers'

15.25 Lifetime gifts to individuals and to certain trusts can provide an effective means of eroding the UK IHT base provided:

- the gift is outright, to a life interest trust or to an accumulation and maintenance trust or a trust for the disabled;
- the donor survives the gift by seven years; and
- the gift is not subject to a level of capital gains tax that would outweigh the other benefits.

15.26 Lifetime gifts to a non-UK domiciled spouse (for IHT purposes) by a UK domiciled spouse, either outright or via a trust in which she has an interest in possession, are not exempt spousal transfers but are potentially exempt transfers (PETs), where the donor is not subject to IHT if he survives the transfer by seven years. Such gifts are therefore an effective way for spouses of mixed domicile to remove assets from IHT exposure.

---

[22] Though not the underlying assets of any holding company which the trustees may own.
[23] TCGA 1992, ss 72–74. The ability to claim hold-over relief depends on the settlement being a UK resident settlement and, therefore, not likely to be commonplace in such situations, as the trust will normally be non-UK resident. However, from 10 December 2003, the ability to claim hold-over relief has been removed generally, even for UK trusts, on transfers into settlement where the settlor or his spouse have, or later acquire, an interest. FA 2004, s 116.

15.27 *Non-domiciliary Planning to Remove Assets from UK Inheritance Tax*

15.27 All gifts are subject to CGT on the market value of the assets given away unless the transferee is a UK resident and either:

- the transfer is also subject to IHT (eg to a discretionary trust);[24] *or*
- the transfer is of property qualifying as a business asset[25]

and in each case a hold-over election is made.

15.28 In addition, outright gifts to a spouse are not subject to CGT (the cost basis of the property in effect carrying over, regardless of the UK domicile or residence status of the spouse)[26] nor to IHT (subject to the seven-year survival period where the donor is UK domiciled and the donee is non-UK domiciled).[27] As a result, for UK sited assets, effective CGT lifetime gift planning is generally limited to outright gifts to spouses or to transfers of sterling cash, non-appreciated assets or, where the donee is UK resident, transfers qualifying for hold-over relief.

15.29 For the non-UK domiciled individual who is not UK resident but who owns UK assets, the planning is fundamentally the same for IHT as in the case of a UK resident non-UK domiciliary. However, for CGT purposes there are fewer constraints since he will not normally be subject to CGT unless he is transferring an asset used in a UK trade or business or he has been resident in the UK previously, and is subject to the temporary non-residence rules which tax disposals during a period of non-residence of less than five tax years, in the year of return.[28]

15.30 Furthermore, the UK 'connected party' disposal rule[29] has interesting consequences for non-UK residents, who are not subject to UK CGT. For example, a non-resident who owns a UK holiday home might make a potentially exempt transfer of such property to an individual, an interest in possession trust or to an accumulation and maintenance (A&M) trust. No CGT would be incurred, although the tax basis of the property for the donee should be re-based to market value for CGT purposes. Nor would any IHT exposure exist if the transferor survived the transfer by seven years and did not retain a benefit in the transferred property within seven years of his death.

---

[24] TCGA 1992, s 260; but note restrictions from 10 December 2003 where the settlor or his spouse can now, or may at some future date, benefit from the trust. The new provisions affect trusts which are not settlor interested trusts at the outset but become so within a period of six years from the beginning of the tax year following the disposal (eg where the transfer into trust is made on 31 July 2004 the period expires from 6 April 2011).

[25] TCGA 1992, s 165, but, again, note the restrictions from 10 December 2003 where the settlor or his spouse can now, or may at some future date, benefit from the trust. As above, the six-year period applies.

[26] TCGA 1992, s 58. It should be noted that, in contrast with outright gifts, transfers to a spousal interest in possession trust do not qualify for tax deferral through 'no-gain, no-loss' treatment. Note also, however, in the case of outright gifts to a non-UK resident during a part-year of residence that the 'split tax year' concession can, in cases of perceived abuse, be withdrawn. Furthermore, the restrictions noted above will apply on or after 10 December 2003.

[27] In which case, the exemption for gifts to a spouse for IHT purposes is limited to £55,000, or 50% of the transfer if treaty 'article 8 relief' applies. See **CHAPTER 7**.

[28] TCGA 1992, s 10A.

[29] See **CHAPTER 11**.

F. Permanent establishment property

15.31 The taxability of such property is discussed in **CHAPTER 14** at **14.108** et seq.

G. Excluded property trusts and offshore holding vehicles

15.32 Under current law, routine planning for non-UK domiciliaries likely to become UK deemed domiciled is to establish an offshore 'excluded property' trust.[30] If such a trust is established and funded prior to acquiring deemed UK domicile, as the law stands[31] all non-UK sited property held in the trust will be indefinitely excluded from IHT. The exclusion will continue to apply even if the settlor or other beneficiaries later become UK domiciled as a matter of general law or deemed UK domiciled. The exclusion also applies even though the trust is revocable (although it will more commonly be irrevocable for other reasons). Further, excluded property status applies whether or not the settlor

- retains an interest in possession; *and/or*
- is a discretionary capital beneficiary.[32]

The above follows from the interaction of the reservation of benefit rules and the excluded property provisions.[33] With respect to any trust from which the settlor is not irrevocably excluded from benefiting, the gift will have been a gift with reservation, but the benefit will be reserved over excluded property, which is outside the inheritance tax charge at death. Clearly, where the trust owns UK sited assets, these will be within the scope of the tax charge regardless of the domicile of the settlor or a life tenant (specific planning may be undertaken with regard to UK property as discussed at **15.13** et seq).

15.33 Similarly, the anti-avoidance rule,[34] which creates grantor ('settlor interested') trust status for capital gains purposes with respect to a UK resident trust

---

[30] IHTA 1984, s 43(3).
[31] As noted previously this is under review.
[32] In excluded property trust planning, it may be desirable that an interest in possession is not held initially by the settlor or his spouse, in order to avoid IHTA 1984, ss 80(1) and 82 which re-tests domicile, for the purposes of the IHT discretionary trust tax regime, on the death of the last such interest in possession holder. See the discussion of this rule in **CHAPTER 6** and **CHAPTER 19**.
[33] See IHTA 1984, s 48(3) and FA 1986, s 102. Despite the Capital Taxes Office having openly accepted this interpretation since 1986, they indicated informally some time ago that they were reviewing whether it was, in fact, the proper interpretation. In the period since they voiced their initial thoughts it would appear that they may have reconsidered. It may be difficult for them to be seen to do a volt-face after more than fifteen years of interpreting and applying the law in a manner generally accepted to be correct by most professionals and academics. However, it remains to be seen whether they will ultimately seek to modify the legislation as part of the two reviews, currently underway, of the taxation of non-UK domiciliaries and of trusts.
More recently interest in possession trusts have been used in the light of these Inland Revenue comments on their possible review of the interpretation of the excluded property provisions and the slightly more robust analysis of the technical position in the case of such trusts as compared with discretionary trusts.
[34] TCGA 1992, s 77.

15.34 *Non-domiciliary Planning to Remove Assets from UK Inheritance Tax*

from which the settlor or his spouse are not irrevocably excluded from all benefit, is not applicable to non-UK resident trusts.[35] The equivalent offshore CGT provisions,[36] which focused on taxing the settlor, do not apply where he is a non-UK domiciliary in the year of assessment.[37] Those CGT provisions may later become relevant where the settlor's domicile changes but only take effect from the year of change.

15.34 UK property not attributable to a UK trade can be sold by a non-UK resident trust free of UK capital gains tax and, in principle, the proceeds can be distributed free of capital gains tax (and possibly IHT) to the settlor, provided he is not then *both* UK domiciled and resident (however, such assets would usually best remain in trust for both practical succession planning reasons and tax efficiency). For this purpose it should be remembered that it is the general law domicile concept which is of relevance and not the 'deemed domicile' IHT concept.

15.35 If the assets are distributed to a beneficiary who is not the settlor, that distribution will escape capital gains tax if the beneficiary is:

- neither UK resident nor ordinarily resident; or
- a non-UK domiciliary in the year of distribution.[38]

15.36 It is usual for the trust to confer wide powers of appointment over capital on the trustees including powers to make payments to the settlor where he is a beneficiary (in substance, making the settlement 'revocable', albeit at the instance of the trustees rather than the settlor). For US settlor individuals, since the lifetime gift tax exemption is limited to $1m per taxpayer (plus $114,000 annual exclusion for gifts to a non-US citizen spouse), a trust which has been settled with a greater sum will usually be structured as an incomplete gift trust for US purposes with a qualified marital trust taking effect at the settlor's death to defer US estate tax until the death of the last spouse to die.

15.37 UK assets can also be protected from IHT provided they are held by an offshore company owned by the trust (see **15.39**) or are encumbered with appropriately structured debt.[39] In the latter case, the trust would not be an excluded

---

[35] TCGA 1992, s 77(7).
[36] TCGA 1992, s 86.
[37] Although from 17 March 1998, UK resident and domiciled beneficiaries receiving direct or indirect capital cash payments, or benefits in kind, can be taxed. TCGA 1992, s 87.
[38] TCGA 1992, s 87(7).
[39] It is not recommended that this structure be used to hold real estate for occupation, in view of the potential income tax charge. The UK Inland Revenue takes the position that an income tax liability arises on the 'benefit' of an individual occupying a home owned by a company in certain circumstances. In a recent criminal case before the House of Lords (*R v Allen [2001] STC 1537*), the Inland Revenue succeeded in establishing that the UK income tax legislation which taxes benefits received by employees (Income Tax (Earnings and Pensions) Act 2003, Pt 3, Ch 5) covers the provision of living accommodation for 'deemed' directors of companies. The definition of 'director' for this purpose is very wide and includes any person in accordance with whose instructions the named directors are accustomed to act. As result of a further court decision' the term may be even wider and include any person in accordance with whose advice the directors habitually act (*Secretary of State for Trade and Industry v Deverell and another [2000] 2All ER 365*). In theory, this could apply where the property is owned by a company which is in turn

G. Excluded property trusts, etc **15.41**

property trust with respect to the UK sited property, which would remain subject to UK IHT, reduced, however, by the value of the debt.[40] If the settlor had a life interest, the cost base of the property would be uplifted to its open market value at the date of the settlor's death without CGT charge.

15.38   Alternative testamentary planning could include:

- reducing the inheritance tax exposure by property ownership as joint tenants or as tenants in common (although no discount in value of property left to a third party at death would apply if it were being valued as related property[41]);

- deferral of inheritance tax by a testamentary bequest outright to, or in an interest in possession trust for, a surviving spouse (or by a lifetime potentially exempt transfer if the donor spouse were UK domiciled and the donee spouse were not UK domiciled for IHT purposes); or

- providing for the liability by term insurance equal to the inheritance tax (preferably written under suitable trusts, so as not to give rise to tax on the proceeds themselves).

15.39   A non-UK resident trust owning an offshore company could be used by a non-UK domiciled settlor to hold UK property. The company (being non-UK sited shares) would avoid UK IHT and the trust would allow tax-free distribution of capital gains under current law to non-UK domiciled or non-UK resident beneficiaries.

15.40   There are limitations however. First, it will not be possible to transfer directly held appreciated UK property (other than a UK principal residence, where generally there are other disadvantages of doing so in any event – see below) to an offshore trust without incurring a capital gains tax charge. Therefore, such trusts should be set up in advance to acquire UK real (and perhaps business) property as an original owner.

15.41   Second, there is an income tax risk to the settlor in placing UK residential property in an offshore company where the settlor is a UK resident and uses the property as his residence.[42] The exposure arises because, as in the US, free use of corporate property by a UK resident director or employee is deemed to be a taxable benefit in kind. In the case of a UK resident settlor of a trust which owns the

---

owned by a trust, although the technical argument here is more difficult in a properly managed structure. The value of the 'benefit' is calculated under a statutory formula and can be substantial in the case of larger properties.

[40]   Care needs to be taken with respect to the provisions which seek to restrict deductions for certain types of debts. See FA 1986, s 103 and **CHAPTER 1**.

[41]   IHTA 1984, s 161. Related property includes any property owned by a spouse or owned by a charity (or a political party, housing association or certain other designated bodies) within the last five years, pursuant to a gift from the settlor or his spouse. Where a higher valuation would arise if the property were valued with related property, it is valued in aggregate and the higher value attributed proportionately to the respective owners.

[42]   See footnote 39. Where the settlor is non-UK domiciled, the Inland Revenue may attempt an assessment on the basis that the taxpayer is carrying out the duties of his deemed office while in the UK.

company, the Inland Revenue may argue that the settlor is a 'shadow director' of the company by virtue of his effective control over the company (see earlier).[43]

15.42 For US purposes, if a non-US offshore holding company is acquired by a US client, either as a direct shareholder, or by his trustees where he is the settlor of a grantor trust, consideration should be given to making a 'check the box' election to treat the entity (solely for US tax purposes) as a disregarded single owner entity or as a foreign partnership. Otherwise, adverse US income tax consequences may arise under the US controlled foreign company, foreign personal holding company or passive foreign investment company rules.

15.43 Alternatively, a US limited liability company (LLC) might be used as such an entity is transparent under US tax rules. If this is considered, the corporate status of the entity should be respected by the Inland Revenue. A US regular corporation, for which Subchapter S tax status has been elected to treat the company as generally transparent for US corporate income tax, is usually not a desirable holding company vehicle, both because of its imperfect transparency for capital gains tax purposes[44] and also because a foreign trust cannot be a shareholder.[45] See also the discussion in **CHAPTER 18** generally and at **16.34** with regard to passive foreign investment companies.

15.44 In implementing lifetime planning through the use of trusts and/or companies to hold UK sited assets, from 6 April 2005, it will be important to have regard to the income tax charge imposed in certain cases where assets previously owned by the settlor have been transferred into trust.[46]

15.45 Subject to certain exceptions, the pre-owned assets regime applies, inter alia, where an individual is in physical occupation of land or is using chattels which he previously owned, but no longer does. It also applies to intangibles which he previously owned but which are now comprised in a trust from which he can benefit. Accordingly, for the US taxpayer benefiting from any such assets it will be a relevant consideration. It should be noted that the provisions are very wide and apply to situations where a gifted asset has been sold and the funds are later reinvested by the donee into the asset which the donor is using. They also to apply to situations where funds have been provided in order to purchase the asset (or a cash gift is, as a matter of fact, so used within specific periods following the gift). The detailed rules are considered in **CHAPTER 1**.

15.46 This charge does not apply in certain excepted cases including where the relevant property (or an asset which derives its value from the relevant property) is deemed to remain comprised in the estate of the donor for inheritance tax purposes under the IHT legislation. Exemption from the pre-owned assets income charge clearly applies in the case of UK sited assets directly owned by trustees where the

---

[43] Income Tax (Earnings and Pensions) Act 2003, Pt III, Ch 5. See also **CHAPTER 2**.
[44] For example, the $250,000/$500,000 gain exemption on the sale of a principal residence (Code § 121) may not apply.
[45] Code § 1361(c)(2)(A).
[46] See **CHAPTER 1** and FA 2004, s 84, Sch 15.

settlor has an interest in possession[47] or where he is a discretionary beneficiary and the trust therefore falls within the reservation of benefit regime.[48]

15.47 It ought also to apply where the assets are owned through a holding company and, accordingly, in each of the following circumstances:

(a) where a UK sited asset is directly owned by a trust with an interest in possession for the settlor, the regime will not apply as he will be deemed to own the assets;[49]

(b) where a UK sited asset is directly owned by a discretionary trust and the settlor is a beneficiary, the regime will not apply as the assets will be deemed to be included in his estate;[50]

(c) where a UK sited asset is held by a non-UK company owned by a trust with an interest in possession for the settlor, the regime will not apply as he will be deemed to own the assets which derive their value from the relevant property;[51]

(d) where a UK sited asset is held by a non-UK company owned by a discretionary trust and the settlor is a beneficiary, he will be deemed to own the assets which derive their value from the relevant property.[52]

H. Grantor trust and US transfer tax issues

15.48 A foreign trust settled by a US income tax resident with a potential US beneficiary will be a grantor trust (income tax transparent) for US income tax purposes.[53] Such trusts are ignored for US income and gains tax purposes (and, if incomplete gift trusts, also for gift and estate tax purposes) with resultant look through US taxation of income (including deductions and credits) to the US settlor of such a trust.

15.49 Under UK tax rules, a US citizen who is a UK resident but non-UK domiciled settlor of a non-UK resident trust from which he or his spouse can benefit, would generally be taxable on:

---

[47] IHTA 1984, s 49 and see **CHAPTER 1**.
[48] FA 1986, s 102 and see **CHAPTER 1**.
[49] IHTA 1984, s 49 and FA 2004, Sch 15, para 11(1)(a).
[50] FA 1986, s 102 and FA 2004, Sch 15, para 11(3) and (5).
[51] FA 2004, Sch 15, para 11(1) and 11(3). The company is deemed comprised within the estate under IHTA 1984, s 49 and it derives its value from the property. FA 2004, Sch 15, para 12(3). This provision preserves the benefit of excluded property status for previously created trusts, after the domicile of the settlor has changed to that of the UK.
[52] FA 2004, Sch 15, para 11(3) and 11(5). The company is deemed comprised within the estate under the reservation of benefit provisions and it derives its value from the property (para 12(3)). This provision preserves the benefit of excluded property status for previously created trusts, after the domicile of the settlor has changed to that of the UK.
[53] Including settlors who are US citizens wherever resident and green card holders whose residence is not treaty tie breaked to the UK. See **CHAPTER 12**. Note that foreign nationals whose US income tax residence is tie breaked to a foreign country, remain US residents for non-income tax computation purposes, such as the Subchapter S and the CFC shareholder ownership provisions. Treas Reg § 301.7701(b)–7(a)(3).

15.50 *Non-domiciliary Planning to Remove Assets from UK Inheritance Tax*

(a) UK source income received by the trust (whether or not discretionary or one in which he had an interest in possession);

(b) on foreign source income distributed to him offshore and directly or indirectly remitted by him to the UK; and

(c) on certain types of income not qualifying for remittance basis taxation (such as gains on the disposition or maturity of an offshore life insurance policy).[54]

15.50 The UK will not tax the gains of such a trust unless distributed to a UK domiciled and resident beneficiary. Furthermore, if the settlor becomes UK domiciled under the general law he will be taxable on all gains which *thereafter* arise to the trustees including past gains to the extent distributed or enjoyed by the settlor as a capital ' payment'.[55]

15.51 A US citizen or US domiciled settlor is subject to US gift tax on transfers into trust, unless the trust is structured as an 'incomplete' gift trust. For asset transfers in excess of the settlor's lifetime gift tax exemption,[56] incomplete gift status can be achieved inter alia by using (i) a revocable trust or by the settlor retaining a (ii) testamentary power of appointment and a life interest or (iii) by the settlor retaining the power to add or remove beneficiaries, with or without the consent of a non-adverse party.[57]

15.52 If the trust is revocable, or if the settlor retains certain other powers and interests, the cost base of the trust assets will generally be re-based to market value on the settlor's death without US tax charge.[58] If structured generally as an incomplete gift trust, the trust assets will be included in the settlor's US estate tax base because the settlor will have retained dominion and control over the transferred assets.[59] It is due to such deemed inclusion, that the trust assets will be re-based to market value.[60]

15.53 Typically, an incomplete gift trust settled by a married individual would contain a qualified marital trust (QTIP or general power of appointment) for any

---

[54] ICTA 1988, s 547.

[55] TCGA 1992, ss 86 and 87. In order to avoid exposure of the trustees themselves to UK income tax, as a UK resident trust, there must be no trustee who is a UK resident if the settlor was, when the funds were settled, UK resident, ordinarily resident or UK domiciled. In order to avoid capital gains taxation as a resident trust the majority of the trustees must be resident overseas and the administration of the trust must be conducted overseas (although the CGT criteria may change with effect from 5 April 2005 to become aligned with the income tax rules). The UK income and CGT consequences of such trusts must be carefully considered and are discussed in **Chapter 13**.

[56] By making a joint gift election under Code § 2513 with a US citizen or domiciled spouse, the settlor can also utilise his spouse's exemption.

[57] Code § 2511. A non-adverse party is essentially an independent person who is not a beneficiary of the trust. It is interesting to note that the US philosophy is to regard independent fiduciaries as being in the 'control' of the settlor and attributes their powers to him, whereas in the UK, the view is that such persons are likely to act impartially in exercising their fiduciary responsibilities.

[58] Code § 1014(b)(1). A number of exceptions apply, eg foreign personal holding companies and 'income in respect of a decedent' items, such as deferred compensation and pension benefits, annuities and third-party life insurance policies, which have a carry-over basis.

[59] See **Chapter 16**.

[60] See **Chapter 11**.

surviving spouse, to defer US estate tax until the death of the last spouse to die. In the case of a non-US citizen surviving spouse, the trust must also be a QDOT to qualify for the deferral. Under the QDOT rules, following the settlor's death, the trust must have a US trustee (a bank, if assets generally exceed $2m), be subject to US trust law and meet other requirements, including withholding of estate tax on distributions of trust principal, including capital gains unless qualifying as 'hardship' distributions.[61]

---

[61] See **CHAPTER 4**.

Chapter 16

US Pre-Immigration Planning

A. Introduction and summary

16.1 Moving from one country to another, to live there indefinitely, can offer some spectacular tax planning opportunities – often the chance to leave one tax jurisdiction but structurally insulate one's assets and/or income from tax in the new country. Pre-immigration planning allows taxpayers to exploit these opportunities and 'fall between the cracks' – a nightmare for tax globalists who believe (wrongly) that all income and all gratuitous transfers should be subject to tax somewhere. This chapter considers the planning for a foreign national's move to live indefinitely in the United States.[1]

16.2 From a US income tax perspective, the foreign national might consider

- realizing income or gains prior to the move (including 'bed and breakfasting' while in a tax haven);
- disposing of troublesome assets;
- examining the US income tax implications of trusts created by the immigrant or for his benefit; and
- consider variable insurance products as ways of sheltering income from US tax.

16.3 An individual might also consider pre-immigration gifts to others (outright or in trust) in order to:

- avoid the US gift tax exemption limits;
- avoid limits on transfers to non US citizen spouses;
- take advantage of an unlimited generation-skipping tax (GST) exemption;
- jettison troublesome assets; and
- otherwise reduce the immigrant's US estate tax exposure.

An immigrant will also need to consider existing trusts that he has established, or for his benefit, to understand the extent to which those trusts create US estate tax exposure.

16.4 Finally, the immigrant might consider transferring a portion of his wealth in what is referred to as a 'drop off trust'. As discussed in more detail at Section I

---

[1] The authors wish to thank Stephen Gray, Esq., Schutts & Bowen, London, for his review of this chapter and comments thereon.

16.5   US Pre-Immigration Planning

(**16.107** et seq), the immigrant could be a discretionary beneficiary of that trust without exposing the trust property to US estate tax at the immigrant's death. To accomplish the tax objectives, the trust property must also be legitimately protected from the claims of the immigrant's creditors (a noble objective in and of itself). This generally requires forming the trust in certain offshore tax havens with favourable legislation.

B.   Domicile – am I there yet?

16.5   US domiciliaries are subject to US transfer taxes on the same basis as US citizens – that is, on all transfers without regard to the location of the transferred assets. Thus, a US-domiciled alien will be subject to:

- US gift tax on gifts of foreign real estate;

- US generation-skipping tax on gifts or bequests of securities in foreign companies to grandchildren (even grandchildren who are not US persons); and

- US estate tax on non-US situated property including real estate, tangibles, and investments owned at death.

16.6   In contrast, a NDA is generally subject only to US gift tax on transfer of US real estate and tangible personal property (including cash). With proper pre-immigration planning, it is possible for an immigrant to minimize or avoid this US tax exposure. Accordingly, it is important to know when the individual is considered to be a US domiciliary.

1.   General principles

16.7   Conceptually, an individual acquires US domicile by living there, even for a brief period of time, with no present intention of later emigrating from the US.[2] A foreign national will generally acquire a US domicile at that time when he or she

---

[2]   Regrettably, the Code and the regulations refer to domicile as 'residence', a use of the term which is very confusing in the transfer tax area since 'residence' for income tax purposes has two objective tests (green card and substantial presence) and is not at all determinative of domicile. In this book we attempt to minimize this confusion by referring to estate and gift tax 'residence' as domicile, and to non 'resident' foreign nationals as 'non-domiciled aliens' or 'NDAs' to distinguish them from income tax non-residents, whom the Code calls 'non-resident aliens' or 'NRAs'. See Treas Reg § 20.0–1(b) (estate tax), which states:

'A "resident" decedent is a decedent who, at the time of his death, had his domicile in the US. A person acquires a domicile in a place by living there, for even a brief period of time, with no definite present intention of later removing therefrom. Residence without the requisite intention to remain indefinitely will not suffice to constitute domicile, nor will intention to change domicile effect such a change unless accompanied by actual removal.'

The same definition applies for gift tax. Treas Reg § 25.2501–1(b). See, generally, Troxell, BNA Tax Management Portfolio 837–1st, *Aliens – Estate, Gift and Generation-Skipping Taxation*. An intention to leave the US in the near to medium term could suffice. *Fara Forni v Comm'r* 22 TC 975 (1954).

Domicile – am I there yet? **16.8**

commences to live in the US indefinitely, as evidenced by a number of factual circumstances including the location of the settlor's:

- 'permanent home', i e principal residence in size, cost, functionality and use;[3]
- immediate family, including spouse and minor children;[4]
- driver's license;[5]
- centre of business and social interests;[6]
- service providers: doctor, dentist, broker, lawyer, accountant;
- pets, boats, planes, vehicles, art collection;[7]
- wills and legal documents, business and financial records;[8]
- business, country and political clubs;
- church burial plot;
- bank, brokerage, cash management and other financial accounts;
- voting registration.[9]

16.8 Visa status is generally not relevant. The legal right of permanent residence (a 'green card' visa) may be one factor indicating US domicile, but will not establish it.[10] Conversely, it is now settled law that US domicile may be acquired even by illegal (or, the current, more politically correct term, 'undocumented') aliens[11] and by limited term non-immigrant visa holders and diplomats.[12]

---

[3] Holiday homes may be disregarded even if always available, see, for example, *Estate of Fokker v Comm'r 10 TC 1225 (1948), acq 1948–2 CB 2 (St Moritz)*; *Rogers v Comm'r 17 BTA 570 (1929)* (Cannes); *Estate of Paquette v Comm'r 46 TCM 1400 (1983)* (Florida 'snowbird' home disregarded even though the taxpayer had sold both Canadian city and country homes, although retaining other ties to Canada).

[4] *Farmer's Loan and Trust Co v US 60 F 2d 618 (SDNY 1932)* (children placed in US school indicated US domicile); *Estate of Nienhuys v Comm'r 17 TC 1149 (1952), acq 1952–1 CB 3* (Holland); *Estate of Khan v Comm'r 75 TCM 1957 (1998)*.

[5] This factor has unusual importance and multiple driving licenses should be retained if possible.

[6] *Estate of Fokker v Comr 10 TC 1225 (1948), acq 1948–2 CB 2; Estate of Khan v Comm'r 75 TCM 1957 (1988)*.

[7] See, for example, *Farmer's Loan & Trust Co v US 60 F 2d 618 (SDNY 1932)*.

[8] See, for example, *Estate of Fokker Est v Comm'r 10 TC 1225 (1948), acq 1948–2 CB 2; Estate of Bloch-Sulzberger v Comm'r 6 TCM 1201 (1947); Frederick Rodiek, Ancillary Executor 33 BTA 1020 (1936), non acq XV-2 CB 35, aff'd 87 F 2d 328 (2d Cir 1937)*: self-serving statements may not be given effect and statements in visa, financial applications, letters and oral statements may be used adversely to the taxpayer.

[9] See Cassell, Karlin, McCaffrey & Streng, 'US Estate Planning for Non-resident Aliens Who Own Partnership Interests', Tax Notes (16 June 2003), at pp 1683, 1685.

[10] *Estate of Lyons Est v Comm'r 4 TC 1202, 1208 (1945)*.

[11] Rev Rul 80–209, 1980–2 CB 248.

[12] *Estate of Jack v US 2002–2 USTC ¶ 60,452 (Ct Cl 2002)* (deceased Canadian dentist could be shown by factual circumstances to have formed an intent to remain in the US beyond the expiration of his limited term visa). Most non-immigrant visas, for example:
- B (business and pleasure);
- F (full time study);
- E (treaty trader or investor);
- L (inter company managerial transferees);
- H (temporary employment for training or where US workers unavailable);

16.9 *US Pre-Immigration Planning*

16.9 For many immigrants there will be a factually bright line set of controllable facts defining the acquisition of US domicile, eg the sale of a UK residence, moving the family to US, acquisition of a Florida home, driver's license, bank and financial accounts. For others – including some Canadian snowbirds and many Latin Americans who have dual homes, families and existences in the US (such as Florida or New York) and their home country – the adviser (and client) will face a more challenging task. Ultimately, the client will need to understand the factual and legal issues (and often uncertainties) regarding his US domicile status and the US tax risks from making certain pre-immigration transfers when the individual might, in fact, be considered US domiciled.

2. Domicile of UK emigrants

16.10 The UK also taxes its domiciliaries on worldwide gifts and estates. A UK domiciliary moving to the US must accordingly consider the UK tax implications of any pre-immigration/emigration planning. The UK also has a common law concept of domicile – the place of an individual's permanent residence. CHAPTER 2 discusses the various nuances of the UK domicile rules, including the reversion to a domicile of origin upon abandonment of a domicile of choice.

16.11 There are two other UK domicile rules applicable only to inheritance tax that can be relevant to a UK domiciliary planning to move to the US. First, an individual will be considered domiciled in the UK if he or she had been domiciled in the UK at any time within the preceding three calendar years.

Example

A person leaving the UK for permanent residence abroad on 1 July 2004 would not lose his UK domicile for inheritance tax purposes until 1 July 2007.

16.12 Second, an individual is deemed domiciled if she had been a UK income tax resident for all, or any, part of 17 or more years in the 20-year period where the 20th year is the year in which the given event falls.[13]

- J (students and scholars); and
- O (extraordinary ability in science, art education, business or athletics),

are issued for a limited time, generally six months to three years.

Following the Supreme Court's decision in *Elkins v Moreno 435 US 647 (1978)*, that a non-immigrant alien has the legal capacity to form the requisite intent to establish domicile in the US, the IRS reversed prior rulings and held that non-immigrant visa holders could acquire US domicile in Rev Rul 80–363, (international organization employee with G-4 non-immigrant visa held US domiciled).

[13] IHTA 1984, s 267(1). Interestingly, both of these rules are disapplied as regards their exemption from tax as 'excluded property', for certain designated government securities (owned by an individual or held in trust) and government sponsored savings products (IHTA 1984, ss 6(2), (3) and 48(4)). They are also disapplied in the case of certain older double taxation conventions. IHTA 1984, s 158(6). See CHAPTER 7.

Example
>A person leaving the UK on 1 July 2004 would not, under this rule, lose his deemed UK domicile until 6 April 2008, since it is UK tax years and not calendar years which are relevant.

As will be seen, a person who is a UK domiciliary under the general law but who has also been a UK resident in more than 17 years out of the prior 20 years, will be subject to the second, more stringent, of these rules.

16.13 Because of the nuanced differences in the US and UK common law domicile rules, and because of the two special UK IHT rules just described, an immigrant to the US from the UK might be considered domiciled in both countries for a period of time. That contingency is, fortunately, addressed in the 1979 US/UK Estate and Gift Tax treaty (the 'US/UK treaty'). Domicile is first determined under local law.[14] If a person is considered to be domiciled in both countries under local law,[15] two special treaty tie-breaker rules apply.

16.14 First, a UK *national* who continues to maintain his UK domiciliary status will be treated as a UK domiciliary (and not a US domiciliary) if – at the time of the relevant transfer – he had not been a US income tax resident in seven or more of the ten taxable years including the year of the relevant transfer.[16] There are two corollaries to this rule:

- **six-year grace period** – A UK national who actually retains ties to the UK and remains UK domiciled under the UK common law cannot be considered a US domiciliary for the first six years of US income tax residence;

- **three-year grace period** – A UK national/domiciliary who immigrates to the US will continue to be treated as a UK (and not a US) domiciliary during the three-year period that he is deemed under UK tax law to continue to be a UK domiciliary, even if he retains no ties to the UK and would not have been considered a UK domiciliary under UK common law.

16.15 Second, if, after application of local law and the first treaty rule, the individual is still considered domiciled in both countries, the treaty's general tie-breaker rules treat the individual as domiciled in:

(a) the country in which the individual has his 'permanent home',[17] or if such home is in both or neither country;

---

[14] US/UK treaty article 4(1).
[15] US/UK treaty article 4(1).
[16] US/UK treaty article 4(2). This rule only applies if the individual is not also a US citizen.
[17] Note that the term 'home' can include a house, condo or an apartment, owned or rented. 'Permanent' means the accommodation is always available to the taxpayer, and not just on a seasonal or short-term basis. See Clutton, 'Inheritance Double Taxation Agreements', published as Chapter 7 of Tolley's *International Personal Tax Planning* (2002, Dixon and Finney eds) at p 7–5. The IRS adopts the same definitions in Form 8840, which is used to claim a closer connection to a foreign country in tie-breaking US residence to a foreign country. Under this definition, a Florida home which is occupied by its NDA owner 5½ months in the winter should not be a permanent home.

16.16 *US Pre-Immigration Planning*

(b) the country which is the 'centre of his vital interests', or, if that cannot be determined;

(c) the country in which he has a 'habitual abode', or, if the individual has a habitual abode in both or neither country;

(d) the country of his nationality, or, if he is a dual US/UK national, then by agreement of competent authority.[18]

3. Summary

16.16 So what does all this mean? Simply this: a UK domiciliary planning to move to the US will not be considered domiciled in the US during the following periods:

- prior to becoming a US domiciliary under US common law (that is, prior to moving to the US with the intention to make the US his permanent home);

- at all times the individual is able to maintain his UK domicile under the US/UK treaty's general tie-breaker rules;

- during the US/UK treaty's six-year grace period if the individual is a UK national and maintains UK domicile during this period; and

- otherwise during the three-year grace period if the UK national severs ties to the UK but nonetheless remains a UK domiciliary under the UK's three-year continuing domicile rule.[19]

16.17 During the relevant period, the individual can make 'pre-immigration' transfers of non-US property without exposure to US gift tax.[20] Instead, during the relevant grace period, the UK domiciliary or national will only be subject to US gift (and estate) tax on transfers of US real and business property.[21] This result applies

---

[18] US/UK treaty article 4(4).
[19] Technically, 'domicile' for UK purposes refers to that status within a jurisdiction with its own laws, e g a country such as England and Wales, Scotland or Northern Ireland, or a province, state or canton such as Quebec, Florida or Vaud. Loss of 'UK' domicile after the relevant period would, therefore, require factual abandonment of, say, English domicile and acquisition of a new domicile of choice in, say, Florida, from the outset and thereafter continuously throughout the tail-off period. UK advice would prudently be sought that there is no reversion to a UK domicile of origin if the new domicile of choice is changed during this three-year period, e g by the client moving from Florida to California. The shorter the duration of the stay in the first state, the more likely the Revenue are to argue that, in fact, no permanent change has been made to the prior UK domicile status. It should be noted that the burden of proof is on the person asserting the change.
[20] US/UK treaty article 5.
[21] US/UK treaty articles 5 (taxing rights), 6 (real estate) and 7 (permanent establishment property). Note that under US/UK treaty article 5(1), a situs country can only tax a domiciliary of the other on real property and permanent establishment property located in that country – provided that both the US and the UK can tax their nationals on other property under local law but have to give credit for the domiciliary country tax (limited to UK-sited property in the case of a UK national domiciled in the US). Credit is only given if the tax is actually paid to the other country. Under US/UK treaty article 5(2), subject to articles 6 and 7, property of nationals of one but not both countries who are third-country domiciliaries can only be taxed in the country of nationality. A person who is a US citizen and a resident of a US possession at death shall not be considered a US citizen or domiciliary if he acquired that status solely by reason of being a citizen of the

even though, in the last three exceptions described above, the individual moves to the US and becomes a US income tax resident and a domiciliary under US common law.

16.18 While local tax consequences must be considered, in the UK and a number of other jurisdictions, such gifts can often be made as a practical matter without local gift tax (see further Section G at **16.85** et seq).[22]

C. US income tax resident – am I there yet?

16.19 Some pre-immigration income tax planning (such as realizing gain on appreciated property) might be necessary prior to the individual becoming a US income tax resident. So when does an individual become a US income tax resident?

16.20 As discussed in more detail in **CHAPTER 9**, a non-citizen is considered a US income tax resident under one of two objective tests:

- the green card test; and
- the substantial presence test.

The green card is an immigrant visa granting the individual a right to permanent US residence. The substantial presence test is based on a mathematical formula of the number of days the individual is physically present in the US during the current calendar year (and, in some cases, the prior two calendar years).

16.21 If an individual was not a US income tax resident during the prior calendar year, then special rules in the US tax regulations dictate the individual's US residency start date. The green card residency start date is the first date the individual is physically present in the US with a green card.[23] The substantial presence residency start date is the first date the individual is physically present in the US during the calendar year in which he satisfies the substantial presence test.[24]

16.22 For purposes of the substantial presence start date, up to ten days of 'nominal' physical presence can be ignored if the individual has a tax home in, and

---

[22] possession and his birth or residence within such possession, consistent with Code §§ 2208 and 2209.

Care needs to be taken, as noted earlier, in the context of the UK as certain gifts into trust made by a UK domiciliary can continue to attract UK taxes long after the settlor has ceased to be UK domiciled. However, many lifetime gifts are tax free. For example, gifts to a spouse are IHT exempt unless the donor is UK domiciled and the donee is non-UK domiciled (IHTA 1984, s 18), while outright gifts to anyone, to a trust providing for an interest in possession or to an Accumulation and Maintenance Trust (see **CHAPTER 13**) are exempt if the donor survives the gift by seven years. Under the laws of a number of Swiss cantons, gifts to spouses or lineal descendants are subject to nil or very low rates of tax. Hong Kong, Singapore, South Africa and a number of other countries have an estate tax, but no gift tax. Canada, Italy and Australia have neither tax. Note that in civil law countries, barring a separate property agreement, the spouses may own assets equally as community property.

[23] Code § 7701(b)(2)(A)(ii); Treas Reg § 301.7701(b)-4(a).

[24] Code § 7701(b)(2)(A)(iii); Treas Reg § 301.7701(b)-4(a).

closer connection to, a foreign country. However, the individual may not ignore any days during a period of consecutive days present in the US unless all days during that period are ignored under this rule.[25]

Example

Nigel Nuworld plans to move to the US in 2004. He visits the US on 4 January 2004 on a house-hunting trip, staying for seven days. He returns again on 10 February and stays for three days. He and his family move to the US on 1 March and remain in the US for the rest of the year. Nigel's residency start date is 1 March, the prior ten days being ignored. If, however, on his second trip Nigel stayed for four days, his first three February days could not be excluded and his residency start date would be 10 February 2004.

16.23 If an individual is considered an income tax resident under both tests, the individual will be considered a US income tax resident on the first of the two start dates.[26]

Example

Nigel's substantial presence residency start date is 1 March 2004 but he obtained his green card on 10 February 2004, thus making 10 February his green card residency start date. Nigel is considered a US income tax resident as of 10 February 2004.

16.24 For immigrants who wish to establish US income tax residence in the immigration year, even though they meet neither the green card nor the substantial presence tests of income tax residence, there is also a special 'first year' election to establish residence towards the end of an arrival year. Such an election might be made if US tax rates were lower than the UK.[27] Under Code § 7701(b)(4), an immigrant who is:

(a) continually present in the US for at least 31 consecutive days (with a grace period allowed of up to five days absence); *and*

(b) who is present in the US at least 75% of the total days from the start of such continuous US residence period until 31 December,

can elect to be a US income tax resident from the start of such continuous residence period.

16.25 Here again, US income tax residence can be affected by a tax treaty between the US and another country, such as the UK. Under article 4 of the 2001 US/UK Income Tax treaty, an individual who is an income tax resident of both countries will be deemed resident in the country in which he has his sole

---

[25] Treas Reg § 301.7701(b)-4(c)(1).
[26] Treas Reg § 301.7701(b)-4(a).
[27] This pre-supposes that the individual continued to be regarded as UK tax resident and that a tie break to the US on the relevant criteria could be substantiated in these circumstances. The more likely scenario is that on leaving the UK permanently, the individual would cease to be UK tax resident and would have a period during which he was resident in neither jurisdiction.

'permanent home', failing which, the country which is the center of his 'vital interests', failing which, the country in which he has an 'habitual abode', failing which, the country of his nationality.

D. Pre-immigration US income tax planning

16.26 Pre-immigration US income tax planning generally involves five areas:

- consider the advisability of realizing or deferring gains, income or deductions prior to or after becoming a US income tax resident;

- where appropriate and possible, realize gains through 'bed and breakfasting' to establish a new tax basis;

- consider steps to avoid falling into the penal US 'anti-avoidance' rules on investments in foreign companies, including on commonly found investments such as foreign mutual funds;

- examine US income tax implications to avoid pitfalls with respect to foreign trusts created by the immigrant or for his benefit; and

- for individuals expecting to be only temporarily resident in the US (for example, an executive expecting to work in the US for three to five years) consider investing in variable insurance or annuity products as a way of mitigating current US income tax and deferring income tax until after departing the US.

1. Realize gains, income or deductions before or after becoming a US income tax resident

16.27 A UK taxpayer who plans to immigrate to the US should consider the merits of realizing gain, income (such as taking dividends from a privately-held company, receiving deferred compensation or bonuses) or deductions prior to becoming a US income tax resident.

16.28 Consideration should obviously be given to a variety of factors, including the relative tax rates in the two countries. For example, the US tax rate on long-term capital gains and dividends is currently only 15%, compared to a possible top rate of 40% in the UK. The different rules for determining the tax basis for assets are also relevant when comparing relative levels of taxation, with the US generally using a historical cost basis and the UK adjusting the cost basis for inflation prior to 1998 and offering taper relief to reduce the taxable gain thereafter. With respect to tax basis, the immigrant should consider the countries' different tax basis rules that apply to property received by gifts or bequests. Finally, the immigrant needs to consider the different exemptions in effect in each country. For example, in the UK an individual is entitled to exempt an unlimited amount of gain from the sale of his primary residence from tax, while in the US, a taxpayer is only able to exempt $250,000 of gain ($500,000 if married) every five years.

16.29 In some instances, a taxpayer would be advised to realize gains or recognize income while still a UK income tax resident. For example, a UK resident

16.30 US Pre-Immigration Planning

planning to sell his UK home, which has appreciated in value, should consider doing so prior to becoming a US income tax resident if the amount of the inherent gain exceeds the US exemption limits. In other instances, an immigrant might save overall taxes by deferring realization of income (including capital gains and dividend income) until becoming a US resident given the lower US tax rates.

2. Bed and breakfasting

16.30 As noted above, prior to immigration the taxpayer should consider realizing current portfolio gains. Unlike Canada and Australia (and potentially the UK as to property transferred to a trust or to another individual, although not to a spouse),[28] the US does not assign a new fair market value tax basis to an immigrant's assets. As a consequence, built in gains which the client brings with her to the US will be taxed if and when realized while she is a US tax resident.

16.31 Traditionally, US immigrant clients have been advised to eliminate pre-entry gains by 'bed and breakfasting'. This could involve a sale and repurchase of market securities, in a tax haven after the immigrant has terminated his old foreign tax residence and prior to his US residency start date.[29]

3. Avoiding onerous US 'anti-avoidance' rules (CFCs, FPHCs and PFICs)

16.32 The US income tax laws include a number of anti-avoidance rules designed to minimize the US tax benefits of using a foreign company to earn certain types of income. These rules subject a US taxpayer to current taxation on certain passive and other earnings realized by US controlled foreign corporations (CFCs)[30] and by foreign personal holding companies (FPHCs).[31] The CFC and FPHC rules both require a certain degree of US direct or indirect ownership (including through attribution from family members, trusts, corporations and partnerships). The third anti-avoidance rule – related to holdings in passive foreign investment companies (PFICs), including foreign mutual funds – requires no aggregate US ownership and imposes onerous income tax and interest charges on certain distributions and gains from PFICs.[32]

---

[28] This follows from the fact that all gifts constitute disposals for UK capital gains tax purposes, although in limited cases, the gain can be deferred by using 'hold over relief' or by reason of the transaction taking effect on a 'no gain no loss' basis.

[29] The US 'wash-sale' rule (requiring carry-over basis) only applies to *loss* sales and not to gains. Code § 1091.

[30] Code § 951 et seq. A CFC is a foreign corporation which is controlled more than 50% by vote or value by 10% US shareholders, applying attribution rules, for more than 30 days of the year. Foreign family ownership is not attributed to US family members. Generally, passive, related party, shipping, downstream oil and insurance earnings are taxed on an arising basis to 10% US shareholders as 'Subpart F' income, whether or not distributed, with exceptions for high taxed, de minimis and 'same country' income.

[31] Code § 551 et seq.

[32] Code § 1291 et seq. A PFIC is any foreign corporation which in *any* year has either:
- gross income consisting 75% or more of passive income; or

16.33 CFC or FPHC income is taxed to the US owner (or deemed owner) as ordinary income at rates of up to 35%. Although the CFC rules treat so-called 'subpart F' income as if it had been distributed as a dividend, the special 15% dividend rates will generally not apply to this income.[33] Note that taxing CFC and FPHC income at ordinary income rates produces an even worse result than if the US taxpayer had owned the foreign company's underlying investments directly and earned tax-rate advantaged income such as capital gains and dividends taxable in the US currently at a maximum rate of 15%. Taxes paid by the CFC or FPHC are effectively only taken as a deduction in computing the net earnings of the foreign company that are taxable to the US shareholder: had the company's investments been directly owned, the foreign taxes would have been available as a *credit* against US taxes. CFC or FPHC losses are unavailable to the US shareholder personally. A US shareholder's principal residence held through a foreign company will not qualify for the $250,000 personal residence gain relief.

16.34 Any investment in foreign mutual funds will be exposed to adverse taxation under the PFIC rules.[34] Excess distributions from the PFIC – more than 125% of the last three years' average distribution – and gains from the sale of the PFIC's shares are allocated on a daily pro-rata basis over the shareholder's holding period.[35] PFIC income allocated to the current year is treated as ordinary income and taxed along with the US taxpayer's other current income.[36] PFIC income thrown back to prior years results in a 'deferred tax amount' determined by reference to the highest marginal tax bracket in effect during those prior years *plus* an interest charge.[37]

Example

Georgina Bush, a US taxpayer, liquidates her investment in a foreign mutual fund at the end of the 10th year of her ownership, realizing $1m of capital gains. $100,000 of this PFIC gain is allocated to each of years 1 to 9. The PFIC gain allocated to year 1 is subject to an income tax based on the highest marginal *ordinary* income tax rate in effect in year 1 – even if the US tax rates in year 10 are higher or lower. The tax so imposed on year 1 gain is subject to an interest charge for 9 years' worth of deferral (from 15 April of year 2, when the taxes would have been due, until 15 April of year 11 when Georgina pays taxes on year 10's PFIC gain). The same procedure is followed for PFIC gains allocated to years 2 to 9. The PFIC gain allocated to the year of sale is treated as ordinary income (not capital gains income) and added to Georgina's other income in year 10 to determine her year 10 tax liability.

- assets consisting 50% or more of passive assets (generally by value).

  US control is irrelevant. The provision catches, but is not limited to, foreign mutual funds. Priority rules apply (albeit imperfectly) so that a CFC is not also taxed as a PFIC (post-1998) and a so that a CFC is not also taxed as a FPHC.

[33] Code § 1(h)(11). The lower 15% rate only applies to dividends from domestic companies and certain 'qualified foreign corporations', which will generally not include most CFCs. In addition, actual dividends from FPHCs will not qualify for these lower rates. Code § 1(h)(11)(c)(iii).
[34] Code § 1291 et seq.
[35] Code § 1291(a)(1) and (2).
[36] Code § 1291(a)(1)(B).
[37] Code § 1291(a)(1)(C) and (c).

16.35 US Pre-Immigration Planning

16.35 There are two alternative methods of taxing PFIC earnings. First, in limited situations the US taxpayer can make a Qualified Electing Fund (QEF) election and be taxed currently on his share of the PFIC's net income and gains.[38] In most cases, however, it will be impossible to make this election because most foreign mutual funds cannot provide the US taxpayer the data to determine his share of PFIC earnings as their information reporting systems are understandably not aligned with the US requirements. Further, many foreign funds are themselves invested in underlying PFIC funds for which separate QEF elections must be made.

16.36 Second, if the PFIC is publicly traded the US taxpayer can make an election to be taxed on the 'mark to market' increase (ordinary income) or decrease (ordinary loss, to the extent of prior increases) in fund net asset value.[39] This is an unwelcome alternative to the QEF election because it taxes the taxpayer on both realized *and unrealized* fund gains. Further, in contrast to US mutual funds where the taxpayer's allocable share of long-term gains are currently taxed at a maximum rate of 15%, the mark to market election for PFICs will subject the deemed earnings to tax at ordinary income rates of up to 35%.[40]

16.37 Immigrating to the US with a PFIC investment can create significant adverse tax implications to the immigrant. As noted at **16.34**, 'excess distributions' (including PFIC gain) are allocated over the taxpayer's holding period, which could include a significant period of time prior to the immigrant becoming a US taxpayer. Nevertheless, a US taxpayer who has PFIC income allocable to prior tax years is subject to a 'deferred tax amount' which (as noted) is determined based on the highest marginal tax rate in effect in the prior years. Importantly, the deferred tax amount is determined without reference to the US taxpayer's particular tax situation, including (it appears) the fact that the individual might not have been a US taxpayer in those prior years.

Example

Nigel Nuworld moves to the US and immediately liquidates his holdings in a PFIC he owned for ten years. Nigel is slapped with a PFIC deferred tax (and interest) on PFIC income allocated to prior years when he was not even a US resident. How fair is that?

16.38 If these rules are not bad enough, the US shareholder of a foreign corporation will have to file a battery of annual forms to report the income or gains of a CFC, FPHC and/or PFIC.[41]

16.39 It is possible to establish a market value US tax basis for all corporate held assets and elimination of underlying earnings prior to becoming a US income tax resident – including while 'bed and breakfasting' – by liquidating an offshore holding company. Under US tax rules, a liquidating corporation is deemed to sell all of its assets at market value – provided the corporation is not owned 80% or more by

---

[38] Code §§ 1293 and 1295.
[39] Code § 1296.
[40] Code § 1296(c).
[41] See Form 5471 and instructions (CFCs and FPHCs) and Form 8621 (applicable to a PFIC, if a QEF election is made), available on the IRS website www.irs.gov under Forms & Instructions.

Pre-immigration US income tax planning **16.45**

another corporation and the liquidated assets are not re-incorporated in the same form in another corporation (which could be viewed as a basis 'rollover' foreign to foreign re-incorporation).[42] The liquidation would also eliminate accumulated earnings, which disappear with the liquidating distribution.

16.40 Since 1997, US tax regulations have offered immigrants a simple and efficient strategy for both bed and breakfasting foreign entity-held gains and earnings *and* removing such entities from the CFC and FPHC rules during the client's US tax residency.[43] Under entity classification regulations applicable to most foreign companies, an authorized director of the company can file a 'check the box' tax election with the IRS Philadelphia office to treat the entity for *all* US tax purposes as a foreign partnership (if the entity has two or more owners) or as a single owner 'foreign disregarded entity' (if it has only one owner).[44]

16.41 The election, which does not apply to trusts or to public companies, can be made retroactive for a period of up to 75 days or prospective for a period of up to one year after filing. *The election is only effective for US federal tax purposes (income, gift, estate and GST)*. The entity continues to exist for all other purposes: it retains its assets and remains subject to its liabilities, it can shelter shareholders from corporate liabilities, and can remain subject to local tax all as if this election had never been made.

16.42 Finally, immigrants wishing to invest in offshore mutual funds without PFIC taxation might consider the planning alternative of 'wrapping' such investments in a qualified variable insurance policy – discussed below. This could be an effective way to avoid the onerous PFIC tax rules while permitting indirect investment, for example, in a number of offshore hedge and long-short equity funds that have been attractive to some investors.

4. Examine income tax implications of existing trusts

16.43 If the immigrant client or family members were settlors or are beneficiaries of existing trusts, those trusts should be reviewed for US income, gift and estate tax purposes. This section summarizes some of the relevant income tax issues.

16.44 First, if the immigrant was the settlor of the trust, it should be determined if (after becoming a US income tax resident) the settlor will be taxed under the US grantor trust rules as the owner of the trust. As discussed in detail in **CHAPTER 12**, the grantor trust rules determine the circumstances in which a settlor can be taxed on trust income and gains essentially as if he owned the trust's underlying assets.

16.45 Foreign trusts formed within five years of the settlor becoming a US resident are particularly susceptible to grantor trust treatment. Under Code § 679,

---

[42] Code §§ 331–37 (liquidation) and 361, 368(a)(1)(F) (re-incorporation).
[43] Treas Reg § 301.7701–2 (defining eligible entities) and Treas Reg § 301.7701–3 (default entity classification rules and mechanics of 'check the box' elections).
[44] Treas Reg § 301.7701–3. As if the IRS didn't have enough information already, in December 2003, it proposed a new Form 8858 reporting earnings of 'foreign disregarded entities' (FDEs).

16.46 *US Pre-Immigration Planning*

the immigrant will be treated as having formed the trust immediately upon becoming a US tax resident. Under the general rules of that section, a US taxpayer will be considered the owner of a foreign trust that he funds for the current or future benefit of US taxpayers. Therefore, unless the foreign trust precludes US persons from being beneficiaries, the immigrant will likely be considered the grantor/owner.

16.46 Code § 679 does not apply to trusts funded *more than five years* prior to the settlor's becoming US income tax resident. This offers an opportunity for an immigrant – with some foresight and patience – to create an irrevocable trust that could have US beneficiaries, but still be considered a non-grantor trust if the immigrant can wait five years after funding to move to the US. Whilst unlikely to be an attractive option to a UK immigrant for the reasons stated previously, an individual planning to move to the US in the medium term could settle an irrevocable, discretionary pre-immigration trust and then take up residence in the Bahamas or in Canada during the five-year period.

Even if the immigrant/settlor is able to escape the claws of Code § 679, he can also be considered the grantor/owner of a trust under the other grantor trust provisions, discussed in more detail in **CHAPTER 12**. Examples include:

- trusts for the current or future benefit of the settlor and/or his spouse;
- trusts that are revocable by the settlor;
- trusts granting the settlor the right to substitute assets;
- trusts where the settlor has borrowed funds; and
- trusts subject to a retained power to add beneficiaries.

16.47 It is apparently possible, with careful planning, for the settlor or settlor's spouse to be discretionary beneficiaries of a trust that is considered to be a non-grantor trust. There are two relevant provisions. Code § 677 generally provides that the settlor will be considered the 'owner' of a trust if the income can be distributed to (or accumulated for future distribution to) the settlor or the settlor's spouse. However, if the distribution is subject to the consent of an adverse party, then this rule does not apply. An adverse party is a person with a substantial beneficial interest in the trust that would be adversely affected – in this case – by the distribution to the settlor or settlor's spouse.[45] For example, requiring the consent of a child/beneficiary could do the trick.

16.48 Code § 673 also treats the settlor as owner if the settlor (or his spouse) has a 'reversionary' interest in the trust that is valued at more than 5% of the value of the trust property. For the purpose of this rule, one must assume the trustee's maximum exercise of discretion in favour of the settlor (or settlor's spouse).[46] Importantly, there is no 'adverse party' exception in Code § 673 and many had believed that the 'maximum exercise' rule would cause the settlor to be treated as owner in all discretionary trusts where the trustee could exercise immediate discretion to terminate the trust and distribute all trust assets to the settlor (or

---

[45] Code § 672(a).
[46] Code § 673(c).

Pre-immigration US income tax planning **16.52**

settlor's spouse). However, the IRS has not apparently agreed with that interpretation, ruling in two instances that Code § 673 would not apply.[47] It is understood from counsel who were responsible for at least one of these rulings that the IRS does not consider a settlor's discretionary beneficial interest to be a 'reversionary interest' in the legal sense of that term, thus limiting the application of this section to situations where the trust property reverts to the settlor (or settlor's spouse) at the termination of a prior interest.

16.49 Second, the immigrant also needs to consider the possible implications under Code § 684 if he would be considered the grantor/owner of a foreign trust after becoming a US resident. As discussed in CHAPTER 8 (see 8.15 et seq), the regulations under that section treat a US taxpayer as having sold property to a foreign trust when the trust ceases to be considered a grantor trust. All gains (but no losses) are recognized and subject to US tax. There are a variety of circumstances that cause a US taxpayer to cease to be considered the owner of the trust, including death and (under many circumstances) ceasing to be a US resident. Under the regulations, if the foreign trust ceases to be a grantor trust at the settlor's death and the basis of the property is determined under Code § 1014 (generally, a basis adjustment to fair market value for property included in the decedent's estate), then no gain is realized.

16.50 In CHAPTER 8 the authors expressed their dismay at the apparent application of Code § 684 to foreign trusts created by an immigrant *prior to* becoming a US taxpayer. The language and purpose of that section (as well as the related special provisions of Code § 679) could be read to extend the reach to foreign trusts created by immigrants. Further, as noted in CHAPTER 8 (see 8.44 et seq), there is some risk the interaction of Code §§ 679 and 684 could cause an immigrant to immediately recognize gain on appreciated property held in a foreign trust created by the immigrant within five years if the trust is *not* considered a grantor trust (for example, if established for a non-US beneficiary).

16.51 Third, the immigrant should consider the US income tax implication (to the immigrant or other US beneficiaries) of distributions from foreign trusts, particularly the taxation of undistributed taxable income (UNI). Under complex rules discussed at **12.85** et seq, UNI distributed from a foreign trust to a US beneficiary is taxed under the so-called 'throwback' rules. These rules generally tax the income as if it had been distributed in three of the prior five tax years (discarding the years with the highest and lowest income). The tax so determined is then subject to an interest charge based on the weighted age of the accumulations. If UNI has accumulated for many years, the interest charge can be considerable.

16.52 Depending on the circumstances, a variety of planning strategies should be considered. These include:

- create or modify foreign trusts so they will not be considered grantor trusts once the immigrant/settlor becomes a US resident;
- create, modify or re-establish foreign trusts for the benefit of the immigrant so that a foreign non-immigrant settlor will be respected as grantor owner;

---

[47] PLR 200148028 (27 August 2001) and PLR 9016079 (25 January 1990).

16.53 *US Pre-Immigration Planning*

- prior to the settlor becoming a US resident, a foreign trust to which the settlor contributed assets should realize inherent gains and losses so as to minimize the impact of code § 684;[48]

- a foreign trust settled by the immigrant could distribute trust assets to beneficiaries prior to his immigration and avoid all grantor trust and Code § 684 issues;

- prior to immigration – perhaps while bed and breakfasting – distribute sufficient assets to remove the UNI of a foreign non-grantor trust.[49]

16.53 In all cases it is essential to check the local laws of the country in which the immigrant is residing prior to arrival and also any other relevant laws, such as those of his domicile or of the situs of the assets or of the residence of any relevant trustees.

5. Income tax planning using variable insurance products

16.54 Properly designed cash value variable life insurance products can defer (and, in some cases, avoid) US income tax and also avoid the adverse implications of the US anti-avoidance rules described above.

16.55 The premiums paid for a cash value variable life policy will substantially exceed the policy underwriting (the pure insurance cost) and other charges, leaving the excess cash available to invest within the policy. For example, a $1m cash premium might have deducted from it only $15,000 of annual underwriting and policy charges, leaving $985,000 for investment. This excess cash is held in a 'segregated asset account', which means the policy account assets are protected from the insurance company's creditors. The policyholder determines the allocation of the policy investments among a limited choice of 'subaccount' funds.[50] The amount

---

[48] This would be particularly important if the immigrant settlor had transferred property to the trust within five years because of the interaction of Code § 679(a)(4) and Code § 684. See **8.44** et seq. Although there are considerably stronger arguments that Code § 684 should not apply to pre-immigration trusts funded earlier than five years before the settlor's immigration, caution would suggest minimizing any risks under this section by having the trust realize all gains prior to the settlor's immigration.

[49] This strategy might not be necessary. Code § 667 provides that distributions of previously accumulated income are taxed to the beneficiary to the extent that income would have been taxed to the beneficiary if distributed in the year of accumulation. As discussed in **CHAPTER 12**, there is a reasoned argument that this provision would effectively exempt an immigrant from tax on foreign income accumulated in a trust prior to his becoming a US income tax resident, since a non-US person is only subject to US income tax on US-sourced income. See **12.99**. While this position is advocated by one of the most respected commentators on US taxation of trusts and estates, the IRS might argue that the statute is ambiguous, as discussed in **CHAPTER 12**. As the issue is not entirely free from doubt, an immigrant would be better advised to receive an accumulation distribution *prior to* becoming a US taxpayer, rather than waiting until afterwards and arguing for a literal interpretation of the Code § 667.

[50] Where the taxpayer is a UK person or he may return eventually to the UK, care needs to be taken since certain insurance arrangements which give the taxpayer the ability to influence investment decisions are categorized as Personal Portfolio Bonds, which suffer disadvantageous tax treatment.

Pre-immigration US income tax planning **16.60**

of the premiums and return on the variable life policy investment ultimately determine the amount of insurance coverage required by the applicable Code provisions.

16.56 A properly designed multiple premium variable life policy offers the following US income tax benefits:

- no current tax on income/gains realized within the policy's investment accounts;
- tax-free withdrawals from the policy up to the amount of the premiums invested;
- tax-free loans from the policy which need not be repaid prior to death;
- income tax-free proceeds at death.

16.57 If the policy is cashed out prior to death, the US taxpayer will be subject to US income tax on the difference between his cost basis in the policy (his premiums) and the amount of cash received on liquidation. This amount is taxed at ordinary income rates (of up to 35%), not at capital gains rates (currently capped at 15%). A US taxpayer (or soon-to-be US taxpayer) considering a variable life policy as a tax-deferral investment vehicle, therefore needs to consider the relative benefits of deferral against the differential in applicable rates.

16.58 For an immigrant planning to live in the US for only a limited period, an offshore variable life policy can offer an opportunity to avoid US taxes altogether. If the immigrant needs access to the cash in the policy while still a US tax resident, he can take tax-free withdrawals (up to his investment in the policy) and tax-free loans of a substantial part of policy cash value.[51]

16.59 The CFC, FPHC and PFIC rules all impose tax on US taxpayers who directly or indirectly own shares in the foreign company. A complex set of attribution rules attribute shares owned by family members, corporations, partnerships, trusts and estates to other family members, shareholders, partners and beneficiaries. These attribution rules do not, however, attribute foreign company shares owned by a properly designed variable life policy to the policy's US owner. These policies, therefore, offer an opportunity for US taxpayers to indirectly own shares in foreign mutual funds – taxed as PFICs if directly held – without being subject to the onerous tax implications and reporting requirements.

16.60 To achieve these tax benefits, the policy must comply with a series of requirements under Code §§ 7702 and 7702A. In addition, to achieve income tax deferral, the policy must comply with both the portfolio diversification rules of Code § 817(h) and the 'self-directed investor control' rulings.[52]

---

[51] As above.
[52] Rev Rul 2003–91, IRB 2003–33; Rev Rul 2003–92, IRB 2003–33; Rev Rul 82–54, 1982–1 CB 11; Rev Rul 81–225, 1981–2 CB 12; Rev Rul 80–274, 1980–2 CB 27; Rev Rul 77–85, 1977–1 CB 12. See *Christofferson v United States* 749 F 2d 513 (8th Cir 1984), cert denied, 473 US 905; see also PLR 200420017 (2 February 2004) (acceptability of fund-of-funds planning in private placement life insurance). Prior to the 2003 Revenue Rulings just cited, some practitioners believed that the

16.61 *US Pre-Immigration Planning*

16.61 The portfolio diversification rules basically require that no more than 55% of an insurance-wrapped fund be invested in any one equity or fund, no more than 70% in any two equities or funds, no more than 80% in any three equities or funds and not more than 90% in any four equities or funds.[53] For this purpose, the underlying investments of a fund or partnership – rather than the fund or partnership itself – would be considered if the fund or partnership is only available by investing in the insurance policy.[54]

16.62 The regulations had originally applied a similar 'look through' rule for private (non-US registered) investment partnerships, even if the investment partnership were available to the 'public' on a private placement basis. However, the IRS announced that the partnership look-through rule was inconsistent with the self-directed investor rule and would accordingly be modified to apply only if the partnership were not otherwise available to the public.[55]

16.63 The self-directed investor rulings basically hold that a policyholder cannot direct the insurance company to invest the cash value in specific equities or funds that are available to the public. For example, the insured cannot simply wrap a policy around an investment in Cisco stock or Fidelity's Magellan Fund, since these assets can be directly purchased by the public without buying the policy.

16.64 To achieve these tax benefits, an immigrant could purchase a qualified policy from a domestic US insurer. There are also several major international insurance companies that offer US tax compliant insurance policies through offshore subsidiaries. Aside from the added flexibility of the foreign insurers, the offshore policy offers an immigrant who is planning to be resident in the US for only a temporary period a substantial US tax benefit: upon leaving the US, the immigrant/emigrant can cash out the policy without any US tax exposure. In contrast, unless otherwise excepted by treaty, a non-US person who cashes out a US policy is considered to have US-sourced income subject to a 30% tax withheld at the source by the insurance company.[56]

E. Pre-immigration gift planning

16.65 Once an immigrant becomes domiciled in the US, he will be subject to US gift tax on worldwide transfers. Prior to becoming US domiciled, the non-citizen's

---

portfolio diversification rules superseded the prior self-directed investor rulings. However, in these rulings the IRS clearly stated otherwise: if both the portfolio diversification rules and the self-directed investor rulings are not complied with, there is no income tax deferral and annual increases in policy cash value will be taxed to the policy holder.

[53] Treas Reg § 1.817–5(b).
[54] Treas Reg § 1.817–5(f)(2)(i) and (ii). The regulations had originally applied this 'look through' rule to private placement (non-US registered) investment partnerships, even if individuals could make direct investment in the partnership. Many private placement hedge funds were structured as partnerships and 'wrapped' in insurance policies. However, the IRS announced that these regulations were inconsistent with the self-directed investor rule and would accordingly be modified to apply only if the partnership were not otherwise available to the public. Rev Rul 2003–92, IRB 2003–33.
[55] Rev Rul 2003–92, IRB 2003–33.
[56] Rev Rul 64–51, 1964–1 CB 322; Rev. Rul. 2004–75, IRB 2004–31. In choosing an offshore insurance policy, care should be taken that the offshore issuer has not made a section 953(d) election to be taxed as a US insurance company. This will be stated in the tax section of the offering document.

exposure to US gift tax is generally limited to US real property and (unless further limited by treaty) tangible personal property (including cash). For a variety of reasons, and subject to considering local law considerations, an immigrant to the US should consider transferring non-US property – free from US tax – prior to becoming a US domiciliary and achieving unparalleled US tax benefits. Some of these reasons are summarized below.

1. Avoid limits to US gift tax exemption

16.66 A US citizen or domiciliary can only make lifetime, tax-free gifts totaling $1m. (This is in addition to annual exclusion gifts and certain non-taxable gifts to charity and to US citizen spouses.) Unlike the US estate tax exemption, the gift tax exemption is not scheduled to increase in coming years (and the gift tax is not repealed, albeit temporarily, in 2010). An immigrant who wishes to make larger gifts – for example, to his children – should obviously consider doing so prior to becoming US domiciled.

> **Example**
>
> Nigel Nuworld has a £20m estate and would like to give each of his four children £1m each. If Nigel waited until he was a US domiciliary, only $1m of his gift would be exempt and he would owe gift taxes on the remaining gifts. If, however, Nigel were to make the gifts (using non-US property) prior to becoming US domiciled he would avoid the substantial US tax.[57]

2. Avoid marital deduction restrictions on gifts to non-citizen spouses

16.67 Gifts to non-US citizen spouses (whether by US citizens, domiciliaries or NDAs) do not qualify for the gift tax marital deduction. Instead, a donor is entitled to an annual exclusion of $114,000 (adjusted annually for inflation) for gifts to a non-US citizen spouse. An immigrant wishing to make a substantial gift to his non-US citizen spouse should accordingly consider doing so – using non-US property – prior to becoming a US domiciliary.[58]

16.68 An immigrant might consider making a large pre-immigration gift to his non-citizen spouse in order to balance the couple's respective estates. Effective US estate planning for married couples typically includes ensuring that the first spouse to die sets aside a portion of his or her estate equal to the US estate tax exemption so

---

[57] If Nigel were a UK domiciliary, he could give unlimited amounts outright and free of UK inheritance tax provided he survived seven years thereafter. Care would need to be taken, however, as to whether any UK capital gains taxes were applicable to the gift.
[58] Note that if he is a UK domiciled person then gifts to his UK domiciled spouse would be tax free. If the spouse is not UK domiciled then the gifts may still be inheritance tax free if he survives the gift by more than seven years.

16.69 *US Pre-Immigration Planning*

that this property will not be taxed in the survivor's estate.[59] The US estate tax applicable exclusion is currently $1.5m and is scheduled to increase to $3.5m by 2009. Assuming the exemptions remain as high as $3.5m, a married couple can effectively pass $7m to their heirs without US estate tax. To do so, however, the first spouse to die must have sufficient assets in his or her estate to take advantage of the estate tax applicable exclusion. Assume for purposes of the following examples that the US Congress has frozen the estate tax exemption at $3.5m.

Example

Nigel Nuworld and his wife, Noreen, have a combined estate of $7m – all in Nigel's name. The couple immigrate to the US and Noreen dies first. Since she has no assets, her estate plan cannot take advantage of the US estate tax exemption otherwise available to her. At Nigel's later death, the full $7m will be taxed in his estate and his $3.5m exemption will shelter only half of his estate from tax.

Example

Same facts as in the example above, but assume Nigel gave Noreen half of his assets prior to immigrating to the US. At Noreen's death, she is able to shelter her entire $3.5m estate from US estate tax, placing her property in a special trust for Nigel's benefit. No US estate tax is imposed on this trust at Noreen's death because of her applicable exclusion credit; no tax is imposed at Nigel's death because of the design of this trust. Nigel later then dies with only a $3.5m taxable estate, all of which is exempt from US estate tax. Had Nigel waited until after becoming domiciled in the US to make gifts to Noreen to build up her estate, he would be limited to annual exclusion gifts of only $114,000 per year.

3. Take advantage of the unlimited GST exemption

16.69 The GST exemption permits grandparents to make a certain level of tax-free gifts and bequests to grandchildren – either directly or through trusts for the interim generation. The GST exemption is $1.5m in 2004 and climbs to $3.5m in 2009. The GST exemption is available to citizens, domiciliaries and NDAs alike, and can be applied against relevant gifts or bequests subject to the US gift or estate tax. With respect to NDAs, this is accordingly limited to gifts or bequests of US situated property. Importantly, a NDA who makes a gift of non-US situated property – thus not subject to US gift tax – will not be subject to the GST. If the gift is in trust, the NDA will not be considered the all-important 'transferor' and, therefore, later events – such as distributions to grandchildren or the death of a child/beneficiary – will not be considered taxable generation-skipping transfers. Effectively, a NDA is granted an unlimited GST exemption for gifts of non-US property. An immigrant might thus consider making pre-immigration gifts of non-US situated property in order to take advantage of this unlimited GST exemption.

---

[59] See **CHAPTER 20**.

Pre-immigration gift planning **16.72**

Example

Christopher Cumbria has a £20m estate and five adoring grandchildren (and one 'black sheep' grandson, Spike, who has spiked hair, a pierced tongue and drug addiction). Prior to becoming US domiciled, Christopher buys each of his 'good' grandchildren a cottage in the Cotswolds. No US gift tax – or US GST – is imposed on these gifts. Christopher also still has his full GST exemption remaining, which he could use if and when Spike cleans up his act and is deemed worthy of a similar gift.

4. Transfer troublesome assets

16.70 Earlier in this chapter we described the US anti-avoidance rules and the adverse tax problems associated with a US income tax resident's ownership of interests in certain foreign corporations. Of particular concern is the application of the PFIC rules to a US resident's ownership of foreign mutual funds. Rather than immigrating to the US with the tax baggage associated with such investments, the immigrant might consider gifting those investments to family members who are not immigrating to the US.

5. Estate freeze

16.71 Prior to October 1990, a common US estate planning technique involved re-capitalizing a closely-held business investment into common and preferred shares. 90% (or more) of the company's value would be attributed to the preferred shares – with dividend and liquidation preferences. The common shares would represent a relatively small portion of the company's current value, but would, essentially, be entitled to all of the future growth. The senior generation would then keep the preferred shares and gift away the common, essentially freezing the value of his interest in the company to its current value.

Example

George Washington re-capitalizes his privately owned company – Valley Forge Realty Inc – into common and preferred shares. The company is appraised at $10m. The preferred have a $9.5m liquidation preference and provide for a non-cumulative dividend preference of $100 per share. In 1985, George gifts to his children the common shares valued at $500,000. Ten years later, George dies still holding the preferred shares. At that time, the company's value has increased to $15m. George's preferred shares (which are taxed in his estate) are still valued at only $9.5m, while the common shares (which he gifted away years earlier) have enjoyed all of the value growth.

16.72 In 1990, Congress enacted so-called 'special valuation' rules. These rules were designed to prevent estate freezing techniques and other perceived abuses. Under these rules, unless the preferred shares are properly designed (for example, with cumulative dividend rights), they will be considered as having no value for the purpose of determining the value of gifted common shares. In effect, the entire value of the company could be assigned to the common shares, ignoring the economic value attributed to the preferred.

> **Example**
>
> Same example as above, but George re-capitalizes Valley Forge Inc in 2004 and makes a gift of the common shares. George's gift is valued at $10m because his retained preferred shares are considered to have no value for purposes of valuing the gifted common. George owes substantial gift tax.

16.73 The special valuation rules apply for the purpose of determining the value of an individual's US taxable gift. These rules accordingly do not apply to gifts by NDAs of property not subject to US gift tax. Therefore, it would appear to still be possible for an immigrant to accomplish an effective estate freeze prior to becoming a US domiciliary.

> **Example**
>
> Christopher Cumbria, a UK domiciliary, owns New World Inc, a US company valued at $10m. Prior to moving to the US, Christopher re-capitalizes the company and is issued common and preferred shares. Christopher gifts the common shares to his children and retains the preferred. Even though New World Inc is a US company, Christopher's interest in that company is considered to be intangible personal property, gifts of which are not subject to US gift tax. The US special valuation rules thus would not apply to Christopher's pre-immigration gift. If Christopher later dies while a US domiciliary, his estate will include only his 'frozen' preferred shares.

6. Estate planning

16.74 Pre-immigration gifts have the effect of reducing the size of the donor's estate, thus reducing his or her exposure to US estate tax. See Section I (at **16.107** et seq) for a detailed discussion on additional pre-immigration US estate planning involving the creation of a so-called 'drop off trust' for the immigrant's benefit but designed to be excluded from the immigrant's US-taxable estate.

F. Pre-immigration gifts (to others) in trust

16.75 The previous section discussed a number of US tax benefits that might be enjoyed by an immigrant making gifts to others prior to becoming a US domiciliary. Many – if not all – of these tax benefits can be enjoyed for gifts made in trust. Caution is needed to ensure the trust achieves the US transfer tax (and, where relevant, income tax) objectives. If so, not only will the funding of the trust escape US gift tax but distributions from the trust will also be free of US transfer tax and assets remaining in the trust will escape estate tax and the GST.

1. Completed gift

16.76 The first objective is to ensure that the gift is considered complete for US gift tax purposes. A gift is *not* considered complete for US gift tax purposes if the donor retains dominion and control.[60] This can include:

- the power to revoke the trust;[61]
- the power as trustee to make discretionary distributions;[62]
- the power to name new beneficiaries;[63]
- the power to remove and replace 'related and subordinate' trustees;[64]
- a testamentary power to appoint the remainder interest;[65] and
- a beneficial interest in the trust such that, under relevant local law, the settlor's creditors can break the trust and attach trust assets.[66]

16.77 The settlor is deemed to have retained dominion or control even if the retained power can only be exercised in conjunction with a person not having a 'substantial adverse interest' in the trust.[67] For example, a power to revoke a trust only with the consent of a trustee or Protector who has no beneficial interest in the trust will cause the gift to be incomplete. Conversely, a power exercisable only in conjunction with an adverse party would make the gift complete.

2. Excluded from US taxable estate

16.78 Since one of the primary objectives of the pre-immigration gift is to remove the gifted property from the settlor/immigrant's US estate, the trust needs to be designed so as not to be included in the immigrant's estate. The factors (see **16.76**) that cause an immigrant's pre-immigration gift to a trust to be incomplete would also cause the trust to be included in US taxable estate if the immigrant dies while domiciled in the US. Other factors that could cause the pre-immigration gift trust to be included in the immigrant's US estate include:

- the trustee's power to make distributions that discharge the settlor's legal obligations (including the obligation of support);[68]

---

[60] Treas Reg § 25.2511–2(a).
[61] Treas Reg § 25.2511–2(c).
[62] Treas Reg § 25.2511–2(c) unless the power is limited by an ascertainable standard; Treas Reg § 25.2511–2(g).
[63] Treas Reg § 25.2511–2(c).
[64] Rev Rul 95–58, 1995–1 CB 191.
[65] Treas Reg § 25.2511–2(b).
[66] See Rev Rul 76–103, 1976–1 CB 293; *Comm'r v Vander Weele* 254 F 2d 895 (6th Cir 1958); *Paxton v Comm'r* 86 TC 785 (1986) (applying Washington law); *Outwin v Comm'r* 76 TC 153 (1981), acq 1981–2 CB 2 (applying Massachusetts law); and *Paolozzi v Comm'r* 23 TC 182 (1954).
[67] Treas Reg § 25.2511–2(e). The term 'substantial adverse interest' generally means a beneficial interest in the trust income or principal that is capable of monetary valuation and that would be adversely affected by the exercise of the power. See *Comm'r v Prouty* 115 F 2d 999 (1st Cir 1940); *Camp v Comm'r* 195 F 2d 999 (1st Cir 1952); Rev Rul 58–395, 1958–2 CB 398.
[68] Code § 2036; see *Estate of McKeon* 25 TC 697 (1956).

- retained power (even in conjunction with an adverse party) to control beneficial enjoyment of the trust property;[69]
- retained power to vote stock in certain closely-held corporations;[70]
- a retained reversionary interest valued at greater than 5%;[71]
- a retained general or limited power of appointment;[72]
- an 'incident of ownership' with respect to a trust-owned life insurance policy on the settlor's life (for example, the right to change beneficiaries).[73]

16.79 If the trust beneficiaries are (or might some day become) US domiciliaries or citizens, then it is also critical to design the gift trust so that their rights, powers and interests in the trust will not cause the property to be taxed in their estates. This issue is discussed in more detail at Section I (**16.107** et seq).

3. Grantor trust considerations

16.80 An immigrant creating a pre-immigration trust needs to also consider the US income tax implications of the gift trust, including whether the trust will be considered a grantor trust. If so, the immigrant settlor will be subject to US income tax as if she continued to own the underlying trust property.

16.81 In some circumstances, grantor trust status might have some indirect benefits. If the immigrant settlor is taxed as the grantor/owner of the trust, the settlor (not the trust or the beneficiaries) will be taxed on the trust income and gains. This technique indirectly confers further economic benefit on the trust and its beneficiaries while simultaneously reducing the settlor's estate. Even so, conventional wisdom in the US is that the settlor's payment of these taxes should not be considered taxable gifts. The settlor of a grantor trust is not paying the trust's taxes – he is paying his own taxes imposed by the grantor trust rules. Further, the IRS has ruled that the settlor will not be considered to have retained an interest in the trust (and thus will not be subject to estate tax exposure) even if the trust agreement allows the trustee to pay the settlor's US additional income taxes caused by the trust's grantor trust status.[74]

16.82 In other circumstances, the settlor might not wish to remain subject to continued US income taxes. For example, if the settlor has gifted an interest in a PFIC to a trust in order to escape the adverse US income tax implications of continued ownership, a gift into a grantor trust would not achieve the objective.

16.83 CHAPTER 12 discusses the grantor trust rules in some detail. Factors that could cause a trust to be considered a grantor trust include:

---

[69] Code § 2036(a)(2).
[70] Code § 2036(b).
[71] Code § 2037(a)(2).
[72] Code § 2036(a)(2) for a limited power and Code § 2041 for a general power.
[73] Code § 2042.
[74] Rev. Rul. 2004–64, 2004–27 IRB 7; see also PLR 199922062 (26 February 1999).

- power by the a trustee (other than an adverse or independent party) to make discretionary distributions;[75]
- power by a trustee to add to the class of beneficiaries;[76]
- the settlor's spouse as a beneficiary;[77]
- the power to substitute assets, even for assets of equal value;[78]
- a foreign trust with current (or potential) US beneficiaries created by:
    (a) a NRA within five years of the settlor becoming a US income tax resident; or
    (b) a US taxpayer (regardless when created).[79]

Careful consideration of these rules will be required to avoid (or, where desired, create) grantor trust status. If the pre-immigration trust is a foreign trust, the immigrant will need to consider the implications of Code §§ 679 and 684, discussed at **16.50** et seq. See also **CHAPTER 8** and **CHAPTER 12**.

16.84 To avoid the possible adverse implications of Code § 684 as well as the onerous reporting obligations that accompany foreign grantor trusts, the immigrant might fund a US (rather than foreign) pre-immigration trust. Unless the settlor or the settlor's spouse were a beneficiary of the US trust, it should be possible to design the trust to be a non-grantor trust (if this is important). The US trust will be subject to current US tax on its current income and gains, but this should typically not result in more tax than if the trust were a foreign trust and the wealthy US immigrant/settlor were taxed as the grantor/owner.

G. UK (and other foreign) tax considerations to pre-US immigration gift planning

16.85 The pre-immigration gift planning (discussed at Section E, **16.65** et seq) generally applies to any foreign national intending to take up permanent residence in the United States whether emigrating from the UK or another country.

16.86 Most emigrants from non-UK Commonwealth countries come from civil law countries where the Anglo-American concept of domicile is not generally recognized. Instead, civil law countries generally impose inheritance and/or gift taxation on the basis of income tax residency under civil code rules. In civil law countries, an income tax resident may, therefore, be subject to inheritance or gift taxation on a global basis even though he or she is not a domiciliary of that country within the Anglo-American concept.

---

[75] Code § 674.
[76] Code § 674(b)(5)–(7) and (c).
[77] Code § 677.
[78] Code § 675.
[79] Code § 679.

16.87   *US Pre-Immigration Planning*

16.87   Civil law countries are increasingly applying 'tail off' rules for emigrating nationals. Both Sweden and the Netherlands have ten-year tail off rules for inheritance tax purposes, Germany has a five-year tail off rule[80] and Japan is understood to tax distributions from trusts if, within five years, either the settlor or the distributee was a domiciled national. Further, some civil law countries (including Germany and Spain) impose transfer tax on the *donee* and not the donor.

16.88   A number of specific planning considerations are relevant to emigrants from civil law countries. These include community ownership of property, which may apply upon marriage in such country or according to subsequent election in, or out, rather than automatically by residence. Also relevant are the potential continuing effect of forced heirship provisions in the country of former residence, recognition of trusts and, with respect to real and personal property, the availability (or not) of probate in the US (prior to acquiring a domicile there). Also relevant is the applicability of the law of situs, domicile, residence or nationality with regard to the formal and essential validity of wills, including the application of the *renvoi* doctrine. These considerations will not be further discussed here but must be specifically addressed in any such planning situation.

16.89   For immigrants who are UK domiciliaries, complex integrated US/UK planning is required to ensure optimum structuring and to avoid potential pitfalls.

16.90   The optimum US planning may involve setting up pre-immigration trusts prior to arrival. The main difficulty here is that creating such a trust would permanently attribute to it the settlor's current UK domicile for UK inheritance tax purposes, with the consequence that a distribution of assets or termination of any interest in possession could potentially or actually attract UK inheritance tax. This is notwithstanding that the settlor may at that time have ceased to be UK domiciled himself and that the trust assets are invested outside the UK.[81]

16.91   The treaty does not change this taxation[82] for UK nationals or domiciliaries emigrating to the US.

16.92   The optimum structure will:

---

[80]   ErbStG, § 2, para 1, no 1b.

[81]   For example, if the settlor had an interest in possession which terminated at his death, while domiciled in the US, the trustees would be liable for UK inheritance tax (IHT) – even though had he owned the assets outright, the settlor's non-UK sited free estate would have been exempt from UK IHT by reason of the settlor's non UK domicile at his death. Similarly, if the trustees terminated the settlor's interest in possession during his life and no other person had an interest in possession thereafter, the trust would become a discretionary trust subject to a 20% IHT charge at that time and the decennial charges regime subsequently. See IHTA 1984, Pt III, Ch III and see generally **CHAPTER 13**.

[82]   Treaty article 5(4) preserves UK IHT taxing authority over trusts unless, at the time of settlement, the settlor was not a UK national and was domiciled in the US (in such case, IHT exposure would be limited to UK real and business property held by the trust). Treaty article 5(3), which contains a corresponding provision relating to the continuing right of the US to tax generation skipping trusts, is now moot – both because the GST then in effect has since been repealed and replaced by a different GST and because regulations limit the current GST's application to NDA transfers to a trust which are either subject to US gift or estate tax; under treaty article 5(1), such transfers by a UK domiciled NDA are only subject to US gift or estate tax (and hence GST) if the gifted property is US real estate or business property.

G. Tax considerations to pre-US immigration gift planning   16.96

1. allow a pre-immigration trust to be fully funded while the settlor is still UK domiciled, but protected by the treaty from being US domiciled; *and*

2. allow for exempt or potentially IHT exempt trust distributions or transfers of assets.

16.93 If a pre-immigration trust is warranted, the two primary ways which the UK legislation permits avoidance of the tax disadvantage of the trust's attributed UK domicile of the settlor at time of funding are:

- potentially exempt distributions (which become tax free where the holder of the interest in possession survives for a further seven years); and

- investment in a range of permitted exempt assets.

In this regard, to remove the trust assets from US gift and estate tax, the settlor himself cannot retain a life interest or an interest in possession in trust assets (unless such interest is terminated more than three years before his death).[83] Further, any distributions to US citizens or domiciliaries (though potentially exempt from UK inheritance tax) will obviously be subject to US estate tax at the death of such person if still a citizen or domiciliary.

16.94 If the settlor's spouse were given an interest in possession in a pre-immigration trust and she died first, UK IHT could be deferred if her surviving husband had a sequential interest in possession in the trust assets. Whilst for UK purposes this could be built into any trust at the outset, for US purposes this should be achieved by conferring on her a special testamentary power of appointment under which she has the ability to create such an interest. Whilst UK IHT would arise at his subsequent death, it is possible during his lifetime for the trust to make potentially exempt distributions to other beneficiaries who are not likely to be US citizens or domiciliaries at their death, or who are US citizens or domiciliaries, but who have available US estate/GST tax exclusions (up to $3.5m per spouse in 2009) which could be used to remove such assets from US transfer taxes.

16.95 Given the vagaries of such planning, the trustees might instead consider mitigating any potential UK inheritance tax by investing, at an appropriate time, in assets designated as exempt by the IHT legislation (such as UK government securities qualifying as excluded property where owned by certain discretionary or interest in possession trusts).[84] While individual ownership must be avoided – in order to avoid US gift and estate tax exposure – such assets can be owned in trust if a qualifying person has in interest in possession or if all beneficiaries are qualifying persons.[85]

16.96 Since the pre-immigration trust will retain its UK attributed domicile if distributions cannot be made to persons without potential subsequent exposure to US transfer taxes, other viable distributees must therefore be found.

---

[83] Code §§ 2036 (retained life interests) and 2035 (taxing 'string' interests held by the settlor within three years of death).
[84] Under IHTA 1984, s 6(2), a non UK domiciled individual is exempt from UK tax where he owns such assets outright.
[85] IHTA 1984, s 48(4).

16.97 Less complex issues arise where the taxpayer is able to make outright gifts prior to arrival in the US. The UK legislation permits a variety of opportunities for giving without triggering IHT,[86] although care is always required where CGT may be in point.

- Outright gifts are unlimited when made to a spouse in the case where either both parties are non-UK domiciled or the donee spouse is UK domiciled. Furthermore, unlike most other transfers, gifts may generally be made between spouses (irrespective of domicile status) without triggering UK CGT concerns.

- Outright gifts of unlimited amounts by a UK domiciliary to his non UK domiciled spouse or gifts to his children or other third-party individuals can give rise to IHT. However, if the donor survives for seven years the gifts become exempt.[87]

- Any desire to make gifts for the benefit a UK charity should also be addressed prior to arrival in the US since the gifts will be exempt for UK IHT purposes but not for US purposes.

H. Examine existing trusts for US estate tax exposure

16.98 Prior to becoming a US domiciliary, an immigrant will also want to examine existing trusts – created by the immigrant or others – to determine if the retained or conferred powers would cause the trust to be included in his or her US taxable estate. This issue can be relevant to members of the immigrant's family who are also moving to the US who might also acquire a US domicile.

1. Trusts funded by the settlor/immigrant

16.99 An immigrant who funded a trust prior to becoming a US domiciliary – including trusts funded many years before with no US planning objectives – will need to examine the trusts to determine whether the trust creates any US estate tax exposure.

16.100 The factors that would cause transfers to a trust to be considered incomplete for US gift tax purposes (summarised at **16.76**), include retained powers to revoke the trust, or name new beneficiaries or to appoint the trust property at death. If, under US gift tax rules, the settlor's gift to the trust would be considered incomplete, then the trust would be included in the settlor's US taxable estate if he dies while a US domiciliary.

16.101 Also, as noted at **16.78**, other factors could also cause the trust to be taxed in the settlor's estate include:

---

[86] See **CHAPTER 3** and **CHAPTER 4**.
[87] In the event of death within seven years the legislation treats the original gift as taxable at the time when it was made. Accordingly, the fact that the transferor later loses his UK domicile is unlikely to be of assistance in mitigating the tax due on the original gift.

- the trustee's power to make distributions that discharge the settlor's legal obligations (including the obligation of support);
- retained power (even in conjunction with an adverse party) to control beneficial enjoyment of the trust property;
- retained power to vote stock in certain closely-held corporations;
- a retained reversionary interest valued at greater than 5%;
- a retained general or limited power of appointment;
- an 'incident of ownership' with respect to a trust-owned life insurance policy on the settlor's life (for example, the right to change beneficiaries).

2. Trusts funded by others

16.102 The immigrant might also be a beneficiary, trustee or even protector of a trust funded by others. For example, the immigrant's deceased parents might have established a trust for his benefit. In those instances, the concern is whether the interests or powers of the immigrant would cause the trust to be included in his US taxable estate if he dies while a US domiciliary. Here the primary concern is whether the immigrant would be considered to have a general power of appointment.[88]

16.103 A general power of appointment is defined as a power to appoint trust property to oneself, one's estate, one's creditors or creditors of one's estate. This could include both a testamentary power to appoint trust property to an unlimited class or a power during life to withdraw all trust property. If the immigrant is trustee of a trust formed by another and has the authority to make distributions to himself, the immigrant would be considered to have a general power of appointment unless his distribution authority as trustee were limited by an ascertainable standard.

16.104 A beneficiary might also be considered to have a general power of appointment if he can remove and replace trustees, for example, in his capacity as protector. The IRS takes the position that the power to replace trustees indirectly confers the powers of the trustee on the power holder – even if the power holder cannot name himself as trustee. If the power holder is a beneficiary and can replace trustees, the power holder/beneficiary could thus be considered to have an indirect power to make distributions to himself – a general power of appointment.

16.105 There are two relevant exceptions. First, if the trustee's power to make distributions to the beneficiary is limited by an ascertainable standard related to health, maintenance, support and education, the beneficiary will not be considered to have a general power of appointment.[89] Second, if the beneficiary can only

---

[88] Code § 2041.
[89] See, for example, PLR 9310012 (10 December 1992), citing Code § 2041(b)(1) and Treas Reg § 20.2041–1(c)(2).

remove and replace independent trustees – more specifically, trustees who are not 'related and subordinate' to the beneficiary – the powers of the trustee will not be attributed to the beneficiary.[90]

16.106 Therefore, if:

(a) an immigrant serves as Protector of a trust for the benefit of others;

(b) the Trustee has the authority to add to the class of beneficiaries, and

(c) the Protector is not precluded from being named as beneficiary,

the convergence of these factors could cause US estate tax exposure in an otherwise innocent situation.

Example

Nigel Nuworld's business partner, Marcus Rich, established an offshore trust for the primary benefit of Mr Rich's family. Nigel was named as protector, with authority, among other things, to remove and replace trustees without limitations. The trustee has a broad discretion to distribute among beneficiaries and has the authority to add to the class of beneficiaries with the consent of the protector. While the trust prohibits a trustee from being appointed as beneficiary, the deed does not preclude the protector from being appointed. Under principles discussed at **16.104**, Nigel's power as protector to replace trustees will attribute the trustee's powers to Nigel. Therefore, Nigel would be considered to have the indirect power to:

- name himself as beneficiary; and
- make distributions to himself as beneficiary.

Nigel would thus be considered to possess a general power of appointment.

Rather than risking adverse US estate tax implications, an immigrant serving as protector for another person's trust should seriously consider resigning that post prior to becoming a US domiciliary.

I. Pre-immigration estate planning – drop off trusts

16.107 OK. The immigrant has examined all pre-existing trusts to ensure that he has no retained or conferred interests or powers that would cause the trust to be included in his estate were he later to die a US domiciliary. The immigrant has also gifted to others (outright or in trust) all property that he feels comfortable parting with and retaining sufficient assets for his own personal benefit. He has also made gifts to his wife to ensure that she will have sufficient assets to fully utilize her US estate tax exemption credit if she dies first (again, while a US domiciliary). What is

---

[90] PLR 9735023 (30 May 1997), citing Rev Rul 95–58, 1995–1 CB 191, in which the settlor's power to remove and replace trustees who are not related and subordinate to the settlor will not cause trust to be included in settlor's estate.

I. Pre-immigration estate planning   **16.110**

left to do? Depending on the size of the immigrant's estate (and, if married, his spouse's estate), the immigrant might consider a 'drop off trust'.

16.108 The estate tax objective of a drop off trust (so called because the immigrant 'drops off' assets in the trust before moving to the US) is to set aside a portion of the immigrant's assets in a trust that will both:

- benefit the immigrant/settlor; *and*
- keep the property from being taxed in the settlor's estate if he dies while a US domiciliary.

A properly drafted trust can also legitimately offer significant protection of assets from future speculative claims – a paramount consideration for an individual of means living in the highly litigious United States. However, if the settlor also wishes to be a beneficiary, only a properly structured and funded *offshore* trust has the potential to legitimately protect trust-held assets from both speculative litigants and US estate, gift and GST taxes.

16.109 Before examining the concept of the drop off trust in more detail, the immigrant should consider whether such planning is necessary or desirable. Factors relevant to this consideration include the following.

- **The size of the immigrant's estate relative to the US estate tax applicable exclusion** – currently that exclusion is $1.5m but is scheduled to increase to $3.5m by 2009. If the immigrant's estate is likely to be less than the exclusion, the drop off trust might be overkill.

- **The projections regarding the permanence of US estate tax repeal** – that tax is scheduled to be repealed in 2010 – for one year – but Congress is likely to act before then to enact some sort of permanent relief either in the form of permanent repeal (unlikely in our view) or frozen high exemptions (more likely). If the immigrant has faith in Congress to repeal the estate tax – and has faith in his own longevity to see it out until repeal is made permanent – then the drop off trust is unnecessary.

- **The immigrant's desire to transfer substantial wealth to his family** – in many instances, wealthy families find that – through prior planning and good fortune – substantial wealth has already been bestowed on the next generations. 'How rich (or richer) do I want to make my kids?', they ask. If the answer is that the immigrant is planning to leave his estate to charity at death, then no fancy, pre-immigration planning should be required unless the desired beneficiary is not a US charity.

- **An understanding of the immigrant's lack of guaranteed benefits from or control over the drop off trust assets** – In order to get something (estate tax mitigation) the settlor must give up something (control, unlimited use and benefit of the assets). Just how comfortable is the immigrant with this idea? Many wealthy individuals are control freaks – it can be what made them wealthy – and the notion of losing even an ounce of control of the hard-earned (or, in some cases, easily-inherited) wealth makes the immigrant nauseous.

16.110 After considering and carefully weighing the possible benefits and real drawbacks of the drop off trust, the immigrant decides that some of this pre-immigration planning is warranted. So what is required and possible in the trust's design? First, the immigrant/settlor's transfer to the trust must be considered a completed gift. This issue is discussed at **16.76** and applies with equal force where the immigrant/settlor is intended to be trust beneficiary. Accordingly, the settlor cannot retain the power to amend or revoke the trust, the power to add beneficiaries, or a testamentary power of appointment.

16.111 Second, the settlor should not retain any 'strings' over the trust that would cause US estate tax inclusion of trust assets should the settlor die domiciled in the US. The principal 'string' interests or powers which must be avoided overlap with many of the completed gift principles and include:

- revocability of the trust;
- a settlor retained rights to trust income or assets (such as a settlor retained life interest or annuity interest); and
- the settlor's *possession* of such a retained power of appointment (regardless of with whom such power is shared).[91]

16.112 Careful drafting of an irrevocable drop off trust must also avoid other string interests which would also cause estate tax inclusion, including a settlor retained 'reversionary' interest exceeding 5% of trust assets or the settlor's retention of 'incidents of ownership' (such as the power to change policy beneficiaries) with respect to a life insurance policy on the settlor's life owned by the trust.[92]

16.113 Third – for the control-freak immigrant – the immigrant settlor can retain a right to remove and replace independent trustees. The IRS had originally taken the position that a settlor's power to replace trustees (even independent institutional trustees) would cause the settlor to be treated as retaining the power of the trustee.[93] This, in turn, could cause the trust to be taxed in the settlor's estate. After losing this issue in the courts, the IRS relented, conceding only that estate tax inclusion would not result if the settlor could replace the trustee only with an independent trustee – defined as one that is not 'related and subordinate' to the settlor.[94] The term 'related and subordinate' is borrowed – for lack of originality – from the income tax grantor trust rules, and generally means certain family members, subordinate employees or closely held companies.[95]

16.114 Fourth, as noted above, the settlor cannot retain a *right* to trust income or corpus. But we have said that the settlor can be a beneficiary. What gives? The key is distinguishing a 'right' from a beneficial interest. Rights are bad, *discretionary*

---

[91] Code §§ 2035–2038.
[92] Code §§ 2037 (reversionary interests), 2041(special and general powers of appointment) and 2042 (life insurance).
[93] Rev Rul 79–353, 1979–2 CB 325.
[94] Rev Rul 95–58, 1995–1 CB 191.
[95] Code § 672(c) defined the following 'related' persons as presumably 'subordinate' to the grantor: the power holder's spouse (if living with the settlor), parents, issue, siblings, and any employee of the settlor, of a company in which the settlor's and the trust's voting control is significant or a subordinate employee of a company of which the settlor is an executive.

beneficial interests are okay. The courts have ruled – albeit years ago – that a settlor's retained interests in a discretionary trust do not rise to the level of a 'right' such as would cause estate tax inclusion.[96]

16.115   There are a number of exceptions to this rule:

- where there is an agreement with the trustees that the settlor would be allowed continued enjoyment of transferred property or trust income.[97] The ability to benefit is probably assumed by most settlors, but to avoid a *de facto* retained interest, an independent, professional trustee should be used and care taken in drafting trust deeds, letters of wishes and correspondence with trustees not to erroneously imply that such an agreement exists;

- where the settlor is trustee or retains the power to remove and replace trustees, unless only a person other than 'related or subordinate party' can be appointed;[98]

- where the trustee's discretion is subject to a standard that can be enforced by the settlor as beneficiary.[99] For example, if the settlor retains discretionary income as needed for his support and maintenance, and relevant local law would give local courts the ability to enforce this standard and direct the trustee to make distributions for the stated purposes, the settlor would be considered to have a retained 'right';

- where, under applicable creditors rights laws, the settlor's creditors can reach the trust income to pay the settlor's debts.[100]

16.116   This last factor is potentially the most troublesome. Virtually every discretionary trust has a 'spendthrift' provision that purports to prevent the trust assets from being diverted from the intended beneficiaries to pay the claims of

---

[96] *Comm'r v Irving Trust Co 147 F 2d 946 (2d Cir 1945)*; *Sherman v Comm'r 9 TC 594 (1947)*.
[97] Dodge, BNA Tax Management Portfolio 50–5, *Transfers with Retained Interests and Powers* at note 868.
[98] *US v O'Malley 383 US 627 (1966)*; Rev Rul 73–142, 1973–1 CB 405; Rev Rul 95–58, 1995–1 CB 191.
[99] *Estate of Boardman v Comm'r 20 TC 871 (1953)*, acq 1954–1 CB 3, holding that distribution of income to settlor as trustees determined necessary for her 'comfort, support and/or happiness' was a retained interest.
[100] Rev Rul 76–103, 1976–1 CB 293; *Comm'r v Vander Weele 254 F 2d 895 (6th Cir 1958)*; *Paxton v Comm'r 86 TC (1986)* (applying Washington Law); *Outwin v Comm'r 76 TC 153 (1981)*, acq 1981–2 CB 2 (applying Massachusetts law); and *Paolozzi v Comm'r 23 TC 182 (1954)*. See also, Rev Rul 77–378, 1977–2 CB 347 (no state law specified), PLR 9332006 (20 August 1992) and *Estate of German v Comm'r 85–1 USTC ¶ 13,610 (1985)*, hold that a transfer to an irrevocable discretionary trust of which the settlor is a beneficiary may result in the transfer's being a completed gift and not includible in the settlor's estate *if under state law the settlor's creditors could not reach the assets transferred to the trust*. A contrary result follows if they can. See Restatement (Second) of Trusts § 156(2) (where local fraudulent conveyance law applies, trustee is presumed to exercise its maximum discretion in favor of the settlor as a discretionary beneficiary). As a consequence of the maximum discretion rule, a settlor is generally deemed to have retained rights to trust assets for both gift and estate tax purposes. Cf PLR 9332006 (20 August 1992) (foreign trust was a completed gift because under the trust's proper law creditors could not reach assets); PLR 9837007 (10 June 1998) (completed gift under Alaska Asset Protection Statute, but the IRS refused to rule on the absence of a settlor retained interest for estate tax purposes); PLR 199917001 (15 January 1999) (no completed gift because under California law creditors could reach discretionary trust assets).

16.117 *US Pre-Immigration Planning*

beneficiaries' creditors. But do those provisions prevent claims by the settlor's creditors? Here, the laws of the US and certain foreign trust jurisdictions differ in an important way.

1. US asset protection trusts

16.117 The law in most US states is that a 'self-settled' trust (that is, where the settlor is a beneficiary) will not be exempt from the claims of the settlor/beneficiary's creditors.[101] Such *domestic* trusts can also be exposed to claims of creditors under the Uniform Fraudulent Conveyances Act or the Uniform Fraudulent Transfers Act.[102] As noted at **16.115**, there is precedent that a settlor-beneficiary of a *domestic* trust has a retained interest in trust assets (under such local law) and hence all the trust assets are exposed not only to creditors, but also to estate tax. Further, if the settlor's creditor can reach trust asset, then (as noted at **16.76**) the settlor's gift to the trust will be considered incomplete and distributions from the trust to others during the settlor's life would be considered taxable gifts.

16.118 Since 1997, a few states – Alaska, Delaware, Nevada, Rhode Island and Utah – have enacted statutes overruling, in varying fashion, the 'self-settled' exception to the spendthrift trust rule.[103] Generally, these statutes are intended to create a domestic 'asset protection trust' alternative and specifically apply even though the settlor is a discretionary beneficiary.[104] Each statute has its own restrictions, limitations and exceptions.

16.119 These statutes are primarily intended for US citizens and domiciliaries who are seeking asset protection. Although some estate planning benefits are touted by practitioners and lawyers in these jurisdictions, estate tax planning is typically of secondary importance to the domestic settlor.

16.120 It would be unwise for an immigrant to attempt to create a pre-immigration Drop Of Trust under any of these domestic statutes. To the extent the relevant domestic statutes carve out exceptions for certain creditors – for example, for tort claims, spousal and child support obligations – the domestic trust remains subject to certain creditor claims and thus arguably could be included within the settlor's taxable estate. Further, there are serious and yet unresolved conflict of law

---

[101] See eg Cal Probate Code § 15304.
[102] See eg Cal Civil Code § 3439 et seq, applicable to creditor claims arising before *or after* transfer of assets to the trust, with a seven year statute of limitations.
[103] See eg AS 34.40.110 (Alaska 1997), 12 Del CS 3570 et seq (Delaware 1997), NRS 166 (Nevada 1999) and RS Chapter 18–9 (Rhode Island 1999), discussed in 'Current Asset Protection Techniques', a 2003 memorandum prepared by Gideon Rothschild, Moses and Singer LLP, New York.
[104] The Delaware, Nevada and Rhode Island statutes allow the settlor power to veto distributions and retain a testamentary special power of appointment (to appoint by will trust assets to persons other than the settlor or his creditors). Under the Delaware statute, a settlor may retain:
- current income;
- annual annuity payments from a charitable remainder trust;
- annual 'unitrust' payments of up to 5% of current trust value; and
- principal payments under an ascertainable standard (for the settlor's maintenance, education, support or health).

I. Pre-immigration estate planning   **16.122**

issues where the creditors, settlor or even some of the trust assets are located in jurisdictions that follow the old 'self-settled' rule. The US Constitution requires the states to give 'full faith and credit' to judgments in another state,[105] but does that require a state like California to respect the asset protection trust laws of Alaska or for Alaska to respect the judgment of a California creditor against a California debtor? One suspects that assets and custodians located outside of Alaska are at risk.

2. Foreign asset protection trusts

16.121 The 'self-settled' exception to the US spendthrift trust rule is found in some, but not all, non-US trust law. Further, a number of offshore jurisdictions otherwise subject to the English common law – including the 1571 Statute of Elizabeth which is the basis for the American uniform fraudulent transfer acts – have enacted statutes which impose statutory limitations in time and effect on a creditor's right to challenge a trust settled under such law.[106] A properly planned and structured *foreign* trust should, therefore, allow the settlor to be both a discretionary beneficiary of the pre-immigration trust *and* preserve the benefit of removing assets from both estate and gift tax and the reach of future unknown creditors.

16.122 Generally, if an immigrant fully settles a trust subject to an appropriate foreign proper law with foreign professional trustees prior to immigrating to the US, foreign creditor rights law, if any, should apply to any subsequent challenge to the trust by a US resident creditor.[107] Even though a subsequent US creditor might assert that US state law should apply under 'conflicts of law' principles (eg subsequent residence of the settlor and trust beneficiaries in a US state), such a creditor should be generally precluded from reaching trust assets due to a US court's lack of *in personam* jurisdiction over a foreign trustee and lack of *in rem* jurisdiction over trust assets (with the possible exception of trust-owned US real property which has benefited from the US creditor's services).[108]

---

[105] United States Constitution, article IV, section 1
[106] See Rothschild, 'Establishing and Drafting Offshore Asset Protection Trusts', 23 Estate Planning 65 (February 1996), listing as of 1996 the following jurisdictions with favorable asset protection laws: Anguilla, Antigua, Bahamas, Barbados, Belize, Bermuda, Cayman Islands, Cook Islands, Cyprus, Gibraltar, Labuan, Marshall Islands, Mauritius, Nevis, Niue, St Vincent, St Lucia, Seychelles, Turks and Caicos. Offshore island jurisdictions generally do not impose gift, inheritance or capital gains taxes and most do not impose income, sales or VAT taxes.
[107] Restatement (Second) of Conflicts of Laws § 273, gives effect to a settlor's choice of foreign law with respect to the assignability of a beneficiary's interest in *movables* owned by the trust.
[108] For example, see *In re Portnoy, 201 BR 685 (1996 Bankr SDNY)*, discussed at **6.21**, in which the court applied, under conflict of law principles, New York law in determining whether the transfer was fraudulent, but lacked *in personam* jurisdiction over the Jersey trustee to set aside the trust assets (*in rem* jurisdiction over the assets would also generally be lacking, particularly if the custodian were not a US resident). Under Jersey law, which does not contain an 'asset protection' statute (making it a *favored* jurisdiction since such statutes could be viewed as a 'badge of fraud' for UFTA purposes), relief would have been limited to the Jersey bankruptcy statute, which would not apply to a non resident bankrupt where there were no Jersey sited assets. See generally, Rothschild, Rubin and Blattmachr, 'Self-Settled Spendthrift Trusts: Should a Few Bad Apples Spoil the Bunch', 32 Vanderbilt Journal of Transnational Law 763 (May 1999).

J. UK tax implications for drop off trusts

16.123 For US estate tax purposes, any interest in possession, life interest or legal life estate held by a person *other than the settlor* simply lapses in value and is not exposed to US estate tax on death of the life tenant. Such an interest (if indefeasible) does have value, according to IRS actuarial tables, for US gift tax purposes and will be subject to gift tax if *voluntarily* relinquished inter vivos *by* the life tenant.

16.124 In contrast, for UK inheritance tax purposes, the holder of an interest in possession is deemed to own the trust principal, as well as the income, with the result that termination of the interest results in an inheritance tax chargeable event, with exceptions for excluded property trusts, exempt assets and certain successive interests in possession. Further, a chargeable event can occur even if the *trustees* terminate an interest in possession (a power which is typically given trustees in UK interest in possession trusts). The inheritance tax position of the holder of the interest in possession can be impacted (for example, in effect, his nil-rate band may be allocated to the transfer) even though he is powerless to prevent the termination of his interest. However, the tax attributable is paid out of the trust assets.

16.125 If a person immigrating to the US is a UK domiciled settlor, the pre-immigration trust will almost always have at least one interest in possession holder – to qualify the transfer into the trust as a potentially exempt transfer. For US estate tax purposes, an interest in possession should never initially (or prudently, ever) be held by the settlor, even though terminable by the trustees.[109] Retained interests subject to a condition *subsequent* (eg terminable by the trustees) could subject trust assets to estate tax inclusion under the statutory language which includes interests retained by the settlor 'for his life or for any period not ascertainable without reference to his death or for any period which does not in fact end before his death'.[110] Further, retained interests or powers held by the settlor within three years of his death cause inclusion of trust held assets.[111]

16.126 Arguably, an interest in possession *subsequently* conferred on the settlor by the trustees acting in their independent discretion should not fall within the concept of a legal interest or the enjoyment of property which was 'retained' by the settlor.[112] However, retained interests subject to a condition precedent (eg where the settlor has a successive life interest) are generally caught if possessed at death.[113]

---

[109] With respect to an interest in possession held by persons *other than* the settlor, it would seem that the trustee's termination of such interest in possession in pre-immigration trust (which would have been a *completed* gift trust) arguably would not be subject to US gift tax. The holder of the defeasible interest is not making a voluntary disposition of his trust interest; the interest is terminated by the trustee. Even if the interest in possession beneficiary were somehow treated as having made a gift of his trust interest, the valuation of that interest would arguably be negligible given its defeasible nature.

[110] Code § 2036(a).

[111] Code § 2035(a) includes transfers or relinquishment of an interest in property *by the settlor* within three years of death.

[112] Stephens, Maxfeld, Lind & Calfee *Federal Estate and Gift Taxation* (7th edn, 1997) Warren, Gorham & Lamont, at p 4–154, n 42.

[113] Code § 2036(a).

16.127 Although in certain existing trusts it may be necessary to evaluate the risk in terminating the settlor's retained interest in possession or subsequently granting such an interest, in normal pre-immigration trust planning the settlor's interest in a foreign trust should at most be limited to inclusion in a discretionary class of beneficiaries (eg with respect to capital). Further, in planning for larger estates, or where a US trust is used, it may be advisable not to name the settlor as a beneficiary at all (although he could be added) or to exclude him and establish a separate pre-immigration trust of which he would be a member of the beneficial class.[114]

16.128 Since under UK inheritance law, an immigrant who severs his ties to the UK and moves to the US permanently will only retain UK domicile for three full UK tax years, the treaty double domicile tie-breaker rules could cause him to become solely US domiciled after three rather than six years, eg on 6 April 2008 if, for example, he were to leave in June 2004.[115] Such an immigrant would have to fully fund a pre-immigration trust prior to this tie-breaker date in order to avoid US gift tax on funding the trust.

16.129 However such a trust would permanently acquire the settlor's UK domicile for UK inheritance tax purposes with the consequence that a distribution from the trust or termination of any interest in possession would potentially, or actually, attract UK inheritance tax.[116] As discussed in Section G (**16.85** et seq), UK inheritance tax exit strategies include exempt and potentially exempt distributions, as well as the trust's investing in exempt assets.

---

[114] It should be noted that for UK purposes the various tax anti-avoidance legislation will generally apply to tax the settlor in circumstances where he (and in the case of income and gains taxes, also his spouse) has not been fully excluded from all possible benefit. Where this has not occurred, he will at all times be regarded as potentially capable of benefiting. Inclusion in a class of potential discretionary beneficiaries would generally cause the trust to fall within the UK reservation of benefit rules. This would cause ongoing inclusion of the trust assets in the settlor's UK inheritance taxable estate. See **CHAPTER 1**.

[115] Technically, 'domicile' for UK purposes refers to that status within a jurisdiction with its own laws, eg a country such as England and Wales, Scotland or Northern Ireland, or a province, state or canton such as Quebec, Florida or Vaud. Loss of 'UK' domicile after the relevant period would, therefore, require factual abandonment of, say, English domicile and acquisition of a new domicile of choice in, say, Florida, from the outset and thereafter continuously throughout the tail-off period. UK advice would prudently be sought that there is no reversion to a UK domicile of origin if the new domicile of choice is changed during this three-year period, eg by the client moving from Florida to California. The shorter the duration of the stay in the first state, the more likely the Revenue are to argue that, in fact, no permanent change has been made to the prior UK domicile status. It should be noted that the burden of proof is on the person asserting the change.

[116] For example, if the settlor's wife had an interest in possession that terminated at her death while domiciled in the US, the trustees would be liable for UK inheritance tax under the treaty if the trust then became a discretionary trust – even though had the wife owned the assets outright, her non-UK sited free estate would have been exempt from UK inheritance tax by reason of the wife's non-UK domicile at her death. Similarly, if the trustees terminated the wife's interest in possession during her life and no other person had an interest in possession thereafter, the trust would become a discretionary trust subject to a 20% IHT charge at that time and the decennial charges regime subsequently. See IHTA 1984, Pt III, Ch III and see generally **CHAPTER 13** and Section G (**16.85** et seq).

16.130 *US Pre-Immigration Planning*

K. Pre-immigration GST planning

16.130   In previous sections of this chapter, we have examined strategies – some involving pre-immigration transfers – in order to mitigate US gift and estate tax exposure. If all works as planned, the US GST should also be avoided.

1. Pre-immigration gifts

16.131   An immigrant who makes a completed gift of non-US property prior to becoming a US domiciliary will not be considered the 'transferor' for GST purposes. Such gifts directly to grandchildren (or in trust for their benefit) – even if the grandchildren are US citizens or domiciliaries – will not be considered direct skips and not subject to GST. If the immigrant is not considered the 'transferor' with respect to gifts in trust, then events that would otherwise be considered GST taxable terminations or distributions will not be taxed.

2. Trusts excluded from immigrant settlor/beneficiary's estate

16.132   If a pre-immigration trust is drafted so that the trust property will not be included in the immigrant's estate (either because of retained rights or powers as settlor or because of rights, powers or interests conferred on the immigrant as beneficiary), the immigrant settlor/beneficiary will not become the GST 'transferor' at death. As a result, property can skip generations or remain in trust for generations without exposure to the GST.

L. Pre-immigration strategies for US real property

16.133   US real property is US sited property for gift and estate tax purposes. Thus, a NDA pre-immigration gift of US real estate would be subject to US gift tax.

16.134   With respect to US real estate which the immigrant already directly owns and wants to transfer to a drop off trust, there are basically three pre-immigration methods of transferring such property without gift tax to a trust which will not be subject to US estate tax:

- sale of the US real property to a drop off trust for market value consideration;
- sale of the property to a *foreign* holding company which is owned by or later transferred to a drop off trust;[117] or

---

[117]   A contribution of US real property to a foreign holding company would be a deemed sale at market value under Code §§ 897 (foreign resident transferor) or 367(a) (US resident transferor) and would also result in gift tax if the company were owned by a drop off trust. An exchange for shares would also be subject to income tax, although not gift tax.

- a rollover transfer of the property to a *US* corporation[118] followed by a later NDA gift of the shares to a drop off trust.[119]

16.135 The simplest of these three methods is sale to a pre-immigration trust. If the individual is then non-US income tax resident, the sale arguably should be respected even if a note is received (if intended to be repaid). The note will be includible in the individual's US estate (resulting in an estate freeze), but if sufficient time elapses before the individual becomes US domiciled, the note proceeds might be later contributed in an unrelated transaction to the trust as a non-taxable NDA gift. If the sale occurs while the individual is US income tax resident, it will not be respected for income tax purposes (as the trust is transparent) but should be respected for gift tax purposes (ie as not a taxable gift because market value consideration is received).[120]

16.136 Under the second method, sale of the property to an offshore company for market value consideration, gain, if any, will be taxable, although under current rules a 15% maximum long-term capital gain rate may apply.[121] The company itself must be transferred to a drop off trust prior to the individual acquiring US domicile as otherwise the company's shares would be potentially subject to US gift and estate tax in the hands of the shareholder once US domiciled.

16.137 If the individual were a US income tax resident when these transfers occur, unless the company had cash and the two steps were not integrated, 'step transaction' regulations could recast the transfer as first a gratuitous transfer to the trust followed by a drop down sale to the company and distribution of the note.[122] This recharacterization is for income tax purposes only and intended to make the transaction reportable on Form 3520 as a transfer to the trust.[123] It should not cause the transfer to be a taxable gift (due to the contemporaneous receipt of market value consideration).

16.138 Once the individual becomes US resident, the drop off trust will be transparent[124] and a foreign holding company deemed a controlled foreign corporation[125] which is subject to annual financial reporting rules.[126] Corporate ownership

---

[118] Code § 351.
[119] The gain is not taxable under FIRPTA because nothing is 'realized' on the gift. Treas Reg § 1.897–1(g), (h).
[120] Code § 679(a)(4). Property sold to the trust should have a contemporaneous written valuation. If the transfer occurs when the settlor is non-US resident, the trust will generally be a non-grantor trust, the transferor will be subject to tax under FIRPTA (Code § 897) and the purchaser required to withhold 10% of the transfer proceeds unless prior to this the transferor files Form 8288B with the IRS to avoid withholding (eg if the property has nil or little gain). If the transfer occurs when the settlor is US resident, the consideration should be paid in cash (as a note will be disregarded under IRS Notice 97–34) and since the trust will be a grantor trust the transfer will not be a taxable sale for income tax purposes, but should be reported on Form 3520 (to avoid a 35% excise tax) and on Form 709 (to set the clock running on gift tax valuation). Whether a note or cash is received, the transfer should avoid gift tax if the note is for the property's fair market value and actually paid plus interest – since section 679 only applies for income tax purposes.
[121] Code § 1(h).
[122] Treas Reg § 1.679–3(f).
[123] Code §§ 679 and 6048.
[124] Code § 679(a)(4).
[125] Code § 951 et seq.

16.139 *US Pre-Immigration Planning*

will also subject the individual to a potentially higher gains tax cost on a future sale of the property by the company (34–35% versus 15%) and, if the property is occupied as a principal residence, the individual will lose the $250,000–$500,000 gains exemption on sale of a principal residence.[127]

16.139 However, if the company has no actual realized earnings, there should be no constructive dividend arising from the individual's rent-free occupation of the property.[128] In time, and without pre-arrangement, the company might be liquidated for US tax purposes by making a 'check the box' election to treat the company as a disregarded foreign entity (which will result in gain taxed as ordinary income).[129]

16.140 Under the third alternative method, the individual might first transfer the real property to a *US* real property holding corporation, a rollover transaction for gains tax purposes, followed by an independent and non pre-arranged later NDA gift of the shares to the drop off trust. This planning has the same step transaction risks as the offshore company, except that the US company is not subject to reporting rules and a 'check the box' liquidation cannot be made for it (although it can be liquidated with corporate level gain taxed as ordinary income).

16.141 Ordinarily, offshore trustees will not want to hold US real estate directly and will want a limited liability holding company. If a foreign holding company is used, the company, rather than an occupying individual, should pay ownership expenses (property tax and insurance) to avoid creating deemed rental were an occupying individual to pay these items, and the individual should pay his own utility expenses, to avoid reportable distributions for excise tax purposes.

16.142 A simpler alternative would be for the trustees to use a US limited liability company (LLC). An LLC is transparent for all US income tax purposes,[130] and as the drop off trust is also transparent for income tax purposes, there should generally be no income tax or reporting issues arising from the individual's permitted rent-free occupation of the property, although there is an estate tax issue relating to the settlor's possible de facto retention of an interest in trust owned property.

16.143 On balance, trust ownership of US real property for a US resident settlor of a drop off trust can be an expensive proposition with potential fiscal risk in creating the structure with respect to previously owned property. A pragmatic alternative could be for the immigrating individual to retain direct ownership of US real estate and other lifestyle and portfolio assets approximating the individual's anticipated estate tax exemption ($7m combined for US domiciled married individuals as of 2009).

---

[126] IRS Form 5471.
[127] Code § 121.
[128] See Bittker and Eustice *Federal Income Taxation of Corporations and Shareholders* (7th edn, 2000) Warren, Gorham & Lamont at para 8.05(4) and pp 8–46 and 8–47; *Eisner v Macomber 252 US 189 (1920)*.
[129] Treas Reg § 301.7701–2 and 3; IRS Form 8832.
[130] Treas Reg § 301.7701–3(b)(1).

Chapter 17

US or Foreign Trust Providing for UK Beneficiary

A. Summary of relevant income and capital gains tax planning considerations

17.1 A non-UK resident trust created by a UK domiciled and resident individual is subject to wide ranging anti-avoidance legislation, in particular, related to capital gains taxation and, accordingly, only rare circumstances will warrant the use of a non-UK resident trust for purely domestic UK planning.[1] However, a non-resident trust settled by a non-UK domiciled settlor, can defer capital gains taxation of UK domiciled beneficiaries, and distribute gains, including UK source gains, without UK taxation to non-UK resident or non-UK domiciled beneficiaries. A discussion of planning issues in this chapter relating to foreign trust distributions to UK beneficiaries presumes a background knowledge of the UK trust residence rules, taxation of trusts, settlors and beneficiaries, which is provided in **CHAPTER 13**.

17.2 For income tax purposes, if a non-resident trust is one from which the settlor or his spouse can benefit in any circumstance whatsoever,[2] the tax position is largely neutral compared with outright ownership of assets – providing arising basis taxation in the case of a UK domiciled settlor and remittance basis for a non-UK domiciled settlor. However, where the settlor or his spouse are excluded from all possible benefit, there can be *income tax* deferral advantages of using a non-UK resident trust as opposed to a UK resident trust – including where there is a UK domiciled and resident settlor (although the capital gains tax disadvantages of such a structure are likely to outweigh the benefits in the latter case).

17.3 As can be seen from the above, creation of a non-UK resident trust providing for a UK beneficiary, will normally contemplate a situation where the settlor is non-UK domiciled. This chapter therefore focuses on planning for a non-resident trust settled by a non-UK domiciled settlor.[3]

---

[1] See **CHAPTER 13** for a detailed consideration of residence as it applies to trusts. A UK domiciled and resident settlor is taxed on gains as they arise to non-UK resident trustees where he, his children, his grandchildren, any spouses of the foregoing, or any companies controlled by them can benefit. This generally covers all persons for the benefit of whom such a trust is likely to be created (s 86 of the Taxation and Chargeable Gains Act 1992).

[2] Ie if they are not irrevocably excluded from benefit now and in the future.

[3] Certain pre-1991 non-UK resident trusts created by UK domiciled settlors (largely in the late 1980s) are still in existence. These often contain significant deferred capital gains, realised prior to changes in the legislation. The challenge in such cases is how to distribute the 'locked in' gains without triggering the penal tax charges that can now apply in such circumstances. A variety of strategies were developed over recent years, taking advantage of loopholes in the legislation, but

17.4 *US or Foreign Trust Providing for UK Beneficiary*

17.4 The residence status of the trust itself does not affect the inheritance tax (IHT) position, which depends on the domicile status of the settlor and the location of the assets.

B. Planning income and capital gains distributions with respect to UK resident beneficiaries

17.5 Non-UK resident trusts have capital gains tax favoured status in that both UK and offshore gains realised by such a trust may be distributed capital gains tax free to UK resident but non-UK domiciled persons.[4] For this purpose, it is general law domicile which is relevant, and not the IHT concept of deemed domicile.

17.6 Prior to 17 March 1998, offshore trust gains were effectively exempted from tax whether or not distributed to UK domiciled and resident beneficiaries, provided that the settlor was not UK domiciled either at any time in the year of assessment when the trust was made or in the year of assessment when the distribution was made. However, since 17 March 1998, the charge to capital gains tax on capital payments by offshore trusts to UK resident *and domiciled* beneficiaries applies irrespective of the domicile status of the settlor.

17.7 In contrast, a non-resident trust may make tax-free capital payments, representing UK and foreign sited gains, to UK resident beneficiaries who are non-UK domiciled, provided that this does not invoke the application of certain income tax anti-avoidance provisions. Broadly speaking, these should not apply if either:

(a) the trust creates an interest in possession such that no income has been retained or accumulated; or

(b) any trust and underlying company income is annually distributed offshore to non-UK domiciled beneficiaries and/or to non-UK resident beneficiaries.[5]

See **CHAPTER 13**. The term ' capital payment' includes direct or indirect 'payments' or the 'conferring of any other benefit', for example, the value attributed to the benefit of using assets in specie.

17.8 UK income and capital gains tax consequences of distributions to, or the use of trust or company property by, UK resident beneficiaries are not always well understood in transatlantic situations, or with respect to other trusts established in overseas countries many years previously for reasons wholly unconnected with the

---

new legislation has generally been used to close them down one by one. A detailed discussion is beyond the scope of this book.

[4] In principle, this is also the case where the settlor is UK domiciled and resident but the probability is that (save in relation to old stockpiled gains) he will already have been taxed under the relevant anti-avoidance legislation. TCGA 1992, s 86.

[5] As an alternative to this strategy it may be desirable from an income tax perspective to ensure that trusts intending to confer benefits in kind (eg use of assets in specie) do not also hold income-producing assets. Therefore, to the extent practicable, separate trusts should be used for these two separate asset classes.

B. Planning for UK resident beneficiaries **17.9**

UK and therefore without regard to possible UK implications. Accordingly, in today's environment of global families and estates, it is important for trustees of non-UK resident trusts to understand the potential wider implications of the actions which they take for their UK resident beneficiaries.

Example

Mogadishu Tuthree, a Kenyan resident and domiciled settlor, sets up an irrevocable discretionary Jersey, Channel Islands trust. The trust owns a Jersey investment holding company, Discrete Investments Ltd. Both the trust and company have substantial portfolio assets. In addition, the trust owns a residence in Surrey in the UK, in which the settlor's niece is allowed to live rent free. No one has paid any attention to UK tax planning and both the trust and the company have accumulated portfolio income.

If the establishment of this arrangement were considered by the Inland Revenue to have been UK tax motivated, they could use s 740 of the Income and Corporation Taxes Act 1988 (ICTA 1988) to subject the niece to UK income tax to the extent of the lesser of the fair rental value of the Surrey residence (the capital benefit) and the aggregate of the undistributed income of the company and trust.

To avoid this exposure, the trustees prudently should have considered a policy of distributing the earnings of the company to the trust and distributing the income of the trust (assuming it is all non-UK source income) to the offshore accounts of UK resident but non-UK domiciled beneficiaries or to non-UK resident beneficiaries.

17.9 The key to successful UK tax planning for these trusts is to achieve tax deferral and additionally to mitigate any 'penalty' taxes which might otherwise arise. Trustees should consider the following relevant planning issues.

- A beneficiary in receipt of a distribution must be UK resident or ordinarily resident in order for the capital gains tax charge to apply to distributions and, therefore, if payment is received at a time when he is not, no charge arises. However, accumulated trust income, and then stockpiled gains may, in appropriate cases, be reduced.[6]

- Capital gains tax is potentially subject to 'supplementary charges' (broadly equivalent to an interest charge) of up to 24% which counters the benefits of deferral of the tax through non-distribution of stockpiled trust gains.[7] Income tax does not suffer the same penalty charges and therefore where the trustees wish to retain funds, ensuring that the disposal of the trust asset triggers

---

[6] TCGA 1992, s 2(1). See **CHAPTER 9** regarding UK residence for capital gains tax purposes.
[7] TCGA 1992, s 91. This can increase the tax rate on distributions to 64% after six years (the maximum penalty period) since a 10% 'interest' charge is imposed on the 40% tax rate for each year since the gain was realised. Note that the effective tax rate may be less, due to taper relief applicable to the taxable gain (see **CHAPTER 10**). The supplementary charge commences with effect from 1 December in the tax year following the disposal. For example, if the trustees make a disposal on 31 March 2004, the charge commences with effect from 1 December 2004, although it will not apply provided that a distribution is made by the end of that tax year, ie 5 April 2005.

17.9   US or Foreign Trust Providing for UK Beneficiary

- *income* tax, rather than gains tax, can reduce the eventual tax rate on distribution to 40%, rather than 64%.[8]

- Since non-UK residence for income tax may currently be achievable more easily under the UK income tax rules (given the five-year rule applicable to capital gains tax for temporary non-residents[9]), distribution of income at a time of non-UK tax residence can also offer tax mitigation opportunities.

- The supplementary interest charges on realised gains can also be avoided or reduced where the asset disposals are made within a suitable tax approved 'wrapper', such that the gains do not arise to the trustees until disposal or part disposal of the 'wrapper' itself. It should be noted that an offshore holding company will not normally suffice to achieve this objective in view of the relevant anti-avoidance rules which attribute the company gains through to the trustees and potentially onward to beneficiaries.[10] UK planning often utilises collective investments (such as unit or investment trust type vehicles) for this purpose, some of which are taxed in the UK on disposal as income and some as gains. This can offer significant UK flexibility but may have adverse US tax consequences under the PFIC rules with respect to US taxable beneficiaries who have either an interest in possession or are viewed as having a proportionate interest in trust assets.[11]

- Insurance arrangements can offer an alternative 'wrapper' in appropriate cases. The cash premium paid for an offshore insurance bond can be allocated to funds offered by the company and provided the personal portfolio bond legislation is avoided,[12] the policy holder can withdraw 5% of premium investment annually by encashment, which is treated as a non-taxable return of premium for the first 20 years. The 5% threshold amount, if unused in one year, can be carried over to the next. While the death of the settlor can result in an income tax charge to a then UK resident settlor[13] such taxation can normally be deferred by using a policy with multiple insured lives, including younger generations.[14]

---

[8] Various specific anti-avoidance provisions tax the gains on disposal of certain assets as 'income' rather than capital gain. For example, the disposal of an offshore 'non-distributor status' collective investment fund, results in the gain being taxable as income. In contrast, an offshore trust's sale of a fund with 'distributor status' results in capital gain which, if retained becomes a part of trust 'stockpiled' gains, potentially taxable when a UK resident and domiciled beneficiary later receives a distribution or a 'capital payment' from the trust. If the gain is undistributed for six years, the maximum charge of up to 64% may apply. Capital payments (including enjoyment of a capital benefit) are deemed to be attributed to 'relevant income' in the trust (taxable under ICTA 1988, s 740) prior to trust stockpiled capital gains (taxable under TCGA 1992, s 87) (see **CHAPTER 13**). Careful selection of trust investments by the trustees may therefore itself determine the relevant tax applicable.

[9] TCGA 1992, s 10A and see **CHAPTER 9**.

[10] TCGA 1992, s 13. See also **CHAPTER 16**.

[11] See the discussion at **16.32** et seq on the US Passive Foreign Investment Company (PFIC) rules of Code § 1291 et seq.

[12] Under these rules an overt attempt to wrap private investments could subject the policy holder to a 15% deemed taxable income with respect to the premium.

[13] ICTA 1988, s 547.

[14] Care needs to be taken in adopting a strategy to use the 5% capital 'tax free' withdrawals. If the original funds used to purchase the policy would have been taxable on remittance, depending on the circumstances, this may still be the case, irrespective of the 'tax free' character of the encashment itself. Furthermore, if trustees are seeking to use the 5% capital withdrawals to

C. UK tax consequences of US living trusts **17.11**

- The UK capital payments regime attributes the gains (on a first-in, first-out basis), to beneficiaries in sequence with their capital payments and up to the amount of such payments received. Where there is a mix of UK taxable and non-UK taxable beneficiaries, payments can be made to the non-UK taxable beneficiaries in priority to the UK taxable beneficiaries.[15] Save in certain limited cases, this attributes the gains to non-UK taxable persons, since they are allocated to all beneficiaries irrespective of their tax status.[16] Distributions to non-UK taxable beneficiaries should be made in a tax year prior to distributions to taxable beneficiaries since gains attributed to distributions made in the same tax year are pro-rated between the recipients.[17]

- Careful consideration should be given to possible adverse income and capital gains tax consequences of using an excluded property trust owning investment holding companies. While the gains of such companies qualify for indexation relief, they are attributed by TCGA 1992, s 13 to the trustees on an arising basis, without taper relief and subject to the supplementary capital gains tax charge of up to 24% under TCGA 1992, s 87, if such attributed gains remain in the trust up to six years. Furthermore, double taxation can result since a later dividend distribution of such gains to the trust can result in income at the trust level, in addition to the deemed gain which has previously arisen to the trustees.

17.10 Non-UK resident trusts may be established by non-UK domiciliaries (whether residents of the UK or not) for the traditional purposes of conservation and preservation of assets for the benefit of younger generation beneficiaries or other dependents. Further, the excluded property rules allow wide flexibility in the design of the trust, permitting even a revocable trust to qualify as an excluded property trust for purposes of removing assets from IHT. (See the discussion of excluded property trust planning in **CHAPTERS 6, 13, and 15**.)

C. UK tax consequences of US living trusts – a trap for unwary US expatriates

17.11 The prevalent practice of American expatriates living in Britain to serve as trustees or co-trustees of their own US revocable trusts (lifetime trusts which are 'will substitute' trusts, sometimes called 'living trusts') can cause such a UK

---

distribute as 'annual income' to a beneficiary, this may, in some cases, be characterised and taxed as income in the beneficiary's hands (irrespective of the source). *Brodie v IRC (1933) 17 TC 432*; *Stevenson v Wishart [1987] 59 TC 740*.

[15] Distributions of a part of a trust's assets to another trust will generally simply transfer a *proportionate* part of the transferor trust's gains to the distributee trust, and thus will not be effective to strip out trust gains to a transferee holding trust, as could be done under US tax rules (TCGA 1992, s 90), subject to anti avoidance exceptions – see below.

[16] TCGA 1992, Sch 4C, para 8(3) and (4), as amended by Finance Act 2003, s 163. An anti avoidance provision exists which disapplies this rule where certain types of transfers have occurred. This affects a specific planning strategy which the measure was introduced to counter, involving transfers linked with borrowings undertaken by the trustees. This anti-avoidance provision was introduced with respect to certain borrowings of the trustees to fund a new trust in an attempt to strip the old trust of assets which could carry out taxable gains.

[17] TCGA 1992, s 87(5).

17.12 *US or Foreign Trust Providing for UK Beneficiary*

resident, but non-domiciled settlor, to be taxable on otherwise non-taxable offshore trust gains, on an arising basis. This is due to the UK trustee status of the settlor and/or his wife, which can make the trust UK resident for capital gains tax purposes. Unlike the income tax settlor interested ('grantor') trust rules, the comparable capital gains rule of TCGA 1992, s 77 (applicable to UK resident trust gains) does not attribute trust gains to the settlor on a 'look through' basis, but rather taxes him on an 'amount equal to' the gains realised by the trust. Since this rule does not attribute the underlying source of offshore gains to the settlor, he loses the remittance basis of taxation and hence becomes taxable on an amount equal to the worldwide gains of the UK resident trust. Furthermore, rectifying the position by resignation of the UK resident trustees will trigger the deemed disposal and tax charge on exit from the UK.[18] See **CHAPTER 13** for a discussion of these provisions.

17.12 The above differences in the residence and settlor interested trust rules for income and gains pose a number of difficulties in establishing a routine US revocable trust and probate avoidance planning for Americans residing in the UK. None the less, some general planning considerations may make such trusts and planning feasible.

- If an offshore trust is to be used only for capital gains, a majority of its trustees must be non-UK resident and its administration must be offshore. In practice, this requires two non-resident trustees if a UK resident settlor wishes to be a trustee. To avoid any question of continued direction by the settlor or of administration taking place in the UK, it is preferable that there be *no* UK trustee.[19]

- If an offshore trust also receives *income,* generally it will be preferable that none of its trustees are UK resident, whether or not the settlor was UK resident when the trust was settled.

- The non-resident trustees must, in fact, exercise effective and independent trustee powers and cannot be seen to be mere nominees of the UK resident settlor and acting at his direction. The place of trust administration must be outside the UK. In practice, the non-resident trustee would prudently be an independent trust company and or professional advisor resident in an acceptable low tax jurisdiction.

- Where married spouses are domiciled in one of the nine US community property states[20] and the trust is settled with community funds, the UK would most likely regard, for example, California law as determining the ownership of assets (being the state of domicile) *other than* UK real property (being

---

[18] TCGA 1992, s 80. Where any persons with such trusts are taking up residence in the UK it will be advisable to resign all trusteeships, preferably in the UK tax year prior to their arrival.

[19] Since most trusts of the type under discussion are tax-neutral in the US, advisers in that country normally have no real concerns around the perceived involvement of the settlor, since he is taxable in any event. The relevant US tax anti-avoidance provisions tend to simply ignore the existence of the trust. This is in marked contrast with the UK position where, generally, the natural consequences of the facts and circumstances, and of transactions, will continue to be relevant, the tax exposure of a settlor being superimposed and relief being granted in the event of double taxation, for example, see TCGA 1992, s 70.

[20] Idaho, Washington, California, Nevada, Arizona, New Mexico, Texas, Louisiana and Wisconsin.

C. UK tax consequences of US living trusts **17.13**

governed by the country of situs). The trust would then be substantially viewed as two trusts, with each spouse the settlor of his or her trust (being half of the total trust).[21]

17.13 The costs of the above structures will make such trusts impracticable for all but cases involving substantial estates. For a general discussion of non-UK resident trust planning for non-UK domiciled settlors see also **CHAPTER 15**.

---

[21] Prior to effecting any planning it is generally prudent, to avoid any dispute over ownership, for the parties to enter into a marital agreement under the terms of which they clearly set out and agree the ownership of their respective assets.

Chapter 18

UK or Foreign Trusts Providing for a US Beneficiary

A. Introduction

18.1 As noted previously, a non-UK resident trust settled by a non-UK domiciled settlor can distribute gains free from capital gains tax to a UK resident beneficiary who is not domiciled in the UK.[1] However, care needs to be taken that this does not trigger any UK income taxes with respect to income which may have been retained by the trustees.[2]

18.2 In contrast, if the settlor is UK domiciled and resident, he is taxable on gains realized by the trustees as they arise.[3] If the settlor is UK domiciled and resident, he or she may also be taxed on income under anti-avoidance rules (the latter of which are generally the same for a non-UK domiciled person, although subject to the advantage of the remittance basis of assessment for overseas income[4]). If gains are not taxable to a UK resident settlor (whether UK domiciled or not), they are stockpiled within the trust and taxable to a UK resident and *domiciled* beneficiary in receipt of a capital payment, potentially at a rate of up to 64% (being 40% tax and a supplementary charge of up to 24%, depending on the time since the gain was realized by the trustees). To the extent that a capital distribution is made to such a beneficiary, he or she is deemed taxable first on an amount representing undistributed trust income (whether or not it has been formally accumulated) and then on such stockpiled gains.

18.3 The US tax regime provides similar tax results for distributions to US beneficiaries through the operation of the grantor trust rules and the accumulation distribution rules applicable to non-grantor trust distributions. In contrast, these results can be even more dramatic since the US rules:

(a) allow tax-free distributions to US beneficiaries of both income and gains of a grantor trust with a foreign grantor; and

---

[1] Taxation of Chargeable Gains Act 1992 (TCGA 1992), s 87. See also **CHAPTER 13**.
[2] Income and Corporation Taxes Act 1988 (ICTA 1988), s 740. See also **CHAPTER 13**.
[3] TCGA 1992, s 86, Sch 5, para 2(3) and (7). This provision only applies where the settlor has an interest in the trust. However, the definition of the circumstances in which he is deemed to have such an interest are so broad as to encompass most, if not all, of the situations which merit the use of family trusts. This will be the case where any of the settlor, his spouse, child or grandchild are beneficiaries or where they receive de facto benefit. In addition, the provisions will apply if the settlement can benefit any company controlled by any of the foregoing persons or a company associated with such a company (ie one has control of the other or both are under the control of the same persons).
[4] ICTA 1988, Pt XV, s 739 and see **CHAPTER 13**.

18.4 *UK or Foreign Trusts Providing for a US Beneficiary*

(b) permit rent-free use of property held in a foreign non-grantor trust without adverse tax implications to the US beneficiary.

Conversely, the accumulation distribution rules can result in a tax bite higher than the maximum 64% tax imposed by the UK stockpiled gain rules.

18.4 This chapter discusses planning for such distributions to US beneficiaries, *first* in the context of distributions from grantor trusts and *second* in the context of distributions from non-grantor trusts. This sequence addresses:

- 'pre-planning' opportunities where the adviser will always want to consider the establishment of a grantor trust by a foreign settlor if there is a US spouse or family member beneficiary; and

- 'post-planning' situations where the adviser may be confronted with a dead settlor or an existing inter vivos non-grantor trust which cannot be changed under trust law or without adverse local law consequences.

Where there is flexibility, the adviser might consider amending or more likely distributing out and separately establishing a trust that does have grantor trust status.

18.5 Understanding this planning requires a thorough understanding of the US grantor trust and non-grantor trust rules, the taxation of grantors, trusts and beneficiaries, the residence of trusts, the excise tax reporting rules and the taxation of foreign estates – all of which are summarized in **CHAPTER 12**. In all cases it is assumed that the trust was settled by a NDA settlor who, in the case of a grantor trust, is still alive. Obviously, should the settlor subsequently decide to become US resident, the structure should be revisited and **CHAPTER 16** pre-immigration planning should be considered well in advance.

18.6 It should be remembered, in the context of the observations below, that the characteristics of a trust which determine whether or not it is taxable as to the settlor differ between the UK and the US. Generally, the UK rules look to whether the settlor, his spouse or, in certain cases, his children (and connected entities) can benefit from the assets. The US rules tend, in addition, to consider whether there are powers by virtue of which a settlor has, or may be deemed to have, continued control of who may benefit. This can mean that a settlor may be exposed to US gift and estate tax with respect to an incomplete gift trust or to US income tax with respect to a grantor trust in circumstances where the equivalent provisions in the UK are inapplicable since the assets can never revert to the settlor or his spouse. However, as Section B (18.8 et seq) contemplates trusts from which the settlor or his spouse are not excluded, the UK anti-avoidance legislation will be relevant (see **CHAPTER 13**) and any offsetting UK tax cost should be borne in mind.

18.7 A further point which needs to be taken into account is the possibility of a mismatch of any potential tax credits in the case where the applicable tax in different jurisdictions may fall on different persons (eg the settlor in one case and the beneficiaries or trustees in the other) or different entities (eg a company in one jurisdiction and its shareholders in the other). The new 2001 US/UK Income Tax treaty and the 2002 Protocol attempt to address such mismatches, but treaty relief may not be provided in all cases.

B. Foreign grantor trusts with foreign grantors

18.8 To the extent the settlor is treated as the grantor/owner of the trust under the US grantor trust rules, US beneficiaries can receive tax-free distributions from the trust.[5] This is true whether or not the grantor is a US taxpayer or the trust is a domestic or foreign trust. If the grantor is not a US taxpayer, however, then the US will generally only be able to tax certain kinds of US-source income.[6]

18.9 The other advantage of a grantor trust with a foreign grantor is that any US-sourced trade or business income, which includes gains from the sale of US property investments under the Foreign Investment in Real Property Tax Act (FIRPTA) rules, will be taxed at rates applicable to individuals rather than the compressed rate structure that applies for trusts. US tax law changes in 1996 (with effective dates reaching back to 1995 in some instances) have substantially limited the circumstances in which a foreign settlor will be respected as the grantor/owner of a foreign trust.

1. Existing 'grandfathered' grantor trusts

18.10 A foreign settlor will be respected as the grantor/owner of certain trusts settled prior to 19 September 1995. These trusts are said to be 'grandfathered' (that is, not subject to the new rules). To qualify, either:

(a) the settlor and/or the settlor's spouse must be permissible beneficiaries to whom distributions could be made without the consent of an adversely affected beneficiary; or

(b) the settlor must retain the power to revoke the trust (again, without the consent of an adverse party).

Other 'tweaks' often used to make a foreign settlor the grantor/owner under prior law – such as the right of the settlor to substitute assets of equal value or the right of a non-adverse party to add to the class of beneficiaries – will not work.

18.11 Grandfathered status only applies to funds contributed to the trust prior to 19 September 1995. If assets have been contributed after this date, the portion of the trust attributed to the contributed assets will either be:

(a) a grantor trust (if qualifying under one of the exceptions discussed below); or

(b) a non-grantor trust (if not so qualifying).

The trust's status as a grandfathered trust does not entitle the grantor to funnel additional assets to the trust.

---

[5] Rev Rul 69–70, 1969–1 CB 182.
[6] As discussed in **CHAPTER 12**, this includes:
- US-sourced fixed or determinable annual or periodic income (such as dividends, rents and interest income);
- income effectively connected with a US trade or business;
- gain from the sale of US real property interests.

18.12 *UK or Foreign Trusts Providing for a US Beneficiary*

18.12 Further, the regulations require that amounts contributed to a grandfathered trust before and after 19 September 1995 must be separately accounted for in order to preserve the grandfathered status of the pre-19 September 1995 portion.[7] If this is not done, then the foreign grantor's status as owner *of the entire trust* (including the pre-19 September 1995 portion) will be determined under the general rules summarized below. The regulations do not require physical segregation of the trust assets into separate brokerage accounts, provided that the trust's books and records adequately identify the assets, income and gains of each fund. As a practical matter, Trustees will want to file separate withholding tax forms, eg W8-BENs for the non-grantor fund and for the grantor fund and separate Form 3520s should be filed with respect to distributions from the respective funds. If separate accounting has not been done to date, it should be attempted on a reconstructed basis and maintained going forward.

2. Revocable trusts

18.13 A foreign settlor will also be respected as the grantor/owner of a trust created (or funded) after 20 August 1996 if the settlor can revoke the trust. This exception applies only if the settlor can revoke the trust on his own or with the consent of a family member or other related or subordinate party. As discussed in **CHAPTER 14**, a revocable trust will not – in and of itself – offer any shelter from US estate tax for US assets held in the trust at the foreign settlor's death. To shelter the trust's underlying US assets from US estate tax, the settlor must use a variation of this theme, in which US assets are held within a wholly owned offshore holding company. Used for many Latin American settlors, this structure is discussed at **14.45** et seq.

18.14 The US tax benefits of properly implementing and funding this structure include:

- grantor trust status (income and gains realized during the settlor's lifetime can be distributed income tax free to US beneficiaries);
- removal of assets from US estate and gift tax; and
- market value re-basing of structure assets within the trust on the settlor's death.

The funding and, in particular, planning immediately following the settlor's death require expert US tax advice at the time to avoid pitfalls.

3. Settlor and spouse only trusts

18.15 A third category of qualifying trusts are those created after 20 August 1996 from which, at all times by the terms of the trust, no person can benefit during

---

[7] Treas Reg § 1.672-f(3)(e).

the settlor's life other than the settlor and/or his spouse. These trusts would typically be irrevocable, otherwise they would qualify under the exception discussed at **18.13**.

18.16 While these irrevocable trusts do not offer an opportunity for current, tax-free distributions to US beneficiaries (except perhaps the US spouse of a foreign settlor), income and gains earned and accumulated in these trusts will not become part of undistributed net income (UNI). As such, distributions to the US beneficiaries after the grantor trust status ends that are attributed to this accumulated income will not attract any US tax liability.

4. Planning for the post-grantor trust phase

18.17 Although a trust which is a grantor trust can make income tax-free distributions to US beneficiaries of income and gains realized during the settlor's life, two possible traps for the unwary arise at the settlor's death.

18.18 First, any distribution after grantor trust status terminates is treated as coming from current income (DNI) or accumulated income (UNI) that has been earned and/or accumulated after the trust's grantor trust status terminates.

Example

A foreign grantor trust has $150,000 of accumulated income and gains for a period prior to grantor trust status terminating (at the settlor's death) in June 2004. Between the date of the settlor's death and the end of 2004, the trust earns $20,000 of income and gains, which are also accumulated. In 2005, when the trust earns $25,000 of income and gains, the trust distributes $50,000 to its US beneficiary. The distribution is treated as coming (i) first from 2005's DNI of $25,000 and (ii) next from 2004's UNI of $20,000. Only after the trust's DNI and UNI have been fully distributed can the trust's capital (including earnings accumulated during the trust's grantor trust status) be distributed tax-free. In this example, the additional $5,000 distribution is free of tax.

18.19 Second, if the trust's assets do not receive a basis adjustment at death (see **CHAPTER 11**), then the inherent gains in the trust asset will be exposed to US tax if and when those gains are later realized and distributed to US beneficiaries. This exposure can be minimized if the trust were to periodically sell its appreciated assets during the trust's grantor trust phase; the gains do not become part of DNI or UNI and the trust takes a new cost basis in the assets acquired with the reinvested proceeds.

18.20 The problem can be exacerbated when an irrevocable trust owns a holding company, which in turn owns appreciated investments. Even if the trust were able to get a basis step-up on its interest in the corporation, the inherent gain in the underlying corporate investments will still be locked in and thus potentially taxable on post-death realization (unless the company can be liquidated post-mortem without exposure to the US CFC, FPHC and PFIC rules, as discussed in **16.32** et seq). The same applies to income earned and accumulated in the company prior to the termination of grantor trust status To minimize these risks, gains can be realized periodically within the company and income/gains distributed to the grantor trust.

18.21 *UK or Foreign Trusts Providing for a US Beneficiary*

This flushes out the company's earnings and, if the dividends are reinvested within the company, provides the trust with an additional cost basis. Other planning might involve bed and breakfasting or creative use of the entity classification election rules.[8]

18.21 Further, both revocable and certain irrevocable trusts can be amended prior to the settlor's death to mandate certain distributions of specific trust assets or cash legacies to US beneficiaries. These trusts – which are known as 'capital first' trusts (and which are discussed in more detail at **18.34** et seq) – effectively permit tax-free distributions to US beneficiaries from non-grantor trusts despite the existence of DNI or UNI earned or accumulated after the settlor's death.

C. Foreign non-grantor trusts with US beneficiaries

18.22 The following sections explore a number of strategies for planning for foreign non-grantor trusts, including trusts that were once but have ceased to be grantor trusts. The concern here is the potentially adverse tax implications of accumulation distributions (ie those deemed to come from earnings accumulated after the trust ceases to be a grantor trust). As discussed in **CHAPTER 12**, these adverse consequences include:

- taxation of accumulated gains at ordinary income rates; and
- the imposition of an interest charge on this tax depending on the weighted age of the accumulations.

1. Domesticate the foreign trust

18.23 Although this option has been listed first, it is actually not high on our 'recommended' list. But it is easy to understand. If a foreign trust 'migrates' to the US (ie controlled by US persons and subject to supervision by US courts), then the trust will be considered a US trust (and not a foreign trust). The trust will accordingly be taxed on all realized income and gains (subject to a deduction for distributions made to its beneficiaries).

18.24 Any income or gains accumulated prior to domestication (and after grantor trust status terminates) will remain as part of the trust's UNI. Further, distributions of UNI that has accumulated in a foreign, non-grantor trust after the trust becomes a US trust remains subject to the throwback rules (discussed in **CHAPTER 12**) and the interest charge (which effectively continue to accrue). First, the throwback tax specifically applies to domestic trusts that were once foreign

---

[8] Ie the rules that permit a taxpayer to make a 'check the box' election to determine whether taxation is on an opaque basis (as a corporate entity) or on a look-through basis (as a partnership). See the discussion at **16.40**.

trusts.[9] Second, the IRS has ruled that the interest charge continues to apply to accumulation distributions attributed to UNI accumulated while the US trust had been a foreign trust.[10]

18.25 Finally, all undistributed trust income and gains will be subject to US income tax on a going forward basis and US courts will have *in personam* jurisdiction over the trustee. If properly designed, the assets in the domesticated trust can be protected from US transfer tax to the same degree they would have been protected in the offshore trust; the key is limiting the US beneficiary's rights in, and powers over, the trust. For US beneficiaries unwilling to put up with the potential problems and headaches of foreign trusts (but who are also willing to forgo the possible benefits), domestication is clearly an option.

2. *Rhythm method distributions of accumulated income*

18.26 If a foreign, non-grantor trust remains foreign and has both US and foreign beneficiaries, the trustees should consider timing distributions to foreign beneficiaries to flush out current and (more importantly, accumulated) income, followed by a subsequent year distribution of current income and tax-free capital to US beneficiaries. In effecting this planning, it should be borne in mind that:

(a) there is no 'first in time' rule for distributions in the current year (a $50,000 distribution to beneficiary A on 1 January is treated as carrying out the same portion of DNI or UNI as a $50,000 distribution to beneficiary B on 31 December),

(b) all current year distributions carry out income at the end of the current year, and

(c) a '65 day election' can be made to carry out the prior year's DNI but not UNI accumulated in years prior.[11]

Example

A revocable trust had $10m of securities at the foreign settlor's death in 1994. In 2004, the trustees propose to distribute all $17m of the trust's assets (consisting of $7m of current and accumulated income) to the settlor's four children, two of whom are resident in the US, one of whom is a resident in the UK (but non-domiciled) and one is a UK resident/domiciliary. Before the end of 2004, the trustees distribute $8.5m to a new trust for the benefit of the UK children.[12] This has the effect of

---

[9] Code § 665(c)(2)(A).
[10] Rev Rul 91–6, 1991–1 CB 89.
[11] Treas Reg § 1.663(b)-1(a)(2). The 65-day election *cannot*, therefore, cause a distribution to be treated as an accumulation distribution and subject to throwback tax.
[12] Depending on the type of trust and whether there has been significant accumulation of income over the years, if the increase relates substantially to capital gains, arguably the better strategy for the UK resident non-UK domiciled beneficiary could be an outright distribution, since this is clearly not taxable under TCGA 1992, s 87. Where assets are transferred between trustees this leaves the possibility of future distributions being taxable to beneficiaries with the appropriate UK tax status at that time.

18.27 *UK or Foreign Trusts Providing for a US Beneficiary*

stripping out the trust's $7m of current and accumulated income. On 2 January 2005, the trustees wire the remaining $8.5m in cash to the US beneficiaries and wind up the existing trust. The US beneficiaries must report the 2005 distribution on Form 3520, but should have no taxable income.

3. Distribution of all current trust income and net gains

18.27 Once a foreign trust ceases to be a grantor trust (typically upon the settlor's death), the trustees can distribute all current income and net gains to the US beneficiaries (or to a US distribution trust for the benefit of US beneficiaries). Because all of the trust's DNI is currently distributed to a US person, the foreign trust will not have any UNI and thus will not be subject to the potentially onerous accumulation distribution rules.

18.28 Under this technique, all income and gains will thus be subject to current US tax (the same result if the trust had become a domestic trust on the settlor's death). The offshore trust is not subject to US *in personam* jurisdiction and (depending on the jurisdiction) the beneficiaries should have increased asset protection with respect to principal remaining in the offshore trust (though not as to any funds actually distributed to them). The trustees could retain the flexibility of switching to a US tax deferred distribution strategy if warranted by planning considerations or changes in family lifestyle patterns (eg a US beneficiary's marriage to a non-resident alien and emigration to the UK as non-UK domiciled residents).

18.29 Assets remaining in the offshore trust can also be protected from US transfer tax exposure if the rights and powers of the US beneficiaries are appropriately limited. This protection can also extend to a US distribution trust (ie a trust formed to receive current DNI distributions from the foreign trust) if the US trust is properly structured.

4. UNI accumulations followed by DNI 'annuity' distributions

18.30 Another strategy involves allowing the trust to accumulate income and gains after the trust ceases to be a grantor trust. Distributions (if any are needed) should come only from current income (DNI) so as not to attract the throwback tax and interest charge penalties. If the foreign trust is established in a tax haven, income (except for certain income taxed at the source) and gains can effectively accumulate tax free for many years.

18.31 If the foreign trust is successfully invested, it can grow to substantial values after a number of years. At that point, the foreign trust can begin to make current and periodic distributions to US beneficiaries (or US trusts for their benefit), again, out of only current income.

Example

Assume a foreign trust has $10m at the settlor's death when the trust's grantor trust status terminates. If the trust is domesticated, it will pay current US taxes on all income and gains. Assume a 10% rate of return (net of expenses) and a blended tax rate of 25%. After 20 years, the domesticated trust (assuming no distributions) would have grown to about $42.5m.

If the trust remained offshore and grew tax free, after the same 20 years the foreign trust would be valued at about $67.3m. At that point, assume the foreign trust begins distributing all of its current earnings – $6.73m annually – to a domestic US trust for the US beneficiaries. Those distributions attract current US tax but, because the distribution does not exceed current DNI, there is no accumulation distribution of UNI and no interest charge. After taxes, the annual distribution from the foreign trust amounts to about $5m. If those distributions are reinvested domestically along with similar distributions from the foreign trust in later years, by year 36 the domestic distribution trust will have grown to $146m. And it should not be forgotten that the foreign trust still has $67.3m, which is still producing $6.7m of annual income that can be distributed without adverse tax implications each year. Effectively, at the end of year 36, a combined $213.3m is held in the foreign and domestic trusts.

In contrast, after 16 more years of accumulated after-tax earnings, the foreign trust that domesticated in year 1 would have grown to a value of $135m.

18.32 The obvious disadvantage of this technique is the inability to make distributions from the foreign trust beyond the current year's DNI. To do so many years out would be considered an accumulation distribution, subjecting the UNI to a throwback tax and corresponding interest charge that could wipe out the entire distribution. The original $10m of corpus, as well as the UNI accumulated through year 20 in the prior example, will effectively be trapped within the foreign trust.

18.33 There are two caveats. First, the trust could be designed to make a 'capital first' distribution in some later year. As discussed at **18.34**, that distribution would be free of tax, even though the trust had UNI accumulations. Second, even if the UNI cannot itself be distributed tax free from the foreign trust, it can continue indefinitely to make annual DNI distributions without adverse tax consequences. One might consider the foreign trust's UNI to be a *premium* payment on an annuity contract that pays the US distribution trust $6.7m annually. Not a bad investment. The gap between the values in the originally-domesticated trust and the domestic distribution trust will grow wider in later years as the domestic distribution trust continues to receive these annuity payments from the foreign trust.

5. *'Capital First' trust distributions*

18.34 Code § 663(a)(1) provides that US beneficiaries are not required to recognise income or gain on the certain distributions mandated by the terms of the

18.35 *UK or Foreign Trusts Providing for a US Beneficiary*

trust instrument.[13] To qualify for this exception, the trust must mandate the distribution of a fixed sum or of specific property to a beneficiary that is payable in three or fewer installments. Distributions can be made to more than one beneficiary, as long as the total mandated distributions to each do not exceed three. Amounts payable only out of income do not qualify for this exception. There is no requirement that the mandated distribution occur upon the settlor's death. This rule applies regardless of whether the trust is domestic or foreign.

Example

A foreign trust provides that, upon the settlor's death, the trustees shall distribute $1m to each of the settlor's children. The US children will not be taxed on this distribution (even if, in the year of distribution and after the settlor's death, the trust had DNI). The US beneficiary must report the distribution from the foreign trust using Form 3520 even though it is not taxable.

Example

The foreign accumulation trust described in the Example at **18.31** provides for a distribution of $30m to a US domestic distribution trust in year 20. Assuming the other requirements of Code § 663(a)(1) are met, this distribution will be tax free, even though the foreign trust at that time had over $57m of accumulated earnings. In fact, the trust could have mandated that $65m be distributed to the domestic distribution trust, and no US tax would be imposed.

Example

However, if the terms of the foreign trust direct that it terminates in year 20 and distributes all of its assets to a domestic distribution trust, the accumulated UNI would then be taxed (and the tax would be subject to an interest charge). Again, to qualify for the benefits of Code § 663(a)(1), the distribution must be a fixed amount. A mandate to terminate the trust and distribute whatever is left at that time is obviously not of a fixed amount.

6. *Depleting a trust using the default distribution rule*

18.35 In situations in which there is no other exit strategy and large unknown UNI balances in a foreign trust, it might make sense to take advantage of the 'default' distribution rule found in Part IIIA of Form 3520. Under that rule, an amount equal to 125% of the average distributions in the prior three years will be treated as coming from current – rather than accumulated – income. The good news is that there will be no UNI, no throwback tax, and no interest charge. The bad news is:

---

[13] Where such a trust also falls within the UK income tax anti-avoidance legislation, if there is any accumulated income, the possible UK tax consequences need to be addressed when distributing to US citizens and domiciliaries who are resident in the UK.

(a) the election is irrevocable;

(b) the entire distribution is taxed as ordinary income (even if part of the foreign trust's current earnings are attributed to capital gains);

(c) distributions are taxable even if they would have been attributed to the trust's original corpus; and

(d) distributions in excess of 125% of the prior three years' distributions will be taxed under the accumulation distribution rules, with the accumulation attributed to the earliest years of the trust.

Example

A foreign trust has unknown accumulations from past years as a non-grantor trust. The value in 2004, when it begins annual distributions to US beneficiaries (or a US distribution trust) is $10m. The trust earns $1m of DNI in each of 2004 to 2006, and distributes that amount to the US. In 2007, the trust can distribute $1.25m (a 25% increase over the average distribution in 2004 to 2006). Regardless of the trust's current DNI, the beneficiaries can elect to treat the distribution as a DNI distribution of ordinary income. In 2008, the three-year average increases to $1.083m ($3.25m divided by 3); a default DNI distribution of $1.354m (125% of $1.083m) could be made that year. This pattern could continue annually until all assets of the trust (including untaxed UNI and what could have been tax-free capital) have been distributed and taxed.

7. Beneficiary's rent free use of trust owned property

18.36 A trust can acquire property such as a primary or seasonal residence, yacht or plane, and make it available rent free for the use of a beneficiary. Under current US practice, such use is not considered income or a gift and is not reportable by the beneficiary under the excise tax reporting rules. While the beneficiary can be required to pay current operating expenses under a license agreement with the trustees, the trustees should themselves pay capital expenses, taxes, fire insurance and other liabilities of an owner, as the beneficiary's payment of such expenses could result in taxable rental income to the trustees.[14]

8. Beneficiary's sale of assets to trust

18.37 A foreign trust with substantial UNI can alternatively make available cash assets to US beneficiaries by acquiring substantial assets from them in a purchase transaction which results in no, or minimal, income tax cost to the beneficiary. For example, a beneficiary could sell a substantial residence to the trustees and pay little

---

[14] In the case of a UK resident US citizen, free use of assets can trigger income taxation under ICTA 1988, s 740 and capital gains taxation under TCGA 1992, s 87, however, the latter will not be relevant if such a beneficiary is not UK domiciled as a matter of general law and, in such a case, nor should the former apply if the benefit is conferred outside the UK.

18.38   *UK or Foreign Trusts Providing for a US Beneficiary*

income tax due to the $500,000 exempt gain on sale of a principal residence. A formal property valuation should be required and care should be taken that the transaction is structured at market value.

9. Distribution of trust assets to settlor followed by a gift over

18.38   Settlors resident in certain jurisdictions can receive and make gifts offshore without substantial adverse income or gift tax consequences. For example, a UK resident individual who is not domiciled in the UK may make gifts out of his non-UK sited assets free of UK taxes provided that such gifts are fully completed offshore.

18.39   In such a situation, it is possible to avoid the accumulation distribution rules by making periodic distributions to the settlor's personal, non-UK account. The settlor can, if he wishes, subsequently direct the payment of gifts from his account to his US-taxpayer children.

18.40   Indirect distributions through a settlor are not subject to the US automatic tracing rule of Code § 643(h).[15] Properly structured, such distributions are:

- not reportable under the excise tax rules unless they exceed $100,000 annually; and
- not subject to income tax.

18.41   If UK taxes are also in point, then from a UK perspective it would be fundamental that any distribution to a settlor was wholly independent of a later decision that he may take to make gifts, in order to avoid any contention that the distribution was an indirect distribution to other UK taxable beneficiaries.

10. Distribution to other non-US beneficiaries followed by a gift over

18.42   Families with only US beneficiaries may, at some point in time, acquire a well-liked non-resident alien spouse or perhaps a foreign national beneficiary who is, or becomes, a non-resident of the US. Once a beneficiary is no longer subject to US income or transfer tax jurisdiction – depending on local law consequences – it may be possible to resettle the assets of a foreign trust by a distribution of its assets to such beneficiary. Such a distribution would cleanse the trust of its current DNI and accumulated UNI, facilitating later tax-favored distributions from that trust to US beneficiaries (as discussed at **18.26**).

---

[15]   As discussed in **CHAPTER 12**, a US beneficiary could be treated as having received a distribution from a foreign trust that is made through an intermediary *other than the settlor*. In view of this codified exception for distributions 'through' the grantor, it is highly questionable if the IRS could successfully assert that the step-transaction doctrine applied where trust distributions to a US beneficiary are routed through the settlor.

C. Foreign non-grantor trusts: US beneficiaries   18.47

18.43 If the foreign beneficiary much later and independently were to decide to settle a portion of those distributed assets into a new trust (hopefully one in which the foreign beneficiary/settlor is considered the grantor/owner), the US family members could benefit from the new trust in substantially tax enhanced ways.

18.44 The biggest hurdle with this planning is the tracing rules for distributions from foreign trusts through intermediaries found in Code § 643(h), as discussed above and in **CHAPTER 12**. The regulations clarify that this rule applies if the intermediary had received the initial trust distribution as part of a plan to avoid US taxes.[16] Tax avoidance will be assumed if the US person is related to the trust's grantor[17] and the intermediary transfers the property to the US person within 24 months before, or after receiving, a distribution from a foreign trust.[18] The following example was given in **CHAPTER 12**.

Example

A wealthy lady forms a foreign non-grantor trust for the benefit of her descendants. One of her grandchildren, Nigel Nuworld, is a US income tax resident. Rather than Nigel receiving a direct distribution from the foreign trust, Nigel suggests to the trustee that a distribution be made to Nigel's brother – Sunny – who currently resides in a Caribbean tax haven. Sunny pays no local taxes on the trust distribution and is not subject to any transfer taxes on his gifts, including gifts to his dear brother Nigel. Under Code § 643(h), Nigel can be taxed as if he received the distribution directly from the foreign trust.

18.45 The intermediary rule effectively shifts the burden of proof back to the taxpayer to prove the absence of a tax avoidance scheme. Under prior law, the IRS could attempt to tax the US person by arguing that the intermediary was serving as the US person's agent or by applying the 'step-transaction' doctrine, but the IRS had the burden of proof. Now, it is the US taxpayer who needs to prove that the intermediary was acting independently of the grantor and trustee and was not the US person's agent.[19]

18.46 Any resettlement should clearly not be contemplated at the time of the distribution. The trustees should be cautioned against getting indemnities from the other beneficiaries (as if the assets are later settled the indemnity process may make them constructive settlors or taint the independence of the transactions).

18.47 There should also be no understandings, conditions, or 'locks' imposed on the distributed assets. The new settlor should act independently, should have total freedom of disposition, should spend or retain some of the distributed assets and should be a beneficiary of the new trust. There should be a sufficient passage of time between the original distribution and the settlement of the new trust. The objective here is to survive scrutiny under rigorous US substance over form rules (including

---

[16] Treas Reg § 1.643(h)-1(a)(1).
[17] Treas Reg § 1.643(h)-1(a)(2); the US person is deemed to be related to the grantor under rules set out in Code § 643(i)(2)(B), with some modifications.
[18] Treas Reg § 1.643(h)-1(a)(2)(ii).
[19] Treas Reg § 1.643(h)-1(a)(2)(iii).

18.47 *UK or Foreign Trusts Providing for a US Beneficiary*

agency, nominee and, possibly, the step transaction doctrines) as well as sustaining the US taxpayer's burden of proof under Code § 643(h).

Chapter 19

US Spouse Providing for a UK Spouse

A. Introduction

19.1 This chapter considers integrated tax planning for a US citizen spouse providing for a UK national spouse. There are a number of possible planning situations depending on the residence and domicile of the spouses, but the main focus is circumventing the many pitfalls which can arise in such cases, potentially giving rise to double taxation. If the US spouse is UK domiciled, additional objectives are to ensure that the tax burden in both countries is deferred to the latest possible time, to match credits and allow the survivor access to maximum resources, and to allocate that tax burden to whichever of the relevant countries has the lower tax rate at the time.[1] Any plan should remain sufficiently flexible that modifications can be made to take account of changes.

19.2 The general planning considerations applicable in a variety of situations are discussed in this chapter, including (in the most complicated of settings, where the US citizen spouse is also a UK domiciliary). The US tax objectives in the US spouse's estate plan will be to:

- maximise the tax benefit of the US lifetime gift tax exclusion (capped at $1m);

- maximise the effective use of the US estate tax exemption (currently $1.5m as at 2004 and rising to an anticipated $3.5m by 2009); and

- secure a US marital deduction for the remainder of her estate.

19.3 Where the US spouse is also a UK domiciliary (or deemed domiciliary) or, if not UK domiciled, where the US spouse owns UK-taxable property, the UK tax objectives will also be to:

- use the UK lifetime planning options effectively;

- minimise the US spouse's exposure to UK inheritance tax (IHT) by funding an excluded property trust prior to become a UK IHT domiciliary;

- maximise the effective use of the inheritance tax nil rate band amount of £263,000 (2004/05); and

- secure a UK spouse exemption for the remainder of the US spouse's UK taxable estate.

---

[1] See **CHAPTER 15** (at **15.10** et seq). Assuming an exchange rate of $1.75 = £1, the UK generally has a lower overall tax on 2004 estates below $6.5m. Because the US rules provide for a staged increase in the estate tax exemption and a staged decrease in the top marginal rates, the crossover point (where US rates become higher than UK rates) is likely to climb to over $27m by 2009.

19.4 *US Spouse Providing for a UK Spouse*

B. Lifetime gifts to the UK spouse by the US spouse

19.4 A US spouse making a lifetime gift to a UK spouse will need to be concerned about the:

(a) US gift tax implications of the gift;

(b) UK IHT implications to the US donor spouse;

(c) potential US estate tax implications to the UK donee spouse; and

(d) UK tax implications to the UK donee spouse.

1. US gift tax implications to the US donor spouse

19.5 The US gift tax implications of the US citizen spouse's gift to her UK spouse will depend on:

- whether or not the UK spouse is also US citizen;
- the structure of the gift; and *possibly*
- the size of gift.

If the UK donee spouse is also a US citizen, the gift will qualify for the US unlimited marital deduction if properly structured. Outright gifts qualify, as do gifts in certain marital deduction trusts that generally grant the donee spouse a right to all income (see **CHAPTER 4**).

19.6 If the UK donee spouse is not a US citizen (even if the UK donee spouse is a US domiciliary), the US donor spouse's gift will not qualify for the US marital deduction. Instead, a properly structured gift will qualify for the expanded annual gift tax exclusion, which in 2004 is $114,000.[2]

19.7 If the gift to the UK donee spouse (who is not a US citizen) exceeds the expanded gift tax annual exclusion limit or does not otherwise qualify for the annual exclusion (for example, because the gift is in a non-qualifying trust), the gift will still be exempt from current gift tax if, and to the extent, the US donor spouse has remaining gift tax applicable exclusion. If not, the gift will cause an immediate gift tax.

Example

Cannes Ritz, a spoiled American cracker heiress, is married to Harrison Bosworth III, member of the moderately successful UK boys' band, Space Boyz. Harrison (referred to in the press as 'Lucky Space') is a UK

---

[2] Code §§ 2523(i)(2) and 2503. Outright gifts to a non-citizen spouse qualify for the expanded annual exclusion. Gifts in trust also qualify, but only if the trust would have qualified for the marital deduction had the spouse been a US citizen, and the spouse has a 'present interest' in that trust as required by the annual exclusion rules.

national and not a US citizen. For Lucky's 30th birthday, Cannes surprises him with keys (and title) to a 460 bhp Aston Martin V12 Vanquish – price tag $235,000. Since the gift exceeds Cannes's $114,000 annual exclusion, her gift will use up $121,000 of her $1m lifetime exemption. To some extent, this would be a waste of her exemption, which is generally best used in passing property down to the next generation. If Cannes had already used her $1m lifetime exemption on prior gifts, the $121,000 net taxable gift in this example would result in a gift tax of about $50,000. Cannes might be advised to keep title to the car in her name and let Lucky 'borrow' the keys (or perhaps purchase something a bit more reasonable, such as a $115,000 400 bhp Jaguar XKR convertible).

2. *UK IHT implications to US donor spouse*

19.8 The UK IHT implications to the US donor spouse will, in the first instance, depend on the domicile of the US donor spouse and the situs of the gifted asset.

19.9 First, the following summarises the scope of UK IHT depending on the donor spouse's domicile.

- If the US donor spouse is US domiciled at the time of the gift, the US/UK treaty will generally limit the UK IHT to gifts of only article 6 (real estate) and article 7 (permanent establishment) property. Thus a gift by a US citizen/domiciliary spouse of stock in a UK company would not be subject to UK IHT.

- If the US donor spouse is domiciled outside the US (but not in the UK), then IHT will generally apply to her gift of all UK-situated property. However, a gift of non-UK property (for example, stock in a US company) would not be subject to IHT.

- If the US donor spouse is domiciled (or deemed domiciled) in the UK, IHT would apply to all gifts, regardless of the situs of the gifted property.

19.10 If the US donor spouse is UK domiciled or (if non-domiciled) makes a gift of UK-taxable property, the next question is whether that gift will qualify for the UK spouse exemption. This will depend, in part, on the domicile of the UK donee spouse.

- If the UK donee spouse is UK domiciled, then an outright gift or a gift into a life interest trust of an unlimited amount will qualify for the UK spouse exemption.

- The identical rule applies if the UK donee spouse *and the US donor spouse* are both not UK domiciled.

- In the admittedly rare situation where the US donor spouse is UK domiciled but the UK donee spouse is not, the UK spouse exemption is limited to £55,000. In that situation, however, a properly structured gift could qualify as a potentially exempt transfer (PET) (as discussed in **CHAPTER 1**).

19.11 *US Spouse Providing for a UK Spouse*

19.11 For primarily US tax purposes, the US spouse might decide to fund an irrevocable discretionary trust for the benefit of her UK husband and children. Funding such a trust could cause adverse UK tax implications if either:

(a) the US donor spouse were domiciled (or deemed domiciled) in the UK at the date of the gift (in which event, all property transferred to the trust would be subject to IHT); or

(b) the US donor spouse funded the trust with UK-taxable property.

In that event, an immediate IHT (at a rate of 20%, with possible upward revision to 40% if she dies within seven years of the gift) would be imposed on the portion of the UK-taxable transfer in excess of the nil-rate band.

Example

Cannes (a UK domiciliary) funds a $1m irrevocable discretionary trust for the benefit of Lucky and the couple's twins (christened, in true celebrity fashion, Grapefruit and Kiwi). If Cannes is a UK domiciliary at the time, an immediate 20% IHT will be imposed on the value of the property in excess of the nil-rate band. If Cannes were not a UK domiciliary, but funded the trust with UK-taxable property, the IHT would only be imposed on the value of the UK-situated (and taxable) property transferred to this trust.

If Cannes' objective was to use her $1m gift tax exemption (and shelter future appreciation from US tax), she should consider funding a PET gift (in an interest in possession (IIP) trust or an accumulation and maintenance trust) for the benefit of Grapefruit and Kiwi. No US gift tax or IHT would be imposed on the formation of the trust. The funding will be completely exempt from IHT if Cannes survives by seven years.

If Cannes were not UK domiciled (nor deemed domiciled), no IHT would be imposed if she simply funds the gift on discretionary trusts for Lucky, Grapefruit and Kiwi with non-UK assets (such as stock in the family cracker company).

3. *US estate tax implications to the UK donee spouse*

19.12 If the UK donee spouse is a US citizen or domiciliary at death, any property that he has received as an outright gift from the US donor spouse and not otherwise consumed or disposed of will be included in the UK donee spouse's US taxable estate.

19.13 If the UK donee spouse is not a US citizen or domiciliary at death, then his exposure to US estate tax will generally be limited to US situated property. If the UK donee spouse is a domiciliary of the UK at death, the US/UK treaty will generally limit his US estate tax exposure to article 6 (real estate) and article 7 (permanent establishment) property.

4. UK IHT implications to the UK donee spouse

19.14 If the UK donee spouse is (or at some later time becomes) a UK domiciliary, then any property gifted outright from the US spouse will generally be subject to IHT on the UK spouse's later death or disposition of that property. If the UK donee spouse is not a UK domiciliary, then his IHT exposure will be limited to only UK-situated property.

19.15 If the US donor spouse established a marital deduction trust (only if the UK spouse is a US citizen) or qualifying annual exclusion trust for the UK donee spouse, either of which will provide the UK spouse with a life estate, the UK IHT exposure at the UK donee spouse's death is summarised as follows:

- if the US spouse were domiciled (or deemed domiciled) in the UK at the date of the gift, IHT will be imposed on this trust at the UK beneficiary spouse's later death;

- if the US spouse were not UK domiciled (or deemed domiciled) at the date of the gift and the trust holds non UK sited property the trust will be an excluded property trust. As a consequence, no IHT will be imposed at the UK spouse's later death unless the trust holds UK-situated property at that time.

C. Provisions for the UK surviving spouse at the US spouse's death

19.16 At a US spouse's earlier death, the traditional US domestic estate plan would divide his estate into two shares as follows.

- The estate plan would first allocate to a so-called 'by-pass trust' an amount that is exempt from federal estate taxes by reason of the estate tax applicable exclusion credit. (That amount is currently (2004) $1.5m and rises to $3.5m in 2009, but is effectively reduced by certain large lifetime gifts.) The by-pass trust could either confer a life interest on the surviving spouse or be in the form of a discretionary trust. If properly designed, the by-pass trust will escape (or, in other words, by-pass) US estate taxes in the survivor's estate, thus avoiding US taxes in the spouses' generation.

- The balance of the first spouse's estate would then pass to the surviving spouse in a form qualifying for the US estate tax *marital deduction* (either an outright gift or a gift in a qualifying trust), thus avoiding taxes at the first death. The marital deduction is a tax-deferral tool, not a tax-avoidance tool. At the survivor's death, any property remaining from the marital gift or in the marital trust will generally be taxed in the survivor's US estate.[3]

---

[3] This division is typically mandated by a 'formula' clause and takes into account all relevant facts, including the effective use of the US decedent's estate tax exemption on large lifetime gifts and bequests to others at the US spouse's death. For example, a bequest of $50,000 to each of the US spouse's children at his earlier death would reduce the amount that could be set aside tax-free in the by-pass trust.

19.17 *US Spouse Providing for a UK Spouse*

19.17 The next section of this chapter will examine:

- the US estate tax implications to the US decedent spouse;
- the UK IHT implications to the US decedent spouse;
- the US estate tax implications to the UK surviving spouse; and
- the UK tax implications to the UK surviving spouse.[4]

1. US estate tax implications to the US decedent spouse

19.18 The by-pass trust, marital deduction plan outlined above is designed to avoid US estate taxes at the first death. Funding the by-pass trust will not cause any US estate tax at the US spouse's death, because the amount passing to that trust is sheltered by the US estate tax applicable exclusion credit. Funding the marital deduction transfer will likewise be exempt from current tax, because of the US marital deduction.

19.19 If the UK surviving spouse is not a US citizen (and regardless of whether he is a US domiciliary), the US spouse's bequest to the surviving spouse will only qualify for the marital deduction if that bequest is placed in a so-called qualified domestic trust (QDOT).[5] The QDOT must be governed by US law, have at least one US trustee from whom the US can collect the deferred taxes and incorporate other safeguards designed to ensure collection of the deferred US taxes.

19.20 In UK tax planning, the trustees are often given the power to terminate the surviving spouse's interest in possession in a spousal exemption trust. For IHT purposes, the termination would be treated as a gift by the spouse and, if properly structured, a PET (exempt from IHT if the spouse survives by seven years). However, for US estate tax purposes, the QDOT would not qualify for the US marital deduction if the trustees had the authority to terminate the spouse's income interest.

2. UK IHT implications to the US decedent spouse

a. US decedent spouse not UK domiciled

19.21 If the US decedent spouse is not domiciled (or deemed domiciled) in the UK at death, his exposure to UK IHT will be limited to UK-situated property. If

---

[4] Note that Figures 1 to 3 in Appendix VIII illustrate common planning structures and the US/UK tax implications at the UK spouse's later death.

[5] An outright bequest of assets to the UK spouse would qualify for the UK spouse exemption. However, if the surviving spouse is not a US citizen, an outright bequest to the surviving spouse would only qualify for the US marital deduction if the surviving spouse settled those assets in a post-death QDOT within the time for filing the US spouse's estate tax return. A QDOT trust settled by the surviving spouse would be a grantor trust for US income tax purposes (see **CHAPTER 12** and the equivalent UK income and gains tax provisions – see **CHAPTER 13**) and would result in the assets remaining in the surviving spouse's estate for UK IHT purposes, unless such post-death QDOT had been effected in a manner also qualifying for the special IHT treatment of post-death variations. IHTA 1984, s 142. See **CHAPTER 3**.

C. Provisions for the UK surviving spouse **19.24**

the US decedent spouse is domiciled in the US and thus entitled to treaty protection, only UK-situated property under article 6 (real property) and article 7 (permanent establishment property) would be subject to IHT. If the US decedent is domiciled outside the US (but not in the UK), then all UK-situated property would be subject to IHT.

19.22 If the UK-taxable property were directed to the UK surviving spouse (or to a QDOT in which the surviving spouse had a life interest), this bequest of UK property should qualify for the unlimited UK spouse exemption. Since, in this chapter, we assume the US decedent spouse is not a UK domiciliary, the bequest would so qualify regardless of whether the UK surviving spouse were a UK domiciliary or a non-UK domiciliary.

19.23 The US decedent's UK-taxable property could also be left to a discretionary by-pass trust and still be exempt from IHT, but only to the extent of the nil-rate band (£263,000 in 2004/05). If, and to the extent, UK-taxable property in excess of the nil-rate band were allocated to a discretionary by-pass trust, a 40% IHT would be imposed at the US spouse's earlier death (not a pleasant sight for the UK surviving spouse to see).

Example

Wally Wealthy, a US citizen and domiciliary, is married to Wanda Wimbledon, a UK national and domiciliary. Wally's worldwide estate is valued at $10m, including $3.5m of UK real estate. Wally dies in 2009, when the US estate tax exemption is $3.5m and the UK nil-rate band is assumed still to be £263,000. Wally's estate plan provides for the creation of a by-pass trust (funded with the US estate tax exempt amount) and a QDOT marital trust (funded with the balance of his estate). If Wally's estate plan directed all of his UK real property to the discretionary by-pass trust, no US estate taxes would be imposed on funding. However, because the amount of UK-taxable property transferred to the by-pass trust exceeds the nil-rate band, IHT of $1.2m (40% of $3m value in excess of the nil rate band) would be imposed at Wally's death.

19.24 As in the prior example, if the amount of UK-taxable property allocated to the by-pass trust would exceed the UK nil-rate band, the terms of the trust could direct the division of the by-pass trust into two sub-trusts. The first (a discretionary by-pass trust) would be funded with all property not subject to UK tax, including an amount of UK property equal to the nil-rate band. This trust would be exempt from both US and UK taxes at both deaths. The second sub-trust would be funded with an amount of UK-taxable property in excess of the nil-rate band and would confer a life estate (an interest in possession) on the UK surviving spouse. The objective of the IIP by-pass trust would be to qualify for the UK spouse exemption, and thus deferral of UK taxes.

Example

Same as the example above, but assume Wally's estate plan directed that any UK property transferred to the by-pass trust in excess of the

19.25 *US Spouse Providing for a UK Spouse*

nil-rate band would be set aside in an IIP by-pass sub-trust for Wanda's sole benefit. Wally's estate would accordingly be divided as follows (see Illustration 1 below):

- £263,000 (or approximately $500,000) of UK property to a discretionary by-pass trust; and
- $3m (the balance of Wally's $3.5m US estate tax exemption in excess of the nil-rate band) of UK property to an IIP by-pass trust; and
- the balance of his estate ($6.5m of non-UK property) to a QDOT for his wife's sole benefit.

Illustration 1

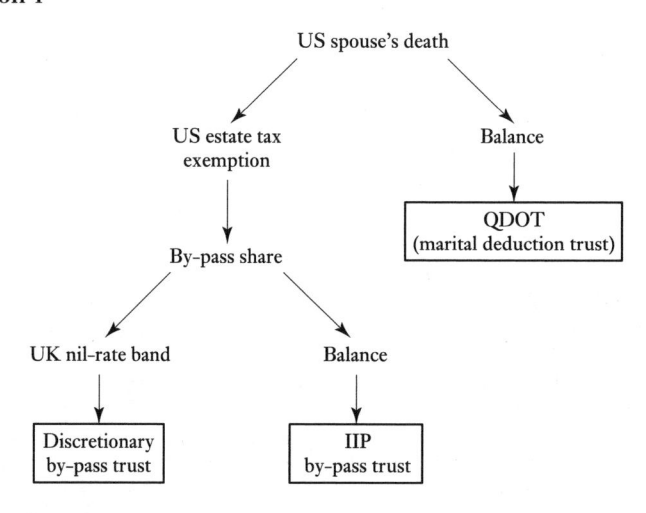

```
                        US spouse's death
                       /                \
              US estate tax            Balance
               exemption                  |
                   |                      v
                   v              ┌──────────────────┐
              By-pass share       │      QDOT        │
              /          \        │(marital deduction│
             /            \       │      trust)      │
            v              v      └──────────────────┘
      UK nil-rate band   Balance
            |               |
            v               v
      ┌───────────┐   ┌───────────┐
      │Discretionary│ │    IIP    │
      │by-pass trust│ │by-pass trust│
      └───────────┘   └───────────┘
```

19.25 If the US domiciled spouse settles UK assets which are later sold during the lifetime of his surviving spouse and reinvested outside the UK, there will be no UK IHT at her later death.

If the US decedent spouse's estate were sufficiently large, it might be beneficial (depending on the nature of the assets) simply to pass the UK-taxable property in excess of the nil-rate band to the surviving spouse in a form qualifying for both the US marital deduction and the UK spouse exemption.

Example

Same as the examples above, but Wally's estate plan instead provides as follows (see Illustration 2):

- $3.5m of property not subject to IHT (for example, a US stock portfolio) to a discretionary by-pass trust; and
- the balance of his estate (including the UK-taxable property) to a QDOT for his wife's sole benefit.

Illustration 2

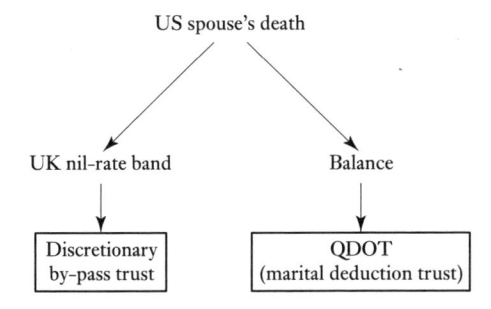

```
                    US spouse's death
                   /                \
                  /                  \
           UK nil-rate band        Balance
                  |                  |
                  ↓                  ↓
          ┌──────────────┐    ┌──────────────────────┐
          │ Discretionary│    │        QDOT          │
          │ by-pass trust│    │(marital deduction    │
          │              │    │       trust)         │
          └──────────────┘    └──────────────────────┘
```

19.26 The QDOT will qualify for the US marital deduction. In addition, the UK property transferred to the QDOT will qualify for the UK spouse exemption. The benefit of this structure is that, at Wanda's death, foreign tax credits will likely be available to limit the total tax to the higher of the two.[6] The discretionary by-pass trust, in turn, will be exempt from both US estate tax as well as IHT at both deaths. The disadvantage is that the UK exemptions will be lost, though that may not be crucial if the US tax is the higher overall.

b. US decedent spouse UK domiciled

19.27 The planning becomes even more complicated if the US citizen spouse is also domiciled (or deemed domiciled) in the UK at death. In that event, the US decedent's worldwide estate (other than property set aside in an excluded property settlement) would be subject to IHT.

(i) Excluded property strategy

19.28 Where the US spouse has become UK domiciled (or deemed domiciled), the couple's IHT exposure can be substantially limited if the US spouse had previously established an excluded property trust (see **CHAPTER 6** at **6.62** et seq). This requires that:

- the US spouse not be domiciled (or deemed domiciled) in the UK at the date of funding, and
- the trust not hold any UK-situated property.

The type of trust is largely irrelevant (though the type of trust can impact the UK tax exposure in succeeding generations).

19.29 The inter vivos excluded property trust would typically be designed as an 'incomplete gift' for US gift tax purposes. As a result, the excluded property assets would be included in the US settlor spouse's US taxable estate and (for US income

---

[6] In a letter dated 7 September 1990 from DJ Ferley of the Capital Taxes Office (CTO) to Paul Knox of Ernst & Young, it was indicated that whilst the treaty did not make any specific provision, the CTO would consider any application for relief sympathetically.

19.30 *US Spouse Providing for a UK Spouse*

tax purposes) re-based to market value.[7] If the excluded property trust provides at the US settlor's death for a discretionary by-pass trust and a QDOT:

- the discretionary bypass trust assets are removed from both US estate tax (due to her lifetime exclusion) and from UK IHT due to excluded property trust status; and
- the QDOT defers US estate tax until the surviving spouse's death and totally avoids UK IHT due to the trust's excluded property status.

19.30 There are two primary tax benefits from the US spouse's funding of the excluded property trust prior to becoming a UK domiciliary. First, the US spouse would be able to preserve sufficient assets to fully fund a discretionary by-pass trust at her earlier death, without concerns about (and the added complications from) the more limited UK nil-rate band. Second, in the possible (but, in the authors' view, somewhat unlikely) event that the US repealed the estate tax, the excluded property trust will avoid the only transfer tax imposed at the US spouse's death – the IHT.

19.31 Since the excluded property trust is an incomplete gift, the by-pass and marital trusts may (but need not necessarily) be specified in the original deed. The trust could subsequently be amended to allocate trust property at the settlor's death to be held in separate bypass and marital trust 'funds', which will be treated as separate trusts for US purposes.

19.32 Care needs to be taken to ensure that the excluded property trust effectively excludes the trust property from IHT at the UK spouse's later death. To this end, the trust should not hold UK assets at the US spouse's death, nor at his spouse's later death.

(ii) If no excluded property trust had been formed

19.33 If the US spouse had not created an excluded property settlement prior to becoming a UK domiciliary (or deemed domiciliary), the US decedent spouse's estate plan is significantly more complicated and worldwide tax saving more difficult to accomplish.

19.34 Since the UK-domiciled US citizen spouse's worldwide estate will be subject to IHT, funding a discretionary by-pass trust with the amount exempt from US estate tax (again, for 2004 $1.5m but climbing to $3.5m in 2009) would result in an IHT being imposed at the US spouse's death. This is a result of the different size

---

[7] See **CHAPTER 11** and **16.76**. An 'incomplete gift' excluded property trust may be used effectively in conjunction with a US lifetime revocable trust created as a will planning substitute to avoid probate. The revocable or 'living' trust is also an incomplete gift trust and technically could itself serve as an excluded property trust (if funded when the settlor was not UK IHT domiciled). As stated in **CHAPTER 13**, for UK gains tax purposes, a UK resident settlor and spouse of an excluded property trust should avoid being trustees, since their UK residence could cause the settlor to be taxable on worldwide trust gains under the Taxation of Chargeable Gains Act 1992 (TCGA 1992), s 77.

of the transfer tax exemptions in the two countries – for 2004 this is $1.5m in the US (climbing to $3.5m in 2009) and £263,000 in the UK (subject to annual adjustments).

19.35   There are two alternatives to avoid IHT at the UK-domiciled, US spouse's death. Both involve funding a discretionary by-pass trust with only an amount exempt from IHT by reason of the nil-rate band.[8]

19.36   Under the first alternative, the amount of the US estate tax exemption in excess of the UK nil-rate band would simply be added to and incorporated in the QDOT.

Example

Wally Wealthy (a US citizen domiciled in the UK) dies in 2009 with a UK-citizen spouse (Wanda) and a $10m worldwide estate. Wally's estate plan directs for his estate to be divided between the following two trusts:

- £263,000 (or approximately $500,000) to a discretionary by-pass trust; and
- the balance of his estate ($9.5m) to a QDOT for his wife's sole benefit.

The QDOT qualifies for the UK spouse exemption (assuming, as is likely the case, that Wanda is also UK domiciled or deemed domiciled). The discretionary by-pass trust is exempt from IHT because of the nil-rate band. No IHT would be imposed at Wally's death. Importantly, even though Wally's estate plan only funds the by-pass trust with the lower nil-rate band amount, his estate will still effectively use the entire US estate tax exemption (albeit the balance over the nil-rate band is used at the survivor's death, as discussed at **19.38** et seq).

19.37   Under the second alternative, the estate plan of the UK-domiciled, US citizen decedent spouse could provide for the full funding of the by-pass trust with the US estate tax exempt amount, but a subdivision of that trust between:

(a)   a discretionary by-pass trust (equal to the UK nil rate band); and

(b)   a by-pass trust in which the UK surviving spouse had as a life estate (interest in possession), qualifying for the UK spouse exemption.

Example

Same as above, but Wally's estate plan directs that his estate be divided as follows:

- £263,000 (or approximately $500,000) to a discretionary by-pass trust; and

---

[8]   To have maximum effect this is best achieved by using a formula to ensure the use of the maximum nil-rate sum applicable at death, taking account of upward adjustments in the exemption and any necessary deductions as a result of gifts within the prior seven years.

19.38 *US Spouse Providing for a UK Spouse*

- $3m (the balance of Wally's $3.5m estate tax exemption in excess of the nil-rate band) to an IIP by-pass trust; and
- the balance of his estate ($6.5m) to a QDOT for his wife's sole benefit.

The QDOT and IIP by-pass trust would qualify for the UK spouse exemption. The discretionary by-pass trust would also be exempt from IHT, again, because of the nil-rate band. Thus, no IHT at Wally's death.

The US implications of these two alternatives are discussed below.

3. US estate tax implications at UK surviving spouse's death

19.38 If the US decedent spouse had established a QDOT for the UK spouse, then a deferred US estate tax (referred to in **CHAPTER 4** as the 'QDOT estate tax') is imposed on:

(a) a distribution of principal (including capital gains) from the QDOT; and

(b) the balance of the assets remaining in the QDOT at the survivor's death.

The tax is computed as if the property had been included in the US spouse's estate (at the rates and subject to the exemptions available at the US spouse's earlier death). Property remaining in the by-pass trust will not be subject to US estate tax at the survivor's death.

19.39 Paragraphs 19.33 et seq describe the possible need for the US decedent spouse to limit the amount funding a discretionary by-pass trust to only an amount sheltered by the UK nil-rate band. This would be particularly important if the US spouse were UK domiciled at death and had not established an excluded property trust, thus exposing his worldwide estate to IHT. Two alternative structures were suggested. In one, all property in excess of the nil-rate band would be set aside in a QDOT. In the other, an IIP by-pass trust would be funded with the difference between the US estate tax exempt amount and the UK nil-rate band. The US tax implications of these two alternatives are illustrated in the following examples.

Example (big QDOT)

Wally Wealthy is a US citizen who died domiciled in the UK in 2009. Assume his estate plan directed for the funding of the following trusts:

- £263,000 (or approximately $500,000) to a discretionary by-pass trust; and
- the balance of his estate ($9.5m) to a QDOT for his wife's sole benefit.

At Wanda's later death, assume the QDOT assets had appreciated by 50% to $14.25m. Because Wally's estate only used $500,000 of his estate tax exemption at his earlier death (in funding the discretionary by-pass trust), the balance of his exemption ($3m = $3.5m less $500,000) would

C. Provisions for the UK surviving spouse **19.42**

be available to reduce QDOT estate taxes at Wanda's later death. The balance of the QDOT ($11.25m = $14.25m less $3m) would be subject to an estate tax of about $5.1m.

Example (IIP by-pass trust)

As an alternative, Wally's estate plan could have directed the following without any UK or US taxes being imposed at his earlier death:

- £263,000 (or approximately $500,000) to a discretionary by-pass trust; and
- $3m (the balance of Wally's $3.5m estate tax exemption in excess of the nil-rate band) to an IIP by-pass trust; and
- the balance of his estate ($6.5m) to a QDOT for his wife's sole benefit.

Assume the smaller QDOT had similarly appreciated by 50%, in this case to $9.75m. The US estate tax on that amount would be about $4.4m. The $700,000 of US tax savings ($4.4m versus $5.1m) results from excluding the appreciation on the IIP by-pass trust from US estate tax at Wanda's later death.

19.40 If the UK surviving spouse were a US citizen or domiciliary at her later death, the property remaining in the QDOT would also be subject to US estate tax in her estate. Similarly, if the UK spouse were not a US citizen or domiciliary at her later death, any *US property* held in the QDOT (limited to article 6/7 property if the survivor were a UK domiciliary) would be taxed in her US estate because of the estate tax situs rules. The *QDOT estate tax* is credited against any US estate tax imposed on the survivor's estate. The objective of this credit is to ensure that there is only one US tax on this property in the couple's generation – not a double tax. In most instances, the QDOT estate tax will be higher than any US estate tax imposed on the survivor's estate.

19.41 As noted, the QDOT estate taxes can also be imposed on a distribution of principal from the QDOT to the surviving spouse. Such a distribution would not, however, be a taxable event for IHT purposes. Even though the distributed property might be subject to IHT at the UK spouse's later death, the UK would not grant a foreign tax credit for US estate taxes imposed on this earlier QDOT distribution. Thus, to avoid double tax (without offsetting credits), it may be advisable not to make any principal distributions to the UK spouse.

4. *UK IHT implications at the UK surviving spouse's later death*

a. **IHT exposure depends on whether QDOT (or IIP by-pass trust) is an excluded property trust**

19.42 The UK surviving spouse's exposure to IHT on property held in a QDOT (or an IIP by-pass trust) depends on whether the trust is considered an excluded property trust. If it is (and holds no UK assets at the survivor's death), it

19.43 *US Spouse Providing for a UK Spouse*

will be exempt from IHT, regardless of the survivor's domicile. If not, it will be subject to IHT, again, regardless of the survivor's domicile.

Example

Davey Breckman (a US citizen and domiciliary) was a famed hairstylist at the posh London hair salon, Loreal Madrid. There he met, treated and married one of his more famous UK customers, Vikki S. Pyce. Davey was killed in a freak honeymoon accident while attempting to 'straighten it like Breckman' – a hair straightening technique he created involving mayonaise, leather and banjo wire (don't ask). Prior to his marriage, Davey had prepared a US estate plan that provided for all of his non-UK assets to pass into a QDOT marital trust for Vikki's benefit. The trust will be considered an excluded property trust and exempt from IHT at Vikki's later death. This would be true even though Vikki was domiciled in the UK at Davey's death and even if she were still UK domiciled at her later death. To maintain this excluded property status, the trust must not have any UK-situated property at Vikki's later death. Her UK domicile may, however, impact the ongoing UK IHT position on any subsequent discretionary trusts.

Example

Julie Robins, an American stage actress, moves to London to further her stage career in a West End musical (Andy Floyd Webster's political masterpiece, *Hillary*). There Julie meets and later marries a UK bookseller, Grant Hew. The couple remain in the UK and Julie eventually becomes a UK domiciliary (or deemed domiciliary). Julie does not create an excluded property trust. At her death (as a US citizen domiciled in the UK), her estate plan establishes a QDOT (and perhaps an IIP by-pass trust) for Grant's benefit. Grieving Julie's death and bitten by the acting bug, Grant moves permanently to Hollywood (where he later takes US citizenship after remarrying) and becomes domiciled there. Grant's interest in the QDOT (and IIP by-pass trust) will be subject to IHT at his later death, even though he is a US citizen and domiciliary at death.

19.43 Note the 'all or none' consequence of IHT domicile in settling a trust. An excluded property trust will be attributed with the settlor's non-UK domicile (Davey) at the time of funding. Its non-UK assets will be excluded property and thus exempt from UK IHT under either the IIP[9] or discretionary trust[10] IHT regimes. This holds true even if the settlor were to later be UK IHT domiciled at death, and even if the surviving spouse (Vikki) who possesses a life interest in the trust is UK IHT domiciled.

19.44 Conversely, a trust settled when the settlor (Julie) was UK IHT domiciled (or deemed UK domiciled) itself acquires a status by reference to the settlor's then UK domicile. This status continues even after the settlor's death and even if the surviving spouse becomes non-UK domiciled (Grant's move to the US).[11] This

---

[9] IHTA 1984, ss 49–57A, Ch II.
[10] IHTA 1984, ss 58–85, Ch III.
[11] IHTA 1984, ss 48(3) and 52.

C. Provisions for the UK surviving spouse   **19.46**

results in ongoing potential inheritance tax exposure throughout the trust's existence. The tax is payable by the trustees out of the trust property.

b. Foreign tax credit issues

19.45   Unless the QDOT were an excluded property trust for IHT purposes, a US estate tax (the QDOT estate tax) and an IHT could both be imposed at the UK surviving spouse's death. If both US estate tax and IHT is imposed on the QDOT at the UK spouse's death, the foreign tax credits granted by each country should essentially result in the higher of the two taxes applying. There is a technical risk that credit relief may not apply (because the US and UK taxes are viewed as imposed on separate events, eg separate deaths and with respect to different estates) and hence a risk of double taxation. Generally, however, it is understood that the UK Capital Taxes Office may not take this point and hence allow for relief in appropriate circumstances.[12] The US would clearly give a foreign death tax credit for any UK taxes imposed on the QDOT property.[13]

19.46   The effect of the foreign tax credit is to subject the QDOT (or IIP by-pass trust) to tax at the highest effective rate in the two countries.

Example

Julie Robins (a US citizen, domiciled in the UK at death) dies in 2009 and leaves a $10m estate. Her estate plan directs an amount equal to the nil-rate band (£263,000, or about $500,000 at relevant exchange rates) to a by-pass trust and the balance of her estate (about $9.5m) to a QDOT for her UK husband, Grant. No US or UK taxes would be imposed at her death.

Assume the QDOT had appreciated by 50% to $14.25m at Grant's death. He has no personal assets apart from his interest in the trust. In computing the QDOT estate tax, the balance of Julie's US estate tax exemption ($3m = $3.5m less $500,000 used in funding the by-pass trust) is still available. Effectively, only $11.25m of the QDOT ($14.25m less Julie's remaining $3m estate tax exemption) would be taxed. The QDOT estate tax (at an assumed rate of 45%) would be $5.1m.

The IHT on the $14.25m QDOT would be $5.5m (at an assumed rate of 40% after taking into account an assumed nil-rate band that exempts only $500,000 of the QDOT). If the US gives full credit for the UK taxes imposed on the QDOT (per treaty article 9(3)(c)) the total taxes would be $5.5m (the amount of the UK IHT).

The same worldwide taxes would be imposed if Julie's estate plan had provided for the funding of an IIP by-pass trust with the difference

---

[12]   See footnote 6.
[13]   Code § 2056A(b)(10)(A) allows the QDOT estate tax to be computed after taking into account certain deductions (such as the marital deduction and charitable deduction) and credits (such as foreign death tax credit and, until 2005, the state death tax credit) that would otherwise have been available to the *survivor* had he or she been a US citizen.

19.47 *US Spouse Providing for a UK Spouse*

between the nil-rate band and the US estate tax exemption (about $3m in this example). Julie's estate would thus be divided as follows:

- £263,000 (or about $500,000) to a discretionary by-pass trust;
- $3m to a IIP by-pass trust for Grant's benefit; and
- $6.5m to an IIP QDOT, qualifying for both the US/UK.

This IIP by-pass sub-trust would be designed to qualify for the UK spouse exemption, but Julie's estate would not need to make a QDOT election for that trust to escape US taxes at her death. As a result, the IIP by-pass trust would be subject to only UK tax at Grant's later death. The QDOT estate tax on the smaller $9.75m QDOT (appreciated by 50% from Julie's death) would be $4.4m. However, both the QDOT and the IIP by-pass trust would be subject to IHT. Assuming those combined trusts had appreciated by 50%, the total value subject to IHT would be $14.25m. The IHT would be $5.5m, which would be fully credited in the US to offset the lower US taxes. Again, however, the worldwide tax bill would be $5.5m.

As shown, regardless of whether Julie's plan funded a larger QDOT or an IIP by-pass trust, the same $5.5m of worldwide taxes would be imposed at Grant's later death. The UK tax in these examples exceeds the US tax, therefore, worldwide tax is effectively paid at the higher UK rate at Grant's later death.

The benefits of excluded property trust planning can be readily quantified. Assume Julie had sufficiently funded an excluded property trust so that, at her death, her by-pass trust could be fully funded from property that was exempt from IHT. The QDOT would accordingly need to be funded with $6.5m at her death to avoid US and UK tax. At Grant's later death, only the smaller QDOT (then appreciated to $9.75m) would be subject to IHT and US estate tax. The QDOT estate tax would again be $4.4m, while the IHT would drop to $3.7m; $9.75m less $500,000 – representing the UK nil-rate band assuming there is no free estate – at 40% (completely offset by a foreign tax credit for the US taxes). Excluded property planning thus reduces the worldwide tax imposed at Grant's death by $1.1m in this example ($4.4m versus $5.5m).

c. Excluded property planning: final thoughts

19.47 There are three possible strategies for a US citizen planning to fund an incomplete gift, excluded property trust. The first strategy would be to design the trust as a 'discretionary trust' from a US perspective but a defeasible interest in possession trust from a UK perspective, that is, one in which the US citizen settlor retains a life estate, terminable at the discretion of the trustees.[14] Typically this could

---

[14] The preference is that the independent trustees are given all appropriate powers rather than the settlor, and that the settlor's involvement with the trust following settlement remains simply in his capacity as beneficiary. If necessary for US purposes, the settlor could be given a testamentary power of appointment which, of itself, should not cause inclusion of the trust assets in his UK taxable estate.

C. Provisions for the UK surviving spouse **19.49**

be followed by a life interest for the spouse and then either life interests for the children or discretionary trusts for them. The disadvantage of this trust is that either the domicile of the settlor will be retested at the date of his death, or at the later death of a surviving spouse her domicile will be retested. In either case, if the last life tenant to die has a UK domicile, the discretionary trusts for the children will not fall into the excluded property trust regime.[15] The disadvantage of the latter can be overcome if the trust never becomes discretionary and the children are given sequential life interests after the deaths of both spouses (any desired 'accumulation' or retention of income for trust law purposes, being achieved through suitable investment vehicles such as mutual funds rather than the terms of the trust). One of the benefits of the interest in possession is that there will be an uplift in cost basis of the assets at the date of death of the life tenant, which may be advantageous as far as unrealised gains are concerned.[16]

19.48 The second strategy would be to design the trust as a fully discretionary trust from the outset, but followed at the settlor's death by a life interest for the spouse and, following the spouse's death, either life interests for the children or discretionary trusts for them. In principle, the discretionary trust, as an excluded property trust, should be exempt from UK IHT as to non-UK assets with respect to all beneficiaries for as long as the trust subsists. However, discretionary trusts have been somewhat out of favour in view of certain recent indications that the Inland Revenue may be reviewing its position on the interaction of the reservation of benefit legislation and excluded property trusts where the settlor continues to benefit.[17] The other disadvantage of such a discretionary trust is that there will be no uplift in cost basis of the assets for UK capital gains tax purposes, at the date of death of any of the beneficiaries.

19.49 The third strategy would be to design the trust as in **19.47** but, assuming there are practical reasons for doing so, with an initial discretionary period following which the trust is converted into a life interest trust. The objective of this route is to ensure that there is no initial interest in possession of the spouse or settlor and therefore the domicile re-testing, which occurs in **19.47**, is avoided. Arguably, this route offers the most advantageous combination if the desire is ultimately to have a

---

[15] IHTA 1984, ss 80(1) and 82(3).
[16] If the UK domiciled spouse is the husband, then the children will also take his domicile as their domicile of origin. Therefore, potential distributions to any of these beneficiaries carry the risk of attribution of taxable gains under TCGA 1992, s 87.
[17] The Inland Revenue indicated informally in Autumn 2001 that it may be about to change its view on the interaction of these two sets of rules. They contended that revised legal advice was that their interpretation of the rules in 1986 may have been faulty and that a reservation of benefit did arise. On the analysis of the legislation, it seemed to practitioners that the 1986 interpretation was correct and that the excluded property rules did prevail. However, as the technical analysis seemed to be marginally clearer in the case of interest in possession trusts than discretionary trusts, a more recent trend has been to use the former as a matter of caution. However, no formal Inland Revenue statement has been issued on this. The recent background paper on Residence and Domicile indicated that there has been no change in the Inland Revenue's stance on this ('Reviewing the residence and domicile rules as they affect the taxation of individuals; a background paper', April 2003).

19.49 *US Spouse Providing for a UK Spouse*

discretionary trust for the children. This is subject always in appropriate circumstances, to the possibility of the Inland Revenue seeking to disregard the initial discretionary period.[18]

Example

On the advice of UK counsel, Julie Robins (US citizen and not yet UK domiciled) puts her non-UK sited assets into an irrevocable discretionary trust which is at some time thereafter converted into a life interest trust. The trust qualifies as an excluded property trust. The purpose is to protect those assets from UK IHT should she later become domiciled (or deemed domiciled) in the UK. The trustees' powers of appointment would enable the funds to be appointed back to her, at their discretion, if the US estate tax was repealed or if warranted by any other change in family circumstances. The trustees exercise their powers to provide that excluded property trust assets should be divided into two funds on Julie's death if she is survived by her UK husband (Grant):

(a) a discretionary by-pass trust funded with the amount of her unused lifetime estate tax exclusion (eg $3.5m as of 2009); and

(b) the remainder to be held in a QDOT for Grant for his life, with potential discretionary distributions of capital to Grant only.

At Grant's death, the unspent principal of the two trusts can either be held in a discretionary trust for children or on life interest trusts for the children. The irrevocable trust, as an excluded property trust, will be exempt from UK IHT as to non-UK assets with respect to Julie and all beneficiaries for as long as the trust subsists.

---

[18] On the basis it is a step inserted with no purpose other than to avoid the IHTA 1984, s 80 provisions. If the trust is converted at some later date and not as part of any pre-conceived plan, this should not be in point. If this point were to be taken, however, the discretionary children's trust could be converted into a life interests for the children going forward and thereby preserve the excluded property status and avoid the adverse implications of the discretionary trust regime.

Chapter 20

A UK Spouse Providing for a US Spouse

A. Introduction

20.1 This chapter considers integrated tax planning for a UK spouse providing for a US citizen spouse. As in **CHAPTER 19**, there are a number of possible planning situations depending on the residence and domicile of the spouses, but the main focus is circumventing the many pitfalls which can arise in such cases, potentially giving rise to double taxation. Again, any plan should remain sufficiently flexible that modifications can be made to take account of changes.

20.2 The general planning considerations applicable in a variety of situations are discussed, including (in the most complicated of settings, where the US citizen spouse is also a UK domiciliary). The UK tax objectives in the UK spouse's estate plan will generally be to:

- use the UK lifetime planning options effectively;
- maximise the effective use of the inheritance tax nil rate band amount of £263,000 (2004/05); and
- secure a UK spouse exemption for the remainder of the UK spouse's estate.

Where the spouse is a US citizen, the planning should also (if possible and practicable) minimise US estate tax in the US spouse's estate.

B. Lifetime gifts to the US spouse by the UK spouse

20.3

A UK spouse making a lifetime gift to a US spouse will need to be concerned about:

- the UK IHT implications to the UK donor spouse;
- the US gift tax implications of the gift;
- the UK tax implications to the US donee spouse; and
- the potential US estate tax implications to the US donee spouse.

1. UK IHT implications to the UK donor spouse

20.4 A donor spouse who is domiciled in the UK (or IHT deemed domiciled) will be subject to IHT on his worldwide gifts. A donor spouse who is not UK domiciled (regardless of nationality) will only be subject to IHT on gifts of UK-situated property. If the donor spouse is domiciled in the US (including under

20.5 A UK Spouse Providing for a US Spouse

the treaty tie-breaker rules), only gifts of UK-situated article 6 (real estate) and article 7 (permanent establishment) property will be subject to IHT.

20.5 If a donor spouse makes a gift of UK-taxable property to his US donee spouse (either outright or in an interest in possession trust), the gift will qualify for the UK spouse exemption if either:

(a) the US donee spouse is UK domiciled (or deemed domiciled); or

(b) both spouses are domiciled outside the UK.

Example

Charles Princely (a UK domiciliary) gives his wife, Amanda Columbus (a US citizen, domiciled in the UK), title to the couple's Cotswold cottage, valued at £500,000. Since both spouses are UK domiciled, the gift qualifies for the UK spouse exemption.

Example

Charles (a UK national who is domiciled in the US) makes a gift of his Cotswold cottage to Amanda (his US wife, also domiciled in the US). Since neither spouse is UK domiciled, the gift qualifies for the spouse exemption.

Example

Charles (a UK national who is still domiciled in the UK), gives his wife Amanda (a US citizen and domiciliary) $200,000 to start a store in Miami, where the couple currently resides. The gift does not qualify for the UK spouse exemption, because Charles is a UK domiciliary and Amanda is not.

20.6 If the UK donor spouse makes a gift of UK-taxable property to his US spouse and that gift does not qualify for the UK spouse exemption, the gift might still be currently exempt from IHT if structured as a potentially exempt transfer (PET). Outright gifts and gifts to interest in possession (IIP) trusts will qualify as PETs. If the donor survives the gift by seven years, the 'potential' is realised, so to speak, and the transfer is fully exempt. If the UK donor spouse dies within seven years, the transfer will be taxable, but the amount of the tax will reduce depending on the length of time the donor has survived since making the gift.

20.7 If a UK donor spouse is making a gift to a US citizen spouse, the couple should be aware of the US estate tax implications to the US donee spouse. As noted at **20.25** et seq, any property received outright by the US donee spouse will be included in her US estate at death. In contrast, it is possible to structure a gift to an IIP trust that qualifies for the UK spouse exemption or as a PET, but will be exempt from US tax at the US spouse's death. Potentially this can be important because of the higher US marginal estate tax rates for larger estates.

2. US gift tax implications to the UK donor spouse

20.8 A UK donor will only need to be concerned with the US gift tax implications of the gift if:

- he is a US citizen or domiciliary at the time of the gift; or
- if not a US citizen or domiciliary, he makes a gift of US situated property.

If the UK donor is a US citizen (regardless of his domicile) or a US domiciliary, the gift will have US gift-tax implications regardless of the situs of the gifted property. If the UK donor is not a US citizen or domiciliary, then only US-situated property will be taxed. If the UK donor is a UK domiciliary, then the US/UK Treaty will generally limit his US gift tax exposure to gifts of US-situated article 6 (real property) and article 7 (permanent establishment) property.

20.9 If the UK donor makes a gift of US-taxable property to his US citizen spouse, the gift will qualify for the US marital deduction (and thus be exempt from US gift tax) if it is either made outright to the US spouse or in a trust that qualifies for the US marital deduction (generally, a life interest trust). The fact that the *donor* spouse is not a US citizen or domiciliary is irrelevant to the qualification of the gift for the US marital deduction. The key issue is the citizenship of the *donee* spouse. If the donee spouse is a US citizen, then gifts to her can qualify for the deduction. If the donee spouse is not a US citizen (even if she is US domiciled), the gifts will not qualify for the deduction; instead, the gift will only be exempt to the extent it is within the expanded gift tax annual exclusion for gifts to non-citizen spouses (which, in 2004, is $114,000).

20.10 Finally, if the UK donor is a US citizen or domiciliary, the UK donor can make a gift to the US spouse by a discretionary trust of which she is a beneficiary, that does not qualify for the US marital deduction (or annual exclusion) but which would none the less be exempt from US gift tax because of the US gift tax lifetime exclusion (capped at $1m). If a US citizen but a UK domiciliary, the donor needs to take care as a gift to a discretionary trust will be a lifetime chargeable transfer for UK IHT, even if his spouse is a beneficiary.

3. UK IHT implications to the US donee spouse

20.11 A US donee spouse who receives an outright gift will potentially be exposed to UK IHT at her later death depending on:

- her domicile at death; and
- the situs of the property.

If the US spouse is UK domiciled, all property owned by her (wherever situated) will be subject to IHT. If the US donee spouse is not UK domiciled, the US donee spouse will only be subject to IHT on UK-situated property (which, if the US donee spouse is US domiciled, is limited by the US/UK Treaty to article 6/7 property).

20.12 A UK Spouse Providing for a US Spouse

20.12 In cases where the UK donor spouse's gift qualifies for the UK spouse exemption, the gifted property will not necessarily be subject to IHT at the US donor spouse's death. These rules effectively offer a US donee spouse a relatively 'easy' opportunity to escape UK IHT.

Example

Amanda (a US citizen and domiciliary, who is not a deemed UK domiciliary) received a gift of a Cotswold cottage from Charles, her UK citizen, but US domiciled spouse. The gift qualified for the UK spouse exemption, because both spouses were non-domiciled at the time of the gift. If Amanda later sells the UK residence (pays UK CGT, if any, and US capital gains tax) and then re-invests the proceeds in non-UK assets (such as a villa in Portugal), no UK IHT will be imposed at her later death. The same would apply if Amanda invested in UK securities, since the US/UK Treaty will generally allow only the US (her country of domicile) to tax her portfolio investments.

Example

Amanda (a US citizen domiciled in the UK) received a gift of stock in a UK company (Cotswold Crafts, Ltd) from her UK domiciled spouse. The gift was exempt from IHT because both spouses were UK domiciled. Upon the couple's later divorce, Amanda moves back to the US (abandoning her domicile of choice and reverting to her domicile of origin). Although Amanda still owns the UK securities at her death (and even though she received those securities as a gift qualifying for the UK spouse exemption), they will not be subject to IHT at her death, because, at that time, she is US domiciled (thus limiting her IHT exposure to article 6/7 property).

20.13 The same rules would apply if the US spouse had received an outright gift that was exempt from IHT because of the PET rules.

Example

Amanda (a US citizen, domiciled in the US and not deemed UK domiciled) received an outright PET gift of a Cotswold cottage from her UK-domiciled husband. The gift does not qualify for the UK spouse exemption, but is a PET. If Amanda later dies owning that property, it will be subject to IHT at her death. If, however, she sells the property and invests in property that would not be subject to IHT at her death (for example, real property outside the UK or, if she is US domiciled, UK securities), no IHT will be imposed at her death.

Example

Amanda received an outright PET gift of Cotswold Crafts Ltd (a UK company) and later dies a US domiciliary. No IHT is imposed on her ownership interest of this property because of the treaty.

20.14 A US spouse otherwise exposed to IHT on gifted property can also avoid IHT by herself making a PET gift of that property and surviving the gift by seven years.

Example

Amanda (a US citizen domiciled in the UK) had received an outright gift from her UK husband. After her husband's death, Amanda remains in the UK (and thus remains domiciled there). However, to reduce her IHT exposure, she makes a PET gift to her children, thus avoiding IHT if she survives that gift by seven years. (Of course, the US gift tax implications would have to be considered.)

20.15 If the UK spouse made a gift, qualifying as a PET or exempt by reason of the spouse exemption, to the US spouse by way of a trust giving the US spouse an interest in possession, the trust's exposure to IHT on death of the US spouse will depend on whether or not the trust is an excluded property trust. As discussed in CHAPTER 6, an excluded property trust must be funded by a person who is a non-UK domiciliary at the time of funding, and will be exempt from IHT regardless of the eventual domicile of the settlor or beneficiary spouse. The only exception is if the trust holds UK-situated property at the taxable event, ie the US donee spouse's death.

Example

Charles (a UK national domiciled in the Cayman Islands) creates an IIP trust for the benefit of Amanda, his US citizen spouse. Charles transfers title to a London flat to that trust, but has no current IHT exposure because the gift qualifies for the spouse exemption. Because Charles is not domiciled in the UK, the trust is also an excluded property trust, and will be exempt from IHT at Amanda's later death, to the extent of its non-UK property. If the trust continued to own the London flat, that property would be subject to IHT (collected from the trustees) at Amanda's death. If the flat were sold prior thereto and the proceeds reinvested in non-UK taxable property (including UK authorised unit trusts if Amanda were a US domiciliary), no IHT would be imposed.

20.16 If the UK donor spouse was UK domiciled at the date the IIP trust was created, the trust will *not* be an excluded property trust and will not be exempt from IHT at Amanda's later death, regardless of the situs of the trust's assets and regardless of the US beneficiary spouse's domicile. In this context, exposure results from the donor's domicile at the time of funding the trust, not the domicile of the interest in possession holder.

Example

Charles (a UK national and domiciliary) creates an IIP trust for the benefit of Amanda, his US citizen spouse. The trust qualifies for the UK spouse exemption because, at the time of the gift, Amanda was UK-deemed domiciled. If Amanda relinquishes her UK domicile, the trust will still be subject to IHT at her later death.

Example

Charles transfers title to his London flat to an IIP trust for the benefit of Amanda, his US-domiciled spouse. The gift does not qualify for the UK spouse exemption, but is a PET. Even if the trust later sells the UK property and reinvests the proceeds outside the UK, and even though

20.17   *A UK Spouse Providing for a US Spouse*

Amanda is not a UK domiciliary at her later death, the trust will be taxed at that time. Again, this is because of the donor's UK domicile at the time of funding.

20.17 If a trust was created by a UK domiciliary for his US spouse, with the benefit of the UK spouse exemption or if it qualified as a PET, IHT can still be avoided at the US spouse's later death.

20.18 First, if the US spouse is not UK domiciled, the trust property could be distributed to her outright. In that event, the US spouse's IHT exposure will be limited to UK situated property.

Example

Amanda is the beneficiary of an IIP trust created by her UK domiciled spouse. To avoid IHT at Amanda's death, the trustees liquidate the trust's UK investments and distribute the cash proceeds to Amanda. If Amanda is a US domiciliary at her death, IHT would only be imposed on her UK article 6/7 property.

20.19 Second, the trustees could terminate the US spouse's interest in possession (in full or in part) in favour of the couple's children as an outright gift, or on trusts in their favour (either IIP or accumulation and maintenance (A&M) trusts). For UK purposes, the termination of the spouse's interest would be taxed as if it were a gift by the spouse (although tax being paid, if any, by the trustees). However, if that 'gift' is properly structured (as outlined above), it would also qualify as a PET. Again, the taxability of a gift on the termination of the US *donee* spouse's IIP is a result of the original settlor spouse's UK domicile at the time the trust was funded. However, the donee spouse's deemed gift can still qualify as a PET by her. If the US donee spouse (the 'donor' of the PET gift at the termination of her IIP) survives that gift by seven years, no IHT will be imposed.

20.20 In the examples above, given that Amanda, and probably the children, will be US citizens, PET transfers out of the trust during Amanda's life can avoid UK IHT while not being subject to US estate tax, provided that the estates of the beneficiaries remain within the amount of the US applicable exclusion. Amanda *and each child* (and potentially *each spouse of each child*) will *each* be able to benefit from the 2001 Tax Act increases in US transfer tax exemptions (currently $1.5m rising to $3.5m by 2009 for estate and GST taxes). It should, however, be noted that the children will be general law domiciliaries of the UK as a result of their father's UK domicile at the date of their birth – the planning consequence being that the children will have to have a defensible non UK domicile of choice at any relevant time in order to avoid being subject to global UK inheritance tax.[1]

20.21 The incentive for PET distributions is of further significance since if Amanda does not survive the seven-year period, the gift is brought back into the

---

[1]   Assuming an exchange rate of $1.75 = £1, the UK generally has a lower overall tax on 2004 estates below $6.5m. Because the US rules provide for a staged increase in the estate tax exemption and a staged decrease in the top marginal rates, the crossover point (where US rates become higher than UK rates) is likely to climb to over $27m by 2009.

IHT charge but still has the benefit of taper relief (eg the IHT is only 20% of the death tax rate – 8% – if she survives the gift by six years). Further, the taxable value of the gift is frozen at the time of the gift, so that future appreciation is taken out of the charge to IHT. Finally, if the IHT rate is then lower than the rate at the time of the gift, the lower IHT rate applies and, furthermore, will probably also reflect a then larger indexed nil-rate band amount.

20.22 In addition, the nil-rate band is renewed every seven years so that, in fact, defeasance of the surviving spouse's life interest by way of chargeable gifts (eg to a discretionary trust) can also be done within the nil-rate band. If the donor survives such gifts by seven years she acquires a new nil-rate band which can then be used to cover further taxable gifts.

20.23 In summary, with respect to lifetime trusts, given lower US estate tax rates for smaller estates and the wife's US general law domicile status, depending on the size of the estate it can, therefore, make sense for the husband to use the more flexible UK IHT regime for inter vivos exempt spousal transfers and potentially exempt transfers (either outright or via life interest or A&M settlements). Such planning mitigates both US and UK transfer taxation (with respect to trusts for multiple generations) and, in appropriate circumstances, may also result in capital gains taxes being applied at the favourable US 15% rate (assuming the assets do not qualify for the lower 10% UK tax rate on business assets).

20.24 In this sense, the UK interest in possession trust, taking advantage of the spouse exemption, offers more flexibility for posthumous tax planning than the US QTIP and QDOT marital trusts. The US marital deduction is not allowed unless an election is made to have the trust assets irrevocably deemed comprised in the taxable estate of the surviving spouse (taxable in the case of QDOT trusts with reference to the first spouse to die) and taxable on any principal distributions to the surviving spouse, or on assets held by the trust at her death. Unlike the UK rules, the US marital trust rules require that the surviving spouse's income interest cannot be capable of being defeated, nor may other persons receive discretionary distributions during her lifetime.

4. US estate tax implications to the US donee spouse

20.25 If the US donee spouse is a US citizen (or a US domiciliary), then her worldwide estate will be subject to US estate tax at her death. This includes property (whether or not UK property) that she received as an outright gift from her UK spouse. Importantly, as discussed in **CHAPTER 1** and throughout this book, a US citizen's exposure to US estate tax applies regardless of his or her domicile and regardless of the situs of his or her assets.

> **Example**
>
> Amanda, a US citizen domiciled in the UK, owns at her death 100 shares of Cotswold Crafts Ltd (a UK company) and a London flat that had been gifted to her years earlier from her UK husband. This stock is taxed in Amanda's US estate, even though she is domiciled outside the US and even though the property is not situated in the US.

20.26 *A UK Spouse Providing for a US Spouse*

20.26 A US citizen's rights as a life tenant of an IIP trust, however, will not, in and of itself, subject her to US estate tax. Instead, 'something more' is needed. If properly designed so that the US spouse is not considered to have a so-called 'general power of appointment' (for example, a right to withdraw principal,[2] a right to appoint principal to her estate or creditors, or even a right to replace related party trustees who could make discretionary distributions to her), the US donee spouse's taxable estate will not include property held in an IIP trust funded by her UK husband.

20.27 Because of the potentially higher US estate tax rates (currently 48% compared with 40% in the UK), this point is of critical importance. Simply put, by placing a US spouse's gift in an IIP trust (rather than making an outright gift to her), the couple can limit her tax exposure to only the lower UK tax at her later death.

20.28 Relative tax rates are not the only relevant factor. As discussed in **CHAPTER 14** and **CHAPTER 15**, there is a crossover point below which the US taxes are actually lower than in the UK, because of the considerably higher US exemptions (and despite the higher US tax rates). As discussed in the previous section, assets deferred from IHT in a spousal IIP trust can be removed from IHT exposure without US tax exposure through trustee appointments qualifying as PETs to a number of family beneficiaries who can each benefit from the substantially higher US exemptions.

20.29 Whether worldwide taxes will be lower if the US spouse's gift is held in an IIP trust or outright will additionally depend on a variety of other factors, including the expected size of her estate, her expected domicile, the likely nature/situs of the gifted assets at her later death and the tax rules (rates, exemptions, etc) likely in effect at her death. But keep this point in mind: property gifted outright to the US spouse cannot be reallocated by the US spouse to an IIP trust in order to later save US taxes; in contrast, property originally funding an IIP trust can be distributed to the US spouse (as illustrated above) if so doing would subject that property to lower US tax.

20.30 Finally, the relative US/UK tax implications of the outright gifts versus gifts in IIP trusts might be of secondary importance to a UK spouse looking to provide for his US spouse. Property gifted outright to her is subject to her complete control, including an ability to direct that property to anyone at her later death (including a new spouse or the hairdresser). Property placed in an IIP trust for her benefit can be protected for ultimate distribution to the UK donor spouse's children (perhaps at some early date by the trustee's exercise of their discretion to terminate the US donee spouse's interest in possession). This can be of critical importance to a donor spouse with children from an earlier marriage.

---

[2] Unless the power is limited by an ascertainable 'MESH' standard (allowing objectively determinable sums to be distributed for the maintenance, education, support or heath of the beneficiary). Code §§ 2041 and 2014. If she holds such a MESH power as trustee, the power to make any non MESH appointments to her should be placed solely in an independent co-trustee.

C. Provision for the US surviving spouse at the UK spouse's death[3]

1. UK IHT implications to the UK decedent spouse

a. General principles

20.31 The IHT implications at the UK decedent spouse's death are similar to those outlined at **20.4** et seq. The UK decedent's exposure to IHT will first depend on the UK decedent's domicile and, if not UK, then on the situs of the property.

20.32 If some, or all, of the UK decedent's estate is subject to IHT, then the qualification of a bequest to a US spouse for the UK spouse exemption will again depend on her domicile and perhaps the couple's domicile. If she is UK domiciled, a properly structured bequest (outright or in an IIP trust for her sole benefit) will qualify. If neither is domiciled, then the bequest also qualifies.

20.33 Planning for long-term UK residents will generally involve spouses both of whom are deemed domiciled in the UK with the American spouse retaining her general law US domicile. In this situation, the children will generally also be US citizens (although they may have a UK domicile of origin dependent on their father's domicile at their birth).

20.34 With regard to assets held at the UK spouse's death, his testamentary plan would first dispose of his estate as desired to the extent of the £263,000 UK nil-rate band (as of 2004/05). As a matter of tax effectiveness, gifts in this band should not be made to the surviving spouse but rather to children, friends or other legatees not benefiting from exemptions or reliefs. Alternatively, the gift may be made to a discretionary trust of which the spouse is a discretionary beneficiary.

20.35 As to the balance of the estate, whether or not it is passed outright to the spouse or to a trust for her will depend on a number of things including her life expectancy, the size of the estate, the likely appreciation in the assets and if, and when, she may return to the US. For smaller estates where the overall US estate tax exposure may be lower, it may be desirable simply to pass assets to the survivor outright, giving the flexibility to limit future taxes to the US estate tax net following her return.[4] Alternatively, a transfer into an IIP trust for her may be preferable since this will have the potential advantages set at **20.15** et seq, but will nevertheless retain the option of transferring assets to her or the children (who will generally have their own generous US exemptions) outright at a later stage.

20.36 For larger estates where the US estate tax is likely to be the higher of the two, the key feature of the estate plan of the UK spouse will be for the UK spouse to transfer the balance of his property in trust (lifetime or testamentary) with the UK-deemed domiciled US spouse receiving a life interest and the children the

---

[3] Figure 4 in APPENDIX VIII illustrates a common planning structure where both spouses are UK domiciled and shows the UK and the US taxes imposed at the US spouse's death.
[4] Subject to expiry of the three-year tail off period. IHTA 1984, s 267(1)(b).

remainder. This transfer qualifies for the UK spouse deduction (the US marital deduction not being relevant with respect to property other than US real or permanent establishment property).

20.37 On the surviving spouse's death, the trust property will be deemed to be included in the UK taxable estate of the surviving spouse.[5] However, provided the spouse has no general power of appointment, the assets will not be included in her estate for US estate tax purposes (since the value of her life interest will dissipate at death). Accordingly, where the UK tax regime is the lower, this can enable her to have access to the assets whilst limiting the ultimate tax exposure to the lower taxing country (in this example, the UK).

20.38 As discussed above, the UK tax can be further reduced in appropriate cases, if the spouse does not, in fact, need all of the assets, by the trustees making appointments out of the trust fund to or for the benefit of others. These appointments are deemed to be transfers by the life tenant spouse and can be free of IHT if she survives them by seven years and assuming they qualify as potentially exempt transfers.

20.39 Clearly, this testamentary trust cannot be a discretionary trust during the wife's lifetime as otherwise the UK spouse exemption would not be permitted. Whether the children's remainder is held in a fixed income or discretionary trust depends on the assessment whether it is preferable to generation skip (and pay the UK decennial inheritance tax on the trust assets at up to 6%) or have fixed income interests which are IHT taxable and aggregated (for the purposes of computing that tax) with the children's free estates at their death.

b. 'Nightmare on Planning Street' – a UK domiciled decedent and a US spouse who is not domiciled in the UK

20.40 If the UK decedent is UK domiciled (or deemed domiciled) but the spouse is not, then only £55,000 of the UK decedent's taxable bequest will qualify for the UK spouse exemption. This fact pattern (UK decedent, non-UK spouse) creates the biggest international tax headaches for 'mixed marriage' couples. An outright bequest from a UK domiciled decedent to a US citizen, but non-UK domiciled spouse could potentially be subject to a large UK tax (to the extent that bequest exceeds the UK spouse exemption and the UK nil-rate band). The inherited property will then eventually be subject to US estate tax at the survivor's death, without any foreign tax credit for the taxes imposed at the UK decedent's earlier death. Double tax in the same generation – not a good result for the kids.

20.41 Placing the US spouse's inheritance in a testamentary IIP trust might not change that result. First, the bequest will still not qualify for the UK spouse exemption, because the survivor is not a UK domiciliary (while the decedent was). Second, although the IIP trust (if properly structured) will not be subject to US

---

[5] This is because the taxation of the trust remains governed by the UK domicile of the settlor. Therefore, even if the surviving spouse is not UK domiciled at her death, the trustees will be liable to pay the IHT charge out of trust assets on her death.

C. Provision for the US surviving spouse **20.47**

estate taxes in the US spouse's estate, it would be subject to IHT at the US spouse's death, because the trust is not considered an excluded property trust (the settlor being domiciled at the date of funding, in this case, at his death). Thus, two IHTs would be imposed in the couple's generation. The one tax benefit to this planning is the opportunity for the trustees to terminate the spouse's interest in possession prior to her death. This would be a deemed IHT gift by the US surviving spouse, but (if properly structured) could be a PET, exempt from IHT if the US spouse survives the deemed gift by seven years.

20.42 As an alternative, the UK decedent spouse with a US surviving spouse might opt for placing the US-domiciled spouse's inheritance in a discretionary trust. This structure does not affect the IHT imposed at the UK decedent's death. However, rather than subjecting that trust to IHT at the survivor's death (in the case of an IIP) or to a US estate tax at the survivor's death (in the case of an outright gift), the discretionary trust will instead be subject to a 6% decennial tax in the UK. (Again, care would be needed to ensure that the surviving spouse did not directly or indirectly have a 'general power of appointment' under US principles such as would cause the property in this trust to be included in her US taxable estate.)

20.43 Provided that the family circumstances permit, a UK domiciled taxpayer with a non-UK domiciled US spouse might consider making a lifetime PET gift to her (outright or in an IIP trust). If the UK donor survives by seven years, the gift will not be subject to IHT (and thus the UK spouse could make adequate provision for the US spouse without a tax being imposed on that transfer). At the US spouse's later death, the gifted property could be subject to US estate tax (in the case of an outright gift) or a UK IHT (in the case of an IIP), or perhaps both (subject to tax credit relief).

20.44 If the UK spouse has been able to adequately fund the US spouse through lifetime PET gifts, the US spouse can then leave the balance of his estate to the children (or in trust for their benefit). Double tax is thus avoided.

20.45 In a sense, this scenario is like 'pick your poison' – none of the alternatives seem attractive and each has its potential drawbacks. Couples finding themselves in this peculiar fact pattern will need to carefully weigh their options. This might include having the US spouse adopt a UK domicile – or reside in the UK long enough to be considered UK deemed domiciled – so as to qualify her inheritance for the UK spouse exemption.

2. *US estate tax implications to the UK decedent spouse*

20.46 The US estate tax implications of a bequest from a UK decedent spouse to a US surviving spouse will mirror those discussed at **20.8** et seq for gifts by a UK spouse to a US spouse. The US estate tax exposure will depend on whether the UK decedent spouse is a US citizen or domiciliary and, if neither, whether his estate includes US-situated property.

20.47 If the UK decedent's estate is subject to US estate tax, then his bequest to his US citizen spouse can qualify for the US marital deduction. A UK decedent (who is not a US citizen or domiciliary) also has a relatively small estate tax

20.48 *A UK Spouse Providing for a US Spouse*

exemption ($60,000), which could be transferred to a discretionary trust and avoid US taxes in both estates – but this seems a lot of trouble for not much benefit. A UK decedent who is a US citizen or domiciliary should consider by-pass trust planning (to take advantage of the higher US estate tax exemption) as outlined at CHAPTER 19 (19.16 et seq).

3. UK IHT implications to the US surviving spouse

20.48 The UK tax implications to the US surviving spouse are identical to those outlined at **20.11** et seq. As discussed in that section, a variety of factors will determine the US surviving spouse's IHT exposure on her inheritance, including:

- whether she received the gift outright or in trust;
- the situs of the property;
- her domicile at her death; and
- the possible qualification of the trust as an excluded property trust.

20.49 As at **20.16**, if the US spouse's inheritance were placed in an IIP trust that qualified for the UK spouse exemption, it is possible to mitigate the IHT exposure at the US spouse's later death by

- trust distributions to her; and/or
- the trustee's termination of the spouse's interest in possession in a manner that would be treated as a PET.

4. US estate tax implications to the US surviving spouse

20.50 The eventual US estate tax exposure of a US surviving spouse with respect to her inheritance from her UK spouse will again mirror the discussion at **20.25** et seq.

20.51 If properly structured, a US spouse's interest in an IIP trust will not be subject to US estate tax at her later death, which could be a good result if the US would have imposed a higher effective tax on that property. Similarly, if the UK decedent spouse were to leave a portion of his estate in a discretionary trust for his US spouse's benefit (for example, to take advantage of the nil-rate band or to accept the 6% decennial tax in the 'nightmare' planning situation involving a UK domiciled decedent and a non-UK domiciled spouse), the US spouse's interest in that trust can similarly be designed to escape US taxes at her death.

Appendix I

UK Tax Tables 2004/05

Income tax reliefs

	Principal reliefs
Persons under age 65	
Personal allowance	£4,745
Persons aged 65 to 74	
Personal allowance	£6,830
Married couple's allowance*	£5,725
Persons aged 75 and over	
Personal allowance	£6,950
Married couple's allowance*	£5,795
Married couple's allowance*	minimum amount £2,210
Income limit for age allowance	£18,900
* relief is restricted to 10% of figure quoted	
Other reliefs	
Blind person	£1,560
Life assurance premiums (pre 14 March 1984 only)	£12.5%

Personal pension schemes

Age on 6 April	Percentage of NRE
35 or less	17.5%
36–45	20%
46–50	25%
51–55	30%
56–60	35%
61 or over	40%

Retirement annuity schemes

Age on 6 April	Percentage of NRE
50 or less	17.5%
51–55	20.0%

UK Tax Tables 2004/05

56–60	22.5%
61 or over	27.5%

Note: Net relevant earnings, subject to maximum £102,000.

Income tax rates

Taxable income band	Rate	Tax on band
£0–£2,020	10%	£202.00
£2,021–£31,400	22%	£6,463.60
Excess	40%	

Tax on savings income, other than dividends, is 10% for income within the starting rate band, 20% for all basic rate taxpayers and 40% for taxable income above that. A 32.5% rate will apply on dividend income where taxable income exceeds £31,400. Dividend income within the starting or basic rate bands is taxed at 10%. The tax rate for discretionary and accumulation trusts is 40% for ordinary income and 32.5% for dividend income.

Corporation tax rates

Full rate (profits > £1,500,000)*	30%
Upper marginal rate†	32.75%
Small companies' rate (profits £50,001 – £300,000)*	19%
Lower marginal rate^	23.75%
Starting rate (profits < £10,000)*	Nil

* Limits are reduced proportionately for the number of associated companies

Close investment-holding companies are liable to corporation tax at the full rate.

Marginal relief is given for profits between £10,001 and £50,000^ and for profits between £300,001 and £1,500,000.†

Inheritance tax

Rates on cumulative transfers

First £263,000 at nil %
Excess at 40%

Stamp taxes

Exemptions

Annual gifts per donor	£3,000
Small gifts per donee	£250
For marriage:	
– parent	£5,000
– grandparent	£2,500
– other	£1,000

Gifts to individuals and certain trusts made more than seven years before death

Charge on gifts within seven years of death

Intervening years	0–3	3–4	4–5	5–6	6–7
Percentage of full charge	100%	80%	60%	40%	20%

Capital gains tax

Gains are taxed at the individual's marginal income tax rate on savings income (excluding dividends) of 10%, 20% or 40%. Trust gains are also taxed at 40%.

Annual exemptions

Individuals	£8,200
Trusts	£4,100

Taper relief is available depending on the length of ownership and type of asset.

Stamp taxes

Transfers of land and buildings (consideration paid)

	Land in disadvantaged areas		All other land in the UK	
	Disadvantaged Areas – Residential	Non-residential	Other Land – Residential	Non-residential
Rate	Value of total consideration	Value of total consideration	Value of total consideration	Value of total consideration
0%	£0–£150,000	All	£0–£60,000	£0–£150,000
1%	£150,001–£250,000	N/A	£60,001–£250,000	£150,001–£250,000
3%	£250,001–£500,000	N/A	£250,001–£500,000	£250,001–£500,000
4%	Over £500,000	N/A	Over £500,000	Over £500,000

UK Tax Tables 2004/05

New leases (lease duty)

Rate	Net present value (NPV) of rent Residential *Slice of NPV*	Non-residential *Slice of NPV*
0%	£0–£60,000	£0–£150,000
1%	Over £60,000	Over £150,000

The rate of stamp duty reserve tax on the transfer of shares and securities is unchanged at 0.5%.

Value added tax

Standard rate 17.5% (7/47 VAT inclusive price).

Registration limit from 1 April 2004: £58,000 of annual taxable turnover (10 April 2003: £56,000).

Appendix II

US Tax Tables 2004

Income tax rates – individuals

Single

Taxable income	Tax on lower amount	Rate on excess
$0–$7,150	$0.00	10%
$7,150–$29,050	$715.00	15%
$29,050–$70,350	$4,000.00	25%
$70,350–$146,750	$14,325.00	28%
$146,750–$319,100	$35,717.00	33%
Over $319,100	$92,592.50	35%

Married – filing jointly

Taxable income	Tax on lower amount	Rate on excess
$0–$14,300	$0	10%
$14,300–$58,100	$1,430	15%
$58,100–$117,250	$8,000	25%
$117,250–$178,650	$22,788	28%
$178,650–$319,100	$39,980	33%
Over $319,100	$86,328	35%

Additional rate schedules for:

- married individuals filing separately; and
- heads of household unmarried individual who maintains his/her home for a dependent.

Capital gains and dividends: 15% maximum tax on net capital gain and dividends from US issuer and publicly traded or OECD treaty resident foreign issuer.

US Tax Tables 2004

Income tax rates – trusts

Taxable income	Tax on base ($)	Rate on excess
$0–$1,950	$0.00	15%
$1,950–$4,600	$292.50	25%
$4,600–$7,000	$955.00	28%
$7,000–$9,550	$1,627.00	33%
Over $9,550	$2,468.50	35%

Income tax rates – corporations

Taxable income	Tax on lower amount	Rate on excess
$0–$50,000	$0	15%
$50,001–$75,000	$7,500	25%
$75,001–$100,000	$13,750	34%
$100,001–$335,000	$22,250	39%
$335,001–$10,000,000	$113,900	34%
$10,000,001–$15,000,000	$3,400,000	35%
$15,000,001–$18,333,333	$5,150,000	38%
Over $18,333,334	$6,416,667	35%

Transfer tax rates

Gift and estate tax rate table

Value of cumulative transfers		Tax on first amount	Rate on excess
$0	$10,000	$0	18%
$10,000	$20,000	$1,800	20%
$20,000	$40,000	$3,800	22%
$40,000	$60,000	$8,200	24%
$60,000	$80,000	$13,000	26%
$80,000	$100,000	$18,200	28%
$100,000	$150,000	$23,800	30%
$150,000	$250,000	$38,800	32%
$250,000	$500,000	$70,800	34%
$500,000	$750,000	$155,800	37%
$750,000	$1,000,000	$248,300	39%

Value of cumulative transfers		Tax on first amount	Rate on excess
$1,000,000	$1,250,000	$345,800	41%
$1,250,000	$1,500,000	$448,300	43%
$1,500,000	$2,000,000	$555,800	45%
$2,000,000	and over	$780,800	48% in 2004
			47% in 2005
			46% in 2006
			45% in 2007 to 2009

2011 and thereafter Value of cumulative transfers		Tax on first amount	Rate on excess
$2,000,000	$2,500,000	$780,800	49%
$2,500,000	$3,000,000	$1,025,800	53%
$3,000,000	and over	$1,290,800	55%

GST Rate: Highest marginal estate tax rate: 48% (2004), 47% (2005), 46% (2006), 45% (2007–2009), 55% (2011 and thereafter).

Transfer tax exemptions

US citizens and domiciliaries

Gift tax	$1m
Estate and GST tax	$1.5m increasing to $2m (2006) and $3.5m (2009)

Non-domiciled aliens

Gift tax	nil
Estate tax	$60,000
GST tax	$1.5m increasing to $2m (2006) and $3.5m (2009)

Gift tax exclusions (all taxpayers)

$11,000 per year per donee.

$114,000 to spouse who is not a US citizen.

Unlimited to US citizen donee spouse.

US Tax Tables 2004

Note: The information contained above is believed to be accurate at the time of writing and is intended for general guidance only.

Appendix III

2001 United Kingdom-United States Income Tax Treaty (conformed to include the 2002 Protocol)

Convention Between the Government of the United States of America and the Government of the United Kingdom of Great Britain and Northern Ireland for the Avoidance of Double Taxation and the Prevention of Fiscal Evasion with Respect to Taxes on Income and on Capital Gains

The Government of the United States of America and the Government of the United Kingdom of Great Britain and Northern Ireland;

Desiring to conclude a new Convention for the avoidance of double taxation and the prevention of fiscal evasion with respect to taxes on income and capital gains;

Have agreed as follows:

Article 1

General Scope

1. Except as specifically provided herein, this Convention is applicable only to persons who are residents of one or both of the Contracting States.

2. This Convention shall not restrict in any manner any benefit now or hereafter accorded:

   a) by the laws of either Contracting State; or

   b) by any other agreement between the Contracting States.

3.
   a) Notwithstanding the provisions of sub-paragraph b) of paragraph 2 of this Article:

      (i) any question arising as to the interpretation or application of this Convention and, in particular, whether a taxation measure is within the scope of this Convention, shall be determined exclusively in accordance with the provisions of Article 26 (Mutual Agreement Procedure) of this Convention; and

      (ii) the provisions of Article II and Article XVII of the General Agreement on Trade in Services shall not apply to a taxation measure unless the competent authorities agree that the measure is not within the scope of Article 25 (Non-discrimination) of this Convention.

   b) For the purposes of this paragraph, a 'measure' is a law, regulation, rule, procedure, decision, administrative action, or any similar provision or action.

4. Notwithstanding any provision of this Convention except paragraph 5 of this Article, a Contracting State may tax its residents (as determined under Article 4 (Residence)), and by reason of citizenship may tax its citizens, as if this Convention had not come into effect.

2001 UK-US Income Tax Treaty

5. The provisions of paragraph 4 of this Article shall not affect:

    a) the benefits conferred by a Contracting State under paragraph 2 of Article 9 (Associated Enterprises), sub-paragraph b) of paragraph 1 and paragraphs 3 and 5 of Article 17 (Pensions, Social Security, Annuities, Alimony, and Child Support), paragraphs 1 and 5 of Article 18 (Pension Schemes) and Articles 24 (Relief From Double Taxation), 25 (Non-discrimination), and 26 (Mutual Agreement Procedure) of this Convention; and

    b) the benefits conferred by a Contracting State under paragraph 2 of Article 18 (Pension Schemes) and Articles 19 (Government Service), 20 (Students), 20A (Teachers), and 28 (Diplomatic Agents and Consular Officers) of this Convention, upon individuals who are neither citizens of, nor have been admitted for permanent residence in, that State.

6. A former citizen or long-term resident whose loss of citizenship or long-term resident status had as one of its principal purposes the avoidance of tax (as defined under the laws of the Contracting State of which the person was a citizen or long-term resident) shall be treated for the purposes of paragraph 4 of this Article as a citizen of that Contracting State but only for a period of 10 years following the loss of such status. This paragraph shall apply only in respect of income from sources within that Contracting State (including income deemed under the domestic law of that State to arise from such sources). Paragraph 4 of this Article shall not apply in the case of any former citizen or long-term resident of a Contracting State who ceased to be a citizen or long-term resident of that State at any time before February 6th, 1995.

7. Where under any provision of this Convention income or gains arising in one of the Contracting States are relieved from tax in that Contracting State and, under the law in force in the other Contracting State, a person, in respect of the said income or gains, is subject to tax by reference to the amount thereof which is remitted to or received in that other Contracting State and not by reference to the full amount thereof, then the relief to be allowed under this Convention in the first-mentioned Contracting State shall apply only to so much of the income or gains as is taxed in the other Contracting State.

8. An item of income, profit or gain derived through a person that is fiscally transparent under the laws of either Contracting State shall be considered to be derived by a resident of a Contracting State to the extent that the item is treated for the purposes of the taxation law of such Contracting State as the income, profit or gain of a resident.

Article 2

Taxes Covered

1. This Convention shall apply to taxes on income and on capital gains imposed on behalf of a Contracting State irrespective of the manner in which they are levied.

2. There shall be regarded as taxes on income and on capital gains all taxes imposed on total income, or on elements of income, including taxes on gains from the alienation of property.

3. The existing taxes to which this Convention shall apply are:

    a) in the case of the United States:

        (i) the Federal income taxes imposed by the Internal Revenue Code (but excluding social security taxes); and

        (ii) the Federal excise taxes imposed on insurance policies issued by foreign insurers and with respect to private foundations;

    b) in the case of the United Kingdom:

2001 UK-US Income Tax Treaty

       (i)   the income tax;

       (ii)   the capital gains tax;

       (iii) the corporation tax; and

       (iv) the petroleum revenue tax.

4. This Convention shall apply also to any identical or substantially similar taxes that are imposed after the date of signature of this Convention in addition to, or in place of, the existing taxes. The competent authorities of the Contracting States shall notify each other of any changes that have been made in their respective taxation or other laws that significantly affect their obligations under this Convention.

Article 3

General Definitions

1. For the purposes of this Convention, unless the context otherwise requires:

    a) the term 'person' includes an individual, an estate, a trust, a partnership, a company, and any other body of persons;

    b) the term 'company' means any body corporate or any entity that is treated as a body corporate for tax purposes;

    c) the term 'enterprise' applies to the carrying on of any business;

    d) the term 'business' includes the performance of professional services and of other activities of an independent character;

    e) the terms 'enterprise of a Contracting State' and 'enterprise of the other Contracting State' mean respectively an enterprise carried on by a resident of a Contracting State, and an enterprise carried on by a resident of the other Contracting State;

    f) the term 'international traffic' means any transport by a ship or aircraft, except when the ship or aircraft is operated solely between places in the other Contracting State;

    g) the term 'competent authority' means:

        (i) in the United States: the Secretary of the Treasury or his delegate; and

        (ii) in the United Kingdom: the Commissioners of Inland Revenue or their authorised representative;

    h) the term 'United States' means the United States of America, and includes the states thereof and the District of Columbia; such term also includes the territorial sea thereof and the sea bed and sub-soil of the submarine areas adjacent to that territorial sea, over which the United States exercises sovereign rights in accordance with international law; the term, however, does not include Puerto Rico, the Virgin Islands, Guam or any other United States possession or territory;

    i) the term 'United Kingdom' means Great Britain and Northern Ireland, including any area outside the territorial sea of the United Kingdom which in accordance with international law has been or may hereafter be designated, under the laws of the United Kingdom concerning the Continental Shelf, as an area within which the rights of the United Kingdom with respect to the sea bed and sub-soil and their natural resources may be exercised;

    j) the term 'national' of a Contracting State, means:

        (i) in relation to the United States,

- A) any individual possessing the citizenship of the United States; and
- B) any legal person, partnership, association or other entity deriving its status as such from the laws in force in the United States;

(ii) in relation to the United Kingdom,

- A) any British citizen, or any British subject not possessing the citizenship of any other Commonwealth country or territory, provided he has the right of abode in the United Kingdom; and
- B) any legal person, partnership, association or other entity deriving its status as such from the laws in force in the United Kingdom;

k) the term 'qualified governmental entity' means:

(i) a Contracting State, or a political subdivision or local authority of a Contracting State;

(ii) a person that is wholly owned, directly or indirectly, by a Contracting State or a political subdivision or local authority of a Contracting State, provided

- A) it is organized under the laws of the Contracting State;
- B) its earnings are credited to its own account with no portion of its income inuring to the benefit of any private person;
- C) its assets vest in the Contracting State, political subdivision or local authority upon dissolution; and
- D) it does not carry on a business;

l) the term 'Contracting State' means the United States or the United Kingdom, as the context requires;

m) the term 'real property' means any interest (other than an interest solely as a creditor) in land, crops or timber growing on land, mines, wells and other places of extraction of natural resources, as well as any fixture built on land (buildings, structures, etc.) and other property considered real or immovable property under the law of the Contracting State in which the property in question is situated. The term shall in any case include livestock and equipment used in agriculture and forestry, rights to which the provisions of general law respecting landed property apply, usufruct of real property and rights to variable or fixed payments as consideration for the working of, or the right to work, mineral deposits and other natural resources; ships, boats and aircraft shall not be regarded as real property.

n) the term 'conduit arrangement' means a transaction or series of transactions:

(i) which is structured in such a way that a resident of a Contracting State entitled to the benefits of this Convention receives an item of income arising in the other Contracting State but that resident pays, directly or indirectly, all or substantially all of that income (at any time or in any form) to another person who is not a resident of either Contracting State and who, if it received that item of income direct from the other Contracting State, would not be entitled under a convention for the avoidance of double taxation between the state in which that other person is resident and the Contracting State in which the income arises, or otherwise, to benefits with respect to that item of income which are equivalent to, or more favourable than, those available under this Convention to a resident of a Contracting State; and

(ii) which has as its main purpose, or one of its main purposes, obtaining such increased benefits as are available under this Convention.

o) the term 'pension scheme' means any plan, scheme, fund, trust or other arrangement established in a Contracting State which is:

(i) generally exempt from income taxation in that State; and

(ii) operated principally to administer or provide pension or retirement benefits or to earn income for the benefit of one or more such arrangements.

2. As regards the application of this Convention at any time by a Contracting State, any term not defined therein shall, unless the context otherwise requires, or the competent authorities agree on a common meaning pursuant to the provisions of Article 26 (Mutual Agreement Procedure) of this Convention, have the meaning which it has at that time under the law of that State for the purposes of the taxes to which this Convention applies, any meaning under the applicable tax laws of that State prevailing over a meaning given to the term under other laws of that State.

Article 4

Residence

1. Except as provided in paragraphs 2 and 3 of this Article, the term 'resident of a Contracting State' means, for the purposes of this Convention, any person who, under the laws of that State, is liable to tax therein by reason of his domicile, residence, citizenship, place of management, place of incorporation, or any other criterion of a similar nature. This term, however, does not include any person who is liable to tax in that State in respect only of income from sources in that State or of profits attributable to a permanent establishment in that State.

2. An individual who is a United States citizen or an alien admitted to the United States for permanent residence (a 'green card' holder) is a resident of the United States only if the individual has a substantial presence, permanent home or habitual abode in the United States and if that individual is not a resident of a State other than the United Kingdom for the purposes of a double taxation convention between that State and the United Kingdom.

3. The term 'resident of a Contracting State' includes:

a) a pension scheme;

b) a plan, scheme, fund, trust, company or other arrangement established in a Contracting State that is operated exclusively to administer or provide employee benefits and that, by reason of its nature as such, is generally exempt from income taxation in that State;

c) an organization that is established exclusively for religious, charitable, scientific, artistic, cultural, or educational purposes and that is a resident of a Contracting State according to its laws, notwithstanding that all or part of its income or gains may be exempt from tax under the domestic law of that State; and d) a qualified governmental entity that is, is a part of, or is established in, that State.

4. Where by reason of the provisions of paragraph 1 of this Article, an individual is a resident of both Contracting States, then his status shall be determined as follows:

a) he shall be deemed to be a resident only of the State in which he has a permanent home available to him; if he has a permanent home available to him in both States, he shall be deemed to be a resident only of the State with which his personal and economic relations are closer (centre of vital interests);

b) if the State in which he has his centre of vital interests cannot be determined, or if he does not have a permanent home available to him in either State, he shall be deemed to be a resident only of the State in which he has an habitual abode;

c) if he has an habitual abode in both States or in neither of them, he shall be deemed to be a resident only of the State of which he is a national;

d) if he is a national of both States or of neither of them, the competent authorities of the Contracting States shall endeavour to settle the question by mutual agreement.

5. Where by reason of the provisions of paragraph 1 of this Article a person other than an individual is a resident of both Contracting States, the competent authorities of the Contracting States shall endeavour to determine by mutual agreement the mode of application of this Convention to that person. If the competent authorities do not reach such an agreement, that person shall not be entitled to claim any benefit provided by this Convention, except those provided by paragraph 4 of Article 24 (Relief from Double Taxation), Article 25 (Non-discrimination) and Article 26 (Mutual Agreement Procedure).

6. A marriage before January 1st, 1974 between a woman who is a United States national and a man domiciled within the United Kingdom shall be deemed to have taken place on January 1st, 1974 for the purpose of determining her domicile for United Kingdom tax purposes, on or after the date on which this Convention first has effect in relation to her.

Article 5

Permanent Establishment

1. For the purposes of this Convention, the term 'permanent establishment' means a fixed place of business through which the business of an enterprise is wholly or partly carried on.

2. The term 'permanent establishment' includes especially:

    a) a place of management;

    b) a branch;

    c) an office;

    d) a factory;

    e) a workshop; and

    f) a mine, an oil or gas well, a quarry, or any other place of extraction of natural resources.

3. A building site or construction or installation project constitutes a permanent establishment only if it lasts for more than twelve months.

4. Notwithstanding the preceding provisions of this Article, the term 'permanent establishment' shall be deemed not to include:

    a) the use of facilities solely for the purpose of storage, display or delivery of goods or merchandise belonging to the enterprise;

    b) the maintenance of a stock of goods or merchandise belonging to the enterprise solely for the purpose of storage, display or delivery;

    c) the maintenance of a stock of goods or merchandise belonging to the enterprise solely for the purpose of processing by another enterprise;

d) the maintenance of a fixed place of business solely for the purpose of purchasing goods or merchandise, or of collecting information, for the enterprise;

e) the maintenance of a fixed place of business solely for the purpose of carrying on, for the enterprise, any other activity of a preparatory or auxiliary character;

f) the maintenance of a fixed place of business solely for any combination of the activities mentioned in sub-paragraphs a) to e) of this paragraph, provided that the overall activity of the fixed place of business resulting from this combination is of a preparatory or auxiliary character.

5. Notwithstanding the provisions of paragraphs 1 and 2 of this Article, where a person – other than an agent of an independent status to whom paragraph 6 of this Article applies – is acting on behalf of an enterprise and has and habitually exercises in a Contracting State an authority to conclude contracts that are binding on the enterprise, that enterprise shall be deemed to have a permanent establishment in that State in respect of any activities that the person undertakes for the enterprise, unless the activities of such person are limited to those mentioned in paragraph 4 of this Article that, if exercised through a fixed place of business, would not make this fixed place of business a permanent establishment under the provisions of that paragraph.

6. An enterprise shall not be deemed to have a permanent establishment in a Contracting State merely because it carries on business in that State through a broker, general commission agent, or any other agent of an independent status, provided that such person is acting in the ordinary course of his business as an independent agent.

7. The fact that a company that is a resident of a Contracting State controls or is controlled by a company that is a resident of the other Contracting State, or that carries on business in that other State (whether through a permanent establishment or otherwise), shall not constitute either company a permanent establishment of the other.

Article 6

Income From Real Property

1. Income derived by a resident of a Contracting State from real property, including income from agriculture or forestry, situated in the other Contracting State may be taxed in that other State.

2. The provisions of paragraph 1 of this Article shall apply to income derived from the direct use, letting, or use in any other form of real property.

3. The provisions of paragraphs 1 and 2 of this Article shall also apply to the income from real property of an enterprise.

Article 7

Business Profits

1. The business profits of an enterprise of a Contracting State shall be taxable only in that State unless the enterprise carries on business in the other Contracting State through a permanent establishment situated therein. If the enterprise carries on business as aforesaid, the business profits of the enterprise may be taxed in the other State but only so much of them as are attributable to that permanent establishment.

2. Subject to the provisions of paragraph 3 of this Article, where an enterprise of a Contracting State carries on business in the other Contracting State through a permanent establishment situated therein, there shall in each Contracting State be attributed to that permanent establishment the business profits that it might be expected to make if it were a distinct and separate enterprise engaged in the same or similar activities under the same or similar conditions and dealing wholly independently with the enterprise of which it is a permanent establishment. For this purpose,

the business profits to be attributed to the permanent establishment shall include only the profits derived from the assets used, risks assumed and activities performed by the permanent establishment.

3. In determining the business profits of a permanent establishment, there shall be allowed as deductions expenses that are incurred for the purposes of the permanent establishment, including executive and general administrative expenses so incurred, whether in the State in which the permanent establishment is situated or elsewhere.

4. For the purposes of the preceding paragraphs, the profits to be attributed to the permanent establishment shall be determined by the same method year by year unless there is good and sufficient reason to the contrary.

5. The United States excise tax on insurance policies issued by foreign insurers shall not be imposed on insurance or reinsurance policies, the premiums on which are the receipts of a business of insurance carried on by an enterprise of the United Kingdom. However, if such policies are entered into as part of a conduit arrangement, the United States may impose excise tax on those policies, unless the premiums in respect of those policies are, or are part of, the income of a permanent establishment that the enterprise of the United Kingdom has in the United States.

6. Where business profits include items of income that are dealt with separately in other Articles of this Convention, then the provisions of those Articles shall not be affected by the provisions of this Article.

7. In applying this Article, paragraph 5 of Article 10 (Dividends), paragraph 3 of Article 11 (Interest), paragraph 3 of Article 12 (Royalties), and paragraph 2 of Article 22 (Other Income) of this Convention, income or profits attributable to a permanent establishment may, notwithstanding that the permanent establishment has ceased to exist, be taxed in the Contracting State in which it was situated.

Article 8

Shipping and Air Transport

1. Profits of an enterprise of a Contracting State from the operation of ships or aircraft in international traffic shall be taxable only in that State.

2. For the purposes of this Article, profits from the operation of ships or aircraft include profits derived from the rental of ships or aircraft on a full (time or voyage) basis. They also include profits from the rental of ships or aircraft on a bareboat basis if the rental income is incidental to profits from the operation of ships or aircraft in international traffic. Profits derived by an enterprise from the inland transport of property or passengers within either Contracting State shall be treated as profits from the operation of ships or aircraft in international traffic if such transport is undertaken as part of international traffic conducted by such enterprise.

3. Profits of an enterprise of a Contracting State from the use, maintenance, or rental of containers (including trailers, barges and related equipment for the transport of containers) used in international traffic shall be taxable only in that State.

4. The provisions of paragraphs 1 and 3 of this Article shall also apply to profits from participation in a pool, a joint business, or an international operating agency.

Article 9

Associated Enterprises

1. Where:

a) an enterprise of a Contracting State participates directly or indirectly in the management, control or capital of an enterprise of the other Contracting State; or

b) the same persons participate directly or indirectly in the management, control, or capital of an enterprise of a Contracting State and an enterprise of the other Contracting State,

and in either case conditions are made or imposed between the two enterprises in their commercial or financial relations that differ from those that would be made between independent enterprises, then any profits that, but for those conditions, would have accrued to one of the enterprises, but by reason of those conditions have not so accrued, may be included in the profits of that enterprise and taxed accordingly.

2. Where a Contracting State includes in the profits of an enterprise of that State, and taxes accordingly, profits on which an enterprise of the other Contracting State has been charged to tax in that other State, and the other Contracting State agrees that the profits so included are profits that would have accrued to the enterprise of the first-mentioned State if the conditions made between the two enterprises had been those that would have been made between independent enterprises, then that other State shall make an appropriate adjustment to the amount of the tax charged therein on those profits. In determining such adjustment, due regard shall be paid to the other provisions of this Convention and the competent authorities of the Contracting States shall if necessary consult each other.

Article 10

Dividends

1. Dividends paid by a company which is a resident of a Contracting State to a resident of the other Contracting State may be taxed in that other State.

2. However, such dividends may also be taxed in the Contracting State of which the company paying the dividends is a resident and according to the laws of that State, but if the dividends are beneficially owned by a resident of the other Contracting State, the tax so charged shall not exceed, except as otherwise provided,

   a) 5 per cent. of the gross amount of the dividends if the beneficial owner is a company that owns shares representing directly or indirectly at least 10 per cent. of the voting power of the company paying the dividends;

   b) 15 per cent. of the gross amount of the dividends in all other cases.

   This paragraph shall not affect the taxation of the company in respect of the profits out of which the dividends are paid.

3. Notwithstanding the provisions of paragraph 2 of this Article, dividends shall not be taxed in the Contracting State of which the company paying the dividends is a resident if the beneficial owner of the dividends is a resident of the other Contracting State and either:

   a) a company that has owned shares representing 80 per cent. or more of the voting power of the company paying the dividends for a 12-month period ending on the date the dividend is declared, and that:

      (i) owned shares representing, directly or indirectly, at least 80 per cent. of the voting power of the company paying the dividends prior to October 1st, 1998; or

      (ii) is a qualified person by reason of sub-paragraph c) of paragraph 2 of Article 23 (Limitation on Benefits) of this Convention; or

(iii) is entitled to benefits with respect to the dividends under paragraph 3 or paragraph 6 of that Article; or

b) a pension scheme, provided that such dividends are not derived from the carrying on of a business, directly or indirectly, by such pension scheme.

4. Sub-paragraph a) of paragraph 2 and sub-paragraph a) of paragraph 3 of this Article shall not apply in the case of dividends paid by a pooled investment vehicle which is a resident of a Contracting State. Sub-paragraph b) of paragraph 2 and sub-paragraph b) of paragraph 3 of this Article shall apply in the case of dividends paid by a pooled investment vehicle, the assets of which consist wholly or mainly of shares, securities or currencies or derivative contracts relating to shares, securities or currencies. In the case of dividends paid by a pooled investment vehicle not described in the preceding sentence, sub-paragraph b) of paragraph 2 and sub-paragraph b) of paragraph 3 of this Article shall apply only if:

a) the beneficial owner of the dividends is an individual or pension scheme, in either case holding an interest of not more than 10 per cent. in the pooled investment vehicle;

b) the dividends are paid with respect to a class of stock that is publicly traded and the beneficial owner of the dividends is a person holding an interest of not more than 5 per cent. of any class of the stock of the pooled investment vehicle; or

c) the beneficial owner of the dividends is a person holding an interest of not more than 10 per cent. in the pooled investment vehicle and that vehicle is diversified.

5. The previous provisions of this Article shall not apply if the beneficial owner of the dividends, being a resident of a Contracting State, carries on business in the other Contracting State, of which the payer is a resident, through a permanent establishment situated therein, and the dividends are attributable to such permanent establishment. In such case, the provisions of Article 7 (Business Profits) of this Convention shall apply.

6. A Contracting State may not impose any tax on dividends paid by a company which is a resident of the other Contracting State, except insofar as the dividends are paid to a resident of the first-mentioned State or the dividends are attributable to a permanent establishment situated in that State, nor may it impose tax on a company's undistributed profits, except as provided in paragraph 7 of this Article, even if the dividends paid or the undistributed profits consist wholly or partly of profits or income arising in that State.

7. A company that is a resident of a Contracting State and that has a permanent establishment in the other Contracting State, or that is subject to tax in that other State on a net basis on its income or gains that may be taxed in that other State under Article 6 (Income from Real Property) or under paragraph 1 of Article 13 (Gains) of this Convention, may be subject in that other State to a tax in addition to any tax that may be imposed by that other State in accordance with the other provisions of this Convention. Such tax, however, may be imposed on only the portion of the business profits of the company attributable to the permanent establishment, and the portion of the income or gains referred to in the preceding sentence that is subject to tax under Article 6 or under paragraph 1 of Article 13, that, in the case of the United States, represents the dividend equivalent amount of such profits, income or gains and, in the case of the United Kingdom, is an amount that is analogous to the dividend equivalent amount. This paragraph shall not apply in the case of a company which:

a) prior to October 1st, 1998 was engaged in activities giving rise to profits attributable to that permanent establishment or to income or gains to which the provisions of Article 6 or, as the case may be, paragraph 1 of Article 13 apply;

b) is a qualified person by reason of sub-paragraph c) of paragraph 2 of Article 23 (Limitation on Benefits) of this Convention; or

2001 UK-US Income Tax Treaty

    c)   is entitled to benefits under paragraph 3 or paragraph 6 of that Article with respect to an item of income, profit or gain described in this paragraph.

8. The additional tax referred to in paragraph 7 of this Article may not be imposed at a rate in excess of the rate specified in sub-paragraph a) of paragraph 2 of this Article.

9. The provisions of this Article shall not apply in respect of any dividend paid under, or as part of, a conduit arrangement.

10. For the purposes of this Article:

    a)   the term 'dividends' means income from shares or other rights, not being debt-claims, participating in profits, as well as income from other corporate rights and any other item which, under the laws of the Contracting State of which the company paying the dividend is a resident, is treated as a dividend or a distribution of a company;

    b)   the term 'pooled investment vehicle' means a person:

        (i)   whose assets consist wholly or mainly of real property, or of shares, securities or currencies, or of derivative contracts relating to shares, securities or currencies or real property;

        (ii)   whose gross income consists wholly or mainly of dividends, interest, gains from the alienation of assets and rents and other income and gains from the holding and alienation of real property; and

        (iii)   which, in respect of its income, profits or gains, is exempt from, or is not chargeable to, tax in the State of which it is a resident, or is subject to tax at a special rate in that State, or which is entitled to a deduction for dividends paid to its shareholders in computing the amount of its income, profits or gains;

    c)   a pooled investment vehicle is 'diversified' if the value of no single interest in real property exceeds 10 per cent. of the pooled investment vehicle's total interests in real property. For the purposes of this rule, foreclosure property shall not be considered an interest in real property. Where a pooled investment vehicle holds an interest in a partnership, it shall be treated as owning directly a proportion of the partnership's interests in real property corresponding to the proportion of its interest in the partnership.

Article 11

Interest

1. Interest arising in a Contracting State and beneficially owned by a resident of the other Contracting State shall be taxable only in that other State.

2. The term 'interest' as used in this Article means income from debt-claims of every kind, whether or not secured by mortgage, and whether or not carrying a right to participate in the debtor's profits, and, in particular, income from government securities and income from bonds or debentures, including premiums or prizes attaching to such securities, bonds or debentures, and all other income that is subjected to the same taxation treatment as income from money lent by the taxation law of the Contracting State in which the income arises. Income dealt with in Article 10 (Dividends) of this Convention and penalty charges for late payment shall not be regarded as interest for the purposes of this Article.

3. The provisions of paragraph 1 of this Article shall not apply if the beneficial owner of the interest, being a resident of a Contracting State, carries on business in the other Contracting State, in which the interest arises, through a permanent establishment

situated therein, and the interest is attributable to such permanent establishment. In such case, the provisions of Article 7 (Business Profits) of this Convention shall apply.

4. Where, by reason of a special relationship between the payer and the beneficial owner or between both of them and some other person, the amount of the interest exceeds, for whatever reason, the amount which would have been agreed upon by the payer and the beneficial owner in the absence of such relationship, the provisions of this Article shall apply only to the last-mentioned amount. In such case, the excess part of the payments shall remain taxable according to the laws of each State, due regard being had to the other provisions of this Convention.

5.
   a) Notwithstanding the provisions of paragraph 1 of this Article, interest paid by a resident of a Contracting State and determined by reference to receipts, sales, income, profits or other cash flow of the debtor or a related person, to any change in the value of any property of the debtor or a related person or to any dividend, partnership distribution or similar payment made by the debtor to a related person, may also be taxed in the Contracting State in which it arises, and according to the laws of that State, but if the beneficial owner is a resident of the other Contracting State the gross amount of the interest may be taxed at a rate not exceeding the rate prescribed in sub-paragraph b) of paragraph 2 of Article 10 (Dividends) of this Convention.

   b) Sub-paragraph a) of this paragraph shall not apply to any interest solely by reason of the fact that it is paid under an arrangement the terms of which provide:
      (i) that the amount of interest payable shall be reduced in the event of an improvement in the factors by reference to which the amount of interest payable is determined; or
      (ii) that the amount of interest payable shall be increased in the event of a deterioration in the factors by reference to which the amount of interest payable is determined.

6. Notwithstanding the provisions of paragraph 1 of this Article, a Contracting State may tax, in accordance with its domestic law, interest paid with respect to the ownership interests in a vehicle used for the securitisation of real estate mortgages or other assets, to the extent that the amount of interest paid exceeds the return on comparable debt instruments as specified by the domestic law of that State.

7. The provisions of this Article shall not apply in respect of any interest paid under, or as part of, a conduit arrangement.

Article 12

Royalties

1. Royalties arising in a Contracting State and beneficially owned by a resident of the other Contracting State shall be taxable only in that other State.

2. The term 'royalties' as used in this Article means:
   a) any consideration for the use of, or the right to use, any copyright of literary, artistic, scientific or other work (including computer software and cinematographic films) including works reproduced on audio or video tapes or disks or any other means of image or sound reproduction, any patent, trade mark, design or model, plan, secret formula or process, or other like right or property, or for information concerning industrial, commercial or scientific experience; and

b) any gain derived from the alienation of any right or property described in sub-paragraph a) of this paragraph, to the extent that the amount of such gain is contingent on the productivity, use, or disposition of the right or property.

3. The provisions of paragraph 1 of this Article shall not apply if the beneficial owner of the royalties, being a resident of a Contracting State, carries on business in the other Contracting State, in which the royalties arise, through a permanent establishment situated therein, and the royalties are attributable to such permanent establishment. In such case, the provisions of Article 7 (Business Profits) of this Convention shall apply.

4. Where, by reason of a special relationship between the payer and the beneficial owner or between both of them and some other person, the amount of the royalties paid exceeds, for whatever reason, the amount which would have been agreed upon by the payer and the beneficial owner in the absence of such relationship, the provisions of this Article shall apply only to the last-mentioned amount. In such case, the excess part of the payments shall remain taxable according to the laws of each Contracting State, due regard being had to the other provisions of this Convention.

5. The provisions of this Article shall not apply in respect of any royalty paid under, or as part of, a conduit arrangement.

Article 13

Gains

1. Gains derived by a resident of a Contracting State that are attributable to the alienation of real property situated in the other Contracting State may be taxed in that other State.

2. For the purposes of this Article the term 'real property situated in the other Contracting State' shall include:

    a) rights to assets to be produced by the exploration or exploitation of the sea bed and sub-soil of that other State and their natural resources, including rights to interests in or the benefit of such assets;

    b) where that other State is the United States, a United States real property interest; and c) where that other State is the United Kingdom:

    (i) shares, including rights to acquire shares, other than shares in which there is regular trading on a stock exchange, deriving their value or the greater part of their value directly or indirectly from real property situated in the United Kingdom; and

    (ii) an interest in a partnership or trust to the extent that the assets of the partnership or trust consist of real property situated in the United Kingdom, or of shares referred to in clause (i) of this sub-paragraph.

3. Gains from the alienation of property (other than real property) forming part of the business property of a permanent establishment that an enterprise of a Contracting State has or had in the other Contracting State, including gains from the alienation of such a permanent establishment (alone or with the whole enterprise), may be taxed in that other State, whether or not that permanent establishment exists at the time of the alienation.

4. Gains derived by an enterprise of a Contracting State from the alienation of ships or aircraft operated in international traffic by the enterprise, or of containers used in international traffic, or of property (other than real property) pertaining to the operation or use of such ships, aircraft or containers, shall be taxable only in that State.

5. Gains from the alienation of any property other than property referred to in the preceding paragraphs of this Article shall be taxable only in the Contracting State of which the alienator is a resident.

6. The provisions of paragraph 5 of this Article shall not affect the right of a Contracting State to levy according to its law a tax on gains from the alienation of any property derived by an individual who is a resident of the other Contracting State and has been a resident of the first-mentioned Contracting State at any time during the six years immediately preceding the alienation of the property.

Article 14

Income From Employment

1. Subject to the provisions of Articles 15 (Directors' Fees), 17 (Pensions, Social Security, Annuities, Alimony, and Child Support) and 19 (Government Service) of this Convention, salaries, wages, and other similar remuneration derived by a resident of a Contracting State in respect of an employment shall be taxable only in that State unless the employment is exercised in the other Contracting State. If the employment is so exercised, such remuneration as is derived therefrom may be taxed in that other State.

2. Notwithstanding the provisions of paragraph 1 of this Article, remuneration derived by a resident of a Contracting State in respect of an employment exercised in the other Contracting State shall be taxable only in the first-mentioned State if:

    a) the recipient is present in the other State for a period or periods not exceeding in the aggregate 183 days in any twelve-month period commencing or ending in the taxable year or year of assessment concerned;

    b) the remuneration is paid by, or on behalf of, an employer who is not a resident of the other State; and

    c) the remuneration is not borne by a permanent establishment which the employer has in the other State.

3. Notwithstanding the preceding provisions of this Article, remuneration described in paragraph 1 of this Article that is derived by a resident of a Contracting State in respect of an employment as a member of the regular complement of a ship or aircraft operated in international traffic shall be taxable only in that State.

Article 15

Directors' Fees

Directors' fees and other similar payments derived by a resident of a Contracting State for services rendered in the other Contracting State in his capacity as a member of the board of directors of a company that is a resident of the other Contracting State may be taxed in that other State.

Article 16

Entertainers and Sportsmen

1. Income derived by a resident of a Contracting State as an entertainer, such as a theatre, motion picture, radio, or television artiste, or a musician, or as a sportsman, from his personal activities as such exercised in the other Contracting State, which income would be exempt from tax in that other State under the provisions of Article 7 (Business Profits) or 14 (Income from Employment) of this Convention, may be taxed in that other State, except where the amount of the gross receipts derived by that resident, including expenses reimbursed to him or borne on his behalf, from such

activities does not exceed twenty thousand United States dollars ($20,000) or its equivalent in pounds sterling for the taxable year or year of assessment concerned.

2. Income in respect of activities exercised by an entertainer or a sportsman in his capacity as such which accrues not to the entertainer or sportsman himself but to another person may, notwithstanding the provisions of Article 7 (Business Profits) or 14 (Income from Employment) of this Convention, be taxed in the Contracting State in which the activities of the entertainer or sportsman are exercised, unless that other person establishes that neither the entertainer or sportsman nor persons related thereto participate directly or indirectly in the profits of that other person in any manner, including the receipt of deferred remuneration, bonuses, fees, dividends, partnership distributions, or other distributions.

Article 17

Pensions, Social Security, Annuities, Alimony, and Child Support

1.
   a) Pensions and other similar remuneration beneficially owned by a resident of a Contracting State shall be taxable only in that State.

   b) Notwithstanding sub-paragraph a) of this paragraph, the amount of any such pension or remuneration paid from a pension scheme established in the other Contracting State that would be exempt from taxation in that other State if the beneficial owner were a resident thereof shall be exempt from taxation in the first-mentioned State.

2. Notwithstanding the provisions of paragraph 1 of this Article, a lump-sum payment derived from a pension scheme established in a Contracting State and beneficially owned by a resident of the other Contracting State shall be taxable only in the first-mentioned State.

3. Notwithstanding the provisions of paragraph 1 of this Article, payments made by a Contracting State under the provisions of the social security or similar legislation of that State to a resident of the other Contracting State shall be taxable only in that other State.

4. Any annuity derived and beneficially owned by an individual ('the annuitant') who is a resident of a Contracting State shall be taxable only in that State. The term 'annuity' as used in this paragraph means a stated sum paid periodically at stated times during the life of the annuitant, or during a specified or ascertainable period of time, under an obligation to make the payments in return for adequate and full consideration (other than in return for services rendered).

5. Periodic payments, made pursuant to a written separation agreement or a decree of divorce, separate maintenance, or compulsory support, including payments for the support of a child, paid by a resident of a Contracting State to a resident of the other Contracting State, shall be exempt from tax in both Contracting States, except that, if the payer is entitled to relief from tax for such payments in the first-mentioned State, such payments shall be taxable only in the other State.

Article 18

Pension Schemes

1. Where an individual who is a resident of a Contracting State is a member or beneficiary of, or participant in, a pension scheme established in the other Contracting State, income earned by the pension scheme may be taxed as income of that individual only when, and, subject to paragraphs 1 and 2 of Article 17 (Pensions, Social Security,

Annuities, Alimony, and Child Support) of this Convention, to the extent that, it is paid to, or for the benefit of, that individual from the pension scheme (and not transferred to another pension scheme).

2. Where an individual who is a member or beneficiary of, or participant in, a pension scheme established in a Contracting State exercises an employment or self-employment in the other Contracting State:

   a) contributions paid by or on behalf of that individual to the pension scheme during the period that he exercises an employment or self-employment in the other State shall be deductible (or excludable) in computing his taxable income in that other State; and

   b) any benefits accrued under the pension scheme, or contributions made to the pension scheme by or on behalf of the individual's employer, during that period shall not be treated as part of the employee's taxable income and any such contributions shall be allowed as a deduction in computing the business profits of his employer in that other State.

   The reliefs available under this paragraph shall not exceed the reliefs that would be allowed by the other State to residents of that State for contributions to, or benefits accrued under, a pension scheme established in that State.

3. The provisions of paragraph 2 of this Article shall not apply unless:

   a) Contributions by or on behalf of the individual, or by or on behalf of the individual's employer, to the pension scheme (or to another similar pension scheme for which the first-mentioned pension scheme was substituted) were made before the individual began to exercise an employment or self-employment in the other State; and

   b) the competent authority of the other State has agreed that the pension scheme generally corresponds to a pension scheme established in that other State.

4. Where, under sub-paragraph a) of paragraph 2 of this Article, contributions to a pension scheme are deductible (or excludable) in computing an individual's taxable income in a Contracting State and, under the laws in force in that State, the individual is subject to tax in that State, in respect of income, profits or gains, by reference to the amount thereof which is remitted to or received in that State and not by reference to the full amount thereof, then the relief that would otherwise be available to that individual under that sub-paragraph in respect of such contributions shall be reduced to an amount that bears the same proportion to that relief as the amount of the income, profits or gains in respect of which the individual is subject to tax in that State bears to the amount of the income, profits or gains in respect of which he would be subject to tax if he were so subject in respect of the full amount thereof and not only in respect of the amount remitted to or received in that State.

5.
   a) Where a citizen of the United States who is a resident of the United Kingdom exercises an employment in the United Kingdom the income from which is taxable in the United Kingdom and is borne by an employer who is a resident of the United Kingdom or by a permanent establishment situated in the United Kingdom, and the individual is a member or beneficiary of, or participant in, a pension scheme established in the United Kingdom,

      (i) contributions paid by or on behalf of that individual to the pension scheme during the period that he exercises the employment in the United Kingdom, and that are attributable to the employment, shall be deductible (or excludable) in computing his taxable income in the United States; and

(ii) any benefits accrued under the pension scheme, or contributions made to the pension scheme by or on behalf of the individual's employer, during that period, and that are attributable to the employment, shall not be treated as part of the employee's taxable income in computing his taxable income in the United States. This paragraph shall apply only to the extent that the contributions or benefits qualify for tax relief in the United Kingdom.

b) The reliefs available under this paragraph shall not exceed the reliefs that would be allowed by the United States to its residents for contributions to, or benefits accrued under, a generally corresponding pension scheme established in the United States.

c) For purposes of determining an individual's eligibility to participate in and receive tax benefits with respect to a pension scheme established in the United States, contributions made to, or benefits accrued under, a pension scheme established in the United Kingdom shall be treated as contributions or benefits under a generally corresponding pension scheme established in the United States to the extent reliefs are available to the individual under this paragraph.

d) This paragraph shall not apply unless the competent authority of the United States has agreed that the pension scheme generally corresponds to a pension scheme established in the United States.

Article 19

Government Service

1. Notwithstanding the provisions of Articles 14 (Income from Employment), 15 (Directors' Fees) and 16 (Entertainers and Sportsmen) of this Convention:

    a) salaries, wages and other similar remuneration, other than a pension, paid from the public funds of a Contracting State or a political subdivision or a local authority thereof to an individual in respect of services rendered to that State or subdivision or authority shall, subject to the provisions of sub-paragraph b) of this paragraph, be taxable only in that State;

    b) such salaries, wages and other similar remuneration, however, shall be taxable only in the other Contracting State if the services are rendered in that State and the individual is a resident of that State who:

        (i) is a national of that State; or

        (ii) did not become a resident of that State solely for the purpose of rendering the services.

2. Notwithstanding the provisions of paragraphs 1 and 2 of Article 17 (Pensions, Social Security, Annuities, Alimony, and Child Support) of this Convention:

    a) any pension paid by, or out of funds created by, a Contracting State or a political subdivision or a local authority thereof to an individual in respect of services rendered to that State or subdivision or authority shall, subject to the provisions of sub-paragraph b) of this paragraph, be taxable only in that State;

    b) such pension, however, shall be taxable only in the other Contracting State if the individual is a resident of, and a national of, that State.

3. The provisions of Articles 14 (Income from Employment), 15 (Directors' Fees), 16 (Entertainers and Sportsmen) and 17 (Pensions, Social Security, Annuities, Alimony, and Child Support) of this Convention shall apply to salaries, wages and other similar

remuneration, and to pensions, in respect of services rendered in connection with a business carried on by a Contracting State or a political subdivision or a local authority thereof.

Article 20

Students

Payments received by a student or business apprentice who is, or was immediately before visiting a Contracting State, a resident of the other Contracting State, and who is present in the first-mentioned State for the purpose of his full-time education at a university, college or other recognised educational institution of a similar nature, or for his full-time training, shall not be taxed in that State, provided that such payments arise outside that State, and are for the purpose of his maintenance, education or training. The exemption from tax provided by this Article shall apply to a business apprentice only for a period of time not exceeding one year from the date he first arrives in the first-mentioned Contracting State for the purpose of his training.

Article 20A

Teachers

1. A professor or teacher who visits one of the Contracting States for a period not exceeding two years for the purpose of teaching or engaging in research at a university, college or other recognised educational institution in that Contracting State and who was immediately before that visit a resident of the other Contracting State, shall be exempted from tax by the first-mentioned Contracting State on any remuneration for such teaching or research for a period not exceeding two years from the date he first visits that State for such purpose.

2. The exemption provided in this Article may be applied by the Contracting State in which the teaching or research is performed to current payments to such professor or teacher in anticipation or fulfillment of the requirements of paragraph 1 or by way of withholding and refund, but in either case exemption shall be conditional upon fulfillment of the requirements of paragraph 1.

3. This Article shall apply to income from research only if such research is undertaken by the professor or teacher in the public interest and not primarily for the benefit of some other private person or persons.

Article 21

Offshore Exploration and Exploitation Activities

1. The provisions of this Article shall apply notwithstanding any other provision of this Convention where activities are carried on offshore in a Contracting State in connection with the exploration (hereinafter called 'exploration activities') or exploitation (hereinafter called 'exploitation activities') of the sea bed and sub-soil and their natural resources situated in that State.

2. An enterprise of a Contracting State which carries on exploration activities or exploitation activities in the other Contracting State shall, subject to paragraph 3 of this Article, be deemed to be carrying on business in that other State through a permanent establishment situated therein.

3. Exploration activities which are carried on by an enterprise of a Contracting State in the other Contracting State for a period or periods not exceeding in the aggregate 30 days within any period of twelve months shall not constitute the carrying on of business through a permanent establishment situated therein. For the purposes of determining such period or periods:

a) where an enterprise of a Contracting State carrying on exploration activities in the other Contracting State is associated with another enterprise carrying on substantially similar exploration activities there, the former enterprise shall be deemed to be carrying on all such activities of the latter enterprise, except to the extent that those activities are carried on at the same time as its own activities;

b) An enterprise shall be regarded as associated with another enterprise if one participates directly or indirectly in the management, control or capital of the other or if the same persons participate directly or indirectly in the management, control or capital of both enterprises.

4. Salaries, wages and other similar remuneration derived by a resident of a Contracting State from an employment in respect of exploration activities or exploitation activities carried on in the other Contracting State may be taxed in that other State, to the extent that the duties are performed offshore in that other State. However, income derived by a resident of a Contracting State in respect of such employment performed in the other Contracting State shall not be taxable in that other State if the employment is performed in that other State for a period or periods not exceeding in the aggregate 30 days within any period of twelve months.

Article 22

Other Income

1. Items of income beneficially owned by a resident of a Contracting State, wherever arising, not dealt with in the foregoing Articles of this Convention (other than income paid out of trusts or the estates of deceased persons in the course of administration) shall be taxable only in that State.

2. The provisions of paragraph 1 of this Article shall not apply to income, other than income from real property, if the beneficial owner of the income, being a resident of a Contracting State, carries on business in the other Contracting State through a permanent establishment situated therein, and the income is attributable to such permanent establishment. In such case, the provisions of Article 7 (Business Profits) of this Convention shall apply.

3. Where, by reason of a special relationship between the resident referred to in paragraph 1 of this Article and some other person, or between both of them and some third person, the amount of the income referred to in that paragraph exceeds the amount (if any) which would have been agreed upon between them in the absence of such relationship, the provisions of this Article shall apply only to the last-mentioned amount. In such a case, the excess part of the income shall remain taxable according to the laws of each Contracting State, due regard being had to the other applicable provisions of this Convention.

4. The provisions of this Article shall not apply in respect of any income paid under, or as part of, a conduit arrangement.

Article 23

Limitation on Benefits

1. Except as otherwise provided in this Article, a resident of a Contracting State that derives income, profits or gains from the other Contracting State shall be entitled to all the benefits of this Convention otherwise accorded to residents of a Contracting State only if such resident is a 'qualified person' as defined in paragraph 2 of this Article and satisfies any other specified conditions for the obtaining of such benefits.

2. A resident of a Contracting State is a qualified person for a taxable or chargeable period only if such resident is either:

- a) an individual;
- b) a qualified governmental entity;
- c) a company, if
  - (i) the principal class of its shares is listed or admitted to dealings on a recognized stock exchange specified in clauses (i) or (ii) of sub-paragraph a) of paragraph 7 of this Article and is regularly traded on one or more recognized stock exchanges; or
  - (ii) shares representing at least 50 per cent. of the aggregate voting power and value of the company are owned directly or indirectly by five or fewer companies entitled to benefits under clause (i) of this sub-paragraph, provided that, in the case of indirect ownership, each intermediate owner is a resident of either Contracting State;
- d) a person other than an individual or a company, if:
  - (i) the principal class of units in that person is listed or admitted to dealings on a recognized stock exchange specified in clauses (i) or (ii) of sub-paragraph a) of paragraph 7 of this Article and is regularly traded on one or more recognized stock exchanges; or
  - (ii) the direct or indirect owners of at least 50 per cent. of the beneficial interests in that person are qualified persons by reason of clause (i) of sub-paragraph c) or clause (i) of this sub-paragraph;
- e) a person described in sub-paragraph a), b) or c) of paragraph 3 of Article 4 (Residence) of this Convention, provided that, in the case of a person described in sub-paragraph a) or b) of that paragraph, more than 50 per cent. of the person's beneficiaries, members or participants are individuals who are residents of either Contracting State;
- f) a person other than an individual, if:
  - (i) on at least half the days of the taxable or chargeable period persons that are qualified persons by reason of sub-paragraphs a), b), clause (i) of sub-paragraph c), clause (i) of sub-paragraph d), or sub-paragraph e) of this paragraph own, directly or indirectly, shares or other beneficial interests representing at least 50 per cent. of the aggregate voting power and value of the person, and
  - (ii) less than 50 per cent. of the person's gross income for that taxable or chargeable period is paid or accrued, directly or indirectly, to persons who are not residents of either Contracting State in the form of payments that are deductible for the purposes of the taxes covered by this Convention in the State of which the person is a resident (but not including arm's length payments in the ordinary course of business for services or tangible property and payments in respect of financial obligations to a bank, provided that where such a bank is not a resident of a Contracting State such payment is attributable to a permanent establishment of that bank located in one of the Contracting States); or
- g) a trust or trustee of a trust in their capacity as such if at least 50 per cent. of the beneficial interest in the trust is held by persons who are either:
  - (i) qualified persons by reason of sub-paragraphs a), b), clause (i) of sub-paragraph c), clause (i) of sub-paragraph d), or sub-paragraph e) of this paragraph; or
  - (ii) equivalent beneficiaries, provided that less than 50 per cent. of the gross income arising to such trust or trustee in their capacity as such for the

taxable or chargeable period is paid or accrued, directly or indirectly, to persons who are not residents of either Contracting State in the form of payments that are deductible for the purposes of the taxes covered by this Convention in the Contracting State of which that trust or trustee is a resident (but not including arm's length payments in the ordinary course of business for services or tangible property and payments in respect of financial obligations to a bank, provided that where such a bank is not a resident of a Contracting State such payment is attributable to a permanent establishment of that bank located in one of the Contracting States).

3. Notwithstanding that a company that is a resident of a Contracting State may not be a qualified person, it shall be entitled to the benefits of this Convention otherwise accorded to residents of a Contracting State with respect to an item of income, profit or gain if it satisfies any other specified conditions for the obtaining of such benefits and:

   a) shares representing at least 95 per cent. of the aggregate voting power and value of the company are owned, directly or indirectly, by seven or fewer persons who are equivalent beneficiaries; and

   b) less than 50 per cent. of the company's gross income for the taxable or chargeable period in which the item of income, profit or gain arises is paid or accrued, directly or indirectly, to persons who are not equivalent beneficiaries, in the form of payments that are deductible for the purposes of the taxes covered by this Convention in the State of which the company is a resident (but not including arm's length payments in the ordinary course of business for services or tangible property and payments in respect of financial obligations to a bank, provided that where such a bank is not a resident of a Contracting State such payment is attributable to a permanent establishment of that bank located in one of the Contracting States).

4.
   a) Notwithstanding that a resident of a Contracting State may not be a qualified person, it shall be entitled to the benefits of this Convention with respect to an item of income, profit or gain derived from the other Contracting State, if the resident is engaged in the active conduct of a trade or business in the first-mentioned State (other than the business of making or managing investments for the resident's own account, unless these activities are banking, insurance or securities activities carried on by a bank, insurance company or registered securities dealer), the income, profit or gain derived from the other Contracting State is derived in connection with, or is incidental to, that trade or business and that resident satisfies any other specified conditions for the obtaining of such benefits.

   b) If a resident of a Contracting State or any of its associated enterprises carries on a trade or business activity in the other Contracting State which gives rise to an item of income, profit or gain, sub-paragraph a) of this paragraph shall apply to such item only if the trade or business activity in the first-mentioned State is substantial in relation to the trade or business activity in the other State. Whether a trade or business activity is substantial for the purposes of this paragraph shall be determined on the basis of all the facts and circumstances.

   c) In determining whether a person is engaged in the active conduct of a trade or business in a Contracting State under sub-paragraph a) of this paragraph, activities conducted by a partnership in which that person is a partner and activities conducted by persons connected to such person shall be deemed to be conducted by such person. A person shall be connected to another if one possesses at least 50 per cent. of the beneficial interest in the other (or, in the case of a company, shares representing at least 50 per cent. of the aggregate voting power and value of the company or of the beneficial equity interest in the company) or another person possesses, directly or indirectly, at least 50 per cent. of the beneficial interest (or, in the case of a company, shares representing at least 50 per cent. of the aggregate voting power and value of the company or of the beneficial equity interest in the company) in each person. In any case, a person shall be considered to be connected to another if, on the basis of all the facts and circumstances, one has control of the other or both are under the control of the same person or persons.

5. Notwithstanding the preceding provisions of this Article, if a company that is a resident of a Contracting State, or a company that controls such a company, has outstanding a class of shares:

   a) which is subject to terms or other arrangements which entitle its holders to a portion of the income, profit or gain of the company derived from the other Contracting State that is larger than the portion such holders would receive in the absence of such terms or arrangements; and

   b) 50 per cent. or more of the voting power and value of which is owned by persons who are not equivalent beneficiaries,

the benefits of this Convention shall apply only to that proportion of the income which those holders would have received in the absence of those terms or arrangements.

6. A resident of a Contracting State that is neither a qualified person nor entitled to benefits with respect to an item of income, profit or gain under paragraph 3 or 4 of this Article shall, nevertheless, be granted benefits of this Convention with respect to such item if the competent authority of the other Contracting State determines that the establishment, acquisition or maintenance of such resident and the conduct of its operations did not have as one of its principal purposes the obtaining of benefits under this Convention.

The competent authority of the other Contracting State shall consult with the competent authority of the first-mentioned State before refusing to grant benefits of this Convention under this paragraph.

7. For the purposes of this Article the following rules and definitions shall apply:

   a) the term 'recognized stock exchange' means:

      (i) the NASDAQ System and any stock exchange registered with the U.S. Securities and Exchange Commission as a national securities exchange under the U.S. Securities Exchange Act of 1934;

      (ii) the London Stock Exchange and any other recognised investment exchange within the meaning of the Financial Services Act 1986 or, as the case may be, the Financial Services and Markets Act 2000;

      (iii) the Irish Stock Exchange, the Swiss Stock Exchange and the stock exchanges of Amsterdam, Brussels, Frankfurt, Hamburg, Johannesburg, Madrid, Milan, Paris, Stockholm, Sydney, Tokyo, Toronto and Vienna; and

      (iv) any other stock exchange which the competent authorities agree to recognise for the purposes of this Article;

   b)
      (i) the term 'principal class of shares' means the ordinary or common shares of the company, provided that such class of shares represents the majority of the voting power and value of the company. If no single class of ordinary or common shares represents the majority of the aggregate voting power and value of the company, the 'principal class of shares' is

that class or those classes that in the aggregate represent a majority of the aggregate voting power and value of the company;

    (ii) the term 'shares' shall include depository receipts thereof or trust certificates thereof;

c) the term 'units' as used in sub-paragraph d) of paragraph 2 of this Article includes shares and any other instrument, not being a debt-claim, granting an entitlement to share in the assets or income of, or receive a distribution from, the person. The term 'principal class of units' means the class of units which represents the majority of the value of the person. If no single class of units represents the majority of the value of the person, the 'principal class of units' is those classes that in the aggregate represent the majority of the value of the person;

d) an equivalent beneficiary is a resident of a Member State of the European Community or of a European Economic Area state or of a party to the North American Free Trade Agreement but only if that resident:

    (i)

        A) would be entitled to all the benefits of a comprehensive convention for the avoidance of double taxation between any Member State of the European Community or a European Economic Area state or any party to the North American Free Trade Agreement and the Contracting State from which the benefits of this Convention are claimed, provided that if such convention does not contain a comprehensive limitation on benefits article, the person would be a qualified person under paragraph 2 of this Article (or for the purposes of sub-paragraph g) of paragraph 2, under the provisions specified in clause (i) of that sub-paragraph) if such person were a resident of one of the Contracting States under Article 4 (Residence) of this Convention; and

        B) with respect to income referred to in Article 10 (Dividends), 11 (Interest) or 12 (Royalties) of this Convention, would be entitled under such convention to a rate of tax with respect to the particular class of income for which benefits are being claimed under this Convention that is at least as low as the rate applicable under this Convention; or

    (ii) is a qualified person by reason of sub-paragraphs a), b), clause (i) of sub-paragraph c), clause (i) of sub-paragraph d), or sub-paragraph e) of paragraph 2 of this Article.

For the purposes of applying paragraph 3 of Article 10 (Dividends) in order to determine whether a person, owning shares, directly or indirectly, in the company claiming the benefits of this Convention, is an equivalent beneficiary, such person shall be deemed to hold the same voting power in the company paying the dividend as the company claiming the benefits holds in such company.

e) For the purposes of paragraph 2 of this Article, the shares in a class of shares or the units in a class of units are considered to be regularly traded on one or more recognized stock exchanges in a chargeable or taxable period if the aggregate number of shares or units of that class traded on such stock exchange or exchanges during the twelve months ending on the day before the beginning of that taxable or chargeable period is at least six per cent. of the average number of shares or units outstanding in that class during that twelve-month period.

f) A body corporate or unincorporated association shall be considered to be an insurance company if its gross income consists primarily of insurance or reinsurance premiums and investment income attributable to such premiums.

Article 24

Relief from Double Taxation

1. In accordance with the provisions and subject to the limitations of the law of the United States (as it may be amended from time to time without changing the general principle hereof), the United States shall allow to a resident or citizen of the United States as a credit against the United States tax on income

   a) the income tax paid or accrued to the United Kingdom by or on behalf of such citizen or resident; and

   b) in the case of a United States company owning at least 10 per cent. of the voting stock of a company that is a resident of the United Kingdom and from which the United States company receives dividends, the income tax paid or accrued to the United Kingdom by or on behalf of the payer with respect to the profits out of which the dividends are paid.

For the purposes of this paragraph, the taxes referred to in sub-paragraph b) of paragraph 3 and in paragraph 4 of Article 2 (Taxes Covered) of this Convention shall be considered income taxes.

2. For the purposes of applying paragraph 1 of this Article,

   a) subject to sub-paragraph b) of this paragraph, an item of gross income, as determined under the laws of the United States, derived by a resident of the United States that, under this Convention, may be taxed in the United Kingdom shall be deemed to be income from sources in the United Kingdom;

   b) however, gains derived by an individual while that individual was a resident of the United States, that are taxed in the United States in accordance with this Convention, and that may also be taxed in the United Kingdom by reason only of paragraph 6 of Article 13 (Gains) of this Convention, shall be deemed to be gains from sources in the United States.

3. Notwithstanding the provisions of paragraph 1 of this Article, the amount of United Kingdom petroleum revenue tax allowable as a credit against United States tax shall be limited to the amount attributable to the United Kingdom source taxable income in the following way, namely:

   a) the amount of United Kingdom petroleum revenue tax on income from the extraction of minerals from oil or gas wells in the United Kingdom to be allowed as a credit for a taxable year shall not exceed the amount, if any, by which the product of the maximum statutory United States tax rate applicable to a corporation for such taxable year and the amount of such income exceeds the amount of other United Kingdom tax on such income;

   b) the amount of United Kingdom petroleum revenue tax on income from the extraction of minerals from oil or gas wells in the United Kingdom that is not allowable as a credit under sub-paragraph a) of this paragraph, shall be deemed to be income taxes paid or accrued in the two preceding or five succeeding taxable years, to the extent not deemed paid or accrued in a prior taxable year, and shall be allowable as a credit in the year in which it is deemed paid or accrued subject to the limitation in sub-paragraph a) of this paragraph;

   c) the provisions of sub-paragraphs a) and b) of this paragraph shall apply separately, *mutatis mutandis*, to the amount of United Kingdom petroleum revenue tax on income from initial transportation, initial treatment and initial storage of minerals from oil or gas wells in the United Kingdom.

4. Subject to the provisions of the law of the United Kingdom regarding the allowance as a credit against United Kingdom tax of tax payable in a territory outside the United Kingdom (which shall not affect the general principle hereof):

   a) United States tax payable under the laws of the United States and in accordance with this Convention, whether directly or by deduction, on profits, income or chargeable gains from sources within the United States (excluding, in the case of a dividend, United States tax in respect of the profits out of which the dividend is paid) shall be allowed as a credit against any United Kingdom tax computed by reference to the same profits, income or chargeable gains by reference to which the United States tax is computed;

   b) in the case of a dividend paid by a company which is a resident of the United States to a company which is a resident of the United Kingdom and which controls directly or indirectly at least 10 per cent. of the voting power in the company paying the dividend, the credit shall take into account (in addition to any United States tax for which credit may be allowed under the provisions of sub-paragraph a) of this paragraph) the United States tax payable by the company in respect of the profits out of which such dividend is paid;

   c) United States tax shall not be taken into account under sub-paragraph b) of this paragraph for the purpose of allowing credit against United Kingdom tax in the case of a dividend paid by a company which is a resident of the United States if and to the extent that

      (i) the United Kingdom treats the dividend as beneficially owned by a resident of the United Kingdom; and

      (ii) the United States treats the dividend as beneficially owned by a resident of the United States; and

      (iii) the United States has allowed a deduction to a resident of the United States in respect of an amount determined by reference to that dividend;

   d) the provisions of paragraph 2 of Article 1 (General Scope) of this Convention shall not apply to sub-paragraph c) of this paragraph.

   For the purposes of this paragraph, the income taxes referred to in clause (i) of sub-paragraph a) of paragraph 3 and in paragraph 4 of Article 2 (Taxes Covered) of this Convention shall be considered United States tax.

5. For the purposes of paragraph 4 of this Article, profits, income and chargeable gains owned by a resident of the United Kingdom which may be taxed in the United States in accordance with this Convention shall be deemed to arise from sources within the United States.

6. Where the United States taxes, in accordance with paragraph 4 of Article 1 (General Scope) of this Convention, a United States citizen, or a former United States citizen or long-term resident, who is a resident of the United Kingdom:

   a) the United Kingdom shall not be bound to give credit to such resident for United States tax on profits, income or chargeable gains from sources outside the United States as determined under the laws of the United Kingdom;

   b) in the case of profits, income or chargeable gains from sources within the United States, the United Kingdom shall take into account for the purposes of computing the credit to be allowed under paragraph 4 of this Article only the amount of tax, if any, that the United States may impose under the provisions of this Convention on a resident of the United Kingdom who is not a United States citizen;

c) for the purposes of computing United States tax on the profits, income or chargeable gains referred to in sub-paragraph b) of this paragraph, the United States shall allow as a credit against United States tax the income tax and capital gains tax paid to the United Kingdom after the credit referred to in sub-paragraph b) of this paragraph; the credit so allowed shall not reduce the portion of the United States tax that is creditable against the United Kingdom tax in accordance with sub-paragraph b) of this paragraph; and

d) for the exclusive purpose of relieving double taxation in the United States under sub-paragraph c) of this paragraph, profits, income and chargeable gains referred to in sub-paragraph b) of this paragraph shall be deemed to arise in the United Kingdom to the extent necessary to avoid double taxation of such profits, income or chargeable gains under sub-paragraph c) of this paragraph.

Article 25

Non-Discrimination

1. Nationals of a Contracting State shall not be subjected in the other Contracting State to any taxation or any requirement connected therewith that is more burdensome than the taxation and connected requirements to which nationals of that other State in the same circumstances, particularly with respect to taxation on worldwide income, are or may be subjected.

2. The taxation on a permanent establishment that an enterprise of a Contracting State has in the other Contracting State shall not be less favourably levied in that other State than the taxation levied on enterprises of that other State carrying on the same activities.

3. Except where the provisions of the second sentence of paragraph 5 of Article 7 (Business Profits), paragraph 1 of Article 9 (Associated Enterprises), paragraph 9 of Article 10 (Dividends), paragraphs 4 and 7 of Article 11 (Interest), paragraphs 4 and 5 of Article 12 (Royalties), or paragraphs 3 and 4 of Article 22 (Other Income) of this Convention apply, interest, royalties, and other disbursements paid by a resident of a Contracting State to a resident of the other Contracting State shall, for the purpose of determining the taxable profits of the first-mentioned resident, be deductible under the same conditions as if they had been paid to a resident of the first-mentioned State.

4. Enterprises of a Contracting State, the capital of which is wholly or partly owned or controlled, directly or indirectly, by one or more residents of the other Contracting State, shall not be subjected in the first-mentioned State to any taxation or any requirement connected therewith that is more burdensome than the taxation and connected requirements to which other similar enterprises of the first-mentioned State are or may be subjected.

5. Nothing in this Article shall be construed as obliging either Contracting State to grant to individuals not resident in that State any of the personal allowances, reliefs and reductions for tax purposes which are granted to individuals so resident or to its nationals.

6. Nothing in this Article shall be construed as preventing either Contracting State from imposing a tax as described in paragraph 7 of Article 10 (Dividends) of this Convention.

7. The provisions of this Article shall, notwithstanding the provisions of Article 2 (Taxes Covered) of this Convention, also apply to taxes of every kind and description imposed by each Contracting State or by its political sub-divisions or local authorities.

Article 26

Mutual Agreement Procedure

1. Where a person considers that the actions of one or both of the Contracting States result or will result for him in taxation not in accordance with the provisions of this Convention, he may, irrespective of the remedies provided by the domestic law of those States, present his case to the competent authority of the Contracting State of which he is a resident or national. The case must be presented within three years from the first notification of the action resulting in taxation not in accordance with the provisions of this Convention or, if later, within six years from the end of the taxable year or chargeable period in respect of which that taxation is imposed or proposed.

2. The competent authority shall endeavour, if the objection appears to it to be justified and if it is not itself able to arrive at a satisfactory solution, to resolve the case by mutual agreement with the competent authority of the other Contracting State, with a view to the avoidance of taxation which is not in accordance with this Convention. Any agreement reached shall be implemented notwithstanding any time limits or other procedural limitations in the domestic law of the Contracting States, except such limitations as apply for the purposes of giving effect to such an agreement.

3. The competent authorities of the Contracting States shall endeavour to resolve by mutual agreement any difficulties or doubts arising as to the interpretation or application of this Convention. In particular the competent authorities of the Contracting States may agree:

    a) to the same attribution of income, deductions, credits, or allowances of an enterprise of a Contracting State to its permanent establishment situated in the other Contracting State;

    b) to the same allocation of income, deductions, credits, or allowances between persons;

    c) to the same characterization of particular items of income, including the same characterization of income that is assimilated to income from shares by the taxation law of one of the Contracting States and that is treated as a different class of income in the other Contracting State;

    d) to the same characterization of persons;

    e) to the same application of source rules with respect to particular items of income;

    f) to a common meaning of a term;

    g) that the conditions for the application of the second sentence of paragraph 5 of Article 7 (Business Profits), paragraph 9 of Article 10 (Dividends), paragraph 7 of Article 11 (Interest), paragraph 5 of Article 12 (Royalties), or paragraph 4 of Article 22 (Other Income) of this Convention are met; and

    h) to the application of the provisions of domestic law regarding penalties, fines, and interest in a manner consistent with the purposes of this Convention.

    They may also consult together for the elimination of double taxation in cases not provided for in this Convention.

4. The competent authorities of the Contracting States may communicate with each other directly for the purpose of reaching an agreement in the sense of the preceding paragraphs.

Article 27

Exchange of Information and Administrative Assistance

1. The competent authorities of the Contracting States shall exchange such information as is necessary for carrying out the provisions of this Convention or of the domestic laws of the Contracting States concerning taxes covered by this Convention insofar as the taxation thereunder is not contrary to this Convention, including for the purposes of preventing fraud and facilitating the administration of statutory provisions against legal avoidance. This includes information relating to the assessment or collection of, the enforcement or prosecution in respect of, or the determination of appeals in relation to, the taxes covered by this Convention. The exchange of information is not restricted by paragraph 1 of Article 1 (General Scope) of this Convention. Any information received by a Contracting State shall be treated as secret in the same manner as information obtained under the domestic laws of that State but may be disclosed to and only to persons or authorities (including courts and administrative bodies) involved in the assessment, collection, or administration of, the enforcement or prosecution in respect of, or the determination of appeals in relation to, the taxes covered by this Convention or the oversight of the above. Such persons or authorities shall use the information only for such purposes. They may disclose the information in public court proceedings or in judicial decisions.

2. If information is requested by a Contracting State in accordance with this Article, the other Contracting State shall obtain that information in the same manner and to the same extent as if the tax of the first-mentioned State were the tax of that other State and were being imposed by that other State, notwithstanding that the other State may not, at that time, need such information for the purposes of its own tax.

3. In no case shall the provisions of paragraphs 1 and 2 of this Article be construed so as to impose on a Contracting State the obligation:

    a) to carry out administrative measures at variance with the laws and administrative practice of that or of the other Contracting State;

    b) to supply information that is not obtainable under the laws or in the normal course of the administration of that or of the other Contracting State;

    c) to supply information that would disclose any trade, business, industrial, commercial, or professional secret or trade process, or information the disclosure of which would be contrary to public policy.

4. If specifically requested by the competent authority of a Contracting State, the competent authority of the other Contracting State shall provide information under this Article in the form of authenticated copies of unedited original documents (including books, papers, statements, records, accounts, and writings), to the same extent such documents can be obtained under the laws and administrative practices of that other State with respect to its own taxes.

5. Each of the Contracting States shall endeavour to collect on behalf of the other Contracting State such amounts as may be necessary to ensure that relief granted by this Convention from taxation imposed by that other State does not inure to the benefit of persons not entitled thereto. This paragraph shall not impose upon either of the Contracting States the obligation to carry out administrative measures that would be contrary to its sovereignty, security, or public policy.

6. The competent authority of a Contracting State intending to send officials of that State to the other Contracting State to interview individuals and examine books and records with the consent of the persons subject to examination shall notify the competent authority of the other Contracting State of that intention.

7. The competent authorities of the Contracting States shall consult with each other for the purpose of cooperating and advising in respect of any action to be taken in implementing this Article.

Article 28

Diplomatic Agents and Consular Officers

Nothing in this Convention shall affect the fiscal privileges of diplomatic agents or consular officers under the general rules of international law or under the provisions of special agreements.

Article 29

Entry Into Force

1. This Convention shall be subject to ratification in accordance with the applicable procedures of each Contracting State and instruments of ratification shall be exchanged as soon as possible.
2. This Convention shall enter into force upon the exchange of instruments of ratification and its provisions shall have effect:
    a) in the United States:
        (i)   in respect of taxes withheld at source, for amounts paid or credited on or after the first day of the second month next following the date on which this Convention enters into force;
        (ii) in respect of other taxes, for taxable periods beginning on or after the first day of January next following the date on which this Convention enters into force; and
    b) in the United Kingdom:
        (i)   in respect of taxes withheld at source, for amounts paid or credited on or after the first day of the second month next following the date on which this Convention enters into force;
        (ii) in respect of income tax not described in clause (i) of this sub-paragraph and capital gains tax, for any year of assessment beginning on or after the sixth day of April next following the date on which this Convention enters into force;
        (iii) in respect of corporation tax, for any financial year beginning on or after the first day of April next following the date on which this Convention enters into force;
        (iv) in respect of petroleum revenue tax, for chargeable periods beginning on or after the first day of January next following the date on which this Convention enters into force.
3.
    a) The Convention between the Government of the United States of America and the Government of the United Kingdom of Great Britain and Northern Ireland for the Avoidance of Double Taxation and the Prevention of Fiscal Evasion with Respect to Taxes on Income and Capital Gains, signed at London on December 31st, 1975, as modified by subsequent notes and protocols ('the prior Convention') shall cease to have effect in relation to any tax with effect from the date on which this Convention has effect in relation to that tax in accordance with paragraph 2 of this Article. In relation to tax credits in respect of dividends paid by companies which are residents of the United Kingdom, the prior Convention

shall terminate and cease to be effective in respect of dividends paid on or after the first day of the second month next following the date on which this Convention enters into force.

b) Notwithstanding sub-paragraph a) of this paragraph, where any person entitled to benefits under the prior Convention would have been entitled to greater benefits thereunder than under this Convention, the prior Convention shall, at the election of such person, continue to have effect in its entirety with respect to that person for a twelve-month period from the date on which the provisions of this Convention otherwise would have effect under paragraph 2 of this Article. The prior Convention shall terminate on the last date on which it has effect in relation to any tax or to any entitlement to tax credits in accordance with the foregoing provisions of this sub-paragraph.

4. Notwithstanding the entry into force of this Convention, an individual who is entitled to the benefits of Article 21 (Students and Trainees) of the prior Convention at the time of entry into force of this Convention shall continue to be entitled to such benefits as if the prior Convention had remained in force.

Article 30

Termination

This Convention shall remain in force until terminated by a Contracting State. Either Contracting State may terminate this Convention by giving notice of termination to the other Contracting State through diplomatic channels. In such event, this Convention shall cease to have effect:

a) in the United States:

   (i) in respect of taxes withheld at source, for amounts paid or credited after the date that is six months after the date on which notice of termination was given; and

   (ii) in respect of other taxes, for taxable periods beginning on or after the date that is six months after the date on which notice of termination was given.

b) in the United Kingdom:

   (i) in respect of taxes withheld at source, for amounts paid or credited after the date that is six months after the date on which notice of termination was given;

   (ii) in respect of income tax not described in clause (i) of this sub-paragraph and capital gains tax, for any year of assessment beginning on or after the date that is six months after the date on which notice of termination was given;

   (iii) in respect of corporation tax, for any financial year beginning on or after the date that is six months after the date on which notice of termination was given; and

   (iv) in respect of petroleum revenue tax, for chargeable periods beginning on or after the date that is six months after the date on which notice of termination was given.

In witness whereof, the undersigned, being duly authorised thereto by their respective Governments, have signed this Convention.

Done at London in duplicate, this twenty-fourth day of July, 2001.

For the Government of the United States of America:

For the Government of the United Kingdom of Great Britain and Northern Ireland:

Appendix IV

1978 United Kingdom-United States Estate and Gift Tax Treaty

Convention Between the Government of the United States of America and the Government of the United Kingdom of Great Britain and Northern Ireland for the Avoidance of Double Taxation and the Prevention of Fiscal Evasion with Respect to Taxes on Estates of Deceased Persons and on Gifts

The Government of the United States of America and the Government of the United Kingdom of Great Britain and Northern Ireland;

Desiring to conclude a new Convention for the avoidance of double taxation and the prevention of fiscal evasion with respect to taxes on estates of deceased persons and on gifts;

Have agreed as follows:

Article 1

Scope

This Convention shall apply to any person who is within the scope of a tax which is the subject of this Convention.

Article 2

Taxes Covered

(1) The existing taxes to which this Convention shall apply are:

    (a) in the United States: the Federal gift tax and the Federal estate tax, including the tax on generation-skipping transfers; and

    (b) in the United Kingdom: the capital transfer tax.

(2) This Convention shall also apply to any identical or substantially similar taxes which are imposed by a Contracting State after the date of signature of the Convention in addition to, or in place of, the existing taxes. The competent authorities of the Contracting States shall notify each other of any changes which have been made in their respective taxation laws.

Article 3

General Definitions

(1) In this Convention:

    (a) the term 'United States' means the United States of America, but does not include Puerto Rico, the Virgin Islands, Guam or any other United States possession or territory;

    (b) the term 'United Kingdom' means Great Britain and Northern Ireland;

    (c) the term 'enterprise' means an industrial or commercial undertaking;

    (d) the term 'competent authority' means:

(i) in the United States: the Secretary of the Treasury or his delegate, and

(ii) in the United Kingdom: the Commissioners of Inland Revenue or their authorized representative;

(e) the term 'nationals' means:

(i) in relation to the United States, United States citizens, and

(ii) in relation to the United Kingdom, any citizen of the United Kingdom and Colonies, or any British subject not possessing that citizenship or the citizenship of any other Commonwealth country or territory, provided in either case he had the right of abode in the United Kingdom at the time of the death or transfer;

(f) the term 'tax' means:

(i) the Federal gift tax or the Federal estate tax, including the tax on generation-skipping transfers, imposed in the United States, or

(ii) the capital transfer tax imposed in the United Kingdom, or

(iii) any other tax imposed by a Contracting State to which this Convention applies by virtue of the provisions of paragraph (2) of Article 2,

as the context requires; and

(g) the term 'Contracting State' means the United States or the United Kingdom as the context requires.

(2) As regards the application of the Convention by a Contracting State, any term not otherwise defined shall, unless the context otherwise requires and subject to the provisions of Article 11 (Mutual Agreement Procedure), have the meaning which it has under the laws of that Contracting State relating to the taxes which are the subject of the Convention.

Article 4

Fiscal Domicile

(1) For the purposes of this Convention an individual was domiciled:

(a) in the United States: if he was a resident (domiciliary) thereof or if he was a national thereof and had been a resident (domiciliary) thereof at any time during the preceding three years; and

(b) in the United Kingdom: if he was domiciled in the United Kingdom in accordance with the law of the United Kingdom or is treated as so domiciled for the purposes of a tax which is the subject of this Convention.

(2) Where by reason of the provisions of paragraph (1) an individual was at any time domiciled in both Contracting States, and

(a) was a national of the United Kingdom but not of the United States, and

(b) had not been resident in the United States for Federal income tax purposes in seven or more of the ten taxable years ending with the year in which that time falls,

he shall be deemed to be domiciled in the United Kingdom at that time.

(3) Where by reason of the provisions of paragraph (1) an individual was at any time domiciled in both Contracting States, and:

(a) was a national of the United States but not of the United Kingdom, and

(b) had not been resident in the United Kingdom in seven or more of the ten income tax years of assessment ending with the year in which that time falls, he shall be deemed to be domiciled in the United States at that time. For the purposes of this paragraph, the question of whether a person was so resident shall be determined as for income tax purposes but without regard to any dwelling-house available to him in the United Kingdom for his use.

(4) Where by reason of the provisions of paragraph (1) an individual was domiciled in both Contracting States, then, subject to the provisions of paragraphs (2) and (3), his status shall be determined as follows:

(a) the individual shall be deemed to be domiciled in the Contracting State in which he had a permanent home available to him. If he had a permanent home available to him in both Contracting States, or in neither Contracting State, he shall be deemed to be domiciled in the Contracting State with which his personal and economic relations were closest (centre of vital interest);

(b) if the Contracting State in which the individual's centre of vital interests was located cannot be determined, he shall be deemed to be domiciled in the Contracting State in which he had an habitual abode;

(c) if the individual had an habitual abode in both Contracting States or in neither of them, he shall be deemed to be domiciled in the Contracting State of which he was a national; and

(d) if the individual was a national of both Contracting States or of neither of them, the competent authorities of the Contracting States shall settle the question by mutual agreement.

(5) An individual who was a resident (domiciliary) of a possession of the United States and who became a citizen of the United States solely by reason of his

(a) being a citizen of such possession, or

(b) birth or residence within such possession, shall be considered as neither domiciled in nor a national of the United States for the purposes of this Convention.

Article 5

Taxing Rights

(1)

(a) Subject to the provisions of Articles 6 (Immovable Property (Real Property)) and 7 (Business Property of a Permanent Establishment and Assets Pertaining to a Fixed Base Used for the Performance of Independent Personal Services) and the following paragraphs of this Article, if the decedent or transferor was domiciled in one of the Contracting States at the time of the death or transfer, property shall not be taxable in the other State.

(b) Sub-paragraph (a) shall not apply if at the time of the death or transfer the decedent or transferor was a national of that other State.

(2) Subject to the provisions of the said Articles 6 and 7, if at the time of the death or transfer the decedent or transferor was domiciled in neither Contracting State and was a national of one Contracting State (but not of both), property which is taxable in the Contracting State of which he was a national shall not be taxable in the other Contracting State.

(3) Paragraphs (1) and (2) shall not apply in the United States to property held in a generation-skipping trust or trust equivalent on the occasion of a generation-skipping transfer; but, subject to the provisions of the said Articles 6 and 7, tax shall not be

imposed in the United States on such property if at the time when the transfer was made the deemed transferor was domiciled in the United Kingdom and was not a national of the United States.

(4) Paragraphs (1) and (2) shall not apply in the United Kingdom to property comprised in a settlement; but, subject to the provisions of the said Articles 6 and 7, tax shall not be imposed in the United Kingdom on such property if at the time when the settlement was made the settlor was domiciled in the United States and was not a national of the United Kingdom.

(5) If by reason of the preceding paragraphs of this Article any property would be taxable only in one Contracting State and tax, though chargeable, is not paid (otherwise than as a result of a specific exemption, deduction, exclusion, credit or allowance) in that State, tax may be imposed by reference to that property in the other Contracting State notwithstanding those paragraphs.

(6) If at the time of the death or transfer the decedent or transferor was domiciled in neither Contracting State and each State would regard any property as situated in its territory and in consequence tax would be imposed in both States, the competent authorities of the Contracting States shall determine the situs of the property by mutual agreement.

Article 6

Immovable Property (Real Property)

(1) Immovable property (real property) may be taxed in the Contracting State in which such property is situated.

(2) The term 'immovable property' shall be defined in accordance with the law of the Contracting State in which the property in question is situated, provided always that debts secured by mortgage or otherwise shall not be regarded as immovable property. The term shall in any case include property accessory to immovable property, livestock and equipment used in agriculture and forestry, rights to which the provisions of general law respecting landed property apply, usufruct of immovable property and rights to variable or fixed payments as consideration for the working of, or the right to work, mineral deposits, sources and other natural resources; ships, boats, and aircraft shall not be regarded as immovable property.

(3) The provisions of paragraphs (1) and (2) shall also apply to immovable property of an enterprise and to immovable property used for the performance of independent personal services.

Article 7

Business Property of a Permanent Establishment and Assets Pertaining to a Fixed Base Used for the Performance of Independent Personal Services

(1) Except for assets referred to in Article 6 (Immovable Property (Real Property)), assets forming part of the business property of a permanent establishment of an enterprise may be taxed in the Contracting State in which the permanent establishment is situated.

(2)
- (a) For the purposes of this Convention, the term 'permanent establishment' means a fixed place of business through which the business of an enterprise is wholly or partly carried on.
- (b) The term 'permanent establishment' includes especially:
    - (i) a branch;

(ii) an office;

(iii) a factory;

(iv) a workshop; and

(v) a mine, an oil or gas well, a quarry, or any other place of extraction of natural resources.

(c) A building site or construction or installation project constitutes a permanent establishment only if it lasts for more than twelve months.

(d) Notwithstanding the preceding provisions of this paragraph, the term 'permanent establishment' shall be deemed not to include:

(i) the use of facilities solely for the purpose of storage, display, or delivery of goods or merchandise belonging to the enterprise;

(ii) the maintenance of a stock of goods or merchandise belonging to the enterprise solely for the purpose of storage, display or delivery;

(iii) the maintenance of a stock of goods or merchandise belonging to the enterprise solely for the purpose of processing by another enterprise;

(iv) the maintenance of a fixed place of business solely for the purpose of purchasing goods or merchandise, or of collecting information, for the enterprise;

(v) the maintenance of a fixed place of business solely for the purpose of carrying on, for the enterprise, any other activity of a preparatory or auxiliary character; or

(vi) the maintenance of a fixed place of business solely for any combination of activities mentioned in paragraphs (i)–(v) of this sub-paragraph.

(e) Notwithstanding the provisions of sub-paragraphs (a) and (b) where a person – other than an agent of an independent status to whom sub-paragraph (f) applies – is acting on behalf of an enterprise and has, and habitually exercises, in a Contracting State an authority to conclude contracts in the name of the enterprise, that enterprise shall be deemed to have a permanent establishment in that State in respect of any activities which that person undertakes for the enterprise, unless the activities of such person are limited to those mentioned in sub-paragraph (d) which, if exercised through a fixed place of business, would not make this fixed place of business a permanent establishment under the provisions of that sub-paragraph.

(f) An enterprise shall not be deemed to have a permanent establishment in a Contracting State merely because it carries on business in that State through a broker, general commission agent or any other agent of an independent status, provided that such persons are acting in the ordinary course of their business.

(g) The fact that a company which is a resident of a Contracting State controls or is controlled by a company which is a resident of the other Contracting State or which carries on business in that other State (whether through a permanent establishment or otherwise) shall not of itself constitute either company a permanent establishment of the other.

(3) Except for assets described in Article 6 (Immovable Property (Real Property)), assets pertaining to a fixed base used for the performance of independent personal services may be taxed in the Contracting State in which the fixed base is situated.

Article 8

Deductions, Exemptions, Etc

(1) In determining the amount on which tax is to be computed, permitted deductions shall be allowed in accordance with the law in force in the Contracting State in which tax is imposed.

(2) Property which passes to the spouse from a decedent or transferor who was domiciled in or a national of the United Kingdom and which may be taxed in the United States shall qualify for a marital deduction there to the extent that a marital deduction would have been allowable if the decedent or transferor had been domiciled in the United States and if the gross estate of the decedent had been limited to property which may be taxed in the United States or the transfers of the transferor had been limited to transfers of property which may be so taxed.

(3) Property which passes to the spouse from a decedent or transferor who was domiciled in or a national of the United States and which may be taxed in the United Kingdom shall, where:

 (a) the transferor's spouse was not domiciled in the United Kingdom but the transfer would have been wholly exempt had the spouse been so domiciled, and

 (b) a greater exemption for transfers between spouses would not have been given under the law of the United Kingdom apart from this Convention,

be exempt from tax in the United Kingdom to the extent of 50 per cent of the value transferred, calculated as a value on which no tax is payable and after taking account of all exemptions except those for transfers between spouses.

(4)
 (a) Property which on the death of a decedent domiciled in the United Kingdom became comprised in a settlement shall, if the personal representatives and the trustees of every settlement in which the decedent had an interest in possession immediately before death so elect and subject to subparagraph (b), be exempt from tax in the United Kingdom to the extent of 50 per cent of the value transferred (calculated in paragraph (3)) on the death of the decedent if:

 (i) under the settlement, the spouse of the decedent was entitled to an immediate interest in possession,

 (ii) the spouse was domiciled in or a national of the United States,

 (iii) the transfer would have been wholly exempt had the spouse been domiciled in the United Kingdom, and

 (iv) a greater exemption for transfers between spouses would not have been given under the law of the United Kingdom apart from this Convention.

 (b) Where the spouse of the decedent becomes absolutely and indefeasibly entitled to any of the settled property at any time after the decedent's death, the election shall, as regards that property, be deemed never to have been made and tax shall be payable as if on the death such property had been given to the spouse absolutely and indefeasibly.

(5) Where property may be taxed in the United States on the death of a United Kingdom national who was neither domiciled in nor a national of the United States and a claim is made under this paragraph, the tax imposed in the United States shall be limited to the amount of tax which would have been imposed had the decedent become domiciled in the United States immediately before his death, on the property which would in that event have been taxable.

Article 9

Credits

(1) Where under this Convention the United States may impose tax with respect to any property other than property which the United States is entitled to tax in accordance with Article 6 (Immovable Property (Real Property)) or 7 (Business Property of a Permanent Establishment and Assets Pertaining to a Fixed Base Used for the Performance of Independent Personal Services) (that is, where the decedent or transferor was domiciled in or a national of the United States), then, except in cases to which paragraph (3) applies, double taxation shall be avoided in the following manner:

    (a) Where the United Kingdom imposes tax with respect to property in accordance with the said Article 6 or 7, the United States shall credit against the tax calculated according to its law with respect to that property an amount equal to the tax paid in the United Kingdom with respect to that property.

    (b) Where the United Kingdom imposes tax with respect to property not referred to in subparagraph (a) and the decedent or transferor was a national of the United States and was domiciled in the United Kingdom at the time of the death or transfer, the United States shall credit against the tax calculated according to its law with respect to that property an amount equal to the tax paid in the United Kingdom with respect to that property.

(2) Where under this Convention the United Kingdom may impose tax with respect to any property other than property which the United Kingdom is entitled to tax in accordance with the said Article 6 or 7 (that is, where the decedent or transferor was domiciled in or a national of the United Kingdom), then, except in the cases to which paragraph (3) applies, double taxation shall be avoided in the following manner:

    (a) Where the United States imposes tax with respect to property in accordance with the said Article 6 or 7, the United Kingdom shall credit against the tax calculated according to its law with respect to that property an amount equal to the tax paid in the United States with respect to that property.

    (b) Where the United States imposes tax with respect to property not referred to in subparagraph (a) and the decedent or transferor was a national of the United Kingdom and was domiciled in the United States at the time of the death or transfer, the United Kingdom shall credit against the tax calculated according to its law with respect to that property an amount equal to the tax paid in the United States with respect to that property.

(3) Where both Contracting States impose tax on the same event with respect to property which under the law of the United States would be regarded as property held in a trust or trust equivalent and under the law of the United Kingdom would be regarded as property comprised in a settlement, double taxation shall be avoided in the following manner:

    (a) Where a Contracting State imposes tax with respect to property in accordance with the said Article 6 or 7, the other Contracting State shall credit against the tax calculated according to its law with respect to that property an amount equal to the tax paid in the first-mentioned Contracting State with respect to that property.

    (b) Where the United States imposes tax with respect to property which is not taxable in accordance with the said Article 6 or 7, then

        (i) where the event giving rise to a liability to tax was a generation-skipping transfer and the deemed transferor was domiciled in the United States at the time of that event,

(ii) where the event giving rise to a liability to tax was the exercise or lapse of a power of appointment and the holder of the power was domiciled in the United States at the time of that event, or

(iii) where (i) or (ii) does not apply and the settlor or grantor was domiciled in the United States at the time when the tax is imposed, the United Kingdom shall credit against the tax calculated according to its law with respect to that property an amount equal to the tax paid in the United States, with respect to that property.

(c) Where the United States imposes tax with respect to property which is not taxable in accordance with the said Article 6 or 7 and subparagraph (b) does not apply, the United States shall credit against the tax calculated according to its law with respect to that property an amount equal to the tax paid in the United Kingdom with respect to that property.

(4) The credits allowed by a Contracting State according to the provisions of paragraphs (1), (2) and (3) shall not take into account amounts of such taxes not levied by reason of a credit otherwise allowed by the other Contracting State. No credit shall be finally allowed under those paragraphs until the tax (reduced by any credit allowable with respect thereto) for which the credit is allowable has been paid. Any credit allowed under those paragraphs shall not, however, exceed the part of the tax paid in a Contracting State (as computed before the credit is given but reduced by any credit for other tax) which is attributable to the property with respect to which the credit is given.

(5) Any claim for a credit or for a refund of tax founded on the provisions of the present Convention shall be made within six years from the date of the event giving rise to a liability to tax or, where later, within one year from the last date on which tax for which credit is given is due. The competent authority may, in appropriate circumstances, extend this time limit where the final determination of the taxes which are the subject of the claim for credit is delayed.

Article 10

Non-Discrimination

(1)

(a) Subject to the provisions of sub-paragraph (b), nationals of a Contracting State shall not be subjected in the other State to any taxation or any requirement connected therewith which is other or more burdensome than the taxation and connected requirements to which nationals of that other State in the same circumstances are or may be subjected.

(b) Sub-paragraph (a) shall not prevent the United States from taxing a national of the United Kingdom, who is not domiciled in the United States, as a non-resident alien under its law, subject to the provisions of paragraph (5) of Article 8 (Deductions, Exemptions Etc).

(2) The taxation on a permanent establishment which an enterprise of a Contracting State has in the other Contracting State shall not be less favourably levied in that other State than the taxation levied on enterprises of that other State carrying on the same activities.

(3) Nothing contained in this Article shall be construed as obliging either Contracting State to grant to individuals not domiciled in that Contracting State any personal allowances, reliefs and reductions for taxation purposes which are granted to individuals so domiciled.

(4) Enterprises of a Contracting State, the capital of which is wholly or partly owned or controlled, directly or indirectly, by one or more residents of the other Contracting State, shall not be subjected in the first-mentioned Contracting State to any taxation or any requirement connected therewith which is other or more burdensome than the taxation and connected requirements to which other similar enterprises of the first-mentioned State are or may be subjected.

(5) The provisions of this Article shall apply to taxes which are the subject of this Convention.

Article 11

Mutual Agreement Procedure

(1) Where a person considers that the actions of one or both of the Contracting States result or will result in taxation not in accordance with the provisions of this Convention, he may, irrespective of the remedies provided by the domestic laws of those States, present his case to the competent authority of either Contracting State.

(2) The competent authority shall endeavour, if the objection appears to it to be justified and if it is not itself able to arrive at an appropriate solution, to resolve the case by mutual agreement with the competent authority of the other Contracting State, with a view to the avoidance of taxation not in accordance with the Convention. Where an agreement has been reached, a refund as appropriate shall be made to give effect to the agreement.

(3) The competent authorities of the Contracting States shall endeavour to resolve by mutual agreement any difficulties or doubts arising as to the interpretation or application of the Convention. In particular the competent authorities of the Contracting States may reach agreement on the meaning of the terms not otherwise defined in this Convention.

(4) The competent authorities of the Contracting States may communicate with each other directly for the purpose of reaching an agreement as contemplated by this Convention.

Article 12

Exchange of Information

The competent authorities of the Contracting States shall exchange such information (being information available under the respective taxation laws of the Contracting States) as is necessary for the carrying out of the provisions of this Convention or for the prevention of fraud or the administration of statutory provisions against legal avoidance in relation to the taxes which are the subject of this Convention. Any information so exchanged shall be treated as secret and shall not be disclosed to any persons other than persons (including a court or administrative body) concerned with the assessment, enforcement, collection, or prosecution in respect of the taxes which are the subject of the Convention. No information shall be exchanged which would disclose any trade, business, industrial or professional secret or any trade process.

Article 13

Effect on Diplomatic and Consular Officials and Domestic Law

(1) Nothing in this Convention shall affect the fiscal privileges of diplomatic or consular officials under the general rules of international law or under the provisions of special agreements.

(2) This Convention shall not restrict in any manner any exclusion, exemption, deduction, credit, or other allowance now or hereafter accorded by the laws of either Contracting State.

Article 14

Entry into Force

(1) This Convention shall be subject to ratification in accordance with the applicable procedures of each Contracting State and instruments of ratification shall be exchanged at Washington as soon as possible.

(2) This Convention shall enter into force immediately after the expiration of thirty days following the date on which the instruments of ratification are exchanged, and shall thereupon have effect:

    (a) in the United States in respect of estates of individuals dying and transfers taking effect after that date; and

    (b) in the United Kingdom in respect of property by reference to which there is a charge to tax which arises after that date.

(3) Subject to the provisions of paragraph (4) of this Article, the Convention between the Government of the United States of America and the Government of the United Kingdom of Great Britain and Northern Ireland for the Avoidance of Double Taxation and the Prevention of Fiscal Evasion with respect to Taxes on the Estates of Deceased Persons signed at Washington on 16 April 1945 (hereinafter referred to as 'the 1945 Convention') shall cease to have effect in respect of property to which this Convention in accordance with the provisions of paragraph (2) of this Article applies.

(4) Where on a death before 27 March 1981 any provision of the 1945 Convention would have afforded any greater relief from tax than this Convention in respect of

    (a) any gift inter vivos made by the decedent before 27 March 1974, or

    (b) any settled property in which the decedent had a beneficial interest in possession before 27 March 1974 but not at any time thereafter, that provision shall continue to have effect in the United Kingdom in relation to that gift or settled property.

(5) The 1945 Convention shall terminate on the last date on which it has effect in accordance with the foregoing provisions of this Article.

Article 15

Termination

(1) This Convention shall remain in force until terminated by one of the Contracting States. Either Contracting State may terminate this Convention, at any time after five years from the date on which the Convention enters into force provided that at least six months' prior notice has been given through the diplomatic channel. In such event the Convention shall cease to have effect at the end of the period specified in the notice, but shall continue to apply in respect of the estate of any individual dying before the end of that period and in respect of any event (other than death) occurring before the end of that period and giving rise to liability to tax under the laws of either Contracting State.

(2) The termination of the present Convention shall not have the effect of reviving any treaty or arrangement abrogated by the present Convention or by treaties previously concluded between the Contracting States.

In witness whereof the undersigned, duly authorized thereto by their respective Governments, have signed this Convention.

Done in duplicate at London this 19th day of October 1978.

For the Government of the United States of America:

For the Government of the United Kingdom of Great Britain and Northern Ireland:

Appendix V

1995 Protocol to 1980 Canada-United States Income Tax Treaty

Protocol Amending the Convention Between the United States of America and Canada with Respect to Taxes on Income and on Capital Signed at Washington on September 26, 1980, as Amended by the Protocols Signed on June 14, 1983 and March 28, 1984

The United States of America and Canada, desiring to conclude a Protocol to amend the Convention with Respect to Taxes on Income and on Capital signed at Washington on September 26, 1980, as amended by the Protocols signed on June 14, 1983 and March 28, 1984 (hereinafter referred to as 'the Convention'), have agreed as follows:

Article 1

Paragraphs 2 to 4 of Article II (Taxes Covered) of the Convention shall be deleted and replaced by the following:

'2. Notwithstanding paragraph 1, the taxes existing on March 17, 1995 to which the Convention shall apply are:

(a) in the case of Canada, the taxes imposed by the Government of Canada under the Income Tax Act; and

(b) in the case of the United States, the Federal income taxes imposed by the Internal Revenue Code of 1986. However, the Convention shall apply to:

(i) the United States accumulated earnings tax and personal holding company tax, to the extent, and only to the extent, necessary to implement the provisions of paragraphs 5 and 8 of Article X (Dividends);

(ii) the United States excise taxes imposed with respect to private foundations, to the extent, and only to the extent, necessary to implement the provisions of paragraph 4 of Article XXI (Exempt Organizations);

(iii) the United States social security taxes, to the extent, and only to the extent, necessary to implement the provisions of paragraph 2 of Article XXIV (Elimination of Double Taxation) and paragraph 4 of Article XXIX (Miscellaneous Rules); and

(iv) the United States estate taxes imposed by the Internal Revenue Code of 1986, to the extent, and only to the extent, necessary to implement the provisions of paragraph 3(g) of Article XXVI (Mutual Agreement Procedure) and Article XXIX B (Taxes Imposed by Reason of Death).

3. The Convention shall apply also to:

(a) any taxes identical or substantially similar to those taxes to which the Convention applies under paragraph 2; and

(b) taxes on capital; which are imposed after March 17, 1995 in addition to, or in place of, the taxes to which the Convention applies under paragraph 2.'

Protocol to 1980 Canada-US Income Tax Treaty

Article 2

Subparagraphs (c) and (d) of paragraph 1 of Article III (General Definitions) of the Convention shall be deleted and replaced by the following:

- '(c) The term "Canadian tax" means the taxes referred to in Article II (Taxes Covered) that are imposed on income by Canada;

- (d) The term "United States tax" means the taxes referred to in Article II (Taxes Covered), other than in subparagraph (b)(i) to (iv) of paragraph 2 thereof, that are imposed on income by the United States;'

Article 3

1. Paragraph 1 of Article IV (Residence) of the Convention shall be deleted and replaced by the following:

'1. For the purposes of this Convention, the term "resident" of a Contracting State means any person that, under the laws of that State, is liable to tax therein by reason of that person's domicile, residence, citizenship, place of management, place of incorporation or any other criterion of a similar nature, but in the case of an estate or trust, only to the extent that income derived by the estate or trust is liable to tax in that State, either in its hands or in the hands of its beneficiaries. For the purposes of this paragraph, an individual who is not a resident of Canada under this paragraph and who is a United States citizen or an alien admitted to the United States for permanent residence (a "green card" holder) is a resident of the United States only if the individual has a substantial presence, permanent home or habitual abode in the United States, and that individual's personal and economic relations are closer to the United States than to any third State. The term "resident" of a Contracting State is understood to include:

- (a) the Government of that State or a political subdivision or local authority thereof or any agency or instrumentality of any such government, subdivision or authority, and

- (b)
  - (i) A trust, organization or other arrangement that is operated exclusively to administer or provide pension, retirement or employee benefits; and
  - (ii) A not-for-profit organization that was constituted in that State and that is, by reason of its nature as such, generally exempt from income taxation in that State.'

2. A new sentence shall be added at the end of paragraph 3 of Article IV (Residence) of the Convention as follows:

'Notwithstanding the preceding sentence, a company that was created in a Contracting State, that is a resident of both Contracting States and that is continued at any time in the other Contracting State in accordance with the corporate law in that other State shall be deemed while it is so continued to be a resident of that other State.'

Article 4

Paragraphs 3 and 4 of Article IX (Related Persons) of the Convention shall be deleted and replaced by the following:

'3. Where an adjustment is made or to be made by a Contracting State in accordance with paragraph 1, the other Contracting State shall (notwithstanding any time or procedural limitations in the domestic law of that other State) make a corresponding adjustment to the income, loss or tax of the related person in that other State if:

- (a) It agrees with the first-mentioned adjustment; and

(b) Within six years from the end of the taxable year to which the first-mentioned adjustment relates, the competent authority of the other State has been notified of the first-mentioned adjustment. The competent authorities, however, may agree to consider cases where the corresponding adjustment would not otherwise be barred by any time or procedural limitations in the other State, even if the notification is not made within the six-year period.

4. In the event that the notification referred to in paragraph 3 is not given within the time period referred to therein, and the competent authorities have not agreed to otherwise consider the case in accordance with paragraph 3(b), the competent authority.'

Article 5

1. The references in paragraphs 2(a) and 6 of Article X (Dividends) of the Convention to a rate of tax of '10 per cent' shall be deleted and replaced by references to a rate of tax of '5 per cent'.

2. Paragraph 7 of Article X (Dividends) of the Convention shall be deleted and replaced by the following:

'7. Notwithstanding the provisions of paragraph 2:

(a) Dividends paid by a company that is a resident of Canada and a non-resident-owned investment corporation to a company that is a resident of the United States, that owns at least 10 per cent of the voting stock of the company paying the dividends and that is the beneficial owner of such dividends, may be taxed in Canada at a rate not exceeding 10 per cent of the gross amount of the dividends;

(b) Paragraph 2(b) and not paragraph 2(a) shall apply in the case of dividends paid by a resident of the United States that is a Regulated Investment Company; and

(c) Paragraph 2(a) shall not apply to dividends paid by a resident of the United States that is a Real Estate Investment Trust, and paragraph 2(b) shall apply only where such dividends are beneficially owned by an individual holding an interest of less than 10 per cent in the trust; otherwise the rate of tax applicable under the domestic law of the United States shall apply. Where an estate or a testamentary trust acquired its interest in a Real Estate Investment Trust as a consequence of an individual's death, for the purposes of the preceding sentence the estate or trust shall for the five-year period following the death be deemed with respect to that interest to be an individual.'

Article 6

1. The reference in paragraph 2 of Article XI (Interest) of the Convention to '15 per cent' shall be deleted and replaced by a reference to '10 per cent'.

2. Paragraph 3(d) of Article XI (Interest) of the Convention shall be deleted and replaced by the following:

'(d) The interest is beneficially owned by a resident of the other Contracting State and is paid with respect to indebtedness arising as a consequence of the sale on credit by a resident of that other State of any equipment, merchandise or services except where the sale or indebtedness was between related persons; or'

3. A new paragraph 9 shall be added to Article XI (Interest) of the Convention as follows:

'9. The provisions of paragraphs 2 and 3 shall not apply to an excess inclusion with respect to a residual interest in a Real Estate Mortgage Investment Conduit to which Section 860G of the United States Internal Revenue Code, as it may be amended from time to time without changing the general principle thereof, applies.'

Article 7

1. Paragraph 3 of Article XII (Royalties) of the Convention shall be deleted and replaced by the following:

'3. Notwithstanding the provisions of paragraph 2:
   (a) Copyright royalties and other like payments in respect of the production or reproduction of any literary, dramatic, musical or artistic work (other than payments in respect of motion pictures and works on film, videotape or other means of reproduction for use in connection with television);
   (b) Payments for the use of, or the right to use, computer software;
   (c) Payments for the use of, or the right to use, any patent or any information concerning industrial, commercial or scientific experience (but not including any such information provided in connection with a rental or franchise agreement); and
   (d) Payments with respect to broadcasting as may be agreed for the purposes of this paragraph in an exchange of notes between the Contracting States,

arising in a Contracting State and beneficially owned by a resident of the other Contracting State shall be taxable only in that other State.'

2. Paragraph 6 of Article XII (Royalties) of the Convention shall be deleted and replaced by the following:

'6. For the purposes of this Article,
   (a) Royalties shall be deemed to arise in a Contracting State when the payer is a resident of that State. Where, however, the person paying the royalties, whether he is a resident of a Contracting State or not, has in a State a permanent establishment or a fixed base in connection with which the obligation to pay the royalties was incurred, and such royalties are borne by such permanent establishment or fixed base, then such royalties shall be deemed to arise in the State in which the permanent establishment or fixed base is situated and not in any other State of which the payer is a resident; and
   (b) Where subparagraph (a) does not operate to treat royalties as arising in either Contracting State and the royalties are for the use of, or the right to use, intangible property or tangible personal property in a Contracting State, then such royalties shall be deemed to arise in that State.'

Article 8

Paragraph 8 of Article XIII (Gains) of the Convention shall be deleted and replaced by the following:

'8. Where a resident of a Contracting State alienates property in the course of a corporate or other organization, reorganization, amalgamation, division or similar transaction and profit, gain or income with respect to such alienation is not recognized for the purpose of taxation in that State, if requested to do so by the person who acquires the property, the competent authority of the other Contracting State may agree, in order to avoid double taxation and subject to terms and conditions satisfactory to such competent authority, to defer the recognition of the profit, gain or income with respect to such property for the purpose of taxation in that other State until such time and in such manner as may be stipulated in the agreement.'

Protocol to 1980 Canada-US Income Tax Treaty

Article 9

1. Paragraph 3 of Article XVIII (Pensions and Annuities) of the Convention shall be deleted and replaced by the following:

'3. For the purposes of this Convention, the term "pensions" includes any payment under a superannuation, pension or other retirement arrangement, Armed Forces retirement pay, war veterans pensions and allowances and amounts paid under a sickness, accident or disability plan, but does not include payments under an income-averaging annuity contract or any benefit referred to in paragraph 5.'

2. Paragraph 5 of Article XVIII (Pensions and Annuities) of the Convention shall be deleted and replaced by the following:

'5. Benefits under the social security legislation in a Contracting State (including tier 1 railroad benefits but not including unemployment benefits) paid to a resident of the other Contracting State (and in the case of Canadian benefits, to a citizen of the United States) shall be taxable only in the first-mentioned State.'

3. A new paragraph 7 shall be added to Article XVIII (Pensions and Annuities) of the Convention as follows:

'7. A natural person who is a citizen or resident of a Contracting State and a beneficiary of a trust, company, organization or other arrangement that is a resident of the other Contracting State, generally exempt from income taxation in that other State and operated exclusively to provide pension, retirement or employee benefits may elect to defer taxation in the first-mentioned State, under rules established by the competent authority of that State, with respect to any income accrued in the plan but not distributed by the plan, until such time as and to the extent that a distribution is made from the plan or any plan substituted therefor.'

Article 10

1. Paragraphs 2 and 3 of Article XXI (Exempt Organizations) of the Convention shall be deleted and replaced by the following:

'2. Subject to the provisions of paragraph 3, income referred to in Articles X (Dividends) and XI (Interest) derived by:

(a) A trust, company, organization or other arrangement that is a resident of a Contracting State, generally exempt from income taxation in a taxable year in that State and operated exclusively to administer or provide pension, retirement or employee benefits; or

(b) A trust, company, organization or other arrangement that is a resident of a Contracting State, generally exempt from income taxation in a taxable year in that State and operated exclusively to earn income for the benefit of an organization referred to in subparagraph (a);

shall be exempt from income taxation in that taxable year in the other Contracting State.

3. The provisions of paragraphs 1 and 2 shall not apply with respect to the income of a trust, company, organization or other arrangement from carrying on a trade or business or from a related person other than a person referred to in paragraph 1 or 2.'

2. A new sentence shall be added at the end of paragraph 5 of Article XXI (Exempt Organizations) of the Convention as follows:

'For the purposes of this paragraph, a company that is a resident of Canada and that is taxable in the United States as if it were a resident of the United States shall be deemed to be a resident of the United States.'

3. Paragraph 6 of Article XXI (Exempt Organizations) of the Convention shall be deleted and replaced by the following:

'6. For the purposes of Canadian taxation, gifts by a resident of Canada to an organization that is a resident of the United States, that is generally exempt from United States tax and that could qualify in Canada as a registered charity if it were a resident of Canada and created or established in Canada, shall be treated as gifts to a registered charity; however, no relief from taxation shall be available in any taxation year with respect to such gifts (other than such gifts to a college or university at which the resident or a member of the resident's family is or was enrolled) to the extent that such relief would exceed the amount of relief that would be available under the Income Tax Act if the only income of the resident for that year were the resident's income arising in the United States. The preceding sentence shall not be interpreted to allow in any taxation year relief from taxation for gifts to registered charities in excess of the amount of relief allowed under the percentage limitations of the laws of Canada in respect of relief for gifts to registered charities.'

Article 11

A new paragraph 3 shall be added to Article XXII (Other Income) of the Convention as follows:

'3. Losses incurred by a resident of a Contracting State with respect to wagering transactions the gains on which may be taxed in the other Contracting State shall, for the purpose of taxation in that other State, be deductible to the same extent that such losses would be deductible if they were incurred by a resident of that other State.'

Article 12

1. Paragraphs 2(a) and 2(b) of Article XXIV (Elimination of Double Taxation) of the Convention shall be deleted and replaced by the following:

   '(a) Subject to the provisions of the law of Canada regarding the deduction from tax payable in Canada of tax paid in a territory outside Canada and to any subsequent modification of those provisions (which shall not affect the general principle hereof):

      (i) income tax paid or accrued to the United States on profits, income or gains arising in the United States; and

      (ii) in the case of an individual, any social security taxes paid to the United States (other than taxes relating to unemployment insurance benefits) by the individual on such profits, income or gains,

   shall be deducted from any Canadian tax payable in respect of such profits, income or gains;

   (b) Subject to the existing provisions of the law of Canada regarding the taxation of income from a foreign affiliate and to any subsequent modification of those provisions – which shall not affect the general principle hereof – for the purpose of computing Canadian tax, a company which is a resident of Canada shall be allowed to deduct in computing its taxable income any dividend received by it out of the exempt surplus of a foreign affiliate which is a resident of the United States; and'

2. Paragraph 5 of Article XXIV (Elimination of Double Taxation) of the Convention shall be deleted and replaced by the following:

'5. Notwithstanding the provisions of paragraph 4, where a United States citizen is a resident of Canada, the following rules shall apply in respect of the items of income referred to in Article X (Dividends), XI (Interest) or XII (Royalties) that arise (within the meaning of paragraph 3) in the United States and that would be subject to United States tax if the resident of Canada were not a citizen of the United States, as long as the law in force in Canada allows a deduction in computing income for the portion of any foreign tax paid in respect of such items which exceeds 15 per cent of the amount thereof:

(a) The deduction so allowed in Canada shall not be reduced by any credit or deduction for income tax paid or accrued to Canada allowed in computing the United States tax on such items;

(b) Canada shall allow a deduction from Canadian tax on such items in respect of income tax paid or accrued to the United States on such items, except that such deduction need not exceed the amount of the tax that would be paid on such items to the United States if the resident of Canada were not a United States citizen; and

(c) For the purposes of computing the United States tax on such items, the United States shall allow as a credit against United States tax the income tax paid or accrued to Canada after the deduction referred to in subparagraph (b). The credit so allowed shall reduce only that portion of the United States tax on such items which exceeds the amount of tax that would be paid to the United States on such items if the resident of Canada were not a US citizen.'

3. Paragraph 7 of Article XXIV (Elimination of Double Taxation) of the Convention shall be deleted and replaced by the following:

'7. For the purposes of this Article, any reference to "income tax paid or accrued" to a Contracting State shall include Canadian tax and United States tax, as the case may be, and taxes of general application which are paid or accrued to a political subdivision or local authority of that State, which are not imposed by that political subdivision or local authority in a manner inconsistent with the provisions of the Convention and which are substantially similar to the Canadian tax or United States tax, as the case may be.'

4. A new paragraph 10 shall be added to Article XXIV (Elimination of Double Taxation) of the Convention as follows:

'10. Where in accordance with any provision of the Convention income derived or capital owned by a resident of a Contracting State is exempt from tax in that State, such State may nevertheless, in calculating the amount of tax on other income or capital, take into account the exempted income or capital.'

Article 13

1. Paragraph 3 of Article XXV (Non-Discrimination) of the Convention shall be deleted and replaced by the following:

'3. In determining the taxable income or tax payable of an individual who is a resident of a Contracting State, there shall be allowed as a deduction in respect of any other person who is a resident of the other Contracting State and who is dependent on the individual for support the amount that would be so allowed if that other person were a resident of the first-mentioned State.'

2. Paragraph 10 of Article XXV (Non-Discrimination) of the Convention shall be deleted and replaced by the following:

'10. Notwithstanding the provisions of Article II (Taxes Covered), this Article shall apply to all taxes imposed by a Contracting State.'

Article 14

1. Paragraphs 3(f) and (g) of Article XXVI (Mutual Agreement Procedure) of the Convention shall be deleted and replaced by the following:

    '(f) To the elimination of double taxation with respect to a partnership;

    (g) To provide relief from double taxation resulting from the application of the estate tax imposed by the United States or the Canadian tax as a result of a distribution or disposition of property by a trust that is a qualified domestic trust within the meaning of section 2056A of the Internal Revenue Code, or is described in subsection 70(6) of the Income Tax Act or is treated as such under paragraph 5 of Article XXIX B (Taxes Imposed by Reason of Death), in cases where no relief is otherwise available; or

    (h) To increases in any dollar amounts referred to in the Convention to reflect monetary or economic developments.'

2. A new paragraph 6 shall be added to Article XXVI (Mutual Agreement Procedure) of the Convention as follows:

'6. If any difficulty or doubt arising as to the interpretation or application of the Convention cannot be resolved by the competent authorities pursuant to the preceding paragraphs of this Article, the case may, if both competent authorities and the taxpayer agree, be submitted for arbitration, provided that the taxpayer agrees in writing to be bound by the decision of the arbitration board. The decision of the arbitration board in a particular case shall be binding on both States with respect to that case. The procedures shall be established in an exchange of notes between the Contracting States. The provisions of this paragraph shall have effect after the Contracting States have so agreed through the exchange of notes.'

Article 15

A new Article XXVI A (Assistance in Collection) shall be added to the Convention as follows:

'Article XXVI A

Assistance in Collection

1. The Contracting States undertake to lend assistance to each other in the collection of taxes referred to in paragraph 9, together with interest, costs, additions to such taxes and civil penalties, referred to in this Article as a "revenue claim".

2. An application for assistance in the collection of a revenue claim shall include a certification by the competent authority of the applicant State that, under the laws of that State, the revenue claim has been finally determined. For the purposes of this Article, a revenue claim is finally determined when the applicant State has the right under its internal law to collect the revenue claim and all administrative and judicial rights of the taxpayer to restrain collection in the applicant State have lapsed or been exhausted.

3. A revenue claim of the applicant State that has been finally determined may be accepted for collection by the competent authority of the requested State and, subject to the provisions of paragraph 7, if accepted shall be collected by the requested State as though such revenue claim were the requested State's own revenue claim finally determined in accordance with the laws applicable to the collection of the requested State's own taxes.

4. Where an application for collection of a revenue claim in respect of a taxpayer is accepted

(a) By the United States, the revenue claim shall be treated by the United States as an assessment under United States laws against the taxpayer as of the time the application is received; and

(b) By Canada, the revenue claim shall be treated by Canada as an amount payable under the Income Tax Act, the collection of which is not subject to any restriction.

5. Nothing in this Article shall be construed as creating or providing any rights of administrative or judicial review of the applicant State's finally determined revenue claim by the requested State, based on any such rights that may be available under the laws of either Contracting State. If, at any time pending execution of a request for assistance under this Article, the applicant State loses the right under its internal law to collect the revenue claim, the competent authority of the applicant State shall promptly withdraw the request for assistance in collection.

6. Subject to this paragraph, amounts collected by the requested State pursuant to this Article shall be forwarded to the competent authority of the applicant State. Unless the competent authorities of the Contracting States otherwise agree, the ordinary costs incurred in providing collection assistance shall be borne by the requested State and any extraordinary costs so incurred shall be borne by the applicant State.

7. A revenue claim of an applicant State accepted for collection shall not have in the requested State any priority accorded to the revenue claims of the requested State.

8. No assistance shall be provided under this Article for a revenue claim in respect of a taxpayer to the extent that the taxpayer can demonstrate that:

(a) where the taxpayer is an individual, the revenue claim relates to a taxable period in which the taxpayer was a citizen of the requested State; and

(b) where the taxpayer is an entity that is a company, estate or trust, the revenue claim relates to a taxable period in which the taxpayer derived its status as such an entity from the laws in force in the requested State.

9. Notwithstanding the provisions of Article II (Taxes Covered), the provisions of this Article shall apply to all categories of taxes collected by or on behalf of the Government of a Contracting State.

10. Nothing in this Article shall be construed as:

(a) limiting the assistance provided for in paragraph 4 of Article XXVI (Mutual Agreement Procedure); or

(b) imposing on either Contracting State the obligation to carry out administrative measures of a different nature from those used in the collection of its own taxes or that would be contrary to its public policy (ordre public).

11. The competent authorities of the Contracting States shall agree upon the mode of application of this Article, including agreement to ensure comparable levels of assistance to each of the Contracting States.'

Article 16

1. Paragraph 1 of Article XXVII (Exchange of Information) of the Convention shall be deleted and replaced by the following:

'1. The competent authorities of the Contracting States shall exchange such information as is relevant for carrying out the provisions of this Convention or of the domestic laws of the Contracting States concerning taxes to which the Convention applies insofar as the taxation thereunder is not contrary to the Convention. The exchange of information is not restricted by Article I (Personal Scope). Any information received by a Contracting State shall be treated as secret in the same manner as information obtained under the taxation laws of that State and shall be disclosed only to persons or authorities (including courts and administrative bodies) involved in the assessment or collection of, the administration and enforcement in respect of, or the determination of appeals in relation to the taxes to which the Convention applies or, notwithstanding paragraph 4, in relation to taxes imposed by a political subdivision or local authority of a Contracting State that are substantially similar to the taxes covered by the Convention under Article II (Taxes Covered). Such persons or authorities shall use the information only for such purposes. They may disclose the information in public court proceedings or in judicial decisions. The competent authorities may release to an arbitration board established pursuant to paragraph 6 of Article XXVI (Mutual Agreement Procedure) such information as is necessary for carrying out the arbitration procedure; the members of the arbitration board shall be subject to the limitations on disclosure described in this Article.'

2. Paragraph 4 of Article XXVII (Exchange of Information) of the Convention shall be deleted and replaced by the following:

'4. For the purposes of this Article, the Convention shall apply, notwithstanding the provisions of Article II (Taxes Covered):

(a) To all taxes imposed by a Contracting State; and

(b) To other taxes to which any other provision of the Convention applies, but only to the extent that the information is relevant for the purposes of the application of that provision.'

Article 17

1. Paragraph 3(a) of Article XXIX (Miscellaneous Rules) of the Convention shall be deleted and replaced by the following:

'(a) Under paragraphs 3 and 4 of Article IX (Related Persons), paragraphs 6 and 7 of Article XIII (Gains), paragraphs 1, 3, 4, 5, 6(b) and 7 of Article XVIII (Pensions and Annuities), paragraph 5 of Article XXIX (Miscellaneous Rules), paragraphs 1, 5 and 6 of Article XXIX B (Taxes Imposed by Reason of Death), paragraphs 2, 3, 4 and 7 of Article XXIX B (Taxes Imposed by Reason of Death) as applied to the estates of persons other than former citizens referred to in paragraph 2 of this Article, paragraphs 3 and 5 of Article XXX (Entry into Force), and Articles XIX (Government Service), XXI (Exempt Organizations), XXIV (Elimination of Double Taxation), XXV (Non-Discrimination) and XXVI (Mutual Agreement Procedure);'

2. Paragraphs 5 to 7 of Article XXIX (Miscellaneous Rules) of the Convention shall be deleted and replaced by the following:

'5. Where a person who is a resident of Canada and a shareholder of a United States S corporation requests the competent authority of Canada to do so, the competent authority may agree, subject to terms and conditions satisfactory to such competent authority, to apply the following rules for the purposes of taxation in Canada with respect to the period during which the agreement is effective:

(a) the corporation shall be deemed to be a controlled foreign affiliate of the person;

(b) all the income of the corporation shall be deemed to be foreign accrual property income;

(c) for the purposes of subsection 20(11) of the Income Tax Act, the amount of the corporation's income that is included in the person's income shall be deemed not to be income from a property; and

(d) each dividend paid to the person on a share of the capital stock of the corporation shall be excluded from the person's income and shall be deducted in computing the adjusted cost base to the person of the share.

6. For purposes of paragraph 3 of Article XXII (Consultation) of the General Agreement on Trade in Services, the Contracting States agree that:

(a) a measure falls within the scope of the Convention only if:

(i) the measure relates to a tax to which Article XXV (Non-Discrimination) of the Convention applies; or

(ii) the measure relates to a tax to which Article XXV (Non-Discrimination) of the Convention does not apply and to which any other provision of the Convention applies, but only to the extent that the measure relates to a matter dealt with in that other provision of the Convention; and

(b) notwithstanding paragraph 3 of Article XXII (Consultation) of the General Agreement on Trade in Services, any doubt as to the interpretation of subparagraph (a) will be resolved under paragraph 3 of Article XXVI (Mutual Agreement Procedure) of the Convention or any other procedure agreed to by both Contracting States.

7. The appropriate authority of a Contracting State may request consultations with the appropriate authority of the other Contracting State to determine whether change to the Convention is appropriate to respond to changes in the law or policy of that other State. Where domestic legislation enacted by a Contracting State unilaterally removes or significantly limits any material benefit otherwise provided by the Convention, the appropriate authorities shall promptly consult for the purpose of considering an appropriate change to the Convention.'

Article 18

A new Article XXIX A (Limitation on Benefits) shall be added to the Convention as follows:

'Article XXIX A

Limitation on Benefits

1. For the purposes of the application of this Convention by the United States:

(a) A qualifying person shall be entitled to all of the benefits of this Convention; and

(b) Except as provided in paragraphs 3, 4 and 6, a person that is not a qualifying person shall not be entitled to any benefits of the Convention.

2. For the purposes of this Article, a qualifying person is a resident of Canada that is:

(a) A natural person;

(b) The Government of Canada or a political subdivision or local authority thereof, or any agency or instrumentality of any such government, subdivision or authority;

(c) A company or trust in whose principal class of shares or units there is substantial and regular trading on a recognized stock exchange;

Protocol to 1980 Canada-US Income Tax Treaty

- (d) A company more than 50 per cent of the vote and value of the shares (other than debt substitute shares) of which is owned, directly or indirectly, by five or fewer persons each of which is a company or trust referred to in subparagraph (c), provided that each company or trust in the chain of ownership is a qualifying person or a resident or citizen of the United States;

- (e)
  - (i) a company 50 per cent or more of the vote and value of the shares (other than debt substitute shares) of which is not owned, directly or indirectly, by persons other than qualifying persons or residents or citizens of the United States, or
  - (ii) a trust 50 per cent or more of the beneficial interest in which is not owned, directly or indirectly, by persons other than qualifying persons or residents or citizens of the United States,

  where the amount of the expenses deductible from gross income that are paid or payable by the company or trust, as the case may be, for its preceding fiscal period (or, in the case of its first fiscal period, that period) to persons that are not qualifying persons or residents or citizens of the United States is less than 50 per cent of its gross income for that period;

- (f) An estate;

- (g) A not-for-profit organization, provided that more than half of the beneficiaries, members or participants of the organization are qualifying persons or residents or citizens of the United States; or

- (h) An organization described in paragraph 2 of Article XXI (Exempt Organizations) and established for the purpose of providing benefits primarily to individuals who are qualifying persons, persons who were qualifying persons within the five preceding years, or residents or citizens of the United States.

3. Where a person that is a resident of Canada and is not a qualifying person of Canada, or a person related thereto, is engaged in the active conduct of a trade or business in Canada (other than the business of making or managing investments, unless those activities are carried on with customers in the ordinary course of business by a bank, an insurance company, a registered securities dealer or a deposit-taking financial institution), the benefits of the Convention shall apply to that resident person with respect to income derived from the United States in connection with or incidental to that trade or business, including any such income derived directly or indirectly by that resident person through one or more other persons that are residents of the United States. Income shall be deemed to be derived from the United States in connection with the active conduct of a trade or business in Canada only if that trade or business is substantial in relation to the activity carried on in the United States giving rise to the income in respect of which benefits provided under the Convention by the United States are claimed.

4. A company that is a resident of Canada shall also be entitled to the benefits of Articles X (Dividends), XI (Interest) and XII (Royalties) if

  - (a) Its shares that represent more than 90 per cent of the aggregate vote and value represented by all of its shares (other than debt substitute shares) are owned, directly or indirectly, by persons each of whom is a qualifying person, a resident or citizen of the United States or a person who:
    - (i) Is a resident of a country with which the United States has a comprehensive income tax convention and is entitled to all of the benefits provided by the United States under that convention;

(ii) Would qualify for benefits under paragraphs 2 or 3 if that person were a resident of Canada (and, for the purposes of paragraph 3, if the business it carried on in the country of which it is a resident were carried on by it in Canada); and

(iii) Would be entitled to a rate of United States tax under the convention between that person's country of residence and the United States, in respect of the particular class of income for which benefits are being claimed under this Convention, that is at least as low as the rate applicable under this Convention; and

(b) The amount of the expenses deductible from gross income that are paid or payable by the company for its preceding fiscal period (or, in the case of its first fiscal period, that period) to persons that are not qualifying persons or residents or citizens of the United States is less than 50 per cent of the gross income of the company for that period.

5. For the purposes of this Article:

(a) The term "recognized stock exchange" means:

(i) the NASDAQ System owned by the National Association of Securities Dealers, Inc. and any stock exchange registered with the Securities and Exchange Commission as a national securities exchange for purposes of the Securities Exchange Act of 1934;

(ii) Canadian stock exchanges that are "prescribed stock exchanges" under the Income Tax Act; and

(iii) Any other stock exchange agreed upon by the Contracting States in an exchange of notes or by the competent authorities of the Contracting States;

(b) The term "not-for-profit organization" of a Contracting State means an entity created or established in that State and that is, by reason of its not-for-profit status, generally exempt from income taxation in that State, and includes a private foundation, charity, trade union, trade association or similar organization; and

(c) The term "debt substitute share" means:

(i) A share described in paragraph (e) of the definition "term preferred share" in the Income Tax Act, as it may be amended from time to time without changing the general principle thereof; and

(ii) Such other type of share as may be agreed upon by the competent authorities of the Contracting States.

6. Where a person that is a resident of Canada is not entitled under the preceding provisions of this Article to the benefits provided under the Convention by the United States, the competent authority of the United States shall, upon that person's request, determine on the basis of all factors including the history, structure, ownership and operations of that person whether:

(a) Its creation and existence did not have as a principal purpose the obtaining of benefits under the Convention that would not otherwise be available; or

(b) It would not be appropriate, having regard to the purpose of this Article, to deny the benefits of the Convention to that person.

The person shall be granted the benefits of the Convention by the United States where the competent authority determines that subparagraph (a) or (b) applies.

7. It is understood that the fact that the preceding provisions of this Article apply only for the purposes of the application of the Convention by the United States shall not be construed as restricting in any manner the right of a Contracting State to deny benefits under the Convention where it can reasonably be concluded that to do so otherwise would result in an abuse of the provisions of this Convention.'

Article 19

A new Article XXIX B (Taxes Imposed by Reason of Death) shall be added to the Convention as follows:

'Article XXIX B

Taxes Imposed by Reason of Death

1. Where the property of an individual who is a resident of a Contracting State passes by reason of the individual's death to an organization referred to in paragraph 1 of Article XXI (Exempt Organizations), the tax consequences in a Contracting State arising out of the passing of the property shall apply as if the organization were a resident of that State.

2. In determining the estate tax imposed by the United States, the estate of an individual (other than a citizen of the United States) who was a resident of Canada at the time of the individual's death shall be allowed a unified credit equal to the greater of:

- (a) The amount that bears the same ratio to the credit allowed under the law of the United States to the estate of a citizen of the United States as the value of the part of the individual's gross estate that at the time of the individual's death is situated in the United States bears to the value of the individual's entire gross estate wherever situated; and

- (b) The unified credit allowed to the estate of a nonresident not a citizen of the United States under the law of the United States.

The amount of any unified credit otherwise allowable under this paragraph shall be reduced by the amount of any credit previously allowed with respect to any gift made by the individual. A credit otherwise allowable under subparagraph (a) shall be allowed only if all information necessary for the verification and computation of the credit is provided.

3. In determining the estate tax imposed by the United States on an individual's estate with respect to property that passes to the surviving spouse of the individual (within the meaning of the law of the United States) and that would qualify for the estate tax marital deduction under the law of the United States if the surviving spouse were a citizen of the United States and all applicable elections were properly made (in this paragraph and paragraph 4 referred to as "qualifying property"), a non-refundable credit computed in accordance with the provisions of paragraph 4 shall be allowed in addition to the unified credit allowed to the estate under paragraph 2 or under the law of the United States, provided that:

- (a) The individual was at the time of death a citizen of the United States or a resident of either Contracting State;

- (b) The surviving spouse was at the time of the individual's death a resident of either Contracting State;

- (c) If both the individual and the surviving spouse were residents of the United States at the time of the individual's death, one or both was a citizen of Canada; and

- (d) The executor of the decedent's estate elects the benefits of this paragraph and waives irrevocably the benefits of any estate tax marital deduction that would be allowed under the law of the United States on a United States Federal estate tax return filed for the individual's estate by the date on which a qualified domestic trust election could be made under the law of the United States.

4. The amount of the credit allowed under paragraph 3 shall equal the lesser of:

   (a) The unified credit allowed under paragraph 2 or under the law of the United States (determined without regard to any credit allowed previously with respect to any gift made by the individual); and

   (b) The amount of estate tax that would otherwise be imposed by the United States on the transfer of qualifying property.

The amount of estate tax that would otherwise be imposed by the United States on the transfer of qualifying property shall equal the amount by which the estate tax (before allowable credits) that would be imposed by the United States if the qualifying property were included in computing the taxable estate exceeds the estate tax (before allowable credits) that would be so imposed if the qualifying property were not so included. Solely for purposes of determining other credits allowed under the law of the United States, the credit provided under paragraph 3 shall be allowed after such other credits.

5. Where an individual was a resident of the United States immediately before the individual's death, for the purposes of subsection 70(6) of the Income Tax Act, both the individual and the individual's spouse shall be deemed to have been resident in Canada immediately before the individual's death. Where a trust that would be a trust described in subsection 70(6) of that Act, if its trustees that were residents or citizens of the United States or domestic corporations under the law of the United States were residents of Canada, requests the competent authority of Canada to do so, the competent authority may agree, subject to terms and conditions satisfactory to such competent authority, to treat the trust for the purposes of that Act as being resident in Canada for such time as may be stipulated in the agreement.

6. In determining the amount of Canadian tax payable by an individual who immediately before death was a resident of Canada, or by a trust described in subsection 70(6) of the Income Tax Act (or a trust which is treated as being resident in Canada under the provisions of paragraph 5), the amount of any Federal or state estate or inheritance taxes payable in the United States (not exceeding, where the individual was a citizen of the United States or a former citizen referred to in paragraph 2 of Article XXIX (Miscellaneous Rules), the amount of estate and inheritance taxes that would have been payable if the individual were not a citizen or former citizen of the United States) in respect of property situated within the United States shall:

   (a) To the extent that such estate or inheritance taxes are imposed upon the individual's death, be allowed as a deduction from the amount of any Canadian tax otherwise payable by the individual for the taxation year in which the individual died on the total of:

      (i) Any income, profits or gains of the individual arising (within the meaning of paragraph 3 of Article XXIV (Elimination of Double Taxation)) in the United States in that year; and

      (ii) Where the value at the time of the individual's death of the individual's entire gross estate wherever situated (determined under the law of the United States) exceeded 1.2 million U.S. dollars or its equivalent in Canadian dollars, any income, profits or gains of the individual for that year from property situated in the United States at that time; and

   (b) To the extent that such estate or inheritance taxes are imposed upon the death of the individual's surviving spouse, be allowed as a deduction from the amount of any Canadian tax otherwise payable by the trust for its taxation year in which that spouse dies on any income, profits or gains of the trust for that year arising (within the meaning of paragraph 3 of Article XXIV (Elimination of Double Taxation)) in the United States or from property situated in the United States at the time of death of the spouse.

For purposes of this paragraph, property shall be treated as situated within the United States if it is so treated for estate tax purposes under the law of the United States as in effect on March 17, 1995 subject to any subsequent changes thereof that the competent authorities of the Contracting States have agreed to apply for the purposes of this paragraph. The deduction allowed under this paragraph shall take into account the deduction for any income tax paid or accrued to the United States that is provided under paragraph 2(a), 4(a) or 5(b) of Article XXIV (Elimination of Double Taxation).

7. In determining the amount of estate tax imposed by the United States on the estate of an individual who was a resident or citizen of the United States at the time of death, or upon the death of a surviving spouse with respect to a qualified domestic trust created by such an individual or the individual's executor or surviving spouse, a credit shall be allowed against such tax imposed in respect of property situated outside the United States, for the federal and provincial income taxes payable in Canada in respect of such property by reason of the death of the individual or, in the case of a qualified domestic trust, the individual's surviving spouse. Such credit shall be computed in accordance with the following rules:

(a) A credit otherwise allowable under this paragraph shall be allowed regardless of whether the identity of the taxpayer under the law of Canada corresponds to that under the law of the United States.

(b) The amount of a credit allowed under this paragraph shall be computed in accordance with the provisions and subject to the limitations of the law of the United States regarding credit for foreign death taxes (as it may be amended from time to time without changing the general principle hereof), as though the income tax imposed by Canada were a creditable tax under that law.

(c) A credit may be claimed under this paragraph for an amount of federal or provincial income tax payable in Canada only to the extent that no credit or deduction is claimed for such amount in determining any other tax imposed by the United States, other than the estate tax imposed on property in a qualified domestic trust upon the death of the surviving spouse.

8. Provided that the value, at the time of death, of the entire gross estate wherever situated of an individual who was a resident of Canada (other than a citizen of the United States) at the time of death does not exceed 1.2 million U.S. dollars or its equivalent in Canadian dollars, the United States may impose its estate tax upon property forming part of the estate of the individual only if any gain derived by the individual from the alienation of such property would have been subject to income taxation by the United States in accordance with Article XIII (Gains).'

Article 20

1. The appropriate authorities of the Contracting States shall consult within a three-year period from the date on which this Protocol enters into force with respect to further reductions in withholding taxes provided in the Convention, and with respect to the rules in Article XXIX A (Limitation on Benefits) of the Convention.

2. The appropriate authorities of the Contracting States shall consult after a three-year period from the date on which the Protocol enters into force in order to determine whether it is appropriate to make the exchange of notes referred to in Article XXVI (Mutual Agreement Procedure) of the Convention.

Article 21

1. This Protocol shall be subject to ratification in accordance with the applicable procedures in Canada and the United States and instruments of ratification shall be exchanged as soon as possible.

2. The Protocol shall enter into force upon the exchange of instruments of ratification, and shall have effect:

    (a) For tax withheld at the source on income referred to in Articles X (Dividends), XI (Interest), XII (Royalties) and XVIII (Pensions and Annuities) of the Convention, except on income referred to in paragraph 5 of Article XVIII of the Convention (as it read before the entry into force of this Protocol), with respect to amounts paid or credited on or after the first day of the second month next following the date on which the Protocol enters into force, except that the reference in paragraph 2(a) of Article X (Dividends) of the Convention, as amended by the Protocol, to '5 per cent' shall be read, in its application to amounts paid or credited on or after that first day:

    (i) Before 1996, as '7 per cent'; and

    (ii) After 1995 and before 1997, as "6 per cent"; and

    (b) For other taxes, with respect to taxable years beginning on or after the first day of January next following the date on which the Protocol enters into force, except that the reference in paragraph 6 of Article X (Dividends) of the Convention, as amended by the Protocol, to '5 per cent' shall be read, in its application to taxable years beginning on or after that first day and ending before 1997, as '6 per cent'.

3. Notwithstanding the provisions of paragraph 2, Article XXVI A (Assistance in Collection) of the Convention shall have effect for revenue claims finally determined by a requesting State after the date that is 10 years before the date on which the Protocol enters into force.

4. Notwithstanding the provisions of paragraph 2, paragraphs 2 through 8 of Article XXIX B (Taxes Imposed by Reason of Death) of the Convention (and paragraph 2 of Article II (Taxes Covered) and paragraph 3(a) of Article XXIX (Miscellaneous Rules) of the Convention, as amended by the Protocol, to the extent necessary to implement paragraphs 2 through 8 of Article XXIX B (Taxes Imposed by Reason of Death) of the Convention) shall, notwithstanding any limitation imposed under the law of a Contracting State on the assessment, reassessment or refund with respect to a person's return, have effect with respect to deaths occurring after the date on which the Protocol enters into force and, provided that any claim for refund by reason of this sentence is filed within one year of the date on which the Protocol enters into force or within the otherwise applicable period for filing such claims under domestic law, with respect to benefits provided under any of those paragraphs with respect to deaths occurring after November 10, 1988.

5. Notwithstanding the provisions of paragraph 2, paragraph 2 of Article 3 of the Protocol shall have effect with respect to taxable years beginning on or after the first day of January next following the date on which the Protocol enters into force.

IN WITNESS WHEREOF, the undersigned, duly authorized thereto by their respective Governments, have signed this Protocol.

Done in two copies at Washington this seventeenth day of March, 1995, in the English and French languages, each text being equally authentic.

FOR THE GOVERNMENT OF THE UNITED STATES OF AMERICA:

Protocol to 1980 Canada-US Income Tax Treaty

RICHARD E HECKLINGER

FOR THE GOVERNMENT OF CANADA:

ROBERT C WRIGHT

Appendix VI

A Decedent's Exposure to UK/US Transfer Tax

Note that all the examples in the table below assume that no other bilateral transfer tax treaties apply.

A Decedent's Exposure to UK/US Transfer Tax

Citizenship and domicile status	Column 1 US citizen (not US domiciled)	Column 2 US domiciliary (not US citizen)	Column 3 Both a US citizen and a US domiciliary	Column 4 Neither a US citizen nor a US domiciliary
Row A UK national (but not UK domiciliary)	1. UK tax on all UK situated property[1] 2. US tax on worldwide estate with credit for UK tax[4]	1. UK tax on all UK situated property (with credit for US tax on UK property other than UK article 6/7 property)[2] 2. US tax on worldwide estate (with credit for UK tax on UK article 6/7 property)[5]	1. UK tax on all UK-situated property (with credit for US tax on UK property other than UK article 6/7 property)[2] 2. US tax on worldwide estate (with credit for UK tax on UK article 6/7 property)[6]	1. UK tax on all UK situated property[3] 2. US tax on all US-situated property (but US estate tax potentially limited by article 8(5) of the US/UK treaty)[7]

Row B
UK domiciliary (but not UK national)
	1. UK tax on worldwide estate (with credit for US tax on US article 6/7 property)[8]	1. If US/UK treaty tie-breaker rules results in person deemed to be UK domiciled:
		  (a) UK tax on worldwide estate (with credit for US tax on US article 6/7 property)[8]
		  (b) US tax on US article 6/7 property[9]
			1. If US/UK treaty tie-breaker rules results in person deemed to be *UK* domiciled:
			  (a) UK tax on worldwide estate (with credit for US tax on US article 6/7 property)[8]
			  (b) US tax on worldwide estate (with credit for UK taxes)[10]
				1. UK tax on worldwide estate (with credit for US tax on US article 6/7 property)[8]

A Decedent's Exposure to UK/US Transfer Tax

Citizenship and domicile status	Column 1 US citizen (not US domiciled)	Column 2 US domiciliary (not US citizen)	Column 3 Both a US citizen and a US domiciliary	Column 4 Neither a US citizen nor a US domiciliary
	2. US tax on worldwide estate (with credit for UK taxes)[10]	2. If US/UK treaty tie-breaker rules results in person deemed to be *US* domiciled: (a) UK tax on UK article 6/7 property[11] (b) US tax on worldwide estate (with credit for UK tax on UK article 6/7 property)[5]	2. If US/UK treaty tie-breaker rules results in person deemed to be *US* domiciled: (a) UK tax on UK article 6/7 property[11] (b) US tax on worldwide estate (with credit for UK tax on UK article 6/7 property)[6]	2. US tax on US article 6/7 property[9]
Row C Both a UK national and a UK domiciliary	1. UK tax on worldwide estate (with credit for US tax on US article 6/7 property)[8]	1. If US/UK treaty tie-breaker rules results in person deemed to be *UK* domiciled: (a) UK tax on worldwide estate (with credit for US tax on US article 6/7 property)[8] (b) US tax on US article 6/7 property (but US estate tax potentially limited by article 8(5) of the US/UK treaty)[12]	1. If US/UK treaty tie-breaker rules results in person deemed to be *UK* domiciled: (a) UK tax on worldwide estate (with credit for US tax on US article 6/7 property)[8] (b) US tax on worldwide estate (with credit for UK taxes)[10]	1. UK tax on worldwide estate (with credit for US tax on US article 6/7 property)[8]

493

Citizenship and domicile status	Column 1 US citizen (not US domiciled)	Column 2 US domiciliary (not US citizen)	Column 3 Both a US citizen and a US domiciliary	Column 4 Neither a US citizen nor a US domiciliary
	2. US tax on worldwide estate (with credit for UK taxes)[10]	2. If US/UK treaty tie-breaker rules results in person deemed to be *US domiciled*: (a) UK tax on all UK situated property (with credit for US tax on UK property other than UK article 6/7 property)[2] (b) US tax on worldwide estate (with credit for UK tax on UK article 6/7 property)[5]	2. If US/UK treaty tie-breaker rules results in person deemed to be *US domiciled*: (a) UK tax on all UK situated property (with credit for US tax on UK property other than UK article 6/7 property)[2] (b) US tax on worldwide estate (with credit for UK tax on UK article 6/7 property)[6]	2. US tax on US article 6/7 property (but US estate tax potentially limited by article 8(5) of the US/UK treaty)[12] 0.
Row D Neither a UK national nor a domiciliary	1. UK tax on UK article 6/7 property[13] 2. US tax on worldwide property (with credit for UK tax on UK article 6/7 property)[6]	1. UK tax on UK article 6/7 property[11] 2. US tax on worldwide estate (with credit for UK tax on UK article 6/7 property)[5]	1. UK tax on UK article 6/7 property[11] 2. US tax on worldwide estate (with credit for UK tax on UK article 6/7 property)[6]	1. UK tax on all UK-situated property[14] 2. US tax on all US-situated property[14]

A Decedent's Exposure to UK/US Transfer Tax

1. The US/UK treaty does not restrict the ability of the UK to tax a person who is domiciled outside the US. Accordingly, the UK would (under its domestic rules) have the right to tax a domiciliary of a third country (whether or not a UK national) on all UK-situated property. Article 5(2) of the US/UK treaty does not apply in this example, because the decedent would be a national of both countries. The UK will not give a credit as it is only taxing UK sited property and the treaty does not require the UK to credit US tax on UK sited property where the taxpayer is a non-US domiciliary.

2. Even though the domiciliary country (the US) generally has sole taxing rights (except for article 6/7 property), this rule does not apply where the decedent was a national of the non-domiciliary country (the UK in this example). US/UK treaty article 5(1)(b). Accordingly, the UK can continue to tax all UK situated property under its domestic rules. The US must grant credit for UK taxes imposed on UK article 6/7 property (US/UK treaty article 9(1)(a)). The UK must give credit for US taxes on all other UK property (such as UK securities). US/UK treaty article 9(2)(b).

3. The US/UK treaty does not restrict the ability of the UK to tax a person who is domiciled outside the US. Accordingly, the UK would (under its domestic rules) have the right to tax a domiciliary of a third country (whether or not a UK national) on all UK-situated property.

4. The US taxes its citizens on their worldwide estates. Code § 2001. Treaty article 9(1)(a) requires the US to credit the UK tax on UK article 6/7 property against the US tax on such property. Treaty article 9(1)(b) does not require the US to credit UK tax on other UK sited property since the decedent is not UK domiciled; however, under US unilateral credit rules, the US would give a credit for UK taxes on UK sited property (determined under US rules).

5. The US taxes a US *domiciliary* on his worldwide estate (Code § 2001) but gives credit for UK taxes imposed on UK-situated property. US/UK treaty article 9(1)(a).

6. The US taxes a US *citizen* on his worldwide estate (Code § 2001) but gives credit for UK taxes imposed on UK-situated article 6/7 property. US/UK treaty article 9(1)(a).

7. Where a non-domiciled alien (NDA) of the US is also not a UK domiciliary, the US/UK treaty imposes no restrictions on the US's ability to tax the NDA's estate. Accordingly, under US domestic rules (Code § 2106(a)) the US can tax all US-situated property owned by the decedent at death.

8. In the case of a UK domiciliary (including a dual domiciliary who is considered to be a UK domiciliary under the treaty tie-breaker rules), the US has first taxing rights with respect to US-situated article 6/7 property, but the UK can tax the decedent's worldwide estate (US/UK treaty articles 5(1), 6 and 7). However, the UK must give credit for US taxes imposed on the US article 6/7 property. US/UK treaty article 9(2)(a).

8. Where a person who is not a US citizen is domiciled in the UK (including a dual domiciliary who is considered to be a UK domiciliary under the treaty tie-breaker rules), the US can only tax US-situated articles 6 and 7 property. US/UK treaty articles 5(1), 6 and 7.

10. The US taxes its citizens on their worldwide estate. Code § 2001. Where a US citizen is domiciled in the UK, the US must give credit for:
    (a) UK tax imposed on UK article 6/7 property (US/UK treaty article 9(1)(a); and
    (b) all other property subject to UK tax. US/UK article 9(1)(b).

11. Where a person who is not a UK national is domiciled in the US (including a dual domiciliary who is considered to be a US domiciliary under the treaty tie-breaker rules), the UK can only tax UK-situated articles 6 and 7 property. US/UK treaty articles 5(1), 6 and 7.

12. See footnote 9 above. Also see US/UK treaty article 8(5) for possible limitation of US tax imposed on UK national.

13. If a decedent is domiciled in neither the US or UK but is a national of one state (the US in this case), the other state (the UK) is precluded to tax property (other than UK-situated article 6/7 property) that is taxed by the US. US/UK treaty article 5(2). Thus, because the US will tax its citizens on their worldwide estates, the UK could only tax its article 6/7 property and cannot tax other UK-situated property (such as stock in a UK company).

14. The US/UK treaty has no impact where an individual is neither a citizen nor a domiciliary in either country. Under domestic US and UK laws, both countries can, therefore, tax all property situated in that country at death.

Appendix VII

UK Business Property Relief for Holdings of Unlisted Shares and Securities (including UK AIM listed shares)

	Inheritance tax business property relief	Capital gains tax business asset taper relief	Capital gains tax hold-over relief
Relief	100% deduction for IHT on death or on a lifetime gift. But if either the donor or the donee die within the seven years following the gift, the property must still be relevant business property in the donee's hands at the date of the death, and must have been owned by him throughout the period from the first transfer.	On disposal of the assets a reduced percentage of the gain is taxed – making the effective tax rate either 20% or 10% (instead of 40%).	Where a gift is made, the donor and donee (or the donor alone if the donee is a trustee) can elect to hold over the gains into the hands of the donee, who takes over the donor's cost base for the purposes of future disposals. The taxable (held-over) gain arises on the subsequent sale of the asset or, where the assets transferred then form part of an interest in possession, upon the death of the life tenant. Note that clawback does not arise in the event of the death of an individual donee.

A hold over relief claim cannot be made in respect of a settlement in which settlor or his spouse has an interest.

Nor can it be made to a non-UK resident donee (or a company controlled by such a person) and there are clawback provisions where the donee emigrates within six tax years of the gift. |

UK Business Property Relief for Holdings of Unlisted Shares and Securities (including UK AIM listed)

	Inheritance tax business property relief	Capital gains tax business asset taper relief	Capital gains tax hold-over relief
Owner-ship period	• Two years immediately preceding the transfer; or	• One whole calendar year – 50% of gain is taxed.	Not relevant
		• Two whole calendar years – 25% of gain is taxed.	
	• if it replaced other qualifying property, in aggregate both properties were owned during two years out of the five immediately before the transfer.	• If less than one whole calendar year – no reduction in gain to be taxed.	
Qualifying holding	Shares in any company not listed on a recognised Stock Exchange (eg AIM listed shares qualify but, for example, NASDAQ do not).	All unlisted shares in trading companies or the holding company of a trading group.	All unlisted shares in trading companies or the holding company of a trading group.
	Unlisted securities which either alone or together with other unlisted securities or shares gave the transferor control of company.	Non trading company (or holding company) shares held by an employee (or by the trustees of a trust, where a beneficiary with an interest in possession is an employee) who does not have more than 10% of the shares, voting rights, or rights to more than 10% of the income or assets.	

UK Business Property Relief for Holdings of Unlisted Shares and Securities (including UK AIM listed)

	Inheritance tax business property relief	Capital gains tax business asset taper relief	Capital gains tax hold-over relief
Qualifying business	Excludes a business wholly or mainly dealing in securities, stocks, shares, land or building (unless the business also includes building construction or land development), or the making or holding of investments, save for: • a UK market maker or discount house; • a holding company of a company whose business does so qualify.	A trading company is as understood for income tax purposes (see opposite). To qualify as a trading company it must not have activities which are to any substantial extent non-trading (generally considered by the Inland Revenue as more than 20%). Limited investment income is not necessarily inconsistent with trading activities.	A trading company as for income tax purposes. A trade being every manufacture, adventure, concern in the nature of a trade, conducted on a commercial basis with a view to realising profits and excluding purely investment holding activities. A trade includes furnished holiday lettings in the UK and farming or market gardening in the UK but normally excludes rents and other income from land. Where a company owns assets not used for trading purposes, hold over relief is restricted (on a pro-rata basis) for a transferor who has voting rights of at least 5% (and in the case of trustees 25%). No restriction occurs for ownership below these limits provided the company meets the trading tests as described.
Note:	*Listed shares and securities can qualify if they gave the transferor control of the company but the relief in this case is 50% rather than 100%.* IHTA 1984, Pt V, Ch 1	*Listed shares can qualify if the shareholder has voting rights of at least 5%, or is an employee of the company (and in the case of a trust, if the employee is a beneficiary with an interest in possession) regardless of his percentage ownership.* TCGA 1992, s 2A and Sch A1	*Listed company shares can qualify if the transferor has voting rights of at least 5% (and in the case of trustees 25%).* TCGA 1992, s 165

Appendix VIII
Illustrations

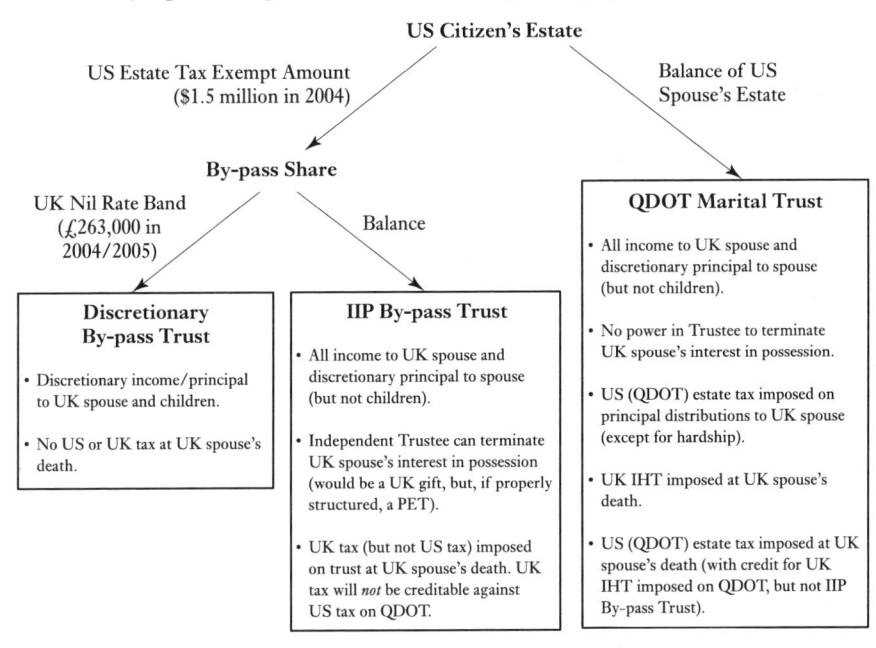

Figure 1: Illustration of estate plan of US citizen spouse (who is UK domiciled) – providing for a UK national spouse (Option 1)

US Citizen's Estate

- US Estate Tax Exempt Amount ($1.5 million in 2004) → **By-pass Share**
- Balance of US Spouse's Estate → **QDOT Marital Trust**

By-pass Share splits into:
- UK Nil Rate Band (£263,000 in 2004/2005) → **Discretionary By-pass Trust**
- Balance → **IIP By-pass Trust**

Discretionary By-pass Trust
- Discretionary income/principal to UK spouse and children.
- No US or UK tax at UK spouse's death.

IIP By-pass Trust
- All income to UK spouse and discretionary principal to spouse (but not children).
- Independent Trustee can terminate UK spouse's interest in possession (would be a UK gift, but, if properly structured, a PET).
- UK tax (but not US tax) imposed on trust at UK spouse's death. UK tax will *not* be creditable against US tax on QDOT.

QDOT Marital Trust
- All income to UK spouse and discretionary principal to spouse (but not children).
- No power in Trustee to terminate UK spouse's interest in possession.
- US (QDOT) estate tax imposed on principal distributions to UK spouse (except for hardship).
- UK IHT imposed at UK spouse's death.
- US (QDOT) estate tax imposed at UK spouse's death (with credit for UK IHT imposed on QDOT, but not IIP By-pass Trust).

Figure 2: Illustration of estate plan of US citizen spouse (who is UK domiciled) – providing for a UK national spouse (Option 2)

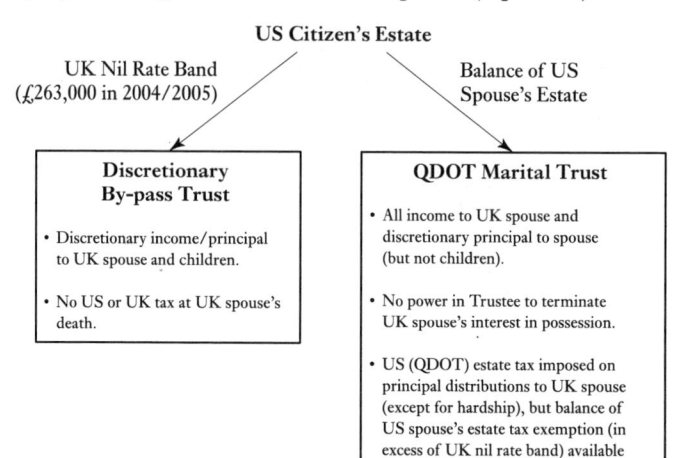

US Citizen's Estate

UK Nil Rate Band (£263,000 in 2004/2005) → **Discretionary By-pass Trust**

- Discretionary income/principal to UK spouse and children.
- No US or UK tax at UK spouse's death.

Balance of US Spouse's Estate → **QDOT Marital Trust**

- All income to UK spouse and discretionary principal to spouse (but not children).
- No power in Trustee to terminate UK spouse's interest in possession.
- US (QDOT) estate tax imposed on principal distributions to UK spouse (except for hardship), but balance of US spouse's estate tax exemption (in excess of UK nil rate band) available to reduce US taxes.
- UK IHT imposed at UK spouse's death.
- US (QDOT) estate tax imposed at UK spouse's death (with credit for UK IHT imposed on QDOT, but not IIP By-pass Trust); balance of US estate tax exemption in excess of nil rate band and not used on principal distributions to spouse available to reduce US taxes at UK spouse's death.

Figure 3: Illustration of estate plan of US citizen spouse (who is not UK domiciled or who has established an excluded property trust to mitigate UK tax exposure) – providing for a UK national spouse

US Citizen's Estate

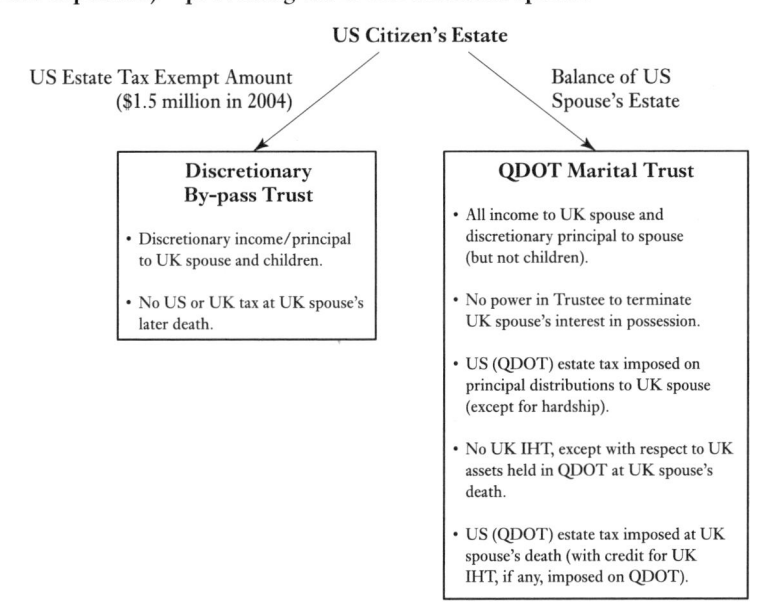

├── US Estate Tax Exempt Amount ($1.5 million in 2004) → **Discretionary By-pass Trust**
│   - Discretionary income/principal to UK spouse and children.
│   - No US or UK tax at UK spouse's later death.
│
└── Balance of US Spouse's Estate → **QDOT Marital Trust**
    - All income to UK spouse and discretionary principal to spouse (but not children).
    - No power in Trustee to terminate UK spouse's interest in possession.
    - US (QDOT) estate tax imposed on principal distributions to UK spouse (except for hardship).
    - No UK IHT, except with respect to UK assets held in QDOT at UK spouse's death.
    - US (QDOT) estate tax imposed at UK spouse's death (with credit for UK IHT, if any, imposed on QDOT).

Figure 4: Illustration of estate plan of UK domiciled spouse – providing for a US Citizen spouse (who is UK deemed domiciled)

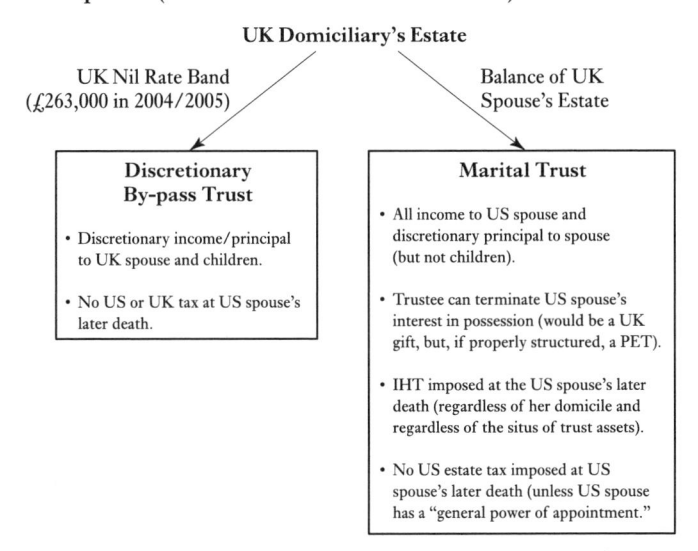

UK Domiciliary's Estate

├── UK Nil Rate Band (£263,000 in 2004/2005) → **Discretionary By-pass Trust**
│   - Discretionary income/principal to UK spouse and children.
│   - No US or UK tax at US spouse's later death.
│
└── Balance of UK Spouse's Estate → **Marital Trust**
    - All income to US spouse and discretionary principal to spouse (but not children).
    - Trustee can terminate US spouse's interest in possession (would be a UK gift, but, if properly structured, a PET).
    - IHT imposed at the US spouse's later death (regardless of her domicile and regardless of the situs of trust assets).
    - No US estate tax imposed at US spouse's later death (unless US spouse has a "general power of appointment."

Appendix IX

The American Jobs Creation Act of 2004

As this book was going to press, the US Congress enacted the American Jobs Creation Act of 2004 ('AJCA', HR 4520). Two of the sections of the AJCA have sufficient impact on certain discussions in the book to warrant summary here and reference to the principal sections of the book affected by such legislative changes.

1. Anti-Expatriation

For years, the US Tax Code has included special rules that apply to tax-motivated expatriates. These rules originally applied to only US citizens who relinquished their citizenship in order to save US taxes. In 1996, Congress extended these rules to certain long-term green card holders who relinquished their green cards. For the purpose of this appendix, former citizens and departed long-term green card holders are referred to as 'expatriates'.

a. A new purely objective test

The anti-expatriation rules originally had required a determination of the expatriate's subjective intent. In 1996, HIPAA provided the first objective standard by creating a presumption (rebuttable in limited circumstance) that certain wealthy individuals were tax motivated. (See **2.22**.) AJCA adopts a purely objective test: a citizen who expatriates or a long-term green card holder who relinquishes his green card is subject to the anti-expatriation rules (regardless of his motivation), with three exceptions. The taxpayer's intent is thus no longer relevant. In effect, the anti-expatriation rules now apply to all expatriates, regardless of their motivation, unless falling within one of the limited (but objective) exceptions.

The first exception is for an individual who demonstrates that (i) his average annual net income tax liability for the previous five years does not exceed $124,000, and (ii) his net worth does not exceed $2 million. Second, the anti-expatriation rules do not apply to certain dual nationals who have had no substantial contacts with the US (including a requirement that the individual never have had a US passport). Finally, these rules do not apply to an individual who became a US citizen at birth to non-US parents and who loses his citizenship before turning age 18½. An individual falling within one of the three exceptions must also certify to the IRS that he has complied with US tax laws for the prior five years and submit evidence of that compliance (eg, his US tax returns).

These exceptions supplant the prior rules (loathed by the IRS) that had allowed certain individuals (for example, departing green card holders returning to their country of nationality) to petition the IRS for a determination that their decision to leave was not primarily motivated by tax savings.

In addition, AJCA also provides that an individual continues to be treated as a citizen or resident until he properly notifies the US immigration and tax authorities of his expatriation or the relinquishment of his green card. No more slipping out quietly in the middle of the night.

b. Expanded application of gift tax to US property owned through certain foreign companies

AJCA extends the US gift tax to an expatriate's gift of shares of certain controlled foreign companies, but only to the extent of his portion of the foreign company's underlying US assets. This expands the scope of an expatriate's exposure to US gift tax (discussed in **2.24**) and mirrors a similar estate tax rule (discussed in **2.25**). This rule applies only to gifts made within ten years of expatriation.

c. Sanctions for expatriates who spend 'too much' time in the US

AJCA imposes special sanctions on expatriates who spend over 30 days in the US during any of the ten years following expatriation. Under new rules, such an expatriate will be deemed to be a US citizen (in the case of former US citizens) or a US 'resident' (in the case of former long-term green card holders) during that year. Presumably a former green card holder caught within these rules is considered to be a US resident for both income and transfer tax purposes.

The intended effect of this potentially controversial rule is to re-expose the expatriate to all relevant US income and transfer taxes, without regard for the situs of the income or transferred assets.

For purposes of determining if an individual is physically present in the US for more than 30 days, various general exceptions (applicable to diplomats, students, teachers and persons in transit) do not apply. The only exception is for the narrow class of individuals who return to the US on business for an unrelated employer. Even then, only 30 days of presence in the US for an employer will be excepted. (In some instances, former green card holders who are considered to be US residents under this new provision of the Code might escape the harshness of this new rule if they are residents of a treaty country and, under the relevant tie-breaker provision, are treated a resident of the other country.)

If an expatriate is treated by this special rule as a citizen or domiciliary in a subsequent year, the transfer tax deductions, exclusions, exemptions and credits applicable to US citizens and domiciliaries (and discussed in Chapter 3) would apply for taxable transfers during that year.

Presumably a former US citizen spouse who is treated as if she were a US citizen during a year she spent 31 or more days in the US would be entitled to receive during that year a gift or bequest that qualifies for the marital deduction, without being subject to the restrictions described in **4.4**.

There are other ancillary income tax consequences of an expatriate's being taxed as a citizen or resident for spending as little as 31 days in the US. First, an expatriate could be deemed under Code § 679 to be the grantor/owner of certain foreign trusts funded by the expatriate within the prior five years. (See **12.49** et seq.) In addition to being taxed as the trust's owner, the expatriate would have special reporting obligations under Code § 6048 (see **12.54**) and be subject to severe penalties for failure to file the relevant report. Second, an expatriate could also be exposed to tax under Code § 684 when his deemed citizenship/residency expires at the end of that calendar year. (See the discussion at **8.34** et seq and **9.1** et seq.)

d. Effective date

This rule applies to US citizens who expatriate or long-term green card holders who terminate their US residency after 3 June 2004.

e. The bright side

It could have been worse. AJCA adopted the House proposals in dealing with tax-motivated expatriates. The Senate proposal would have subjected an expatriate to an exit tax on any unrealized gain and subjected a US person who receives a gift or bequest from a tax-motivated expatriate as having income taxable at the highest marginal gift and estate tax rates.

Principal affected sections of the book: **2.21** et seq, **3.16** et seq, **3.32** et seq, **3.54** et seq, **4.4**, **8.34** et seq, **9.1** et seq, and **12.49** et seq.

2. Repeal of Foreign Personal Holding Company (FPHC) Rules

AJCA repeals the foreign personal holding company ('FPHC') rules, generally for tax years beginning after 31 December 2004.

Conforming amendments are made to numerous provisions of the Code. Perhaps the most important of which is that Code § 1014(b)(5) – which limits a person's inherited basis in an FPHC to the lower of the decedent's basis or the estate tax value (generally, the date of death value) – will not apply to FPHCs inherited after 1 January 2005.

Principal affected sections of the book: **11.11**, **14.49** (footnote 35) and **16.32–16.42**.

Index

[All references are to paragraph number.]

A

Accumulation and maintenance trusts
trustees' liability for tax, 6.47–6.55
Accumulation distributions
computation of throwback tax, 12.90–12.98
foreign trusts, and, 12.104–12.117
generally, 12.85–12.89
immigrants, and, 12.99–12.103
Agricultural property relief
generally, 3.71–3.73
introduction, 3.63
Annual exclusion
generation-skipping tax
citizens, 3.35
domiciliaries, 3.35
non-domiciled aliens, 3.52–3.53
tax-motivated expatriates, 3.54–3.55
gift tax
citizens, 3.7–3.8
domiciliaries, 3.7–3.8
non-domiciled aliens, 3.14
tax-motivated expatriates, 3.16–3.17
Annual exemption
capital gains tax, 10.6
inheritance tax, 3.75
Annuity insurance policies
capital gains tax, 10.5
Anti-avoidance
pre-immigration planning, 16.32–16.42
Applicable credit
See also Nil-rate band
estate tax
citizens, 3.22–3.23
domiciliaries, 3.22–3.23
non-domiciled aliens, 3.30
tax-motivated expatriates, 3.32–3.33
gift tax
citizens, 3.12
domiciliaries, 3.12
non-domiciled aliens, 3.15
tax-motivated expatriates, 3.16–3.17

B

Bare trusts
capital gains tax, 13.30–13.31
income tax, 13.20
Bed and breakfasting
pre-immigration planning, 16.30–16.31
Beneficiaries (UK)
capital gains tax, 13.70–13.81
income tax, 13.63–13.69
Beneficiaries (income taxation) (US)
distributions from non-grantor trusts, and
accumulation distributions, 12.85–12.117
complex trusts, 12.79–12.84
introduction, 12.71–12.73
loans from foreign trusts, 12.118–12.119
simple trusts, 12.74–12.78
transfers through intermediaries, 12.120–12.123
foreign non-grantor trust/NRA beneficiary, 12.8
foreign non-grantor trust/US beneficiary, 12.7
introduction, 12.4
US non-grantor trust/NRA beneficiary, 12.6
US non-grantor trust/US beneficiary, 12.5
Business property relief
generally, 3.64–3.70
introduction, 3.63
rates and reliefs, Appendix 7

C

Canada/US tax treaty
generally, 7.20–7.30
text, Appendix 5
'Capital first' trust distributions
foreign non-grantor trusts, 18.34
Capital gains distributions
US trust providing for UK beneficiary, 17.5–17.10

509

Index

Capital gains tax (United Kingdom)
annual exemption,	10.6
annuity insurance policies,	10.5
charitable gifts,	10.7
connected persons,	11.28–11.39
debts,	10.5
deductions and exclusions	
exempt assets,	10.5
exempt disposals,	10.7
exempt gains,	10.6
introduction,	10.4
tax reliefs,	10.8–10.24
enterprise investment schemes,	10.6
gifts and bequests, and	
connected persons,	11.28–11.39
general rules,	11.19–11.27
introduction,	11.17–11.18
market value rebasing,	11.20–11.21
matching rules,	11.24–11.27
'wholly and exclusively' rule,	11.22–11.23
hold-over relief	
business assets,	10.16–10.17
general,	10.19–10.22
gifts subject to inheritance tax,	10.18
introduction,	10.15
reinvestment,	10.23–10.24
indexation relief,	10.8–10.14
individuals	
domicile,	9.27–9.29
ordinary residence,	9.24–9.26
residence,	9.17–9.23
temporary non-residents,	9.30–9.32
introduction,	8.69–8.83
market value rebasing,	11.20–11.21
matching rules,	11.24–11.27
motor vehicles,	10.5
Personal Equity Plans,	10.6
personal representatives,	8.33–8.40
principal residence,	10.5
property acquired by gift,	11.30–11.32
property acquired from decedent,	11.33–11.39
rates and reliefs,	Appendix 1
reinvestment relief,	10.23–10.24
settlements for benefit of employees,	10.7
spousal transfers,	10.7
tangible moveable property,	10.5
taper relief,	10.8–10.14
tax reliefs	
hold-over relief,	10.15–10.24
indexation relief,	10.8–10.14

Capital gains tax (United Kingdom) – *contd*
tax reliefs – *contd*	
table of rates,	Appendix 1
taper relief,	10.8–10.14
taxable persons	
individuals,	9.17–9.32
introduction,	9.15–9.16
personal representatives,	9.33–9.40
trustees,	9.33–9.40
trusts, and	
And see Capital gains taxation on trusts	
generally,	13.1–13.102
venture capital trusts,	10.6
'wholly and exclusively' rule,	11.22–11.23
woodland,	10.6

Capital gains tax (United States)
deductions and exclusions,	10.1–10.3
distributions from trusts and estates	
introduction,	8.4
property in kind,	8.5
property sold to beneficiary,	8.6–8.7
entities,	9.14
foreign entities,	9.1
foreign trusts,	8.11
gifts and bequests, and	
GST transfers,	11.15–11.16
introduction,	11.1
property acquired by gift,	11.2–11.6
property acquired from decedent,	11.7–11.14
grantor trust rules,	8.10–8.11
grantor's departure from US,	8.34–8.43
'green card' test,	9.4–9.5
GST transfers,	11.15–11.16
individuals	
capital gains tax 'trap',	9.10–9.13
generally,	9.2–9.3
'green card' test,	9.4–9.5
introduction,	9.1
'substantial presence' test,	9.6–9.9
introduction,	8.1–8.7
legislative basis	
grantor's departure from US,	8.34–8.43
introduction,	8.8–8.15
loss of US beneficiary,	8.17
pre-immigration trusts,	8.44–8.54
release of powers,	8.16
settlor's death,	8.18–8.23
loss of US beneficiary,	8.17
non-resident aliens,	9.1

510

Index

Capital gains tax (United States) – *contd*
pre-immigration trusts
  generally, 8.44–8.50
  other legislative application, 8.51–8.54
principal residence, 10.2
property acquired by gift, 11.2–11.6
property acquired from decedent, 11.7–11.14
release of powers, 8.16
resident entities, 9.14
resident individuals
  capital gains tax 'trap', 9.10–9.13
  generally, 9.2–9.3
  'green card' test, 9.4–9.5
  introduction, 9.1
  'substantial presence' test, 9.6–9.9
settlor's death
  generally, 8.18–8.23
  insurance, 8.24–8.33
strategies for dealing with Code § 684 exposure
  emigration strategies, 8.62–8.65
  immigration strategies, 8.66–8.67
  property held in foreign grantor trust, 8.55–8.61
'substantial presence' test, 9.6–9.9
taxable persons, 9.1–9.14

Capital gains taxation of trusts, etc. (United Kingdom)
bare trusts, of, 13.30–13.31
beneficiaries, of, 13.70–13.81
discretionary trusts, of, 13.21–13.38
fixed interest trusts, of, 13.21–13.38
rate tables, Appendix 1
reform proposals, 13.82–13.102
residence of trusts, 13.11–13.12
resident settlor, of
  introduction, 13.39–13.41
  non-UK resident trusts, 13.55–13.62
  UK resident trusts, 13.52–13.54
resident trusts, of
  distribution or resettlement, 13.27–13.28
  exit charges on emigration, 13.32–13.38
  hold-over relief, 13.29
  generally, 13.22
  introduction, 13.21
  taper relief, 13.23–13.26
  summary, 13.1–13.9
trustees, of, 13.21–13.38

Charitable deduction
estate tax
  citizens, 3.18

Charitable deduction – *contd*
estate tax – *contd*
  domiciliaries, 3.18
  non-domiciled aliens, 3.29
  tax-motivated expatriates, 3.32–3.33
gift tax
  citizens, 3.5–3.6
  domiciliaries, 3.5–3.6
  non-domiciled aliens, 3.13
  tax-motivated expatriates, 3.16–3.17

Charitable gifts
capital gains tax, 10.7
inheritance tax, 3.58

Charitable remainder trusts
marital deduction trusts, 4.27

Citizens (United Kingdom)
liability to tax, 2.32

Citizens (United States)
deductions, exclusion, exemptions and credits
  estate tax, 3.18–3.28
  generation-skipping tax, 3.35–3.51
  gift tax, 3.4–3.12
  introduction, 3.1–3.3
liability to tax
  estate tax, 2.2–2.6
  generation-skipping tax, 2.7
  gift tax, 2.2–2.6

Complex trusts
distributions from non-grantor trusts, 12.79–12.84

Connected persons
capital gains tax, 11.28–11.39

Conservation easements
estate tax, 3.19

Controlled foreign corporations
pre-immigration planning, 16.32–16.42

Corporation tax
rates, Appendix 1

Credits (United States)
and see Deductions, exclusion, exemptions and credits
introduction, 3.1–3.3

D

Debts and expenses
capital gains tax, 10.5
estate tax, 3.20
generation-skipping tax, 3.50

Decedent's exposure to tax
generally, 7.71
summary, Appendix 6

Index

Deductions, exclusion, exemptions and credits (United Kingdom)
agricultural property relief
  generally, 3.71–3.73
  introduction, 3.63
annual exemption, 3.75
business property relief
  generally, 3.64–3.70
  introduction, 3.63
capital gains tax, and
  exempt assets, 10.5
  exempt disposals, 10.7
  exempt gains, 10.6
  introduction, 10.4
  tax reliefs, 10.8–10.24
charitable gifts, 3.58
dispositions not intended to confer gratuitous benefit, 3.79
excluded property, 3.82
family maintenance dispositions, 3.78
gifts in consideration of marriage, 3.77
introduction, 3.56
nil-rate band, 3.61–3.62
normal expenditure out of income, 3.74
political parties, gifts to, 3.59–3.60
post death variations, 3.83–3.87
reallocation of, 3.81
spouse exemption, 3.62
summary, 3.57–3.62
£250 exemption, 3.76
transfers to spouses
  historical background, 4.29–4.32
  introduction, 4.28
  qualifying transfers, 4.33–4.47
US/UK tax treaty
  credits, 7.68–7.70
  deductions and exemptions, 7.58–7.67
waiver of dividend, 3.80

Deductions, exclusion, exemptions and credits (United States)
capital gains tax, 10.1–10.3
estate tax
  citizens, 3.18–3.28
  domiciliaries, 3.18–3.28
  non-domiciled aliens, 3.29–3.31
  tax-motivated expatriates, 3.32–3.33
generation-skipping tax
  citizens, 3.35–3.51
  domiciliaries, 3.35–3.51
  introduction, 3.34
  non-domiciled aliens, 3.52–3.53
  tax-motivated expatriates, 3.54–3.55

Deductions, exclusion, exemptions and credits (United States) – *contd*
gift tax
  citizens, 3.4–3.12
  domiciliaries, 3.4–3.12
  non-domiciled aliens, 3.13–3.15
  tax-motivated expatriates, 3.16–3.17
introduction, 3.1–3.3
transfers to spouses
  historical background, 4.2–4.5
  introduction, 4.1
  qualifying transfers, 4.6–4.27
US/UK tax treaty
  credits, 7.68–7.70
  deductions and exemptions, 7.58–7.67

Deemed domicile
United Kingdom, 2.41–2.44

Default distribution rule
foreign non-grantor trusts, 18.35

Departure from US
capital gains tax, 8.34–8.43

Depleting trust
foreign non-grantor trusts, 18.35

Direct ownership
removal of assets from estate tax, 14.120

Discretionary trusts
capital gains tax, 13.21–13.38
income tax, 13.13–13.17
trustees' liability for tax, 6.34–6.46

Dispositions not intended to confer gratuitous benefit
exemptions and reliefs, and, 3.79

Distributable net income (DNI)
domestic non-grantor trusts, 12.57–12.64
foreign non-grantor trusts, 18.30–18.33

Distribution from trusts and estates
introduction, 8.4
property in kind, 8.5
property sold to beneficiary, 8.6–8.7

Distribution of assets
non-US beneficiaries followed by gift over, 18.42–18.47
settlor followed by gift over, 18.38–18.41

Distribution of current trust income and net gains
foreign non-grantor trusts, 18.27–18.29

DNI annuity distributions
foreign non-grantor trusts, 18.30–18.33

Domestic non-grantor trust (income taxation)
distribution deduction, 12.57–12.64
introduction, 12.55–12.56
rates, 12.65–12.66

Domestic non-grantor trust (income taxation) – *contd*
summary, 12.3

Domesticate the foreign trust
foreign non-grantor trusts, 18.23–18.25

Domicile
pre-immigration planning
  general principles, 16.7–16.9
  introduction, 16.5–16.6
  summary, 16.16–16.18
  UK emigrants, of, 16.10–16.15

Domiciliaries (United Kingdom)
liability to tax, 2.33–2.45

Domiciliaries (United States)
deductions, exclusion, exemptions and credits
  estate tax, 3.18–3.28
  generation-skipping tax, 3.35–3.51
  gift tax, 3.4–3.12
  introduction, 3.1–3.3
liability to tax
  estate tax, 2.2–2.6
  generation-skipping tax, 2.7
  gift tax, 2.2–2.6

Double tax treaties
United Kingdom
  France, 7.37
  generally, 7.35–7.36
  India, 7.38
  introduction, 7.31–7.34
  Ireland, 7.42
  Italy, 7.38
  Netherlands, 7.43
  Pakistan, 7.40
  South Africa, 7.44
  Sweden, 7.45
  Switzerland, 7.46
United States
  introduction, 7.1–7.2
  OECD treaties, 7.10–7.19
  post-1979 treaties, 7.10–7.19
  pre-1970 treaties, 7.3–7.9
  US/Canadian treaty, 7.20–7.30
US/UK estate and gift tax treaty
  credits, 7.68–7.70
  decedent's exposure to tax, 7.71
  deductions and exemptions, 7.58–7.67
  exceptions, 7.54–7.56
  fiscal domicile, 7.51–7.53
  introduction, 7.47
  non-domicile in either country, 7.57
  scope, 7.48–7.50
  taxes covered, 7.48–7.50

'Drop off' trusts
foreign asset protection trusts, 16.121–16.122
generally, 16.107–16.116
introduction, 16.4
UK tax implications, 16.123–16.129
US asset protection trusts, 16.117–16.120

Dynasty trusts
generation-skipping tax, 3.46

E

Effectively connected income (ECI)
income taxation of grantor, 12.47

Employer identification numbers (EINs)
income taxation reporting obligations, 12.153–12.159

Enterprise investment schemes
capital gains tax, 10.6

Entities
capital gains tax, 9.14

Estate administration expenses
estate tax, 3.21

Estate freezes
corporate estate freeze, 14.98–14.99
formation of corporation, 14.100–14.101
introduction, 14.95–14.97
split-interest purchase, 14.100–14.101
split-interest purchase of real estate, 14.102–14.105

Estate tax
deductions, exclusion, exemptions and credits
  citizens, 3.18–3.28
  domiciliaries, 3.18–3.28
  non-domiciled aliens, 3.29–3.31
  tax-motivated expatriates, 3.32–3.33
introduction, 1.2–1.12
removal of assets from
  And see Removal of assets
  alternative structures for holding income-producing real estate, 14.117–14.140
  introduction, 14.1–14.9
  marital deduction planning, 14.21–14.32
  rate crossover point, 14.15–14.20
  scope of person's exposure to tax, 14.10–14.12
  tax reduction techniques, 14.33–14.116
  US/UK treaty, 14.13–14.14
repeal proposals, 1.31–1.33

Index

Estate tax – *contd*
  tax rates and computation
    applicability to taxable persons, 5.6–5.8
    generally, 5.2–5.5
    prior taxable gifts, 5.9–5.14
    tables, Appendix 2
    'tax-on-tax' effect, 5.15–5.16
  taxable persons
    citizens, 2.2–2.6
    domiciliaries, 2.2–2.6
    introduction, 2.1
    non-domiciled aliens, 2.13–2.18
    residents, 2.2–2.6
    tax-motivated expatriates, 2.21–2.31
  transfers to spouses
    historical background, 4.2–4.5
    introduction, 4.1
    qualifying transfers, 4.6–4.27
  trustees' liability
    introduction, 6.1
    jurisdictional issues, 6.18–6.31
    QDOT, 6.6–6.7
    QTIP marital trust, 6.2–6.5
    statutory executor, 6.10–6.13
    transferee liability, and, 6.14–6.17
  UK spouse providing for US spouse
    implications to UK decedent spouse, 20.46–20.47
    implications to US donee, 20.25–20.30
    implications to US surviving spouse, 20.50–20.51
  UK/US Tax Treaty 1978, Appendix 4
  US spouse providing for UK spouse
    implications to UK donee, 19.12–19.13
    implications to UK surviving spouse, 19.38–19.41
    implications to US decedent spouse, 19.18–19.20

Excluded property
  exemptions and reliefs, and, 3.82

Excluded property trusts
  removal of assets from inheritance tax, 15.32–15.47
  trustees' liability for tax, 6.62–6.66

Exclusions (United States)
  and see Deductions, exclusion, exemptions and credits
  introduction, 3.1–3.3

Exempt transfers
  generation-skipping tax, 3.41–3.46

Exemptions (United Kingdom)
  and see Deductions, exclusion, exemptions and credits
  introduction, 3.56
  summary, 3.57

Exemptions (United States)
  and see Deductions, exclusion, exemptions and credits
  introduction, 3.1–3.3

Existing trusts
  income tax implications, 16.43–16.53
  introduction, 16.98
  trusts funded by others, 16.102–16.106
  trusts funded by settlor, 16.99–16.101

Expanded annual exclusion
  citizens, 3.9
  domiciliaries, 3.9
  non-domiciled aliens, 3.14
  tax-motivated expatriates, 3.16–3.17

F

Family maintenance dispositions
  exemptions and reliefs, and, 3.78

Fiscal domicile
  US/UK tax treaty, 7.51–7.53

Fixed interest trusts
  capital gains tax, 13.21–13.38
  income tax, 13.18–13.19
  trustees' liability for tax, 6.56–6.61

Fixed or determinable annual or periodic income (FDAPI)
  income taxation of trusts, etc., 12.46

Foreign beneficiaries on distributions from non-grantor trusts
  income taxation of trusts, etc., 12.124–12.131

Foreign company owning RPHC
  removal of assets from estate tax, 14.126

Foreign death tax credit
  citizens, 3.26
  domiciliaries, 3.26
  non-domiciled aliens, 3.31
  tax-motivated expatriates, 3.33

Foreign entities
  capital gains tax, 9.1

Foreign grantor trusts with foreign grantors
  existing 'grandfathered' grantor trusts, 18.10–18.12
  introduction, 18.8–18.9
  post-grantor trust phase, 18.17–18.21
  revocable trusts, 18.13–18.14

Index

Foreign grantor trusts with foreign grantors – *contd*
settlor and spouse only trusts, 18.15–18.16
Foreign non-grantor trusts for US beneficiary
'capital first' trust distributions, 18.34
default distribution rule, 18.35
depleting trust, 18.35
distribution of assets to settlor followed by gift over, 18.38–18.41
distribution of assets to non-US beneficiaries followed by gift over, 18.42–18.47
distribution of current trust income and net gains, 18.27–18.29
DNI annuity distributions, 18.30–18.33
domesticate the foreign trust, 18.23–18.25
introduction, 18.22
rent free use of trust owned property, 18.36
rhythm method distributions of accumulated income, 18.26
sale of assets to trust, 18.37
UNI accumulations, 18.30–18.33
Foreign holding company
removal of assets from estate tax, 14.125
Foreign investment in real property (FIRPTA)
income taxation of trusts, etc., 12.47
Foreign non-grantor trust (income tax)
generally, 12.67–12.70
summary, 12.3
Foreign personal holding companies
pre-immigration planning, 16.32–16.42
Foreign tax considerations
pre-immigration planning, 16.85–16.97
Foreign trusts providing for UK beneficiary
capital gains distributions, 17.5–17.10
income distributions, 17.5–17.10
summary, 17.1–17.4
US living trusts, 17.11–17.13
Foreign trusts providing for US beneficiary
foreign grantor trusts with foreign grantors
existing 'grandfathered' grantor trusts, 18.10–18.12
introduction, 18.8–18.9
post-grantor trust phase, 18.17–18.21
revocable trusts, 18.13–18.14

Foreign trusts providing for US beneficiary – *contd*
foreign grantor trusts with foreign grantors – *contd*
settlor and spouse only trusts, 18.15–18.16
foreign non-grantor trusts
'capital first' trust distributions, 18.34
default distribution rule, 18.35
depleting trust, 18.35
distribution of assets to settlor followed by gift over, 18.38–18.41
distribution of assets to non-US beneficiaries followed by gift over, 18.42–18.47
distribution of current trust income and net gains, 18.27–18.29
DNI annuity distributions, 18.30–18.33
domesticate the foreign trust, 18.23–18.25
introduction, 18.22
rent free use of trust owned property, 18.36
rhythm method distributions of accumulated income, 18.26
sale of assets to trust, 18.37
UNI accumulations, 18.30–18.33
introduction, 18.1–18.7
Foreign trusts
capital gains tax, 8.11
removal of assets from estate tax, 14.127–14.140
Funeral expenses
estate tax, 3.20

G

Gains tax
And see Capital gains tax
deductions and exclusions
United Kingdom, 10.4–10.24
United States, 10.1–10.3
gifts and bequests, and
United Kingdom, 11.17–11.39
United States, 11.1–11.16
introduction
United Kingdom, 8.69–8.83
United States, 8.1–8.68
taxable persons
United Kingdom, 9.15–9.40
United States, 9.1–9.14

515

Index

General power of appointment trusts
marital deduction trusts, 4.7–4.8

Generation-skipping tax (GST)
deductions, exclusion, exemptions and credits
citizens, 3.35–3.51
domiciliaries, 3.35–3.51
introduction, 3.34
non-domiciled aliens, 3.52–3.53
tax-motivated expatriates, 3.54–3.55
introduction, 1.26–1.30
pre-immigration planning
excluded trusts, 16.132
gifts, 16.131
introduction, 16.130
repeal proposals, 1.31–1.33
tax rates and computation, 5.17–5.23
taxable persons
citizens, 2.7
domiciliaries, 2.7
introduction, 2.1
non-domiciled aliens, 2.19–2.20
residents, 2.7
tax-motivated expatriates, 2.26–2.31
trustees' liability for tax, 6.8–6.9

Gift of US intangibles
removal of assets from estate tax, 14.34–14.35

Gift of US tangibles
removal of assets from estate tax, 14.36–14.38

Gift tax
deductions, exclusion, exemptions and credits
citizens, 3.4–3.12
domiciliaries, 3.4–3.12
non-domiciled aliens, 3.13–3.15
tax-motivated expatriates, 3.16–3.17
introduction, 1.13–1.25
pre-immigration planning
estate freeze, 16.71–16.73
estate planning, 16.74
GST exemption, 16.69
introduction, 16.65
limits to lifetime, tax-free gifts, 16.66
marital deduction restrictions, 16.67–16.68
troublesome assets, 16.70
tax rates and computation
applicability to taxable persons, 5.6–5.8
generally, 5.2–5.5
prior taxable gifts, 5.9–5.14

Gift tax – *contd*
tax rates and computation – *contd*
tables, Appendix 2
taxable persons
citizens, 2.2–2.6
domiciliaries, 2.2–2.6
introduction, 2.1
non-domiciled aliens, 2.9–2.12
residents, 2.2–2.6
tax-motivated expatriates, 2.21–2.31
transfers to spouses
historical background, 4.2–4.5
introduction, 4.1
qualifying transfers, 4.6–4.27
trustees' liability
introduction, 6.1
jurisdictional issues, 6.18–6.31
QDOT, 6.6–6.7
QTIP marital trust, 6.2–6.5
statutory executor, 6.10–6.13
transferee liability, and, 6.14–6.17
UK spouse providing for US spouse, 20.8–20.10
UK/US Tax Treaty 1978, Appendix 4
US spouse providing for UK spouse, 19.5–19.7

Gift tax credit
citizens, 3.27
domiciliaries, 3.27
non-domiciled aliens, 3.30
tax-motivated expatriates, 3.33

Gifts and bequests (CGT)
United Kingdom
connected persons, 11.28–11.39
general rules, 11.19–11.27
introduction, 11.17–11.18
market value rebasing, 11.20–11.21
matching rules, 11.24–11.27
property acquired by gift, 11.30–11.32
property acquired from decedent, 11.33–11.39
'wholly and exclusively' rule, 11.22–11.23
United States
GST transfers, 11.15–11.16
introduction, 11.1
property acquired by gift, 11.2–11.6
property acquired from decedent, 11.7–11.14

Gifts in consideration of marriage
exemptions and reliefs, and, 3.77

Gifts in trust
completed gift, 16.76–16.77

516

Index

Gifts in trust – *contd*
  exclusion from taxable estate, 16.78–16.79
  grantor trusts, 16.80–16.84
  introduction, 16.75

Grandfathered' grantor trusts
  foreign grantor trusts with foreign grantors, 18.10–18.12

Grantor (income tax)
  ECI, 12.47
  FDAPI, 12.46
  FIRPTA rules, 12.47
  foreign trusts, 12.49–12.54
  grantor trust rules, 12.22–12.31
  introduction, 12.19–12.21
  owner, as, 12.32–12.39
  respect of NRA as owner of trust, 12.40–12.48
  summary, 12.2

Grantor retained annuity trust
  estate tax, 3.27

Grantor trusts
  capital gains tax, 8.10–8.11
  removal of assets from inheritance tax, 15.48–15.53

'Green card' test
  capital gains tax, 9.4–9.5

GST exemption
  generation-skipping tax, 3.41–3.46

GST transfers
  capital gains tax, 11.15–11.16

H

Hold-over relief
  business assets, 10.16–10.17
  general, 10.19–10.22
  gifts subject to inheritance tax, 10.18
  introduction, 10.15
  reinvestment, 10.23–10.24

Holding US property
  corporation, in
    Anstalts, 14.56–14.57
    Code §§ 2036 and 2038 provisions, 14.58–14.68
    domestic corporation, 14.51–14.54
    FIRPTA, 14.71
    foreign corporation, 14.55
    foreign hybrid entities, 14.69–14.70
    foundations, 14.56–14.57
    introduction, 14.50
    Stiftungs, 14.56–14.57

Holding US property – *contd*
  partnership, in
    aggregate theory, 14.74–14.76
    entity theory, 14.77
    family limited partnerships, and, 14.85–14.88
    introduction, 14.72–14.73
    limited precedent, 14.78–14.84
    summary, 14.89
  trust, in, 14.39–14.49

I

Immovable property
  US/UK tax treaty, 7.54–7.55

Incidence of tax
  inheritance tax, 5.38–5.42

Income distributions
  US trust providing for UK beneficiary, 17.5–17.10

Income taxation of trusts, etc. (United Kingdom)
  bare trusts, of, 13.20
  beneficiaries, of, 13.63–13.69
  discretionary trusts, of, 13.13–13.17
  enjoyment of property previously owned, and
    chattels, 1.60
    excluded transactions, 1.55
    exemptions from charge, 1.56–1.58
    intangible assets, 1.61–1.66
    introduction, 1.51–1.54
    land, 1.59
  fixed interest trusts, of, 13.18–13.19
  interest in possession trusts, of, 13.18–13.19
  rate tables, Appendix 1
  reform proposals, 13.82–13.102
  residence of trusts, 13.10
  resident settlor, of
    introduction, 13.39–13.41
    settlor-interested trust, 13.42–13.46
    transfer of assets abroad, 13.47–13.51
  summary, 13.1–13.9
  trustees, of
    bare trusts, 13.20
    discretionary trusts, 13.13–13.17
    fixed interest trusts, 13.18–13.19
    interest in possession trusts, 13.18–13.19
  UK/US Tax Treaty 2001, Appendix 3

Index

Income taxation of trusts, etc. (United States)
accumulation distributions
  computation of throwback tax, 12.90–12.98
  foreign trusts, and, 12.104–12.117
  generally, 12.85–12.89
  immigrants, and, 12.99–12.103
beneficiaries, of
  foreign non-grantor trust/NRA beneficiary, 12.8
  foreign non-grantor trust/US beneficiary, 12.7
  introduction, 12.4
  US non-grantor trust/NRA beneficiary, 12.6
  US non-grantor trust/US beneficiary, 12.5
beneficiaries on distributions from non-grantor trusts, of
  accumulation distributions, 12.85–12.117
  complex trusts, 12.79–12.84
  introduction, 12.71–12.73
  loans from foreign trusts, 12.118–12.119
  simple trusts, 12.74–12.78
  transfers through intermediaries, 12.120–12.123
Canada/US Tax Treaty 1980
  generally, 7.20–7.30
  text, Appendix 5
complex trusts, 12.79–12.84
distributable net income (DNI), 12.57–12.64
domestic non-grantor trust, of
  distribution deduction, 12.57–12.64
  introduction, 12.55–12.56
  rates, 12.65–12.66
  summary, 12.3
effectively connected income, 12.47
employer identification numbers, 12.153–12.159
estates, of, 12.132–12.136
fixed or determinable annual or periodic income, 12.46
foreign beneficiaries on distributions from non-grantor trusts, 12.124–12.131
foreign investment in real property, 12.47
foreign non-grantor trust, of
  generally, 12.67–12.70
  summary, 12.3

Income taxation of trusts, etc. (United States) – *contd*
grantor, of
  ECI, 12.47
  FDAPI, 12.46
  FIRPTA rules, 12.47
  foreign trusts, 12.49–12.54
  grantor trust rules, 12.22–12.31
  introduction, 12.19–12.21
  owner, as, 12.32–12.39
  respect of NRA as owner of trust, 12.40–12.48
  summary, 12.2
loans from foreign trusts, 12.118–12.119
loans treated as distributions, 12.9
non-grantor trust, of
  beneficiaries on distributions, 12.71–12.123
  domestic trust, 12.55–12.66
  foreign beneficiaries on distributions, 12.124–12.131
  foreign trust, 12.67–12.70
  summary, 12.3
pre-immigration planning
  avoiding anti-avoidance rules, 16.32–16.42
  bed and breakfasting, 16.30–16.31
  implications of existing trusts, 16.43–16.53
  introduction, 16.26
  realizing gains, income or deductions, 16.27–16.29
  variable insurance products, 16.54–16.64
rate tables, Appendix 2
reporting obligations
  domestic trusts, 12.144
  EINs, 12.153–12.159
  Form 90–22.1, 12.151–12.152
  generally, 12.137
  introduction, 12.9
  penalties, 12.145
  procedure, 12.146–12.150
  reportable events, 12.138–12.143
  special obligations, 12.138–12.150
residence of trusts
  'control' test, 12.16–12.18
  'court' test, 12.12–12.15
  introduction, 12.9–12.11
simple trusts, 12.74–12.78
Subchapter S rules, 12.9
summary, 12.1–12.8

Index

Income taxation of trusts, etc. (United States) – *contd*
 'throwback' tax
  computation of throwback tax, 12.90–12.98
  foreign trusts, and, 12.104–12.117
  generally, 12.85–12.89
  immigrants, and, 12.99–12.103
  introduction, 12.9
 transfers through intermediaries
  generally, 12.120–12.123
  introduction, 12.9
 UK/US Tax Treaty 2001
  generally, 7.47–7.71
  text, Appendix 3

Indexation relief
 capital gains tax, 10.8–10.14

Inheritance tax
 deductions, exclusion, exemptions and credits
  agricultural property relief, 3.71–3.73
  annual exemption, 3.75
  business property relief, 3.64–3.70
  charitable gifts, 3.58
  dispositions not intended to confer gratuitous benefit, 3.79
  excluded property, 3.82
  family maintenance dispositions, 3.78
  gifts in consideration of marriage, 3.77
  introduction, 3.56
  nil-rate band, 3.61–3.62
  normal expenditure out of income, 3.74
  political parties, gifts to, 3.59–3.60
  post death variations, 3.83–3.87
  reallocation of, 3.81
  spouse exemption, 3.62
  summary, 3.57–3.62
  £250 exemption, 3.76
  waiver of dividend, 3.80
 incidence of tax, 5.38–5.42
 introduction, 1.38–1.50
 removal of assets from
  And see Removal of assets
  excluded property trusts, 15.32–15.47
  grantor trusts, 15.48–15.53
  introduction, 15.1
  offshore holding vehicles, 15.32–15.47
  permanent establishment property, 15.31
  potentially exempt transfers, 15.25–15.30
  rate crossover point, 15.7–15.12

Inheritance tax – *contd*
 removal of assets from – *contd*
  scope of UK tax exposure, 15.2–15.6
  spouse exemption planning, 15.13–15.24
 tax rates and computation
  generally, 5.25
  incidence of tax, 5.38–5.42
  introduction, 5.24
  prior gifts, 5.26–5.34
  table, Appendix 1
  'tax-on-tax' effect, 5.35–5.37
 taxable persons
  citizens, 2.32
  domiciliaries, 2.33–2.45
  introduction, 2.32
  liability for payment, 2.51–2.53
  non-domiciliaries, 2.46–2.50
 transfers to spouses
  historical background, 4.29–4.32
  introduction, 4.28
  qualifying transfers, 4.33–4.47
 UK spouse providing for US spouse
  inheritance tax implications to UK decedent spouse, 20.31–20.45
  inheritance tax implications to UK donor, 20.4–20.7
  inheritance tax implications to US donee, 20.11–20.24
  inheritance tax implications to US surviving spouse, 20.48–20.49
 US spouse providing for UK spouse
  implications to UK donee, 19.14–19.15
  implications to UK surviving spouse, 19.42–19.49
  implications to US decedent spouse, 19.21–19.37
  implications to US donor, 19.8–19.11

Insurance products
 pre-immigration planning, 16.54–16.64

Interest in possession trusts
 income tax, 13.18–13.19

J

Joint ownership
 removal of assets from estate tax, 14.90–14.94

Index

L

Lease for life
trustees' liability for tax,   6.67

Life insurance
removal of assets from estate tax,   14.115–14.117

Lifetime gifts
deductions, exclusion, exemptions and credits
  agricultural property relief,   3.71–3.73
  annual exemption,   3.75
  business property relief,   3.64–3.70
  charitable gifts,   3.58
  dispositions not intended to confer gratuitous benefit,   3.79
  excluded property,   3.82
  family maintenance dispositions,   3.78
  gifts in consideration of marriage,   3.77
  introduction,   3.56
  nil-rate band,   3.61–3.62
  normal expenditure out of income,   3.74
  political parties, gifts to,   3.59–3.60
  post death variations,   3.83–3.87
  reallocation of,   3.81
  spouse exemption,   3.62
  summary,   3.57–3.62
  £250 exemption,   3.76
  waiver of dividend,   3.80
incidence of tax,   5.38–5.42
introduction,   1.67–1.77
tax rates and computation
  generally,   5.25
  incidence of tax,   5.38–5.42
  introduction,   5.24
  prior gifts,   5.26–5.34
  'tax-on-tax' effect,   5.35–5.37
taxable persons
  citizens,   2.32
  domiciliaries,   2.33–2.45
  introduction,   2.32
  liability for payment,   2.51–2.53
  non-domiciliaries,   2.46–2.50
transfers to spouses
  historical background,   4.29–4.32
  introduction,   4.28
  qualifying transfers,   4.33–4.47
UK spouse providing for US spouse
  estate tax implications to US donee,   20.25–20.30

Lifetime gifts – *contd*
UK spouse providing for US spouse – *contd*
  gift tax implication to UK donor,   20.8–20.10
  inheritance tax implications to UK donor,   20.4–20.7
  inheritance tax implications to US donee,   20.11–20.24
  introduction,   20.3
US spouse providing for UK spouse
  estate tax implications to UK donee,   19.12–19.13
  gift tax implications to US donor,   19.5–19.7
  inheritance tax implications to UK donee,   19.14–19.15
  inheritance tax implications to US donor,   19.8–19.11
  introduction,   19.4

Living trusts
US trust providing for UK beneficiary,   17.11–17.13

Loans from foreign trusts
distributions from non-grantor trusts,   12.118–12.119

Loans treated as distributions
income taxation of trusts, etc.,   12.9

Loss of beneficiary
capital gains tax,   8.17

M

Marital deduction
See also Spouse exemption
estate tax
  citizens,   3.18
  domiciliaries,   3.18
  non-domiciled aliens,   3.29
  tax-motivated expatriates,   3.32–3.33
generation-skipping tax,   3.48
gift tax
  citizens,   3.4
  domiciliaries,   3.4
  non-domiciled aliens,   3.14
  tax-motivated expatriates,   3.16–3.17
removal of assets from estate tax, and
  estate tax,   14.26–14.29
  gift tax,   14.22–14.25
  inheritance tax,   14.30–14.32
  introduction,   14.21

Index

Marital deduction – *contd*	
transfers to spouses, and	
historical background,	4.2–4.5
introduction,	4.1
qualifying transfers,	4.6–4.27
Marital deduction trusts	
charitable remainder trust,	4.27
general power of appointment trusts,	4.7–4.8
historical background,	4.2–4.5
generally,	4.1
introduction,	4.6
marital lead trust,	4.27
QDOTs,	4.16–4.26
QTIP trusts,	4.9–4.15
Marital lead trusts	
marital deduction trusts,	4.27
Market value rebasing	
capital gains tax,	11.20–11.21
Marriage gifts	
exemptions and reliefs, and,	3.77
Matching rules	
capital gains tax,	11.24–11.27
Medical expenses, gifts of	
generation-skipping tax	
citizens,	3.35–3.37
domiciliaries,	3.35–3.37
non-domiciled aliens,	3.52–3.53
tax-motivated expatriates,	3.54–3.55
gift tax	
citizens,	3.10
domiciliaries,	3.10
non-domiciled aliens,	3.14
tax-motivated expatriates,	3.16–3.17
Motor vehicles	
capital gains tax,	10.5

N

Nil-rate band	
exemptions and reliefs, and,	3.61–3.62
Non-domiciled aliens (NDAs)	
capital gains tax,	9.1
deductions, exclusion, exemptions and credits	
estate tax,	3.29–3.31
generation-skipping tax,	3.52–3.53
gift tax,	3.13–3.15
introduction,	3.1–3.3
liability to tax	
estate tax,	2.13–2.18
generation-skipping tax,	2.19–2.20
gift tax,	2.9–2.12

Non-domiciled aliens (NDAs) – *contd*	
liability to tax – *contd*	
introduction,	2.8
removal of assets from US estate tax	
And see Removal of assets	
alternative structures for holding income-producing real estate,	14.117–14.140
introduction,	14.1–14.9
marital deduction planning,	14.21–14.32
rate crossover point,	14.15–14.20
scope of US tax exposure,	14.10–14.12
tax reduction techniques,	14.33–14.116
US/UK treaty,	14.13–14.14
Non-domiciliaries (United Kingdom)	
liability to tax,	2.46–2.50
Non-domiciliary planning	
removal of assets from estate tax	
And see Removal of assets	
alternative structures for holding income-producing real estate,	14.117–14.140
introduction,	14.1–14.9
marital deduction planning,	14.21–14.32
rate crossover point,	14.15–14.20
scope of US tax exposure,	14.10–14.12
tax reduction techniques,	14.33–14.116
US/UK treaty,	14.13–14.14
removal of assets from inheritance tax	
And see Removal of assets	
excluded property trusts,	15.32–15.47
grantor trusts,	15.48–15.53
introduction,	15.1
offshore holding vehicles,	15.32–15.47
permanent establishment property,	15.31
potentially exempt transfers,	15.25–15.30
rate crossover point,	15.7–15.12
scope of UK tax exposure,	15.2–15.6
spouse exemption planning,	15.13–15.24
Non-grantor trust (income tax)	
beneficiaries on distributions,	12.71–12.123
domestic trust,	12.55–12.66
foreign beneficiaries on distributions,	12.124–12.131
foreign trust,	12.67–12.70
summary,	12.3

521

Index

Non-resident trust providing for UK beneficiary
capital gains distributions,	17.5–17.10
income distributions,	17.5–17.10
summary,	17.1–17.4
US living trusts,	17.11–17.13

Normal expenditure out of income
exemptions and reliefs, and,	3.74

O

Offshore holding vehicles
removal of assets from inheritance tax,	15.32–15.47

Orphan's exclusion
generation-skipping tax,	3.38–3.40

Outright gifts to spouses
historical background,	4.2–4.5
generally,	4.6
introduction,	4.1

P

Passive foreign investment companies
pre-immigration planning,	16.32–16.42

Permanent establishment property
removal of assets from estate tax,	14.108–14.114
removal of assets from inheritance tax,	15.31
US/UK tax treaty,	7.54–7.55

Personal Equity Plans
capital gains tax,	10.6

Personal representatives
capital gains tax,	8.33–8.40

Political parties, gifts to
exemptions and reliefs, and,	3.59–3.60

Post death variations
exemptions and reliefs, and,	3.83–3.87

Potentially exempt transfers (PETs)
removal of assets from inheritance tax,	15.25–15.30

Pre-immigration planning
See also Pre-immigration trusts
avoiding anti-avoidance rules,	16.32–16.42
bed and breakfasting,	16.30–16.31
controlled foreign corporations,	16.32–16.42

Pre-immigration planning – *contd*
domicile
general principles,	16.7–16.9
introduction,	16.5–16.6
summary,	16.16–16.18
UK emigrants, of,	16.10–16.15

'drop off' trusts
foreign asset protection trusts,	16.121–16.122
generally,	16.107–16.116
introduction,	16.4
UK tax implications,	16.123–16.129
US asset protection trusts,	16.117–16.120

existing trusts
income tax implications,	16.43–16.53
introduction,	16.98
trusts funded by others,	16.102–16.106
trusts funded by settlor,	16.99–16.101

foreign personal holding companies,	16.32–16.42
foreign tax considerations,	16.85–16.97

generation-skipping trust planning
excluded trusts,	16.132
gifts,	16.131
introduction,	16.130

gift tax planning
estate freeze,	16.71–16.73
estate planning,	16.74
GST exemption,	16.69
introduction,	16.65
limits to lifetime, tax-free gifts,	16.66
marital deduction restrictions,	16.67–16.68
troublesome assets,	16.70

gifts in trust
completed gift,	16.76–16.77
exclusion from taxable estate,	16.78–16.79
grantor trusts,	16.80–16.84
introduction,	16.75

income tax planning
avoiding anti-avoidance rules,	16.32–16.42
bed and breakfasting,	16.30–16.31
implications of existing trusts,	16.43–16.53
introduction,	16.26
realizing gains, income or deductions,	16.27–16.29
variable insurance products,	16.54–16.64

income tax resident,	16.19–16.25
insurance products,	16.54–16.64

522

Index

Pre-immigration planning – *contd*
  introduction, 16.1–16.4
  passive foreign investment
    companies, 16.32–16.42
  real property strategies, 16.133–16.143
  realizing gains, income or
    deductions, 16.27–16.29
  renvoi doctrine, 16.88
  variable insurance products, 16.54–16.64
Pre-immigration trusts
  generally, 8.44–8.50
  other legislative application, 8.51–8.54
Principal residence (CGT)
  United Kingdom, 10.5
  United States, 10.2
Prior taxable gifts
  United Kingdom, 5.26–5.34
  United States, 5.9–5.14
Property acquired by gift
  United Kingdom, 11.30–11.32
  United States, 11.2–11.6
Property acquired from decedent
  United Kingdom, 11.33–11.39
  United States, 11.7–11.14

Q

Qualified domestic trusts (QDOTs)
  citizens, 3.18
  domiciliaries, 3.18
  marital deduction trusts, and, 4.16–4.26
  non-domiciled aliens, 3.29
  tax-motivated expatriates, 3.32–3.33
  trustees' liability for tax, 6.6–6.7
Qualified terminable interest property (QTIP) trusts
  generally, 4.9–4.15
  trustees' liability for tax, 6.2–6.5

R

Rate crossover point
  removal of assets from estate tax, 14.15–14.20
  removal of assets from inheritance tax
    US citizen domiciled in UK, 15.10–15.12
    US taxpayer with article 6/7 property, 15.7–15.9

Real property holding corporation (RPHC)
  removal of assets from estate tax, 14.121–14.124
Reallocation of exemptions and reliefs
  generally, 3.81
Recent inheritances credit
  estate tax
    citizens, 3.28
    domiciliaries, 3.28
    non-domiciled aliens, 3.31
  generation-skipping tax, 3.51
Recourse mortgages
  removal of assets from estate tax, 14.106–14.107
Reinvestment relief
  capital gains tax, 10.23–10.24
Release of powers
  capital gains tax, 8.16
Reliefs (United Kingdom)
  and see Deductions, exclusion, exemptions and credits
  introduction, 3.56
  summary, 3.57
Removal of assets from estate tax
  alternative structures for holding income-producing real estate
    direct ownership, 14.120
    foreign company owning RPHC, 14.126
    foreign holding company, 14.125
    foreign trust, 14.127–14.140
    introduction, 14.117–14.118
    real property holding corporation, 14.121–14.124
    relevant income taxes, 14.119
  direct ownership, 14.120
  estate freezes
    corporate estate freeze, 14.98–14.99
    formation of corporation, 14.100–14.101
    introduction, 14.95–14.97
    split-interest purchase, 14.100–14.101
    split-interest purchase of real estate, 14.102–14.105
  foreign company owning RPHC, 14.126
  foreign holding company, 14.125
  foreign trust, 14.127–14.140
  gift of US intangibles, 14.34–14.35
  gift of US tangibles, 14.36–14.38
  holding US property
    corporation, in, 14.50–14.71
    partnership, in, 14.72–14.89

523

Index

Removal of assets from estate tax – *contd*
holding US property – *contd*
  trust, in, 14.39–14.49
holding US property in corporation
  Anstalts, 14.56–14.57
  Code §§ 2036 and 2038 provisions, 14.58–14.68
  domestic corporation, 14.51–14.54
  FIRPTA, 14.71
  foreign corporation, 14.55
  foreign hybrid entities, 14.69–14.70
  foundations, 14.56–14.57
  introduction, 14.50
  Stiftungs, 14.56–14.57
holding US property in partnership
  aggregate theory, 14.74–14.76
  entity theory, 14.77
  family limited partnerships, and, 14.85–14.88
  introduction, 14.72–14.73
  limited precedent, 14.78–14.84
  summary, 14.89
introduction, 14.1–14.9
joint ownership, 14.90–14.94
life insurance, 14.115–14.117
marital deduction planning
  estate tax, 14.26–14.29
  gift tax, 14.22–14.25
  inheritance tax, 14.30–14.32
  introduction, 14.21
moving US tangibles out of the US, 14.36–14.38
permanent establishment property, 14.108–14.114
rate crossover point, 14.15–14.20
real property holding corporation, 14.121–14.124
recourse mortgages, 14.106–14.107
scope of person's exposure to tax, 14.10–14.12
split-interest purchase
  generally, 14.100–14.101
  real estate, of, 14.102–14.105
tax reduction techniques
  estate freezes, 14.95–14.105
  introduction, 14.33
  joint ownership, 14.90–14.94
  life insurance, 14.115–14.117
  permanent establishment property, 14.108–14.114
  recourse mortgages, 14.106–14.107

Removal of assets from estate tax – *contd*
tax reduction techniques – *contd*
  US intangibles, 14.34–14.35
  US property in corporation, 14.50–14.71
  US property in partnership, 14.72–14.89
  US property in trust, 14.39–14.49
  US tangibles, 14.36–14.38
  US/UK treaty, Article 8(5), 14.13–14.14

Removal of assets from inheritance tax
excluded property trusts, 15.32–15.47
grantor trusts, 15.48–15.53
introduction, 15.1
offshore holding vehicles, 15.32–15.47
permanent establishment property, 15.31
potentially exempt transfers, 15.25–15.30
rate crossover point
  US citizen domiciled in UK, 15.10–15.12
  US taxpayer with article 6/7 property, 15.7–15.9
scope of UK tax exposure
  introduction, 15.2
  US citizen domiciled in UK, 15.3
  US domiciliary, 15.4–15.6
spouse exemption planning, 15.13–15.24

Rent free use of trust owned property
foreign non-grantor trusts, 18.36

***Renvoi* doctrine**
pre-immigration planning, 16.88

Reporting obligations (income tax)
domestic trusts, 12.144
EINs, 12.153–12.159
Form 90–22.1, 12.151–12.152
generally, 12.137
introduction, 12.9
penalties, 12.145
procedure, 12.146–12.150
reportable events, 12.138–12.143
special obligations, 12.138–12.150

Residence of trusts
United Kingdom
  capital gains tax, 13.11–13.12
  income tax, 13.10
United States
  'control' test, 12.16–12.18
  'court' test, 12.12–12.15
  introduction, 12.9–12.11

Index

Resident entities
  capital gains tax, 9.14
Resident settlor
  introduction, 13.39–13.41
  non-UK resident trusts, 13.55–13.62
  UK resident trusts, 13.52–13.54
Revocable trusts
  foreign grantor trusts with foreign grantors, 18.13–18.14
Rhythm method distributions of accumulated income
  foreign non-grantor trusts, 18.26

S

Sale of assets to trust
  foreign non-grantor trusts, 18.37
Settlements for benefit of employees
  capital gains tax, 10.7
Settlor and spouse only trusts
  foreign grantor trusts with foreign grantors, 18.15–18.16
Settlor's death
  generally, 8.18–8.23
  insurance, 8.24–8.33
Simple trusts
  distributions from non-grantor trusts, 12.74–12.78
Split gifts election
  citizens, 3.11
  domiciliaries, 3.11
  non-domiciled aliens, 3.14
  tax-motivated expatriates, 3.16–3.17
Split-interest purchase
  generally, 14.100–14.101
  real estate, of, 14.102–14.105
Spouse exemption
  See also Marital deduction
  capital gains tax, 10.7
  inheritance tax
    generally, 3.62
    historical background, 4.29–4.32
    introduction, 4.28
    qualifying transfers, 4.33–4.47
  removal of assets from inheritance tax, 15.13–15.24
Stamp taxes
  rates, Appendix 1
State tax credit
  estate tax
    citizens, 3.24–3.25
    domiciliaries, 3.24–3.25
    non-domiciled aliens, 3.31

State tax credit – *contd*
  generation-skipping tax, 3.49
Statutory executor
  trustees' liability for tax, 6.10–6.13
Subchapter S rules
  income taxation of trusts, etc., 12.9
'Substantial presence' test
  capital gains tax, 9.6–9.9
£250 exemption
  generally, 3.76

T

Tangible moveable property
  capital gains tax, 10.5
Taper relief
  capital gains tax, 10.8–10.14
Tax rates and computation (United Kingdom)
  inheritance tax
    generally, 5.25
    incidence of tax, 5.38–5.42
    prior gifts, 5.26–5.34
    'tax-on-tax' effect, 5.35–5.37
    introduction, 5.24
    lifetime gifts, 5.24
Tax rates and computation (United States)
  estate tax
    applicability to taxable persons, 5.6–5.8
    generally, 5.2–5.5
    prior taxable gifts, 5.9–5.14
    'tax-on-tax' effect, 5.15–5.16
  generation-skipping tax, 5.17–5.23
  gift tax
    applicability to taxable persons, 5.6–5.8
    generally, 5.2–5.5
    prior taxable gifts, 5.9–5.14
  introduction, 5.1
Tax treaties
  United Kingdom
    France, 7.37
    generally, 7.35–7.36
    India, 7.38
    introduction, 7.31–7.34
    Ireland, 7.42
    Italy, 7.38
    Netherlands, 7.43
    Pakistan, 7.40
    South Africa, 7.44
    Sweden, 7.45

Index

Tax treaties – *contd*
  United Kingdom – *contd*
    Switzerland, 7.46
  United States
    introduction, 7.1–7.2
    OECD treaties, 7.10–7.19
    post-1979 treaties, 7.10–7.19
    pre-1970 treaties, 7.3–7.9
    US/Canadian treaty, 7.20–7.30
  US/UK estate and gift tax treaty
    credits, 7.68–7.70
    decedent's exposure to tax, 7.71
    deductions and exemptions, 7.58–7.67
    exceptions, 7.54–7.56
    fiscal domicile, 7.51–7.53
    introduction, 7.47
    non-domicile in either country, 7.57
    scope, 7.48–7.50
    taxes covered, 7.48–7.50

Taxable persons
  capital gains tax
    individuals, 9.17–9.32
    introduction, 9.15–9.16
    personal representatives, 9.33–9.40
  inheritance tax
    citizens, 2.32
    domiciliaries, 2.33–2.45
    introduction, 2.32
    liability for payment, 2.51–2.53
    non-domiciliaries, 2.46–2.50

Taxable persons (United States)
  capital gains tax
    entities, 9.14
    individuals, 9.2–9.13
    introduction, 9.1
  citizens
    estate tax, 2.2–2.6
    generation-skipping tax, 2.7
    gift tax, 2.2–2.6
  domiciliaries
    estate tax, 2.2–2.6
    generation-skipping tax, 2.7
    gift tax, 2.2–2.6
  introduction, 2.1
  non-domiciled aliens
    estate tax, 2.13–2.18
    generation-skipping tax, 2.19–2.20
    gift tax, 2.9–2.12
    introduction, 2.8
  residents
    estate tax, 2.2–2.6
    generation-skipping tax, 2.7
    gift tax, 2.2–2.6

Taxable persons (United States) – *contd*
  tax-motivated expatriates
    estate tax, 2.21–2.31
    generation-skipping tax, 2.26–2.31
    gift tax, 2.21–2.31

Tax-motivated expatriates
  deductions, exclusion, exemptions and credits
    estate tax, 3.32–3.33
    generation-skipping tax, 3.54–3.55
    gift tax, 3.16–3.17
    introduction, 3.1–3.3
  liability to tax
    estate tax, 2.21–2.31
    generation-skipping tax, 2.26–2.31
    gift tax, 2.21–2.31

'Tax-on-tax' effect
  United Kingdom, 5.35–5.37
  United States, 5.15–5.16

Tax tables
  United Kingdom, Appendix 1
  United States, Appendix 2

'Throwback' tax
  computation, 12.90–12.98
  foreign trusts, and, 12.104–12.117
  generally, 12.85–12.89
  immigrants, and, 12.99–12.103
  introduction, 12.9

Transfer on death
  introduction, 1.38–1.50

Transferee liability
  appointed property, 6.17
  introduction, 6.14
  life insurance proceeds, 6.17
  state law, under, 6.16
  unpaid gift and estate taxes, for, 6.15

Transfers through intermediaries
  generally, 12.120–12.123
  introduction, 12.9

Transfers to spouses (United Kingdom)
  capital gains tax, 10.7
  inheritance tax
    historical background, 4.29–4.32
    introduction, 4.28
    qualifying transfers, 4.33–4.47

Transfers to spouses (United States)
  historical background, 4.2–4.5
  introduction, 4.1
  marital deduction trusts
    charitable remainder trust, 4.27
    general power of appointment trusts, 4.7–4.8

Index

Transfers to spouses (United States) – *contd*
  marital deduction trusts – *contd*
    introduction, 4.6
    marital lead trust, 4.27
    QDOTs, 4.16–4.26
    QTIP trusts, 4.9–4.15
  outright gifts, 4.6
  qualifying transfers, 4.6–4.27
Trustees
  capital gains tax
    generally, 13.21–13.38
    introduction, 9.33–9.40
  income tax
    bare trusts, 13.20
    discretionary trusts, 13.13–13.17
    fixed interest trusts, 13.18–13.19
    interest in possession trusts, 13.18–13.19
Trustees' liability (United Kingdom)
  accumulation and maintenance trusts, 6.47–6.55
  discretionary trusts, 6.34–6.46
  excluded property trusts, 6.62–6.66
  fixed interest trusts, 6.56–6.61
  introduction, 6.32–6.3
  lease for life, 6.67
Trustees' liability (United States)
  generation-skipping tax, 6.8–6.9
  introduction, 6.1
  jurisdictional issues
    in rem jurisdiction over trust assets in US courts, 6.26
    introduction, 6.18
    personal jurisdiction in US courts, 6.19–6.22
    personal jurisdiction over custodian of US assets, 6.23–6.25
    trustee in foreign courts, 6.27–6.31
  liability of transferee, and appointed property, 6.17
  introduction, 6.14
  life insurance proceeds, 6.17
  state law, under, 6.16
  unpaid gift and estate taxes, for, 6.15
  QDOT, 6.6–6.7
  QTIP marital trust, 6.2–6.5
  statutory executor, 6.10–6.13
Tuition expenses, gifts of
  generation-skipping tax
    citizens, 3.35–3.37
    domiciliaries, 3.35–3.37
    non-domiciled aliens, 3.52–3.53

Tuition expenses, gifts of – *contd*
  generation-skipping tax – *contd*
    tax-motivated expatriates, 3.54–3.55
  gift tax
    citizens, 3.10
    domiciliaries, 3.10
    non-domiciled aliens, 3.14
    tax-motivated expatriates, 3.16–3.17
Types of tax (United Kingdom)
  income tax by reference to enjoyment of property previously owned
    chattels, 1.60
    excluded transactions, 1.55
    exemptions from charge, 1.56–1.58
    intangible assets, 1.61–1.66
    introduction, 1.51–1.54
    land, 1.59
  inheritance tax, 1.38–1.50
    introduction, 1.34–1.37
    lifetime transfers, 1.67–1.77
    transfer on death, 1.38–1.50
Types of tax (United States)
  estate tax
    generally, 1.2–1.12
    repeal proposals, 1.31–1.33
  generation-skipping tax
    generally, 1.26–1.30
    repeal proposals, 1.31–1.33
  gift tax, 1.13–1.25
  introduction, 1.1

U

UK spouse providing for US spouse
  death
    estate tax implications to UK decedent spouse, 20.46–20.47
    estate tax implications to US surviving spouse, 20.50–20.51
    inheritance tax implications to UK decedent spouse, 20.31–20.45
    inheritance tax implications to US surviving spouse, 20.48–20.49
  introduction, 20.1–20.2
  lifetime gifts
    estate tax implications to US donee, 20.25–20.30
    gift tax implication to UK donor, 20.8–20.10
    inheritance tax implications to UK donor, 20.4–20.7

527

Index

UK spouse providing for US spouse – *contd*
  lifetime gifts – *contd*
    inheritance tax implications to
      US donee,   20.11–20.24
    introduction,   20.3

UK trusts providing for US beneficiary
  foreign grantor trusts with foreign grantors
    existing 'grandfathered' grantor trusts,   18.10–18.12
    introduction,   18.8–18.9
    post-grantor trust phase,   18.17–18.21
    revocable trusts,   18.13–18.14
    settlor and spouse only trusts,   18.15–18.16
  foreign non-grantor trusts
    'capital first' trust distributions,   18.34
    default distribution rule,   18.35
    depleting trust,   18.35
    distribution of assets to settlor followed by gift over,   18.38–18.41
    distribution of assets to non-US beneficiaries followed by gift over,   18.42–18.47
    distribution of current trust income and net gains,   18.27–18.29
    DNI annuity distributions,   18.30–18.33
    domesticate the foreign trust,   18.23–18.25
    introduction,   18.22
    rent free use of trust owned property,   18.36
    rhythm method distributions of accumulated income,   18.26
    sale of assets to trust,   18.37
    UNI accumulations,   18.30–18.33
  introduction,   18.1–18.7

UNI accumulations
  foreign non-grantor trusts,   18.30–18.33

US living trusts
  US trust providing for UK beneficiary,   17.11–17.13

US spouse providing for UK spouse
  death
    estate tax implications to UK surviving spouse,   19.38–19.41
    estate tax implications to US decedent spouse,   19.18–19.20

US spouse providing for UK spouse – *contd*
  death – *contd*
    inheritance tax implications to UK surviving spouse,   19.42–19.49
    inheritance tax implications to US decedent spouse,   19.21–19.37
    introduction,   19.16–19.17
  introduction,   19.1–19.3
  lifetime gifts
    estate tax implications to UK donee,   19.12–19.13
    gift tax implications to US donor,   19.5–19.7
    inheritance tax implications to UK donee,   19.14–19.15
    inheritance tax implications to US donor,   19.8–19.11
    introduction,   19.4

US trust providing for UK beneficiary
  capital gains distributions,   17.5–17.10
  income distributions,   17.5–17.10
  summary,   17.1–17.4
  US living trusts,   17.11–17.13

US/UK estate and gift tax treaty
  credits,   7.68–7.70
  decedent's exposure to tax
    generally,   7.71
    summary,   Appendix 6
  deductions and exemptions,   7.58–7.67
  exceptions,   7.54–7.56
  fiscal domicile,   7.51–7.53
  introduction,   7.47
  non-domicile in either country,   7.57
  scope,   7.48–7.50
  taxes covered,   7.48–7.50
  text,   Appendix 3

V

Value added tax
  rates,   Appendix 1

Variable insurance products
  pre-immigration planning,   16.54–16.64

Venture capital trusts (VCTs)
  capital gains tax,   10.6

W

Waiver of dividend
  exemptions and reliefs, and,   3.80

'Wholly and exclusively' rule
  capital gains tax, 11.22–11.23

Woodland
  capital gains tax, 10.6